FORCE MAJEURE AND FRUSTRATION OF CONTRACT

SECOND EDITION

LLOYD'S COMMERCIAL LAW LIBRARY

Interests in Goods
by Norman Palmer and
Ewan McKendrick
(1993)

The Law of Insurance Contracts
second edition
by Malcolm A. Clarke
(1994)

EC Banking Law
second edition
by Marc Dassesse, Stuart Isaacs QC
and Graham Penn
(1994)

Appeals from Arbitration Awards
by D. Rhidian Thomas
(1994)

*Force Majeure and Frustration
of Contract*
second edition
Edited by Ewan McKendrick
(1995)

FORCE MAJEURE AND FRUSTRATION OF CONTRACT

EDITED BY
EWAN McKENDRICK
Fellow of St. Anne's College, Oxford
Linnells Lecturer in Law in the University of Oxford

SECOND EDITION

FOREWORD BY THE HON. ANDREW ROGERS QC

|L|L|P|

LONDON NEW YORK HAMBURG HONG KONG
LLOYD'S OF LONDON PRESS LTD
1995

Lloyd's of London Press Ltd.
Legal Publishing Division
27 Swinton Street
London WC1X 9NW

USA AND CANADA
Lloyd's of London Press Inc.
Suite 308, 611 Broadway
New York, NY 10012 USA

GERMANY
Lloyd's of London Press GmbH
59 Ehrenbergstrasse
2000 Hamburg 50, Germany

SOUTH EAST ASIA
Lloyd's of London Press (Far East) Ltd.
Room 1101, Hollywood Centre
233 Hollywood Road
Hong Kong

First published in Great Britain, 1991
Second edition 1995

British Library Cataloguing in Publication Data
A catalogue record for this book is
available from the British Library

ISBN 1-85044-819-1

Text set in 10/12pt Times by
Interactive Sciences, Gloucester
Printed in Great Britain by
Hartnolls Ltd,
Bodmin, Cornwall

FOREWORD

BY THE HON. ANDREW ROGERS Q.C.

With greater or lesser justification, it has been the age-old cry of businessmen that the law fails to meet the legitimate needs of commerce. In the field of frustration this is a justified complaint in the English system and in most common law systems which still adhere to its basic principles in the field of contract. As the chapter by Mr Parker demonstrates, the European Court of Justice is also oscillating in the search for an acceptable doctrine. Yet, of necessity, particularly in long term contracts, there will be changes in circumstances ranging from the minor to the most fundamental. Changes which were not in the contemplation of the drafters of the contracts and were not catered for have embroiled the courts in difficulties and, as the law reports evidence, continue to do so.

It is only in relatively recent times that the English courts relented in their demand that the strict words of the contract be adhered to, notwithstanding changes in circumstance. The resulting doctrine of frustration has not worked satisfactorily. The courts found it difficult to determine its doctrinal foundation or the limits for its application. This is graphically illustrated by the first of Mr McKendrick's contributions.

The statutory provisions which have attacked the problem in a piecemeal fashion are neither complete nor satisfactory. As Professor Diamond points out, the Sale of Goods Act 1979 is restrictive in its application to contracts for specific goods which perish before the risk has passed. Yet as Professor Bridge has shown, contracts for the sale of unascertained goods may also become impossible of performance owing to supervening events. The Law Reform (Frustrated Contracts) Act 1943 excludes from its coverage contracts which are addressed by section 7 of the Sale of Goods Act.

Mr McKendrick, in his second contribution, throws into high relief the criticisms not only of the English Act dealing with frustrated contracts, but also of the various Commonwealth prototypes it has spawned. In the light of his analysis, it is open to conclude that it is better to reject the legislative assistance offered by the various statutes and exclude their operation. Thereupon the businessman and his advisers are driven back to the general law. In today's burgeoning international trade, that can hardly be described as a satisfactory system to present to a foreign trader. What may be even more unsatisfactory is that frustration under the general law brings in its train automatic discharge. To avoid such results, the parties to the contract are required to draft their own particular code. That in turn means a substantial increase in transaction costs.

Notwithstanding the costs involved, in an effort to meet the difficulty many contractors have undertaken fairly detailed contractual risk allocation. The use of *force majeure* clauses attempts to cater for the unanticipated and unforeseeable. It is hardly surprising in the circumstances that Donaldson J., speaking of such clauses, pointed out that "the precise meaning of this term, if it has one, has eluded lawyers for years" (*Thomas Borthwick (Glasgow) Limited* v. *Faure Fairclough Limited* [1968] 1 Lloyd's Rep. 16, at p. 28).

It is therefore a field of law of paramount importance to the commercial world, and to the advisors who work in it, that the contributions undertake to survey. The survey is thorough and analytical. In the result, the authors have done the commercial community a signal service.

For the second edition the structure of the book has been recast and four valuable new essays added. The reader is taken on a scholarly survey of the field, viewed first from general aspects, and then in its impact on various fields of commercial activity, concluding with remedies and international and comparative aspects. Mr McInnis points out that most *force majeure* clauses are drafted in two parts. One limb will enumerate a series of individual events, the other will seek to cover all others "howsoever arising" and then go on to indicate the consequences. Mr Swadling examines the treatment that *force majeure* clauses and those incorrectly categorised as such (cf. *The Super Servant Two* [1990] 1 Lloyd's Rep. 1) have received at the hand of the courts. Until courts decide on a coherent philosophy towards frustration and *force majeure*, they will be bedevilled by the difficulty of determining whether to construe such provisions strictly and in the same way as exclusion clauses. Surely there is merit in the argument that a *force majeure* clause is simply a risk allocation provision that should be construed in the same fashion as any other ordinary contractual clause.

Following upon the examinations of general principle, authors examine the principal areas, other than sale of goods, where frustration has its major impact. By reference to shipping cases, Mr Howard Q.C. points out that the courts have never subjected to any rigorous analysis the question whether a wholly objective test should be applied in determining whether frustration has brought the contract to an end. Professor Palmer deals with the disabling effects of industrial action in bringing principles of frustration into play and calls for risk allocation by means of *force majeure* clauses. Professor Palmer argues that industrial disruption is of particular significance to frustration. An interesting feature of his discussion is the illustration of judges being drawn into an assessment of the conduct of parties in an industrial dispute. The evident difficulty felt by judges does not seem to be replicated in their consideration of commercial situations which may be just as threatening to the particular litigants or the community at large.

One of the most interesting features of the book is in Part VI, which includes a discussion of the role of frustration in the Vienna Sales Convention, under the Uniform Commercial Code and in EU law. It is the expectation of Professor Hudson that, most likely, parties will exclude the relevant provision, Article 79 of the Vienna Convention, in day-to-day practice.

What this volume demonstrates beyond argument is that the law on the topic shrieks for attention. Whilst practitioners, academics and judges generally bemoan the state of the law, nothing appears to be happening. One of the great virtues of a publication such as this is that it may serve as the impetus for action. Indeed, it is not too much to say that it serves the purpose of a discussion paper by a Law Reform Commission around which ideas for reform can be built. In the meantime, it will save untold hours of sweat to judges and practitioners confronted with a problem in the field.

ANDREW ROGERS

PREFACE

Force majeure and frustration are subjects of considerable commercial interest, yet they have been rather neglected by English textbook writers. This book, which has its origins in a conference organised by Professor Norman Palmer in Colchester in November 1988, is an attempt to remedy this deficiency. Our aim is not, however, to write an exhaustive treatise on *force majeure* and frustration; rather, we have attempted to evaluate critically the general principles relating to *force majeure* and frustration and to examine some of the difficulties which arise when seeking to apply these principles in particular contexts. In terms of critical evaluation no one consistent line is adopted throughout the book; each author has been left free to express his or her own views as to the current state of the law and the desirability or otherwise of reform. We do not seek to provide a simple all-encompassing solution to the problems identified in this book; rather, our aim has been to stimulate debate on these important issues.

While the stated aims of this edition remain the same as those of the first edition, I am pleased to be able to welcome four new authors to the team for this edition: Barry Nicholas, Alan Berg, Simon Curtis and Sukhnam Digwa-Singh. The addition of four new chapters (as well as revisions to existing chapters) has necessitated some re-structuring of the book. It is now divided into six parts. The first part is essentially introductory. We have chosen to focus on *force majeure* (in both a common law and a civilian context) because *force majeure* tends to be rather less familiar to the English legal mind than the doctrine of frustration. In this part we also attempt to assess the relationship between frustration and *force majeure* in English law. The second part has as its focus the drafting of *force majeure* clauses, both in terms of general guidelines which ought to be borne in mind by the contract draftsman and in terms of a more detailed, practical analysis of the real difficulties which can arise when seeking to draft such clauses. The third part begins to put the general principles of *force majeure* and frustration to work: here in the context of shipping law. The fourth part continues to look at the practical applications of *force majeure* and frustration, this time in the context of industrial action and building contracts. The fifth part shifts attention towards the remedial aspects of frustration, both in terms of a critical analysis of the Law Reform (Frustrated Contracts) Act 1943 and the intriguing suggestion by Andrew Rogers that some frustration cases might usefully be re-analysed in terms of estoppel. The final part deals with international and comparative aspects of frustration and *force majeure*. It ranges over a wide area, including the Vienna Convention, the Uniform Commercial Code, EU law and international sales contracts.

PREFACE

The contributors to this volume are drawn from both the practising and the academic world and they bring their own specialist knowledge to bear on their chosen subjects. I would like to express my gratitude to them all for the considerable time and effort which they have devoted to this project (in particular to the new contributors who have had to comply with rather tight deadlines). I would also like to thank Andrew Rogers who generously agreed to write the foreword and to contribute a chapter to the book. The staff of Lloyd's of London Press have, as always, provided invaluable support and encouragement at all stages in the preparation of this edition. My final and greatest debt is to my wife, Rose, and our children, Jenny, Sarah, Rachel and Katie, who, once again, have had to put up with the obsessions of authorship.

We very much regret that Professor Treitel's important new book *Frustration and Force Majeure* was published just as the page proofs of this edition were being returned to the publishers. While we have been able to incorporate one or two references in the footnotes, this work undoubtedly deserved, if space and time had permitted, much greater consideration in the text.

Unless otherwise stipulated, the law is stated on the basis of the materials available to us as at 31 July 1994, although it has, on occasion, been possible to take account of subsequent developments at proof stage.

1 November 1994 EWAN MCKENDRICK

CONTRIBUTORS

ALAN BERG is a solicitor with Watson, Farley & Williams, London. He is the author of *Drafting Commercial Agreements* (Butterworths, 1991) and has written a number of articles on matters of contract law, equity and banking law.

MICHAEL BRIDGE is the Hind Professor of Commercial Law in the University of Nottingham and a barrister. Formerly, he was legal counsel to the Alberta Law Reform Agency and Professor of Law at McGill University, Montreal. He is the author of *Sale of Goods* (Toronto, 1988) and the co-author of *Sales and Sales Financing in Canada: Cases and Materials* (Toronto, 1981). In addition, he has written a text on *Personal Property Law* (1993), is a contributor to *Palmer's Company Law* and *Emden's Construction Law* and has written articles on the subjects of contract, tort, sale and credit and security.

SIMON CURTIS is a solicitor and partner with Watson, Farley & Williams, an international firm of lawyers specialising in shipping. He is the author of *The Law of Shipbuilding Contracts* (1991) and of numerous articles on shipbuilding and other maritime matters.

BRIAN DAVENPORT was called to the Bar by Gray's Inn in 1960 and thereafter practised at the Bar, specialising in maritime and commercial law. From 1970 to 1980 he was also standing junior counsel to various government departments, including the Export Credit Guarantees Department and the Board of land Revenue (common law). He became a Q.C. in 1980, and from 1981 to 1988 was a Law Commissioner. He is now Director of Research Services at Norton Rose, London.

AUBREY DIAMOND is Emeritus Professor of Law in the University of London, Professor of Law at the University of Notre Dame and a consultant with a London firm of solicitors. He has been a Law Commissioner and the Director of the Institute of Advanced Legal Studies (University of London). He is the author of *Commercial and Consumer Credit: An Introduction* and joint author of *The Consumer, Society and the Law*, and has contributed to various legal and medical symposia. He is a Deputy Chairman of the Data Protection Tribunal and was a Chairman of Industrial Tribunals. He has been a visiting professor in the United States, Australia and Africa.

SUKHNAM DIGWA-SINGH is a Legal Researcher. She has previously worked as a consultant in the Legal Division at the Commonwealth Secretariat and as a merchant banker. She studied law and was awarded a Ph.D. at Pembroke College, Cambridge, and has contributed a number of articles to various journals on the subjects of contract law, US and Soviet commercial law and international banking fraud.

MICHAEL FURMSTON is Professor of Law at the University of Bristol and a Bencher of Gray's Inn. He previously lectured at Birmingham and Belfast and was a Fellow of Lincoln College, Oxford, from 1964 to 1978. He was Dean of the Law Faculty at Bristol from 1980 to 1984 and Pro-Vice-Chancellor of the University from 1986 to 1989. His books include the editorship of *Cheshire, Fifoot & Furmston on Contract*; joint authorship of Beale, Bishop & Furmston, *Cases and Materials on Contract*; and a book on *Sale of Goods* (1990).

M. N. HOWARD is a Queen's Counsel based in London, practising in the field of commercial and maritime law. He is the senior editor of *Phipson on Evidence* and from 1987–1992 was Visiting Professor of Law at the University of Essex.

CONTRIBUTORS

A. H. HUDSON is Emeritus Professor of Common Law in the University of Liverpool, having previously held appointments in the Universities of Hull, Birmingham and Manchester. He has contributed on commercial topics to a number of books and legal periodicals.

J. ARTHUR MCINNIS is a Lecturer at the University of Hong Kong who holds common and civil law degrees. He has practised as a barrister and solicitor in Canada and practises as a consultant with Baker & McKenzie in Hong Kong.

EWAN MCKENDRICK is a Fellow of St. Anne's College, Oxford, and Linnells Lecturer in Law in the University of Oxford, having previously held lectureships at the Universities of Central Lancashire and Essex and the London School of Economics and Political Science. He is an editor of *Chitty on Contracts*, the author of *Contract Law* (2nd Edn., 1994, Macmillan) and has written a number of articles on various aspects of the law of obligations.

BARRY NICHOLAS was successively Professor of Comparative Law at the University of Oxford and Principal of Brasenose College. He has written mainly on Roman law and comparative law. His books include *The French Law of Contract* (2nd Edn., 1992). He is a Fellow of the British Academy, an Honorary Bencher of the Inner Temple and an Honorary Doctor of the University of Paris V.

NORMAN PALMER is Rowe & Maw Professor of Commercial Law at University College London and a practising barrister, formerly having held chairs at the Universities of Reading, Essex and Southampton. He is the author of *Bailment* (2nd Edn., 1991) and co-editor of Emden's *Construction Law* (1990) and *Crossley Vaines on Personal Property* (1973). He is also a contributor to the 4th edition of *Halsbury's Laws of England*. He is a director of the International Cultural Property Society, and the editor of the International Journal of Cultural Property.

MICHAEL PARKER is a solicitor and partner with Clyde & Co., a leading international law firm. He studied law at Magdalene College, Cambridge, and has contributed a number of articles to various journals on matters of EC law.

ANDREW ROGERS QC was appointed a Judge of the Supreme Court of New South Wales in 1979 and Chief Judge of the Commercial Division of that Court until 1993. He is now an Arbitrator, Mediator and Corporate and Legal Consultant. He has written on a wide range of topics, ranging from *Mareva* injunctions through arbitration to the application of the Companies Code in family law disputes.

WILLIAM SWADLING is a lecturer in law at University College London, having previously held lectureships at the University of Southampton and Queen Mary and Westfield College, University of London. He also teaches on a part-time basis at Trinity College, Cambridge. He is a contributor to the 4th edition of *Halsbury's Laws of England* and is the author of a number of articles on the law of property and the law of restitution. He is also an editor of *Trust Law International* and managing editor of the *Restitution Law Review*.

CONTENTS

PART II—THE DRAFTING OF FORCE MAJEURE CLAUSES

PART V—FRUSTRATION, REMEDIES AND RE-APPRAISAL

PART VI—FRUSTRATION AND FORCE MAJEURE—INTERNATIONAL AND COMPARATIVE ASPECTS

TABLE OF CASES

TABLE OF CASES

TABLE OF LEGISLATION, CONVENTIONS ETC.

AUSTRALIA

CANADA

PART I

FORCE MAJEURE AND FRUSTRATION: INTRODUCTION AND INTERRELATIONSHIP

CHAPTER 1

THE JUDICIAL CONSTRUCTION OF FORCE MAJEURE CLAUSES

1. INTRODUCTION

The common law of contract proceeds from the basis that liability for non-performance of contractual obligations is strict. Apart from those cases where the promise is to provide personal services, where the presumption is that the promisor undertakes only to exercise reasonable care in performing his or her duties under the contract,[1] failure to bring about the state of affairs promised in the contract will, without more, amount to a breach of contract and give rise to a claim for damages. The rationale for such a rule was given by the Court of King's Bench as long ago as 1647 in *Paradine* v. *Jane*[2]: "When the party by his own contract creates a duty or charge upon himself, he is bound to make it good, if he may, notwithstanding any accident by inevitable necessity, because he might have provided against it by his contract."[3]

Proof of breach is not dependent on the promisee showing that the promisor was in some way at fault in failing to perform as promised.[4] As Lord Edmund-Davies said in *Raineri* v. *Miles*[5]: "It is axiomatic that, in relation to claims for damages for breach of contract, it is, in general, immaterial why the defendant failed to fulfil his obligation, and certainly no defence to plead that he had done his best." By contrast, the law of tort generally finds a defendant liable to compensate another for harm that he has caused only where the victim shows that the defendant was in some way at fault in causing that harm. Where the defendant's conduct is not shown to have fallen below a certain standard, generally that of the reasonable man, he will not be called upon to compensate the plaintiff for the harm which he has inflicted. The rationale for this distinction rests in the source of the different obligations. Contractual obligations, unlike tortious duties, are freely assumed[6]: if

1. See, for example, *Eyre* v. *Measday* [1986] 1 All E.R. 488; *Thake* v. *Maurice* [1986] Q.B. 644; *George Hawkins* v. *Chrysler* (UK) *Ltd. & Burne Associates* (1986) 38 Build.L.R. 36, 50.
2. (1647) Aleyn 26.
3. *Ibid*. at p. 27.
4. One limited exception was provided by the rule in *Bain* v. *Fothergill* (1874) L.R. 7 H.L. 158 which, while not denying the existence of a breach, limited the damages payable by a vendor who through no fault of his own was unable to deduce a good title to the estate in land he had contracted to sell. With the advent of modern conveyancing practices the rule was considered anomalous and it has since been abolished by the Law of Property (Miscellaneous Provisions) Act 1989, s. 3.
5. [1981] A.C. 1050, 1086.
6. This is not to say that to be actionable an assumption of responsibility must always be contractual, as *Hedley Byrne & Co. Ltd.* v. *Heller & Partners Ltd.* [1964] A.C. 465 demonstrates. But the House of Lords also made clear in that case that a person assuming such a responsibility was free unilaterally to

the promisor wants in some way to limit his obligation then he is free to do so; if he chooses not to he bears the risk of non-performance. Such a proposition, which would seem to penalise a promisor for failing to perform the impossible, is easier to accept if we view a contractual promise not as a promise to perform but as a promise to bear the risk of the promised event not coming to pass.[7] The point is well put by Holmes[8] when he says:

"An assurance that it will rain tomorrow, or that a third person shall paint a picture, may as well be promised as one that the promisee shall receive from some source one hundred bales of cotton, or that the promisor shall pay the promisee one hundred dollars."

" . . . the law does not inquire . . . how far the accomplishment of an assurance touching the future is within the power of the promisor . . . In the case of a binding promise that it shall rain tomorrow, the immediate legal effect of what the promisor does is, that he takes the risk of the event . . . as between himself and the promisee. He does no more when he promises to deliver a bale of cotton."[9]

It is this ability to allocate risks which provides a major function of the law of contract: it enables individuals and corporations to plan for the future with a moderate degree of certainty and hence to maximise their freedom of action. Secure in the knowledge that contractual obligations will be performed or compensation given if they are not, a promisee is free to turn his or her attention to some other transaction. Under a standard building contract, for example, the main contractor will subcontract various parts of the task to specialist contractors. Having entered into a binding contract for the installation of the floors of the building he is able to turn his attention to finding someone to provide the roof and so on. Then when the subcontracting process is complete he can turn his attention to another project. And it matters not that the agreements entered into might at any stage be wholly executory: an executory promise is just as effective as an executed one. If it were not possible to both give and receive binding promises any ability to plan for the future by the contractual allocation of risk would be denied.[10]

It may be, however, that a promisor does not wish to assume such an absolute risk and he is free to delimit the extent of the obligation in any way he chooses, subject, of course, to the agreement of the promisee and to mandatory rules of law. As we have already seen, the justification given in *Paradine* v. *Jane* for the imposition of strict liability in contract was that the promisor could have limited his obligation by agreement if he had so wished.[11] In many cases the promisor may be especially

limit the scope of the obligation. Such limitations may, however, now be caught by the Unfair Contract Terms Act 1977: *Smith* v. *Eric S. Bush* [1990] 1 A.C. 831.

7. *Bunge y Born Limitada Sociedad Anonima Comercial Financier y Industrial of Buenos Aires* v. *H. A. Brightman & Co.* [1925] A.C. 799, 816, *per* Lord Sumner.

8. *The Common Law*, (1881) Little Brown & Co.

9. *Ibid.*, at pp. 298–300.

10. Cf. Atiyah, "Contracts, Promises and the Law of Obligations" (1978) 94 L.Q.R. 193, who, in the absence of proof of detrimental reliance by the promisee, argues against the enforcement of purely executory contracts.

11. See also *Southcote* v. *Bennet* (1601) 4 Coke 83b where Coke C.J. has this advice for the bailee of goods: "it is a good policy for him who takes any goods to keep, to take them in a special manner, *scil.* to keep them as he keeps his own goods, or to keep them the best he can at the peril of the party, or, if they happen to be stolen or purloined, that he shall not answer for them; for he who accepteth them ought to take them in such or the like manner, or otherwise he may be charged by his general acceptance."

unwilling to accept the risk of events over which he has no control and a contract may typically provide that "the promisor shall not be responsible for any losses occasioned by any Act of God, strike, lockout, riot or civil commotion, combination of workmen, breakdown of machinery, fire or any cause contemplated in the term *force majeure* . . . ". Such clauses are known generally as *force majeure* clauses. In this chapter we will be concerned with the judicial interpretation of such clauses. It should be pointed out, however, that *force majeure* clauses come in a multitude of forms and, as with all contractual terms, each must be read in the context of the contract as a whole. No definitive answers can therefore be given but some light may be shed by the enquiry as to their treatment by the courts, most especially whether they are subject to the same restrictive interpretation as exception clauses.

To complete the picture, reference must also be made to the doctrine of frustration.[12] Since *Paradine* v. *Jane*, the common law has, in certain limited circumstances, relieved a promisor from liability for failure to bring about the promised state of affairs.[13] The doctrine of frustration, which excuses non-performance where "a contractual obligation has become incapable of being performed because the circumstances in which performance is called for would render it a thing radically different from that which was undertaken by the contract",[14] operates even though the terms of the contract are *prima facie* absolute. But such a doctrine, by relieving a promisor from liability for non-performance, subverts the forward-planning element of contract law outlined above and places the risk of future non-performance on the promisee.[15] It is not surprising, therefore, to find that judges are nowadays generally reluctant to find that a particular contract has been frustrated.[16] A *force majeure* clause, on the other hand, seeks to anticipate such eventualities and settle the allocation of risks beforehand in an agreed, rather than an imposed, manner. For that reason, *force majeure* clauses are common elements of commercial contracts.

2. WHAT IS FORCE MAJEURE?

The concept of *force majeure*, though alien to the common law, is an established doctrine in French law which relieves a promisor from responsibility for non-performance in certain circumstances. Although having a close affinity with the common law doctrine of frustration, it is somewhat narrower in its relieving

12. Treitel, *Law of Contract* (8th Edn., 1991), pp. 763–823.

13. For a general historical discussion of the doctrine of frustration see Stoljar, *A History of Contract at Common Law* (1975) 187–199.

14. *Davis Contractors Ltd.* v. *Fareham U.D.C.* [1956] A.C. 696, 729.

15. The position of the promisee in relation to liabilities incurred *before* the occurrence of the frustrating event has of course been alleviated somewhat by the decision of the House of Lords in *Fibrosa Spolka Akcyjna* v. *Fairbairn, Lawson, Combe, Barbour Ltd.* [1943] A.C. 32, and the enactment of the Law Reform (Frustrated Contracts) Act 1943. The restitutionary aspects of a frustrated contract are discussed in detail in Chapter 11 below.

16. See, e.g., *British Movietonenews Ltd.* v. *London and District Cinemas* [1952] A.C. 166; *Tsakiroglou & Co. Ltd.* v. *Noblee Thorl G.m.b.H* [1962] A.C. 93; *The Nema* [1982] A.C. 724; *J. Lauritzen A.S.* v. *Wijsmuller B.V. (The Super Servant Two)* [1990] 1 Lloyd's Rep. 1; Treitel, *op. cit.*, pp. 763–767.

effects.[17] Many *force majeure* clauses in English contracts actually use the French words and, as an aid to their construction, reference is sometimes made to their meaning in French law.[18] It therefore becomes necessary to examine the meaning of the term in that jurisdiction.

(a) Force majeure in French law[19]

The words *force majeure* appear in article 1148 of the Code Civil which provides: "There is no place for any damages when, as a result of *force majeure* or *cas fortuit*,[20] the debtor has been prevented from conveying or doing that to which he was obliged or has done what was forbidden to him." To invoke successfully a defence of *force majeure* the debtor (promisor) must show that performance has been made impossible and not merely more onerous. In this respect *force majeure* corresponds with the English law of frustration.[21] Where French law differs, however, is in the rule that technical performance excludes the defence. If the contract is capable of technical performance a defence of *force majeure* will not be available, even though the economic foundation of the contract may have disappeared. In this respect the French law of *force majeure* is narrower than the English law of frustration, which does relieve a promisor in such circumstances.[22] French law takes into account only physical or legal impossibility.[23]

To qualify as *force majeure*, the event preventing performance must have been both unforeseeable and irresistible. If the event was foreseeable, provision for it should have been made in the contract or the obligation ought not to have been assumed. So too with the doctrine of frustration in English law, the presumption being that where the parties have foreseen a risk but have made no provision for it in the contract then the loss is intended to lie where it falls.[24] The failure to perform must have been irresistible in the sense that it was both unavoidable and insurmountable; where there is an alternative method of performance or where the obstacle to performance might have been removed, the promisor will not be able to

17. Nicholas, "Force Majeure and Frustration" (1979) 27 Am. J. Comp. Law 231.

18. See, e.g., *Matsoukis* v. *Priestman & Co.* [1915] 1 K.B. 681, 685, where Bailhache J., after hearing evidence from a Belgian lawyer, said that he was not sure whether he was bound or entitled to give the words the full meaning they had on the Continent.

19. A full discussion is contained in Chapter 2 below. See also Smith, "Impossibility of Performance as Excuse in French Law; The Doctrine of *Force Majeure*" (1936) 45 Yale L.J. 452; Amos & Walton, *Introduction to French Law* (3rd Edn., 1967); Nicholas, *French Law of Contract* (2nd Edn., 1992) pp. 200–210; David, *English Law and French Law* (1980) pp. 119–195.

20. The terms *force majeure* and *cas fortuit* are used interchangeably by French lawyers and nothing turns on any distinction between the two.

21. *Davis Contractors Ltd.* v. *Fareham U.D.C.* [1956] A.C. 696.

22. See, e.g., *Krell* v. *Henry* [1903] 2 K.B. 740; *Metropolitan Water Board* v. *Dick Kerr & Co.* [1918] A.C. 119. English courts do, however, make it difficult to establish the defence of frustration of purpose. See, e.g., *Amalgamated Investment & Property Co. Ltd.* v. *John Walker & Son Ltd.* [1977] 1 W.L.R. 164, and generally, Treitel, *op. cit.*, pp. 783–785.

23. This is only true for cases coming before the Cour de Cassation. Where the contract is subject to the jurisdiction of the *droit administratif* then the *théorie de l'imprévision* allows the court to relieve the promisor where the economic basis of the contract has disappeared. See further, Chapter 2 below.

24. *Davis Contractors Ltd.* v. *Fareham U.D.C.* [1956] A.C. 696, 731 *per* Lord Radcliffe; *Wates Ltd.* v. *Greater London Council* (1983) 25 Build.L.R. 1; *Treitel*, op. cit., 799–803. *Contra, W. J. Tatem Ltd.* v. *Gamboa* [1939] 1 K.B. 132; *The Eugenia* [1964] 2 Q.B. 226, 239 *per* Lord Denning M.R.

invoke the doctrine. That this is also the position in English law is illustrated first, by those cases which held that the closure of the Suez canal was not a frustrating event since the goods in question could have been shipped via the Cape of Good Hope[25] and secondly, by the rule that impossibility of performance in one of a number of possible ways of performing the obligation will not amount to frustration.[26]

There are occasions, however, where the French law of *force majeure* can be more generous to the promisor than would the English doctrine of frustration. In one case,[27] a vendor had contracted to deliver wine "by the end of February" but found, on attempting to do so in the last three days of the month, that all roads were impassable owing to flooding. The court held that he was excused performance but it is doubtful whether the vendor could have successfully pleaded frustration in an English court. Unless the goods were specific goods, an English court would have taken the view that such a risk was assumed by the vendor. The vendor could be expected in such a case to provide for delivery from some other source.[28] As Pickford L.J. said in *Blackburn Bobbin Co. Ltd.* v. *Allen & Son*[29]: "Why should a purchaser of goods, not specific goods, be deemed to concern himself with the way in which the seller is going to fulfil his contract by providing the goods he has agreed to sell?"[30]

(b) Force Majeure in English law

Although there is no general doctrine of *force majeure* in English law parties often use the words *force majeure* in their contracts,[31] thus forcing the English courts to attribute to them some meaning. And though Donaldson J., in *Thomas Borthwick (Glasgow) Ltd.* v. *Faure Fairclough Ltd.*,[32] remarked that "the precise meaning of this term, if it has one, has eluded lawyers for years", the words have been considered in a number of cases. One caveat should, however, be entered at this stage. It is rare for the words *force majeure* to appear in a contract otherwise than as part of a longer list of exceptions and, as McCardie J. pointed out in *Lebeaupin* v. *Richard Crispin & Co.*,[33] the words should be construed in each case with a close attention to those which precede or follow them, and with a due regard to the nature and general terms of the contract. What follows, therefore, is a discussion of

25. E.g., *Palmco Shipping Co.* v. *Continental Ore Corp.* [1970] 2 Lloyd's Rep. 21.
26. *The Furness Bridge* [1977] 2 Lloyd's Rep. 367.
27. Cass. req. 28.11.1934, S. 1935.1.105, also discussed at p. 25.
28. Atiyah, *Sale of Goods* (8th Edn., 1990) pp. 329–331.
29. [1918] 2 K.B. 467, 469.
30. It might also be argued that the vendor had the whole month in which to deliver. Before the floods the roads were passable. If he chose to leave it to the last minute to fulfil his obligations then he should bear the risk of any *vis major* preventing performance.
31. There are even instances of the words appearing in English statutory material. In *Hackney Borough Council* v. *Doré* [1922] 1 K.B. 431, an obligation to supply electricity was placed on the appellants by the Hackney Electric Lighting Order, 1893. In the event of default they were liable to a penalty unless the court should be of the opinion "that such default was caused by inevitable accident or force majeure". Sankey J. was forced to comment that he regretted the introduction of foreign words into English statutes and Orders without any definition of them being given.
32. [1968] 1 Lloyd's Rep. 16, 28.
33. [1920] 2 K.B. 714, 720.

what has been held *on the construction of a particular contract* to amount to *force majeure*.

In *Matsoukis* v. *Priestman & Co.*[34] a shipbuilding contract provided for the payment by the defendant builder of liquidated damages for every day's delay past the time stipulated for delivery, "*force majeure* excepted". Delivery of the ship was delayed by a combination of a universal coal-strike, the breakdown of machinery in the defendant's yard, bad weather, and the attendance of the builder's employees at football matches and a funeral. The plaintiffs argued that the words *force majeure* were simply the French rendering of the Latin words *vis major*, which, since they had the same meaning as the term "act of God" in English law, could not cover strikes which where dependent on human intervention. Nor, they argued, did it cover breakdown in machinery which was a usual occurrence and must have been taken into account by the defendants in calculating the length of time required for the building of the ship. Bailhache J., after hearing evidence from a Belgian lawyer, rejected the argument that the words were interchangeable with *vis major* or act of God. He held that no damages were due in respect of days lost by the coal-strike or the breakdown in machinery but held that the term *force majeure* could not extend to such things as bad weather and the attendance of the defendant's workforce at football matches and a funeral since these were usual incidents affecting work, and the defendants in making their contract no doubt took them into account. This interpretation was accepted by McCardie J. in *Lebeaupin* v. *Richard Crispin & Co.*,[35] who held additionally that a promisor could not rely on his own act, or negligence, or omission or default as constituting *force majeure*.[36] That the superior force must amount to physical or legal restraint was accepted by the Privy Council in *The Concadoro*,[37] where it was held that a ship's master who was unable to leave port because he had not been provided with sufficient funds to do so was not restrained by circumstances amounting to *force majeure*.[38] And, in *Brauer & Co.* v. *James Clark & Co.*,[39] the Court of Appeal held that a 20–30 per cent rise in prices did not come within the term *force majeure*.[40]

Thus, with some hesitation, we might say that in English law an event will be a *force majeure* event if it constitutes a legal or physical restraint on the performance of the contract (whether or not occurring through human intervention, although it must not be caused by the act, negligence, omission or default of the contracting party) which is both unforeseen and irresistible.[41]

34. [1915] 1 K.B. 681.

35. [1920] 2 K.B. 714, 719–720. This case contains what is probably the best discussion of the authorities.

36. See also *Yrazu* v. *Astral Shipping Co.* (1904) 9 Com. Cas. 100, where Walton J. held that a miscalculation by the master and engineer of a ship causing the ship to leave with insufficient coals whereby she was compelled to call at another port and thereby suffered delay and depreciation of cargo was not a case of *force majeure*. The result would have been different, he said, if the deficiency of coals had arisen from some accident or casualty.

37. [1916] 2 A.C. 199.

38. The decision actually concerned the meaning of the words *force majeure* in Arts 1 and 2 of the Hague Convention No. IV of 1907.

39. [1952] 2 Lloyd's Rep. 147.

40. See also *Tennants* (*Lancashire*) *Ltd.* v. *C. S. Wilson & Co. Ltd.* [1917] A.C. 495.

41. The assertion in Schmitthoff's, *Export Trade* (9th Edn. 1990), p. 199, that *force majeure* "includes every event which is beyond the control of the parties" is probably too wide.

3. WHAT IS A FORCE MAJEURE CLAUSE? [42]

Force majeure clauses come in many shapes and sizes, ranging from the simple clause providing for cancellation of the contract in the event that performance is prevented by circumstances comprehended within the term *force majeure*, to clauses of immense complexity containing, *inter alia*, a list of excusing events, provisions for notices to be issued to the promisee and detailing the consequences of the *force majeure* event. To take just one example, clause 17 of the Refined Sugar Association Contract provides as follows:

"*Force Majeure*

Should EEC Legislation, Government Intervention, ice, war, strikes, rebellion, political or labour-disturbances, civil commotion, fire, stress of weather, act of God or any cause of *force majeure* (whether or not of like kind to these before mentioned) beyond the Seller's control prevent directly or indirectly within the delivery period stated in the contract:

(a) the supply or delivery in whole or in part of the sugar allocated or to be allocated by the Seller against the contract, or
(b) the means of transport declared or to be declared for loading the sugar and the Seller or his agent be unable to supply other means of transport of equal character to enable him to effect delivery within the contract period,

the Seller shall immediately advise the Buyer by cable or by teleprinter of such fact and the quantity so affected and the delivery period shall be extended by 45 days. If the Seller is prevented from advising immediately through the circumstances beyond his control he shall notify the Buyer as soon as possible. If the delivery is still prevented by the end of the extended period, the contract shall be void for such quantity without penalty payable or receivable."

And the clause may not only protect a promisor who has been prevented from performing by certain events; sometimes a clause may extend protection to a promisor whose performance has merely been hindered[43] or delayed.

The flexibility of such clauses immediately provides us with the answer why, given that English law recognises frustration as a defence to claims for non-performance of contractual obligations, parties may nevertheless incorporate a *force majeure* clause in their contract. Frustration, apart from being a relatively uncertain concept, has the very blunt effect of bringing the contract automatically to an end. Both parties are simply relieved, on the occurrence of a frustrating event, from liability for failure to perform future obligations arising under the contract.[44] A suitably drafted *force majeure* clause, on the other hand, may provide a more subtle response, with the possibility of extensions of time being granted to the promisor, suspension or variation of the contract in certain events, return of moneys paid and, of course, eventual cancellation if performance remains impossible beyond a certain time. It may also be thought desirable to provide for termination of the con-

42. For a discussion of the meaning the words commonly contained in *force majeure* clauses see *Chitty on Contracts*, ed. Guest (27th Edn., 1994) Vol. I, paras 14–121—14–136.

43. As in *Dixon & Sons* v. *Henderson Craig & Co.* [1919] 2 K.B. 778. For the meaning of this word see *Crawford & Rowatt* v. *Wilson Sons & Co.* (1896) 12 T.L.R. 170; *Instone (S.) & Co. Ltd.* v. *Speedy Marshall & Co.* (1915) 114 L.T. 370; *Phosphate Mining Co.* v. *Ranklin Gilmour & Co.* (1915) 21 Com. Cas. 248; *Benjamin's Sale of Goods,* ed. Guest (4th Edn., 1992) para. 8–088.

44. Treitel, *op. cit.*, pp. 807–818.

tract in conditions which would not amount to frustrating circumstances.[45] So, for example, the contract may provide for cancellation in the event of an abnormal increase in prices and wages,[46] it being well settled that a mere increase in price is not a ground of frustration.[47] Yet it is this flexibility which makes it difficult, if not impossible, to define exactly what is meant by a *force majeure* clause[48]; suffice it to say that we are concerned with a clause which makes provision for non-performance or varied performance in circumstances which are beyond the control of the promisor.

4. ARE FORCE MAJEURE CLAUSES EXCLUSION CLAUSES?

The question which must be addressed is whether a *force majeure* clause is merely a variant of that other well-known device excusing non-performance, the exclusion or exemption clause. The question is important because on it depend a number of issues.[49] First, the answer will determine whether the strict rules of construction applicable to exclusion clauses,[50] now somewhat less rigorously employed following the introduction of the statutory controls of the Unfair Contract Terms Act 1977,[51] should apply to *force majeure* clauses or whether, as the House of Lords has held in the case of clauses limiting the time in which a claim may be brought or the amount of damages recoverable for breach,[52] a more generous construction should

45. As was the case in *Intertradex S.A.* v. *Lesieur Torteaux S.A.R.L.* [1978] 2 Lloyd's Rep. 509. where a breakdown of machinery at the only factory at which the goods contracted to be sold were produced did not amount to a frustrating circumstance, such events being commonplace in the world of affairs, but nevertheless did come within the scope of the *force majeure* clause so as to relieve the seller from liability. See too *J. Lauritzen A.S.* v. *Wijsmuller B.V.* (*The Super Servant Two*) [1990] 1 Lloyd's Rep. 1 where the Court of Appeal held that the sinking of the barge by which the defendant intended to transport the plaintiffs' oil rig, although not a frustrating event, was, unless caused by the defendants' own negligence, within the provisions of a *force majeure* clause in the contract, entitling the defendants to cancel the contract they had made with the plaintiffs.

46. As in *J. Lauritzen A.S.* v. *Wijsmuller B.V.* (*The Super Servant Two*) [1990] 1 Lloyd's Rep. 1.

47. *Davis Contractors Ltd.* v. *Fareham U.D.C.* [1956] A.C. 696; *Tsakiroglou & Co.* v. *Noblee & Thorl G.m.b.H.* [1962] A.C. 93, 115, *per* Lord Simonds; *Wates Ltd.* v. *Greater London Council* (1983) 25 Build.L.R. 1. Cf. the judgment of Lord Denning M.R. in *Staffordshire Area Health Authority* v. *South Staffordshire Waterworks Co.* [1978] 1 W.L.R. 1387.

48. So much so that a term "the usual *force majeure* clauses to apply" has been held void for uncertainty: *British Electrical and Associated Industries* (*Cardiff*) *Ltd.* v. *Patley Pressings Ltd.* [1953] 1 W.L.R. 280. Use of a too widely drawn *force majeure* clause may also deprive the transaction of any contractual effect, as happened in *MacRobertson Miller Airline Services* v. *Commissioner of State Taxation* (*W.A.*) (1975) 133 C.L.R. 125.

49. The distinction may also be important for other reasons: see, e.g., *G. H. Renton & Co. Ltd.* v. *Palmyra Trading Corp. of Panama* [1957] A.C. 149 where a clause in the bill of lading provided for discharge of the goods at any convenient port if industrial disputes prevented delivery at the named port. The House of Lords held that the clause was not one relieving the carrier from liability and so not rendered void by the Hague Rules. The clause merely went to define the extent of the carrier's obligation; it did not operate as a defence to a breach.

50. Treitel, *op. cit.*, 202–223; Yates, *Exclusion Clauses in Contracts* (2nd Edn., 1982) 123–160.

51. *Photo Production Ltd.* v. *Securicor Ltd.* [1980] A.C. 827; *Scottish Special Housing Association* v. *Wimpey Construction U.K. Ltd.* 1986 S.L.T. 173. See generally, Palmer [1983] L.M.C.L.Q. 557; Lewison, *Interpretation of Contracts* (1989) 251–282.

52. *Ailsa Craig Fishing Co. Ltd.* v. *Malvern Fishing Co. Ltd.* [1983] 1 W.L.R. 964; Palmer (1982) 45 M.L.R. 327; *George Mitchell* (*Chesterhall*) *Ltd.* v. *Finney Lock Seeds Ltd.* [1983] 2 A.C. 803.

apply. Secondly, it may be relevant to determine where the burden of proof in such cases lies. Is it for the promisor to prove that he comes within the terms of the *force majeure* clause or is it for the promisee to prove that he does not? Finally, there is the question of the applicability of the Unfair Contract Terms Act 1977. Does the Act apply to *force majeure* clauses and thereby subject them to a test of reasonableness or are such clauses exempt from its provisions?[53] The argument might be made that a *force majeure* clause simply defines the extent of the promisor's obligation, rather than excludes or restricts liability for breach and that the provisions of the 1977 Act can have no application to it.[54] But just as there is a difficulty in drawing a distinction between exception clauses and limitation clauses,[55] the dividing line between a *force majeure* clause and an exception clause may be equally hard to find.

In order to differentiate between an exclusion clause and a *force majeure* clause we must first define exactly what we mean by exclusion clauses and examine their effect on the contractual relations of the parties. We might then usefully compare the operation of exception clauses to that of *force majeure* clauses.

A tripartite distinction between different types of clause was made by Donaldson J. (as he then was) in *Kenyon, Son & Craven Ltd.* v. *Baxter Hoare & Co. Ltd.*[56] as follows:

> "Protective conditions are of three distinct types: first those which limit or reduce what would otherwise be the defendant's duty; second, those which exclude the defendant's liability for breach of specified aspects of that duty, and third, those which limit the extent to which the defendant is bound to indemnify the plaintiff in respect of the consequences of breaches of that duty."

The difference between the first two categories is said to be this: in the first case there is no breach of contract since there is no obligation to perform in the circumstances which have arisen, whilst in the second case there is a breach but the liability to pay damages in respect of it has been removed. One consequence of the latter approach is that if a clause falls within the second category it is construed separately from the rest of the contract. As Denning L.J. said in *Karsales (Harrow) Ltd.* v. *Wallis*[57]: "The thing to do is to look at the contract apart from the exempting clauses and see what are the terms, express or implied, which impose an obli-

53. S. 3(2)(a) being the provision most likely to be invoked in this context.

54. Treitel, *op. cit.*, at pp. 228, 232. If there is no breach then s. 3(2)(a) cannot be invoked. Nor will s. 3(2)(b)(ii) be of any assistance. This provides that the reasonableness test also applies to any contract term by which a party claims to be entitled "in respect of the whole or any part of his contractual obligation, to render no performance at all". *Ex hypothesi*, if the *force majeure* clause is applicable there will be no contractual obligation that the promisor will be claiming not to have to perform. Although s. 13(1) of the Act provides that terms which exclude or restrict duties rather than liabilities are also subject to a test of reasonableness, the operation of this section does not extend to s. 3 because it is specifically limited to negligence liability and implied terms in contracts for the sale of goods.

55. In *Atlantic Shipping Ltd.* v. *Louis Dreyfus & Co.* [1922] A.C. 250, 260 Lord Sumner said: "There is no difference in principle between words which save [the defendants] from having to pay at all and words which save them from having to pay as much as they would otherwise have to pay." Any distinction between exclusion clauses and limitation clauses was rejected in Australia in *Darlington Futures Ltd.* v. *Delco Australia Pty. Ltd.* (1987) 61 A.L.J.R. 76, where the High Court preferred to apply a natural and ordinary construction to both types of clause.

56. [1971] 1 W.L.R. 519, 522.

57. [1956] 1 W.L.R. 936.

gation on the party."[58] Only then should the court go on to consider whether the clause provides a defence to a breach of those obligations.

The logic of such an analysis is difficult to defend and depends, as Professor Coote[59] has pointed out, on the possibility of there being "a category of legal, contractual rights which have effect as such despite the intention of the parties that they shall never be enforceable".[60] In his view, exclusion clauses should be seen as defining the extent of the obligation assumed by the promisor to the promisee[61] and treated in the same way as any other term of the contract.[62] Unfortunately, judicial opinion differs on this matter and, although both approaches can be detected in the case law, the current of judicial authority is heavily in favour of the view that exclusion clauses act as a defence to a breach, with only the occasional glimpse of the Coote thesis being accepted.[63]

The position is only slightly clearer when it is *force majeure* clauses which are under consideration. Although both strands of reasoning can again be detected in the case law, the balance of judicial opinion instead favours the view that *force majeure* clauses come within the first of Donaldson J.'s categories; they define the obligation assumed rather than excuse or limit the consequences of breach. For example, Parker L.J., in *J.H. Vantol Ltd.* v. *Fairclough Dodd & Jones Ltd.*[64] said that a *force majeure* clause operated to "prevent what otherwise might be a breach from being a breach".[65]

The only extended discussion of the nature of *force majeure* clauses is that of Kerr J. in *Trade & Transport Inc.* v. *Iino Kaiun Kaisha Ltd.* (*The Angelia*),[66] a case involving the relationship between a *force majeure* clause and the doctrine of fundamental breach.[67] Consistent with the general hostility of the courts to exclusion clauses, the Court of Appeal, in *Harbutt's "Plasticine" Ltd.* v. *Wayne Tank Co. Ltd.*,[68] held that, as a matter of law and not merely of construction, an exclusion

58. *Ibid.*, at p. 940. This statement was admittedly made in the context of a discussion of the now discredited doctrine of fundamental breach described more fully below in the text at fn. 69.
59. *Exception Clauses* (1964).
60. *Ibid.*, at p. 5.
61. As the House of Lords did in *G. H. Renton & Co. Ltd.* v. *Palmyra Trading Corp. of Panama* [1957] A.C. 149.
62. One obvious exception must be clauses which seek not to limit the contractual duty owed by the promisor but to take away rights of action which exist independently of the contract and are not voluntarily assumed. A clause such as that used in *Adler* v. *Dickson* [1955] 1 Q.B. 158, which sought to absolve the carrier from the usual consequences of the tortious conduct of its servants, could in no sense be described as one defining the extent of the obligation assumed by the defendant: the duty to take care in tort, being one imposed by law whether the defendant desires it or not, exists outside of the contract, although the plaintiff's rights may of course be cut down by it. Such a clause does not seek to excuse non-performance but to take away pre-existing rights of action. As such, it should necessarily receive a restrictive interpretation.
63. This difference of approach is to be found in a comparison of the judgments of Lord Diplock and Lord Wilberforce in *Photo Production Ltd.* v. *Securicor Transport Ltd.* [1980] A.C. 827.
64. [1955] 1 W.L.R. 1302.
65. *Ibid.*, at p. 1312. Although the decision of the Court of Appeal in this case was later reversed by the House of Lords ([1957] 1 W.L.R. 136), no doubt was cast on this statement.
66. [1973] 1 W.L.R. 210. The decision was subsequently overruled by the House of Lords in *The Nema* [1982] A.C. 724 but on a point not relevant to the discussion.
67. It should also be remarked that Donaldson J.'s tripartite classification in *Kenyon, Son & Craven Ltd.* v. *Baxter Hoare & Co. Ltd.* [1971] 1 W.L.R. 519 referred to above was made at a time when the doctrine of fundamental breach was binding on him and forms part of a valiant attempt to reconcile the conflicting views of the House of Lords and the Court of Appeal on the subject.
68. [1970] 1 Q.B. 447.

clause, no matter how widely drafted, could never apply to exempt a promisor from liability for a fundamental breach of contract. This erroneous notion has since been corrected,[69] but when *The Angelia* was decided in 1973 it still had some currency.[70] In that case the plaintiff shipowners chartered a ship, the *Angelia*, to the defendants to carry phosphate from the port of Eilat in Israel to Japan. By clause 2 of the charterparty

> "... shortage of cars, wagons ... or other unavoidable hindrances in mining, transporting, loading, discharging or receiving the phosphate ... and any other causes or hindrances happening without the fault of the charterer, shippers or suppliers of cargo, preventing or delaying the mining, supplying, loading, discharging or receiving of the cargo are excepted and neither charterer nor shippers shall be liable for any loss or damage resulting from any such excepted causes and time lost by reason thereof shall not count as lay days or days on demurrage ..."

Because of a road transport strike in Israel which was beyond the control of the charterer, it was not possible to transport the phosphate to the intended port of shipment. Upon discovering the difficulties, the charterer cabled the shipowner purporting to cancel the charterparty. The shipowner accepted the cancellation but reserved its claim for damages for wrongful repudiation. The charterers relied, *inter alia*, on clause 2 of the charterparty but the shipowner claimed that it could not apply so as to protect the charterer from what was claimed to be a fundamental breach of contract *scil.*, the failure to provide a cargo. Kerr J. rejected the shipowner's contention. He said:

> "The charterer's failure to load a cargo at any time could never be a breach, let alone a fundamental breach, if the failure to supply and load a cargo was due to unavoidable hindrances covered by clause 2 of the charterparty. It is an impossible argument, and one which puts the cart before the horse, for the owners to say that the supply of a cargo is prima facie an absolute and fundamental obligation and that they can therefore get rid of clause 2 by treating the charterer's failure to supply a cargo as a repudiatory and fundamental breach, although clause 2 expressly provides that such failure shall be no breach at all if due to unavoidable hindrances. The correct analysis is that under this charterparty the charterers did not undertake an absolute obligation to supply a cargo, but merely the qualified obligation to do so unless prevented by any unavoidable hindrances within clause 2."[71]

69. Only a few years before *Harbutt's "Plasticine"* the House of Lords, in *Suisse Atlantique Société d'Armement Maritime S.A.* v. *Rotterdamsche Kolen Centrale* [1967] 1 A.C. 361, had denied the existence of any such restriction on the parties' freedom of contract. The common law position was clarified only in 1980 when the House of Lords, in *Photo Production Ltd.* v. *Securicor Transport Ltd.* [1980] A.C. 827, reaffirming its judgment in the *Suisse Atlantique* case and overruling the Court of Appeal authority to the contrary, held that there was no rule of law which prevented the parties from excluding liability for a fundamental breach of contract. The rule was merely a rule of construction; in the absence of clear words to the contrary, the court would presume that the parties did not intend an exclusion clause to apply to a situation involving such a serious breach of the contract.

70. Kerr J. recognised the difficulties generated by *Harbutt's "Plasticine"* but as a first instance judge bound to follow the decision of the Court of Appeal he was content to observe, at p. 234, that "the law should be rationalised at a higher level".

71. *Ibid.*, at p. 230. See also the judgment of Bramwell B. in *Jackson* v. *Union Marine Insurance Co. Ltd.* (1874) L.R. 10 C.P. 125, who, at p. 145, said: "The exception is an excuse for him who is to do the act, and operates to save him from an action and make his non-performance not a breach of contract ..." An approach more reminiscent of that of Denning L.J. in *Karsales (Harrow) Ltd.* v. *Wallis* [1956] 1 W.L.R. 936, 940 is that of Donaldson J. in *Thomas Borthwick (Glasgow) Ltd.* v. *Faure Fairclough Ltd.* [1968] 1 Lloyd's Rep. 16, 26, who said that in construing a contract he found it convenient initially to ignore the *force majeure* clause and then to consider whether the clause affected the legal position.

His lordship's analysis of the *force majeure* clause must, however, be treated with some reservation for our purposes. First, it was made in the context of the doctrine of fundamental breach, a doctrine which has now been finally interred: there would today be no need to classify the clause as a duty-defining one for it to be efficacious. Secondly, and more importantly, his lordship elsewhere in his judgment said that the clause was "properly to be described as an exception clause", with the consequence that it must be strictly construed. On the question of construction, therefore, Kerr J. would have made no distinction between an exception clause and a *force majeure* clause.

One method of resolving this issue might be to approach the question inductively and ask how in fact the courts treat *force majeure* clauses: do they apply to them the strict rules of construction reserved for exclusion clauses, and do they place the burden of proof on the promisor to prove that he or she comes within the words of the clause?

(a) Canons of construction

As a preliminary matter, it may be worth summarising briefly the rules of construction applicable to exclusion clauses. The first rule of construction is that in any case of ambiguity the court will adopt the construction which is least favourable to the party relying on the clause.[72] This is known as the *contra proferentem* rule. However, its applicability does not seem to have been canvassed in any reported case involving the construction of a *force majeure* clause, although as we have seen, there are *dicta* in *The Angelia*[73] to the effect that such clauses must be strictly construed.[74] It may be, however, that the *contra proferentem* rule is a general rule of construction, applicable to all ambiguous terms of a contract. This seems to be the approach adopted by Hirst J. in *Kleinwort Benson Ltd.* v. *Malaysia Mining Corp. Bhd.*,[75] in which case a *force majeure* clause should, like any other term of the contract, be construed in such a manner where the words used admit of more than one meaning.

The second rule of construction is concerned with the exclusion of liability for negligence. The presumption is that a contracting party would not consent to the deprivation of his or her expected contractual benefits which resulted from the

72. *Houghton* v. *Trafalgar Insurance* [1954] 1 Q.B. 247; *Hollier* v. *Rambler Motors* (*A.M.C.*) *Ltd.* [1972] 2 Q.B. 71.

73. [1973] 1 W.L.R. 210, 230.

74. See also *Lebeaupin* v. *Richard Crispin & Co.* [1920] 2 K.B. 714, 718, where McCardie J. said of a *force majeure* clause: "If a seller desires to escape from liability in such a case as the present, he must take care to use words of adequate clearness and width . . . The point was cogently put by Lord Macnaghten in *Elderslie Steamship Co.* v. *Borthwick* [1905] A.C. 93, 96, when he said: 'An ambiguous document is no protection.' " There are a number of cases involving alleged exceptions to demurrage where the courts have placed a very strict interpretation on *force majeure* clauses: e.g., *Compania Naviera Aeolus S.A.* v. *Union of India* (*The Spalmatori*) [1964] A.C. 868; *Islamic Republic of Iran Shipping Lines* v. *Ierax Shipping Company of Panama* (*The Forum Craftsman*) [1991] 1 Lloyd's Rep. 81; *Ellis Shipping Corpn.* v. *Voest Alpine Intertrading* (*The Lefthero*) [1992] 2 Lloyd's Rep. 109. But since they concern demurrage, they necessarily concern a party in breach of contract which is looking to exclude its liability for damages. As such they are exclusion clauses and merit the more restrictive interpretation which they receive. They provide no assistance to the question in hand.

75. [1988] 1 All E.R. 714, 722 (overruled on another point [1989] 1 All E.R. 785).

promisor's lack of care.[76] Very stringent requirements need to be satisfied before an exclusion clause will be effective to exclude liability for negligence.[77] At first sight it would appear that the idea of the promisor excluding liability for his or her own negligence is simply inconsistent with the concept of *force majeure*, since we have seen that it only covers events preventing performance which were beyond the control of the promisor. Nevertheless, there are a number of cases where a clause headed "*Force Majeure*" has been held to cover the happening of events within the control of the promisor, thereby necessitating a discussion of the reasonableness of the promisor's conduct.

In *B & S Contracts and Design Ltd.* v. *Victor Green Publications Ltd.*[78] the plaintiff contracted to erect some exhibition stands for the defendant. The plaintiff's workforce, because of a dispute over severance pay, threatened that they would not perform the contract and the defendant, in order to avert this possibility, advanced half the amount in dispute to the plaintiff, though the plaintiff insisted this was not as a part-payment under the contract. The work went ahead but when the plaintiff submitted its bill the defendant deducted the amount previously advanced. When sued for this amount the defendant counterclaimed for restitution of the same amount, arguing that it had been extracted by duress. To this the plaintiff replied that its threat not to perform was not unlawful and that therefore the allegation of duress could not be sustained.[79] It was not unlawful, argued the plaintiff, since what was threatened did not amount to a breach because of a contractual provision in the following form:

> " '*Force Majeure*'
> Every effort will be made to carry out any contract based on an estimate, but the due performance of it is subject to variation or cancellation owing to an act of God, war, strikes, civil commotion, work to rule or go-slow or overtime bans, lock-out, fire, flood, drought or any other cause beyond our control, or owing to our inability to procure materials or articles except at increased prices due to any of the foregoing causes."

The Court of Appeal held that the plaintiff could not rely on the clause because it had not acted reasonably in refusing to pay to its workforce the money demanded by them, which payment could have been facilitated by accepting the defendant's payment as an advance rather than as a gift. This decision has been rightly criticised on the ground of the undesirability of a court pronouncing on the reasonableness of an employer's response to domestic industrial conflict, it being better to construe the clause in the instant case as simply not covering a strike which could have been avoided or settled by the plaintiff, whether by reasonable efforts or otherwise.[80] In

76. *Gillespie Bros Ltd.* v. *Roy Bowles Transport Ltd.* [1973] Q.B. 400.
77. A three-tier test was laid down by Lord Morton of Henryton in *Canada Steamship Lines Ltd* v. *R.* [1952] A.C. 192, 208. If the clause expressly excludes negligence then effect will be given to it. If there is no express reference to negligence the court must consider whether the words are wide enough, in their ordinary meaning, to cover negligence, any doubt on this point being resolved against the party relying on the clause. But even if the words are wide enough for this purpose, they will not be effective to exclude negligence if they could also apply to some other head of damage which is not so fanciful or remote that the promisor cannot be supposed to have desired protection against it.
78. [1984] I.C.R. 419. This case is discussed in detail in Chapter 9 below.
79. It is not of course the case that there is a direct correlation between unlawfulness and illegitimate pressure: *Universe Tankships of Monrovia* v. *International Transport Workers' Federation* (*The Universe Sentinel*) [1983] 1 A.C. 366.
80. Palmer & Catchpole (1985) 48 M.L.R. 102.

light of the fact that the clause was headed "*Force Majeure*" it is submitted that this must be the correct approach.[81]

The reasonableness of the promisor's conduct was also considered relevant in *J. Lauritzen A.S.* v. *Wijsmuller B.V.* (*The Super Servant Two*).[82] The defendants agreed to transport the plaintiffs' oil rig, using at their option either of two self-propelling barges, called *Super Servant One* and *Super Servant Two*. Before the time for performance of the contract, the defendants allocated *Super Servant Two* to the plaintiffs' contract, the other barge being allocated to other concluded contracts. *Super Servant Two* later sank and the plaintiffs' rig was delivered late as a consequence. They claimed damages from the defendants who sought to rely, *inter alia*, on clause 17 of the contract. This entitled the defendants to cancel their performance:

> "in the event of *force majeure*, Acts of God, perils or dangers and accidents of the sea, acts of war, war-like operations, acts of public enemies, restraints of princes, rulers or people or seizure under legal process, quarantine restrictions, civil commotions, blockade, strikes, lockout, closure of the Suez or Panama Canal, congestion of harbours or any other circumstances whatsoever, causing extraordinary periods of delay and similar events and/or circumstances, abnormal increases in prices and wages, scarcity of fuel and similar events, which reasonably may inpede, prevent or delay the performance of this contract."

The question which arose for decision was whether the defendants, focusing on the words "perils or dangers and accidents of the sea", which, in the context of marine insurance, are accepted as including accidents caused by the negligence of the assured himself,[83] could invoke the clause if it was shown that the sinking of *Super Servant Two* was a result of the negligence of either themselves, their servants or their agents. The Court of Appeal held that they could not. Bingham L.J. held that although the clause was not an exception clause it was one which conferred on "one party only a right exercisable in a very wide range of circumstances to nullify the contractual bargain made between the parties at no cost to itself and regardless of the loss which the other party may sustain".[84] To such a clause, said the learned Lord Justice, the broad approach indicated by *Canada Steamship* was appropriate. Applying those rules of construction,[85] Bingham L.J. held that though the words of the clause were wide enough to include the negligence of the defendants, the clause would not be deprived of a sensible application if it were confined to events other than those brought about by the defendants' negligence. His Lordship's extension of the *Canada Steamship* rules to a *force majeure* clause has been described by one commentator as "unfortunate",[86] but it is submitted that if this clause did indeed purport to exempt the defendants from performance when the disabling event was a circumstance within their control then it was not a *force majeure* clause at all. *The Super Servant Two* is not, therefore, authority for the proposition that the rules of construction laid down in *Canada Steamship* are applicable to *force majeure*

81. The reasoning in this case was nevertheless applied by the Court of Appeal in *Channel Island Ferries Ltd.* v. *Sealink U.K. Ltd.* [1988] 1 Lloyd's Rep. 323, although this was because of a concession made at the trial of the action. The proposition made in the text was not argued.
82. [1990] 1 Lloyd's Rep. 1.
83. *Trinder, Anderson & Co.* v. *Thames and Mersey Marine Insurance Co.* [1898] 2 Q.B. 114.
84. [1990] 1 Lloyd's Rep. 1, 7.
85. See fn. 77 above.
86. McKendrick [1990] L.M.C.L.Q. 153, 155.

clauses. Whether the rules should still be applied to exclusion clauses is, of course, another question altogether.

(b) Burden of proof

An answer to the question posited above, whether *force majeure* clauses are treated in the same way as exclusion clauses, might be provided by asking where the burden of proof lies in a case involving a *force majeure* clause.[87] The general rule in English law is that the legal burden of proving all facts essential to his case rests on the plaintiff.[88] Thus, in a claim for damages for breach of contract it will be for the plaintiff to prove that there has in fact been a breach. If, however, the defendant seeks to escape the consequences of his breach by pleading that he is protected by an exception clause, then it will be for him to show that the facts are brought within the exception.[89] If a *force majeure* clause is in truth one which goes merely to defining the extent of the obligation to perform then it will be incumbent on the plaintiff to prove that, in the case of non-performance by the defendant, the obligation to perform has in fact arisen. If, on the other hand, a *force majeure* clause operates as a defence to an action for breach then the burden will be on the defendant to prove that his non-performance is excused by the clause. A survey of the decided cases adopts the latter approach, indicating that, in this respect at least, *force majeure* clauses are no different from exception clauses. Indeed, in *Bremer Handelsgesellschaft m.b.H.* v. *C. Mackprang Jr.*[90] Lord Denning M.R. equated the two types of clause when he said: "If the seller had relied on clause 21 [a prohibition of export clause], on whom is the burden of proof? Plainly the burden is on the seller. At common law a party who relies on an exception clause must prove the facts to support his contention."[91]

Cases in which the court has imposed the burden of proof on the defendant where the contract contains a *force majeure* clause are legion.[92] To take just one example, in *P.J. Van der Zijden* v. *Tucker & Cross*[93] there was a contract for the sale of frozen Chinese rabbits. The contract provided for extension of delivery dates or cancellation in the event that the sellers were unable to deliver by reason of "war, flood, fire, storm, heavy snow or any other causes beyond their control". The sellers were unexpectedly let down by their Chinese supplier but Donaldson J. held

87. For a detailed discussion of the burden of proof of *force majeure* clauses in contracts concerning the sale of goods see *Benjamin's Sale of Goods*, ed. Guest (4th Edn., 1992), para. 8–085.

88. Cross, *Evidence*, ed. Tapper (7th Edn., 1990) pp. 110–159.

89. *The Glendaroch* [1894] P. 226, 231; *The Antwerpen* [1994] 1 Lloyd's Rep. 213, 237–238. Where the plaintiff alleges that the exception clause is inapplicable because of a proviso contained therein it will be for him to show that the proviso applies.

90. [1979] 1 Lloyd's Rep. 221.

91. *Ibid.*, at p. 223.

92. See, for example, *Tradax Export S.A.* v. *André et Cie.* [1976] 1 Lloyd's Rep. 416; *Avimex S.A.* v. *Dewulf & Cie.* [1979] 2 Lloyd's Rep. 57; *André et Cie. S.A.* v. *Ets. Michel Blanc et Fils* [1979] 2 Lloyd's Rep. 427; *Bunge S.A.* v. *Deutsche Conti Handelsgesellschaft m.b.H.* [1979] 2 Lloyd's Rep. 435; *Continental Grain Export Corp.* v. *S.T.M. Grain Ltd.* [1979] 2 Lloyd's Rep. 460; *Toepfer* v. *Schwarze* [1980] 1 Lloyd's Rep. 385; *Thomas P. Gonzalez Corp.* v. *Muller's Muhle, Muller G.m.b.H.* [1980] 1 Lloyd's Rep. 445; *Tradax Export S.A.* v. *Cook Industries Inc.* [1981] 1 Lloyd's Rep. 236. In *Channel Island Ferries* v. *Sealink U.K. Ltd.* [1988] 1 Lloyd's Rep. 323 the point was conceded by counsel for the defendants.

93. [1975] 2 Lloyd's Rep. 240.

that they could not rely on the protective clause because they had failed to prove that it was impossible for them to acquire the goods from another source.[94]

It may be argued, however, that, as a matter of policy, it is right to place the burden of proof on the person seeking to rely on a *force majeure* clause. Where a promise is not performed, the plaintiff will more often than not have no knowledge of the facts which prevent performance. Nor would the plaintiff have the means of discovering the true state of affairs. Knowledge of the circumstances which prevent the defendant from performing will in many cases be peculiar to the defendant. In such circumstances it is not unjust to place on the defendant the burden of proving that he falls within the terms of the *force majeure* clause.[95] The same approach has been taken in bailment cases, such as *Levison* v. *Patent Steam Cleaning Co. Ltd.*,[96] where goods which are entrusted to the bailee undamaged are returned damaged. Where the bailee tries to rely on an exclusion clause in the contract but the bailor alleges a fundamental breach then the burden is on the bailee to show that the goods were not damaged by a breach so serious as to fall outside the scope of the exception clause.

5. CONCLUSION

We have been concerned to discover the way in which *force majeure* clauses are interpreted by the courts, our task being to ask whether they are treated as if they were like any other term of the contract or whether they are properly classified as exclusion clauses and interpreted in a restrictive manner. We also noted that, whatever the answer to that question might be, the courts are presently adopting a more generous approach to the construction of exclusion clauses generally and are less willing than in the past to search for strained constructions by which their application to relieve the promisor can be avoided.

We might summarise our conclusions as follows:

1. *Force majeure* clauses, it seems, go to limit the extent of the obligation assumed by the promisor. They do not operate so as to shield a promisor from liability for a breach of contract. A *force majeure* clause will ensure that non-performance is no breach because no performance was due in the circumstances which have occurred.
2. Since *force majeure* clauses do not exclude or restrict liability, they are not subject to the statutory requirement of reasonableness under the Unfair Contract Terms Act 1977.
3. Although the evidence is scanty, it would appear that *force majeure* clauses properly so called are not given the strained construction previously reserved for exclusion clauses. There is no case in which the *contra proferentem* rule has been applied to a *force majeure* clause, and the one case in which the *Canada Steamship* rules of construction were applied did not

94. This result can be avoided by careful drafting, as was the case in *European Grain & Shipping* v. *J. H. Rayner & Co.* [1970] 2 Lloyd's Rep. 239.
95. Palmer, *Bailment*, (2nd Edn., 1991) 1552–1557; Treitel, *op. cit.*, 222–223.
96. [1978] Q.B. 68.

involve a *force majeure* clause properly so called. However, judicial opinion on this subject is divided.

4. The burden of proving the applicability of a *force majeure* clause rests on the party seeking to invoke it and not, as is the case with the generality of contractual terms, on the party alleging a breach. Although this seems to indicate that *force majeure* clauses are no different from exception clauses, it may be explained as a decision of policy, analogous with the case law on proof of fundamental breach.[97]

WILLIAM SWADLING

97. Ewan McKendrick and Norman Palmer kindly read and made helpful comments on an earlier draft of this chapter. They of course bear no responsiblity for any errors which remain.

CHAPTER 2

FORCE MAJEURE IN FRENCH LAW

1. INTRODUCTION

Whereas *force majeure* as a concept exists in the common law only to the extent that it is imported into a contract by the parties,[1] it plays a central part (together with the related concepts of *cause étrangère* and *cas fortuit*[2]) in the structure of both contractual and delictual liability in French law. It derives from the Roman law term *vis maior*, mediated through the centuries of doctrinal commentary. In the Roman texts its function is to set a limit to the strict liability imposed on certain bailees (to use the common law term) or their equivalent in the case of land. Thus we are told that the strict liability of ships' captains for goods entrusted to them did not extend to losses resulting from shipwreck or seizure by pirates and that the same was true of the liability of innkeepers and stablekeepers for any *vis maior* which occurred on their premises.[3] Here the meaning of the term emerges by inference from the illustration, but elsewhere in the handful of texts in which the term occurs the meaning is left undefined.[4]

The term *force majeure* is likewise undefined where it occurs in the French Civil Code. There is nothing unusual in this, however. The Code is not given to definitions and indeed French statutes generally lack that common feature of English statutes, the definition section. In French legislation the meaning of a term is commonly left to be worked out by *doctrine* and the courts. The results of this working out in the case of *force majeure* are examined below. We must first consider its function.

2. FUNCTION OF FORCE MAJEURE

The function of *force majeure* is essentially the same as it was in Roman law. It sets a limit to strict liability. French law inherited from Roman law the premise that contractual liability was, apart from some exceptional cases of strict liability such as those mentioned above, based on fault. It was only in those exceptional cases that

1. Or in statutory material, cf. McKendrick, *Force Majeure and Frustration of Contract* (1st Edn., 1991), p. 8, fn. 33.
2. See below, p. 23.
3. Dig. 4.9.3.1.
4. In Dig. 19.2.25.6 Gaius says that the corresponding Greek term is "the force of God", which might suggest that it was confined to events occurring without human intervention, but the example of seizure by pirates shows that this was not so.

force majeure could be relevant, since in the ordinary situation all that was necessary to exclude liability was absence of fault. What has changed in the modern law is the range of the situations in which strict liability (i.e. liability subject to the limit of *force majeure*) occurs. We are no longer concerned just with bailments and the like. The law has come to recognise in this connection two broad categories of obligation to which a contract can give rise.[5] In the case of what are called *obligations de moyens* the party in question is obliged only to exercise reasonable care, not to achieve a particular result. The familiar example is that of the doctor, who is obliged to take reasonable steps to cure his patient but is not liable if nevertheless he fails to do so. In the case of what are called *obligations de résultat*, however, the party is obliged not simply to show due diligence, but to achieve the result envisaged. If he fails to do so, he is liable in damages. Thus it has long been settled that a contract for the carriage of goods or persons obliges the transporter to carry the goods or persons safely to the destination. The obligation is not, however, absolute. The party obliged will be exempt from liability if he can show *force majeure*.[6]

The essential difference between the two categories of obligation lies in the burden of proof. In both cases the burden of showing that the party obliged has not performed his obligation lies of course with the other party. Where the obligation in question is *de moyens*, he must prove failure to show due care, i.e. fault,[7] but where the obligation is *de résultat*, he has only to show that the result has not been achieved. It is then for the party obliged to prove *force majeure*. The difference between the two burdens becomes crucial when the cause of the failure to achieve the result is unknown.

It is important for the common lawyer, who thinks in terms of frustration, to notice that the classification is one of obligations, not of contracts. A single contract will commonly give rise to a number of obligations. To take a simple example, a restaurateur is under *obligations de moyens* in regard to the safety of the premises or the safe-keeping of coats left in the cloakroom,[8] or the gastronomic quality of the food he serves, but under an *obligation de résultat* to ensure that the food does not endanger the client's health. In large commercial contracts the number of obligations will obviously be much larger. It is from liability for non-performance of the particular obligation in question that *force majeure* provides exemption. It is only where the performance of the particular obligation or obligations is essential to the performance of the contract as a whole that we can talk of *force majeure* as terminating the contract.[9]

It should likewise be noted that *force majeure* may have only a partial or temporary effect on the obligation and in such a case will provide only a partial or temporary exemption.[10]

5. What follows is no more than an outline. The matter is in detail more complex. See Nicholas, *French Law of Contract* (2nd Edn., 1992) pp. 49–56.

6. There is a category of what may be called absolute obligations in which not even *force majeure* will give exemption. The simplest examples of such obligations can be found in the seller's statutory guarantees against latent defects and against eviction.

7. Of course the circumstances may raise a presumption of fault, which will shift on to the party obliged the burden of showing no fault, but the question is still one of fault, not of proving *force majeure*.

8. The strict liability in this matter referred to above is confined to hotel-keepers.

9. See further the section on the consequences of *force majeure*, below, pp. 26–27.

10. See below, p. 26.

We are here concerned only with the law of contract, but the concept of *force majeure* is not so confined. In its thinking French law makes a much less sharp distinction than does English law between contract and delict or tort. This is partly because it gives prominence to the overarching category of obligations, of which contract and delict are the principal sources. We have seen that *force majeure* serves to set a limit to strict liability for non-performance of an obligation and this is true of delictual obligations as well as contractual. Over the last 100 years the courts have created out of a few lines in the Civil Code[11] a wide area of strict liability for "things which one has under one's control (*sous sa garde*)" and have applied to this liability the limit of *force majeure*. The relevance of this for our purposes here is that decisions of the courts in cases of delict have helped to fill out the meaning of this limit.

3. MEANING OF FORCE MAJEURE

As far as the Civil Code is concerned, the law of *force majeure* has been founded on two articles (which occur in the section entitled "Of damages for non-performance of the obligation"):

> "1147. The debtor is condemned, where appropriate, to the payment of damages, whether for non-performance of the obligation or for delay in its performance, whenever he does not show that the failure to perform derives from an extraneous cause (*cause étrangère*) which cannot be imputed to him, even though there is no bad faith on his part.
>
> 1148. There is no place for any damages when, as a result of a *force majeure* or an accident (*cas fortuit*), the debtor has been prevented from conveying or doing that to which he was obliged or has done what was forbidden to him."

It will be noted that both articles use the term "debtor". This is not confined, as in English law, to a person who owes a money debt, but denotes a person who is under an obligation of any kind. This is normal French legal usage, for which we have no counterpart, and it is used in what follows. The correlative term for the person who is entitled to the performance of the obligation is "creditor".

These articles are regarded as applying to *obligations de résultat*,[12] i.e. to cases of strict liability. They introduce, alongside *force majeure*, two other concepts, *cause étrangère* and *cas fortuit*. Article 1147 is treated as the more general statement, expressed in terms of causation[13] and requiring the debtor to show that the non-performance has a cause which is extraneous to him and for which he is not responsible. Article 1148 appears to give two instances of such a *cause étrangère*, but it is now agreed that no useful distinction can be made between *force majeure* and *cas fortuit* and the former term is almost exclusively used. It does not, however, embrace all forms of *cause étrangère*. It is usual to identify in addition (a) an act of a third party which makes performance impossible and (b) an act or fault of the creditor. Both, however, are governed by the same principles and both (except in so far as legislation may be seen as the act of a third party) are more important in the field

11. Art. 1384.1.
12. Art. 1137, which is formulated in terms of a duty of care, i.e. of fault, is regarded as the basis for *obligations de moyens*; see further, Nicholas, *op.* and *loc. cit.* (above, fn. 5).
13. As always, this gives rise to debate, but lies outside our present scope.

of delict than that of contract. In what follows we shall therefore deal with the general concept of *force majeure*.

The central principles which have been recognised by the courts are that in order to constitute *force majeure* an event (to use a neutral term) must have been (a) irresistible, (b) unforeseeable, and (c) external to the debtor, and must (d) have made performance impossible and not merely more onerous or difficult.

(a) Irresistibility

This applies both to the event and to its consequences and embraces the requirement that they should also have been unavoidable and insurmountable. So in the case of a contract for the delivery of goods which would normally travel by sea, a strike[14] which the debtor could not prevent will satisfy the requirement of irresistibility, but if it is possible to use air transport, there is no *force majeure* (assuming, of course, that the contract does not specify sea transport as the only means to be used).[15] The criterion to be applied is abstract or objective in the sense that a reasonable person could not, in the circumstances in which the event occurred, have resisted or surmounted the obstacle.

(b) Unforeseeability

Little, if anything, is abstractly unforeseeable and therefore to require that the category of event in question (a fire, a hurricane, a strike, legislation) should be unforeseeable in any circumstances would risk converting strict liability into absolute liability. The test which is applied is that the event must have been unforeseeable by a reasonable person at the time of the contract and in the circumstances in which it was made. Administrative delay in the granting of a building permit has been held to be foreseeable,[16] but the order to evacuate in 1940, which caused a garage-owner to leave behind the plaintiff's car, was not.[17]

(c) Externality

This requirement has its primary application in cases of delict, where the defendant cannot escape liability for a thing *sous sa garde* by showing, for example, that the damage was caused by an irresistible and unforeseeable defect in the thing itself. To allow him to do so would drastically curtail the scope of the liability. The same applies to cases of contractual liability in which the cause of the non-performance resides in a thing within the control of the debtor. So a restaurateur who served infected turbot could not plead that the presence of an unforeseeable and insurmountable bacillus constituted *force majeure*.[18] But it is difficult to say how far the requirement applies to cases in which the cause of the non-performance resides in a person. Illness of the debtor himself has been held to constitute *force majeure* where personal performance is essential (a playwright unable to deliver a script in

14. On the problems posed by strikes see below, pp. 25–26.
15. Com. 12.11.1969, J.C.P. 1971.II.16791.
16. Com. 26.10.1954, D.1955.213.
17. Civ.22.12.1954, D.1955.252.
18. Poitiers 16.12.1970, Gaz.Pal. 1971.264.

time because of acute toothache and the resulting dental operation[19]) but, in general, illness is to be foreseen and provided against (e.g. failure to pay the premium on an insurance policy because of a stroke[20]). In general, the fact that the non-performance is due to the fault of persons acting on behalf of the debtor cannot constitute *force majeure*. So the owners of a ship were liable for loss caused by the crew's forcibly taking over the ship. But the considerable number of cases in which strikes were pleaded as constituting *force majeure* causes difficulty. They are considered below.[21]

(d) Impossibility

The principle has been laid down many times[22] that "*force majeure* refers to events which make performance impossible, not to those which only make it more onerous". There is, therefore, no room for a doctrine of frustration[23] or, in American terms, impracticability, or for the German concepts of economic impossibility or disappearance of the basis of the transaction. This narrow principle has in general been rigorously applied, even in the aftermath of the two world wars (though in both cases the legislator intervened to mitigate some of the harshest consequences). Individual decisions may, however, surprise the observer. So a plea of *force majeure* was upheld where a buyer had contracted to collect a quantity of wine from the seller "by the end of February", but found, when he tried to do so during the last three days of the month, that all roads were impassable owing to "diluvian rain" (which was held, surprisingly, to have been unforeseeable).[24] Moreover, there is room for some proportionality in assessing impossibility. While one can be required to exhaust one's fortune to perform a contract, one is not usually required to endanger one's life.[25] So in a nineteenth century case[26] a typhoid epidemic in a town in which an actor had undertaken to appear was held to constitute *force majeure*. More surprisingly, a recent decision of the Paris Court of Appeal upheld a decision that the owner of a cinema who had undertaken to let it for a showing of Jewish films could rely on the danger of a terrorist attack.[27]

4. CAN A STRIKE CONSTITUTE FORCE MAJEURE?

The question whether a strike by the debtor's employees can constitute *force majeure* (a question on which the decisions of the courts have not been consistent) illustrates some of the difficulties in the practical application of the requirements

19. Paris 7.1.1910, D.1910.2.292.
20. Req.15.6.1911, D.P.1912.1.181.
21. Pp. 25–26.
22. E.g. Civ.4.8.1915, S.1916.1.17, D.1916.1.22; Com.18.1.1950, D.1950.227.
23. For *imprévision* in contracts governed by public law see below, pp. 28–29.
24. Req. 28.11.1934, S.1935.1.105.
25. See also the cases in the text below, at fn. 37.
26. Trib. civ. Seine 17.4.1869, D.P.1869.5.221.
27. Paris 14.3.1990, S.1990 IR 84.

which have been outlined in the preceding section. The question raises issues of (a) foreseeability, (b) resistibility and (c) externality.

(a) It can be said that strikes are always foreseeable and therefore that a strike can never constitute *force majeure* and this was at one time the position of the Cour de Cassation,[28] but now it seems that the test is whether a strike on the particular issue was foreseeable when the contract was made.[29] So, in one of a series of cases arising out of strikes against the nationalised *Électricité de France* in 1977 and 1978, it was held that a strike on pay was not foreseeable because several years before the contract was made the government had agreed on a formula for maintaining pay rates and its decision to abandon this formula was not foreseeable.[30]

(b) Where the issue in a strike is within the control of the parties, i.e. does not require the participation of a third party and in particular of the government, it would seem that the dispute can always be settled at a price and the question whether the price is too high is hardly one for the courts. On the other hand, in the same *Électricité de France* case, it was held that the strike was irresistible because the government (which in law was a third party) had sole power to fix pay rates. As a matter of policy the objection has been made that this makes the private sector (in the particular case the plaintiffs were some 4,500 small and medium-sized firms) carry the burden of a decision of the government.[31]

(c) In none of the cases is there a satisfactory reply to the objection that the strikers were employees of the debtor and therefore not external.

5. CONSEQUENCES OF FORCE MAJEURE

As we have seen,[32] articles 1147 and 1148 of the Civil Code say that *force majeure* exempts the debtor from damages. This exemption may, of course, be only partial or temporary. So *Électricité de France* has pleaded *force majeure* as justifying particular interruptions of supply caused by violent storms, objects thrown across the lines etc.[33] Such a plea for exemption from damages has no effect on the continuing existence of the contract.

If, however, *force majeure* makes performance of the obligation or obligations in question wholly and permanently impossible, there is also another consequence. French law shares with all other civil law systems the principle, which the common law does not accept, that an obligation to do the impossible is void (*impossibilium nulla obligatio*).[34] Where therefore the obligation or obligations are essential to the debtor's performance as a whole, the contract itself should necessarily be void[35] and restitution should follow automatically, without recourse to the courts. This is

28. Civ.7.3.66, J.C.P.1966.II.14878.
29. Ch. mixte 4.2.1983, J.C.P.1983.IV.123, D.1984.I.R.165.
30. Paris 4.6.80, J.C.P.1980.II.19411.
31. Cornu (1981) Rev. trim. de droit civ. 171; Viney, *Droit social* (1983) 627.
32. Above, p. 23.
33. Mestre (1991) Rev. trim. de droit civ. 659.
34. The Civil Code contains no explicit statement of the principle, but there are various particular applications (arts. 1722, 1741, 1788, 1790).
35. For the reason of principle for this and for further explanation of what follows see Nicholas, *op. cit.*, above, fn. 5, at pp. 205–208.

the position of principle, but the courts take a different line. They treat the case as, in common law terms, one of breach. They do so because this permits them to introduce a large element of flexibility. Since French law, unlike the common law, does not recognise rescission by the act of a party alone, the creditor must have recourse to a court. And the court, in reaching its decision, has a wide discretion, in this case as in ordinary cases of breach, to grant or not to grant rescission. Where, for example, the contract has been performed in part before the *force majeure* supervenes, or where the *force majeure* does not wholly or permanently prevent performance, the court may indeed rescind the contract and order restitution, but it may also refuse to do so. Of course articles 1147 and 1148 debar it from awarding damages, but it can reduce or vary the creditor's obligation in order to take account of the reduced obligation of the debtor. Moreover, the question whether the effect of the *force majeure* is partial or temporary is one of fact and therefore not subject to review by the Court of Cassation. This introduces a considerable element of flexibility into the apparent rigour or rigidity of the rules of *force majeure*.

For example, where the plaintiff had taken advertising space on an illuminated pillar in a railway station under a long-term contract and on the outbreak of war in 1939 the pillar had to be blacked out at night, the Paris Court of Appeal held that *force majeure* had made performance partially impossible and ordered a reduction of 20 per cent in the amount paid by the plaintiff.[36]

Moreover, the power to vary can be even more extensive than this. There have been a number of cases arising out of a special form of annuity which has been not uncommon in rural France. A party, usually old or disabled, transfers his land to another in return for an undertaking to provide board, lodging and care for the remainder of the transferor's life. The likelihood of friction between the parties to such an arrangement is obvious. Where the courts have found that such friction has made performance of the contract impossible, they have been willing, while rejecting the beneficiary's claim for rescission, to substitute for the other party's obligation of care the payment of a monetary annuity.[37] In these cases the flexibility of the remedy is matched by that of the meaning given to "impossibility". It should be added, however, that since the human problems presented are peculiar, it would be rash to argue by analogy from them to more impersonal business contracts.

The courts' use of the remedy of rescission, contrary to principle though it is, has, therefore, considerable advantages. But it also has a disadvantage. Rescission, if granted, is retrospective to the beginning of the contract. This has the corollary that restitution must be made of benefits received by each party. This, though it may be satisfactory in cases of breach, may be inadequate in cases of non-performance because of *force majeure*. If, for example, one party has incurred expense when total impossibility supervenes, but the other has not yet received any benefit, a simply restitutionary remedy is plainly inequitable. Problems such as this, which are to some extent provided for in English law in the Law Reform (Frustrated Contracts) Act 1943, seem to have attracted no attention in French law. The narrower scope of the doctrine of impossibility does, of course, reduce their practical importance.

36. Paris 13.11.1943, Gaz. Pal. 1943.2.260.
37. Civ. 8.1.1980, D. 1983.307; Civ. 27.11.1950, Gaz. Pal. 1951.1.132; Civ. 6.4.1960, D.1960.629.

6. IMPRÉVISION

The statement made above[38] that French law has nothing to correspond to frustration or impracticability or economic impossibility needs a limited qualification. It is strictly true only of private law contracts.

French law makes a fundamental distinction between public law and private law, which constitute two separate systems, applied by two totally distinct hierarchies of courts.[39] We are here concerned only with the application of the distinction to contracts. The identification of the contracts which are subject to the jurisdiction of the public (or administrative) courts is a matter of considerable complexity and some controversy, but for our purposes it is sufficient to say that the first essential is that one of the parties must be a public body or at least a body providing a public service and the other (private) party must contract to provide such a service. In general the administrative courts apply to public contracts the law of the Civil Code, as applied by the ordinary courts, though with special rules to take account, for example, of the need for public contracts to be duly authorised. The most important differentiating features derive from the need to secure the overriding purpose of all administrative law, which is to ensure the supremacy of the public interest. In the contractual context this means that the rights of the private party, even if they are embodied in the terms of the contract, may not stand in the way of the public interest. The administration may unilaterally modify or abrogate the contract if that is necessary to protect the public interest (and the power to do so will in fact often be expressly stated in the contract). The administration must, however, compensate the private party for any loss which he suffers by the overriding of his rights.

Finally, it is a characteristic of the whole of administrative law that the administration has the privilege of enforcement by executive act, without recourse to the courts (*exécution d'office*). It can take whatever steps are necessary to enforce or supervise the contract, without invoking the assistance of the courts. The private party can take the matter to the administrative courts (which, however, lack the power to grant an interlocutory injunction), but the administration is never the plaintiff.

It is against this background that the principle of *imprévision* was developed. If supervening circumstances make performance of the contract gravely uneconomic for the private party and the administration insists on continuing performance, the private party may go to the administrative court. If the court decides that it is necessary in the public interest that the contract should continue to be performed, it will order that the party be indemnified against the additional cost which he incurs. The principle was finally established by a decision in 1916.[40] The facts were that in 1904 the City of Bordeaux had contracted with a company for the provision of gas-lighting in the streets, the price to be paid for the gas being fixed in the contract. As a result of the overrunning by the Germans in 1914 of a large part of the French coalfields, the price of coal rose steeply (by the time of the hearing it had increased fourfold in 20 months). The company therefore faced collapse, with the

38. P. 25.

39. See Nicholas, *op cit.* (above, fn. 5) pp. 23–27 and (for *imprévision*) pp. 208–210; L.N. Brown and J.S. Bell *French Administrative Law* (4th Edn., 1993) 192–201.

40. C.E. 30.3.1916, S.1916.3.17, D.1916.3.25.

consequence that the streets would be unlit. The court took the view that it was not in the public interest that this should happen and ruled therefore that the company should continue to perform the contract and that an appropriate indemnity should be paid. The question to be asked was not whether performance had become impossible, but whether the "economy of the contract" had been overthrown.

It is possible to draw an analogy between *imprévision* and the English doctrine of frustration, but it is a very superficial one. The foundation of *imprévision* is the need to protect the public interest, a need which is not usually found in ordinary commercial contracts and one which in any event a court would hardly be justified in meeting at the expense of one of the parties.

7. COMPARISON WITH ENGLISH LAW

If one were to seek an exact parallel in French law to the use of *force majeure* in English law, one would need to know how far the words occur in the express terms of French contracts. No doubt they will be found in international contracts drafted in France,[41] but that throws no light on specifically French practice. I have not found any decisions involving *force majeure* clauses in French domestic contracts, but this is not surprising, for several reasons. Such a clause would be superfluous in view of the express provisions in articles 1147 and 1148 of the Civil Code. French draftsmen do not, on the whole, adopt the elaborate belt-and-braces style of drafting sometimes favoured in common law jurisdictions. They draft their contracts against the background of the Civil Code and associated legislation, which provides a framework both of general principles and of particular rules applicable to specific types of contract.[42]

Moreover, the interpretation of the terms of a contract is a matter of fact outside the control of the Court of Cassation which therefore cannot rule on the meaning even of widely adopted standard terms. Again, a court may not, formally at least, rely on a decision by another court as to the meaning of a term before it.[43]

One may more profitably ask what parallel there is in English law for the French use of *force majeure* as a limit on strict liability. French law, as we have seen, starts from fault liability as the norm, with strict liability subject to *force majeure* as the occasional exception, and moves to a position in which each form of liability is recognised to have its appropriate place. English law, by contrast, is normally assumed to have started with absolute liability, subject to no limit, and to have moved only after *Taylor* v. *Caldwell*[44] to a position of strict liability up to the limit of frustration. It is now, however, generally accepted that the picture of universal absolute liability can never have been entirely correct,[45] at least in cases where performance becomes illegal after the contract is made or the contract requires performance by the promisor himself and he dies or is incapacitated. In cases such as these the liability is not absolute, but strict, in that the supervening impossibility

41. M. Fontaine, *Droit des Contrats Internationaux: Analyse et Rédaction des Clauses* (1989) collects a number of examples, but without indication of origin.
42. See further Nicholas, *op cit.* (above, fn. 5) pp. 56–58.
43. On all this see Nicholas, *op cit.* (above fn. 5) at pp. 48–49 and 15 n. 30.
44. (1863) 3 B. & S. 826.
45. Treitel, *The Law of Contract* (8th Edn.) p. 763; Farnsworth, *Contracts* (1991) §9.5.

exempts the promisor from liability. There is, in French terms, an *obligation de résultat*.

Moreover, there are other situations which cannot at any time have given rise to even strict liability. In the paradigm instance of the *obligation de moyens*, the doctor's obligation to his patient, it was long ago clear that in English law also the doctor's duty was only to exercise reasonable skill and care[46] and the same was declared to be true of "a skilled labourer, artizan or artist", such as "an apothecary, a watchmaker, or an attorney".[47] The instrument used to achieve this result was the characteristic common law device of the implied term,[48] applied casuistically, whereas French law proceeds by establishing a rule which applies to categories of contract. The practical result, however, is similar. The liability is for fault.

The same device was employed to justify the limit established in cases of strict liability. The leading case before *Taylor* v. *Caldwell*[49] was *Hall* v. *Wright*,[50] in which the plaintiff contended that the defendant had failed to perform a promise to marry her within a reasonable time. The case turned on the defendant's plea that he was now affected by a dangerous disease which made him incapable of marrying without great danger to his life. There was a majority of four to three for the plaintiff in the Exchequer Chamber, but in the present context the important judgments are those of Pollock C.B. and Bramwell B., both of whom were in the minority and both of whom spoke in terms of an implied exception or excuse which relieved the promisor from liability.[51] In French terms the promisor's obligation was *de résultat* and the risk to his life constituted *force majeure*, which excused him or exempted him from liability in damages.[52]

It was the judgment of Blackburn J. in *Taylor* v. *Caldwell*[53] which diverted the stream of English law. He retained indeed the language of excuses, but in place of an implied term which limits the promisor's liability for the breach which has occurred he introduced the device of an implied term which automatically terminates the whole contract.[54]

Of course, in most cases the difference between the two approaches is without practical importance, but automatic termination does have the consequence that either party can invoke the frustrating event.[55] More widely, it stunted the development of a doctrine of excuses to parallel those based on *force majeure* in French law. A particular consequence is the discomfort in which English law finds itself when faced with partial impossibility, i.e. impossibility which affects only one of the

46. *Lauphier* v. *Phipos* (1838) 8 C. & P. 475.

47. *Harmer* v. *Cornelius* (1858) 5 C.B. N.S. 236 *per* Willes J.; cf. *Smith* v. *Bush* [1990] A.C. 831, 843 *per* Lord Templeman.

48. Nicholas, "Rules and Terms—Civil Law and Common Law", 48 Tul. L.R. (1974) 946ff; *id.* "Fault and Breach of Contract" in Beatson and Friedmann (eds.), *Good Faith and Fault in Contract Law* (1995, Oxford).

49. (1863) 3 B. & S. 826.

50. (1858) 3 B. & E. 746.

51. For more detailed discussion see Nicholas (above, fn. 48) at pp. 962–965.

52. Cf. above, text at fn. 25.

53. (1863) 3 B. & S. 826.

54. For an examination of the confusions which led to this see Nicholas (above, fn. 48), pp. 959–966.

55. Treitel, *op. cit.* (above, fn. 45) p. 808; Nicholas, *op. cit.* (above, fn. 48), pp. 956–957. It should also logically follow that the party whose performance has become impossible is under no duty to inform the other of that fact.

promisor's obligations (not being one which affects the main purpose of the contract so as to satisfy the requirements of frustration).[56]

In short, French law sees impossibility not in terms of the single catastrophic consequence of termination of the contract, but in terms of a doctrine of excuses leading to a considerable flexibility in the powers of the courts to adjust the consequences to the nature of the impossibility.[57] French law has not, however (in principle at least and leaving aside the doctrine of *imprévision*), ventured into the area of frustration. The author of the leading treatise has, however, recently argued that the time has come to embark even on this venture.[58]

BARRY NICHOLAS

56. See, for example, *Chitty on Contracts* (26th Edn.) para. 643; *Eyre* v. *Johnson* [1946] K.B. 481; *Sainsbury* v. *Street* [1972] 1 W.L.R. 834.

57. See above, p. 27.

58. Ghestin, *Traité de droit civil—Les obligations: les effets du contrat* (1992) ss. 302–314.

CHAPTER 3

FORCE MAJEURE AND FRUSTRATION—THEIR RELATIONSHIP AND A COMPARATIVE ASSESSMENT

1. INTRODUCTION

The focus of the opening two chapters has been upon *force majeure*, both in a domestic and a civilian context. To an English contract lawyer this emphasis must appear unusual because English lawyers have traditionally been brought up to believe that *force majeure* is a continental doctrine which is alien to the English common law. English contract law, broadly speaking, employs the doctrine of frustration to do the work which would be done on the continent by *force majeure*. While it is true to say that English law recognises no *doctrine* of *force majeure* as such, it is undoubtedly true that *force majeure clauses* have become an increasingly significant component of many commercial contracts and that such clauses have played an important role in cases which have recently been litigated in the English courts. The question which now arises for consideration is why this should be so.

To some extent it is due to the fact that many international standard form contracts, such as the GAFTA and FOSFA forms, employ the language of *force majeure* and provide for English law as the law applicable to the contract or are subject to arbitration in London.[1] Secondly, *force majeure* is a doctrine which is "alive and vibrant" in EU law and the importance of EU law will undoubtedly increase in the future and have a greater impact upon the drafting of commercial contracts.[2] But the rise in the importance of *force majeure* clauses cannot be attributed solely to international and European factors: there must be some domestic agents at work. The principal domestic factor relates to the scope of the doctrine of frustration. Frustration is a doctrine which operates within very narrow confines in English law: it is difficult to persuade a court to invoke the doctrine, its juridical basis is unclear, and the consequences of its invocation remain, despite the intervention of statute, drastic.

In this chapter we shall seek to assess the relationship between *force majeure* clauses and the doctrine of frustration. We shall commence our analysis by asking whether the presence of a *force majeure* clause in a contract is sufficient of itself to exclude (either in whole or in part) the operation of the doctrine of frustration. We shall then turn to a broader consideration of the advantages which can be obtained by the incorporation into a contract of a suitably drafted *force majeure* clause rather than simply invoke the doctrine of frustration when an unforeseen event occurs

1. Some of these cases are discussed in more detail in Chapter 15.
2. See further Chapter 17.

which makes performance of the contract more onerous or which destroys the basis upon which the parties have contracted.

2. THE RELATIONSHIP BETWEEN FORCE MAJEURE AND FRUSTRATION

The principal question which must be considered here is whether the presence of a *force majeure* clause in a contract is sufficient of itself to exclude the operation of the doctrine of frustration. Such an argument was in fact put to Mocatta J. in the case of *Bremer Handelsgesellschaft m.b.H.* v. *Vanden Avenne-Izegem P.V.B.A.*[3] when it was contended that "there was no room for the doctrine of frustration to apply" because of the elaborate *force majeure* clauses included in the contract. Mocatta J. was of the opinion that there was "much to be said for this submission". In principle one can agree and, indeed, one commentator has stated that it "is perhaps time to take up the suggestion of Mocatta J." and conclude that "if two companies draw up a comprehensive contract complete with *force majeure* clause, then the courts should take them at their word and entirely refuse to apply the doctrine of frustration. Parties strong enough to strike equal bargains should be allowed to do so".[4] Although there may be much to be said for this proposition as a matter of principle, it must be conceded that, as a matter of authority, the presence of a *force majeure* clause in a contract does not, of itself, exclude the operation of the doctrine of frustration.[5] Further, this dictum of Mocatta J. provides very weak support for the proposition that a *force majeure* clause should, of itself, exclude the operation of the doctrine of frustration. This is so for a number of reasons. The first is that "very little" was said about this issue in argument and so the dictum is not grounded in an exhaustive consideration of the authorities or the competing arguments. The second is that the argument was not unequivocally accepted; there was simply "much to be said for it". The third is that reliance was placed by Mocatta J. upon the implied term theory of frustration; the argument being that, in the light of the detailed clauses in the contract, there was no room for the implication of a term that the contract had been frustrated. Yet, as we shall see,[6] the implied term theory has been largely abandoned as an explanation for the doctrine of frustration.

3. EXPRESS PROVISION

So the presence of a *force majeure* clause does not of itself exclude the operation of the doctrine of frustration. But a *force majeure* clause may be relied upon as evidence that the parties have made express provision for the alleged frustrating event or at least that the event was one which was within their reasonable contem-

3. [1977] 1 Lloyd's Rep. 133, at p. 163, *per* Mocatta J.
4. Hedley, "Carriage by Sea—Frustration and Force Majeure" [1990] C.L.J. 209, at p. 211.
5. See, for example, *J. Lauritzen A.S.* v. *Wijsmuller B.V.* (*The Super Servant Two*) [1990] 1 Lloyd's Rep. 1.
6. See pp. 38–39 (below).

plation at the time of entry into the contract. Here the English contract lawyer is on more familiar ground because it is generally accepted that a contract is not frustrated where express provision has been made in the contract for the alleged frustrating event[7] or where the event was foreseen (or was foreseeable) by the parties at the time of entry into the contract.[8] A frustrating event is a supervening, unforeseen event and not an event which has been anticipated in the contract itself.[9]

Although the courts do accept that, supervening illegality apart,[10] express provision for the alleged frustrating event excludes the operation of the doctrine of frustration, they have generally subjected to a narrow interpretation clauses which, it has been alleged, make provision for what would otherwise be a frustrating event.[11] In particular, the mere fact that the contract deals with events of the same general nature as the alleged frustrating event does not mean that the contract deals with every event in that class.

A good example of this restrictive approach is provided by the case of *Metropolitan Water Board* v. *Dick Kerr and Co.*[12] In 1914 contractors agreed to construct a reservoir to be completed within six years. In 1916 the contractors were required by Government Order to stop the work and sell their plant. In these circumstances the contractors claimed that the contract had been frustrated. The Water Board argued that the contract had not been frustrated because express provision had been made in the contract for delay "whatsoever and howsoever occasioned". In the event of "undue delay", they argued, the procedure laid down in the contract was for the contractors to apply to the engineer for an extension of time. The House of Lords rejected the Water Board's argument and held that the contract was frustrated because the delay clause was not intended to apply to such a fundamental change of circumstances. The clause was intended to cover only temporary difficulties; it did not "cover the case in which the interruption is of such a character and duration that it vitally and fundamentally changes the conditions of the contract, and could not possibly have been in the contemplation of the parties to the contract when it was made".[13] Yet, on their ordinary or literal meaning, the words "whatsoever and howsoever occasioned" were apt to cover the delay because they stated that the cause of the delay was irrelevant. On the other hand, the House of Lords regarded it as inherently unlikely that a contractor would promise to complete performance within six years even if it became impossible to do so. The magnitude of the delay was such that the clause could not reasonably have been intended to cover it. On the same reasoning, a clause which makes provision for "strikes" or "wars" may be held not to cover a protracted national strike, such as a general strike,[14] or a war of

7. *Metropolitan Water Board* v. *Dick, Kerr and Co.* [1918] A.C. 119.

8. *Walton Harvey Ltd.* v. *Walker and Homfrays Ltd.* [1931] 1 Ch. 274; cf. *W.J. Tatem Ltd.* v. *Gamboa* [1939] 1 K.B. 132 and *Ocean Tramp Tankers Corporation* v. *V/O Sovfracht (The Eugenia)* [1964] 2 Q.B. 226.

9. *Paal Wilson & Co. A/S* v. *Partenreederei Hannah Blumenthal* (*The Hannah Blumenthal*) [1983] 1 A.C. 854, at p. 909.

10. *Ertel Bieber & Co.* v. *Rio Tinto Co. Ltd.* [1918] A.C. 260.

11. See generally McElroy and Williams *Impossibility of Performance* pp. 204–218; Benjamin's *Sale of Goods* (4th Edn.) paras. 6-046–6-047 and Treitel *The Law of Contract* (8th Edn.) pp. 795–799.

12. [1918] A.C. 119. See also *Acetylene Co. of G.B.* v. *Canada Carbide Co.* (1922) 8 Ll.L.Rep. 456.

13. *Ibid.*, p. 126, *per* Lord Finlay L.C.

14. *The Penelope* [1928] P. 180, although note the doubts expressed by Lord Brandon in *Pioneer Shipping Ltd.* v. *B.T.P. Tioxide Ltd. (The Nema)* [1982] A.C. 724, at p. 754.

the magnitude of the first or second world wars.[15] The courts insist that provision for the event be "full and complete"[16] and, the greater the magnitude of the event, the less likely it is that it will be encompassed within a general clause or even a clause which covers that event "whatsoever and howsoever occasioned".

A further example of this restrictive approach to construction is provided by the *The Playa Larga*.[17] The parties entered into a contract for the sale of bagged Cuban raw sugar. The vendors were a Cuban state trading enterprise and the buyers were a Chilean company, whose major shareholder was a Chilean state trading organisation. After the conclusion of the contract but before deliveries had been completed, there was a coup d'état in Chile and the left-wing government of Dr Allende was overthrown by the military. The response of the Cuban government to the coup d'état was to break off diplomatic relations with Chile and to pass a law (Law 1256) which, in substance, froze all property belonging to Chilean official and semi-official agencies and to judicial persons in which the Chilean state had a direct or indirect interest. This law rendered further performance of the contract illegal by Cuban law. The sellers therefore ceased delivery of the sugar and the buyers claimed damages for breach of contract and for conversion of the goods. The sellers responded by arguing that the contract had been frustrated by the passing of Law 1256 which rendered further performance of the contract illegal. The buyers countered that the contract had not been frustrated, because express provision had been made in rule 120 of their contract for a delay in shipment caused by, *inter alia*, "government intervention". The Court of Appeal rejected the buyers' argument and held that the contract had been frustrated. It was held that rule 120 contemplated a "temporary interruption" and that it was not directed at events which struck at the contract as a whole and rendered further performance by either party "unthinkable".[18] A vital factor which persuaded the court to conclude that rule 120 applied to temporary interruptions was that its effect was to make provision for an extension of the shipping period by 30 days and, if, at the end of the 30 days, the sellers were still unable to deliver, then the buyers were given an option to cancel the contract. Such a provision is obviously more apt to cover a temporary difficulty which may be resolved within 30 days rather than a catastrophic event which immediately renders further performance of the contract "unthinkable".

It is, therefore, extremely difficult, if not impossible, to draft a *force majeure* clause which shuts out the doctrine of frustration completely, because even the widest of clauses may be held not to cover a particular catastrophic event and, further, a *force majeure* clause which makes provision for an extension of time may indicate to the court that the scope of the clause is confined to temporary interruptions in performance. On the other hand, it may yet be possible to argue that, at

15. *Pacific Phosphate Co. Ltd.* v. *Empire Transport Co. Ltd.* (1920) 36 T.L.R. 750; *Coppee* v. *Blagden, Waugh & Co.* (1921) 6 Ll.L.Rep. 319; *Fibrosa Spolka Akcyjna* v. *Fairbairn Lawson Combe Barbour Ltd.* [1943] A.C. 32, at pp. 40–41; *Denny Mott & Dickson Ltd.* v. *James B. Fraser & Co. Ltd.* [1944] A.C. 265, at p. 284.

16. *Bank Line Ltd.* v. *Arthur Capel & Co.* [1919] A.C. 435, at p. 455, *per* Lord Sumner, qualifying the judgment of Bailhache J. in *Admiral Shipping Co. Ltd.* v. *Weidner Hopkins Co.* [1916] 1 K.B. 429, at p. 438. Cases can, however, be found in which provision has been sufficiently full and complete, see *Banck* v. *Bromley* (1920) 37 T.L.R. 71 and *In re Comptoir Commercial Anversois and Power, Son & Co.* [1920] 1 K.B. 681.

17. [1983] 2 Lloyd's Rep. 171.

18. *Ibid.*, p. 189.

least where the parties are of equal bargaining power, the courts should be more prepared to conclude that a clause which expressly covers "delays whatsoever and howsoever occasioned" covers even a delay caused by the most catastrophic of events; in other words, the courts should give up their restrictive rules of construction and subject *force majeure* clauses to a more natural construction.

4. WHY DRAFT A FORCE MAJEURE CLAUSE?

If a *force majeure* clause does not of itself exclude the operation of the doctrine of frustration and if, as the law presently stands, it is subjected to a restrictive interpretation, a question arises as to whether any advantage can be obtained by reliance upon a *force majeure* clause. Why not simply invoke the doctrine of frustration whenever an unforeseen event occurs which renders performance more hazardous than was anticipated at the moment of entry into the contract? The answer to that question lies in the fact that the doctrine of frustration in English law operates within very narrow confines and cannot be invoked simply because contractual performance has become more onerous. To appreciate this point we must now turn to a consideration of the doctrine of frustration.

5. FRUSTRATION—A MODERN DEFINITION

Although the doctrine of frustration is of respectable antiquity, it is nevertheless a doctrine the limits of which are difficult to define. But such a task was recently undertaken by Bingham L.J. (as he then was) in *J. Lauritzen A.S.* v. *Wijsmuller B.V.* (*The Super Servant Two*).[19] He outlined five fundamental "propositions" pertaining to the doctrine of frustration which he held were "established by the highest authority" and were "not open to question".[20] But, as we shall see, each of these propositions gives rise to practical difficulties and the question which we must consider is whether these practical difficulties can be eliminated or reduced by the incorporation into a contract of a suitably drafted *force majeure* clause. We shall set out the five propositions and then consider the difficulties to which they give rise.

The first proposition of Bingham L.J. was that the doctrine of frustration had evolved in an effort to "mitigate the rigour of the common law's insistence on literal performance of absolute promises"[21] and that the object of the doctrine was "to give effect to the demands of justice, to achieve a just and reasonable result, to do what is reasonable and fair, as an expedient to escape from injustice where such would result from enforcement of a contract in its literal terms after a significant change in circumstances".[22] The second proposition was that frustration operates

19. [1990] 1 Lloyd's Rep. 1.

20. *Ibid.*, p. 8.

21. Citing *Hirji Mulji* v. *Cheong Yue Steamship Co. Ltd.* [1926] A.C. 497, at p. 510; *Denny Mott & Dickson Ltd.* v. *James B. Fraser & Co. Ltd.* [1944] A.C. 265, at p. 275; *Joseph Constantine Steamship Line Ltd.* v. *Imperial Smelting Corp. Ltd.* [1942] A.C. 154, at p. 171.

22. Citing *Hirji Mulji* v. *Cheong Yue Steamship Co. Ltd.* [1926] A.C. 497, at p. 510; *Joseph Constantine Steamship Line Ltd.* v. *Imperial Smelting Corp. Ltd.* [1942] A.C. 154, at pp. 183, 193; *National Carriers Ltd.* v. *Panalpina (Northern) Ltd.* [1981] A.C. 675, at p. 701.

to "kill the contract and discharge the parties from further liability under it" and that therefore it cannot be "lightly invoked" but must be kept within "very narrow limits and ought not to be extended".[23] His third proposition was that frustration brings a contract to an end "forthwith, without more and automatically".[24] The fourth proposition was that the "essence of frustration is that it should not be due to the act or election of the party seeking to rely on it"[25] and it must be some "outside event or extraneous change of situation".[26] His final proposition was that a frustrating event must take place "without blame or fault on the side of the party seeking to rely on it".[27] We shall now subject these propositions to closer analysis.

(a) The basis of the doctrine of frustration

The first proposition of Bingham L.J. locates the basis of the doctrine of frustration in the need to give effect to the demands of justice by mitigating the commitment of the law to the literal performance of absolute promises. Such a proposition is not without support in the authorities but it must not be forgotten that the juridical basis of frustration has long been a source of debate.[28] Traditionally, it rested upon the implication of a term into the contract to the effect that, in the circumstances which have occurred, the contract should cease to be binding.[29] But this theory has been criticised on the ground that it "is artificial and often fictitious in its operation, since there would seldom be a genuine common intention to terminate the contract upon the occurrence of the particular event in question"[30] and it has been largely abandoned by the judiciary.[31] The theory which commands most judicial acceptance today was set out by Lord Radcliffe in the following terms:

"frustration occurs whenever the law recognises that, without default of either party, a contractual obligation has become incapable of being performed because the circumstances in which performance is called for would render it a thing radically different from that which

23. Citing *Bank Line Ltd.* v. *Arthur Capel & Co.* [1919] A.C. 435, at p. 459; *Davis Contractors Ltd.* v. *Fareham U.D.C.* [1956] A.C. 696, at pp. 715, 727; *Pioneer Shipping Ltd.* v. *B.T.P. Tioxide Ltd.* (*The Nema*) [1982] A.C. 724, at p. 752.

24. Citing *Hirji Mulji* v. *Cheong Yue Steamship Co. Ltd.* [1926] A.C. 497, at p. 505; *Maritime National Fish Ltd.* v. *Ocean Trawlers Ltd.* [1935] A.C. 524, at p. 527; *Joseph Constantine Steamship Line Ltd.* v. *Imperial Smelting Corp. Ltd.* [1942] A.C. 154, at pp. 163, 170, 171, 187, 200; *Denny Mott & Dickson Ltd.* v. *James B. Fraser & Co. Ltd.* [1944] A.C. 265, at p. 274.

25. Citing *Hirji Mulji* v. *Cheong Yue Steamship Co. Ltd.* [1926] A.C. 497, at p. 510; *Maritime National Fish Ltd.* v. *Ocean Trawlers Ltd.* [1935] A.C. 524, at p. 530; *Denny Mott & Dickson Ltd.* v. *James B. Fraser & Co. Ltd.* [1944] A.C. 265, at p. 274; *Davis Contractors Ltd.* v. *Fareham U.D.C.* [1956] A.C. 696, at p. 729.

26. Citing *Paal Wilson & Co. A/S* v. *Partenreederei Hannah Blumenthal* (*The Hannah Blumenthal*) [1983] 1 A.C. 854, at p. 909.

27. Citing *Bank Line Ltd.* v. *Arthur Capel & Co.* [1919] A.C. 435, at p. 452; *Joseph Constantine Steamship Line Ltd.* v. *Imperial Smelting Corp. Ltd.* [1942] A.C. 154, at p. 171; *Davis Contractors Ltd.* v. *Fareham U.D.C.* [1956] A.C. 696, at p. 729; *The Hannah Blumenthal* [1983] 1 A.C. 854, at pp. 882, 909.

28. See generally McNair, "Frustration of Contract by War" (1940) 56 L.Q.R. 173; Treitel, *The Law of Contract* (8th Edn.) pp. 818–823; *Chitty on Contracts* (27th Edn.) paras. 23-005–23-013.

29. *F.A. Tamplin S.S. Co. Ltd.* v. *Anglo-Mexican Petroleum Products Co. Ltd.* [1916] 2 A.C. 397, at pp. 403–404, *per* Lord Loreburn.

30. *Chitty on Contracts* (27th Edn.) para. 23-007.

31. *Davis Contractors Ltd.* v. *Fareham U.D.C.* [1956] A.C. 696, at p. 728; *National Carriers Ltd.* v. *Panalpina (Northern) Ltd.* [1981] A.C. 675, at p. 687 and *Pioneer Shipping Ltd.* v. *B.T.P. Tioxide Ltd.* (*The Nema*) [1982] A.C. 724, at pp. 751–752.

was undertaken by the contract. *Non haec in foedera veni*. It was not this that I promised to do."[32]

This theory is not based overtly upon the need to do what is "reasonable and fair" in the changed circumstances but rather it focuses upon the construction of the contract and asks whether the contract which the parties made is "on its true construction, wide enough to apply to the new situation; if not, then it is at an end".[33] The difficulties associated with the "just solution" theory advocated by Bingham L.J. are essentially two-fold. The first is that the theory does not "mean that the courts can do what they think just whenever a change of circumstances causes hardship to one party".[34] Secondly, the House of Lords has rejected the proposition that a court has the power at common law to qualify the absolute, literal terms of a promise in order to do what is just and reasonable.[35] Nevertheless, it must be conceded that the just solution theory does have some support in the authorities.

This debate surrounding the theoretical basis of the doctrine probably does not have many important practical consequences but it does make it very difficult to predict when the courts will invoke the doctrine because, if we are not sure of the basis of the doctrine, we are unlikely to be able to predict with any degree of certainty the circumstances in which the courts will invoke it. Uncertainty is therefore inherent in the doctrine of frustration. This uncertainty can, however, be eliminated to a large extent by the incorporation into a contract of a suitably drafted *force majeure* clause. The clause can specify the circumstances in which it is to operate and the role of the court is then reduced to the interpretation of the clause. Of course, difficulties of interpretation may still arise, but at least the parties can limit the enquiry of the court and focus its attention upon the construction of the particular clause at issue rather than upon the vaguer notion of what is "reasonable and fair" in the changed circumstances.

(b) Contexts and contortions—an excursus

Before considering the second of Bingham L.J.'s propositions, it is suggested that some profit can be gained from noting the rather unusual contexts in which frustration has been invoked in recent cases and the resultant contortions in which the courts have had to engage in order to apply orthodox doctrines to unusual fact situations. Two fact situations illustrate this process. The first line of cases concerned agreements to arbitrate which had "gone to sleep" and one party later attempted to revive the arbitration. The essential problem which gave rise to this particular group of cases was that, until the enactment of section 13A of the Arbitration Act 1950 (as inserted by section 102 of the Courts and Legal Services Act 1990), neither the courts nor arbitrators in England had the power to dismiss an arbitration for want of prosecution.[36] In the absence of such a power, the courts were asked to

32. [1956] A.C. 696, at p. 729.

33. *Ibid.*, p. 721, *per* Lord Reid.

34. Treitel, *The Law of Contract* (8th Edn.), pp. 819–820.

35. *British Movietonews Ltd.* v. *London and District Cinemas Ltd.* [1952] A.C. 166, rejecting the radical approach advocated by Lord Denning in the Court of Appeal ([1951] 1 K.B. 190, at p. 202).

36. *Bremer Vulkan Schiffbau und Maschinenfabrik* v. *South India Shipping Corporation* [1981] A.C. 909 and see generally on these cases Mustill and Boyd, *Commercial Arbitration* (2nd Edn.), pp. 503–517.

employ any common law doctrines which appeared even remotely suitable (and some which were manifestly unsuitable) to enable them to reach a commercially just solution, namely that the agreement to arbitrate had been abandoned. Frustration was one of the contractual doctrines[37] which was dredged up in an effort to reach such a solution. But the invocation of frustration foundered on the rule that a frustrating event must be an "outside event or extraneous change of situation".[38] In these cases the delay was caused by the parties themselves and so could not be said to be due to an "outside event" or "extraneous change of situation". The doctrine of frustration probably emerged unscathed from these cases, but it is suggested that there are two principal dangers revealed by this line of authority and their employment of established common law doctrines such as frustration. The first is that they disguise what the courts are really trying to do, namely dismiss an action for want of prosecution.[39] The second is that they may distort well-established principles of the common law.[40]

The second group of cases, which illustrates the second of these dangers more graphically, concerns an employee who is absent from work for a long period of time, for example because of sickness[41] or imprisonment,[42] and in consequence is "dismissed" by his employer. The employee argues that he has been unfairly dismissed. The employer counters that he has not been dismissed because his contract of employment was frustrated by his long absence from work. Now it is important to appreciate why employers have invoked this argument. It is an attempt to evade the clutches of the employment protection legislation, particularly the unfair dismissal legislation, because such legislation applies only to a *dismissal* by the employer; it has no application to frustrated contracts which are terminated, not by the action of the employer, but by *operation of law*. Employees have sought to meet this argument on two principal grounds. The first is to argue that the contract has not been frustrated. The Employment Appeal Tribunal (EAT) has, on

37. Others were repudiatory breach and an agreement to abandon, the agreement being inferred from the silence of both parties.

38. *Paal Wilson & Co. A/S* v. *Partenreederei Hannah Blumenthal* (*The Hannah Blumenthal*) [1983] 1 A.C. 854, see further below pp. 50–52.

39. The problem should not arise in future cases because, as has already been noted, Parliament was eventually persuaded to intervene in the form of s.13A of the Arbitration Act 1950 which gives to an arbitrator, in the absence of a provision to the contrary in the arbitration agreement, the power to make an award dismissing any claim in a dispute referred to him if it appears to him that there has been an inordinate and inexcusable delay on the part of the claimant in pursuing the claim and that the delay will either give rise to a substantial risk that it is not possible to have a fair resolution of the issues in that claim or that it has caused, or is likely to cause or to have caused, serious prejudice to the respondent. The section came into force on 1 January 1992. The House of Lords has held that, in deciding whether or not there has been an inordinate and inexcusable delay, a court may have regard to delay which occurred before the coming into force of the section (*L'Office Cherifien des Phosphates* v. *Yamashita-Shinnihon Steamship Co. Ltd.* [1994] 1 A.C. 486).

40. Although frustration emerged relatively unscathed, this was not the case with the rules of offer and acceptance. For example in *Cie. Française d'Importation et de Distribution S.A.* v. *Deutsche Continental Handelsgesellschaft* [1985] 2 Lloyd's Rep. 592, at p. 599, Bingham J. stated that the proposition that an agreement to abandon an arbitration can be made by silence on both sides does "some violence . . . to familiar rules of contract such as the requirement that acceptance of an offer should be communicated to the offeror unless the requirement of communication is expressly or impliedly waived".

41. See generally *Notcutt* v. *Universal Equipment Co. (London) Ltd.* [1986] 3 All E.R. 582 and the discussion therein of the leading cases.

42. See generally *F.C. Shepherd & Co. Ltd.* v. *Jerrom* [1987] Q.B. 301 and the discussion therein of the leading cases.

occasions, been sympathetic to this argument, aware that the consequence of allowing such a plea to succeed is to enable employers to defeat the aim of the legislation, which is to subject such terminations of the employment relationship to a test of fairness.[43] As Lord Wedderburn has remarked, we can see here the EAT "struggling to free itself of rigid common law doctrines in order to produce what it judges to be a just solution between an individual employee and the employer".[44] But the Court of Appeal, while suggesting that a cautious approach is appropriate, has refused to conclude that frustration has no application to contracts of employment which can be terminated by the employer upon the giving of relatively short notice.[45] The conclusion that an employment contract can, in principle, be frustrated has led to a second argument, particularly in cases where the cause of the absence from work is the imprisonment of the employee. Employees in such cases have argued that the contract is not frustrated because the frustration was "self-induced". It must be conceded that a deliberate act is generally treated by the courts as self-induced frustration[46] but the courts have refused to accede to this argument in this context. This refusal is difficult to reconcile with general principle, but a number of justifications have been offered in its support. The first is the rather specious one that the cause of the employee's absence from work is not his criminal act but the "outside event" of the court sending him to prison.[47] The second is that in these cases it is not the party who has not performed the deliberate act who is invoking self-induced frustration, which is the usual case, it is the party who is responsible for the act who is invoking it.[48] The third and related justification is that the consequence of allowing the plea of self-induced frustration to succeed is to benefit the party putting forward the argument (the employee) by enabling him to bring his claim within the scope of the employment protection legislation when he would not otherwise be able to do so.[49] Finally, Balcombe L.J. has suggested that the doctrine of self-induced frustration may be inappropriate in this context and he indicated that he was prepared to countenance a degree of inconsistency in this respect between employment contracts and other commercial contracts.[50] There is much to be said for this latter approach, treating these cases as *sui generis*, either by excluding frustration and self-induced frustration completely or, as has been done by the EAT, applying them with a strong dose of industrial good sense. But enough

43. See in particular *Harman* v. *Flexible Lamps Ltd.* [1980] I.R.L.R. 418, disapproved in this respect by the Court of Appeal in *Notcutt* v. *Universal Equipment Co. (London) Ltd.* [1986] 3 All E.R. 582, at p. 586.

44. *The Worker and the Law* (3rd Edn.), p. 145, relying upon cases such as *Converfoam Ltd.* v. *Bell* [1981] I.R.L.R. 195; *Chakki* v. *United Yeast Co. Ltd.* [1982] 2 All E.R. 446 and the decision of the EAT (subsequently reversed by the Court of Appeal) in *F.C. Shepherd & Co. Ltd.* v. *Jerrom* [1985] I.C.R. 552.

45. *Notcutt* v. *Universal Equipment Co. (London) Ltd.* [1986] 3 All E.R. 582.

46. See below pp. 46–52.

47. *Hare* v. *Murphy Bros. Ltd.* [1974] 3 All E.R. 940, at p. 942 (Lord Denning) and *F.C. Shepherd & Co. Ltd.* v. *Jerrom* [1987] Q.B. 301, at p. 334 (Balcombe L.J.).

48. *F.C. Shepherd & Co. Ltd.* v. *Jerrom* [1987] Q.B. 301, 318–319, 326, *per* Lawton L.J. and Mustill L.J. As Lord Mustill has remarked extra-judicially ("Anticipatory Breach of Contract: The Common Law at Work", *Butterworth Lectures 1989–1990*, p. 3), the case produced an "absurd state of affairs, in which the ordinary world was turned upside down, with the party who would normally have been denying his fault in fact asserting it".

49. *Ibid.*, *per* Lawton L.J. and Mustill L.J.

50. *Ibid.*, p. 335.

has been said to make the point that these cases must be treated with great caution and they must not be allowed to distort the principles of the doctrine of frustration, both in relation to the circumstances in which frustration can be invoked and in relation to the scope of self-induced frustration. As we have seen, the juridical basis of the doctrine of frustration is already shrouded in uncertainty and that uncertainty can only be compounded by attempting to accommodate the contortions of the courts in these cases within a general theory of the basis and the limits of the doctrine of frustration. These cases are best regarded as being *sui generis*.

(c) A doctrine with "very narrow limits"

The second proposition of Bingham L.J. is worthy of note because it makes the point that it is no easy task to persuade a court that a contract has been frustrated. Indeed, at one point in time, supervening events were not regarded as an excuse for non-performance because the parties could have provided for such eventualities in their contract. In short, once a party had assumed an obligation he was bound to make it good.[51] Even this rule was not, in all probability, an absolute one: "there remained some scope for the development of a defence of supervening impossibility through Act of God and this was allowed where death, the most dramatic Act of God, intervened".[52] However, beginning with *Taylor* v. *Caldwell*,[53] through cases such as *Jackson* v. *Union Marine Insurance Co. Ltd.*[54] to the "coronation cases",[55] the courts began to adopt a more relaxed approach, being rather more willing to discharge a contract on the ground of frustration.

But today, as the judgment of Bingham L.J. reveals, the pendulum has swung back towards a more restrictive approach. This restrictive approach was classically illustrated by the decision of the House of Lords in *Davis Contractors Ltd.* v. *Fareham U.D.C.*[56] The plaintiff contractors agreed to build 78 houses for the defendants for £94,000. The work was scheduled to last for eight months but, owing to shortages of skilled labour, it took 22 months to complete and cost £115,000. The plaintiffs, in an attempt to recover a sum of money in excess of the contract price, argued that the contract had been frustrated and that they were therefore entitled to claim a sum greater than the contract price on a *quantum meruit*. The plaintiffs' argument was rejected. Lord Radcliffe stated that it was not "hardship or inconvenience or material loss itself which calls the principle of frustration into play. There must be as well such a change in the significance of the obligation that the thing undertaken would, if performed, be a different thing from that contracted for."[57] The restrictive attitude of the modern courts was well summed up by Lord Roskill when he said that the doctrine of frustration was "not lightly to be invoked to relieve contracting parties of the normal consequences of imprudent bargains".[58]

51. *Paradine* v. *Jane* (1647) Aleyn 26.
52. Simpson, "Innovation in Nineteenth Century Contract Law" (1975) 91 L.Q.R. 247, at p. 270, citing *Williams* v. *Hide* (1624) Palmer 548; Jones W. 179.
53. (1863) 3 B. & S. 826.
54. (1874) L.R. 10 C.P. 125.
55. See, for example, *Krell* v. *Henry* [1903] 2 K.B. 740 and *Chandler* v. *Webster* [1904] 1 K.B. 493.
56. [1956] A.C. 696.
57. *Ibid*., p. 729.
58. *Pioneer Shipping Ltd.* v. *B.T.P. Tioxide Ltd.* (*The Nema*) [1982] A.C. 724, at p. 752. This desire to avoid disturbing the normal consequences of imprudent bargains has been particularly evident in

Davis Contractors may be said to be the paradigm example of an "imprudent bargain": the unexpected rise in prices undoubtedly caused hardship to the plaintiffs but it did not result in a radical change in the nature of the obligation assumed and so the contract was not frustrated. Similarly, the closing of the Suez Canal, although making the performance of contracts for the carriage of goods by sea more onerous, did not frustrate such contracts because there was not a sufficiently fundamental change in the nature of the obligation assumed.[59]

In principle, there is much to be said for this restrictive stance.[60] This is so for two principal reasons. The first is that contractual obligations are generally strict,[61] and so it is for a contracting party to qualify the obligation which he has assumed in whatever way he deems necessary. The second is that the one thing which we do know about the future is that it is uncertain; war may suddenly break out, prices may suddenly increase, inflation may rise, labour disputes may break out, etc. Contracting parties are expected to foresee and provide against many such possibilities when entering into a contract and they cannot invoke the doctrine of frustration simply because the going gets rough or because performance has become more onerous than they had anticipated at the time of entry into the contract. When considering the narrowness of the doctrine of frustration it must not be forgotten that the parties have at their disposal a wide range of clauses and techniques to deal with unforeseen events, such as *force majeure* clauses, exception clauses, hardship clauses, intervener clauses[62] and price escalation clauses.

On the other hand, it can be argued that such a narrow doctrine of frustration increases the transaction costs of the parties by compelling them to spend time negotiating and drafting an appropriate *force majeure* clause or price variation clause. But the narrowness of the doctrine of frustration has the advantage that it avoids the uncertainty which would be caused by giving to the courts a general power to review "onerous" contract terms or contracts which have turned out to be more "onerous" as a result of a change in circumstances, and parties are at least given the opportunity to tailor the clause to their own particular needs.

The advantage of a *force majeure* clause is, therefore, that it offers to the parties, should they wish to avail themselves of it, the opportunity to escape from the narrowness of the doctrine of frustration by including within their *force majeure* clause an event which would not, at common law, be sufficient to frustrate the contract. For example, we have noted that the closure of the Suez Canal was held not to constitute a frustrating event, but it is common for *force majeure* clauses to list the "closure of the Suez Canal" as an event which gives to the parties an option to ter-

cases such as *Amalgamated Investment & Property Co. Ltd.* v. *John Walker & Sons Ltd.* [1977] 1 W.L.R. 164 where it has been alleged that the purpose of the contract was frustrated.

59. *Tsakiroglou & Co. Ltd.* v. *Noblee & Thorl G.m.b.H.* [1962] A.C. 93; *Ocean Tramp Tankers Corporation* v. *V/O Sovfracht* (*The Eugenia*) [1964] 2 Q.B. 226. A similar conclusion was reached by the courts in the United States: see, for example, *Transatlantic Financing* v. *U.S.* 363 F. 2d. 312 (1966), discussed in more detail at p. 317 (Digwa-Singh).

60. But for a more liberal view of the role and the scope of frustration and analogous doctrines see Chapters 10 (McInnis) and 12 (Rogers). In the latter chapter it is argued that estoppel is the preferable doctrine to invoke in many of these cases.

61. See Treitel, *Remedies for Breach of Contract: A Comparative Account*, Chapter 2, and Holmes, *The Common Law* pp. 298–300, discussed further at pp. 4 above.

62. On which see generally Schmitthoff, "Hardship and Intervener Clauses" [1980] J.B.L. 82.

minate the contract.[63] Similarly, we have noted that an unexpected rise in prices has been held not to constitute a frustrating event, but again it is common to include within a list of *force majeure* events "abnormal increases in prices and wages". The flexibility given to contracting parties to define their own "*force majeure* events" is a significant advantage over the doctrine of frustration.

(d) The consequences of frustration

The third proposition of Bingham L.J. draws attention to the drastic consequences of a finding that a contract has been frustrated. The contract is immediately and automatically brought to an end, irrespective of the wishes of the parties. A court does not have the power at common law to allow the contract to continue and to adapt its terms to the changed circumstances or to substitute new terms more suitable for the changed situation than the terms contained in the original contract. This is claimed to be a significant weakness given the increasing importance of long-term, relational contracts where it is alleged that the existence of such a power would be extremely valuable.[64] Although the harshness of the common law rules relating to the consequences of frustration has been mitigated to an extent by the enactment of the Law Reform (Frustrated Contracts) Act 1943, we shall see[65] that the Act suffers from a number of deficiencies and is unlikely to meet the needs of contracting parties. In contrast, a *force majeure* clause can make its own provision for the consequences of the occurrence of a *force majeure* event; for example, provision can be made for the availability of extensions of time, the suspension or variation of the contract or even the termination of the contract. The remedial rigidity of the general law contrasts unfavourably with the flexibility which can be obtained by the drafting of an appropriate *force majeure* clause.

A further difficulty is created by the proposition that frustration operates *automatically*, that is to say, irrespective of the wishes of the parties.[66] In the first place it creates difficulties where it is alleged that the contract has been frustrated by delay.[67] Secondly, it appears to "make it impossible for the parties to negotiate after the event"[68] because, even if the parties subsequently seek to negotiate their way out of the situation, one party can always undermine that negotiating process by arguing that the contract was frustrated and that, in determining whether the contract was frustrated, his conduct in entering into the negotiating process is irrel-

63. Of course, difficulties of construction may still arise. See generally on the drafting of such clauses Chapters 4 (Furmston) and 5 (Berg). See also Cartoon, "Drafting an Acceptable *Force Majeure* Clause" [1978] J.B.L. 230.

64. Relational contracts are generally beyond the scope of this book. For a useful discussion of this issue see Bell, "The Effect of Changes in Circumstances on Long-term Contracts" in Harris and Tallon (eds.), *Contract Law Today: Anglo-French Comparisons* and Macneil, "Contracts: Adjustment of Long-term Economic Relations under Classical, Neoclassical and Relational Contract Law" (1978) 72 Northwestern Univ. L. Rev. 854. The claim that long-term contracts require separate regulation is challenged by McKendrick, "The Regulation of Long-Term Contracts in English Law" in Beatson and Friedmann (eds.), *Good Faith and Fault in Contract Law* (Oxford, 1995).

65. Discussed further in Chapter 11.

66. See, for criticism, McElroy and Williams, *Impossibility of Performance* pp. 221–231; Goldberg, "Is Frustration Invariably Automatic" (1972) 88 L.Q.R. 464 and Stannard, "Frustrating Delay" (1983) 46 M.L.R. 738, esp. pp. 744–747.

67. This point is discussed further in Chapter 6.

68. Stannard, *op. cit.*, note 66, p. 746.

evant because frustration operates automatically, irrespective of the conduct of the parties after the occurrence of the frustrating event.[69]

Thirdly, the proposition that frustration operates automatically is difficult to reconcile with the troublesome case of *Howell* v. *Coupland*.[70] There the parties entered into a contract for the sale by the defendant to the plaintiff of "200 tons of regent potatoes grown on land belonging to the defendant in Whaplode". The defendant's crop failed because of the potato blight and he was only able to deliver 80 tons of potatoes. The plaintiff sued in respect of the non-delivery of the other 120 tons. It was held that the contract was for the delivery of a portion of a specified crop and that there was implied into the contract a condition which excused the defendant from the consequences of the non-performance of his obligation to deliver the 120 tons in the events which happened. An interesting question which was not raised on the facts of *Howell* was whether the defendant remained under an obligation to deliver the 80 tons of potatoes. That question was subsequently answered in the affirmative by MacKenna J. in the factually similar case of *H.R. and S. Sainsbury Ltd.* v. *Street*.[71] Such a conclusion is clearly inconsistent with the automatic nature of frustration because the obligation to deliver the portion of the crop which is destroyed is discharged but the obligation to deliver the crop which has grown remains enforceable. This inconsistency has led some commentators to assert that *Howell* is not a frustration case but an example of the courts determining the rights of the parties "by the express or (more usually) implied terms of their bargain".[72] But this reasoning is difficult to support because it does not tell us *why* the courts see fit to imply terms into a contract in certain, largely undefined situations. The suggestion that *Howell* has nothing to do with frustration is also difficult to reconcile with the judgment of Blackburn J. in the case itself because he found support for his judgment in *Taylor* v. *Caldwell*,[73] a leading frustration case, thereby suggesting that he was of the opinion that *Howell* was truly a frustration case. Further, given that frustration was at the time *Howell* was decided thought to be based upon the implication of a term into the contract, the use of the same technique in *Howell* also suggests that it is properly regarded as a frustration case. If this is so, it suggests that the rule that frustration operates automatically is in need of reconsideration. The rule could, however, be saved by explaining *Howell* as a case of partial "frustration": the obligation to deliver the 120 tons was frustrated

69. *Hirji Mulji* v. *Cheong Yue S.S. Co.* [1926] A.C. 497; cf. *The Super Servant Two* [1990] 1 Lloyd's Rep. 1 (the facts of which are discussed in greater detail at pp. 46–50) where Bingham L.J. held that the defendants' argument that the contract was frustrated was fatally flawed because they argued that the contract was frustrated, not when their barge which had been allocated to perform the contract with the plaintiffs sank, but when they communicated to the plaintiffs their decision that they could not perform the contract with the other barge. The argument that the operation of the doctrine was dependent upon the decision of the defendants, Bingham L.J. held to be inconsistent with authority. If this was the argument of the defendants, then it would appear to have been misconceived because the frustrating event, if there was one, was the sinking of the barge and so the date of frustration should have been that date, not the date of their communication with the plaintiffs. The subsequent conduct of the defendants, it could then have been argued, was irrelevant because the contract was frustrated automatically.

70. (1874) L.R. 9 Q.B. 462; affd. (1876) 1 Q.B.D. 258. See also the discussion at pp. 258–259 (Diamond).

71. [1972] 1 W.L.R. 834, although it should be noted that, in such a case, the plaintiff is under no obligation to accept the 80 tons, see Sale of Goods Act 1979, s.30(1).

72. Greig and Davis, *The Law of Contract*, p. 1308.

73. (1863) 3 B. & S. 826.

automatically, but the obligation to deliver the 80 tons remained enforceable. This is a plausible explanation of the case but it suffers from the difficulty that English law does not appear to recognise the existence of a doctrine of partial frustration.[74] Barry Nicholas has already pointed out the "discomfort in which English law finds itself when faced with partial impossibility",[75] which discomfort is caused in large part by the fact that the consequences of frustration are directed towards the contract as a whole and not to the particular obligation which has been affected by the unforeseen event. Yet cases can be found in which the courts have excused a party from the consequences of the non-performance of a particular obligation without holding that the contract was frustrated.[76] In so far as these cases are sometimes classified as cases of "partial frustration", it is suggested that such classification is misleading because it suggests that the contract as a whole has been terminated when, in fact, it is only a particular obligation which has not been performed as a result of the supervening event. What is required is for English law to recognise a separate doctrine under which a contracting party can be excused from the non-performance of a particular obligation (where the non-performance has been caused by a supervening event) without the contract as a whole being discharged. But that task must await another day. Here enough has been said to demonstrate the difficulties which surround the "automatic" nature of frustration, which difficulties can be largely avoided by reliance upon a carefully drafted *force majeure* clause which clearly sets out the consequences of the occurrence of a *force majeure* event.

(e) Self-induced frustration

The fourth and fifth propositions of Bingham L.J. relate to the scope of the doctrine of self-induced frustration. English law has never set out with any clarity the limits of this doctrine,[77] and the fourth proposition of Bingham L.J. was critical on the facts of *Super Servant Two*, to which we must now turn.

The defendants agreed to transport the plaintiffs' oil rig, using, at their option, either *Super Servant One* or *Super Servant Two* (both of which were self-propelling,

74. *Kawasaki Steel Corp*. v. *Sardoil S.P.A*. (*The Zuiho Maru*) [1977] 2 Lloyd's Rep. 552, 555, where Kerr J. stated that a plea of partial frustration "will not do", although he stated on the same page that *Howell* was a case in which the contract was not frustrated in its entirety, thereby suggesting that *Howell* might be classified as a case of partial frustration.

75. See p. 30 above.

76. See, for example, *H.R. & S. Sainsbury Ltd.* v. *Street* [1972] 1 W.L.R. 834; *Cricklewood Property and Development Trust Ltd.* v. *Leighton Investment Trust Ltd.* [1945] A.C. 221, 233–234; *Libyan Arab Foreign Bank* v. *Bankers Trust Co.* [1989] Q.B. 728, 772; *John Lewis Properties plc* v. *Viscount Chelsea* [1993] 2 E.G.L.R. 77, 82.

77. An attempt was, however, made by Hobhouse J. at first instance in *The Super Servant Two* [1989] 1 Lloyd's Rep. 148, at pp. 154–156 (noted by McKendrick [1989] L.M.C.L.Q. 3) to define self-induced frustration as a "label" which has been used to describe "those situations where one party has been held by the courts not to be entitled to treat himself as discharged from his contractual obligations". On this analysis, frustration was self-induced where the alleged frustrating event was caused by a breach or an anticipatory breach of contract by the party claiming that the contract had been frustrated, where an act of the party claiming that the contract has been frustrated broke the chain of causation between the alleged frustrating event and the event which made performance of the contract impossible, and where the alleged frustrating event was not a supervening event, by which he meant "something altogether outside the control of the parties". See also the discussion by Swanton "The Concept of Self-induced Frustration" (1990) 2 J.C.L. 206.

semi-submersible barges especially designed for the transportation of rigs). Prior to the time for performance of the contract, the defendants made an internal decision, which they admitted was not irrevocable, to allocate *Super Servant Two* to the performance of the contract with the plaintiffs. They allocated *Super Servant One* to the performance of other concluded contracts. After the conclusion of the contract, but before the time fixed for performance, *Super Servant Two* sank while transporting another rig in the Zaire River. The plaintiffs' rig could not be transported by *Super Servant One* because of its allocation to the performance of other concluded contracts.[78] At this point the parties entered into "without prejudice negotiations" and it was agreed that the defendants should transport the rig by another, more expensive, method. In these circumstances the plaintiffs sued to recover the losses which they had incurred as a result of this more expensive method of transportation, alleging that the defendants were in breach of contract in failing to transport the rig in the agreed manner. The defendants denied liability on two principal grounds. The first was that the sinking of *Super Servant Two* frustrated the contract between the parties. The second was that the sinking of *Super Servant Two* entitled them to cancel the contract under clause 17 of the contract, which was a *force majeure* clause. Here we shall focus our attention upon the frustration point.

The plaintiffs argued that this was not a case of frustration because the cause of the loss was not the sinking of *Super Servant Two* but the decision of the defendants not to use *Super Servant One* in the performance of the contract with the plaintiffs. In this respect the plaintiffs placed heavy reliance upon the decision of the Privy Council in *Maritime National Fish Ltd.* v. *Ocean Trawlers Ltd.*[79] There the defendants chartered a ship from the plaintiffs but the vessel could only be used for its intended purpose if it was fitted with an otter trawl. An otter trawl could only be used under licence and, although the defendants applied for licences for each of the five vessels which they operated, they were allocated only three. They elected to apply the licences to the trawlers which they owned directly or indirectly rather than to the vessel chartered from the plaintiffs. The plaintiffs sued for the hire due under the charter. The defendants denied that they were liable to pay the hire because they maintained that the charterparty had been frustrated because it was impossible to use the trawler for its stated purpose without a licence. The Privy Council held that the failure of the defendants to obtain a licence did not have the effect of frustrating the contract between the parties; it was a case of self-induced frustration and the defendants were in breach of contract.

The scope of the case has, however, always been a source of some controversy. On the one hand, it could be argued that the crucial factor which led the Privy Council to conclude that it was a case of self-induced frustration was that the defendants elected to allocate the licences to trawlers which they owned directly or indirectly rather than to the trawler chartered from the plaintiffs.[80] On the other hand, it could be argued that the mere fact that the defendants had a choice as to

78. After the loss of *Super Servant Two* the defendants did use *Super Servant One* to carry one of the cargoes which had been scheduled for *Super Servant Two* but otherwise no other alteration was made to their internal scheduling.

79. [1935] A.C. 524.

80. The fact that the defendants had an interest in the trawlers to which they allocated the licences is not clear from the judgment of Lord Wright in the Privy Council but it does emerge from the judgments in the Canadian courts, see [1934] 1 D.L.R. 621, at p. 623 and [1934] 4 D.L.R. 288, at p. 299.

the distribution of the licences was sufficient to turn it into a case of self-induced frustration.

The latter interpretation was the one which was adopted in *Super Servant Two*, both at first instance and in the Court of Appeal. Support for such an interpretation can be found in the judgment of Lord Wright in *Maritime National* when he said that it was "immaterial"[81] to speculate why the defendants had allocated the licences to the three particular trawlers. Applying this analysis to the facts of *Super Servant Two*, it was held that the mere fact that the defendants had a choice as to the allocation of *Super Servant One* meant that this was a case of self-induced frustration because the alleged frustrating event was due to the act or election of the party seeking to invoke the doctrine.

Such a conclusion leaves a seller or supplier of goods in an impossible position where his source of supply partially fails because of an unforeseen event. Indeed, in many ways it would be preferable if the source of supply failed completely because then at least the seller could invoke frustration as an excuse for non-performance. There are, however, a number of possible escape routes for a party, such as the defendants in *Super Servant Two*, whose source of supply partially fails for some unforeseen reason.

The first is to eliminate the choice on the part of the defendants. Thus, Bingham L.J. stated that, had the contract been to perform the contract by the use of *Super Servant Two*, then he felt "sure"[82] that the contract would have been frustrated on the sinking of *Super Servant Two*. Such a stipulation would have brought about a complete rather than a partial failure of supply but only at the cost of giving to the defendants less flexibility in the allocation of their barges.

The second is to argue that *Super Servant Two* was, in fact, wrongly decided. A number of arguments can be put forward in support of this proposition.[83] In the first place it can be argued that it provides an odd contrast with *Howell* v. *Coupland*[84] because, there too there was a partial failure of supply, yet the seller was discharged from his obligation to supply the 120 tons of potatoes. Of course, *Super Servant Two* is factually distinguishable because in *Howell* the defendant had entered into a contract with one buyer whereas in *Super Servant Two* the defendants had entered into a number of different contracts with different parties. But this factor hardly seems to be material.

The second argument is that there is some, albeit slight, authority for the proposition that, in the event of a partial failure of supply, a seller who cannot satisfy all his contractual obligations can seek to share the partial supply among his contractors without being in breach of contract. Suppose, for example, that a potato farmer reasonably believes that his land will yield 500 tons of potatoes and so he agrees to sell 100 tons to each of five different purchasers. But his crop partially fails and the land yields only 200 tons. What is the legal position of the farmer? There are, theoretically, a number of possible solutions. The first view is that all

81. [1935] A.C. 524, at p. 530.
82. [1990] 1 Lloyd's Rep. 1, at p. 9.
83. See also the criticisms levelled against the decision by Treitel, *The Law of Contract* (8th Edn.) pp. 805–806.
84. (1874) L.R. 9 Q.B. 462; affd. (1876) 1 Q.B.D. 258, discussed above at note 70 and associated text.

five contracts are frustrated. But the courts are unlikely to accept such an extreme argument.[85] The second view, and the one apparently taken by the Court of Appeal in *Super Servant Two*,[86] is that none of the contracts are frustrated, so that the farmer is in breach of any contract which he fails to perform fully.[87] But such a solution does seem harsh on the farmer, because there is no obvious reason why he should be released from the consequences of non-performance when the failure is total but not when it is partial or why he should be released when he has only one buyer but not when he has many buyers. A third view is that the farmer has a free choice as to which of the five contracts are to be performed and that the rest are discharged on the ground of frustration. But it is suggested that the courts are unlikely to give to the farmer a free hand in the distribution of the scarce supplies and so may require a particular method of division. The fourth view is that a particular method of distribution will be required and, in so far as any of the farmer's contractual obligations remain unperformed, they are discharged on the ground of frustration. But what method of distribution would the law require? One method would be pro rata division,[88] another would be the satisfaction in full of the contracts which happen to be concluded first in time,[89] yet another would be the satisfaction in full of contracts according to their delivery dates.[90] A wider view is that the farmer should simply be required to act reasonably in the distribution of scarce resources.[91] The latter solution has been adopted in America in the Uniform Commercial Code[92] and there were some signs in recent cases that English law was moving slowly in a similar direction.[93]

But such a development was brought to an abrupt halt in *Super Servant Two* because the cases which appeared to support such a movement were explained as cases which turned upon the construction of a *force majeure* clause.[94] Thus, Hobhouse J. expressly stated that if a promisor wished protection in the event of a partial failure of his supplies "he must bargain for the inclusion of a suitable *force majeure* clause in the contract".[95] It is, however, of some interest to note that a

85. Although on one reading the judgments of the House of Lords in *Tennants (Lancashire) Ltd.* v. *C.S. Wilson & Co. Ltd.* [1917] A.C. 495 are capable of supporting such an argument.

86. Although it should be noted that the full range of options was not available to the Court of Appeal because *Super Servant One* was not physically divisible and so she had to be allocated to the performance of certain selected contracts.

87. See also *Hong Guan & Co. Ltd.* v. *R. Jumabhoy & Sons Ltd.* [1960] A.C. 684, at pp. 701–702 and *Pancommerce S.A.* v. *Veecheema B.V.* [1982] 1 Lloyd's Rep. 645, at p. 651, although note the valuable discussion of the former case by Hudson, "Prorating in the English Law of Frustrated Contracts" (1968) 31 M.L.R. 535, at pp. 539–541.

88. *Bremer Handelsgesellschaft m.b.H.* v. *C. Mackprang Jr.* [1979] 1 Lloyd's Rep. 221, at p. 224.

89. *Intertradex S A.* v. *Lesieur Torteaux S.A.R.L.* [1978] 2 Lloyd's Rep. 509.

90. A view apparently held by Lord Finlay in his dissenting speech in *Tennants (Lancashire) Ltd.* v. *C.S. Wilson & Co. Ltd.* [1917] A.C. 495, at p. 508.

91. *Continental Grain Export Cpn.* v. *S.T.M. Grain Ltd.* [1979] 2 Lloyd's Rep. 460, at p. 473 and *Bremer Handelsgesellschaft m.b.H.* v. *Continental Grain Co.* [1983] 1 Lloyd's Rep. 269, at p. 292.

92. Section 2–615, discussed further in Chapter 16.

93. See the analysis of the relevant cases in Treitel, *The Law of Contract* (8th Edn.), pp. 774–776, *Benjamin's Sale of Goods* (4th Edn.), paras. 6-043 and 18-181; Hudson *op. cit.*, note 87 and Hudson "Prorating and Frustration" (1979) 123 S.J. 137.

94. The cases which were distinguished on this ground were *Intertradex S.A.* v. *Lesieur Torteaux S.A.R.L.* [1978] 2 Lloyd's Rep. 509; *Bremer Handelsgesellschaft m.b.H.* v. *C. Mackprang Jr.* [1979] 1 Lloyd's Rep. 221 and *Bremer Handelsgesellschaft m.b.H.* v. *Continental Grain Co.* [1983] 1 Lloyd's Rep. 269.

95. [1989] 1 Lloyd's Rep. 148.

similar position to that adopted by the Court of Appeal and Hobhouse J. in *Super Servant Two* was once adopted by the courts in America but that gradually they were persuaded to permit prorating even in the case where there was no *force majeure* clause or exception clause in the contract.[96] Thus *Super Servant Two* may yet be open for further examination.

But, at least for the moment, the third and safest method of protection for a seller faced with a partial failure of supplies, and the one actually adopted by the defendants in *Super Servant Two*, is to incorporate into the contract a suitably drafted *force majeure* clause. However, even when such a clause has been incorporated into the contract, it should not be assumed that it will necessarily achieve its purpose. The courts will probably still insist that the seller act reasonably in allocating his available supplies.[97] Thus, the protection afforded by an appropriately drafted *force majeure* clause may be limited, but it is better than having no protection at all because the "frustration" is held to be "self-induced".

(f) Frustration and fault

The final proposition of Bingham L.J. relates to the relationship between frustration and fault. This is a vexed issue and it also arose on the facts of *Super Servant Two*. The plaintiffs argued that it was a case of self-induced frustration because they alleged that the cause of the sinking of *Super Servant Two* was the negligence of the defendants or their employees. It is not entirely clear whether a contract can be frustrated when the alleged frustrating event has been brought about by the negligence or fault of one of the contracting parties.[98] Some have argued that, generally, negligence should exclude frustration,[99] while others have maintained that the presence of fault should not necessarily exclude frustration.[100] The point has never been conclusively resolved.[101] The defendants in *Super Servant Two* argued that it was only when they had acted deliberately or were in breach of a duty of care owed to the plaintiff that they would be precluded from relying upon the doctrine of frustration.[102] But this view was rejected[103] on the ground that it would "confine the law in a legalistic strait-jacket"[104] and obscure the real issue, which was whether "the frustrating event relied upon is truly an outside event or extraneous change of

96. See Hudson, *op. cit.*, note 87, p. 536.

97. See, for example, *Intertradex S.A.* v. *Lesieur Torteaux S.A.R.L.* [1978] 2 Lloyd's Rep. 509; *Continental Grain Export Corp.* v. *S.T.M. Grain Ltd.* [1979] 2 Lloyd's Rep. 460 and *Bremer Handelsgesellschaft m.b.H.* v. *Continental Grain Co.* [1983] 1 Lloyd's Rep. 269, as explained by the Court of Appeal and Hobhouse J. in *Super Servant Two*.

98. The principal authority is the decision of the House of Lords in *Joseph Constantine Steamship Ltd.* v. *Imperial Smelting Corporation Ltd.* [1942] A.C. 154 but even here there are only *obiter dicta* on point.

99. Treitel, *The Law of Contract* (8th Edn.), p. 804.

100. Viscount Simon in *Joseph Constantine S.S. Co.* v. *Imperial Smelting Corporation Ltd.* [1942] A.C. 154, at p. 166.

101. See the rather equivocal remarks of Lord Brandon in *The Hannah Blumenthal* [1983] 1 A.C. 854, at p. 909.

102. Relying upon *Joseph Constantine Steamship Ltd.* v. *Imperial Smelting Corporation Ltd.* [1942] A.C. 154, at p. 166 (Viscount Simon), 195 (Lord Wright) and 202 (Lord Porter), and *Cheall* v. *A.P.E.X.* [1983] 2 A.C. 180, at pp. 188–189.

103. Relying upon the judgment of Griffiths L.J. in *The Hannah Blumenthal* [1983] 1 A.C. 854, at p. 882.

104. [1990] 1 Lloyd's Rep. 1, at p. 10.

situation or whether it is an event which the party seeking to rely on it had the means and opportunity to prevent but nevertheless caused or permitted to come about". The same point was made at first instance by Hobhouse J. when he held that the sinking of *Super Servant Two* was not an event which was outside the control of the defendants; it was an event which was within their control and it did not cease to be within their control simply because they had unreasonably failed to exercise control.[105] The adoption of such an approach is likely to lead to the conclusion that most if not all cases involving negligence on the part of the party claiming that the contract has been frustrated will be treated as cases of self-induced frustration because the alleged frustrating event will be within his reasonable control.

Once again, contracting parties can seek to escape this consequence by drafting a *force majeure* clause which extends to damage caused by the fault of the party relying upon the clause. But such a proposition is a controversial one. On one view, a clause which purports to apply to events within the control of the party relying upon it is not a *force majeure* clause at all.[106] On this argument such a clause is an exception clause, not a *force majeure* clause. But this view was not shared by Bingham L.J. in *Super Servant Two* because he maintained that clause 17, which it was alleged covered the sinking of *Super Servant Two* even when the sinking was caused by the negligence of the defendants or their employees, was a *force majeure* clause, not an exception clause. On the other hand, Bingham L.J. held that the "broad approach" adopted by the Privy Council in *Canada Steamship* v. *R.*,[107] to the construction of exclusion clauses which purported to exclude liability for negligence was also applicable to the interpretation of a *force majeure* clause. Unfortunately, the rules of interpretation enunciated in *Canada Steamship* have been heavily criticised for their artificiality[108] and Donaldson L.J. (as he then was) has warned against treating the rules "as if they were the words of a codifying and, still worse an amending, statute".[109] The extension of these artificial rules to *force majeure* clauses is, therefore, not an approach which can be welcomed, especially when there have been signs, albeit rather limited, of judicial unwillingness to apply the *Canada Steamship* rules to some clauses which have the effect of enabling one contracting party to exclude liability for his own negligence.[110] At a time when a more relaxed and natural approach has been evident in the interpretation of limitation[111]

105. [1989] 1 Lloyd's Rep. 148, at p. 158, although Hobhouse J. conceded that the position would have been otherwise if the contract had contained an exclusion clause which exempted the defendants from liability for their negligence.

106. See pp. 16–17 above.

107. [1952] A.C. 192.

108. See, for example, Palmer, "Negligence and Exclusion Clauses Again" [1983] L.M.C.L.Q. 557.

109. *The Raphael* [1982] 2 Lloyd's Rep. 42, at p. 45.

110. See, for example, *Scottish Special Housing Association* v. *Wimpey Construction U.K. Ltd.* [1986] 2 All E.R. 957, where no mention was made of the *Canada Steamship* rules. Indeed, the Full Supreme Court of Victoria in *Schenker & Co. (Aust) Pty. Ltd.* v. *Malpas Equipment and Services Pty. Ltd.* [1990] V.R. 834, 846 held that the strained approach to construction adopted in *Canada Steamship* was inconsistent with the more natural and ordinary approach to construction adopted by the High Court of Australia in *Darlington Futures Ltd.* v. *Delco Australia Pty. Ltd.* (1986) 161 C.L.R. 500. But such an approach has not yet been adopted in England and the Court of Appeal has recently followed and applied the *Canada Steamship* rules (*EE Caledonia Ltd.* v. *Orbit Valve Co. plc.* [1994] 2 Lloyd's Rep. 239).

111. *Ailsa Craig Fishing Co. Ltd.* v. *Malvern Fishing Co. Ltd.* [1983] 1 W.L.R. 964; *George Mitchell (Chesterhall) Ltd.* v. *Finney Lock Seeds Ltd.* [1983] 2 A.C. 803.

and exclusion clauses,[112] it seems rather unfortunate that Bingham L.J. has seen fit to extend the scope of the artificial *Canada Steamship* rules to *force majeure* clauses.

Apart from this point about the application of the *Canada Steamship* rules of construction to *force majeure* clauses, there is some force in the argument that a *force majeure* clause, by definition, must apply only to events which were beyond the control of the parties. There must, therefore, be some doubt as to whether a *force majeure* clause, properly so called, can ever apply to events which were within the control of the party invoking the clause. But, even if it can so apply, a number of difficulties lie ahead of a party who seeks to draft a *force majeure* clause which covers his own negligence, particularly in the form of the *Canada Steamship* rules of construction and, possibly, even the controls contained in the Unfair Contract Terms Act 1977.[113]

6. CONCLUSION

The theme of this chapter may be said to be, broadly speaking, one of "self-help": that is to say, since the doctrine of frustration operates within narrow confines, considerable advantages can be obtained by the incorporation into a contract of a suitably drafted *force majeure* clause. It may be objected that such an approach adds to the transaction costs of the parties and that a better way of dealing with this issue is to subject the doctrine of frustration to re-examination, with the aim of giving to the courts more extensive powers to re-write contracts which have become more onerous as a result of the occurrence of an unforeseen event. But the latter solution would be costly in terms of the uncertainty which would ensue and it is by no means clear that this uncertainty can be eliminated by enacting specific solutions, because the solutions which will be acceptable to contracting parties are unlikely to be capable of precise identification as they are largely context-dependent.

The proposition that we should not reform the doctrine of frustration is, of course, a contestable one, but it is undeniably true that frustration presently operates within very narrow confines. In the absence of imminent reform two options are available to us. We can either bemoan the present state of the law or we can begin to advise contracting parties as to how they can draft clauses which are suitable to their needs. The latter approach may be acceptable to the party who is legally advised or who can afford legal advice, but what of the contracting party who has not been advised to incorporate a *force majeure* clause into his contract but who finds that his contractual obligations have, as the result of an unforeseen event, become more onerous? As we have seen,[114] he is unlikely to succeed with an argument that the contract has been frustrated. So what can he do?

One obvious step is to give serious consideration to incorporating a *force majeure* clause into his future contracts. But what about his existing contracts? One step

112. See, for example, the speech of Lord Diplock in *Photo Production Ltd.* v. *Securicor Transport Ltd.* [1980] A.C. 827; and, more generally, the decision of the High Court of Australia in *Darlington Futures Ltd.* v. *Delco Australia Pty. Ltd.* (1986) 161 C.L.R. 500.

113. The possible application of the Act to *force majeure* clauses is considered at p. 11 and p. 264.

114. Above, pp. 42–44.

which he can take is to seek to renegotiate the contract in an effort to recover some of the unexpected cost from the other party to the contract. If the other party is willing to pay and does pay, obviously no problem arises. But what if the other party refuses to enter into such negotiations or promises to pay but later refuses? A significant obstacle in the way of a party seeking to renegotiate in such circumstances was the rule that performance of an existing contractual duty owed to the promisor is not good consideration for a fresh promise given in return.[115] But the importance of this hurdle appears to have been radically reduced by the recent decision of the Court of Appeal in *Williams* v. *Roffey Bros. & Nicholls (Contractors) Ltd.*[116] The defendants, who had entered into a contract to renovate a block of flats, subcontracted the carpentry work to the plaintiff for a price of £20,000. During the course of the work the plaintiff ran into financial difficulties, partly because he discovered that he had fixed the price too low. It was in the defendants' interests to ensure that the work was completed on time because, if it was not, they would be liable to pay compensation under a "penalty clause" contained in the main contract. So the defendants arranged a meeting with the plaintiff, at which it was agreed that they would pay the plaintiff an extra £10,300, at the rate of £575 per flat on completion, to ensure that the work was completed on time. The plaintiff sued the defendants to recover some of the additional promised sum, but the defendants argued, *inter alia*, that there was no consideration to support their promise to pay. This argument was rejected by the Court of Appeal. Adopting a pragmatic approach the court held that the defendants had in fact obtained a benefit as a result of the plaintiff's promise to complete the work on time, in that it enabled them to avoid liability under the main contract.

For present purposes our interest lies in whether, prior to the re-negotiations, the plaintiff could have argued that the contract was frustrated. The answer is clear that he could not. And, as Adams and Brownsword have pointed out, this conclusion may render it

> "necessary to review the application of the frustration principle, which . . . firmly sets its face against assisting a contractor to re-negotiate an underpriced contract, despite the underpricing arising through circumstances beyond the control of the parties. Yet, in *Williams* v. *Roffey*, the court bends over backwards to indemnify a contractor against the effects of underpricing in circumstances where the underpricing is entirely within his control."[117]

This does appear at first sight to be rather anomalous but the point can, in fact, be met on two grounds. The first is that *Williams* v. *Roffey* can be reconciled with cases such as *Davis* v. *Fareham U.D.C.*[118] on the ground that the courts in all of these cases were simply concerned to uphold the bargain which the parties had concluded. In *Davis* the original agreement was never consensually varied and the court held the parties to their original agreement. But in *Williams* the parties did reach a new agreement and the effect of the decision of the Court of Appeal was to uphold the validity of the later agreement. The second point of distinction is that it

115. *Stilk* v. *Myrick* (1809) 2 Camp. 317 and 6 Esp. 129.
116. [1991] 1 Q.B. 1.
117. "Contract, Consideration and the Critical Path" (1990) 53 M.L.R. 536, at p. 541 (footnotes omitted).
118. [1956] A.C. 696, discussed in more detail at p. 42 above. *Davis* is, in fact, the case which is relied upon by Adams and Brownsword to draw a contrast with *Williams* v. *Roffey Bros*.

is possible to maintain that the "changed or unforeseen circumstances which would constitute a sufficient basis for an exception to the pre-existing duty rule need not be of the same degree required for actual discharge by impossibility"[119]; it suffices that the changed circumstances created a "reasonable and honest belief that the original duty is discharged".

If *Williams* v. *Roffey* is correct, it would appear that economic duress is now the principal control device which places limits upon the conduct of the parties during the renegotiation of a contract. Renegotiations would thus be liable to be set aside where the party whose performance had become more onerous had employed an "illegitimate"[120] threat which was a (significant[121]) cause[122] of the other party agreeing to the new terms. The difficulty with this formulation of duress, when applied to the facts of *Williams* v. *Roffey*, is that, if the contract was not frustrated (which it was not), there was an illegitimate threat (a breach of contract) which surely was a (not "the") cause of the defendants' agreeing to the new terms.[123] The prerequisites for a successful duress claim would, therefore, appear to have been satisfied, but the Court of Appeal nevertheless concluded that, on the facts, there had been no economic duress. This is rather difficult to explain (and the explanation lies beyond the scope of our present discussion) but it does illustrate, once again, that the courts are willing, within limits, to allow contracting parties to engage in "self-help" in circumstances where it could not be argued that the contract had been frustrated, whether the self-help be in the form of permitting them to draft wider *force majeure* clauses or in upholding the renegotiation of a contract after the occurrence of an unforeseen event. But whether *Williams* v. *Roffey* will, as Adams and Brownsword suggest, result in a "review" of the doctrine of frustration, is a question which only time will answer.[124]

EWAN MCKENDRICK

119. Brody, "Performance of a Pre-existing Contractual Duty as Consideration: The Actual Criteria for the Efficacy of an Agreement Altering Contractual Obligation" (1975) 52 Denver L.J. 433, at p. 461, citing *Michaud* v. *McGregor* 61 Minn. 198, 63 N.W. 479 (1895).

120. *Universe Tankships of Monrovia* v. *International Transport Workers' Federation* (*The Universe Sentinel*) [1983] 1 A.C. 366.

121. *Dimskal Shipping Co. S.A.* v. *International Transport Workers Federation* [1992] 2 A.C. 152, 165H.

122. *Barton* v. *Armstrong* [1976] A.C. 104.

123. See Birks, "The Travails of Duress" [1990] L.M.C.L.Q. 342. Although it would have been harder to show that the threat was a *significant* cause of the new agreement being concluded. See fn. 121 above.

124. Some of the material in this chapter is based on a case-note which was originally published in *Lloyd's Maritime and Commercial Law Quarterly* in 1990. I am grateful to the editor, Professor Francis Rose, for giving permission to draw upon this material.

PART II

THE DRAFTING OF FORCE MAJEURE CLAUSES

CHAPTER 4

DRAFTING OF FORCE MAJEURE CLAUSES—SOME GENERAL GUIDELINES[1]

1. INTRODUCTION

If one considers how much time a commercial lawyer spends on drafting contracts, it is surprising how little by way of useful practical advice has been written. Perhaps this is because the standard practice is to find an example of someone else's drafting and copy it. It is difficult to elevate this into a principle of much generality or nobility. Nevertheless it is, I think, possible to make some observations which have some practical usefulness.

The first step must of course be to define one's object. It would not be appropriate to insert into every contract which needs a *force majeure* clause the same *force majeure* clause. There are two variables which immediately occur to one. The first is whether the draftsman is acting on behalf of the seller, the buyer or some neutral trade association or similar body. (In this chapter I shall use "seller" to include also the supplier of services and manufactured objects. Obviously *force majeure* clauses often find their way into construction contracts.) *Force majeure* clauses are much more commonly aimed at qualifying the seller's obligation to deliver the goods than to qualify the buyer's obligation to pay, but it does not follow that all *force majeure* clauses are drafted on behalf of sellers. A lawyer instructed to draft a *force majeure* clause on behalf of the seller may well wish to draft a clause as wide as he thinks he can get away with, though at least in a rational world, if such a thing ever exists, a buyer may stipulate for a lower price if the seller's obligation to deliver the goods is too elaborately qualified. A lawyer instructed to draft standard conditions of purchase might think that there was no place in them for a *force majeure* clause as to the seller's obligation. On the other hand, one has certainly seen such clauses in a buyer's standard conditions of purchase. Why is this? A practical answer is that a seller who sees in the buyer's standard conditions of purchase a *force majeure* clause may conclude that there is no need to press for the inclusion of such a clause. This will not necessarily be the case if the clause has been tightly drawn with the buyer's interest principally in mind. For example, a clause in a buyer's standard conditions of purchase might say "if delivery is delayed by some cause totally outside the control of the supplier which the supplier could not reasonably foresee or reasonably provide against, then he shall give written notice of such cause within

1. I am particularly indebted to Professor Marcel Fontaine's *Droit des Contrats Internationaux: Analyse et Rédaction de Clauses* and to a paper by David Yates, "Pitfalls in Drafting *Force Majeure* Clauses" delivered at the *Journal of Contract Law* Conference, Sydney, July 1990 and published in (1991) 3 *Journal of Contract Law* 186.

seven days of its commencement and the purchaser may then (but without prejudice to its other rights) allow such extra time for delivery as is reasonable in the circumstances".

A second general consideration is that the *force majeure* clause should make sense in relation to the particular business context in which it is to be employed. Here the draftsman can, with advantage, bear in mind the old army maxim "time spent in recce is never wasted". Careful discussion with the client about typical events which delay performance may be invaluable in drafting a suitable clause.

In the discussion which follows, I am assuming a contract which is subject to English law. The need for a *force majeure* clause may well be different if some other law is the law applicable to the contract. English lawyers tend to write as if the English doctrine of frustration were exceptionally narrow and to assume that all other systems, through the use of concepts such as *force majeure*, have much wider rules. The elaborate comparative survey of frustration and *force majeure* by Denis Philippe[2] suggests that this is much too simple a view. And in practice, as has been shown by the writings of Professor Marcel Fontaine,[3] *force majeure* clauses are to be found in contracts all over the world, whatever the applicable law.

A final general point is that the draftsman of a *force majeure* clause needs to have regard to the way in which the clause may be construed by the courts. The question of construction has already been considered in some detail.[4] We may perhaps, however, point out that there is some authority for the view that *force majeure* clauses are to be treated as a kind of exemption clause and construed *contra proferentem*.[5] It is difficult on any view to see how this could be correct when applied to neutrally drawn trade association terms, and in any case the most recent decisions of the English courts suggest that the *contra proferentem* principle is only to be invoked as a last resort.[6] It is, however, respectfully suggested that, at least in so far as *force majeure* relates to events which are outside the control of the seller, to treat such a clause as a kind of exemption clause is fundamentally misconceived. We need to remind ourselves that the classic justification for the narrow doctrine of frustration in English law is that it is for the parties to agree what the effects of unforeseen events outside their control is to be. It is fundamentally misconceived to start applying to such party-agreed provisions preconceived notions of where the risk of such events should lie derived from a blind application of the doctrine of frustration.

Granted all of these preliminaries it is, I think, possible to identify at least four questions to which any well-drafted *force majeure* clause ought to provide an answer. These are:

1. The definition of the event.
2. Obligations as to reporting.
3. The effect of the event.
4. Questions of adjudication.

2. Denis Philippe, *Changement de Circonstances et Bouleversement de l'Economie Contractuelle* (Emile Bruylant, Brussels, 1986).
3. Fontaine, *op. cit.*, Chapter 6.
4. See Chapter 1 and see further Chapter 5.
5. *Fairclough Dodd & Jones Ltd.* v. *J.H. Vantol Ltd.* [1957] 1 W.L.R. 136.
6. *Ailsa Craig Fishing Co. Ltd.* v. *Malvern Fishing Co. Ltd.* [1983] 1 W.L.R. 964.

2. DEFINITION OF THE EVENT

I am considering here *force majeure* clauses of the classical kind. I consider below, in Section 6, hardship clauses which are to be found in many international commercial contracts and which provide for a mechanism of attempted re-negotiation if there is a change of circumstance which causes substantial hardship to one of the parties. Obviously such clauses have a potential overlap with a *force majeure* clause. There seem to be at least three major alternatives for the definition of the event. These are:

(a) A general reference to "*force majeure*".
(b) A list of specific "*force majeure*" events with or without a wrap-up clause at the end which refers to other unspecified, unforeseen and uncontrollable events.
(c) A general provision for unforeseen and uncontrollable events.

The first course seems clearly wrong given that in English law at the moment *force majeure* is not a term of art and one cannot be sure what meaning a court will give to it. At best a significant amount of time is likely to be wasted in arguing about the proper construction of the clause.

The predominance of authority is that a wrap-up clause in a *force majeure* clause is not to be read *eiusdem generis* with the rest of the clause.[7] If this is correct then there is not much difference between (b) and (c) if the specific list of events in (b) is followed by a general provision, as it usually is. In practice it seems much more common to give a specific list of events, perhaps because this reduces the scope for argument that these particular events are not within the general ambit of the clause.

A not untypical example taken at random from the files provides:

> "the company shall not be liable to the customer for any loss or damage which may be suffered by the customer as a result, directly or however indirectly, of the supply of goods or services by the company being prevented, hindered, delayed or rendered uneconomic by reason of circumstances or events beyond the reasonable control of the company including but not limited to act of God, war, riot, strike, lock-out, trade dispute or labour disturbance, accident, break-down of plant or machinery, fire, flood, storm, difficulty or increased expense in obtaining workmen, materials or transport or other circumstances affecting the supply of the goods or of raw materials thereof by the company's normal source of supply or the manufacture of the goods by the company's normal means or the delivery of the goods by the company's normal route or means of delivery."

Two general questions arise about lists of this kind. First, must the events be unforeseen or unforeseeable? Secondly, do the events have to be outside the control of the seller? Of course, many of the specific examples are outside the seller's control but it is very doubtful whether the mere fact that an event is outside the seller's control should by itself render it a *force majeure* occurrence. This is because the prudent seller needs to provide in his planning against quite a wide range of events which are outside his control. To take an example from a construction contract, a builder is not expected to control the weather but he is expected to know

7. *Ambatielos* v. *Anton Jurgens Margarine Works* [1923] A.C. 175.

that certain types of work are more difficult and more expensive to do in December than in June. In a not dissimilar way, the mere fact that events are not foreseen by the seller is unlikely to give rise to a *force majeure* event where he could have taken steps to guard against the events if he had thought about it. So there is much to be said from the point of view of the buyer on insisting that *force majeure* events should in general be both outside the seller's reasonable foresight and also outside the seller's reasonable control.

3. OBLIGATIONS TO REPORT

Many *force majeure* clauses contain provisions requiring the party who claims that a *force majeure* event has taken place to report it to the other party within a prescribed time. Although this practice is not universal it has much to commend it. There are obvious advantages from the point of view of the other party since, in practical terms, it is much easier to investigate the true extent of the *force majeure* event if it is promptly reported than if it is suddenly revealed several years later. Although an inefficient party may be glad of the possibility of raising an excuse long after the event, it will often also be to the advantage of the party affected by *force majeure* to report promptly since speedy resolution of disputes is in general in the interests of all efficient parties. Furthermore, if the contract provides a mechanism for granting extensions of time in the event of *force majeure*, it is in the interests of the party affected to have this question resolved quickly.

What should be addressed in a reporting clause?

(a) The clause should state to whom the report is to be made. In a contract of sale this would usually be to the other party but in a construction contract it is commonly to the architect or engineer. This is obviously linked with questions of adjudication, which are discussed below.

(b) Within what time-frame should reporting take place? If one is going to have a reporting requirement at all, a relatively short time-span is appropriate. Periods of between seven days and three months have often been seen in such clauses. Much depends on the type of contract and the period over which it is to run.

(c) The contract should provide for the degree of detail with which the report is to be accompanied. This is particularly important if the person to whom the report is to be made has some kind of adjudicating function since rational decision making demands an adequate supply of information. Construction contracts often require the contractor not only to report the extent of the interruption he has suffered but also to give an estimate of its effect on his progress.

(d) The contract ought to make clear whether the requirements set out in (a), (b) and (c) are directory or mandatory. Clauses drafted by buyers or neutrally often make prompt and adequate reporting a condition precedent to the making of a claim. It is extremely desirable that the draftsman consciously address this question and make it clear whether failure to claim in the right time and in the right way is fatal to any claim. Courts have often been rather indulgent to slow claimers in this context and need therefore to have clear guidance from the draftsman as to what is intended.[8]

4. THE EFFECT OF THE EVENT

The contract needs to make clear what the effect on the contract is of a *force majeure* event. In English domestic law the doctrine of frustration, when it operates, operates to bring the contract to an end, although there is certainly a class of events which may excuse non-performance without bringing the contract to an end, for example short-term but serious illness in an employment contract.[9]

Obviously the contract may provide that the happening of a *force majeure* event is to bring the contract to an end, but this will often be too drastic a result, at least in the first instance. So it will often be appropriate to provide that the result of the event is to found a claim for extra time for performance and only in extreme cases to terminate the contract.

If the contract is to provide that the happening of a *force majeure* event may be a ground for the granting of an extension of time, a flexible and well-thought-out definition of an appropriate extension is very important. The critical question is not so much how long a *force majeure* event endures but what its effect is on the seller's ability to perform on time. There will be some cases where there has been a *force majeure* occurrence but the seller can still by a lucky chance quite happily perform. In other cases there will be *force majeure* occurrences which have disruptive effects quite out of proportion to their own duration. Suppose A contracts to build a pipeline across Siberia and because of weather conditions it is only possible to work between April and September. It is possible to envisage that there may be *force majeure* events which force A into the next summer season because a fortnight's delay in September cannot be caught up in October but only in the following April. This problem is, of course, very well known in relation to construction contracts where it is typically resolved by a careful analysis of the effect of the *force majeure* event on the contractor's critical path.

The effect of allowing the seller extra time for performance is to relieve the seller, in whole or in part, from the obligation to pay damages, whether liquidated or unliquidated, for being late. To the extent, therefore, that the seller's lateness causes the buyer loss, that loss falls on the buyer, though of course there may be other loss caused to the seller by the *force majeure* event which falls on him. Such a provision presumably reflects a conscious or unconscious decision that an event which is unforeseen and outside the control of both parties should provoke a sharing of the risk. On the whole, therefore, this reasoning would not suggest that a straightforward *force majeure* event should normally justify a claim by the seller for extra payment, since this would be to transfer the whole of the risk to the buyer. Of course if the seller and the buyer agree that this is to happen they are perfectly free to do so, but such a result needs to be clearly expressed, since a court is likely to find it surprising.

8. *Tersons Ltd.* v. *Stevenage Development Corporation* [1965] 1 Q.B. 37.

9. See, e.g., *Poussard* v. *Spiers and Pond* (1876) 1 Q.B. 410; Stannard, "Frustrating Delay" (1983) 46 M.L.R. 738.

5. QUESTIONS OF ADJUDICATION

Some kinds of *force majeure* clause may simply leave questions to be resolved by the courts in the absence of a negotiated agreement between the parties. In practice, however, there is much to be said for providing an effective mechanism for resolving questions more speedily. Much of the discussion in the earlier sections assumes indeed that the parties will have provided a mechanism for resolving the sorts of questions that arise. In the example given above,[10] the seller reported and the buyer decided, but many sellers would prefer some form of neutral adjudication. The obvious model here is the architect or engineer to whom questions of extensions of time are commonly referred in construction contracts. The architect or engineer is an agent of the employer but it is well understood, both within the industry and in the courts, that in handling such matters as certificates and extensions of time the architect must act independently and reach a fair decision between the parties.[11] If the draftsmen were minded to follow this model there would, no doubt, be much to be said for making this explicitly clear, since it cannot be assumed that the courts will simply carry over into other types of contract the principles which have been worked out in the context of construction contracts.

6. HARDSHIP CLAUSES

Many international commercial contracts contain hardship clauses instead of, or perhaps more commonly as well as, *force majeure* clauses. Such clauses also normally deal with the effects of post-contract developments. The most important difference is that hardship clauses most commonly permit a party which complains of hardship to initiate a phase of renegotiation.

The four questions discussed above in relation to *force majeure* can be considered here too, but the first and third are the most important. As to definition it may perhaps be suggested that there are more widely accepted general notions of what are *force majeure* events than of what amounts to hardship. This suggests that definition of hardship is of great importance but this is clearly connected to the effects of hardship. If the only effect of hardship is to trigger a right to renegotiate, vagueness in definition may be tolerable, but only if the scope of the duty to renegotiate is clear. Is there a duty to negotiate in good faith? Is performance suspended during negotiation and if so, for how long? What happens if negotiations break down? The difficulties which surround the drafting of a hardship clause are discussed in more detail in Chapter 5 below.[12]

Perhaps the most important question is the relationship between *force majeure* and hardship where both clauses exist in the same contract. Are the clauses mutually exclusive? If not, in which order should they be applied? At present, there are no clear answers to these difficult questions.

MICHAEL FURMSTON

10. See above, p. 55.
11. See, e.g., *Hickman* v. *Roberts* [1913] A.C. 229; *Perini Corporation* v. *Commonwealth of Australia* (1969) 12 B.L.R. 82.
12. See, in particular, pp. 105–113.

CHAPTER 5

THE DETAILED DRAFTING OF A FORCE MAJEURE CLAUSE

1. IDENTIFYING THE OBJECTIVES

The "ordinary rule of law is that when *the law* creates a duty and the party is disabled from performing it without any default of his own, by the act of God, or the King's enemies, the law will excuse him[1]; but when a party *by his own contract* creates a duty, he is bound to make it good notwithstanding any accident by inevitable necessity".[2] The common law does not recognise *force majeure* as a defence to an action for breach of contract,[3] unless the terms of the obligation in issue are such as to incorporate an allowance for events beyond the relevant party's control[4]; nor will equity grant relief on the ground that an unforeseen event has prevented a party from fulfilling his obligations[5]; and the doctrine of frustration is confined within "very narrow limits".[6] Hence the need for a *force majeure* clause to relieve a party from liability should his performance of the contract be prevented by an event beyond his control which does not, however, frustrate the contract.

While a classic *force majeure* clause operates only if performance is prevented, more developed clauses apply if performance becomes onerous or even uneconomic and, rather than merely excluding liability, provide for an extension of the time for performance and/or other adjustments to a party's contractual obligations. In

1. See Smith & Hogan, *Criminal Law* (7th Edn., 1992) at pp. 262–263.

2. *Per* Mellish L.J., delivering the judgment of the Court of Appeal in *Nichols* v. *Marsland* (1876) 2 Ex.D. 1 at p. 4 (emphasis added).

3. *Jacobs, Marcus & Co.* v. *Credit Lyonnais* (1884) 12 Q.B.D. 589, but note that in *Ralli Brothers* v. *Compania Naviera Sota y Aznar* [1920] 2 K.B. 287, each member of the Court of Appeal said that the headnote of *Jacobs Marcus & Co.* v. *Credit Lyonnais* was misleading.

4. In *Hick* v. *Raymond & Reid* [1893] A.C. 22, Lord Watson laid down two general propositions. First, where the language of a contract does not expressly, or by necessary implication, fix any time for the performance of a contractual obligation, the law implies that it shall be performed within a reasonable time. Secondly, the condition of reasonable time means "that the party upon whom it is incumbent duly fulfils his obligation, notwithstanding protracted delay, so long as such delay is attributable to causes beyond his control and he has neither acted negligently nor unreasonably". Contrast *Postlethwaite* v. *Freeland* (1880) 5 App.Cas. 599 in which the House of Lords held that if, by the terms of the charterparty, a charterer has agreed to discharge the cargo within a fixed period of time, that is an absolute and unconditional engagement.

5. *Snell's Equity* (29th Edn., 1990), p. 544.

6. See pp. 42–44. But note the implications of *John Lewis Properties plc* v. *Viscount Chelsea* (1993) 67 P. & C.R. 120 in which Mummery J. held that, although events might not constitute sufficiently exceptional circumstances to frustrate a lease (see *National Carriers Limited* v. *Panalpina (Northern) Limited* [1981] A.C.675), yet they might provide an excuse for non-performance of the building covenants contained in the lease. Such events, Mummery J. continued, would provide a defence to an action for forfeiture for breach of the building covenant, but not a defence to a claim for rent.

Fairclough Dodd Ltd. v. *Vantol Ltd.*[7] Lord Tucker[8] rejected an argument that a *force majeure* clause is a provision which only prevents what otherwise might be a breach from being a breach so that it should be construed as applicable only in what would otherwise be a breach situation. Commenting on a clause which extended the time for delivery by two months he said:

"It seems to me to be altogether reasonable to provide in such circumstances for a fixed and definite period of extension which will facilitate commerce rather than to think only in terms of escape from breach or of impossibility of performance. . . . In the case of an exception clause, it is generally true to say that it only operates on the happening of an event which would otherwise result in a breach, but there is nothing to prevent the parties providing for an extension of the time for performance, or for a substituted mode of performance on the occurrence of a '*force majeure*' event, whether or not such event would have prevented performance."[9]

In *British Movietonews Ltd.* v. *London & District Cinemas Ltd.*[10] the House of Lords rejected Denning L.J.'s attempt in the Court of Appeal to introduce a principle that would have given the court power, where there had been "an uncontemplated turn of events" falling short of frustration, to disapply the parties' obligations under the contract and to "do therein what is just and reasonable".[11] In view of this judicial inability to adapt or qualify contractual obligations, some *force majeure* clauses provide for renegotiation of the contract, although, as will be seen, English law presents considerable difficulties in this area. Alternatively, a clause may provide for an arbitrator or expert to determine what modifications to the contract are fair and reasonable in the light of the new circumstances.

A further objective may be to prevent the doctrine of frustration[12] from operating, since frustration discharges a contract automatically, irrespective of the wishes of either party.[13] Moreover, if a contract leaves scope for the doctrine of frustration to apply, uncertainties could well arise about whether or not a particular event has frustrated the contract and, if so, the exact date on which frustration occurred.[14]

However, a *force majeure* clause cannot prevent a contract being automatically discharged[15] for illegality on the outbreak of a war on the ground that the contract involves intercourse with the enemy or confers an immediate or future benefit on the enemy.[16] It should also be noted that the parties do not need to exclude the doctrine of frustration in order to provide their own regime for such matters as the

7. [1956] 3 All E.R. 921.
8. With whom Viscount Simonds and Lord Morton of Henryton agreed.
9. *Ibid.* at p. 926.
10. [1952] A.C. 166.
11. In France, attempts to introduce a theory of *l'imprévision*, similar to Denning L.J.'s principle, have been rejected by the *Cour de Cassation*; see Mazeaud, Mazeaud and Chabas, *Leçons de Droit Civil* (8th Edn., 1991) Tome II, Premier Volume, para. 736.
12. Or to avoid the controversy of whether English law has a doctrine of partial frustration: see pp. 45–46 above.
13. *Joseph Constantine Steamship Line, Limited* v. *Imperial Smelting Corporation, Limited* [1942] A.C. 154, at pp. 170–172 and 187. See also Lord Wright's comments in *Denny, Mott & Dickson Ltd.* v. *James B Fraser & Co. Ltd.* [1944] A.C. 265, at pp. 274–276 and Proposition 3 of Bingham L.J. in *J. Lauritzen A.S.* v. *Wijsmuller B.V. (The Super Servant Two)* [1990] 1 Lloyd's Rep. 1 at p. 8.
14. See pp. 133–134 below.
15. *Ertel Bieber & Co.* v. *Rio Tinto Company* [1918] A.C. 260.
16. *Schering Limited* v. *Stockholms Enskilda Bank* [1946] A.C. 219 at p. 256; see also *Arab Bank Ltd.* v. *Barclays Bank Ltd.* [1954] A.C. 495 and *The Chrysalis* [1983] 1 Lloyd's Rep. 503 at p. 511.

recovery of money paid under the contract, payment for expenditure made in connection with the contract, and payment for non-monetary benefits received under the contract. While allowing the doctrine of frustration to operate, the contract can exclude or modify the provisions of the Law Reform (Frustrated Contracts) Act 1943 which relate to these issues of payment and recovery.[17]

2. THE REQUIREMENT FOR CLEAR WORDS

There appears to be no reported English case in which it was held (as part of the ratio) that there is a principle specifically applicable to *force majeure* clauses which requires a *force majeure* clause to be construed narrowly or against the party seeking to invoke it.[18] However, the general principle which requires an exclusion clause, and to a lesser extent a limitation clause, to be construed strictly is based on the inherent improbability that one party to a contract intended to release the other party from an obligation[19] or liability which the law would otherwise impose on him.[20] The main purpose of an ordinary *force majeure* clause is to relieve a party from a liability to damages for failing to perform a contractual obligation, and such a clause is normally drafted as a statement that a party shall not have any liability or responsibility,[21] rather than a statement that, in a *force majeure* situation, a party shall not be subject to the obligations which the contract would otherwise impose on him.[22] It is therefore considered that a normal *force majeure* clause is subject to the principle requiring an exclusion clause to be expressed in clear express terms if it is to be effective.

(a) The demurrage cases

This view is supported by the cases in which the courts have declined to construe exception clauses as qualifying a charterer's obligation to pay demurrage unless clearly so expressed. Recent examples in the Court of Appeal are *The Lefthero*,[23]

17. See s. 2(3) and pp. 118–119 and 240–242.

18. Treitel, *Frustration and Force Majeure* (1994) at para. 12–018 states that, although there may be a tendency to construe such clauses narrowly, there is no rule of law to this effect.

19. Lord Diplock's observations in *Photo Production Ltd.* v. *Securicor Transport Ltd.* [1980] A.C. 827 at p. 850 show that a clause which excludes a contractual obligation, rather than liability for breach of a contractual obligation, is nevertheless an exclusion clause and subject to strict construction, if the obligation excluded is one implied by law.

20. *Gilbert-Ash (Northern) Ltd.* v. *Modern Engineering (Bristol) Ltd.* [1974] A.C. 689 at p. 717; *Photo Production Ltd.* v. *Securicor Transport Ltd.* [1980] A.C. 827 at p. 850; *Ailsa Craig Fishing Co. Ltd.* v. *Malvern Fishing Co. Ltd.* [1983] 1 W.L.R. 964 at p. 970; *George Mitchell (Chesterhall) Ltd.* v. *Finney Lock Seeds Ltd.* [1983] 2 A.C. 803 at pp. 813–814; *Sonat Offshore S.A.* v. *Amerada Hess Development Ltd.* [1988] 1 Lloyd's Rep. 145 at p. 157; *E.E. Caledonia Ltd.* v. *Orbit Valve p.l.c.* [1994] 2 Lloyd's Rep. 239.

21. See, for example, the International Chamber of Commerce *Force Majeure* (Exemption) Clause which begins: "A party is not liable for a failure to perform any of his obligations . . . ", and clause 22 of GAFTA 100: "Sellers shall not be responsible for delay in shipment."

22. But some clauses qualify a party's obligations, for example, by extending the date for delivery or, in the case of export prohibitions, reducing the quantity to be delivered: see also *Treitel, op. cit.*, note 18 at 12–014.

23. [1992] 2 Lloyd's Rep. 109: see also the decision of Hobhouse J. in *The Forum Craftsman* [1991] 1 Lloyd's Rep. 81.

which concerned an exception for "restraint of princes" and *The Kalliopi A*[24] which concerned an exception for "unavoidable hindrances".

In *The Dias*[25] Lord Diplock gave this explanation:

"Since demurrage is liquidated damages,[26] fixed by agreement between the parties, it is possible by apt words in the charter-party to provide that, notwithstanding the continuance of the breach, demurrage shall not be payable in respect of the period when some event specified in the charter-party is happening; but the effect of such an agreement is to make an exception to the ordinary consequences that would flow in law from the charterer's continued breach of his contract, *viz*. his liability in damages. As was said by Lord Justice Scrutton in a passage in his work on charter-parties that was cited by Lord Reid in the *Union of India* case[27] . . . 'When once a vessel is on demurrage no exceptions will operate to prevent demurrage continuing to be payable unless the exceptions clause is clearly worded so as to have that effect.' This is but an example of the general principle stated by Lord Guest in the same case . . . : ' . . . an ambiguous clause is no protection.[28] "If a party wishes to exclude the ordinary consequences that would flow in law from the contract that he is making he must do so in clear terms." ' [*Szymonowski & Co.* v. *Beck & Co.* [1923] 1 K.B. 457 at p. 466, *per* Lord Justice Scrutton]."[29]

The point is reinforced by *The Saturnia*[30] in which the charterers argued that Lord Justice Scrutton's principle described above should not apply to the Gencon strike clause in view of the statements by Lord Fraser in *Ailsa Craig Fishing Co. Ltd.* v. *Malvern Fishing Co. Ltd.*[31] that the strict rules of construction applied to exceptions clauses are applied with less strictness to clauses which cannot be so described. This argument was rejected by the Court of Appeal, Sir John Donaldson M.R. (with whom Stephen Brown L.J. and Glidewell J. agreed) stating that the Gencon strike clause is "a clause which in all its essentials is in the nature of an exceptions clause". The decision is notable because the strike clause would not have excluded the charterers' liability for demurrage, but merely have reduced it by one-half.[32]

(b) Possible gaps in the ordinary force majeure clause

The appliction of strict rules of construction may well create a gap in the normal type of *force majeure* clause which provides that a party is not "liable" for a failure

24. [1988] 2 Lloyd's Rep. 101.
25. [1978] 1 Lloyd's Rep. 325.
26. *President of India* v. *Lips Maritime Corporation* [1988] A.C. 395 finally established that demurrage is *not* money payable by a charterer as consideration for the exercise by him of a right to detain a chartered ship beyond the stipulated lay days; but "a liability in damages to which a charterer becomes subject because, by detaining the chartered ship beyond the stipulated lay days, he is in breach of his contract. Most, if not all, voyage charters contain a demurrage clause, which prescribes a daily rate at which the damages for such detention are to be quantified. The effect of such a clause is to liquidate the damages payable: it does not alter the nature of the charterer's liability, which is and remains a liability for damages, albeit liquidated damages", *per* Lord Brandon of Oakbrook at p. 422.
27. [1962] 2 Lloyd's Rep. 175 at p. 180; [1964] A.C. 868 at p. 879.
28. This is well illustrated by the speech of Lord Edmund Davies in *The Dias* itself: [1978] 1 Lloyd's Rep. 325 at p. 329.
29. At p. 328.
30. [1987] 2 Lloyd's Rep. 43.
31. [1983] 1 W.L.R. 964 at p. 970.
32. Unfortunately, the charterer's argument was based, in part, on the discredited notion that demurrage is not damages, but money payable by a charterer for the exercise of a right to detain the vessel beyond the stipulated lay days; see the observations of Sir John Donaldson M.R. at [1987] 2 Lloyd's Rep. 43 at p. 45.

to perform caused by *force majeure*.[33] Such a clause, in a contract between A and B, clearly excludes A's liability in damages. However, it is submitted that it does not clearly, and therefore does not effectively, exclude B's right to "terminate" the contract on the ground of A's non-performance. The main effect of such a "termination" is that B "is thereby absolved from future performance of his obligations under the contract".[34] This is not imposing a liability on A. Admittedly there is the further result that those of A's obligations under the contract which remain unperformed are thereby discharged and replaced by a liability to pay damages to compensate B for the non-performance of those unperformed obligations.[35] But there is no reason why a *force majeure* clause could not be construed in a way which would exclude this liability of A to pay damages in respect of these unperformed obligations (as well as any breaches which occurred before "termination"), while leaving intact B's right to treat himself as absolved from future performance.

It is also open to argument that a clause which provides that A shall "not be liable" for non-performance caused by a *force majeure* event will not exclude a common law right of B to deduct from the sum otherwise payable to A the amount of damages which B has sustained as a result of A's non-performance. This right of deduction, or abatement, which is confined to contracts for the sale of goods or for work and labour,[36] entitles B " . . . not to set off, by a proceeding in the nature of a cross action, the amount of damages which he has sustained by breach of the contract, but simply to defend himself by shewing how much less the subject matter of the action was worth, by reason of the breach of contract".[37] It could well be argued that, on a strict construction, a reference to a liability of A should be confined to an obligation of A to make a payment, and does not cover B's common law right of abatement. Some support for this argument is provided by the recent decision of the Court of Appeal in *Connaught Restaurants Ltd.* v. *Indoor Leisure Ltd.*[38] Periodic flooding from the landlords' retained portion of a building disrupted the tenants' business causing them loss. Most of this flooding was caused as a consequence of breaches by the landlords of their covenants in the lease. The tenants withheld payment of the rent, and the landlords brought proceedings for possession of the premises and arrears of rent. The tenants pleaded equitable set-off in defence, but the landlords relied on the covenant to pay rent "without any deduction". The Court of Appeal held that clear words were needed to exclude a tenant's equitable right of set-off; that "deduction" could not be described as a clear word,

33. See, for example, the International Chamber of Commerce *Force Majeure* (Exemption) Clause.

34. See Lord Porter's statement in *Heyman* v. *Darwins Ltd.* [1942] A.C. 356 at p. 399 quoted by Lord Wilberforce in *Johnson* v. *Agnew* [1980] A.C. 367 at p. 393 and in *Photo Production Ltd.* v. *Securicor Transport Ltd.* [1980] A.C. 827 at p. 844; and *Gill & Duffus* v. *Berger* [1984] 1 All E.R. 438 at p. 443.

35. See Lord Diplock's analysis in *Photo Production Ltd.* v. *Securicor Transport Ltd.* [1980] A.C. 827 at p. 849 and propositions 1 and 2 set out by Mustill L.J. in *Lombard North Central P.L.C.* v. *Butterworth* [1987] Q.B. 527 at p. 535.

36. *Aries Tanker Corp.* v. *Total Transport Ltd.* [1977] 1 All E.R. 398 at p. 404.

37. The statement of Parke B. in *Mondel* v. *Steel* (1841) 8 M. & W. 858 at pp. 871–872 quoted by Lord Diplock in *Gilbert-Ash (Northern) Ltd.* v. *Modern Engineering (Bristol) Ltd.* [1974] A.C. 689 at p. 717. See also *Sim* v. *Rotherham Metropolitan Borough Council* [1986] 3 All E.R. 387 at pp. 410–413.

38. [1994] 1 W.L.R. 501. It is thought, however, that the passages in the judgment which are directed to showing that "deduction" is not a clear word can be criticised as reading in an ambiguity by the process of strained construction which was deprecated by Lord Bridge of Harwich in *George Mitchell (Chesterhall) Ltd.* v. *Finney Lock Seeds Ltd.* [1983] 2 A.C. 803 at p. 814. Steyn J.'s decision in *Famous Army Stores* v. *Meehan* [1993] 1 E.G.L.R. 73, disapproved by the Court of Appeal, may be more sound.

since it is heavily dependent on the context in which it is used for an accurate understanding of its meaning; and that in the absence of any context suggesting the contrary the phrase "without any deduction" was insufficient to exclude the tenants' equitable right of set-off. Waite L.J., who delivered the leading judgment, said that there is "a starting presumption that neither party intends to abandon any remedies for breach arising by operation of law, and clear language must be used if this presumption is to be rebutted"[39] and he cited Lord Diplock's statement to that effect in *Modern Engineering (Bristol) Ltd.* v. *Gilbert-Ash (Northern) Ltd.*[40]

The requirement for clear words applies to all aspects of a *force majeure* clause; the specific point about whether a *force majeure* clause will be construed as applying to an event caused by the negligence of the party invoking the clause will be considered later.[41]

3. MAIN COMPONENTS OF A FORCE MAJEURE CLAUSE

A *force majeure* clause should, it is suggested, normally have the following main elements:

(a) a statement of the events in which the clause is capable of being brought into operation; preferably, the clause should be capable of being invoked by a party who apprehends that such an event will occur later;
(b) a statement as to whether or not the event must have been one which the relevant party could not have been expected to take into account at the time of the contract and, if unforeseeability is unnecessary, whether the clause applies to an event already existing at the date of the contract;
(c) a statement of the effect which such an event must have on a party's ability to perform its contractual obligations; for example, the clause may provide that performance must be "prevented" or merely "hindered";
(d) a statement of the affected party's duties in a *force majeure* situation; a key issue here is how far the affected party has to go to attempt to overcome the *force majeure* event's consequences;
(e) the mechanism for bringing the clause into operation;
(f) the consequences of the clause applying, and, in particular, machinery for the adjustment of the contract's terms;
(g) the mechanism for bringing the operation of the clause to an end; and
(h) provisions to prevent the doctrine of frustration from applying.

These elements will now be considered in more detail.

4. A STATEMENT OF THE FORCE MAJEURE EVENTS

(a) Burden of proof

In *Channel Island Ferries Ltd.* v. *Sealink U.K. Ltd.*[42] Parker L.J. laid down several propositions which are relevant to drafting a *force majeure* clause. Parker L.J.'s

39. *Ibid.*, at p. 505.
40. [1974] A.C. 689 at p. 717.
41. At pp. 72–77.
42. [1988] 1 Lloyd's Rep. 323.

first proposition was that "it is for the party relying on a *force majeure* clause to bring himself squarely within that clause".[43] In *Bremer Handelsgesellschaft m.b.H.* v. *C. Mackprang Jr.*,[44] Lord Denning M.R. treated this as an application of the common law principle that "a party who relies on an exception clause must prove the facts to support his exception". The party invoking the clause must show first that one of the events to which the *force majeure* clause applies has occurred, and second that the event was the cause of his being "prevented" or "delayed" (or whatever the relevant expression is) from performing the contract. In *Raiffeisen Hauptgenossenschaft* v. *Louis Dreyfus & Co.*,[45] in which the sellers sought to rely on a clause[46] which provided that "in case of prohibition of export . . . preventing fulfilment, this Contract . . . shall be cancelled", Robert Goff J. (as he then was) said: "It is for the sellers to prove that they could take advantage of the clause, and to do that it is for them to prove that the export control regulations were the cause of their failure to ship, having regard to all the circumstances of the case."[47]

Although not a case on a *force majeure* clause, it is thought that the decision of the House of Lords in *Yorkshire Dale Steamship Co. Ltd.* v. *Minister of War Transport*[48] provides valid guidance about how the question of causation should be handled. The Yorkshire Dale Steamship company owned the vessel *Coxwold* which was requisitioned by the Minister of War Transport on terms which left with the company the responsibility of insuring the vessel "except as otherwise provided". The excepting provision referred *inter alia* to "damage to the ship . . . caused by . . . warlike operations". In May 1940 the *Coxwold* was carrying a cargo of petrol to Norway for the use of British forces and was thus admittedly engaged in a warlike operation. She was in a convoy of merchant vessels under the orders of a naval officer. No navigation lights were shown by the convoy, except that the two leading vessels carried dimmed and shaded stern lights. Owing to poor visibility, the *Coxwold* lost the shaded stern light of her leading ship and an hour later ran aground on the Damsel Rocks. The Court of Appeal held that the cause of the stranding was not the warlike operation on the part of the *Coxwold*, but an unexpected and unexplained set of the tide on the vessel, which would have carried her onto the rocks whatever her destination. This decision was reversed by the House of Lords. Lord Wright, with whom Lord Atkin agreed, said that, although the stranding was undoubtedly a peril of the sea, it was necessary to look behind the stranding to ascertain if the cause of the casualty was a peril which could be described as a consequence of warlike operations. He stated:

"This choice of the real or efficient cause from out of the whole complex of the facts must be made by applying commonsense standards. Causation is to be understood as the man in the street, and not as either the scientist or the metaphysician, would understand it. Cause here

43. See also the statement by Robert Goff J. (as he then was) in *Avimex* v. *Dewulf* [1979] 2 Lloyd's Rep. 57, at p. 67.

44. [1979] 1 Lloyd's Rep. 221.

45. [1981] 1 Lloyd's Rep. 345, at p. 351.

46. The notorious prohibition clause in GAFTA 100. In *Bremer Handelsgesellschaft m.b.H.* v. *Continental Grain Co.* [1983] 1 Lloyd's Rep. 269, at p. 292, Ackner L.J. referred to "the seething cauldron of ingenuity" to which the 1973 US embargo on the export of soya beans and GAFTA 100 had given rise.

47. Discussed in more detail in Chapter 15.

48. [1942] A.C. 691. See also *O' May* on *Marine Insurance* (1993) at pp. 255–256.

means what a business or seafaring man would take to be the cause without too microscopic analysis but on a broad view."[49]

The House of Lords adopted a similar approach in *Monarch Steamship Co. Ltd.* v. *Karlshamns Oljefabriker (A/B)*.[50] The *British Monarch*, a British vessel, was chartered in April 1939 by a British company, and bills of lading signed on behalf of the owners were issued to the charterers in respect of a cargo of soya beans. In June 1939, the charterers nominated a Swedish port as the sole port of discharge. However, there was a delay caused by the *British Monarch's* unseaworthiness, and she was still undergoing repairs at Port Said when war was declared. The British Admiralty prohibited the vessel from proceeding to the Swedish port, and ordered her to proceed to Glasgow. A Swedish company, which had purchased the soya bean cargo from the charterers, became indorsees of the bills of lading, and sued the *British Monarch*'s owners for the losses which they had incurred as a result of the vessel's failure to deliver the cargo at the nominated Swedish port. The owners' defence was based on the war risks clause in the charter which exonerated them in the event of compliance with any orders given by the government of the nation under whose flag the vessel sailed. This defence was rejected by the House of Lords, which held that the cause of the *British Monarch*'s not proceeding to the nominated Swedish port was her unseaworthiness and thus the delay in carrying out the contract of carriage was attributable to the owners' default. Lord Wright said:

"I am not entering upon or discussing any theory of causation. Those interested in philosophy will find modern philosophic views on causation explained in Russell's History of Western Philosophy in the chapter on Hume, Book 3, ch. xvii. The common law however is not concerned with philosophic speculation, but is only concerned with ordinary everyday life and thoughts and expressions, and would not hesitate to think and say that, because it caused the delay, unseaworthiness caused the Admiralty order diverting the vessel. I think the common law would be right in picking out unseaworthiness from the whole complex of circumstances as the dominant cause."[51]

The issue of causation lies at the heart of a seller's obligations where, as a result of an unexpected event, he finds himself with insufficient goods available to fulfil his commitments to all his customers, although he has sufficient goods to meet the order of a particular customer. If the seller fails to deliver the full quantity ordered by that customer, is this failure caused by the *force majeure* event or by the seller's decision to make deliveries to his other customers? In *Westfalische Central-Genossenschaft G.m.b.H.* v. *Seabright Chemicals Ltd.*[52] Robert Goff J. (as he then was) made these observations which were subsequently approved by the Court of Appeal in *Bremer Handelsgesellschaft m.b.H.* v. *Continental Grain Co.*[53]:

" . . . in a case in which a seller can . . . claim the protection of a clause which protects him where fulfilment is hindered by the excepted peril, subsequent delivery of part of his available stock to other customers will not be regarded as an independent cause of shortage, provided that in making such delivery the seller acted reasonably in all the circumstances of the case. This is because, in the absence of any contractual term to the contrary, the buyer under a contract containing such a clause must contemplate that the seller has other customers

49. *Ibid.*, at p. 706.
50. [1949] A.C. 196.
51. *Ibid.*, at p. 228.
52. (1979), unreported.
53. [1983] 1 Lloyd's Rep. 269 at pp. 291–292.

beside himself, and must also contemplate that the seller will take reasonable steps to fulfil the needs of other customers; and reasonable action so taken by the seller should not in these circumstances be regarded as a cause or shortage independent of the excepted peril."[54]

The principle that a party can only invoke a *force majeure* clause if his performance of the contract has, as a matter of commercial reality, been affected is illustrated by the decision of Parker J. (as he then was) in *Tradax Export S.A.* v. *Rocco Giuseppe & Figli*.[55] In that case, the sellers discovered the existence of a circle, that is, that they had repurchased the goods from their buyer (or a subsequent buyer). An exchange of telexes then took place between the sellers and the buyers which replaced the parties' obligations under the existing contracts by an obligation to pay price differences, so that no steps were to be taken to effect physical delivery. It was held that, in these circumstances, the sellers could not invoke the *force majeure* clause on the ground that the United States government had imposed an export embargo.

Where non-performance is attributable to two events, of which only one falls within the *force majeure* clause, it may be sufficient to show that that event was the dominant and proximate cause of the non-performance. In *Leyland Shipping Company, Ltd.* v. *Norwich Union Fire Insurance Society, Ltd*,[56] a ship was insured against perils of the sea by a policy which excluded all consequences of hostilities. The ship was torpedoed by a German submarine 25 miles from Havre, but with the aid of tugs she reached Havre on the evening of the same day. A gale sprang up, and the harbour authorities, fearing that the ship would sink and block the quay, ordered her to a berth inside the outer breakwater, where there was considerable wind and sea. There she was subjected to considerable strain and two days later sank. At first instance Rowlatt J. accepted the insurers' contention that the loss of the ship had been caused by the torpedo. This view was also taken by the Court of Appeal, with Scrutton L.J. doubting but not dissenting. Dismissing the appeal, the House of Lords held that the injury by the torpedo was the proximate cause of the loss. Lord Dunedin[57] stated that the question of which is the proximate cause is not solved by the mere point of order in time.

(b) "Physical or legal impossibility"

Parker L.J.'s second proposition in *Channel Island Ferries Ltd.* v. *Sealink U.K. Ltd.*[58] was that "in most cases, the party relying on a *force majeure* clause must

54. There is a striking similarity between this reasoning and that of Lord Wright M.R. in *The Oropesa* [1943] P. 32. It is thought that the criticism of Robert Goff J.'s reasoning which Dillon L.J. made in *The Super Servant Two* [1990] 1 Lloyd's Rep. 1 at pp. 13 and 14 relates to its validity in a claim that a contract has been frustrated, not in a claim to invoke a *force majeure* clause.

55. [1981] 1 Lloyd's Rep. 353.

56. [1918] A.C. 350; see also *Boiler Inspection and Insurance Company of Canada* v. *Sherwin-Williams Company of Canada Ltd.* [1951] A.C. 319; but note the dicta in *Wayne Tank & Pump Co. Ltd.* v. *Employers Liability Assurance Corporation Ltd.* [1974] 1 Q.B. 57 that insurers can rely on an exceptions clause if the damage is caused by two events of equal causative efficiency, and one is within the general words of the policy and would render the insurers liable but the other is within the exception. Although these are cases on exclusions in insurance policies, they are thought applicable to *force majeure* clauses. Note also *Intertradex S.A.* v. *Lesieur Tourteaux S.A.R.L.* [1978] 2 Lloyd's Rep. 509, discussed at pp. 100–101 below.

57. *Ibid.*, at p. 363.

58. [1988] 1 Lloyd's Rep. 323.

show either legal or physical impossibility".[59] It seems, however, that this only applies if the clause operates on stated events "preventing" performance. A leading case is *In re Comptoir Commerciale Anversois and Power, Son & Co.*[60] where the clause in issue provided: "In case of prohibition of export, *force majeure*, blockade or hostilities preventing shipment, this contract . . . shall be at an end." The Court of Appeal[61] held that, as used in that clause, "prevention" meant either physical or legal prevention of shipment. Scrutton L.J. said: "Economic unprofitability is not 'prevention', though a very high price for the article sold may be evidence of such a physical scarcity due to hostilities as amounts to prevention by hostilities."[62] *Comptoir Commerciale* was cited with approval by Viscount Simonds, Lord Hudson and Lord Guest in *Tsakiroglou & Co. Limited* v. *Noblee Thorl G.m.b.H.*[63] which arose out of the closure of the Suez Canal in 1956. The contract in issue was for the sale of Sudanese groundnuts c.i.f. Hamburg and, when the contract was entered into, the usual route for shipment was via the Suez Canal, both parties then contemplating that shipment would be made by that route. The Suez Canal was blocked, and remained closed, during the period for shipment. But the sellers could have transported the goods via the Cape of Good Hope, although this would have involved a voyage of 11,000 miles as against 4,400 miles via Suez and would have meant a 25 per cent rise in the freight rate above that ruling when the contract was made. The House of Lords held that, although the sellers' profit would have been reduced and might even have disappeared, the c.i.f. contract was not frustrated.[64]

(c) Negligence

A frequent issue is whether a party can invoke a *force majeure* clause in relation to an event caused by the negligence of that party's own employees; one particular point which has been debated is the extent to which a *force majeure* clause is subject to the principles of interpretation laid down in *Canada Steamship Lines Ltd* v. *R.*[65] for clauses that exclude a party's liability for the negligence of its own employees. These principles are (i) if there is no express reference to negligence[66] on the part of the party seeking to rely on the clause, that party must show that the words used in the clause are wide enough, in their ordinary meaning, to cover negligence by

59. [1988] 1 Lloyd's Rep. 323 at p. 327.
60. [1920] 1 K.B. 868.
61. Upholding Bailhache J.
62. *Ibid.*, at p. 898.
63. [1962] A.C. 93.
64. Viscount Simonds stated that "it hardly needs reasserting that an increase of expense is not a ground of frustration".
65. [1952] A.C. 192. For recent applications of the *Canada Steamship* principles see *EE Caledonia Limited* v. *Orbit Valve Co. Europe* [1994] 2 Lloyd's Rep. 239 and *The Fiona* [1994] C.L.C. 808; see also *Dorset County Council* v. *Southern Felt Roofing Co. Ltd.* (1989) 48 B.L.R. 96 (C.A.) discussed Palmer & McKendrick, in *Product Liability in the Construction Industry* (Lloyd's of London Press, 1993) at pp. 205–207; compare Brandon J.'s summary in *The Rossetti* [1972] 2 Lloyd's Rep. 116 at p. 118 of the principles applicable to a clause in a bill of lading which excludes the shipowners' responsibility for unseaworthiness.
66. If, however, there is an express reference to the negligence of a party's employees, it seems that full effect will be given to it, so that even the most culpable negligence by those employees will not render that party liable: *Scrutton on Charterparties* (19th Edn., 1984), at p. 242.

that party's employees; if a doubt arises at this point, it must be resolved against the party invoking the clause; (ii) however, if the words used are wide enough to cover negligence, the court must then consider whether the head of damage may be based on some ground other than that of negligence; (iii) provided that the other ground is not fanciful or remote,[67] the existence of a possible head of damage other than negligence is fatal to an attempt to invoke the clause to protect a party from the consequences of its employees' negligence.[68]

The *Canada Steamship* principles were considered in *The Super Servant Two*[69] in the context of a clause which gave one party the right to cancel the contract if certain *force majeure* events occurred. However, the clause did not expressly limit that party's liability and both Bingham and Dillon L.JJ. stated that it was not an exceptions clause. Bingham L.J. said that the clause was therefore "not . . . directly covered by *Canada Steamship*". But, since it conferred on only one party a right exercisable in a very wide range of circumstances to nullify the contract at no cost to itself and regardless of the loss which the other party might sustain, "the broad approach indicated by *Canada Steamship* is in my judgment appropriate".[70] The main points in Bingham L.J.'s analysis of *The Super Servant Two* clause are relevant to the usual type of *force majeure* clause. He noted, first that the clause did not expressly provide that the relevant party could cancel even though the event in question was one which they could have averted by using reasonable care, and secondly that the language of the clause was wide enough to cover events caused by the relevant party's negligence. However, Bingham L.J. then added these two qualifications:

> "But the general tenor of the clause, opening with a reference to *force majeure* and acts of God and including such events as acts of war, civil commotion, canal closure and harbour congestion, strongly points towards events beyond the direct or indirect control of Wijsmuller.
>
> Clause 17.1 is not deprived of a sensible application if read as excluding events brought about by the negligence of Wijsmuller, their servants or agents. Almost all the events listed could only occur wholly independently of Wijsmuller and there is none which could only occur as a result of Wijsmuller's negligence."[71]

Dillon L.J. seemed to take the view[72] that the *Canada Steamship* principles were not directly applicable because the clause concerned was "a cancellation clause and

67. See Professor N. E. Palmer's reformulation of principle (iii) in [1983] L.M.C.L.Q. 557, at p. 561, commenting on *The Raphael* [1982] 2 Lloyd's Rep. 42: "a clause which is wide enough in its ordinary meaning to cover negligence [is invalidated] only when an alternative head of liability is sufficiently realistic and predictable to enable the court to conclude that the parties intended the clause to apply to that alternative ground alone."

68. Although the *Canada Steamship* principles were originally formulated in the context of clauses excluding liability for employee negligence, and their applicability to such clauses is well established, it is suggested that it is nowadays somewhat unrealistic to subject such clauses to strict construction. It can be argued, particularly in the case of a large company, that the negligent act of an employee below board or senior management level is an "external" event over which the company has no effective control: compare *Tesco Supermarkets Ltd.* v. *Nattrass* [1982] A.C. 153 and *The Safe Carrier* [1994] 1 Lloyd's Rep. 589; but contrast *Tesco Stores Ltd.* v. *Brent London Borough Council* [1993] 1 W.L.R. 1037. Note also *El Ajou v. Dollar Land Holdings* [1994] 2 All E.R. 685.

69. [1990] 1 Lloyd's Rep. 1 at p. 7; see also Chapters 1 and 3.

70. *Ibid.*, at p. 7.

71. *Ibid.*, at p. 7.

72. *Ibid.*, at p. 12.

not an exceptions clause". However, Dillon L.J. referred to a rule, similar to the *Canada Steamship* principles, that, in an exceptions clause in a bill of lading or contract of carriage excepting the shipowner from liability for perils of the sea, there is by necessary inference to be read in an exception upon the exceptions that the exception for perils of the sea is not to apply if the loss was the result of the negligence of the shipowner or his servants.[73] This rule, Dillon L.J. said, applied *prima facie* to a power to cancel a contract where performance of the contract has been impeded, prevented or delayed by perils and accidents of the sea.

Two earlier decisions[74] on the New York Produce Exchange form of time charter support the view that the *Canada Steamship* principles apply to *force majeure* clauses. In *Seven Seas Transportation Ltd.* v. *Pacifico Union Marina Corporation (The Satya Kailash)*,[75] Staughton J. (as he then was) considered that the *Canada Steamship* principles were applicable and that an exception in the *force majeure* clause for "errors of navigation" did not cover negligent errors of navigation. Strictly speaking, however, it was not necessary for Staughton J. to decide the point since he held that the respondents were protected by other provisions. But the decision of Bingham J. (as he then was) in *Industrie Chimiche Italia Centrale S.p.A.* v. *Nea Ninemia Shipping Co. S.A. (The Emmanuel C)*[76] is direct authority for the proposition that the *Canada Steamship* principles are applicable to a *force majeure* clause. However, it is thought that these two decisions should be regarded with some caution since they were decided before *Ailsa Craig Fishing Co. Ltd.* v. *Malvern Fishing Co. Ltd.*, which contains Lord Fraser's statement that the *Canada Steamship* principles are not applicable in their full rigour to limitation clauses, had appeared in the main law reports.[77] In particular, although Bingham J.'s judgment in *The Emmanuel C*[78] contains a list of the main cases relevant to clauses excluding negligence liability, there is no mention of *Ailsa Craig Fishing*.

The *force majeure* clause in *The Super Servant Two*[79] conferred on only one party a right exercisable in a very wide range of circumstances to nullify the contractual bargain made between the parties at no cost to itself and regardless of the loss which the other party might sustain; and it is thought that the more drastic the

73. The main authority cited by Dillon L.J. was *The Glendaroch* [1894] P. 226, particularly the judgment of Lord Esher M.R. at pp. 230–231. See also *Dunn* v. *Bucknall Brothers* [1902] 2 K.B. 614, a claim for damages for delay in the delivery of goods which the plaintiffs had shipped on the defendant's steamship. The bills of lading excepted liability for loss or damage occasioned by restraint of princes. The ship sailed with the plaintiffs' goods on board shortly after the outbreak of war between Britain and the Transvaal. She was arrested by a British warship and found to contain goods consigned to residents in Transvaal. The Prize Court condemned the goods, but released the ship and, as a result of these proceedings, the delivery of the plaintiffs' goods was delayed by several months. One of the findings of the Prize Court was, in effect, that the defendants had been negligent or careless in carrying enemies' goods in the hope of being able to give explanations to the British authorities which would avoid the condemnation of the ship. The Court of Appeal held that the defendants could not rely on the restraint of princes exception "to excuse them from the consequences of a peril which their own negligence has contributed to bring about. The principle is thus stated in Carver on *Carriage by Sea* . . . 'A shipowner will not be exonerated from losses arising from any of these excepted causes when there has been any neglect on his part to take all reasonable steps to avoid them.' " See now *Carver* (13th Edn., 1982) at para. 135.
74. Both decisions related to exceptions, rather than cancellation, clauses.
75. [1982] 2 Lloyd's Rep. 465.
76. [1983] 1 Lloyd's Rep. 310.
77. [1983] 1 W.L.R. 964; [1983] 1 All E.R. 101; (1983) 127 S.J. 508.
78. [1983] 1 Lloyd's Rep. 310.
79. [1990] 1 Lloyd's Rep. 1.

effect of a clause the more likely it is that it will attract the *Canada Steamship* principles. It is, therefore, questionable how far the *Canada Steamship* principles apply to a clause which does not entitle one party to terminate the contract, but, for example, provides a party with a fixed extension of the time for performance. However, it should be kept in mind that in *The Saturnia*[80] the Court of Appeal rejected an argument that a strike clause which would not have excluded liability for demurrage, but merely reduced it by one-half, was not subject to the strict rules of construction applied to exceptions clauses, but should be accorded the less rigorous treatment given to clauses which merely limit liability.[81]

Nevertheless, it is suggested that the issue of whether *Canada Steamship* principles apply to *force majeure* clauses is of limited practical significance. Even if these principles are applicable, they are, as has been said on a number of occasions,[82] no more than guidance, and every contract has to be construed having regard to its own terms and context and the circumstances in which it was made. If the *Canada Steamship* principles are not strictly applicable, a court may well hold, following Bingham L.J. in *The Super Servant Two*, that a broadly similar approach should be adopted. Bingham L.J.'s judgment[83] suggests that the real risk is that a *force majeure* clause which does not expressly cover a party's negligence will, by referring to such events as war, strikes and harbour congestion, strongly point towards events beyond that party's direct or indirect control. A court does not need to invoke the *Canada Steamship* principles in order to adopt such an approach. For example, in *Lloyd* v. *General Iron Screw Collier Company*,[84] decided almost a century before *Canada Steamship*, it was held that an exception in a bill of lading for "accidents or damage of the seas, rivers, and steam navigation, of whatever nature and kind soever," did not exempt the shipowner from responsibility for loss of goods by reason of a collision caused by the negligence of the master or crew. Bramwell B.'s approach was similar to that of Bingham L.J. in *The Super Servant Two*. He said:

"It is to be observed that the exceptions are, 'the act of God, the Queen's enemies, pirates, robbers, thieves'—all of which, I suppose, mean inevitable perils. Then comes 'barratry of master or mariners, restraint of princes and rulers, fire' (which may, no doubt, arise from carelessness or misfortune), 'accident or damage from machinery, boilers, steam' (which cannot apply to an explosion caused by the wilful act of the engineer), 'or from other goods by contact, sweating, leaking or otherwise'. Then comes 'and accidents or damage of the seas, rivers, and steam navigation, of whatever nature or kind soever'. The plaintiff says that the collision was caused by the negligence of the defendants. In common parlance that is certainly not an 'accident.' . . . The words 'accidents or damage of the seas,' &c., have much the same meaning as 'perils of the seas,' and, with the exception of barratry and fire, the whole provision is directed against inevitable accidents, and not against events which might be avoided by prudence and care."[85]

80. [1987] 2 Lloyd's Rep. 43.
81. See *George Mitchell (Chesterhall) Ltd.* v. *Finney Lock Seeds Ltd.* [1983] 2 A.C. 803 at pp. 813–814.
82. Recent examples are the judgment of Hobhouse J. in *EE Caledonia Limited* v. *Orbit Valve Co. Europe* [1994] 1 W.L.R. 221 at p. 227 and that of Steyn L.J. on appeal at [1994] 2 Lloyd's Rep. 239 at p. 245.
83. [1990] 1 Lloyd's Rep. 1 at p. 7; see also Hobhouse J.'s observations at [1989] 1 Lloyd's Rep. 148 at p. 160.
84. (1864) 3 H. & C. 284.
85. *Ibid.*, at p. 292; see also Carver on *Carriage by Sea* (13th Edn., 1982) at para. 137.

Negligence can partially affect a party's right to rely on a *force majeure* clause. In *Elswick Steamship Company Ltd* v. *Montaldi*[86] the defendant was the charterer of the plaintiff's ship and the consignee of the cargo shipped under bills of lading incorporating the charterparty. That provided that the charterer would discharge the ship; that the consignee should take the cargo from alongside at an average of 500 tonnes per working day; and that the consignee should pay demurrage if the ship were detained longer, but that in the case of strikes preventing or delaying the discharge the time lost was not to count unless the ship was already on demurrage. A strike occurred when less than half the cargo had been discharged, but until that point the consignee had been discharging the cargo at less than the contractual rate of 500 tonnes per day. Bigham J. held that the defendant could not rely on the strike as a defence to the demurrage claim, except as regards that quantity of the cargo which would have remained undischarged when the strike commenced if up to that time the defendant had been discharging the cargo at the rate of 500 tonnes per working day.

In cases of alleged negligence, there is an additional point relating to the burden of proof. In a case of an exceptions clause, the position was explained by Lord Esher M.R. in *The Glendarroch*[87]:

> "The plaintiffs would have to prove the contract and the non-delivery. If they leave that in doubt, of course they fail. The defendants' answer is, 'Yes; but the case was brought within the exception—within its ordinary meaning.' That lies upon them. Then the plaintiffs have a right to say there are exceptional circumstances, *viz*., that the damage was brought about by the negligence of the defendants' servants, and it seems to me that it is for the plaintiffs to make out that second exception."[88]

Accordingly, in *The Antwerpen*,[89] where the consignee of 13 containers of whisky sued the operator of the container terminal for damages resulting from the loss of two containers, the New South Wales Court of Appeal held that, once the terminal operator had established that it was entitled to rely on an exemption clause in the bill of lading, the onus of proof moved to the consignee to establish its claim that the containers had been lost through a theft in which the terminal operator's employees had co-operated. The terminal operator did not have to show how the loss of the containers had occurred and was therefore protected by the exemption clause.[90]

A *force majeure* clause which, even on a strict construction, excludes liability for negligence may yet fail under the Unfair Contract Terms Act 1977. *Smith* v. *Bush*[91] makes it impossible to argue that the Act does not apply to a clause which operates by preventing a duty of care from arising in the first place, rather than by excluding liability for breach of it once it has arisen. Moreover, *Stewart Gill Ltd.* v. *Horatio*

86. [1907] 1 K.B. 626.

87. [1894] P. 226; see also *Stag Line Limited* v. *Foscolo, Mango & Co. Limited* [1932] A.C. 328, at p. 340; *The Antwerpen* [1994] 1 Lloyd's Rep. 213 at pp. 237–238; *The Bunga Seroja* [1994] 1 Lloyd's Rep. 455 at p. 460.

88. [1894] P. 226 at p. 231.

89. [1994] 1 Lloyd's Rep. 213.

90. Compare the decision of the Quebec Court of Appeal in *Eisen und Metall A.G.* v. *Ceres Stevedoring Co. Ltd.* [1977] 1 Lloyd's Rep. 665, and the onus of proof in a case of frustration: *Joseph Constantine Steamship Line Ltd.* v. *Imperial Smelting Corporation Limited* [1942] A.C. 154.

91. [1990] 1 A.C. 831: see Lord Templeman's observations at p. 848 and those of Lord Griffiths at pp. 856–857.

Myer & Co. Ltd.[92] establishes that the whole of a clause which is subject to the 1977 Act has to satisfy the requirement of reasonableness, not just that part of the clause which the defendant happens to be relying on to defend the particular claim which has been made. Nevertheless, it should be kept in mind that the Act by no means applies to all contracts; in particular, section 26 excludes international supply contracts; section 27 excludes a contract which, but for an express choice of English, Scottish or Northern Ireland law, would be governed by the law of a country outside the United Kingdom; and Schedule 1 considerably restricts the application of the Act in relation to charterparties and contracts for the carriage of goods by ship. It is clearly possible for a *force majeure* clause to be caught by the Directive on Unfair Terms in Consumer Contracts.[93]

(d) Defaults other than negligence

So far as defaults other than negligence are concerned, it seems clear that there is no rule of law which prevents a *force majeure* clause from providing that it can be invoked by a party in respect of an event caused by a breach of his own obligations under the contract. In *Alghussein Establishment* v. *Eton College*,[94] the House of Lords considered that the weight of authority favours the view that, in general, the principle that a party cannot take advantage of his own wrong is a rule of the construction of contracts, rather than an absolute rule of law. The House of Lords left open the point of whether there are situations such as self-induced frustration where an absolute rule exists.

(e) Circumstances already existing at the date of the contract

In some, but by no means all, cases the courts have held that a party cannot invoke a *force majeure* clause in relation to circumstances which, to that party's knowledge, were in existence when he entered into the contract. For example, in *Safadi* v. *Western Assurance Company*[95] Roche J. said:

> "There is a great deal of doctrine and authority to the effect that you cannot apply language such as 'cause or circumstances or matters beyond the control of the assured' to excuse performance when those . . . matters are represented by . . . matters in existence and known to be in existence by the person relying upon them at the time he makes the contract from the performance of which he seeks to be excused."

However, in *Reardon Smith Line Ltd* v. *Ministry of Agriculture*,[96] Sellers L.J., agreeing with McNair J.'s conclusion at first instance, stated: "There is no settled rule of construction that a specific exception, such as strikes or war, cannot be relied upon if the strike or war was operative at the time when the contract was made or the ship ordered to the affected port. It must depend on a proper construc-

92. [1992] Q.B. 600.
93. Council Directive 93/13/EEC O.J. No. L95/29; see in particular paras. 1(b) and 1(f) in the Annex. See also Reynolds (1994) 110 L.Q.R. 1.
94. [1991] 1 All E.R. 267. See also *Gyllenhammar* v. *Sour Brodogradevna Industrija* [1989] 2 Lloyd's Rep. 403.
95. (1933) 46 Ll.L.Rep. 140 at p. 143.
96. [1962] 1 Q.B. 42.

tion of the contract."[97] The principle was further weakened by Willmer L.J. who, having stated that he did not find it necessary to express any concluded opinion as to the validity of the principle, said that, if it exists, it must be subject to two qualifications:

> "(1) The facts which show that the ship must be inevitably doomed to be subject to the specified cause must be facts in existence when the contract is made. It could not in any case be sufficient merely to prove *ex post facto* that, in the light of events as they in fact turned out, the excepted cause was bound to operate . . . (2) The second qualification, which follows on the first, is that the existence of facts, which show that the excepted cause is bound to operate, must be known to the parties at the time of the contract, or at least to the party who seeks to rely on the exception."[98]

Willmer L.J.'s second qualification was extended by Kerr J. in *Trade and Transport Inc.* v. *Iino Kaiun Kaisha Ltd (The Angelia)*[99]; Kerr J. stated that a party cannot rely on pre-existing facts "if the existence of such facts should reasonably have been known to [that party] . . . and would have been expected by the other party to the contract to be so known". In that case, Kerr J. refused to permit charterers to rely on a *force majeure* clause because they had failed to take "a reasonable business precaution" of making enquiries from which they would have discovered that a *force majeure* event was already in existence.

There are also statements in *Reardon Smith*[100] that strikes are in a special category because they are often ended or settled quickly so that it cannot be said in many cases or, indeed, in any case, that a contract was "doomed" by a strike which existed when the contract was signed.

However, *Navrom* v. *Callitsis Ship Management S.A. (The Radauti)*[101] is probably more representative of current judicial thinking on this issue. In that case, Staughton J. rejected an argument that, since a clause was headed "*Force Majeure*", it would not apply to congestion at the port of Tripoli because the congestion had been in existence when the charter was entered into and it was well known that Tripoli had suffered from congestion for a number of years. Staughton J. was upheld on appeal.[102] Lloyd L.J. (as he then was) quoted the following from *Scrutton on Charterparties*: "Exceptions can be successfully relied upon even though the event preventing performance is operating at the date of the contract."[103] Lloyd L.J. also rejected the argument based on the fact that the clause was headed "*Force Majeure*", stating: "I can see no justification for so limiting the ordinary meaning of the words by reference to the heading. '*Force Majeure*' is clearly used as an omnibus description for a variety of different causes. The rubric

97. *Ibid.*, at p. 83.

98. *Ibid.*, at pp. 107–108. Willmer L.J. cited *Steamship "Induna" Co. Limited* v. *British Phosphate Commissioners* [1949] 2 K.B. 430.

99. [1972] 2 Lloyd's Rep. 154 at p. 163 but note Parker L.J.'s comments in *Channel Island Ferries Ltd.* v. *Sealink Ltd.* [1988] 1 Lloyd's Rep. 323 at p. 328.

100. Particularly by McNair J. at [1960] 1 Q.B. 495–496, by Sellers L.J. at [1962] 1 Q.B. 89 and by Willmer L.J. at [1962] 1 Q.B. 108.

101. [1987] 2 Lloyd's Rep. 276; [1988] 2 Lloyd's Rep. 416.

102. [1988] 2 Lloyd's Rep. 416.

103. 19th Edn., p. 220. Note also that in *Pagnan S.p.A.* v. *Tradax Ocean Transportation S.A.* [1987] 3 All E.R. 565 the quota scheme was introduced shortly before the contract in issue was concluded, but there was no suggestion that this precluded the sellers from relying on the *force majeure* clause.

does not affect the meaning of each individual cause."[104] Croom-Johnson L.J. also said that the heading did not contribute to the interpretation of the clause.

(f) Foreseeability

It can be argued that a party should not be entitled to relief under a *force majeure* clause in respect of an event if, when he entered into the contract, he could reasonably have been expected to take the risk of that event into account and to have made contingency plans to deal with it.[105] However, it is thought that there is no principle of English law to this effect. As noted above[106] there is no rule of English law that prevents a party from invoking a *force majeure* clause in respect of an event which was in operation at the date of the contract. In *The Radauti*[107] the *force majeure* clause in the charterparty referred to "hindrances . . . delaying . . . the discharging of the cargo". Discharge was delayed owing to congestion at Tripoli, and Lloyd L.J. held that the likelihood of congestion was irrelevant: "The phrase 'hindrances . . . delaying . . . the discharging of the cargo' should be given its ordinary meaning, even though on the facts some degree of hindrance was inevitable. The foreseeability of the congestion does not justify attaching an unusual or restricted meaning to the word 'hindrances'."[108]

At first instance Staughton J. referred to a passage in Benjamin's *Sale of Goods*[109] to the effect that, according to French law, one of the necessary elements of *force majeure* is *imprévisibilité*—the event must not be reasonably foreseeable, for the relevant party ought then to have taken steps to prevent or avoid it. Staughton J. said that, in so far as the expression "*force majeure*" had even a general meaning in English law, he doubted whether it necessarily conveyed this element of *imprévisibilité*: "Some wars may be foreseen, some strikes and some abnormal tempests or storms. I would suggest it is more a question of causation: whether the incidence of a particular peril which could have been foreseen can really be said to have caused one party's failure to [perform]."[110] In *The Adolph Leonhardt*,[111] Staughton J. allowed sellers to rely on the Centrocon *force majeure* clause notwithstanding his finding that congestion at the place concerned was "endemic and notorious".[112]

This issue of foreseeability was recently considered by Carruthers J. in the Supreme Court of New South Wales in *The Bunga Seroja*[113] in the context of the perils of the sea exception in the Hague Rules. Carruthers J. contrasted the US–Canadian concept of perils of the sea—which excludes a storm which, in the light of

104. [1938] 2 Lloyd's Rep. 416 at p. 420.
105. See, for example, Art. 79 of the Vienna Convention considered in Chapter 14 below; the International Chamber of Commerce's booklet on *Force Majeure and Hardship*, p. 12, s. 5; and Benjamin's *Sale of Goods* (4th Edn., 1992) at para. 8–085.
106. See page 77.
107. [1988] 2 Lloyd's Rep. 416.
108. [1988] 2 Lloyd's Rep. 416 at p. 420.
109. See now the fourth edition (1992) para. 8–090, fn. 7, and pp. 24–25 above.
110. [1987] 2 Lloyd's Rep. 276 at p. 282.
111. [1986] 2 Lloyd's Rep. 395.
112. [1986] 2 Lloyd's Rep. 395 at p. 401.
113. [1994] 1 Lloyd's Rep. 455.

all the circumstances, was expectable—with the Australian view, based on English authorities.[114] He followed the statement in the judgment of the High Court of Australia in *Shipping Corporation of India Limited* v. *Gamlen Chemical Co. Australasia Pty. Ltd.*[115] that "sea and weather conditions which may reasonably be foreseen and guarded against may constitute a peril of the sea".[116]

(g) Anticipating a force majeure event

The issue here is illustrated by the decision of the House of Lords in *Watts and Company Ltd.* v. *Mitsui & Company Ltd.*[117] The defendants were shipowners who had entered into a charterparty with the plaintiffs which provided that a steamer, the name of which was to be declared at least 21 days before the expected date of readiness, should proceed to Marioupol, on the Sea of Azov, and having there taken on board a cargo, should carry it to Japan. The charter contained an exception for the arrests and restraints of princes. On 1 September 1914, the charterers requested the owners to declare the name of the steamer. On the same day, the owners replied that the charterparty must be considered cancelled, giving as the reason that the British Government had prohibited steamers from going into the Black Sea to load. The owners believed that Turkey would become involved in the war and that the Dardanelles would then be closed. In fact, however, there had been no such closure when the owners gave their cancellation notice, although the closure occurred less than a month later. Lord Finlay L.C., in whose opinion Lord Parker of Waddington concurred, said:

" . . . the contention of the appellants that they could justify the failure to provide a steamship on the ground of the exception for restraint of princes was not made good. There was not, in fact, any restraint of princes to prevent the passage of the steamship through the Dardanelles and to Marioupol until the closing of the Dardanelles on the evening of September 26. There was a reasonable apprehension that the Dardanelles might be closed, but such an apprehension does not constitute a restraint of princes. To bring the case within the exception there must be an actual restraint in existence, and in the present case there was nothing to prevent the steamship from passing the Dardanelles and arriving at the port of loading by the cancelling date (September 20).

It is true that her going there, so far as the actual voyage to Japan was concerned, would have been useless, as the Dardanelles were closed before she could have got out, but if the vessel had arrived at Marioupol the charterers might have insured against war risks."[118]

Lord Dunedin said:

"Restraint of princes, to fall within the words of the exception, must be an existing fact and not a mere apprehension. . . . [I]t may be possible to invoke the exception when a reasonable man in face of an *existing* restraint may consider that the restraint, though it does not affect him at the moment, will do so if he continue the adventure. It would be useless to try to fix by definition the precise imminence of peril which would make the restraint a present

114. *Thames & Mersey Marine Insurance Co.* v. *Hamilton Fraser* (1887) 12 App.Cas. 484; *The Xantho* case (1887) 12 App.Cas. 503; *Hamilton, Fraser* v. *Pandorf* (1887) 12 App.Cas. 518; *Canada Rice Mills, Ltd.* v. *Union Marine & General Insurance Co. Ltd.* [1941] A.C. 55.
115. (1980) 147 C.L.R. 142.
116. *Ibid.*, at p. 166.
117. [1917] A.C. 227.
118. *Ibid.*, at p. 233.

fact as contrasted with a future fear. The circumstances of each particular case must be considered."[119]

These observations suggest that, at least in certain situations, a *force majeure* clause will not adequately protect a party unless it gives him the right to suspend performance if he considers that a *force majeure* event might be imminent.

5. DETAILED DRAFTING POINTS REGARDING THE EVENTS IN WHICH THE CLAUSE IS CAPABLE OF BEING BROUGHT INTO OPERATION

The statement of the events in which the clause is capable of being brought into operation usually comprises (a) a list of specific events, and (b) a general sweeper-up formula; sometimes there is also (c) a statement to the effect that the list of specific events is not to be taken to limit the scope of the sweeper-up formula.

(a) The specific events

GAFTA 100 has two separate clauses dealing with "prohibition" and with "*force majeure*, strikes etc.". The former applies to "prohibition of export, blockade or hostilities or . . . any executive or legislative act done by or on behalf of the country of origin, or of the territory where the port . . . of shipment named herein is . . . situate, restricting export, whether partially or otherwise". The second covers any "Act of God, strike, lockout, riot or civil commotion, combination of workmen, breakdown of machinery, fire or any cause comprehended in the term '*force majeure*' ". The ICC list of events[120] is longer:

"(a) war,[121] whether declared or not, civil war,[121a] riots and revolutions, acts of piracy, acts of sabotage;
(b) natural disasters such as violent storms, cyclones, earthquakes, tidal waves, floods,[122] destruction by lightning;
(c) explosions, fires, destruction of machines,[123] of factories, and of any kind of installations;
(d) boycotts, strikes[124] and lock-outs of all kinds, go-slow, occupation of factories and premises, and work stoppages which occur in the enterprise of the party seeking relief[125];
(e) acts of authority; whether lawful or unlawful, apart from acts for which the party seeking relief has assumed the risk by virtue of other provisions of the contract;"

The ICC clause states that, unless the relevant contract otherwise provides, the

119. *Ibid.*, at p. 238 (emphasis added).
120. ICC Publication No. 421, 1985.
121. See Chapter 8.
121a. See *National Oil Co. of Zimbabwe (Pte) Ltd.* v. *Sturge* [1991] 2 Lloyd's Rep. 281.
122. See *Computer & Systems Engineering p.l.c.* v. *John Lelliott (Ilford) Ltd.* (1990) 54 B.L.R. 1, (C.A.).
123. "Equipment" has a wider meaning: see *Knowles* v. *Liverpool City Council* [1994] 1 Lloyd's Rep. 11 and *Coltman* v. *Bibby Tankers* [1988] A.C. 276.
124. See Chapter 9.
125. It is thought that the words "in the enterprise of the party seeking relief" do not qualify boycotts, strikes etc. but the point is not entirely clear.

clause does not apply to: "lack of authorisations, of licences, of entry or residence permits, or of approvals necessary for the performance of the contract and to be issued by a public authority of any kind whatsoever in the country of the party seeking relief."

However, it seems that three categories of event are seldom covered expressly. The first is a breakdown in communications equipment or computers; for example, a fax line which goes out of order or a computer system which "crashes", loses data or produces incorrect output. The second is a major movement in financial markets, particularly foreign exchange rates, which can make the fulfilment of a contract prohibitively expensive unless it can be delayed until rates have stabilised. However, in the case of an agreement by which banks or securities houses underwrite an issue of shares or bonds, it is a matter of controversy whether a general fall in stock market prices can legitimately be made a *force majeure* event[126]; arguably that would defeat the underwriting agreement's main purpose of insuring the issuing company against disturbances in the financial markets deterring the public from subscribing for the shares or bonds. The third event seldom covered is a breach of contract or the insolvency of a supplier, sub-contractor or other person on whom one of the parties is dependent in order to fulfil its own obligations under the contract.

As already noted,[127] it may be necessary to provide that a *force majeure* clause can be invoked if a party anticipates that one of the specified events is likely to occur in the future. Such a pre-emptive clause should address (a) whether it is sufficient for the apprehension of a future *force majeure* event to be purely subjective or whether it has to be reasonable or based on reasonable grounds; (b) whether the party concerned must consider that the occurrence of a *force majeure* event is "likely" or, for example, "a substantial risk"; and (c) the time period within which the party concerned must consider that a *force majeure* event might occur.

It is proposed to consider just two of the usual *force majeure* events: "acts of authority" and "strikes".[128]

Acts of authority

(i) THE RELEVANT JURISDICTIONS

The effect which "an act of authority" might have on a party's obligations under a contract governed by English law has to be assessed in the light of the common law

126. One of the *force majeure* clauses published by the International Primary Market Association applies "if, in the opinion of the Lead Manager, there shall have been such a change in national or international financial, political or economic conditions or currency exchange rates or exchange controls as would in their view by likely to prejudice materially the success of the offering and distribution of the Securities or dealings in the Securities in the secondary market". It is thought doubtful whether a fall in stock exchange prices which was not caused by some external factor (such as a diplomatic crisis) would, of itself, be "a change in national or international financial . . . conditions" in the context of an underwriting agreement.

127. See p. 80 above.

128. *Scrutton on Charterparties* (19th Edn., 1984) pp. 210–249 contains a detailed list of the shipping cases on such expressions as "arrest and restraint of princes, rulers and peoples", "fire", "collision", "accidents", "accidents to hull", "accidents to cargo", "unavoidable accidents and hindrance".

principle that performance of a contract is excused if (i) it has become illegal by the governing law of the contract, or (ii) it necessarily involves doing an act which is unlawful by the place where the act has to be done.[129] It is an open point whether part (ii) of this principle has survived those provisions of the Rome Convention to which effect has been given in the United Kingdom by the Contracts (Applicable Law) Act 1990.[130] There is also a common law principle that the English courts will not enforce a contract governed by English law which falls to be performed abroad where (i) it relates to an adventure which is contrary to a head of English public policy which is founded on general principles of morality, and (ii) the same public policy applies to the country of performance so that the agreement would not be enforceable under the law of that country.[131] However, in the case of a contract governed by English law which is to be performed in England, it is not a good defence for the defendant to show that performance of his obligation in England would subject him to penal liability in his own country.[132] In *Toprak Mahsulleri Ofisi* v. *Finagrain Compagnie Commerciale Agricole et Financière S.A.*,[133] Turkish buyers of wheat undertook to open a letter of credit with and confirmed by a first class United States or West European bank. The Turkish buyers were unable to obtain exchange control permission from the Turkish Ministry of Finance to open such a letter of credit, and maintained that it was impossible for them to open a letter of credit without exporting money from Turkey. The Court of Appeal held that this was no answer to a claim for damages for non-performance of the contract. Lord Denning M.R. said: "the place of performance was not Turkey. Illegality by the law of Turkey is no answer whatever to this claim. . . . The sellers were not concerned with the machinery by which the Turkish State Enterprise provided that

129. (A) *Libyan Arab Foreign Bank* v. *Bankers Trust Co.* [1989] Q.B. 728 at 743. But note the analysis in Cheshire & North, *Private International Law* (12th Edn., 1992), at pp. 518–519 that (i) an agreement governed by English law to break an *existing* law of a friendly foreign country is against English public policy; but (ii) an agreement governed by English law to perform an act in a foreign country which is prohibited by a law passed in that country *after* the agreement is made is unenforceable under English domestic law's doctrine of frustration, not under English private international law; see also Hill, *International Commercial Disputes* (1994) at 11.4.10. These analyses are based on interpreting *Ralli Brothers* v. *Compania Naviera Sota y Aznar* [1920] 2 K.B. 287 as a case on frustration, although it did not decide that the charter, or even the charterer's obligation to pay freight, had become discharged, but merely that the charterer was not bound to pay freight above the maximum allowed by the law of Spain, the country where the obligation to pay freight was to be performed. But note the comments regarding *Ralli Brothers* made in *The Nile Co. for the Export of Agricultural Crops* v. *H & J M Bennett (Commodities) Ltd.* [1986] 1 Lloyd's Rep. 555. (B) In relation to contracts which are contrary to exchange control regulations of a state which is a member of the International Monetary Fund, the Bretton Woods Agreement overrides the general principles of the conflict of laws; and an English court must refuse to enforce an "exchange contract" which involves the currency of a member state and which is contrary to exchange regulations of a member state maintained or imposed consistently with the Bretton Woods Agreement: see Dicey & Morris, *The Conflict of Laws* (12th Edn., 1993) at pp. 1597 and 1599 and *International Commercial Disputes* at 14.4.1–2. (But note the decision of the Bundesgerichtshof in *Re Exchange Control and a Greek Guarantor* [1993] I.L.Pr. 298.) (C) A contract is unenforceable to the extent that it is prohibited by a mandatory law, or the public policy, of the forum: see Arts. 7(2) and 16 of the Rome Convention.

130. See Dicey & Morris, *The Conflict of Laws* (12th Edn., 1993) at pp. 1245–1247; Plender, *The European Contracts Convention* (1991) at 9.05.

131. *Lemenda Trading Co. Limited* v. *African Middle East Petroleum Co. Limited* [1988] Q.B. 448.

132. See Lord Reid's statement in *Kahler* v. *Midland Bank* [1950] A.C. 24 at p. 51; also Dillon L.J.'s comments in *The Amazonia* [1990] 1 Lloyd's Rep. 236 at p. 249. But this is subject to the overriding effect of the Bretton Woods Agreement noted above.

133. [1979] 2 Lloyd's Rep. 98.

letter of credit at all."[134] In *Libyan Arab Foreign Bank* v. *Bankers Trust Co.*,[135] Staughton J. held that the defendant, a US bank, was not excused from its obligation to transfer funds from the Libyan bank's New York account to its London account by a US Presidential Executive Order which froze all Libyan property in the US or in the possession or control of US persons (including overseas branches of US persons). The US Order provided no defence on the ground of illegality because the relevant part of the contract between the plaintiff and the defendant was governed by English, not US, law. Staughton J. also rejected a claim that the Presidential Order had frustrated the contract between the US bank and the Libyan bank by prohibiting the US bank from repaying the balances on the Libyan bank's account with it.[136]

These cases present additional problems for companies with overseas branches and companies which are members of multinational groups. For example, a US corporation's English subsidiary enters into an English law contract with a company in country X, and subsequently US legislation prohibits US corporations and their subsidiaries from trading with country X. If sued in England, the English subsidiary could not plead the US legislation as a defence, on the ground of illegality, to an action for breach of contract. However, if the contract were closely connected with the US, the English subsidiary might be able to raise such a defence if it is sued in a country, other than the United Kingdom, which has ratified the Rome Convention.[137] Article 7(1) of the Rome Convention, which the United Kingdom has not adopted, empowers a court to give effect to "the mandatory rules of another country with which the situation has a close connection" even though that is the country neither of the governing law nor the place of performance.[138]

The considerations mentioned in the previous paragraph suggest that, if a *force majeure* clause refers to "acts of authority" without specifying the relevant jurisdictions, there is a risk of the clause being confined to "acts of authority" arising in the country of the governing law and the country of performance and, on a favourable interpretation, the country in which the affected party is incorporated or has the branch through which it is to perform the contract. If a *force majeure* clause is to cover "acts of authority" in the country in which a party's main headquarters is located or in which its parent undertaking is incorporated or has its headquarters, that should be stated expressly; and there should also be an express statement if the clause is to cover "acts of authority" in any country in which a party has a branch, subsidiary or joint venture.

134. [1979] 2 Lloyd's Rep. 98 at p. 114. See also *Congimex Companhia Geral de Comercio Importadora e Exportadora, S.A.R.L.* v. *Tradax Export S.A.* [1983] 1 Lloyd's Rep. 250 and Staughton J.'s analysis of *Toprak* in *Libyan Arab Foreign Bank* v. *Bankers Trust Co.* [1989] 1 Q.B. 728 at pp. 743–745. Compare the upholding in *The Amazonia* [1990] 1 Lloyd's Rep. 236 of the *ad hoc* English law arbitration agreement.

135. [1989] 1 Q.B. 728.

136. However, the frustration claim was pleaded as an alternative to two other claims on which the plaintiff succeeded, so that frustration is dealt with only briefly in Staughton J.'s judgment at 771F to 772E.

137. Given effect to in the United Kingdom by the Contracts (Applicable Law) Act 1990.

138. See Dicey & Morris, *The Conflict of Laws* (12th Edn., 1993), at pp. 1242–1243; Collins, *Essays in International Litigation and The Conflict of Laws* (Oxford, 1994) at pp. 410–411; and Plender, *The European Contracts Convention* (London, 1991) at 151–155; but note in particular *Cie. européenne des petroles S.A.* v. *Sensor Nederland B.V.* 1982 (1983) 23 Int. Legal Mat. 66, referred to in Dicey & Morris.

(ii) INTERNATIONAL SANCTIONS

In recent years, perhaps the "acts of authority" which have had the greatest practical impact are the sanctions of the kind imposed in 1990 on Iraq and Kuwait and in 1992 on Serbia and Montenegro. In the latter case, in addition to directions by H.M. Treasury under the Emergency Powers legislation,[139] there was an Order in Council[140] implementing the sanctions imposed by the United Nations Security Council. There were also directly effective Council Regulations of the European Economic Community.[141] In the US, measures were imposed by Executive Orders signed by the President.[142] In the light of this, it is necessary for a clause not only to cover primary and subordinate legislation in the United Kingdom, but also any directives, regulations, decisions or other acts of any institution of the European Union; or any resolution of the United Nations or its Security Council; or any action taken by any institution or authority under any treaty. Since the exact scope of primary legislation or of a statutory instrument is often unclear, a *force majeure* clause should be stated to apply if the transaction is, or on a reasonable interpretation can be considered to be, prohibited by any legislation, directive and so on.[143]

(iii) LICENCES

In addition, the clause should cover specific acts (or non-acts) of a non-legislative nature, such as withdrawal of a licence; or refusal to grant, maintain[144] or renew a licence; or the grant of a licence but on terms difficult or costly to comply with.

The judgments in the Court of Appeal in *Pagnan S.p.A.* v. *Tradax Ocean Transportation S.A.*[145] show the need for a contract to make clear the relationship between the *force majeure* clause and the provisions about licences. The case arose out of a contract for the export of Thai tapioca pellets. Regulations made by the Thai Government under a quota scheme for tapioca exports prevented export of Thai tapioca to the EEC during the shipment period. The contract contained its own special conditions and also incorporated as its general conditions GAFTA 119. The contract provided that its special conditions would prevail over the GAFTA Form in the event of inconsistency. One of the special conditions was "Sellers to provide for export certificate enabling Buyers to obtain import licence into EEC . . . with a 6% import levy". Distinguishing *Coloniale Import-Export* v. *Loumidis Sons*,[146] the Court of Appeal held that this special condition imposed an absolute obligation on the sellers to provide for the export certificate, save in so far as any other clause of the contract might modify the sellers' obligation or relieve

139. The Control of Gold, Securities, Payments and Credits (Serbia and Montenegro) Directions 1992, S.I. 1992/1265.

140. The Serbia and Montenegro (United Nations Sanctions) Order 1992, S.I. 1992/1302.

141. For example, Council Regulation (EEC) No. 1432/92 of 1 June 1992 prohibiting trade between the European Economic Community and the Republic of Serbia and Montenegro.

142. For example, Executive Order 12831 of 15 January 1993 prohibiting transactions related to the transhipment of commodities or products or to ships.

143. See, for example, *Rappaport* v. *London Plywood and Timber Co. Ltd.* [1940] 1 All E.R. 576.

144. See *Czarnikow Ltd.* v. *Rolimpex* [1979] A.C. 351.

145. [1987] 3 All E.R. 565; see also the discussion of this case at p. 263 below.

146. [1978] 2 Lloyd's Rep. 560. This concerned the standard terms of the European Contract for Coffee, art. 30 of which was as follows: "The responsibility in connection with the authority to export from the country of origin shall be that of the sellers and the responsibility in connection with the authority to import into the country of destination shall be that of the buyers." Lloyd J. held that, since these were

him from the consequences of breach.[147] However, the *force majeure* clause in GAFTA 119, which the contract incorporated, provided that in the case of "prohibition of export . . . or any executive or legislative act done by . . . the government of a country of origin . . . restricting export", to that extent the contract or any unfulfilled part of it would be cancelled. The buyers argued that the sellers could not invoke the *force majeure* clause because there was an inconsistency between that clause and the special condition requiring the sellers to provide an export certificate, and the contract provided that in the event of an inconsistency between the special conditions and the general conditions in GAFTA 119, the special conditions would prevail. The Court of Appeal held that there was no such inconsistency; the contract could be construed in a way that would give effect to both of them. The sellers would only be relieved of their contractual obligation if they were unable to provide the export certificate because of an impediment falling within the carefully defined ambit of the *force majeure* clause. Thus the sellers would remain liable if the certificate were not provided as a result of oversight, error, bureaucratic inefficiency or delay, and probably also if the certificate was not provided simply because the Thai authorities failed to issue it.[148]

(iv) PREROGATIVE ACTION, INVALID ACTION AND PUBLIC SECTOR ENTITIES

A *force majeure* clause should probably mention action taken by virtue of the royal prerogative.[149] The royal prerogative was used to acquire the use of British ships to support the Falklands' Task Force in 1982.[150] Analogous powers in countries other than the United Kingdom should also be mentioned.[151]

The clause should state that it applies whether or not the action concerned is lawful or valid so that it would cover, for example, primary or secondary legislation which is incompatible with the EEC Treaty[152] or an unlawful expropriation.[153] The

standard conditions intended to be incorporated in a variety of different contracts governed by a variety of different legal systems, art. 30 was intended to establish whose duty it was to get the licence and to leave open the question of the nature of the obligation. It followed that the nature of the obligation must depend on the implication, and that the only term to be implied was the limited obligation to use best endeavours. Alternatively, Lloyd J. held that if art. 30 were concerned with the nature of the obligation, it still imposed only the more limited "best endeavours" duty, and not an absolute duty. Lloyd J.'s reasons for that view were first they required clear words to impose an absolute obligation, and the word "responsibility" standing on its own was not clear enough; second, the limited "best endeavours" obligation was more consistent with the presence of the *force majeure* clause in the same contract.

147. [1987] 3 All E.R. 565, at p. 572g.

148. [1987] 3 All E.R. 565, at p. 575.

149. See, for example, *Burmah Oil Company Limited* v. *Lord Advocate* [1965] A.C. 75 which arose out of directives given in 1942 by the G.O.C., Burma, for the destruction of the plaintiff's oil installations to prevent them from falling into enemy hands. It was accepted that these demolitions were carried out by an exercise of the royal prerogative.

150. Michael D Miller, *Marine War Risk* (2nd Edn., 1994) at para. 21.14.

151. For example, the Spanish Royal Decree Law expropriating the shares in the Rumasa companies which featured in *Williams & Humbert Ltd.* v. *W. & H. Trade Marks (Jersey) Ltd.* [1986] A.C. 368.

152. For example, *R.* v. *Secretary of State for Transport ex parte Factortame Ltd. (No. 2)* [1991] 1 A.C. 603; *R.* v. *Inland Revenue Commissioners ex parte Commerzbank A.G.* [1994] 1 Q.B. 219; *R.* v. *Secretary of State for Environment ex parte Equal Opportunities Commission* [1994] 2 W.L.R. 409; and *R.* v. *H.M. Treasury, ex parte Centro-Com SRL* [1994] C.L.C. 628 in which the Court of Appeal held that a policy decision by the Bank of England not to permit payments out of Serbian bank accounts for exports to Serbia of authorised medical and humanitarian goods should be referred to the European Court of Justice for a determination of whether it involved a breach of the requirement of uniform export policy under Art. 113 of the EEC Treaty.

153. As in *B.P. Exploration Co. (Libya) Ltd.* v. *Hunt (No. 2)* [1979] 1 W.L.R. 783.

point is illustrated by the judgment of Bailhache J. in *Russian Bank for Foreign Trade* v. *Excess Insurance Co. Ltd.*[154] In 1914 the Russian Bank for Foreign Trade shipped on board a British ship at Novorossisk a parcel of barley for carriage to Falmouth. The bank insured the barley with the defendants against the usual perils, including restraint of princes. While the ship was at Novorossisk, it was requisitioned by the British Admiralty for the use of the Russian government. One of the grounds on which Bailhache J. rejected the Russian bank's claim under the policy was that the order requisitioning this ship was *ultra vires*:

> " . . . The only authority the Admiralty had to requisition ships was given to them by the Proclamation of August 3, 1914, and was confined to the requisitioning for His Majesty's service of vessels of British owners within the British Isles or the waters adjacent thereto. . . . Where restraint takes the form of an order and nothing more, that order must, in my opinion, be one that has behind it the forces of the State, which can, if necessary, be lawfully employed to compel obedience if obedience is refused. Now, an order *ultra vires* the Admiralty could not lawfully be enforced by seizure, detention, or confiscation of the ship, the subject-matter of the order, or by fine or imprisonment of her owner. Obedience to such an order, however praiseworthy in a loyal citizen, is, in my opinion, a voluntary act on his part and not a restraint of princes. It is quite otherwise if the order is accompanied by threats of force, or followed by the use of force.[155] In such a case, disobedience not being illegal, the use of force to compel obedience is illegal, and is a restraint of princes upon which a claim against the underwriters for loss by restraint may be founded."[156]

Where a party is a public sector entity in a particular state, the *force majeure* clause should make it clear whether or not that party is entitled to invoke the clause in respect of legislation introduced in that state or other action taken by its authorities and, if so, under what conditions.[157]

(v) ACTION BY A REGIME NOT CONSIDERED A GOVERNMENT

The clause should also expressly cover action by a regime or body which an English court would not consider to be a government.[158] In *Luigi Monta of Genoa* v. *Cechofracht Co. Ltd*[159] the issue was whether a war risks clause in a charterparty which provided for the ship to have liberty to comply with any directions given "by government" applied where the ship had been ordered to discharge her cargo by a general who said that he came from "the Government of Formosa". The first point

154. [1918] 2 K.B. 123.

155. However, threats of force are unnecessary where the order is *intra vires* andthe government of the nation under whose flag the vessel sails . . . or by any other valid: *British and Foreign Marine Insurance Co Ltd.* v. *Samuel Sanday & Co.* [1916] A.C. 650 at pp. 659 and 669.

156. Arguably, the decision might be different today in view of the greater awareness of the coercive power of the state: compare *Woolwich Building Society* v. *I.R.C.* [1993] A.C. 70.

157. See *Czarnikow* v. *Rolimpex* [1979] A.C. 351 and *The Playa Larga* [1983] 2 Lloyd's Rep. 171.

158. See Hobhouse J.'s important judgment in *Republic of Somalia* v. *Woodhouse Drake & Carey (Suisse) S.A.* [1993] Q.B. 54, which analyses the position following the British government's decision in 1980 to abandon the policy of according recognition to governments, although recognising states in accordance with common international doctrine. This policy change is reflected in the definition of "a recognised State" in s.1(2) of the Foreign Corporations Act 1991.

159. [1956] 2 Q.B. 552. See also *The Silver Sky* [1981] 2 Lloyd's Rep. 95.

decided by Sellers J. was that the clause referred to national governments, as opposed to a municipal or provincial government. "The qualities or character required by the body giving the order . . . must, therefore, include essentially the exercise of full executive and legislative power over an established territory."[160] The umpire (Mr A. A. Mocatta Q.C.) had held that the Government of Formosa did exercise such powers. There were statements from the Foreign Office that the British Government had ceased to recognise the regime in Formosa, but Sellers J. held that these statements were not conclusive.[161] Sellers J. stated that the umpire was entitled to approach the question in the same manner as Goddard J. and the Court of Appeal did in *Kawasaki Kisen Kabushiki Kaisha of Kobe* v. *Bantham Steamship Co. Limited*[162] in which the Court of Appeal, upholding Goddard J., held that the question whether on the true construction of a charterparty war had broken out involving Japan was not conclusively determined by the view of the British Government. Goddard J. was reported as saying that "what he had to determine was what the parties meant by the clause of the charterparty. He thought they were using the word 'war' . . . in the sense in which an ordinary commercial man would use it. He did not think the parties in a case of this sort were going into the niceties of international law."[163]

Strikes[164]

(i) WHAT IS A "STRIKE"?

The exact scope of the term "strike" is unclear. In *The New Horizon*,[165] the Court of Appeal, upholding Ackner J., held that the refusal of crane drivers to work a 24-hour shift was a strike, notwithstanding that they had no legal obligation to work in such shifts, although it was customary for them to do so if requested by the stevedore companies. At first instance Ackner J. (as he then was) said:

> "The word 'strike' is not a readily definable term. . . . I respectfully adopt the non-exhaustive definition provided by Mr Justice Sankey in the case of *Williams Brothers (Hull) (Limited)* v. *Naamlooze Vennootschap, W.H. Berghuys, Kolenhandel*[166] where he said that a strike was 'a general concerted refusal by workmen to work in consequence of an alleged grievance'. That definition was substantially followed by Mr Justice McNair in the case of *The Laga*,[167] save in so far as Mr Justice Sankey's judgment implied that the grievance had to be between the alleged strikers and their employers. In *The Laga*, the motive for the strike did not arise from a grievance between the strikers and their employers but arose out of sympathy with other strikers who had a grievance with their own employers. The concept of a strike was, as the learned Judge noted only too prophetically, a developing one. As Mr Boyd

160. *Ibid.*, at p. 564.
161. See now *Republic of Somalia* v. *Woodhouse Drake & Carey (Suisse) S.A.* [1993] Q.B. 54.
162. [1939] 2 K.B. 544; discussed in more detail at pp. 155–157.
163. *Ibid.*, at p. 549. See also *National Oil Co. of Zimbabwe (Pte) Ltd.* v. *Sturge* [1991] 2 Lloyd's Rep. 281 in which Saville J. held that the expressions "civil war", "rebellion" and "insurrection", when used in marine cargo insurance, bear their ordinary business meanings.
164. See Chapter 9 below; note also Lord Roskill's comment in *The Nema* [1982] A.C. 724 at p. 754 as to the high failure rate of attempts to claim frustration on the basis of a strike.
165. [1974] 2 Lloyd's Rep. 210; [1975] 2 Lloyd's Rep. 314.
166. (1915) 21 Com.Cas. 253.
167. [1966] 1 Lloyd's Rep. 582.

for the charterers observed, a strike does not cease to be a strike whether or not the appropriate epithet is 'general' or 'partial', 'sympathetic' or 'political'."[168]

In the Court of Appeal, Lord Denning M.R. agreed that there was very little guidance in the books as to the meaning of the word "strike", and observed that Sankey J. had taken his definition from the Concise Oxford Dictionary and that ever since *Scrutton on Charterparties* had quoted those words as authoritative. Lord Denning added:

"If I may amplify it a little, I think a strike is a concerted stoppage of work by men done with a view to improving their wages or conditions, or giving vent to a grievance or making a protest about something or other, or supporting or sympathizing with other workmen in such endeavour. It is distinct from a stoppage which is brought about by an external event such as a bomb scare or by apprehension of danger."[169]

The Laga,[170] referred to above, concerned the action taken by stevedores and others at the port of Nantes in refusing to unload or assist vessels carrying coal for discharge at Nantes, the object being to assist French miners who were then on strike. Mr Mustill, for the owners, argued that the ordinary meaning of the word "strike" was a body of men ceasing work in the hope of obtaining concessions from employers. On this basis, nobody had been on strike, since the stevedores had carried on working, the only difference being that they refused to handle coal-carrying ships, and handled other ships instead. Boycott activities, Mr Mustill contended, could not be included: "If housewives stopped buying South African grapefruit because they did not like South African policy, it was not a strike."[171] For the charterers, Mr Goff said that the contract was concerned with the use of a particular ship and whether the workmen refused to work a particular ship.[172] McNair J. held: " . . . the word 'strike' is a perfectly good, appropriate word to use to cover a sympathetic strike and a general strike and there is no need for it to-day to have any ingredient of grievance between those who are refusing to work and their employers."[173] McNair J. also held that it was irrelevant that the port labour continued to accept their employers' instructions and to handle *other* vessels: "You have got to see whether there was a strike *vis-à-vis* the ship with which we are concerned. The problem is: was time lost in respect of this ship by a strike?"[174]

It may be preferable to follow the approach of the ICC clause and to list various kinds of industrial action, including lock-outs. A clause which merely uses the general term "industrial action", without defining that term,[175] should make it clear that this covers (i) action by an employer and (ii) action by a third party's employees or by a third-party employer.

168. [1974] 2 Lloyd's Rep. 210 at p. 214.
169. [1975] 2 Lloyd's Rep. 314 at p. 317: see also *Coates* v. *Modern Methods and Materials* [1983] 1 Q.B. 193.
170. [1966] 1 Lloyd's Rep. 582.
171. *Ibid.*, at p. 586.
172. *Ibid.*, at p. 587.
173. *Ibid.*, at p. 591.
174. *Ibid.*, at p. 591. On this point, McNair J. followed *Seeberg* v. *Russian Wood Agency Ltd.* (1934) 50 Ll.L.Rep. 146, a decision of MacKinnon J.
175. Compare, for example, s.226 of the Trade Union and Labour Relations (Consolidation) Act 1992 which denies the statutory protection from tort liabilities if industrial action is not supported by a ballot.

(ii) THE DUTY TO TAKE REASONABLE STEPS TO SETTLE

The Court of Appeal's decision in *B. & S. Contracts and Design* v. *Victor Green Publications*[176] suggests that a company cannot rely on a *force majeure* exception for strikes if there was available to it a course of action which would have resolved the strike and the company was unreasonable in failing to take that action. The judgments, however, showed some difference of emphasis. Eveleigh and Griffiths L.JJ. stressed that they were far from saying that whenever a contracting party with such a *force majeure* clause is faced with a strike situation he must give in to the strike to perform his contract. As Griffiths L.J. pointed out, if that were the case the clause would be worthless. However, Kerr L.J. said:

> "To rely upon a strike of one's own workforce is difficult for a party seeking to rely on an exception of strikes, but I entirely agree that it is perfectly possible if the circumstances justify such reliance . . . But . . . it is clear that when an exception of strikes is invoked, then like all other exceptions it is subject to the principle that the party seeking to rely on it must show that the strike and its consequences could not have been avoided by taking steps which were reasonable in the particular circumstances.[177] . . . Generally speaking, also, a mere difficulty of additional expense is not a sufficient ground to enable a party to invoke an exception clause."[178]

These observations show that relatively little protection is provided by a clause which simply lists "strikes" as a *force majeure* event and does not relieve the affected party from what may be termed the implied duty to take reasonable steps to settle a strike. For this purpose, it is thought that a provision to the following effect is sufficient: "The Supplier shall be entitled to settle, or refrain from settling, any such dispute and generally to act in relation to any such dispute as the Supplier considers to be in its own interests."[179]

(iii) AFTER-EFFECTS

Channel Island Ferries Limited v. *Sealink U.K. Ltd*[180] indicates that where, as a result of a strike, a company signs an agreement with a trade union the terms of which make it impossible for the company to fulfil its obligations under a contract, the court may hold that the voluntary signature of the agreement with the union was "a completely new causative event", and that therefore the company's fulfilment of the contract was not prevented by a strike within the terms of a *force majeure* clause.

It is, therefore, important to cover the consequences of strikes. To take a further example, if a clause refers only to strikes, the *force majeure* situation may end the moment the strike is settled, whereas the disruption or shortages caused by the strike may prevent a party from resuming work on the contract until considerably

176. [1984] I.C.R. 419, discussed in more detail at pp. 170–173 below.

177. Kerr L.J. cited Carver, *Carriage by Sea* (13th Edn., Vol. 2, 1982), para. 1056 and in particular the judgment of Lord Esher M.R. in *Bulman & Dickson* v. *Fenwick & Co.* [1894] 1 Q.B. 179, at p. 185.

178. Kerr L.J. cited *Brauer & Co. (Great Britain) Limited* v. *James Clark (Brush Materials) Limited* [1952] 2 All E.R. 497.

179. It is thought arguable that such a clause would not be caught by the Unfair Contract Terms Act 1977 since it does not exclude a duty to exercise skill or care in the performance of the contract. However, the clause might, in certain circumstances, be caught by the Directive on Unfair Terms in Consumer Contracts: Council Directive 93/13/EEC O.J. No. L 95/29.

180. [1988] 1 Lloyd's Rep. 323; discussed in more detail at pp. 173–178 below.

later. The need for clear drafting is illustrated by *The Onisilos*.[181] The strikes clause in a charter provided that neither charterers nor owners "shall be responsible for the consequences of any strikes . . . preventing or delaying the fulfilment of any obligations under this contract". At first instance Donaldson J. held that the word "consequences" meant "loss or damage" caused directly by the strike and did not cover its after-effects. However, the Court of Appeal held that the clause covered after-effects, such as congestion in the port of discharge.

(iv) APPREHENSION OF A STRIKE

The point made earlier[182] about the value of providing that a party will be entitled to invoke a *force majeure* clause if he considers that a force majeure event is likely to occur in the future is particularly relevant to strikes. In *Hackney Borough Council* v. *Doré*[183] the council were under a statutory duty to provide a supply of electricity to premises in their district, but the relevant order stated that the council would not be liable for a failure to supply "caused by inevitable accident or *force majeure*". Two of the council's employees refused to connect the electricity supply to Mr. Doré's house because the wiring in that house had been carried out by a man who was not a member of their trade union. The magistrates found that, if the council had dismissed these two employees, the Electrical Trades Union would have caused all their members in the council's employment to resign. If that occurred, the result, as Darling J. put it, would have been that "the whole of Hackney would probably . . . have been plunged in darkness". Nevertheless, the Divisional Court held that the council was not entitled to plead "*force majeure*" since no strike had actually occurred. Sankey J. said: "In my view '*force majeure*' in this case means some physical or material restraint, and does not include a reasonable fear or apprehension of such a restraint."[184]

(b) The general sweeper-up formula

Unless care is taken, a sweeper-up formula designed to extend the range of events covered by a *force majeure* clause will have the opposite effect of cutting down the scope of the events which the clause has previously mentioned. For example, if a clause covers: "natural disasters, strikes, fires, explosions, breakdown of machinery", and there is added: "and any other event beyond the Supplier's control which prevents it from performing this Contract", this will restrict the earlier references to strikes, fires and so on to those which pass the double test of being beyond the supplier's control and preventing—rather than merely hindering or delaying—its performance of the contract.[185]

It is thought unhelpful to use an expression such as "and any other *force majeure* event" in a contract governed by English law. The defence of *force majeure* is alien

181. [1971] 2 Q.B. 500.
182. See p. 80.
183. [1922] 1 K.B. 431.
184. *Ibid.*, at p. 437.
185. See Lord Wrenbury's analysis in *Tennants (Lancashire) Ltd.* v. *C.S. Wilson & Co. Ltd.* [1917] A.C. 495 at pp. 524–525.

to the common law,[186] although it is well established in French civil law. Use of the term *force majeure* in an English law contract might, therefore, in the case of a dispute, necessitate an investigation of French law on the subject. It is also possible that use of the term in the sweeper-up formula might imply that the events specified earlier in the clause are only covered to the extent that they occur in circumstances in which they would qualify as *force majeure* under the French law doctrine.[187] This might exclude, for example, a strike which was on the cards when the contract was signed.[188] The clause should define "event" to include any omission or non-occurrence (such as the failure of a planned event to take place); also any state of affairs.[189]

(c) The *ejusdem generis* rule

It is thought that nowadays it would be unusual for the scope of general sweeper-up words to be cut down under the *ejusdem generis* rule. Although there are cases in the early years of this century in which the rule was applied almost automatically,[190] the more judicial recent tendency is against this.[190a] In *Navrom* v. *Callitsis Ship Management S.A. (The Radauti)*,[191] Staughton J. refused to apply the rule, and quoted the following passage from the judgment of Devlin J. in *Chandris* v. *Isbrandtsen-Moller Co. Inc.*[192]:

"A rule of construction cannot be more than a guide to enable the court to arrive at the true meaning of the parties. The *ejusdem generis* rule means that there is implied into the language which the parties have used words of restriction which are not there. It cannot be right to approach a document with the presumption that there should be such an implication. To apply the rule automatically in that way would be to make it the master and not the servant of the purpose for which it was designed—namely, to ascertain the meaning of the parties from the words they have used."[193]

If, nevertheless, there is a concern that the *ejusdem generis* rule might be applied, Devlin J.'s judgment also contains the following guidance[194] about how to exclude it:

186. This is well illustrated by the judgments in *Jacobs, Marcus & Co.* v. *Credit Lyonnais* (1884) 12 Q.B.D. 589.

187. It is thought that this risk would be considerable if the party whose performance was in issue were based in France or in a jurisdiction which applies the French law concept of *force majeure*. *Treitel, op. cit.,* note 18 at para. 12–017, emphasises the narrowness of the French doctrine and quotes Nicholas, *French Law of Contract* (p. 202) stating that the doctrine is "far narrower" than frustration under English law; see further on this issue Chapter 2.

188. Although in *Matsoukis* v. *Priestman & Co.* [1915] 1 K.B. 681 a *force majeure* clause was held to cover a general coal strike, notwithstanding that, when the contract was made, it was obvious that a strike might take place.

189. Compare *B.F. Caudle* v. *Sharp* [1994] C.L.C. 216 at p. 224.

190. See, for example, *SS Knutsford Limited* v. *Tillmanns & Co.* [1908] A.C. 406 and the other cases cited in *Scrutton on Charterparties* (19th Edn., London 1984) at pp. 218–219.

190a. However, arbitrators seem more inclined to apply the rule: see London Arbitrators 2/94 (L.M.L.N. 385) and 5/94 (L.M.L.N. 386).

191. [1987] 2 Lloyd's Rep. 276.

192. [1951] 1 K.B. 240; compare Lord Scarman's statement in *Quazi* v. *Quazi* [1980] A.C. 744, at pp. 823–824 that the *ejusdem generis* rule is "at best, a very secondary guide to the meaning of a statute. The all-important matter is to consider the purpose of the statute".

193. [1951] 1 K.B. 240, at p. 244.

194. [1951] 1 K.B. 240, at p. 245.

"Legal draftsmen are . . . familiar . . . with the proper signals to hoist if they do not want [the rule] to apply. Phrases such as 'whether or not similar to the foregoing' and 'without prejudice to the generality of the foregoing' are often employed in legal draftsmanship; and if the draftsman has read the report of *Larsen* v. *Sylvester & Co.*,[195] he will know that the addition of 'whatsoever' generally serves the same purpose."[196]

This device was held to be effective in *The Notos*.[197] A charter provided that "demurrage shall not accrue, for any delay caused by strike, lockout, stoppage or restraint of labor of master, officers and crew of the vessel or tugboat or pilots *or any other cause of whatsoever nature or kind over which the charterer has no control*". The vessel's discharge was delayed by the effect of swell which was sufficiently severe to make the only sea-line at the port of discharge unusable. The owners claimed that a limited meaning should be placed upon the last words of the clause (printed in italics), derived from the events expressly excepted, so that those words would be restricted to causes relating to the vessel or her owners or for those for which the owners were responsible. Lord Goff of Chieveley, with whom all the other Law Lords agreed, said: "I can see no basis for so limiting an exception which is expressed to exclude delay caused by— . . . any other cause of whatsoever nature or kind over which the charterer had no control."[198]

However, it does not follow, because the *ejusdem generis* rules does not apply or has been excluded, that a *force majeure* clause will cover whatever event may have occurred. *Metropolitan Water Board* v. *Dick, Kerr & Co. Ltd*[199] arose out of a contract with a water board to construct a reservoir to be completed within six years, subject to a proviso that the engineer could extend the time for completion if by reason of any difficulties, impediments, or obstructions "whatsoever or howsoever occasioned", the contractors should, in the opinion of the engineer, have been unduly delayed or impeded. In 1916, the contractors were served with a notice from the Ministry of Munitions under the Defence of the Realm Acts which required them to cease work forthwith. The House of Lords held that the clause authorising the engineer to grant an extension did not apply to the prohibition of the Ministry of Munitions. Lord Finlay L.C. said:

"This is not a case of a short and temporary stoppage, but of a prohibition in consequence of war, which has already been in force for the greater part of two years, and will, according to all appearances, last as long as the war itself . . . Clause 32 does not cover the case in which the interruption is of such a character and duration that it vitally and fundamentally changes the conditions of the contract, and could not possibly have been in the contemplation of the parties to the contract when it was made."[200]

195. [1908] A.C. 295.
196. See also *Ambatielos* v. *Anton Jurgens Margarine Works* [1923] A.C. 175 in which the *ejusdem generis* rule was held inapplicable to a clause excluding demurrage if the vessel were detained "by causes over which the charterers have no control, *viz*, quarantine, ice, hurricanes, blockade, clearing the steamer after the last cargo is taken over, etc".
197. [1987] 1 Lloyd's Rep. 503.
198. *Ibid.*, at p. 507.
199. [1918] A.C. 119; contrast the decision of the House of Lords, by a bare majority, in *F. A. Tamplin Steamship Co. Limited* v. *Anglo-Mexican Petroleum Products Co. Limited* [1916] 2 A.C. 397 considered at pp. 130–131 below.
200. *Ibid.*, at pp. 125–126.

6. EFFECT ON A PARTY'S ABILITY TO PERFORM THE CONTRACT

Perhaps the most important issue for any *force majeure* clause is: if an event covered by the clause occurs, how difficult does that event need to make a party's performance of the contract in order for the party to be able to invoke the clause? Must performance have become impossible, onerous or merely inpracticable? Conversely, what is the level of the affected party's obligation to try to avoid or mitigate the consequences of the *force majeure* event? Connected with this is the question of whether it is relevant that the action required to counteract the consequences of the *force majeure* event would eliminate the profit which the contract was expected to yield or would result in the affected party incurring a considerable loss.

The difficulties are illustrated by *Tennants (Lancashire) Ltd.* v. *G.S. Wilson & Co. Ltd.*[201] Importers of magnesium chloride agreed to sell to buyers their requirements of magnesium chloride over 1914 estimated at 400 to 600 tons. The contract provided that deliveries "may be suspended pending any contingency beyond the control of the sellers . . . (such as . . . war . . .) causing a short supply of . . . raw material or manufactured produce or otherwise preventing or hindering the manufacture or delivery of the article". The greater part of the supplies of magnesium chloride came from Germany. On 4 August, 1914, on the outbreak of war, the sellers had 17 running contracts and the German source of supply was cut off. The sellers, though able at an increased price to obtain sufficient magnesium chloride to satisfy the particular buyers' contracts if they disregarded their other contracts and the normal requirements of their business, suspended delivery to these buyers. At first instance, Low J. dismissed the buyers' claim for damages for breach of contract. This decision was reversed by a divided Court of Appeal,[202] Lord Cozens-Hardy M.R. and Pickford L.J., with Neville J. dissenting, on the ground that a mere shortage of supply caused by war, which did not also prevent or hinder delivery, did not entitle the defendant to suspend delivery; and that "preventing or hindering" referred to a physical or legal prevention and not to an economic unprofitableness caused by a rise in price. Six Law Lords,[203] Lord Finlay L.C. dissenting, reversed the Court of Appeal. The House of Lords held that, apart from the question of price, the evidence showed a shortage in the supply of the magnesium chloride which hindered delivery by preventing the sellers from fulfilling their obligations to their customers in the ordinary course of their business. Earl Loreburn said that by hindering delivery was meant interposing obstacles which it would be really difficult to overcome, and added: "To place a merchant in a position of being unable to deliver unless he dislocates his business and breaks his other contracts in order to fulfil one, surely hinders delivery."[204]

In the Court of Appeal, Pickford L.J.[205] noted that the price to the sellers rose from 48s to 97s 6d, or a little more than double, against a contractual selling price to the plaintiffs of 63s. However, Pickford L.J. held that this financial loss did not

201. [1917] A.C. 495.
202. [1917] 1 K.B. 208.
203. [1917] A.C. 495.
204. *Ibid.*, at p. 510.
205. [1917] 1 K.B. 208, at pp. 218–219.

"hinder" delivery. On this aspect of the case, Pickford L.J. was upheld by the House of Lords. Earl Loreburn said:

"I do not consider that even a great rise of price hinders delivery.[205a] If that had been intended different language would have been used . . . The argument that a man can be excused from performance of his contract when it becomes 'commercially' impossible, which is forcibly criticised by Pickford L.J., seems to me a dangerous contention, which ought not to be admitted unless the parties have plainly contracted to that effect."[206]

Lord Finlay L.C. agreed:

"I think that Pickford L.J. was right when he pointed out that a rise in price, even if very great, would not amount to a prevention of delivery[206a]. . . . , that 'prevention' in such a clause must refer to physical or legal prevention and not economic unprofitableness, and that 'hindering' must refer to an interference with the manufacture or delivery from the same cause as 'preventing', but interference of a less degree."[207]

The statements in *Tennants* v. *Wilson* about the irrelevance of the large price rise indicate a particularly serious risk of a *force majeure* clause not protecting a party against a *force majeure* event which produces purely financial consequences. This risk materialised in *Exportelisa S.A.* v. *Rocco Giuseppe & Figli Soc. Coll.*[208] The prohibition clause in GAFTA 64 provided for cancellation of the contract "should fulfilment of this contract be rendered impossible by . . . any executive or legislative act done by or on behalf of the Government of the country of origin of the goods". A decree introduced in the Argentine required the sellers to buy the wheat covered by the sale contract from the Argentine state monopoly, precluding them from buying from the source which they had previously intended to use. The Court of Appeal held that the sellers could not invoke the prohibition clause since they could have bought the wheat, albeit at a much higher price, from the Argentine state monopoly.

The difference between "prevent" and "delay" is further illustrated by *Fairclough Dodd & Jones Ltd.* v. *J.H. Vantol Ltd.*[209] One clause in a contract for the sale of Egyptian cottonseed oil provided that in the event of "war, hostilities or blockade preventing shipment" the contract or any unfulfilled part of it would be cancelled. A second clause provided "should shipment be delayed . . . by prohibition of export . . . or any other cause comprehended in the term *force majeure* other than war, hostilities, blockade, the time of shipment shall be extended by two

205a. In *Scheepvaart Maatschappij Gylsen* v. *North African Coating Co.* (1916) 114 L.T. 755 at p. 757 Scrutton J. said of 'interference": "Mere extra expense would not do, if you could get all the ships you wanted by paying extra for them, but if you could not get the ships there would be 'interference' and high freights for those you did get, or in the market generally would be evidence of shortage of ships."

206. [1917] A.C. 495, at p. 510.

206a. In *Blythe & Co.* v. *Richards Turpin & Co.* (1916) 114 L.T. 753 at p. 755 Scrutton J. said: "You are not prevented from buying a thing if you think its cost higher than you can afford, or that it is not worth the price. You are prevented from buying a thing by a given cause if, owing to that cause, there is none to be had." However, in *Bolckow Vaughune* v. *Companania Miaera de Sierra Minera* (1916) 114 L.T. 758 Bailhache J. considered that an "enormous" price rise would constitute "prevention".

207. *Ibid.*, at p. 509. Lord Atkinson said (at p. 518): " 'Preventing' delivery means, in my view, rendering delivery impossible; and 'hindering' delivery means something less than this, namely, rendering delivery more or less difficult, but not impossible." See also *J. H. Vantol Ltd.* v. *Fairclough, Dodd & Jones Ltd.* [1956] 2 Lloyd's Rep. 437.

208. [1978] 1 Lloyd's Rep. 433. The clause in this case was much narrower than that in *Tennants (Lancashire)* v. *Wilson* which referred to "preventing or hindering".

209. [1956] 3 All E.R. 921.

months . . . ". The contract provided for the oil to be shipped during the months of December 1950 and January 1951. In December 1950 the Egyptian Government imposed a ban on the export of cottonseed oil, but the ban was lifted on 3 January 1951 and between 4 January and 31 January oil of the contract description and quantity was available for shipment. The House of Lords held that the sellers were entitled to an extension of the time of shipment, since the use of the word "delayed" in the second clause in contrast to the word "preventing" in the first clause meant that the first clause only applied where shipment remained impossible up to the end of the contract period, while the second clause applied in any case in which shipment was delayed, whether or not the delay persisted until the end of the contract period.[210]

When drafting a *force majeure* clause which is intended to apply to delays, regard should be had to the problems which have arisen in relation to frustration by delay.[211] Pertinent questions are: should a minimum period of delay be specified after which a *force majeure* notice can be served? Should the clause entitle a party to take into account not only the delay which has occurred, but also further delay which is likely to occur? Relevant here are Lord Roskill's comments in *The Nema*[212] regarding frustration by delay:

" . . . where the effect of [an] event is to cause delay in the performance of contractual obligations, it is often necessary to wait upon events in order to see whether the delay already suffered *and the prospects of further delay from that cause*, will make any ultimate performance of the relevant contractual obligations 'radically different' . . . from that which was undertaken by the contract. But . . . businessmen must not be required to await events too long. They are entitled to know where they stand. Whether or not the delay is such as to bring about frustration must be a question to be determined by an informed judgment based upon all the evidence of what has occurred *and what is likely thereafter to occur.* Often it will be a question of degree whether the effect of delay suffered, *and likely to be suffered*, will be such as to bring about frustration of the particular adventure in question."[213]

The discussion in this section suggests that it is preferable to avoid such words as "prevent", "hinder" and "delay"[214] and to provide that a party (A) may invoke the clause:

"if a *force majeure* event and/or its consequences[215] seriously and adversely affect [, or a *force majeure* event and/or its likely consequences are likely seriously and adversely to affect,] A's ability to carry out its obligations under this Contract within the period specified by this Contract and in the manner [provided for by this Contract] [contemplated by the par-

210. See also the comments of Mocatta J. in *European Grain & Shipping* v. *J. H. Rayner* [1970] 2 Lloyd's Rep. 239 at p. 246.

211. See pp. 129–138 below.

212. *Pioneer Shipping* v. *B.T.P. Tioxide* [1982] A.C. 724.

213. *Ibid.*, at p. 752 (emphasis added).

214. Where a clause operates if performance becomes "impracticable", it is thought that "impracticable" would have to be given a narrow meaning in order for the agreement to retain any legal force: compare *Hong Guan & Co. Ltd.* v. *R. Jumabhoy & Sons Ltd.* [1960] A.C. 684. See also *Treitel, op. cit.*, note 18, at paras. 6–021—6–023.

215. "Consequences" should be defined to include indirect consequences, and also effects caused by a *force majeure* event or its consequences operating in conjunction with other events or matters. Ackner J.'s judgment in *Vosper Thornycroft Ltd.* v. *Ministry of Defence* [1976] 1 Lloyd's Rep. 58 contains important observations about the scope of the word "effect". Ackner J. implicitly upheld a submission that the term comprehends direct, indirect and consequential results, provided that they are not too remote to be regarded as the proximate result, they being limited in the same manner as they would be limited if the *force majeure* event had been a product of a breach of contract.

ties at the date of this Contract] or have, or are likely to have, the result that, in order to carry out those obligations within that period and in that manner, A would have to incur increased or additional costs which, in aggregate (after deducting any likely savings) would amount to [50 per cent.] or more of the costs which would otherwise have been attributable to this Contract."

There is a case for a provision to the effect that, where a party invokes the *force majeure* clause on the ground (or mainly on the ground) of substantially increased costs, it shall be relieved of its obligations only if that would be fair and reasonable as regards the other party, balancing the additional costs which the first party would incur in performing the contract against the losses which the second party would incur if the first party did not perform.

It may be prudent for a clause to include wording designed to exclude an argument based on *Wayne Tank & Pump Co. Ltd.* v. *Employers Liability Assurance Corporation Ltd.*[216] that a *force majeure* clause cannot be invoked where a party's ability to perform a contract is affected, by both an event within the clause and an event outside the clause, if each event plays an approximately equal part in preventing performance of the contract.

7. THE AFFECTED PARTY'S DUTIES

In *Channel Island Ferries Ltd.* v. *Sealink U.K. Ltd.*[217] the third proposition laid down by Parker L.J. was that "a party must not only bring himself within the clause but must show that he has taken all reasonable steps to avoid its operation, or mitigate its results."[218] This principle has been applied in embargo cases.[219] In *Continental Grain Export Corporation* v. *STM Grain Ltd*[220] Robert Goff J., as he then was, said that a seller who invokes a prohibition of export clause has to prove (1) that no goods of the contract description were available to him to fulfil his contract and (2) that he could not, following notice of the export prohibition obtain any such goods "by the exercise of any means reasonably open to him". Robert Goff J. noted that it had been established by the House of Lords' decision in *Bremer* v. *Vanden*[221] that it would not be reasonable to require a seller after the United States embargo on the export of soya bean meal to buy goods afloat, since the imposition of such a duty on sellers would result in there being large numbers of buyers chasing very few goods and the price would reach unheard of levels. Robert Goff J. also noted that in *Bunge* v. *Kruse*[221a] Brandon J., as he then was, had held that, by analogy with the decision in *Bremer* v. *Vanden*, relating to goods afloat, there was equally no duty on the sellers to buy goods within one of the "loopholes" of the embargo. Robert Goff J.'s account of a seller's obligations was approved by the Court of Appeal in *André* v. *Tradax Export*.[221b]

216. [1974] 1 Q.B. 57.
217. [1988] 1 Lloyd's Rep. 323.
218. [1988] 1 Lloyd's Rep. 323 at p. 327.
219. And also in the strike cases considered in Chapter 9 below; see also *Michalinos & Co.* v. *Louis Dreyfus & Co.* (1925) 21 Ll.L.Rep. 233.
220. [1979] 2 Lloyd's Rep. 460.
221. [1978] 2 Lloyd's Rep. 109, in particular the statement of Lord Wilberforce at pp. 114–115.
221a. [1979] 1 Lloyd's Rep. 279.
221b. [1983] 1 Lloyd's Rep. 254.

In *The Furness Bridge*[222] a charter for the carriage of a cargo of crude oil stated that the agreed loading ports were "European Mediterranean". Both the owner and the charterer expected the cargo to be shipped from Libya. However, as a result of the Arab–Israel war in 1973, Libya imposed an embargo on shipments of oil to the United States. The charter exempted both the owners and the charterers for any loss resulting from a failure to perform which arose from "restraint of princes". Kerr J. stated that the general principle is that, if a contract provides for alternative methods of performance, and one such method comes to be prevented by an excepted peril, then the party affected must generally perform or seek to perform by one of the alternative methods. It followed that when shipment from Libya became impossible, the charterers had to ship from a European Mediterranean port or to bring themselves within the exception.[223] Kerr J. rejected the charterers' submission that it was sufficient for them to negative the possibility of performing the charter in the way which had been contemplated by both parties—i.e. by shipping from Libya—and that this thereupon required the owners to prove that performance in another permitted way would have been possible. "Merely to negative one method of performance," Kerr J. said, "albeit the anticipated one, is insufficient to shift the burden of proof unless the alternative methods are at least *prima facie* impracticable."[224]

Branson J.'s decision in *Pool Shipping Co. Ltd.* v. *London Coal Co. of Gibraltar Ltd.*[225] suggests that there is an advantage in referring to "the normal working of this contract". The defendants had contracted to supply to the plaintiffs during 1937 such quantities of bunker coal as the plaintiffs' ships might ask for at Gibraltar. The contract provided that, in the event of any circumstances beyond the control of the sellers "which prevents . . . the normal working of this contract", the sellers would be relieved from all obligations under the contract. Branson J. found that the normal practice for that type of contract was to estimate the demand for bunkers that ships were likely to make on the depot at Gibraltar, and then to contract with collieries to supply sufficient coal to meet those requirements. That practice had been followed, and contracts had been placed to buy a quantity of coal equal to the estimated monthly demand plus a margin of 20 per cent. However, in the spring of 1937 the British Government put pressure on the collieries to increase their stocks of coal to full capacity, and it became impossible to obtain coal from Wales or Durham in the quantities normally available. Branson J. rejected the plaintiffs' contention that the defendants could only rely on the *force majeure* clause if they could show that no possible steps would have enabled them to deliver the coal required by the plaintiffs' ships:

"It cannot be . . . that, in the normal working of a contract of this sort, which is, as I have said, to send out monthly coal obtained under contract from collieries, the sellers should have to go round and pick up 200 tons here and 100 tons there and collect it together and send it out, in order to be enabled to say that they have not been prevented by the shortage

222. [1977] 2 Lloyd's Rep. 367.

223. *Ibid.*, at p. 375.

224. *Ibid.*, at p. 378. Contrast *Sociedad Iberica de Molturacion S.A.* v. *Tradax Export S.A.* [1978] 2 Lloyd's Rep. 545 and *Koninklijke Bunge* v. *Compagnie Continentale d'Importation* [1973] 2 Lloyd's Rep. 44.

225. [1939] 2 All E.R. 432, cited in *Hong Guan & Co. Ltd.* v. *R. Jumabhoy & Sons Ltd.* [1960] A.C. 684 at p. 700.

from carrying on the normal working of their contract. So to acquire the coal is not the normal way of working the contract."[226]

However, it is preferable for a clause to give some specific indication of the level of the obligation of the party invoking the clause to find some way of performing the contract despite the *force majeure* event. For example, the clause may require the affected party:

(a) to avoid or mitigate the effects of the *force majeure* situation "so far as reasonably practicable"[227]; or
(b) to use its "best endeavours"[228] to avoid or mitigate those effects;

or to take such steps with a view to avoiding or mitigating those effects as the other party may from time to time reasonably require.

In any event, a *force majeure* clause should impose some obligation on the affected party to provide the other party with any information which it reasonably requests about the *force majeure* event or its consequences or about the action which the affected party—or any other person—is taking or proposing to take to deal with those consequences. It is for consideration whether the clause should require this information to be provided in the form of reports signed by a director of the affected party in terms which would impose on him a duty of care to ensure the correctness and completeness of these reports.[229]

8. MECHANISM FOR BRINGING THE CLAUSE INTO OPERATION

Most *force majeure* clauses require the affected party to serve some form of notice on the other party.[229a]

(a) Mandatory or directory?

The main issue in this area is whether the requirement to serve a notice is mandatory, so that if the notice is not served or does not comply with the clause's requirements, particularly the time limits for service,[230] the affected party is not entitled to the clause's protection; or whether the notice requirement is merely directory, in which case a failure to comply with it will not deprive the affected party of the clause's protection but will only give a right to damages—which might well be

226. [1939] 2 All E.R. 432 at p. 439. Contrast the refusal in *Tsakiroglou & Co. Ltd.* v. *Noblee Thorl G.m.b.H.* [1962] A.C. 93 to imply a term that the goods would be carried by "the customary or usual route". It is thought that referring to performing a contract "in the manner contemplated by the parties" has a broadly similar effect to referring to the normal working of the contract.

227. See *Jordan* v. *Norfolk County Council* [1994] 1 W.L.R. 1353.

228. See *I.B.M. United Kingdom Ltd.* v. *Rockware Glass Ltd.* [1980] F.S.R. 335.

229. Compare *Kuwait Bank* v. *National Nominees Ltd.* [1991] 1 A.C. 187 at pp. 219–222.

229a. *Woodar Investment Development* v. *Wimpey Construction U.K.* [1980] 1 All E.R. 571 implies that a party does not commit a repudiatory breach by serving a *force majeure* notice in good faith if the clause, on its true construction, does not apply to the event thought to justify service of the notice.

230. Compare *United Scientific Holdings Ltd.* v. *Burnley Borough Council* [1978] A.C. 904 and *Bunge Corpn.* v. *Tradax S.A.* [1981] 2 All E.R. 513.

only nominal. This issue arose in *Bremer Handelsgesellschaft m.b.H.* v. *Vanden Avenne-Izegem P.V.B.A.*[231] in connection with two clauses in GAFTA 100. The first was as follows:

"21 *Prohibition*

In case of prohibition of export . . . preventing fulfilment, this contract . . . shall be cancelled. In the event of shipment proving impossible during the contract period by any of the causes enumerated herein, sellers shall advise buyers of the reasons therefor."[232]

The House of Lords held (contrary to the view which Lord Denning M.R. had expressed in *Tradax Export S.A.* v. *André & Cie. S.A.*[233] that the advice provision in the second sentence of the clause was insufficiently precise to be a condition precedent to the seller obtaining the clause's protection. Lord Wilberforce said:

"Automatic and invariable treatment of a clause such as this [as a condition precedent] runs counter to the approach, which modern authorities recognise, of treating such a provision as having the force of a condition (giving rise to rescission or invalidity), or of a contractual term (giving rise to damages only) according to the nature and gravity of the breach. The clause is then categorised as an innominate term. This doctrine emerged very clearly in *Hongkong Fir Shipping Co. Ltd.* v. *Kawasaki Kisen Kaisha Ltd.* [1961] 1 Lloyd's Rep. 478; [1962] 2 Q.B. 26 in relation to the obligation of seaworthiness, and was applied to a contract for sale of goods made on GAFTA form 100 in *The Hansa Nord* [1975] 2 Lloyd's Rep. 445; [1976] Q.B. 44, a decision itself approved by this House in *Reardon Smith Line* v. *Hansen-Tangen* [1976] 2 Lloyd's Rep. 621; [1976] 3 All ER 570. In my opinion the clause may vary appropriately and should be regarded as such an intermediate term; to do so would recognise that while in many, possibly most, instances, breach of it can adequately be sanctioned by damages, cases may exist in which, in fairness to the buyer, it would be proper to treat the cancellation as not having effect. On the other hand, always so to treat it may often be unfair to the seller, and unnecessarily rigid."[234]

The second clause in issue in *Bremer* v. *Vanden* was clause 22, entitled "Force Majeure, Strikes, etc". The first three sentences were as follows:

"1. Sellers shall not be responsible for any delay in shipment of the goods . . . occasioned by any . . . strike, lock-out, riot or civil commotion, . . . or any other cause comprehended in the term *force majeure*.
2. If delay in shipment is likely to occur for any of the above reasons, Shippers shall give notice to their Buyers . . . within seven consecutive days of the occurrence . . .
3. The notice shall state the reason(s) for the anticipated delay."

In contrast to clause 21, all the Law Lords held that clause 22 was a condition, one of the main reasons being that accurate compliance with clause 22 was essential to avoid commercial confusion in view of the possibility of long string contracts being involved.[235]

Bremer v. *Vanden* illustrates the uncertainty which is likely to arise if a *force*

231. [1978] 2 Lloyd's Rep. 109. These cases are discussed in more detail in Chapter 15.
232. In *Bunge Corpn.* v. *Tradax S.A.* [1981] 2 All E.R. 513, at p. 550j, Lord Roskill pointed out that the text of this clause is inaccurately quoted in the headnote of *Bremer* v. *Vanden*, but is correctly quoted in the speech of Viscount Dilhorne [1978] 2 Lloyd's Rep. 109 at p. 121.
233. [1976] 1 Lloyd's Rep. 416.
234. [1978] 2 Lloyd's Rep. 109, at p. 113.
235. See the explanation given by Lord Roskill in *Bunge Corpn.* v. *Tradax S.A.* [1981] 2 All E.R. 513 at pp. 550j–551d.

majeure clause does not state expressly whether or not a requirement to give notice of a *force majeure* event is a condition[235a] of the clause's protection being available.[236] The same point applies to any requirement for the affected party to provide further information about a *force majeure* event or about the action which it is proposing to take in the new circumstances.

Bremer v. *Vanden* also illustrates the risk that, even if a *force majeure* clause expressly specifies that compliance with its requirements is a condition precedent to the clause being validly invoked by a particular party, those requirements may be inadvertently waived by the other party in the course of correspondence exchanged after the *force majeure* event occurs. It is thought doubtful whether the risk of losing, by equitable estoppel or election, the right to reject a notice which does not satisfy the *force majeure* clause's requirements can be excluded by a provision that no act, omission or acquiescence by the party concerned will operate as a waiver of those requirements.

(b) Contents of *force majeure* notice

A clause should make it clear what information a *force majeure* notice must contain. Should it give merely "brief particulars" of the relevant event or must it provide "full details"? In *Intertradax S.A.* v. *Lesieur-Tourteaux S.A.R.L.*,[237] the sellers were prevented from performing their obligations by a breakdown of machinery at their suppliers' factory and by a shortage in the supply of raw materials. But in their notice under the *force majeure* clause, the sellers specified only the breakdown of machinery. Lord Denning M.R., with whom Robert Goff and Cumming-Bruce L.JJ. agreed, said:

"Suppose that during the months of March, April and May, 1973, the breakdown at the factory lasted only six weeks, and that the groundnuts would have been delivered in time: but there was a further delay of another six weeks because it was not possible to get the raw material down by railway. In that event there would have been two causes which operated in succession to prevent production. Suppose next that the loss of production was caused simultaneously by the two causes: partly because of the breakdown of machinery—reducing production by a half—and partly because of the difficulty in getting the raw materials down—reducing production by another half. Those two together might have operated to prevent delivery, but not the breakdown of machinery by itself. In both those instances there would be two causes operating. Taken together they might constitute a case of *force majeure*. But, in order to qualify under cl. 22, the proper notice or notices would have had to be given in regard to both those causes. The second sentence of cl. 22 says that: '. . . shippers shall give notice within seven consecutive days of the occurrence.' [Sentence 3 says that the notice:] 'shall state the reasons for the anticipated delay.' That shows that, if there are two reasons, the notice must give the reasons, stating the occurrences which caused non-performance. If

235a. Compare *Chelsea Building Society* v. *R. & A. Millett (Shops) Ltd* (1993) 67 P. & C.R. 319 in which Rattee J. held that the use of the term "condition precedent" in a rent review clause was sufficient to rebut the presumption that time was not of the essence in relation to the service of the landlord's notice.

236. This point is reinforced by the proceedings in *Secretary of State for Trade and Industry* v. *Langridge* [1991] Ch. 402 in which Mummery J. found that a requirement for a 10-day notice in the Company Directors Disqualification Act 1986 was mandatory, but was reversed by the Court of Appeal, Nourse L.J. dissenting.

237. [1977] 2 Lloyd's Rep. 146; [1978] 2 Lloyd's Rep. 509.

they occur successively, two successive notices must be given. This is necessary so that buyers can check it up to see whether the reasons are valid. The eighth sentence says that 'the sellers shall provide, if required, satisfactory evidence' justifying the delay or non-fulfilment. Hence the necessity for notice of the occurrence."[238]

The Court of Appeal held that the sellers' notice under the *force majeure* clause would be valid only if the breakdown of machinery—the only *force majeure* event specified by the notice—would by itself have been sufficient to prevent delivery. If, however, delivery was prevented by the cumulative effect of the breakdown of machinery and the interruptions of the supply of raw materials to the factory, the sellers' notice would be invalid.[239]

At first instance, Donaldson J. drew attention to the need for an extension clause to make it clear how it is to operate if hazard A is effective so as to extend the period for delivery, but disappears and is replaced by a new hazard B during the extension.[240]

(c) Methods of serving a force majeure notice

The clause should also state how notices are to be given and, in particular, make it clear whether telex or fax notices are permitted; clause 24 of the current GAFTA 100 prohibits notices by fax. If it is intended that it shall be possible to give a notice simply by electronic means, without its being reproduced in written form, this should be stated expressly. An express provision should also be included if it is intended that a notice may be given to the agent of a party or of a group of parties.

(d) Time period for service of force majeure notice

The time periods for a notice also need care. In *Bremer* v. *Vanden*[241] the contract contained a clause which provided that any notices received after 1600 hours on a business day would be deemed to have been received on the business day following; and one of the points in issue was whether a deadline for notices related to the time at which it was despatched or the time at which it was received. The House of Lords held that the terms of GAFTA 100 showed that in the relevant clause the reference to the giving of a notice meant its despatch.

If no time limit is specified, it is likely that a condition will be implied requiring a party to serve a notice within a reasonable time after becoming aware of the relevant *force majeure* event; and it seems that the right to serve a notice will not be saved by a clause providing that no delay in exercising a right shall be operated as a waiver of it, since once a reasonable time has expired, there is no right which such a clause can preserve.[242]

238. [1978] 2 Lloyd's Rep. 509 at p. 514. Compare Art. 79(4) of the Vienna Convention considered at pp. 281–282 below.
239. See the comments of Lord Denning M.R. at p. 514 and of Robert Goff L.J. at p. 580.
240. [1977] 1 Lloyd's Rep. 146 at p. 155.
241. [1978] 2 Lloyd's Rep. 109.
242. Compare *Zeeland Navigation Company Ltd.* v. *Banque Worms*, Rix J. 15 June 1994, unreported.

9. THE CONSEQUENCES OF THE CLAUSE APPLYING

(a) Termination or suspension?[242a]

The main question in this context is, if the *force majeure* clause comes into operation, should the result be:

1. that the parties are thereupon discharged from further performance of their obligations,[243] but without prejudice to (a) any rights which either party has then acquired, including any rights in respect of an earlier breach by the other party, and (b) the obligations of either party to make a payment or repayment for which the *force majeure* clause provides; *or*
2. that the parties' obligations are suspended for the time being?

Many contracts provide for an extension up to a specified maximum period at the end of which the parties' obligations are terminated if performance remains impossible. For example, the *force majeure* clause in GAFTA 100 (clause 22) provides that, if delay in shipment occurs as a result of a *force majeure* event, the shipper can give a notice extending the shipping period; but that if shipment is delayed for more than one month, the buyers may cancel the delayed portion of the contract and that, if the buyers do not cancel, there is a further automatic extension for an additional month. If shipment is still prevented by the end of this additional extension, the contract is then terminated.

A *force majeure* clause which provides that a contract is not to be terminated should suspend performance not only of the affected party's obligations but also of those of the other party. For example, a shipowner has to keep the chartered vessel waiting in port owing to a *force majeure* event. The charter should specify that hire is not payable while the *force majeure* clause is in operation.[244] Where a contract provides for a party to perform several obligations of a different nature, consideration should be given to whether a *force majeure* event might occur that prevents performance of one obligation but not of the others; and, if that could occur, the contract should provide for the unaffected obligations to be performed.

It was suggested[245] that a clause which provides that a party shall "have no liability" in respect of losses caused by a *force majeure* event might well not exclude the other party's right to terminate the contract as a result of the first party's non-performance. It is, therefore, preferable for a clause not only to exclude the affected party's liability, but also to provide that the other party shall not have any rights or

242a. Note also the type of clause which featured in *Johnson Matthey Bankers Ltd.* v. *The State Trading Corporation of India Ltd.* [1984] 1 Lloyd's Rep. 427; the clause, in a contract for the sale of silver bullion, provided that, if the seller were unable to deliver, the contract would be closed by invoicing back to the seller at the market price on the day after the seller's notice; note also *J.F. Adair* v. *Birnbaum* [1939] 2 K.B. 149.

243. It is thought that this formula is preferable to stating that the contract is terminated. It is based on the position which results where a party "terminates" a contract for breach: see the statement of Dixon J. in *McDonald* v. *Dennys Lascelles Limited* (1933) 48 C.L.R. 457 at pp. 476–477 quoted in *Johnson* v. *Agnew* [1980] A.C. 367 at p. 396 and *Bank of Boston Connecticut* v. *European Grain & Shipping Ltd.* [1989] A.C. 1056 at p. 1098. Note also Lord Wright's explanation in *Denny Mott & Dickson* v. *James B Fraser & Co.* [1944] A.C. 265 at p. 274 that frustration discharges "any obligation as to future performance", but not obligations which have accrued.

244. See, for example, clause 11(A) of Baltime 1939.

245. See pp. 66–67 above.

remedies in respect of the *force majeure* event or any of its consequences; and, in particular, shall have no right to terminate the contract or to make any form of withholding or deduction, by way of set-off or otherwise, from the amounts due to the affected party.

(b) Effect on liquidated damages

Hull Central Dry Dock Works Ltd. v. *Ohlson Steamship Ltd.*,[246] a case regarding penalties payable under a building contract for late delivery, establishes that, in the absence of a clear provision, a party cannot rely on a *force majeure* event which occurs *after* the date on which he was required to complete work on a contract in order to reduce the liquidated damages payable in respect of the delay in completion. Bailhache J said:

"It seems to me perfectly plain that the [shipbuilders] cannot rely upon the strike interfering with their work, if at the time the strike began they had exceeded their contract time. They can only rely on the strike clause as being an interference with the work given them or contracted for if at the time of the strike they had committed no breach of contract. That is analogous to the well-known rules as to the demurrage of ships."[247]

The Saturnia[248] is a recent illustration of this principle as it applies to demurrage. The charterers claimed to reduce the rate of demurrage by a half relying on the Gencon strike clause in so far as the vessel was detained after the beginning of the strike. However, the strike had begun after laytime had been exhausted. The Court of Appeal held that the charterers could not invoke the strike clause. Sir John Donaldson M.R., with whom Stephen Brown L.J. and Glidewell J. agreed, said that: " . . . the maxim 'once on demurrage, always on demurrage' . . . is not just something which commercial lawyers mouth. It has a solid basis in common sense, namely that if . . . the ship had been discharged in the laytime, she would not have been in the port of Lagos when the strike occurred and so would have been completely unaffected by it.[249]

In two recent cases[250] the Court of Appeal has held that the principle also applies where the *force majeure* event occurs during laytime.[251] In *The Kalliopi A*[252] the charterers claimed that congestion at Bombay was an "unavoidable hindrance" which prevented discharge of the cargo for a time, and was therefore excepted under the *force majeure* exclusion in the demurrage clause. However, the charterers took the unusual position of *not* contending that the congestion operated as an exception while laytime was running. The charterers' claim was that, after laytime expired, they were excused from any liability to pay demurrage in respect of periods when the vessel was still delayed by congestion. The Court of Appeal held that the principle that, when once a vessel is on demurrage no exceptions will oper-

246. (1924) 19 Ll.L.Rep. 54.
247. *Ibid.*, at p. 56.
248. [1987] 2 Lloyd's Rep. 43.
249. *Ibid.*, at p. 46.
250. *The Kalliopi A* [1988] 2 Lloyd's Rep. 101 and *The Lefthero* [1992] 2 Lloyd's Rep. 109.
251. That is, the period of time which the charter allows the charterer to complete the loading or discharge of the vessel. It is suggested that this corresponds, for example, to the period which a construction contract allows for the completion of the project.
252. [1988] 2 Lloyd's Rep. 101.

ate to prevent demurrage continuing to be payable unless the exceptions clause is clearly worded, was applicable to the case; and this notwithstanding that the vessel was already affected by congestion during laytime and the charterers' breach in failing to discharge her within the laydays did not of itself cause her to be exposed to any subsequent peril.[253] That decision was followed in *The Lefthero*,[254] in which the Court of Appeal held that the maxim "once on demurrage always on demurrage" applied even though the excepted peril, restraint of princes, operated *before* laytime expired.

(c) Allocation of supplies

The position of a seller faced with a partial failure of supplies is discussed in Chapter 3. The uncertain position of such a seller at common law suggests that a *force majeure* clause should provide that a party shall be entitled to allocate its supplies "in any manner which it considers will, so far as reasonably practicable, produce a fair allocation of supplies among its buyers having regard, in particular, to their respective past levels of business with the Seller". If this formula is used, it is thought that the seller would be denied the protection of the *force majeure* clause only if his allocation were shown to have been made in bad faith (for example, that it had been designed to exploit subsequent price rises[254a]) or that it was such that no reasonable person could have considered it fair.[255] It is thought that this judicial review of a seller's allocation would not necessarily be excluded by a formulation entitling the seller to allocate its supplies "in such manner as it may, in its absolute discretion, determine".[256]

By contrast, a clause can prescribe a specific basis on which supplies will be allocated, for example pro rata by reference to the unfilled amount of each outstanding order. However, whatever formulation is adopted, there may be a case for expressly negativing any obligation on the part of the supplier to disclose matters relating to its dealings with other customers and, in particular, the amounts of its deliveries to them, and the provision should specifically exclude any obligation to make such a disclosure in the course of legal proceedings.[257]

253. See the observations of Staughton L.J. at pp. 104 and 106.

254. [1992] 2 Lloyd's Rep. 109.

254a. See *Continental Grain Export Corporation v. S.T.M. Grain Ltd.* [1979] 2 Lloyd's Rep. 460 at p. 473.

255. See the passage in the judgment of Ackner L.J. in *Bremer* v. *Continental Grain* [1983] 1 Lloyd's Rep. 269 which starts at the end of p. 291 and ends at the end of the first para. in col. 2 of p. 292, and fn. 54 above. It is suggested that the test would be similar to, but probably less rigorous than, that applied where an administrative decision is challenged on the ground of "irrationality"; see, for example, *R.* v. *Secretary of State for the Environment, ex parte Nottinghamshire County Council* [1986] A.C. 240, 247; and *R.* v. *Secretary of State for the Environment, ex parte Hammersmith London Borough Council* [1991] 1 A.C. 521, at pp. 595–597.

256 Compare the rejection in the Lloyd's litigation (*Henderson* v. *Merrett Syndicates* [1994] 3 W.L.R. 761 at pp. 778–779) of the claim that, since the agreements between the names and the managing agents conferred on the managing agents powers to be exercised in their "absolute discretion", that excluded the duty ordinarily binding on any professional agent to exercise reasonable care and skill. However, this decision might be distinguished on the basis that the ordinary relationship of seller and buyer does not import any such duty on the seller.

257. It is not certain that such an exclusion would be effective in all circumstances.

10. ADJUSTMENT OF THE CONTRACT

(a) Obligation to negotiate or obligation to use best endeavours to agree amendments

An important issue is how far a clause can bind the parties to negotiate an amendment to the contract to take account of a *force majeure* event or in a situation, not amounting to *force majeure* in the usual sense of the term, in which it has become onerous for a party to perform a contract. A clause which operates in the latter type of situation is often called a hardship clause.[258]

A consideration of this issue must start with the decision of the House of Lords in *Walford* v. *Miles*[259] in which it was held that, where A and B are negotiating for the sale and purchase of a particular property, an undertaking by A to B not to commence negotiations with a third party for the sale of the property is enforceable if, but only if, A's undertaking is limited to a specified period of time.[260] The House of Lords confirmed earlier English decisions[261] that an agreement to negotiate, or an agreement to negotiate "in good faith", is void. Lord Ackner, who delivered the leading speech, distinguished between an agreement to negotiate and an agreement to use best endeavours:

> "The reason why an agreement to negotiate, like an agreement to agree, is unenforceable, is simply because it lacks the necessary certainty. The same does not apply to an agreement to use best endeavours. This uncertainty is demonstrated in the instant case by the provision which it is said has to be implied in the agreement for the determination of the negotiations. How can a court be expected to decide whether, *subjectively*, a proper reason existed for the termination of negotiations? The answer suggested depends upon whether the negotiations have been determined 'in good faith'. However the concept of a duty to carry on negotiations in good faith is inherently repugnant to the adversarial position of the parties when involved in negotiations. Each party to the negotiations is entitled to pursue his (or her) own interest, so long as he avoids making misrepresentations. To advance that interest he must be entitled, if he thinks it appropriate, to threaten to withdraw from further negotiations or to withdraw in fact, in the hope that the opposite party may seek to reopen the negotiations by offering him improved terms. . . . [There is] the vital question—how is a vendor ever to know that he is entitled to withdraw from further negotiations? How is the court to police such an 'agreement'? A duty to negotiate in good faith is as unworkable in practice as it is inherently inconsistent with the position of a negotiating party. It is here that the uncertainty lies. In my judgment, while those negotiations are in existence either party is entitled to withdraw from those negotiations, at any time and for any reason. There can be thus no obligation to continue to negotiate until there is a 'proper reason' to withdraw. Accordingly a bare agreement to negotiate has no legal content.[262]

Walford v. *Miles* has been criticised by Sir Patrick Neill Q.C.,[263] who drew attention to the contrast between that decision and the decision of the Privy Council in

258. See, for example, the hardship provisions suggested in the ICC's booklet on *Force Majeure and Hardship*.

259. [1992] 2 A.C. 128.

260. This assumes that there is either good consideration or that A's undertaking is contained in a deed; as to consideration, see *Pitt* v. *P.H.H. Asset Management Ltd.* [1994] 1 W.L.R. 327 at p. 332.

261. Notably, *Courtney & Fairbairn Limited* v. *Tolaini Brothers (Hotels) Limited* [1975] 1 W.L.R. 297 and *Mallozzi* v. *Carapelli S.p.A.* [1976] 1 Lloyd's Rep. 407.

262. *Ibid.*, at p. 138.

263. (1992) 108 L.Q.R. 405.

Queensland Electricity Generating Board v. *New Hope Collieries Pty. Ltd.*[264] which, it seems, was not cited to the House of Lords in *Walford* v. *Miles*. The *Queensland Electricity* case concerned a 15-year supply contract by which the colliery company agreed to supply coal to the generating board. For the first five-year period the contract contained a scale of base prices and "escalation" or "price variation" provisions for adjusting the base prices for changes in the colliery company's costs. For purchases after the first five years the general terms of the agreement were to continue, and the agreement provided: "The base price and provisions for variations in prices . . . shall be agreed by the parties . . ." There was also an arbitration clause. The Privy Council refused the generating board's application for a declaration that, in relation to the period after the first five years, the agreement constituted nothing more than an agreement to agree. Sir Robin Cooke, delivering the advice of the Privy Council, said:

" . . . their Lordships have no doubt that here, by the agreement, the parties undertook implied primary obligations to make reasonable endeavours to agree on the terms of supply beyond the initial 5-year period and, failing agreement and upon proper notice, to do everything reasonably necessary to secure the appointment of an arbitrator. Further, it is implicit in a commercial agreement of this kind that the terms of the new structure are to be fair and reasonable between the parties. This is the criterion or standard by which the arbitrator is to be guided."[265]

Sir Robin Cooke referred to the decision of the House of Lords in *Sudbrook Trading Estate Limited* v. *Eggleton*[266] in which specific performance had been granted of an option in a lease to purchase the reversion "at such price not being less than £12,000 as may be agreed upon by two valuers one to be nominated by the lessor and the other by the lessee and in default of such agreement by an umpire appointed by the . . . valuers". The lessees had exercised the option, but the lessors refused to appoint a valuer. The Court of Appeal was obliged by authority binding on it to hold that a court could neither compel a party to appoint a valuer nor order specific performance of an incomplete agreement, so that the option was unenforceable. Reversing the Court of Appeal, the House of Lords held that the lease constituted "a contract for sale at a fair and reasonable price assessed by applying objective standards".[267] It followed that the price was capable of being ascertained and was therefore certain.[268] Accordingly, when the option was exercised, there was constituted a complete contract for sale. The provisions regarding the appointment of the valuers were non-essential and subsidiary to the main purpose of the agreement which was for the sale and purchase of the property at a fair or reasonable value[269]; and there was the general principle that, where the machinery is not essential, if it breaks down for any reason the court will substitute its own machinery.

264. [1989] 1 Lloyd's Rep. 205.
265. *Ibid.*, at p. 210.
266. [1983] 1 A.C. 444, considered by the Privy Council (Lord Goff of Chieveley) in *Money* v. *Ven-Lu-Ree Ltd.* [1989] 3 N.Z.L.R. 133 and by the Court of Appeal in *Saipem S.p.A.* v. *Rafidain Bank* [1994] C.L.C. 254.
267. *Ibid.*, *per* Lord Diplock at p. 479C.
268. *Ibid.*, *per* Lord Fraser of Tullybelton at p. 482B.
269. *Ibid.*, *per* Lord Fraser of Tullybelton at p. 483.

It is therefore clear that a contract can validly provide:

(a) that, in a *force majeure* or hardship situation, the parties will use their best endeavours to agree such an extension to the period for performance, and such an adjustment to the contract price, as will be fair and reasonable in all the circumstances (together with any modifications to the contract which are reasonably necessary as a result of the extension and adjustment); and

(b) that, if the parties do not sign an agreement on these matters by a certain date, they will be referred to arbitration or to the determination of an expert[270] to be appointed by the parties.[271]

The effectiveness of an arbitration clause in this context is established by the decision of Ackner J. (as he then was) in *Vosper Thornycroft Ltd.* v. *Ministry of Defence.*[272] A contract for the construction of a frigate contained the following provision:

"Proviso 6. In the event of exceptional dislocation and delay arising during the construction of the vessel due to modifications . . . or any other cause beyond the Contractors' control, the effect thereof shall be assessed by mutual agreement between the Ministry and the Contractor, failing which the Ministry may pay for the vessel on an 'actual cost' basis, subject to cost investigation by the Ministry, plus a fair and reasonable sum for profit."

There was also the following arbitration clause:

"Any dispute or difference between the parties . . . whether in regard to the carrying out of the work under the contract or as to the construction or meaning of the contract . . . shall be referred to the Controller of the Navy who may enter upon the reference."

The Ministry paid Vosper an additional £2 million in respect of *force majeure* delays, but Vosper claimed a further £4 million. The Ministry claimed that the basis on which Vosper had calculated this amount was incorrect and that Vosper's calculations ignored substantial underestimates in Vosper's tender. Ackner J. held that the provision in proviso 6 for "mutual agreement" was ineffective since the law does not recognise a contract to negotiate.[273] The arbitration clause did not expressly provide that, in the event of a failure to reach mutual agreement under

270. If an expert is appointed, consideration should be given to his powers to examine witnesses and order discovery of documents. Also, the powers which the High Court has under s.12(6) of the Arbitration Act 1950 to give assistance to an arbitrator will not be applicable where a dispute is referred to an expert. In *Channel Tunnel Group Ltd.* v. *Balfour Beatty Construction Ltd.* [1993] A.C. 334 the contract in issue for the construction and operation of the Channel Tunnel provided that, in certain circumstances, the prices for additional works would be agreed between the parties or, failing agreement, fixed by the employer at such prices as in its opinion would be reasonable and proper. If the contractor did not accept any price fixed by the employer as reasonable and proper, the contract provided for a two-stage procedure for settlement. In the first instance, the dispute would be referred to a panel of three experts, and if either the employer or the contractor was dissatisfied with a decision of the experts, it could require the dispute to be referred to arbitration under the Rules of the International Chamber of Commerce. It was common ground that the first stage of the procedure, reference to the panel of experts, was not an arbitration within the Arbitration Act 1975, but that the second stage was an arbitration: see Lord Mustill's account at pp. 344H–347G.

271. The remarks of Lord Fraser of Tullybelton in *Sudbrook* [1983] 1 A.C. 444 at 483–484 indicate that, it is only if the expert is named or identified (e.g. by reference to the holder for the time being of a particular office), and the machinery breaks down, that the court will not make an order for the fair and reasonable adjustments to be assessed by other means; but see *Re Malpass* [1985] Ch. 42.

272. [1976] 1 Lloyd's Rep. 58; see also *Foley* v. *Classic Coaches* [1934] 2 K.B. 1.

273. He cited *Courtney Ltd.* v. *Tolaini Brothers Ltd.* [1975] 1 W.L.R. 297.

proviso 6, the matter would be referred to arbitration. However, Ackner J. pointed out that the arbitration clause referred not only to "disputes" but also to "differences", and that it was common ground that the parties had agreed to differ. He held that, given the existence of agreed machinery for settling their difference, it was essential for the business efficacy of proviso 6 to imply a term that, in default of agreement, the effect of the exceptional dislocation and delay should be determined by arbitration under the arbitration clause. The decision establishes that it is possible to provide for arbitration on an issue which is described in very general terms, in the *Vosper* case, "a fair and reasonable sum for profit".[274] The effectiveness of an experts clause to support a provision providing for adjustments to the contract is established by the Court of Appeal's decision in *Superior Overseas Development Corporation* v. *British Gas Corporation*[275] which is considered in detail in the next section.

Although the *Queensland Electricity*[276] decision can be read as based on the fact that the contract contained an arbitration clause, it is thought that a clause providing, for example, for the parties to agree a fair and reasonable adjustment to the contract price will be upheld even if there is no provision for disputes to be referred to an arbitrator or an expert. In *Sudbrook Trading Estate* v. *Eggleton*[277] the arbitration machinery had broken down; and the Court of Appeal's decision in *Didymi Corporation v. Atlantic Lines and Navigation Co. Inc. (The Didymi)*[278] was not based on an arbitration or expert clause. *The Didymi* arose out of a charterparty containing the following provisions:

"30(1) The . . . speed and fuel consumption of the vessel as stipulated in this charterparty are representations by the owners. Should the actual performance of the vessel . . . show any failure to satisfy one or more of such representations, the hire shall be equitably decreased by an amount to be mutually agreed between owners and charterers . . .

(4) Similarly if it is found that the vessel has maintained . . . a better speed and/or consumption . . . owners shall be indemnified by way of increase of hire, such increase to be calculated in the same way as the reduction [referred to in paragraph (1)]."

The court held that the clause prescribed "a purely objective standard", Dillon L.J. commenting that, in this context, "equitably" meant "fair and reasonable"—"a

274. Ackner J. based his decision on this aspect of the case on *F & G Sykes (Wessex) Ltd.* v. *Fine Fare Ltd.* [1967] 1 Lloyd's Rep. 53 in which an agreement having a minimum term of five years which concerned the sale of broiler fowls to a supermarket provided that, during the first year of the agreement, a specified number of fowls would be sold and thereafter "such other figures as may be agreed between the parties". There was an arbitration clause in general terms. Lord Denning M.R. said (at p. 58): "I am quite satisfied that this phrase '[after the first year] such other figures as may be agreed between the parties hereto', does not introduce such uncertainty into the contract as to render it no contract. Effect can be given to this agreement by saying that in default of agreement, the number of chicks shall be such reasonable number as may be ascertained by an arbitrator under the arbitration clause. You can either imply a term that, in default of agreement, the number shall be a reasonable number, with a subsequent provision that in case of any dispute as to what is reasonable, it should be determined by arbitration: or, alternatively, run the two terms together and say 'such reasonable figures as the arbitrator may determine'. Whichever is adopted, it all comes to the same thing. The provision that figures were to 'be agreed' does not nullify the contract. It can be made certain by reasonable figures being ascertained by an arbitrator."

275. [1982] 1 Lloyd's Rep. 262.

276. [1989] 1 Lloyd's Rep. 205.

277. [1983] 1 A.C. 444.

278. [1988] 2 Lloyd's Rep. 108.

broad concept which is well recognised in law".[279] The procedure for the provision for the increase in hire to be agreed between the owners and the charterers was a subsidiary and non-essential term and, since that machinery had broken down, the amount of the increase could be assessed by other means. Notwithstanding the parties' failure to agree on the amount of the increase of hire, the clause was enforceable.[280]

However, it is thought questionable whether a clause can validly provide, in an entirely general and open-ended manner, that the parties shall use their best endeavours to agree "whatever modifications to the contract may be fair and reasonable". It is considered that the modifications have to be confined to specified matters, such as the period for performance and the price, and any consequential changes.

(b) Hardship clauses—the Superior case

Although decided before *Sudbrook Trading Estate* v. *Eggleton*[281] and *Walford* v. *Miles*,[282] *Superior Overseas Development Corporation* v. *British Gas Corporation*[283] provides a good illustration of some of the issues to be borne in mind when drafting a hardship clause in a long-term contract. The case arose out of an agreement which the Phillips and the Arpet Groups made with British Gas Corporation for the sale to the British Gas Corporation of natural gas extracted from the Hewett Field in the North Sea. The agreement was signed in 1968, and both sides contemplated extraction and delivery designed to exhaust the field in about 25 years. The agreement fixed initial prices for the gas, but provided for adjustment during the life of the contract. The first adjustment mechanism was designed to take account of the effects of future inflation or deflation on the capital and operating costs of producing and delivering the gas. A second adjustment mechanism was designed to ensure that gas maintained a competitive position in comparison with other major fuels. A third mechanism was added to deal with the possibility that the parties had failed to foresee some other factor which would falsify some or all of their assumptions. This third mechanism was set out in clause 7 of the 1968 Agreement:

"7(a) If at any time or from time to time during the contract period there has been *any substantial change in the economic circumstances relating to this Agreement* and (notwithstanding the effect of the other relieving or adjusting provisions of this Agreement) *either party feels that such change is causing it to suffer substantial economic hardship* then the parties shall (at the request of either of them) meet together to consider what (if any) adjustment in the prices then in force under this Agreement or in the price revision mechanism contained in Clauses 4, 5 and 6 of this Article are justified in the circumstances in fairness to the parties *to offset or alleviate the said hardship* caused by such change.

(b) If the parties shall not within ninety (90) days after any such request have reached agreement on the adjustments (if any) in the said prices or price revision mechanism which are to be made then the matter may forthwith be referred by either party for determination by experts to be appointed in the manner set out in Article xviii hereof . . .

279. *Ibid.*, at p. 119.

280. See also *Voest Alpine Intertrading G.m.b.H.* v. *Chevron International Oil Co. Ltd.* [1987] 2 Lloyd's Rep. 547 and *Corson* v. *Rhuddlan Borough Council* (1989) 59 P. & C.R. 185.

281. [1983] 1 A.C. 444.

282. [1992] 2 A.C. 128.

283. [1982] 1 Lloyd's Rep. 262.

(c) The experts shall determine what (if any) adjustments in the said prices or in the said price revision mechanism shall be made for the purposes aforesaid and any reviewed prices or any change in the price revision mechanism so determined by such experts shall take effect six (6) months after the date on which the request for the review was first made."[284]

Donaldson L.J. gave this description of Clause 7:

"In my judgment, cl. 7 is an ultimate safety net. To adopt an analogy which is perhaps appropriate to North Sea gas, the parties contemplated that in most foreseeable economic conditions the course of the joint venture would be dictated by the automatic price revision mechanisms contained in cll. 4, 5 and 6 (the agreed price autopilot). But the parties realized that over a period of 25 years economic storms could arise of such severity that the price autopilot would not be able to keep the venture on course. Clause 7 provides for a manual override if this occurs and the venture goes so far off course as to cause one of the parties to suffer substantial economic hardship. The experts then take over, correct the course and, if appropriate, revise the settings on the price autopilot."[285]

The first issue was the meaning of the word "substantial" as used in clause 7(a). As Waller L.J. pointed out[286] "substantial" was used to qualify both the phrase "economic change", which is an event or process and not easy to quantify, and "hardship", which is more appropriate for describing quality than quantity. Waller L.J. stated:

"A 'substantial' change in economic circumstances means something more than the ordinary everyday variations which were current in the late 60s. 'Substantial hardship'[287] must mean something more than difficulties arising from day to day economic variations. It must have a real impact and not a mere transient effect. I would myself suggest that it must be real hardship. Hardship alone would be something more than that which should be disregarded as *de minimis*, but not sufficiently great as to justify by itself a claim followed by reference to experts. There is support for this use of the word 'real' as a meaning of substantial in that it is one of those given in the Shorter Oxford Dictionary. I would therefore read cl. 7(a) as meaning in the earlier part 'if there has been any real change in the economic circumstances' and in the later part 'causing it to suffer real economic hardship'."[288]

Similar views were expressed by Donaldson L.J. in describing the correct approach for the experts to adopt:

"What is meant by 'substantial' on this view of the parties' intentions? It is a simple English word. The parties could, if they had wished, have produced a formula to define it . . . but they have not done so. In my view it was not for the experts to do so.[289] Their task was akin to that of Lord Mansfield's jury of merchants—in this case a 'special jury of experts'. They had to find the economic facts, both as to the causative change or changes in economic circumstances and the effects of that change or changes on the economic fortunes of the parties. Having found the facts, they had to ask themselves two jury questions: 'Has there been any substantial change in the economic circumstances relating to this Agreement?' and 'Has that change or changes caused either and which party to suffer substantial economic hardship?'

284. Emphasis added.
285. *Ibid.*, at p. 269.
286. *Ibid.*, at p. 266.
287. As to "undue hardship", compare the criteria for an extension of time under s.27 of the Arbitration Act 1950 which were set out in *The Aspen Trader* [1981] 1 Lloyd's Rep. 273 and approved by the House of Lords in *Comdel Ltd.* v. *Siporex S.A.* No. 2 [1991] 1 A.C. 148.
288. [1982] 1 Lloyd's Rep. 262, at p. 266.
289. Compare Lord Mustill's warning in *R.* v. *Monopolies Commission, ex parte South Yorkshire Ltd.* [1993] 1 W.L.R. 23 at p. 29, in which "substantial" was considered in another context, against "the dangers of taking an inherently imprecise word, and by redefining it thrusting on it a spurious degree of precision".

They should not have concerned themselves with insubstantial change or insubstantial hardship. Bearing in mind the nature of this clause—an ultimate corrective—I think that the parties must have used the word 'substantial' in the sense of weighty or serious, rather than merely something more than minimal, but more than that cannot be said without being guilty of redrafting the parties' agreement and usurping the judgment of the experts. No doubt in the border area, one panel might reach one conclusion and another a different one, but that is always true when judgment and, particularly economic judgment, is involved."[290]

Donaldson L.J. also commented that the first part of clause 7(a)[291] could be criticised as "an unholy mixture of the objective and subjective". However, he said that that did not matter since the provision was merely a triggering mechanism. If a party were mistaken in thinking that there had been a substantial change in economic circumstances or that such a change was causing it to suffer substantial economic hardship, the mechanism would produce no change in price.[292]

The second issue was at what point or points in time the "substantial economic hardship" had to exist. Waller L.J. said:

" . . . the words 'substantial economic hardship' refer to a condition or state of affairs which exists at the time of request for a meeting. This condition must have existed for some time as a result of a 'substantial change in economic circumstances" but at the time of the request it must be such that it '*is* causing it to suffer substantial hardship'. It would not be sufficient to look at a period of days before the date of request; it would have to be a longer period of months or in a rare case more than a year."[293]

The third issue, which divided Waller and Donaldson L.JJ. on the one hand and Ackner L.J. and Parker J. (at first instance) on the other hand, was this: at the end of clause 7(a) did the phrase "to offset or alleviate the said hardship" have the effect that the experts could fix adjustments that would completely eliminate all hardship or adjustments that would merely reduce "substantial hardship" to, as it were, ordinary hardship? The following passage from Waller L.J.'s judgment sets out the position taken by the majority in the Court of Appeal:

"In my opinion the said hardship refers to the substantial hardship mentioned earlier in the case, and offsetting or alleviating refers to a condition of normality, that is to say without hardship, not merely without the substantial part of the hardship. It is sensible to devise a clause which has what may be described as having a 'trigger' effect. The parties would wish to avoid frequent applications whenever any slight hardship occurs but to require substantial hardship before any application is made. However, once substantial hardship is shown, there is no good reason for not offsetting or alleviating the whole of the substantial hardship. The parties would not wish one party to be left on the borderline of substantial hardship ready to invoke cl. 7 again as soon as conditions become slightly worse. The experts do not have an easy task in quantifying the effect of substantial hardship. To require a further quantification of unsubstantial hardship merely adds to the difficulties."[294]

However, Ackner L.J. considered that there was no difficulty in separating out substantial hardship from ordinary hardship and making an award which only covered substantial hardship. He also pointed out that, at a previous stage in the proceedings when the parties were represented respectively by Mr Staughton and Mr Mustill, as they then were, it was common ground that only substantial hardship should be redressed.

290. [1982] 1 Lloyd's Rep. 262, at pp. 269–270.
291. Down to and including the words "either party feels that such change is causing it to suffer substantial economic hardship".
292. *Ibid.*, at p. 268.
293. *Ibid.*, at p. 266.
294. *Ibid.*, at p. 266.

The fourth issue was what periods of hardship should be covered by an offset or alleviation. There were three possibilities: (i) from the effective date of any adjustments made by the experts under clause 7(c), i.e. six months after the date on which a party first requested a clause 7 review; (ii) from the date of the request; or (iii) from the beginning of the substantial hardship. After considering each of these three possibilities, Waller L.J. said: "I have come to the conclusion that when adjusting the price there is no good reason for not going back to the beginning of the substantial hardship. The obligation is to offset or alleviate and the overriding duty of fairness to the parties gives the experts the discretion, if they think it right, not to offset in full but to alleviate in part."[295] Donaldson L.J. commented:

"Economic hardship and, *a fortiori*, substantial economic hardship is not something which happens in a flash or is here today and gone tomorrow. At the time of the request the hardship being suffered by the complainant consists of the cumulative adverse effects of the substantial change in economic circumstances together with its prospective effects if there is no change in prices. It is this which the experts are bidden to offset (i.e., eliminate by a fully compensatory change) or to alleviate (i.e., by a partially compensatory change) subject in each case to fairness to the parties."[296]

Although the judgments in *Superior Overseas Development Corporation* v. *British Gas Corporation* show that a hardship clause is liable to give rise to finely balanced issues of construction, they dispel the anxiety that a hardship clause might be void for uncertainty if it does not provide a formula according to which the experts are to determine the adjustment, but merely sets out a broad approach which they are to follow. It is also notable that neither party sought to argue that clause 7(a) was void as a mere agreement to negotiate and that consequently the provisions for determination by experts were unenforceable.[297]

(c) Adjustments to contract to be determined by an expert

Two recent decisions indicate that, where a clause expressly provides for certain specific matters to be determined by an expert, his decision will be difficult to challenge in the courts. In *Jones* v. *Sherwood Computer Services P.L.C.*[298] the terms of a takeover provided for an amount of sales to be determined by an independent firm of chartered accountants, whose determination would be "conclusive and final and binding for all purposes". Dillon L.J. was not prepared to read into the clause an exception that the expert's determination of an issue of law or mixed fact and law would be binding only if the court agreed with it. Moreover, both Dillon and Balcombe L.JJ. considered that a contract can provide that a speaking determination, no less than a determination in which the expert does not give his reasons, shall be conclusive and non-reviewable.[299] Dillon L.J.'s judgment indicates that, where a clause provides that an expert's determination shall be conclusive, it cannot, if made in good faith, be set aside unless the expert has departed from his instructions in a material respect; examples given by Dillon L.J. were a valuer who has valued the wrong number of shares or valued shares in the wrong company. In

295. *Ibid.*, at p. 267. 296. *Ibid.*, at p. 270.

297. Such an argument would have been difficult to advance in view of *F. & G. Sykes (Wessex) Ltd.* v. *Fine Fare Ltd.* [1967] 1 Lloyd's Rep. 53; see also *Smith Ltd.* v. *H & S International Holding Inc.* [1991] 2 Lloyd's Rep. 127 at p. 131. 298. [1992] 1 W.L.R. 277.

299. They rejected the distinction made by Nourse J. in *Burgess* v. *Purchase & Sons (Farms) Limited* [1983] Ch. 216 between a speaking and a non-speaking valuation.

Amoco (U.K.) Exploration Co. v. *Amerada Hess Limited*,[300] Morritt J. granted a stay of proceedings in which the plaintiff sought the determination of the court on a dispute which, Morritt J. held, fell within the terms of a clause requiring certain matters to be referred to an expert. It made no difference that the expert would be involved in considering legal matters as well as scientific, and Morritt J. knew of no principle or authority which lays down that an expert is not entitled to obtain and act on legal advice. However, the decision of Rattee J. in *Neste Production Limited* v. *Shell U.K. Limited*[301] shows that there is a risk of the court assuming jurisdiction as regards any matter of law or of mixed law and fact which the contract does not clearly place within the remit of the designated expert. That case can also be read as authority for the proposition that it is impossible for a contract to provide that an expert shall determine an issue relating to the parameters of his remit, for example whether the parties have validly varied the definition of those parameters. However, it is thought that the issue is one of construction, and that it is at least arguable that there is no objection in principle to a contract providing for any issue regarding an expert's remit to be determined by him.[302]

11. PAYMENT ADJUSTMENTS

Chapter 11 analyses the provisions of the Law Reform (Frustrated Contracts) Act 1943 which relate to the recovery of money paid, and expenses incurred, in connection with a frustrated contract and compensation in respect of non-monetary benefits conferred. That analysis identifies a number of questions to which the 1943 Act gives no clear answer. This section considers how a *force majeure* clause might deal with these questions.

(a) Unjust enrichment or adjustment of loss?

The first is whether the purpose of the 1943 Act is (a) prevention of the unjust enrichment of either party to the contract at the other's expense, or (b) to apportion the loss between the parties or to provide a flexible machinery for the adjustment of loss. A *force majeure* clause can avoid a similar uncertainty by including a first subclause to the following effect: "The following provisions of this clause shall have effect for the purpose of . . . ". It is thought that if the sole specified purpose is the prevention of unjust enrichment, this might not cover appropriately the recovery by one party of amounts which it has expended for the purposes of the contract. On the other hand, if the clause covers only the allocation of loss, this might not cover a party's right to recover in respect of non-monetary benefits conferred on the other party. It may therefore be appropriate to specify both purposes.

300. [1994] 1 Lloyd's Rep. 330.
301. [1994] 1 Lloyd's Rep. 447.
302. See *Norwich Union Life Insurance Society* v. *P & O Property Holdings Ltd.* [1993] 1 E.G.L.R. 164 and *Communications Ltd.* v. *Director General of Telecommunications, The Times*, 3 August 1994; and compare "the presumption in favour of one-stop adjudication" to which Hoffmann L.J. referred in *Harbour Assurance Limited* v. *Kansa Limited* [1993] Q.B. 701 at p. 726; and see Mustill & Boyd, *Commercial Arbitration* (2nd Edn., 1989) at p. 15 and Merkin, *Arbitration Law* (1991) at para. 4.49.

(b) Recovery of money paid

The next question arises in the context of the first half of section 1(2) of the 1943 Act: "All sums paid or payable to any party in pursuance of the contract before the time when the parties were so discharged . . . shall, in the case of sums so paid, be recoverable from him as money received by him for the use of the party by whom the sums were paid, and, in the case of sums so payable, cease to be payable."

It might be thought that the words "for the use of" the payee party indicate that the payee party holds these sums on trust for the paying party so that, in a liquidation of the payee party, these sums would not be available for its general creditors. However, the difficulty with this view is that such a trust would probably prevent the payee from using these funds[303] in its own business to buy materials and so on to perform the contract, although there is authority which indicates that the existence of a trust over a fund is not always incompatible with a power for the trustee to use the fund in his own business.[304] To produce an effective trust, a *force majeure* clause would have to require the payee party to hold payments in a separate trust account and to provide that, if the payee party serves a *force majeure* notice, the paying party will thereupon become absolutely entitled to the balance (including accrued interest) on the trust account. However, unless the payee party actually transfers the payments into a separate trust account, the paying party's equitable interest could well be defeated by the combination of account rights of the bank which runs the account to which the payment was credited or by the rights of a holder of a debenture granted by the payee party.[305]

A clause should use wider language that that contained in section 1(2) and cover sums paid "in pursuance of *or in connection with* the contract"; and it should also cover any sums received on or after the date on which a *force majeure* notice is served.

(c) Recovery for expenses incurred

The second set of issues arises in connection with the proviso to section 1(2): "Provided that, if the party to whom the sums were so paid or payable incurred expenses before the time of discharge in, or for the purpose of, the performance of the contract, the court may . . . allow him to retain or, as the case may be, recover the whole or any part of the sums so paid or payable, not being an amount in excess of the expenses so incurred."

The first point is that, unlike this proviso, a *force majeure* clause should give the party who has incurred expenses a clear right to recover them (or a reasonable proportion of them) by commencing independent proceedings, rather than merely a right of set-off in proceedings commenced by the other party. The second point which should be made clear is whether the party which has incurred expenses will

303. Compare, for example, Lord Brougham's observations in *Foley* v. *Hill* (1848) 2 H.L.C. 28 at p. 44.
304. See the observations of Robert Goff L.J. in *Clough Mill Limited* v. *Martin* [1985] 1 W.L.R. 111 at p. 116.
305. Compare *Mac-Jordan Construction Ltd.* v. *Bookmount Erostin Limited* [1992] B.C.L.C. 350, approved by the Privy Council in *Re Goldcorp Exchange Ltd.* [1994] 3 W.L.R. 199 at p. 218.

be entitled to recover their full amount or only a proportion of them so that the loss will fall on both parties. The third point is to broaden the statutory wording "expenses [incurred] in , or for the purpose of, the performance of the contract" to include expenses incurred in preparatory work which was specifically referable to the contract. The fourth point is that the clause should contain a provision similar to section 1(4) of the 1943 Act, which allows the court to include as recoverable expenses "such sum as appears to be reasonable in respect of overhead expenses and in respect of any work or services performed personally by the [relevant] party". Perhaps some provision should also be made for a reasonable profit margin.

(d) Accounting for benefits obtained

The next set of issues arises in connection with section 1(3). This provides that where a party has "by reason of anything done by any other party . . . in, or for the purpose of, the performance of the contract, obtained a valuable benefit (other than a payment of money to which [section 1(2)] applies) before the time of discharge, there shall be recoverable from him by the said other party such sum (if any), not exceeding the value of the said benefit to the party obtaining it, as the court considers just, having regard to all the circumstances of the case . . . ". The first point here is what constitutes a "benefit": is it the end-product of the services rendered by the party concerned or is it the services themselves? In particular, should a party be entitled to a payment in respect of services which do not result in an end-product, perhaps because the *force majeure* event occurs while performance of the contract is still at a preparatory or uncompleted stage?

The second point relates to the basis for determining the sum which a party should be entitled to recover in respect of a non-monetary benefit. For example, should this be based on the value of the benefit to the party who obtained it or the cost of the benefit to the party who provided it? If the former, should the benefit be valued as at the time it was conferred, that is, before the *force majeure* event; or, if the *force majeure* event has reduced the value of the benefit, should this reduction be taken into account?[306]

In this context, the Court of Appeal's decision in *The Westbourne*[307] is of interest. The plaintiffs were the owners, master and crew of the steamship *Howick*, and the defendants the owners of the steamship *Westbourne*. 260 miles from Gibraltar, and 60 miles from Carthagena, the *Westbourne* was in distress, having lost a propeller. The masters of the *Howick* and the *Westbourne* entered into an agreement[308] by which the *Westbourne* was to be towed to Gibraltar for £600. When the agreement was made, the weather was moderate, but it became much worse the next morning, the wind blowing like a hurricane. The hawsers by which the *Howick* was towing the *Westbourne* broke repeatedly, and the master of the *Howick* decided

306. In *B.P. Exploration Co. (Libya) Limited* v. *Hunt (No. 2)* [1979] 1 W.L.R. 783, Robert Goff J. held that, under s.1(3), the benefit has to be valued as at the date of the frustrating event. S.1(3)(b) requires the court, in fixing the "just" sum to be paid in respect of the benefit, to have regard to "the effect, in relation to the said benefit, of the circumstances giving rise to the frustration of the contract".

307. (1899) 14 P.D. 132.

308. Described by Lord Esher M.R. (at p. 134) as "a towage agreement to do work in the nature of a salvage service".

that it was impossible to take the *Westbourne* to Gibraltar, and instead towed her to Carthagena. The owners, master and crew of the *Howick* sued for £900, but the owners of the *Westbourne* contended that they were entitled only to the £600 originally agreed. The Court of Appeal, upholding the decision of Butt J., held that, when it became "practically impossible" for the *Howick* to carry out the original agreement, that agreement came to an end, and the Court of Admiralty had authority to deal with the question as though no contract had been made. Lord Esher MR said:

> "If that agreement became more difficult to carry out by reason of succeeding circumstances, the Court could not therefore alter it. But if, by reason of circumstances over which the salvors had no control, the difficulty of the service was so far increased as to make it in fact a wholly different service from that which was originally contemplated by the parties, or a service of a wholly different class, then the Court of Admiralty has a right to deal with the case as if the original agreement had not been made, and to make such an award as under the circumstances it may think right."[309]

The Court of Appeal therefore upheld the award of £900, notwithstanding that this exceeded the sum originally fixed, and that this was in respect of services at least partially performed after the original agreement had come to an end.

12. THE MECHANISM FOR BRINGING THE OPERATION OF THE CLAUSE TO AN END

This section is only relevant where a *force majeure* clause does not bring the parties' obligations to an end, but in some way suspends performance of them. The issues which arise are (a) who is to decide whether the *force majeure* situation has ended, so that performance of the contract must be resumed, and (b) whether a party should lose the protection of the *force majeure* clause if it breaches any of its obligations under the clause.

To deal first with the second question, a *force majeure* clause must probably, at a minimum, require the affected party to keep the other party regularly informed about developments affecting the *force majeure* situation and any steps which the affected party is taking in order to resume performance. The clause may go further and require the affected party, for example, to use its best endeavours to mitigate the *force majeure* event's consequences.

If the sanction for breach of these obligations is merely an action in damages, this may well place the non-affected party in the difficult position of having to show, for example, that there were reasonable steps which the affected party could have taken which would have mitigated the effect of the *force majeure* situation; that the non-affected party has suffered loss as a result of the affected party's failure to take those steps; and that the loss is recoverable under one of the two limbs of *Hadley* v. *Baxendale*.[310] On the other hand, if the clause provides that the affected party is entitled to the clause's protection only if it complies with its obligations under the

309. *Ibid*., at p. 134.
310. (1854) 9 Exch. 341.

force majeure clause, the other party's claim would be a more straightforward claim for non-performance of the contract. Moreover, the burden of proof can be placed clearly on the affected party by providing that it is for the affected party to show that it has complied with its obligations under the *force majeure* clause.

As regards the provision for ending the *force majeure* situation, there are basically two choices. Either the clause can provide for the *force majeure* situation to come to an end when the affected party serves a notice stating that the *force majeure* situation has ended—which leaves matters very much in the affected party's control; or the clause can provide an objective test, for example that the clause shall cease to apply when the circumstances are such that the affected party can resume performance of the contract or could, by taking such steps as it is reasonable in all the circumstances to expect to take, put itself into a position in which it could resume performance.

13. EXCLUDING THE DOCTRINE OF FRUSTRATION

Strictly, the issue is not whether the doctrine of frustration is excluded but whether provision was made for an event causing the circumstances of performance to be radically different from that undertaken by the contract.[311] The current consensus[312] is that the basis of frustration is as described by Lord Reid in *Davis Contractors Ltd.* v. *Fareham Urban District Council*.[313] Lord Reid, rejecting the implied term theory of frustration, said that the doctrine depends:

> "on the true construction of the terms which are in the contract read in the light of the nature of the contract and of the relevant surrounding circumstances when the contract was made. . . . In *British Movietonews Ltd.* v. *London and District Cinemas Ltd.*,[314] Viscount Simon said: 'If, on the other hand, a consideration of the terms of the contract, in the light of the circumstances existing when it was made, shows that they never agreed to be bound in a fundamentally different situation which has now unexpectedly emerged, the contract ceases to bind at that point—not because the court in its discretion thinks it just and reasonable to qualify the terms of the contract, but because on its true construction it does not apply in that situation. . . . The question is whether the contract which they did make is, on its true construction, wide enough to apply to the new situation: if it is not, then it is at an end.' "[315]

It follows that frustration will not apply[316] if the contract contains a provision which, on its true construction, covers the new situation which has unexpectedly arisen. This is reflected by the terms of the Law Reform (Frustrated Contracts) Act 1943 which provides that the court shall give effect to any provision in a contract to which that Act applies "which, upon the true construction of the contract, is

311. Lord Scarman in *Wong Lai Ying* v. *Chinachem Investment Co. Ltd.* (1979) 13 B.L.R. 81 at p. 95.

312. See Chapter 3; and, for example, the observations of Evans L.J. in *William Sindall plc* v. *Cambridgeshire County Council* [1994] 1 W.L.R. 1016 at pp. 1039–1040; but note Smith, *Mistake, Frustration and Implied Terms* (1994) 110 L.Q.R. 400.

313. [1956] A.C. 696.

314. [1952] A.C. 166, at p. 185.

315. [1956] A.C. 696, at pp. 720–721.

316. Except where a contract is extinguished or prohibited by legislation in the country of the governing law or is frustrated, under the governing law, for reasons of public policy; see *Ertel Bieber & Co.* v. *Rio Tinto Company* [1918] A.C. 260.

intended to have effect in the event of circumstances arising which operate, or which would but for the said provision operate, to frustrate the contract . . . ".[317]

There is, however, a risk that a court will hold that, although the event which has occurred falls within the literal wording of the *force majeure* clause, the event so fundamentally changes the character of the contract performance that the parties must be presumed not to have made provision for it.[318] This situation occurs not uncommonly when the contrast is between events, such as war or strikes, causing mere delay and such events causing a frustrating delay.[319] The risk of a clause being held not to make provision for a particular event increases with the generality of the words which are claimed to cover the event.[320] In the *Fibrosa* case[321] the sale contract provided that should despatch of the machinery be delayed "by any cause whatsoever beyond our reasonable control, including . . . war . . . a reasonable extension of time shall be granted". The Polish buyers argued that there could be no frustration by reason of the war which broke out in 1939 because this contingency was expressly provided for by the extension clause in the contract. This argument was rejected by both the Court of Appeal and the House of Lords. Viscount Simon L.C. said:

"The ambit of the express condition is limited to delay in respect of which 'a reasonable extension of time' might be granted. That might mean a minor delay as distinguished from a prolonged and indefinite interruption of prompt contractual performance which the present war manifestly and inevitably brings about. The principle is that where supervening events, not due to the default of either party, render the performance of a contract indefinitely impossible, and there is no undertaking to be bound in any event, frustration ensues, even though the parties may have expressly provided for the case of a limited interruption."[322]

It is thought that the risk of a court holding that a *force majeure* clause has not prevented a particular event from frustrating the contract can be reduced if the general sweeper-up wording in the statement of the *force majeure* events ends with language such as: "any other event or matter of any kind whatsoever,[323] however serious, protracted or exceptional, which and/or the consequences of which, would or might, but for this clause, operate to frustrate this Agreement." In addition, there is some advantage in stating that the obligation which it is sought to preserve is an "absolute" obligation.[324]

It is thought that there is some advantage in attempting in this way to prevent the

317. S.2(3).

318. See *Wong Lai Ying* v. *Chinachem Investment Co. Ltd.* (1979) 13 B.L.R. 86 discussed at pp. 206–207.

319. See the observations of Rix J. in *The Safeer* [1994] 1 Lloyd's Rep. 637.

320. See the observations of Hannen J. quoted by Lord Parmoor in *Metropolitan Water Board* v. *Dick, Kerr & Co. Ltd.* [1918] A.C. 119, at p. 140.

321. [1943] A.C. 32.

322. *Ibid.*, at p. 40.

323. The expression "or in any other wise whatsoever" in the War Risks ("Voywar 1963") clauses in the Gencon charter form played a part in the decision of Rix J. in *The Safeer* [1994] 1 Lloyd's Rep. 637 that a charter to Kuwait had not been discharged by what was, in effect, the theft of the cargo by the Iraqi authorities after the invasion of Kuwait in August 1990.

324. Compare the statement of Hannen J. in *Baily* v. *De Crespigny* (1869) L.R. 4 Q.B. 180 at p. 185 that a person can by "an absolute contract" bind himself to perform things which subsequently become impossible; this statement was approved in *Metropolitan Water Board* v. *Dick, Kerr & Co.* [1918] A.C. 119 by Viscount Finlay L.C. (at p. 126) and by Lord Parmoor (at p. 140), and the description in *Postlethwaite* v. *Freeland* (1880) 5 App.Cas. 599 at p. 608 of the charterer's obligation as "an absolute and unconditional engagement".

doctrine of frustration from applying—although only in exceptional circumstances could an event which falls outside a normal *force majeure* clause nevertheless be the basis for a successful claim that the contract had been frustrated.

ALAN BERG

PART III

FRUSTRATION, FORCE MAJEURE AND SHIPPING LAW

CHAPTER 6

FRUSTRATION AND SHIPPING LAW—OLD PROBLEMS, NEW CONTEXTS

1. INTRODUCTION

The shipping industry is a perennial victim of crises, commercial and political, and shipping cases are a storehouse of ideas about the doctrine of frustration. Two particular applications of the doctrine were the subject of judicial consideration in the 1980s. First, there were several cases concerned with the circumstances in which the obligation to pay freight can be frustrated. Secondly, there were a number of cases in which the courts had to consider whether or not a time charterparty had been terminated as a result of frustrating delay. This problem is by no means confined to shipping cases, although they are a fruitful field for the law on this point. Indeed, this particular group of authorities throws up problems which are significant for the general theory underlying the law of frustration. There is also a third area in which the law of frustration has been affected by modern developments, though this is not apparent from the reported cases. The application of the Law Reform (Frustrated Contracts) Act 1943 now has an impact on international carriage by sea which was probably unforeseen by those who framed that particular statute.

2. FRUSTRATION AND FREIGHT

Some background is appropriate for the benefit of those who have little acquaintance with shipping law. Despite the common use of the word "freight" to describe cargoes carried, its true meaning and its meaning in law is the consideration received by a carrier for the carriage of goods from A to B. There are three main types of contract for the use of ships for the carriage of goods. First, there are time charterparties (or time charters), whereby the shipowner agrees to allow a charterer to use the space on board his ship for a given period. Secondly, there are voyage charterparties (charters) whereby the owner agrees to allow the charterer to use the space on his ship to carry a given cargo on a given voyage. Thirdly, there is the contract contained in the bill of lading which is the negotiable receipt issued by the shipowner to a shipper at or about the time of shipment.[1] The voyage charterer pays freight under the voyage charter. The shipper or consignee pays freight under the bill of lading. (Under a time charter, the charterer pays not freight but hire, although even this is sometimes known as "time freight", even sometimes just as

1. The bill of lading may do no more than *evidence* the contract of carriage; but this is not material to this discussion.

"freight".)[2] For present purposes, it is freight in the true sense of the word with which we are concerned.

The common law rule was that freight was payable on right and true delivery. In one sense, therefore, contracts of affreightment had built into them a notion apparently analogous to that of frustration: if the goods disappeared, payment was unnecessary. The obligation of the charterer under a voyage charter or of the shipper or consignee under a bill of lading came to an end.[3] This was not very satisfactory to shipowners. In every century prior to this, transoceanic navigation was hazardous; cargoes were apt to perish as a result of the length of voyages; predators were common. Though these dangers still exist, they have been greatly moderated or modified. Two solutions to this problem were found by shipowners. One was to make freight expressly payable "goods lost or not lost". The other was to make freight payable in advance; and this had the great charm that the money could be extracted from the charterer or shipper at a time when the shipowner had not yet lost ship and cargo and when the cargo owner still needed the goods to be carried to destination. This method of payment was also recognised as a proper means of, in effect, providing loan capital out of which the voyage could be financed.

The English rule is, therefore, that if advance freight becomes payable, the fact that the goods are lost before the freight is actually paid does not destroy the obligation to pay.[4] English law as to advance freight is in this respect different to the law of most other countries.[5] The basis of the English rule is said to be that the consideration for advance freight is *shipment* rather than *delivery*. If that is so, it might be thought that the law of frustration would have little impact in this area, because the provision of substantial consideration by the shipment of the goods is inconsistent with the destruction of the substance of the obligation undertaken by the carrier if ship and cargo are subsequently lost. The peculiarity of the English rule has led, however, to its being confined within narrow limits; and the doctrine of frustration has been of greater significance than might have been anticipated at first sight, especially in the light of the older cases.

In the old case of *Oriental S.S. Co.* v. *Taylor*,[6] the Court of Appeal had to consider a case where the charterer undertook to pay one third of the freight on the signing of the bills of lading. The charterparty provided that bills of lading were to be signed by the master within 24 hours after the vessel was loaded. Loading finished at 1730 hours on 11 August 1892 (the exact day and hour is crucial in a number of these cases) and the ship left the berth at 1800 hours. Displaying a laud-

2. The protest by Lord Denning M.R. (in *Federal Commerce and Navigation* v. *Molena Alpha* [1978] Q.B. 927 at p. 973) against the use of the term "freight" to describe monies received as consideration for the use of a ship for a period of time rather than the carriage of a cargo on a particular voyage has been quite unavailing and is, perhaps regrettably, inconsistent not only with mercantile but with legal usage. One example of many comes from a case considered in more detail below: in *Tamplin* v. *Anglo-Mexican Petroleum* [1916] 2 A.C. 397 (H.L.), Lord Parker of Waddington said at p. 426 that "the owners [of a time chartered ship] are not concerned in the charterers doing any specific thing beyond the payment of freight as it becomes due".

3. The analogy is not exact. The true position is that the obligation to deliver and the obligation to pay freight are concurrent conditions: the discharge of the obligation to pay freight does not depend on the degree to which the charterer, shipper or consignee was deprived of the substantial benefit of the contract.

4. *Allison* v. *Bristol Marine Insurance Co.* (1876) 1 App. Cas. 209 (H.L.) is the leading authority.

5. See *ibid.*, *per* Lord Selborne, at p. 253.

6. [1893] 2 Q.B. 518 (C.A.).

able taste for legal conundra, the master managed to foul his anchor to such effect that he succeeded in sinking the ship before she reached the lock gates. It was held that the charterers were still obliged to present the bills of lading and that the shipowners were therefore entitled to their one third advance freight. It might be thought that this indicates clearly that the doctrine of frustration has no application in this class of case. Either the goods are shipped and the freight is earned, or the ship and goods are lost prior to shipment, so that the conditions for the freight obligation to arise are never satisfied. This is not the way the cases have gone, however.

The Lorna I[7] was another case where the fates decided to set a problem which looks as if it has been dreamed up by a legal theorist. There, the charterparty provided that 75% of the freight was to be paid within five days of signing bills of lading and that it was to be "non-returnable cargo and/or vessel lost or not lost". The ship was loaded. Bills of lading were issued and signed. The ship sailed and was never heard of again. For the purposes of the appeal, it was agreed that she had not survived for the five days. It was held that the obligation to pay the advance freight had not arisen. In effect, it was held that the charterparty was frustrated; that the obligation to pay did not arise until the end of the five-day period; that because the ship was lost, all obligations came to an end; and that therefore no advance freight was due. There are three things to be noted about the decision. The first is that the decision in *Oriental S.S. Co.* v. *Taylor*[8] does not appear to have been cited to the court. Secondly, the decision maintains the general common law rule that delivery is the consideration for freight. Thirdly, the ship was lost not only before payment was effected but before the five-day period had expired. The rival contentions are set out in the judgment of Sir John Donaldson M.R.[9] The shipowners' principal argument was that the freight was earned or was deemed to be earned on shipment, the charterers being allowed five days' grace for payment. The charterers argued that in the absence of clear words, the consideration for freight is delivery and that though the freight was payable at an earlier time, they would have been able to claim it back if the ship had been lost in the absence of a further term negativing the right to the return of the freight in those circumstances. This argument succeeded. The decision in *The Lorna I*[10] may at first sight appear in accordance with the merits on the facts as they appear.[11] In fact, the rule gives ample scope for different results on slightly different facts. The Court of Appeal also dealt with the situation where the ship survives the period allowed for payment but is lost before she arrives at destination. In such a case, assuming a contract on similar terms, the freight if paid cannot be recovered and, if unpaid, remains due: "frustration excuses further performance of the contract, not prior non-performance."[12] Equally, if the loss had occurred on the sixth day, the shipowner would have been able to sue for the 75% of freight, notwithstanding that he has not provided any part of the consideration. This would have meant that (a) the contract would have been frustrated because the substance of the obligations had been destroyed, (b) the cargo-owner suffered a

7. [1981] 2 Lloyd's Rep. 559 (Robert Goff J.); affd [1983] 1 Lloyd's Rep. 373 (C.A.).
8. [1893] 2 Q.B. 518 (C.A.).
9. [1983] 1 Lloyd's Rep. 373, at p. 374.
10. Above, fn. 7.
11. Though O'Connor L.J. acknowledged that the decision against the owners was the result of a draftsman's failure to give effect to their true intention: *ibid*, at p. 376.
12. *Ibid*, at p. 375, *per* Sir John Donaldson M.R.

total failure of consideration, but (c) he would still be required to pay 75% of the freight.[13] Again, if one supposes the case where the charterers had in fact paid the 75% of freight prior to the loss and prior to the last day for payment, it is clear (and was expressly stated by O'Connor L.J.[14]) that in that case the freight would have been irrecoverable by the charterers even though, on the analysis of the Court of Appeal, the shipowner had not provided consideration and the cargo owner had not yet come under a liability to pay. Again, consider what the position would have been if the agreement had provided expressly "freight deemed earned on shipment" but still with five days' grace for payment and a provision that the freight was "irrecoverable goods lost or not lost". In that case it would be clear that the consideration for the freight was shipment. If the ship had been lost on the fourth day, the shipowners would have provided the consideration for the freight, but the time for payment would not yet have arrived. Given that the court held on the facts as they were in *The Lorna I*[15] that the right to freight would have accrued if the ship had sunk on the sixth day, notwithstanding that the freight had not been earned, they must have treated the provisions governing the time of payment as having primacy. It ought to follow in this hypothetical case that the mere fact that the freight had been earned would not have entitled the shipowner to payment if the obligation to pay had not yet arisen by the time the contract was frustrated. This is not directly inconsistent with the older cases on advance freight, because those concerned situations where the obligation to pay and the provision of the consideration for the payment arose at the same time. Still, such a result would be unexpected. And it does seem likely that the decision of the House of Lords in *The Dominique*[16] will lead to a different result. There it was held, in the context of a repudiatory breach rather than a frustrating event, that, in circumstances similar to the case just postulated, the freight had accrued on shipment, and the fact that the contract had been terminated prior to the expiration of grace had no bearing on the liability of the charterers to pay. The decision was said to be consistent with that in *The Karin Vatis*,[17] where *The Lorna I*[18] had been distinguished. *The Lorna I*[19] had also been invoked directly by the Court of Appeal in *The Dominique*.[20] This is, perhaps, rather ironic. Technically, *The Karin Vatis*[21] distinguished and therefore followed *The Lorna I*[22]: but the two cases exhale different intellectual atmospheres.[23]

In *The Karin Vatis*,[24] the charterparty provided "freight deemed earned as cargo loaded", that 95% of the freight was to be paid within three days of the bills of lading being signed "vessel and/or cargo lost or not lost", and that the remaining 5%

13. *Per* O'Connor L.J. at p. 376. It is not quite clear that Sir John Donaldson M.R. would have taken that view.
14. *Ibid.*
15. Above, fn. 7.
16. [1989] 1 Lloyd's Rep. 431 (H.L.).
17. [1988] 2 Lloyd's Rep. 330 (C.A.).
18. Above, fn. 7.
19. Above, fn. 7.
20. See *per* Mustill L.J. [1988] 3 All E.R. 233 at p. 237. The decision of the Court of Appeal was reversed on other grounds, but upheld on the construction and effect of the contract.
21. Above, fn. 17.
22. Above, fn. 7.
23. Which is no doubt why at first instance in the later case Leggatt J. thought that the earlier decision compelled the opposite result: [1987] 2 Lloyd's Rep. 361.
24. Above, fn. 17.

of freight was to be paid 20 days after delivery. The vessel sank on the voyage, and the shipowners claimed the balance of freight. It was accepted by the charterers that the 95% they had paid was irrecoverable, but they contended that the obligation to pay the balance of freight had been frustrated. The arbitrators and the judge at first instance[25] held that the charterers were entitled to withhold the balance of freight because the ship had never arrived. The Court of Appeal, however, held that the freight was deemed earned on shipment and that therefore the shipowners were entitled to recover. It was said that the phrase "freight deemed earned as cargo loaded" applied to the whole of the freight. The court dealt with the provision for payment of the balance of freight 20 days after discharge by saying that this related only to the *manner* of payment and did not destroy the accrued obligation to pay. This does not altogether meet the difficulty. It is true that in some cases the court can disregard a stipulation as to the mode of performance as not being essential; but that is not true in every case. If the contract is to be performed in a particular way, the fact that it becomes impossible to do so may have the effect of frustrating the agreement, though it will not always do so. Certainly the court in *The Karin Vatis*[26] was forced to rewrite the provisions governing performance. It was held that if one party earned the freight, the other must have a correlative obligation to pay it, *and that that obligation survived an event which both destroyed the substratum of the contract and rendered the payment terms incapable of performance*. The second half of the proposition was treated as following logically from the first, though it might be said that the court had only reached the point of identifying the question which had to be decided. Moreover, though it was right to hold that the phrase "freight deemed earned as cargo loaded" applied to the whole of the freight, the court does not seem to have considered the importance of the phrase "vessel and/or cargo lost or not lost". That part of the clause seems to apply only to the 95% of freight payable within three days, and that strongly suggests that the other payment obligation did not arise if the goods did not arrive.[27]

At the least, these cases provoke one to reflect on the relationship between (1) the provision of consideration, (2) a total failure of consideration, and (3) an event which so radically transforms the parties' obligations as to frustrate their agreement.

3. THE LAW REFORM (FRUSTRATED CONTRACTS) ACT 1943

Another quiddity of the rules relating to frustration and freight is worth noting. The Law Reform (Frustrated Contracts) Act 1943 does not apply to any contracts of carriage by sea except time charterparties.[28] This has the general effect that the rules relating to freight, governing as they do the rights and duties arising under voyage charters and bills of lading, remain governed by the common law. Where a

25. [1987] 2 Lloyd's Rep. 361.
26. *Ibid.*
27. Another consideration which leads to the same conclusion is that one important purpose of clauses which leave a small margin for freight to be paid on delivery is to cater for losses of bulk cargoes in the course of loading, carriage and discharge and for small measurement differences.
28. S.2(5).

time charter is frustrated, section 1(2) discharges the charterer from the obligation to pay future hire and enables him to recover hire already paid, subject to the discretion of the court to permit the shipowner to retain a sum to cover his expenses. By section 1(3), the shipowner is entitled to recover the sum considered by the court to be just in respect of any valuable benefit he has conferred on the charterer. The interrelationship of these rules may give rise to difficult questions, and what is "just" remuneration may differ according to whether a market rate or a contract rate is taken as an appropriate starting point. Equally, in such a case there is room for argument about what constitutes a "valuable benefit" for these purposes. If payment of a daily rate of hire is to be made monthly, and a charter is frustrated after three months, is the charterer to be treated as having three months' use of the vessel? What is the position if a cargo-carrying voyage had been completed after $2\frac{1}{2}$ months? Is the result the same if *no* such voyage at all had been completed?[29] However these questions are answered, the results brought about by the 1943 Act will be very different for time charters from those which the common law would achieve in the case of voyage charters. The existence of these very different regimes was understandable at that time, for the two types of instrument were used for very different commercial objects. This is no longer generally true.

There was formerly a marked contrast between a typical voyage charterparty for one voyage between two named ports laden with a particular cargo and a time charterparty limited only by period, and often lasting for many voyages over several years. Commercial circumstances have changed, however. Over the last two decades, voyage charters have become rather less popular. A common substitute has been "time charter trips", most frequently on the NYPE form of time charterparty. These tend to involve single voyages, with specific ports of loading and discharge being named.[30] The charter is in the form of a time rather than a voyage charter because it provides a time limit and the shipowner is remunerated on a *per diem* basis.[31] The result is that much international trade which would formerly have been carried on by means of voyage charterparties is now the subject of time charter trips, substantially identical in commercial effect, but different in point of legal form. The use of the term "freight" to describe the time charter hire payable in such a case is much more appropriate than it would be in relation to the hire under a period charter of the older type.[32] Nonetheless, the courts have declined to

29. The only case which considers the operation of s.1(3) in depth is *BP Exploration Co. (Libya) Ltd.* v. *Bunker Hunt* [1979] 1 W.L.R. 783, substantially affirmed [1981] 1 W.L.R. 236 (C.A.), [1983] 2 A.C. 352 (H.L.); but it does not provide a final answer to these questions and has not, so far as this part of the decision is concerned, been wholeheartedly approved by the commentators: see Treitel, *The Law of Contract* (8th Edn.), pp. 809–815; Birks, *An Introduction to the Law of Restitution*, 249–256; cf. Goff and Jones, *The Law of Restitution* (4th Edn.), pp. 453–462. These issues are discussed further in Chapter 11.

30. Sometimes the voyage is contractually linked to particular ports; sometimes the ports are named to show the intention without the parties binding themselves to them; and sometimes their names do not appear in the charter at all, though both parties know from negotiations what is envisaged.

31. Market forces also contributed to the change. The use of most standard forms of voyage charters (and several forms of time charterparty which had previously been popular) declined in employment from about the mid-1970s because their exceptions clauses were very stringent. The NYPE form was much more favourable to charterers, and shipowners' market position was too weak for them to resist pressure to employ it.

32. See above, fn. 2.

characterise any time charter trips as being a species of voyage charter.[33] One consequence of the change of commercial practice, therefore, is that transactions which would formerly have fallen outwith the scope of the Law Reform (Frustrated Contracts) Act 1943 are now subject to it.[34]

4. FRUSTRATION BY DELAY[35]

In *The Nema*[36] Lord Roskill said[37] that the principles of the law of frustration were now well and finally settled, so that there was no need to look at the authorities to see what the law was. This was too optimistic a conclusion. So far from providing all the answers, the authorities have not yet identified all the relevant questions.

It is axiomatic that commercial men look to the law for certainty and predictability when ordering their affairs. Yet the question of whether a contract has been frustrated by delay can put the parties to it in a position of extreme doubt. It is not surprising that there is no litmus test which can be applied where a contract becomes impossible to perform, to see if the whole benefit of the contract has been dissipated. It appears that the courts have tried to remove some of those doubts. Their attempts have not been altogether happy, in that the results reached are not particularly clear and consistent. And it is at least arguable that the certainty which the courts have sought to give the parties exceeds that which commercial law ought to provide.

Classically, the shipping cases where this general topic has arisen have been concerned with the effects of either strikes or hostilities. The two operate in essentially the same way, in that the frustrating factor is delay. One of the features which differentiates delay from some other causes of frustration is that the degree of interference with the performance of the contract which it will engender is unpredictable. Where a ship sinks in mid-ocean, a frustrating event has occurred, and it is obvious that it has. Where a ship is prevented from getting out of a port because of warlike operations or strike action by port workers, performance is equally impossible, but it may not be nearly so clear that performance will not become possible at any moment. In general, wars go on for longer than strikes; but this is not necessarily the case. As it happens, the last decade has seen important cases of both types, and to some extent these have brought into the open problems which were latent in the existing body of case law. The chief of these are questions which are closely related but ought nonetheless to be kept distinct. They are (1) at what point of time can it be decided that delay has frustrated a contract intended to be performed over a period of time? (2) is that point of time the same as the date from which the contract is taken to be frustrated? (3) is the question of whether there has been a frustrating delay to be decided by reference to the facts as they

33. *The Eugenia* [1963] 2 Lloyd's Rep. 155, where this was decided by Megaw J., whose decision, reversed on other grounds, was upheld by the Court of Appeal on this point: [1964] 2 Q.B. 226.

34. Treitel, *The Law of Contract* (8th Edn.) perhaps regards this as a more open question: see p. 816, fn. 29.

35. See J. E. Stannard, *Frustrating Delay* (1983) 46 M.L.R. 738, for a more general consideration of the topic.

36. *Pioneer Shipping* v. *B.T.P. Tioxide* [1982] A.C. 724 (H.L.).

37. *Ibid*. at 751E–752B.

were known at the beginning of the period of delay, at the date of frustration (if that is different) or at the date of trial? and (4) is the frustrating event the delay itself or the occurrence which causes the delay? It cannot yet be said to be clear what the answers to these questions are; yet they are of great practical importance.

The cases illustrate and are complicated by a further type of problem. Generally speaking, events which the parties have or should have foreseen as likely or possible do not have the result of frustrating contracts, at least where the result of the event in question is that performance of the contract becomes impossible as opposed to illegal.[38] Delay is a concept with which the shipping industry is extremely familiar. The very nature of the business is such that owners and charterers can expect that time will be lost for one reason or another. The parties can only make their best guess at what those causes are likely to be. Charterparties normally contain elaborate provisions for allocating the risk of some kinds of delay. Sometimes these provisions are limited to specified kinds of delay, but delays which recur frequently in ordinary commercial affairs; sometimes they deal with delay in a completely general and non-specific way; and sometimes they deal with more unusual but by no means exceptional types of delay, such as the risk of war or industrial action. All these features have tended to complicate the problems presented to the courts by cases of this kind.

It is perhaps a matter for surprise that as late as 1916, in *Tamplin* v. *Anglo-Mexican Petroleum*,[39] the House of Lords was invited to hold that a time charterparty could never be frustrated by delay. The argument was rejected; but it was given serious consideration.[40] In that case, the *F.A. Tamplin*, a tanker, had been chartered for five years in December 1912. In December 1914, she was requisitioned for a period which the government said would end in about mid-January. In early February, the requisition not having terminated, she was requisitioned again, the order taking effect on 15 February 1915 when the ship reached her next port. The vessel was subsequently modified by the government so that she could be employed as a troop carrier. The case reached the House of Lords on 24 July 1916, when 19 months of the charterparty still remained.[41] The charterparty was held not to be frustrated, but the basis of the decision was not entirely clear. Two members of the House (Lords Haldane and Atkinson) dissented and would have held that the charterparty was frustrated. Of the majority, Lord Loreburn based his decision on the uncertainty of the length of future delay,[42] whereas Lord Parker and Viscount Buckmaster based their decision in part on the fact that the "restraint of princes" clause made express provision for the situation which had arisen. That is one factor which has tended to obstruct a clear view of the principle for which the case stands. A second is the fact that the argument about frustration was a cloak for a dispute of a different kind altogether. Government compensation for the requisition of ships was generous and was payable to "the owner" of the ship. The ironic origin of the

38. See *Chitty on Contracts* (27th Edn.), para. 23–046; Treitel, *The Law of Contract* (8th Edn.), pp. 799 *et seq*. A typical dictum to this effect may be found in the next case here considered, *Tamplin* v. *Anglo-Mexican Petroleum* [1916] 2 A.C. 397 (H.L.) at p. 426, *per* Lord Parker.

39. [1916] 2 A.C. 397 (H.L.).

40. See especially *per* Lord Parker at pp. 424–45.

41. The proceedings must have been begun very promptly, because the award from which the appeal was taken through the courts was made by the arbitrator on 4 June 1915.

42. *Ibid*., at pp. 405–406.

litigation was the *shipowners'* contention that the contract was frustrated, the reason being that they wished to be able to obtain the whole of that compensation.[43] These factors make the decision confused even on the points with which it purported to deal. It is not, therefore, surprising that the light it shed on frustration by delay in other respects is somewhat crepuscular. Several of their Lordships spoke of the question as being whether the contract was frustrated *by the requisition*. In saying that "the charterparty did not come to an end when the steamer was requisitioned",[44] Lord Loreburn made it clear that if the delay *had* been sufficient to frustrate the charterparty, the frustration would have taken effect from the *beginning* of the period of delay.

The evidence of delay was not however confined to the foreseeable delay as at the date of requisition. One reason for this was that the parties had agreed that the court should look at all the facts up till the date of trial. On one view this was sensible enough, as the contract period had not yet expired and further proceedings could have been brought if it had been held that the contract was not frustrated on 15 February 1915 but might have been at the date of the final appellate judgment. No one seems to have appreciated that this could have led to one or other party being prejudiced by this arrangement if the contract was held to have become frustrated at some intermediate date. No doubt their assumption was the same as what Lord Loreburn impliedly decided, namely, that if the contract was frustrated at all, it was frustrated from the date of the requisition. This meant that the decision contained two assumptions: first, that the question of whether or not the delay was sufficient to frustrate the charterparty was one to be decided in the light of all the evidence, that is objectively; and secondly, that if the contract was frustrated, it was frustrated from the beginning of the period of delay.

The frailty of these assumptions was exposed in *Bank Line* v. *Capel*,[45] the next case on the topic which reached the House of Lords. There too a time-chartered ship had been requisitioned, but the time charter was for only one year. After the ship had been requisitioned, the parties agreed that the contract should be treated as continuing while the owners sought her release, because the parties were "nonplussed as to the effect of the action of the Crown on their own business arrangements".[46] When they failed to obtain the release of the ship from requisition, the shipowners terminated the charterparty, or, more accurately, maintained that it had come to an end. The charterers' action for damages failed when it was held that the charterparty had been frustrated; and it seems that the date of frustration was not the date of requisition, but the date when the shipowners relied on it. No one focused on this point particularly, because neither party sought to argue that the contract had determined at some earlier date. (In any event, the agreement that the

43. It seems that at this time it was thought by some, including apparently the parties to this litigation, that the charterer was "the owner" of the ship for the purposes of receiving the compensation provided pursuant to the Royal Proclamation entitling the Crown to requisition privately owned ships, and that the registered owner was not. *Tamplin*'s case was expected by the parties to answer this question; but Lord Parker pointed out (*ibid.*, p. 428) that the decision did no such thing. He did, however, suggest that the compensation would have to be apportioned between owners and charterers, a view no less surprising than the parties' own. (The charterparty was not a demise charter.)
44. *Ibid.*, at p. 406.
45. [1919] A.C. 435 (H.L.).
46. *Ibid.*, *per* Lord Shaw of Dunfermline at p. 448.

charter should continue after the requisition was a clear bar to the argument that the contract had been frustrated by that event.)

In the *Bank Line* case,[47] this unconscious postponement of the time of frustration to a time of the parties' choosing sowed the seeds of the divergence of view between those who rely on the facts alone and those who treat the expectations of the parties as relevant. Even so, in the *Bank Line* case itself, Lord Finlay L.C.,[48] Lord Shaw of Dunfermline[49] and Lord Wrenbury[50] all appear to have considered the question of whether the contract had been frustrated (as opposed to when) from a wholly objective standpoint. Lord Sumner, however, said this[51]: "The question must be considered at the trial as it had to be considered by the parties when they came to know of the cause and the probabilities of the delay and had to decide what to do." This test involves an assessment of what the reasonably prudent commercial man would have thought. It might be said to exclude factors which were unknown to the parties, even though some others might know of them. There is indeed a spectrum between a simple objective and a simple subjective test; and the various contestants need separate evaluation.

The war between Iran and Iraq which went on through much of the 1980s gave rise to litigation in which many of these problems appeared. But they were not clearly identified, let alone solved. Three factors at least may have contributed to this. First, the reported cases which arose out of the Iran-Iraq conflict all went first to arbitration. The general effect of the Arbitration Act 1979 has been to restrict the degree to which the courts can reconsider the decisions of arbitrators on questions of mixed fact and law. The doctrine of frustration provides paradigms of such questions, and it is no surprise that it was in the context of a case on frustration, indeed of frustration by delay, that the House of Lords laid down this abstentionist principle.[52] Secondly, the contract or the conduct of the parties may give rise to complications which hinder an analysis in terms of simple frustration. Thirdly, the cases have often concerned the date at which a contract terminated, so that the courts' attention has not been focused on the rather different questions of when that can be decided and by reference to what facts.

The first of these matters needs no amplification. The second is merely an aspect of the fact that cases often present legal problems in a regrettably untidy fashion. The terms of the contracts and of the Royal Proclamation relating to requisitions complicated the questions for decision in the *Tamplin* and *Bank Line* cases.[53] In much the same way, the only one of the Gulf cases arising out of the trapping of ships in the Shatt-al-Arab as a result of the Iran-Iraq war to reach the House of Lords was not a case where the issue was a simple one of frustration by delay. In *The Evia (No. 2)*[54] it was argued that a particular clause prevented the doctrine from applying because the contract made elaborate provision for the situation

47. Above, fn. 45.
48. *Ibid.*, at p. 443.
49. *Ibid.*, at p. 445.
50. *Ibid.*, at p. 461.
51. *Ibid.*, at p. 454. Lord Sumner, unlike the rest of the House of Lords, had been a specialist in commercial, indeed in shipping, disputes when in practice at the bar.
52. *The Nema* (*Pioneer Shipping* v. *B.T.P. Tioxide*) [1982] A.C. 724 (H.L.).
53. Above, fns. 39 and 45.
54. [1983] 1 A.C. 736 (H.L.)

which would arise if the vessel were ordered to a war zone. In fact, this point was dealt with fully only in the lower courts[55] where it was held, in essence, that the clause was intended to apply to circumstances other than those which resulted in the frustration of the agreement. The decision is, therefore, relevant to the scope of the doctrine that events which the parties have foreseen cannot frustrate the contract.[56] It illustrates the two related aspects of the rule. Where the terms of the contract deal with the very event which has rendered performance impossible, the doctrine of frustration can have no application: but the mere fact that the contract deals with events of the same general nature as the frustrating event relied on does not mean that the contract deals with every event of that class. Even where the contract deals expressly with war or delay, it is still necessary to ask whether it deals with the particular type or consequences of war which have occurred or with a delay which would otherwise amount to a frustrating delay.[57]

All four of the questions mentioned earlier[58] have been raised by the Gulf cases. Yet most of them have not been mentioned at all; and only in *The Agathon*[59] has one, the degree to which the parties' own views are relevant, been discussed. Those cases show how difficult it is to identify the time when the contract has been frustrated. This is not because the courts have identified the legal question as to the right time to take, but because of the factual problems involved. In determining when a war begins, the evidence is not easy to come by, the participants have an interest in disseminating false information, and the war may impinge on different places at different times. The case of the Gulf War illustrates all this well. In that instance, there was no declaration of war at all. Border clashes of greater and lesser severity occurred throughout September 1980. But it was not until the 17th of that month that Iraq abrogated the 1975 border agreement between Iran and Iraq. That agreement related in particular to the Shatt-al-Arab waterway at the top of the Persian Gulf which divided the two countries. By 20 September no ships could get out. On 23 September, an Iraqi offensive began which was expected, and not just by the Iraqis, to end the conflict within days. On 7 October, the offensive ground to a halt, and there began the war of attrition which was to occupy most of the ensuing decade. At the time, though, it did not seem to everyone that the ships were locked up indefinitely. For a month or two efforts continued to be made by outsiders to get the ships out. Optimism as to their chances waxed and waned throughout that period.

This was the factual context in which a number of arbitrations came before English arbitrators and thence on appeal to the courts. Not surprisingly, different arbitrators gave different effect to the facts outlined above. Indeed, although in time there grew up a body of received wisdom as to what had happened, the evidence in the early cases was not always the same, and was presented from different angles.

55. See [1982] 1 Lloyd's Rep. 334 for the Court of Appeal's analysis.
56. See above, fn. 38.
57. The next Gulf War, which followed Iraq's invasion of Kuwait, threw up a similar type of problem, though not in the context of frustration by delay. In *The Safeer* [1994] 1 Lloyd's Rep. 637, the War Risks Clause was held to have conferred on the owners a liberty to deliver to the Iraqi invaders (as they had been compelled to do) even though that act would otherwise have been held to frustrate the charterparty.
58. Above, pp. 129–130.
59. [1982] 2 Lloyd's Rep. 211 (C.A.), discussed below.

In *The Agathon*,[60] it was held to be arguable that the charterparty was frustrated on or by 17 October. In *The Wenjiang (No. 2)*,[61] Bingham J. upheld an award by an arbitrator who held that the charterparty was frustrated by 24 November but not by 7 October.

The same date, 24 November, was taken in *The Chrysalis*[62]; but in *The Evia (No. 2)*[63] the arbitrator held that the charterparty was frustrated on 4 October, and this was upheld by the courts as being within the bounds of what was a reasonable finding.[64] Yet the discrepancies were not just due to the differences in the evidence put before the arbitrators. Three different things are necessarily hard to distinguish. There are, first, the expectations of the parties; secondly, the reasonable expectations of reasonably well-informed observers; and, thirdly, the actual course of events as seen in the light of the totality of the evidence available to the court. The third of these provides a wholly objective test. Both the other two tests mix objective and subjective considerations. Both suffer from practical defects. It is difficult to try to assess what was reasonably to be expected at some earlier date when the outcome of events is already known. Equally, there is a problem of identifying the date at which certain expectations could reasonably have been held. And there are great complexities to be found in the situation where the parties take a view falsified by subsequent events. Is the contract frustrated if the view was reasonable, though erroneous? Does it become frustrated if, though unreasonable at the time it was held and acted upon, it later becomes reasonable? And what if the situation changes, so that those expectations become again unrealistic or even untenable? Most litigants would say that the trials of their disputes take place only after a frustrating delay. That normally means that either what was probable has actually come about, or its apparent likelihood has been falsified by subsequent events. It might have been expected that these factors would have driven the courts to adopt a set of objective criteria by which to judge whether or not contracts are frustrated. But the decisions have gone the other way. The dictum of Lord Sumner[65] has been used as the foundation for a body of authority which, without much reflection, has applied one or other of the tests based on expectations rather than events. A poignant example of the latter situation is *Court Line* v. *Dant*.[66] There, the *Errington Court* had become trapped 750 miles up the Yangtse by a boom laid across the river by the Chinese on the outbreak of the Sino-Japanese war. It was plain that the ship was not going to get out in time to redeliver in Australia within the contractual period—except that universal expectations were confounded by the Japanese who forced the boom and enabled the *Errington Court* to escape in time for the contract to be performed. By this time, however, the charterers had treated the contract as frustrated, and the question was whether they had thereby committed a breach of contract. A similar example of expectations confounded is to be found in *Embiricos* v. *Sydney Reid*.[67] In both cases, the court held that the contract had been frustrated

60. Above, fn. 59.
61. [1983] 1 Lloyd's Rep. 400.
62. [1983] 1 Lloyd's Rep. 503.
63. [1983] 1 A.C. 736 (H.L.).
64. [1983] 1 Lloyd's Rep. 503 (C.A.).
65. Above, fn. 51.
66. (1939) 44 Com. Cas. 345.
67. [1914] 3 K.B. 45.

on the ground that the question had to be decided by reference to the facts as they seemed at the date of the frustrating event. (To describe it as such is, of course, to beg an important question.) This is a perplexing amalgam of the subjective and the objective.

Part of the problem stems from the failure to identify the frustrating mechanism, that is, whether it is the delay itself or the cause of the delay. It might be thought that whether or not delay has frustrated a contract is something which can be judged *only* with hindsight: it is only the *causes* of delay whose future consequences can be assessed without regard to later acquired knowledge of what was then the future. It is odd that Lord Roskill, who expressed such confidence in the clarity of the doctrine of frustration in *The Nema*,[68] in the same case, in the very next paragraph of his speech, identified one of the possible sources of trouble. He pointed out that in some cases a particular event could be identified as causing or not causing frustration. He went on to say that:

> "In others, where the effect of that event is to cause delay in the performance of contractual obligations, it is *often* necessary to wait upon events in order to see whether the delay already suffered and the prospects of further delay from that cause will make any ultimate performance of the relevant, contractual obligations 'radically different', to borrow Lord Radcliffe's phrase, from that which has been undertaken by the contract."[69]

"Often" is not the same as "always"; but Lord Roskill fails to tell us by what criteria we can decide when we must and when we must not "wait upon events", and whether we ever have a free choice in the matter.

The cases arising out of the Iran-Iraq war all assume that there is no choice; that the delay rather than the cause of the delay is the source of the frustration; and that frustration has to be judged in the light of expectations assessed retrospectively rather than objectively in the light of the information available at the time of trial. It is noteworthy that neither the date of the outbreak of the war nor even that of the sealing of the Shatt-al-Arab was taken in any of the Gulf cases as the date when the contract was frustrated. If the question of whether or not a contract was frustrated could be judged in the light of subsequent events, one would have thought that 20 September, when the waterway was closed, would have been taken as the key date. But this is not what the courts have done. In *The Chrysalis*,[70] where the war was held to have begun on 22 September and the charterers terminated on 14 November, the contract was held to have been frustrated on 24 November. Again, this must be because the court was looking to the reasonable expectations of the parties. On the other hand, in *The Agathon*,[71] where only a short time was left to run on the charter when she was trapped, neither owners nor charterers treated the contract as having been frustrated. When that was later put forward by the shipowners as the basis of their claim for hire, it was held that there was still a triable issue as to whether or not the contract had been frustrated, notwithstanding the beliefs of the parties. One explanation might be that the case concerned only a very narrow question, namely whether the point was arguable at all. Another would be that reasonable expectations as to the future were not settled decisively by the

68. Above, fn 37.
69. [1982] A.C. 724 at p. 752C–D (emphasis added).
70. [1983] 1 Lloyd's Rep. 503. See also above at pp. 133–134.
71. [1982] 2 Lloyd's Rep. 211 (C.A.).

views of the parties. But that does not seem to be what the court had in mind, because Lord Denning M.R. sought to identify two different tests in the cases. He contrasted the dictum of Lord Sumner in *Bank Line* v. *Capel*[72] with another of Lord Roskill in *The Nema*[73] for the purpose of holding that it was arguable that the contract was frustrated. It is at first sight difficult to see a fundamental difference between saying that "rights ought not to be left in suspense or to hang on the chances of subsequent events" (Lord Sumner) and "businessmen must not be required to await events too long. They are entitled to know where they stand" (Lord Roskill). The explanation seems to be that Lord Denning M.R. found a distinction as follows. He treated Lord Sumner's approach, as encapsulated in the observation that "the matter must be considered by the court at the trial as it had to be considered by the parties when they come to know of the cause and the probabilities and had to decide what to do",[74] as wholly subjective. Lord Roskill's observation that "whether or not the delay is such as to bring about frustration must be a question to be determined by an *informed judgment* based upon all the evidence of what has occurred and what is likely thereafter to occur"[75] can be used as the justification for an objective but still retrospective approach. It is doubtful if the speeches bear this difference of interpretation. Neither Lord Sumner nor Lord Roskill appears to have intended to give any precise indication as to whether it was the parties' views or those of informed observers which were relevant. Certainly, in rejecting the beliefs of the parties as decisive of the questions, Lord Denning M.R. appears to have espoused an objective approach, but one which is limited to a consideration of the facts as they were at the date when the parties had to make their decision. None of the other authorities expressly deals with this point. There is surely something odd about a test which requires the court to assess the facts as they objectively (or reasonably) ought to have seemed in preference to the facts as they were perceived by the relevant actors, but to shut its eyes to subsequent events which make all perceptions possibly erroneous and certainly redundant. Either of the first two approaches presents a tribunal with an almost impossible task. It is impossible to determine whether or not a contract is frustrated by reference to expectations unless one is clear how great a part those expectations are to play or whose expectations are to be taken into account. Even if those matters are clear in theory, there are grave evidential difficulties. In a developing situation, the degree of information available will vary from person to person. Even the best informed observer is likely to be slow to appreciate the totality of a situation as compared with one who has the benefit of hindsight. On the other hand, in a volatile situation expert opinion may undergo wild shifts in a short space of time. If, after a week of uncertainty, a strike or a war looks to the well informed as though it will bring about a delay lasting for years, is the contract automatically frustrated at once? Is this so even though a breakthrough occurs unexpectedly on the next day? Is it so irrespective of the knowledge and beliefs of the parties as opposed to those of the pundits? Does the belief have to be held to any particular degree of certainty? A doctrine which has regard to the opinions of the parties or of onlookers has the

72. [1919] A.C. 435 at p. 454. The central part of this dictum is quoted above, fn. 51.
73. *Pioneer Shipping* v. *B.T.P. Tioxide* [1982] A.C. 724, at p. 752C–D.
74. [1919] A.C. at p. 454.
75. [1982] A.C. at p. 752D (emphasis added).

effect that, at the first moment that the view is formed by the appropriate person that there will be a frustrating delay, the contract is forthwith frustrated. This is so, no matter how soon and how decisively such a belief would have been exposed as erroneous. If this is the position, the law is in a most unsatisfactory state. Once a contract is frustrated, it cannot be unfrustrated by the exposure of the error of the expectations of the relevant persons. The application of either a purely subjective test or Lord Denning M.R.'s hybrid test has the result that the contract falls away at the first instant in time when it can be said that a frustrating delay is to be anticipated. This is so even if this appreciation of the situation is dispelled by further knowledge or a change of circumstances the next day.

There is surely much to be said for applying a wholly objective test. That would result in the question of whether or not a contract was frustrated by delay being decided on the basis of all the evidence available at the time of trial. There would be no question then of contracts being held to have been frustrated by delays which were expected to be long but were unexpectedly curtailed. Faced with the possibility of delay because of a strike or a war, commercial men would have to take a view. They would be forced to make a commercial decision whether or not to treat contracts as over, whether or not they invoked legal jargon to treat them as frustrated. Sometimes their decision would be wrong, because they had misread the future; but that is always a risk inherent in normal commercial activity. There is no obvious reason why the law should rescue them from the consequences of one narrowly defined class of wrong decision. It is clear, though, that whatever the true scope of the doctrine of frustration may be in cases involving delay, the objective approach is the one that is ruled out by the modern cases. In neither *The Nema*[76] nor *The Agathon*[77] was the decision in *Hirji Mulji* v. *Cheong Yue*[78] cited. That was a decision where it was clearly held that the intentions, opinions, knowledge and beliefs of the parties were all irrelevant. Like *Tamplin*'s case[79] and the *Bank Line* case,[80] it concerned a dispute which arose out of a requisition during the first world war, and it is notable that the requisition (rather than the delay) was again held to be the frustrating event.[81] The other striking feature of the decision, having regard to the impact of his views on the questions discussed above, is that the opinion of the Privy Council was delivered by Lord Sumner, who adopted a highly objective approach to the ascertainment of whether or not a contract had been frustrated.[82]

The modern authorities make it impossible to apply a completely objective test. This is regrettable, particularly as this part of the problem seems never to have been carefully analysed. There is nothing obviously absurd in a contract having been frustrated without the parties having realised it. And the law of contract is equally capable of reaching sensible results where a contract is not in law frustrated, even though the parties share the erroneous belief that it has been. It is true that businessmen would like to know where they stand; but no formulation of the

76. Above, fn. 36.
77. Above, fn. 59.
78. [1926] A.C. 497 (P.C.).
79. Above, fn. 39.
80. Above, fn. 45.
81. See [1926] A.C. at p. 501 (though it must be said that at p. 502 there is some moderation of this statement).
82. See especially *ibid.*, pp. 507–509.

law would necessarily enable them to do that in every possible case. Businessmen who are not sure about their legal position and wish to terminate a contract only if legally justified in so doing can always seek a speedy arbitration. (This indeed happened in a number of the Gulf cases.) The arbitrator would then have to make an assessment. Of course, the arbitrator would usually in such a case have to decide how long the delay was likely to continue and its likely effect on the contract: but his decision would be a legally binding one, reached on the basis of all the evidence then available. It would be immaterial if *his* decision were subsequently falsified by events, because there would be a *res judicata*. And this would be perfectly just, because the parties would have sacrificed their right to take a commercial gamble for the sake of a certain decision on which they could base their future conduct. Often in such cases, where two commercial organisations recognise that there is a bona fide difference of view of this kind, the parties will continue to perform without prejudice to their rights, pending the outcome of the arbitration. If courts and arbitrators decide whether delay, accrued or prospective, has frustrated a contract by reference to objective criteria, including all the facts known at the time of the hearing, a wide variety of commercial choices can still be accommodated within the framework of the law. One fortuitous benefit of the law's delay so far as this type of case is concerned is that, in the normal case, by the time of trial the future has, so to speak, already occurred. The law of frustration as it presently stands throws away that advantage.

M. N. HOWARD Q.C.

CHAPTER 7

FORCE MAJEURE PROVISIONS IN A SHIPBUILDING CONTEXT[1]

1. INTRODUCTION

As with other large-scale construction ventures, shipbuilding projects typically expose the contractor, or "builder", to significant risks that the performance of his contractual obligations to the purchaser, or "buyer", will be prevented or impeded by events beyond the builder's control. Although recent years have seen a considerable expansion in the number and size of "covered" newbuilding facilities, most commercial vessels are still built in the open air, often in harsh climatic conditions; each project takes at least a year to complete and requires the employment of a large labour force in addition to the efforts of numerous subcontractors and suppliers engaged by the builder.

Accordingly, quite apart from the potential impact upon the construction programme of the purchaser's non-performance of the contract,[2] an almost infinite range of events outside the builder's control may render him incapable of meeting his contractual obligations, either on time or at all. Whilst the doctrine of frustration may in certain limited circumstances wholly discharge the builder from performance of his obligations where these have been radically affected by supervening events, English common law will not normally protect him if he is simply late in delivering the vessel as the result of supervening events over which he has no influence.

Given the scale and complexity of modern shipbuilding projects, it is almost unknown for the builder to be willing to assume all of the risks of delay arising without default on his part. The overwhelming majority of shipbuilding contracts therefore share the potential exposures between the buyer and the builder by:

(a) providing that the agreed date on which the vessel is to be delivered, usually known as the delivery date, will be extended by any periods during which performance of the builder's obligations is impeded or prevented by defined *force majeure* events; and
(b) entitling the buyer to rescind or terminate the contract if claims for postponement of the delivery date by reason of *force majeure* delays exceed in aggregate an agreed number of days over the life of the contract.

This approach to the allocation of *force majeure* risks can be seen in a number of

1. This article reproduces certain material previously published in *The Law of Shipbuilding Contracts* by Simon Curtis, Lloyd's of London Press Limited, 1991.
2. e.g. in failing to pay the instalments of the contract price when these fall due.

shipbuilding standard forms, of which the best known is the 1974 contract of the Shipbuilders' Association of Japan. Apart from its widespread use in relation to contracts actually placed in Japan, the so-called SAJ Form has become the model for similar standard forms in the other major shipbuilding countries, primarily Korea, China and Singapore.

The *force majeure* provisions of the SAJ form are contained in Article VIII, which provides as follows:

"*1. Causes of Delay:*
If, at any time before the actual delivery, either the construction of the VESSEL or any performance required as a prerequisite of delivery of the VESSEL is delayed due to Acts of God; acts of princes or rulers; requirements of government authorities; war or other hostilities or preparations therefor; blockade; revolution, insurrections, mobilisation, civil war, civil commotion or riots; vandalism, sabotages, strikes, lockouts or other labour disturbances; labour shortage; plague or other epidemics; quarantines; flood, typhoons, hurricanes, storms or other weather conditions not included in normal planning; earthquakes, tidal waves; landslides; fires, explosions, collisions or strandings; embargoes; delays or failure in transportation; shortage of materials, machinery or equipment; import restrictions; inability to obtain delivery or delays in delivery of materials, machinery or equipment, provided that at the time of ordering the same could reasonably be expected by the BUILDER to be delivered in time, prolonged failure, shortage or restriction of electric current, oil or gas; defects in materials, machinery or equipment which could not have been detected by the BUILDER using reasonable care; casting or forging rejects or the like not due to negligence; delays caused by the Classification Society or other bodies whose documents are required; destruction of or damage to the Shipyard or works of the BUILDER, its subcontractors or suppliers, or of or to the VESSEL or any part thereof, by any causes herein described; delays in the BUILDER's other commitments resulting from any causes herein described which in turn delay the construction of the VESSEL or the BUILDER's performance under this Contract; other causes or accidents beyond control of the BUILDER, its subcontractors or suppliers of the nature (*sic*) whether or not indicated by the foregoing words; all the foregoing irrespective of whether or not these events could be foreseen at the day of signing this Contract; then and in any such case, the Delivery Date shall be postponed for a period of time which shall not exceed the total accumulated time of all such delays.
2. Notice of Delay:
Within ten (10) days after the date of occurrence of any cause of delay on account of which the BUILDER claims that it is entitled under this Contract to a postponement of the Delivery Date, the BUILDER shall notify the Buyer in writing or by cable confirmed in writing of the date such cause of delay occurred. Likewise, within ten (10) days after the date of ending of such cause of delay, the BUILDER shall notify the Buyer in writing or by cable confirmed in writing of the date such cause of delay ended. The BUILDER shall also notify the Buyer of the period by which the Delivery Date is postponed by reason of such cause of delay, with all reasonable despatch after it has been determined. Failure of the Buyer to object to the BUILDER's claim for postponement of the Delivery Date within ten (10) days after receipt by the Buyer of such notice of claim shall be deemed to be a waiver by the Buyer of its right to object (*sic*) such postponement of the Delivery Date.
3. Definition of Permissible Delay:
Delays on account of such causes as specified in Paragraph 1 of this Article and any other delays of a nature which under the terms of this Contract permits (sic) postponement of the Delivery Date shall be understood to be permissible delays and are to be distinguished from unauthorised delays on account of which the Contract Price is subject to adjustment as provided for in Article III hereof.
4. Right to Rescind for Excessive Delay:
If the total accumulated time of all delays on account of the causes specified in Paragraph 1 of this Article, excluding delays of a nature which under the terms of this Contract permit postponement of the Delivery Date, amounts to Two Hundred and Ten (210) days or more,

then, in such event, the Buyer may rescind this Contract in accordance with the provisions of Article X hereof. The BUILDER may, at any time after the accumulated time of the aforementioned delays justifying rescission by the Buyer, demand in writing that the Buyer shall make an election, in which case the Buyer shall, within twenty (20) days after such demand is received by the Buyer, either notify the BUILDER of its intention to rescind this Contract, or consent to a postponement of the Delivery Date to a specific future date; it being understood and agreed by the parties hereto that, if any further delay occurs on account of causes justifying rescission as specified in this Article, the Buyer shall have the same right of rescission upon the same terms as hereinabove provided.

2. THE DEFINITION OF FORCE MAJEURE

As can be seen, Article VIII defines a range of more than 35 *force majeure* events which are deemed to entitle the builder to a postponement of the delivery date and details the procedure by which claims for postponement are to be presented. It also provides that the buyer may rescind the contract if the builder's claims for postponement of the delivery date by reason of *force majeure* delays aggregate 210 days or more.

It should be noted, however, that, in common with *force majeure* clauses in other standard shipbuilding forms, Article VIII encompasses only events causing delay in the completion of the vessel's construction. Any circumstances causing another form of hindrance to the performance of the builder's obligations (including, for example, an increase in his costs of labour or materials) will not avail him unless delay also results.[3]

Much of the language used in Article VIII.1 is clear as to its meaning and scope but a number of terms call for specific comment.

(a) "Acts of God"

The expression "act of God" has been somewhat inelegantly defined in English law as "such an operation of the forces of nature as reasonable foresight and ability could not foresee or reasonably provide against".[4] Where this exception is included in the contract, the builder must normally prove not only the impact of a natural phenomenon upon the performance of the contract works, but also that he could not reasonably have anticipated or avoided its effects.

Under the SAJ form, however, a number of circumstances which might as a matter of common law constitute acts of God (in particular floods, typhoons, hurricanes and storms) are expressly included within the scope of the protections provided to the builder. Furthermore, Article VIII.1 excludes any requirement that these circumstances should not have been foreseeable at the time the contract was concluded.

The extent to which mere inclement weather, as opposed to specific meteorological events such as storms or lightning strikes, can constitute an act of God has not been finally settled by the English courts. In *Matsoukis* v. *Priestman & Co.*,[5] Bail-

3. *Brauer & Co. (Great Britain) Ltd.* v. *James Clark (Brush Materials) Ltd.* [1952] 2 Lloyd's Rep. 147.
4. *Per* Atkin J. in *Baldwin's Ltd.* v. *Halifax Corporation* (1916) 85 L.J.K.B. 1769 at p. 1774.
5. [1915] 1 K.B. 681.

hache J., having expressed the view that *force majeure* was wider in law than an act of God, held that "bad weather, football matches and funerals" were "usual incidents interrupting work"[6] and did not fall within the terms of a clause excepting the builder from "the cause of *force majeure*, and/or strikes of workmen".

The proposition that inclement weather cannot constitute an act of God was, however, doubted in the subsequent case of *Lebeaupin* v. *Richard Crispin and Co.*[7] In light of this and other authorities,[8] the better view is that bad weather can constitute an act of God where it is so extreme that, judged in the light of the usual conditions at the place of contractual performance, the party affected could not reasonably have expected to encounter it.

As indicated above, Article VIII.1 of the SAJ form expressly permits a claim for *force majeure* delay in the case of "typhoons, hurricanes, storms or other weather conditions not included in normal planning".

(b) "Strikes, lockouts or other labour disturbances"

Strikes and other forms of industrial action represent one of the commonest and most significant causes of delay in the construction of newbuildings. These are also circumstances which the builder, as the employer of the workforce at the shipyard, may sometimes be in a position to influence or control.

For this reason the inclusion of "strikes, lockouts and other labour disturbances" within the scope of the *force majeure* clause frequently represents the most contentious element of the pre-contract negotiations. If, however, these are not to be regarded as *force majeure* events, the builder may be seriously exposed to the consequences of disputes not only with his own workforce but also between his subcontractors and their employees.

The term "strike" has been judicially defined as: "a simultaneous cessation of work on the part of workmen acting in combination or a concerted refusal of any number of persons who are employed to continue to work or to accept employment".[9]

In *Tramp Shipping Corporation* v. *Greenwich Marine Incorporated*[10] a concerted refusal by workmen, seeking to secure improvements in their terms and conditions of employment, to work customary shifts was held to be a strike within a charterparty exceptions clause. Where, however, there is no dispute between employer and employees, but merely a refusal on the part of the latter to work because, for example, an infectious disease is prevalent at the shipyard, this will not constitute a strike[11]; it is equally neither a strike nor a lockout for the builder, responding to economic pressures rather than the existence of a labour dispute, to make part of his workforce redundant.[12]

6. The funeral was, however, that of the shipyard manager; details of the football matches are not reported.

7. [1920] 2 K.B. 714.

8. *Dixon* v. *Metropolitan Board of Works* (1881) 7 Q.B.D. 418.

9. *Farrer* v. *Close* (1869) L.R. 4 Q.B. 602; s.246 of the Trade Union and Labour Relations (Consolidation) Act 1992 defines a strike as "any concerted stoppage of work".

10. [1975] I.C.R. 261.

11. *Stephens* v. *Harris* (1886) 56 L.J.Q.B. 516. The Court of Appeal declined to express a view on this issue but did not overrule the Divisional Court; see (1887) 57 L.J.Q.B. 203.

12. *Re Richardsons and Samuel* (1897) 66 L.J.Q.B. 868.

The most contentious issue in this context is whether it is open to the buyer to contend that the builder has acted unreasonably in his dealings with his workforce and is thus precluded from asserting that a particular strike has truly resulted from events beyond his control. In *B. & S. Contracts and Design Ltd.* v. *Victor Green Publications Ltd.*,[13] the plaintiffs, who were specialist contractors, agreed to erect exhibition stands for the defendants. The contract incorporated a *force majeure* clause which stated that "due performance is subject to variation or cancellation owing to strikes or any other cause beyond the [contractor's] control". In support of long-standing claims for severance pay, the plaintiffs' workforce refused to erect the stands and the defendants, fearing that they would incur substantial liabilities to the exhibitors, offered to advance half the amount in dispute to the plaintiffs, who were able and willing to meet the balance of the workforce's claim. The plaintiffs refused, however, to agree that the monies be treated as an advance, whereupon the defendants made the payment to them regardless and subsequently set off the amount involved against the plaintiffs' invoice for the contract price.

The defendants argued (*inter alia*) that the payment had been made under the threat of non-performance and was therefore recoverable from the plaintiffs as induced by duress; to this, the plaintiffs replied that their actions were not unlawful because the *force majeure* clause excused non-performance resulting from strikes.

On these facts the Court of Appeal experienced no difficulty in deciding that the *force majeure* clause did not protect the plaintiffs. In the view of all three members of the court, the applicable test was whether the employer had acted reasonably in his dealings with his workforce. In the court's view this had not happened; indeed the plaintiffs had acted wholly unreasonably in refusing to settle their workforce's claims; the court found as a fact that such claims could have been met if the defendants' original offer of an advance had been accepted.

A similar view was clearly taken by counsel in *Channel Island Ferries Ltd.* v. *Sealink Ltd.*,[14] in which it was conceded at the outset that the defendants, Sealink, were entitled to rely upon a *force majeure* exception of strikes only if there was nothing they could reasonably have done to avoid the strike in question or to mitigate its consequences.

A "lockout' has been statutorily defined as:

"the closing of a place of employment, or the suspension of work, or the refusal by an employer to continue to employ any number of persons employed by him in consequence of a dispute, done with a view to compelling those persons or to aid another employer in compelling persons employed by him, to accept terms or conditions of or affecting employment".[15]

(c) "Labour shortage"

This expression is plainly intended to extend the scope of the exception of strikes, etc. to the more general circumstance in which sufficient skilled or unskilled labour is for any reason not available to the builder. In *Lindvig* v. *Forth Shipbuilding & Engineering Co., Ltd.*[16] a *force majeure* provision excusing the builder from the

13. [1984] I.C.R. 419, discussed in more detail in Chapter 9.
14. [1987] 1 Lloyd's Rep. 559; [1988] 1 Lloyd's Rep. 323 (C.A.).
15. Employment Protection (Consolidation) Act 1978, Sch. 13, para. 24(1).
16. (1921) 7 Ll.L.Rep. 253.

consequences of "unexpected and exceptional restriction of output" was held by Roche J. to extend to "a restriction of workmen . . . That is to say, the men were not working as they might be expected to work, owing to changes of hours and other matters".[17]

It is nevertheless a primary obligation of the builder under the contract to procure sufficient labour to complete the vessel on time; in line with general principles, he will not, therefore, be entitled to rely upon the exception of a labour shortage where he has, for example, simply underestimated his requirements for the project.

(d) "Explosions"

In *Commonwealth Smelting Ltd.* v. *Guardian Royal Exchange Ltd.*[18] the term "explosion", in the context of the construction of an insurance policy, was held to mean "an event that is violent, noisy and caused by a very rapid chemical or nuclear reaction, or the bursting out of gas or vapour under pressure".[19] It did not encompass the break-up at speed of a large ventilation fan notwithstanding that this produced outward effects similar to that of a chemical explosion.

(e) "Shortage of materials, machinery or equipment . . . delays in delivery . . . "

Ensuring the availability and timely delivery of the materials and equipment needed for the vessel's construction represents one of the builder's principal obligations under the contract; in any major shipbuilding project, he will be expected to supervise and co-ordinate the activities of a substantial number of suppliers and subcontractors located in a variety of different countries.

Given these circumstances, it is not unreasonable that the builder's right to claim *force majeure* delay consequent upon shortages or delays in deliveries should be restricted to situations in which these occur unexpectedly and without fault on his part. The SAJ form therefore expressly limits such claims to cases in which "at the time of ordering [the materials, machinery or equipment] could reasonably be expected by the builder to be delivered in time".

The fact that the market price of the materials in question has risen is not in itself conclusive evidence of a shortage in supply. Conversely, however, where a shortage does arise, the builder is entitled to rely upon the exclusion even if he could have acquired the materials by paying a higher price. In *Tennants (Lancashire), Ltd.* v. *C. S. Wilson and Co. Ltd.*,[20] the defendant sellers failed, following the outbreak of the 1914–1918 war, to supply magnesium chloride to the plaintiffs under a fixed price contract; the defendants had intended to cover the contract requirement from a source of supply in Germany. The evidence indicated that, provided they were prepared to default in the performance of certain other supply contracts, the defendants could have fulfilled their obligations to the plaintiffs by buying in from other sources, albeit at a significantly increased cost. The defendants sought instead to invoke the provisions of a *force majeure* clause entitling them to suspend deliver-

17. *Ibid.*, at p. 257.
18. [1984] 2 Lloyd's Rep. 608.
19. *Ibid.*, at p 612, *per* Staughton J.
20. [1917] A.C. 495.

ies "pending any contingency beyond the control of the sellers (such as war) causing a short supply of raw material or manufactured produce, or otherwise preventing or hindering the manufacture or delivery of the article".

Against this background the House of Lords held[21] that, a general shortage of supply having been proved, the defendants were entitled to rely upon the *force majeure* clause notwithstanding the existence of an alternative source of supply sufficient to permit them to fulfil their obligations to the plaintiffs. Their Lordships were, however, insistent that a mere increase in price would not have been adequate to establish a shortage in supply. Expressing the view of the majority, Lord Dunedin said: "I do not think price as price has anything to do with it. Price may be evidence, but it is only one of many kinds of evidence as to shortage. If the [sellers] had alleged nothing but advanced price they would have failed."[22]

(f) "Defects in materials, machinery or equipment which could not have been detected by the Builder using reasonable care"

In addition to permitting the builder a postponement of the delivery date in the event of shortages or delays in delivery of materials, machinery or equipment, the SAJ form also protects him against the consequences of defects in such items. This general wording is in addition to the separate and specific exception of "casting or forging rejects or the like not due to negligence".

The SAJ form stipulates that the defect must be "latent" in nature, in the sense that it could not have been discovered through the exercise of reasonable care. However, there is nothing in Article VIII.1 to suggest that the builder's duty is limited in time. Thus, where an item installed on board the vessel is found to be defective, he will *prima facie* be entitled to an extension of the delivery date calculated by reference to the date on which, if the required degree of care had been employed, the defect should have been discovered (rather than the date of its installation).

(g) "Delays in the Builder's other commitments which in turn delay construction of the Vessel"

The builder is also entitled under Article VIII.1 to claim a postponement of the delivery date where the completion of his commitments to third parties is delayed as a result of *force majeure* events and this in turn delays his performance of the contract.

In *Matsoukis* v. *Priestman & Co.*[23] the plaintiff's vessel was delayed by reason of a number of events, including delay in completion of an earlier vessel occupying the berth. Completion of this earlier vessel had itself been held up by late delivery of steel plates consequent on the great coal strike of 1912. The court held that, whilst the effect of the strike upon the completion of the plaintiff's vessel was only indirect, the shipbuilder was excused by the terms of a *force majeure* clause from liability

21. Lord Finlay dissenting.

22. *Ibid.*, at p. 516; see also *Peter Dixon & Sons Ltd.* v. *Henderson, Craig & Co. Ltd.* [1919] 2 K.B. 778.

23. [1915] 1 K.B. 681.

to pay liquidated damages for the delay involved. This was so even though at the date when the contract was made it was "obvious that a strike might take place".[24]

Similarly, in *Lockie and Craggs & Sons*,[25] delay in completion of an earlier vessel occupying the berth was caused by a number of events outside the shipbuilder's control. The contract vessel was, as a result, commenced and completed late. The shipbuilder was held entitled to the protection of a clause which, while fixing the delivery date, required the parties to make "due allowance" for various specified *force majeure* events and "other circumstances beyond Builders' control".

However, under the SAJ form it is expressly provided that the builder is entitled to claim an extension of the delivery date only where delay in respect of other commitments has itself resulted from *force majeure* events as defined in Article VIII.1.

(h) "Other causes or accidents beyond the control of the Builder, its subcontractors or suppliers whether or not indicated by the foregoing words"

This wording is intended to operate as a "sweeping-up" provision, extending protection to the builder against any circumstances beyond his control which prevent performance of the contract but are not included within the list of defined events set out in the first part of Article VIII.1.

Prima facie, wording of this type attracts the operation of the *ejusdem generis* rule of construction. This provides that, where general words in a contract follow,[26] and are intended to expand upon, particular language, the former will be construed in light of the latter and will be read as limited to matters *eiusdem generis* (i.e. of the same class) as those for which specific provision has been made.

Thus in *Herman* v. *Morris*[27] a contract for the repair, re-engining and sale of a damaged vessel, which provided for liquidated damages in the event of late delivery, excepted the vendors from the consequences of "strikes, lockouts et cetera, or any cause beyond the vendor's control". Delay was caused by reason of a decision of the vendors' engine suppliers to give priority to another contract and, in answer to the purchasers' claim for liquidated damages, the vendor sought to argue that this circumstance represented a "cause beyond [his] control". The Court of Appeal held, however, on the authority of *Re Richardsons and Samuel & Co.*[28] that these words were to be construed *ejusdem generis* with strikes and lockouts and did not as such encompass non-performance by the vendor's subcontractors; the use of the words "et cetera" made no difference to such interpretation.

The *ejusdem generis* rule is nevertheless merely a rule of construction and is, as such, capable of being displaced by terms of the contract indicating that the parties intended that it should not apply. In *Larsen* v. *Sylvester & Co.*,[29] for example, it was held inapplicable to a charterparty which, in addition to excepting the charterers' liability for non-performance arising from a list of specific events, also extended to "hindrances of what kind soever (*sic*)". Similarly, in *Chandris* v.

24. *Per* Bailhache J. at p. 686.
25. *In the Matter of an Arbitration between Lockie and Craggs & Sons* (1901) 7 Com. Cas. 7.
26. The rule does not apply where the general language precedes specific wording; *Ambatielos* v. *Anton Jurgens Margarine Works* [1922] 2 K.B. 185.
27. (1919) 35 T.L.R. 574.
28. (1897) 66 L.J.Q.B. 868, see further fn. 12 above.
29. [1908] A.C. 295.

Isbrandtsen-Moller Co., Inc.,[30] the words "or other dangerous cargo" in a charter-party clause which exempted the owner from the obligation to carry "acids, explosives, arms or ammunition or other dangerous cargo" were held, on the true interpretation of the agreement as a whole, to be unaffected by the operation of the *eiusdem generis* rule.

The rule is also excluded where it is not possible to synthesise from the given range of specific events a genus of circumstances to which the general language can be limited. As McCardie J. stated in *S.S. Magnhild* v. *McIntyre Brothers & Co.*[31]:

"the rule of *ejusdem generis* cannot be applied at all unless there be some broad test for the ascertainment of genus. So far as I can see the only test seems to be whether the specified things which precede the general words can be placed under some common category. By this I understand that the specified things must possess some common and dominant feature."[32]

Both of these considerations are relevant to the interpretation of Article VIII.1. In particular, the words "whether or not indicated by the foregoing words" appear plainly to convey an intention that the rule should not apply; furthermore, even if the words do not achieve this effect as a matter of law, it is very difficult to establish amongst the broad range of defined *force majeure* events a "common or dominant feature" sufficient to constitute a genus. In claiming an extension of time for performance by reason of a particular event "beyond his control", it appears, therefore, that the builder is not obliged to show that this is similar in nature to one of the specific events listed in Article VIII.1.

Particular difficulties arise in this context where the builder claims *force majeure* delays as a result of quality or performance failures on the part of his own subcontractors. Where the failure by a subcontractor results from circumstances beyond his control, the *force majeure* clause will usually apply to excuse the builder from liability for any delay he may suffer as a consequence; thus the SAJ form refers to "causes and accidents beyond control of the builder, its subcontractors or suppliers". What is the position, however, if the subcontractor simply and inexcusably defaults in the proper performance of his obligations?

While this was clearly regarded in *Herman* v. *Morris* as an aspect of the shipbuilders' project risk, a more sympathetic approach was adopted in *Scott Lithgow Ltd.* v. *Secretary of State for Defence*.[33] In that case a construction contract for two "Oberon" class submarines provided that the shipbuilder should be entitled to recover from the purchaser the additional costs of construction resulting from "exceptional dislocation and delay arising during the construction of the vessel due to any cause beyond the [Builder's] control". The shipbuilder became exposed to significant additional costs by reason of defects in cables supplied by a subcontractor selected from a list approved by the purchaser.

The shipbuilder claimed these costs from the purchaser and the resulting dispute reached the House of Lords, which held that the shipbuilder was entitled to rely upon the subcontractor's default as being "a cause of delay beyond [his] control". Lord Keith, giving the only detailed judgment, expressed the view that:

30. (1950) 83 Ll.L.Rep. 385.
31. [1920] 3 K.B. 321; see also *Sonat Offshore S.A.* v. *Amerada Hess Development Ltd.* [1988] 1 Lloyd's Rep. 145, *per* Saville J. at p. 149.
32. *Ibid.*, at p. 330.
33. (1989) 45 Build.L.R. 1 (H.L.).

"*prima facie* it is not within the power of a contracting party to prevent quality breaches of contract on the part of a supplier or subcontractor such as lead to delay. The contractor has no means in the ordinary case of supervising the manufacturing procedures of his supplier. He specifies his requirements but has no means of securing that they are met . . . Failures by such suppliers or subcontractors, in breach of their contractual obligations to Scott Lithgow are not matters which, according to the ordinary use of language, can be regarded as within Scott Lithgow's control."[34]

Lord Keith's judgment makes clear, however, that whether or not a failure on the part of a subcontractor constitutes an event beyond the builder's control is in each case an issue of fact, rather than law. Where, for example, the builder is in a position to require that his subcontractors employ proper quality assurance techniques, it seems unlikely that he can rely upon the exception where he has chosen not to take this step and a quality failure results.[35]

The *Scott Lithgow* decision also implies, however, that the builder may be in a stronger position under the contract where the buyer selects the subcontractor and insists that the builder employs him in the performance of the contract works. This is *a fortiori* where (as sometimes occurs) an order is placed by the buyer with a subcontractor directly and transferred to the builder upon the subsequent execution of the shipbuilding contract itself.

3. THE EFFECT OF FORCE MAJEURE EVENTS

The contract will normally contain provisions defining the effect of *force majeure* events upon the parties' rights and obligations thereunder. Article VIII.1 of the SAJ form is in this respect curiously worded, providing no specific guidance as to the extent to which the delivery date is to be postponed by reason of *force majeure* events. On the contrary, the article states merely that such postponement "shall not exceed the total accumulated time of all such [i.e. *force majeure*] delays".

This lack of clarity becomes important where the delay in the builder's construction programme resulting from a *force majeure* event is either more or less than the duration of the event itself. Thus a delay of one week in the supply of a particular item of subcontracted equipment may, depending upon the builder's construction programme, delay the vessel by a fortnight. Is the builder entitled to claim one or two weeks' postponement of the delivery date?

Although the position under the SAJ form is not free from doubt, it seems probable that it is the extent of the delay to the construction programme, rather than the duration of the *force majeure* event itself, which is relevant. Such an interpretation is consistent with the notification provisions of Article VIII.2, which require the builder to notify the buyer of the period "by which the Delivery Date is postponed by reason of such cause of delay", with Article VIII.4, which refers to "all delays on account of [*force majeure*] causes" and with the decision of the High Court in *K/S Stasupply A/S* v. *Dae Dong Shipbuilding Co. Ltd.*[36]

34. *Ibid.*, at pp. 12–13.
35. This issue is unlikely to arise under the SAJ form because of the specific *force majeure* exception of "defects in materials, machinery or equipment which could not have been detected by the Builder using reasonable care"; see p. 145 above.
36. Unreported, Q.B.D., 23 October 1986.

Furthermore, the alternative view (i.e. that it is the duration of the *force majeure* event itself which is relevant) gives rise to serious problems in relation to those *force majeure* circumstances (in particular "defects in materials [and] casting or forging rejects") which are not themselves events of specific duration.

It must nevertheless be conceded that, if Article VIII.1 provides for an extension of the delivery date by the sum of the delays caused to the builder's construction programme, the limitation contained in the last part of the paragraph ("the Delivery Date shall be postponed for a period of time which shall not exceed the total accumulated time of all such delays") appears to be wholly redundant.

Finally, it should be noted that the SAJ form expressly entitles the builder to claim *force majeure* delay at any time prior to the "actual delivery" of the vessel. To this extent, the standard form reverses the position at common law by allowing the builder to claim *force majeure* delay even after the delivery date has passed.

4. THE REQUIREMENT OF NOTICE

Most shipbuilding contracts contain strict time limits within which the builder's claims for postponement of the delivery date must be notified to the buyer. This is primarily designed to afford the buyer an immediate opportunity to investigate the circumstances of the delay and, where appropriate, to challenge the builder's claim. The time limit provisions are, however, also of significance in permitting both parties to maintain an accurate running total of the builder's claims for extension of the delivery date; this may be needed (*inter alia*) to establish the date of accrual in the buyer's favour of rights to rescind the contract for delay.

Under Article VIII.2 of the SAJ form, notice of a claim for postponement of the delivery date must be given to the buyer within 10 days from the date of commencement of the circumstances relied upon. The builder is also required to issue a further notice within 10 days of the ending of the alleged *force majeure* event and must, either contemporaneously or at a "later time but with all reasonable despatch"[37] specify "the period of time by which the delivery date is postponed by reason of such delay".

It should be noted that time runs in each case from the date of commencement or cessation of the alleged *force majeure* event, rather than from the date on which the builder first learns of the same; the builder may therefore be unable to give the required notice in time if the event has its immediate impact outside the shipyard, perhaps by affecting a subcontractor or supplier rather than the builder directly. The SAJ wording is for this reason often amended to provide that time shall run only from the date on which the builder first learns of the *force majeure* event in question.

The legal effect of non-compliance with the time limit is unclear. On one view, breach by the builder of his obligation to notify in time sounds only in damages; the builder remains entitled to assert his claim for postponement, although he is liable to the buyer in damages for any loss sustained as a result of the late notification. Given, however, the primary purpose for which the 10-day time limit is incorpor-

37. *Per* Hobhouse J. in *K/S Stasupply A/S* v. *Dae Dong Shipbuilding Company*, fn. 36 above.

ated in Article VIII (i.e. to afford the buyer an immediate opportunity to investigate and, if necessary, challenge the claim), the better view (it is submitted) is that failure to notify in time bars the claim completely.[38]

Article VIII.2 also stipulates that, where the buyer fails to acknowledge the builder's notification within 10 days of receipt, he is deemed to have waived any right to object to the builder's claim for postponement of the delivery date. Even where such an acknowledgment is given, the buyer's conduct may nevertheless preclude him from contending that the builder's notice was formally defective. Thus, in *Finance for Shipping Ltd.* v. *Appledore Shipbuilding Ltd.*,[39] where the contract required that notice of *force majeure* claims should be given after the occurrence of the event on which they were based, prospective notices of delay were almost certainly defective. The purchaser's equivocal response to the notices was, however, held by the Court of Appeal to give rise to an "arguable defence" that he had waived his rights to treat these as invalid.

5. EXCESSIVE DELAY

The buyer will usually require that the contract should permit him a right to rescind in the event of excessive delay in delivery howsoever occurring. This objective can be achieved by incorporating in the contract a right of rescission exercisable either:

(a) on a fixed future date, often called the "drop dead" date, which is not capable of extension by reference to *force majeure* delays[40]; or

(b) when the builder's aggregate claims for postponement of the delivery date by reason of *force majeure* delays exceed an agreed figure.

The SAJ form adopts the second approach; a right of rescission arises in the buyer's favour under Article VIII.4 where *force majeure* delays amount to 210 days or more. Specifically, the right of rescission is triggered: "If the total accumulated time of all delays on account of the causes specified in Paragraph 1 of this Article, *excluding delays of a nature which, under the terms of this Contract, permit postponement of the Delivery Date*, amounts to Two Hundred and Ten (210) days or more." Given that "delays on account of causes specified in Paragraph 1" expressly permit postponement of the delivery date, it is difficult to understand the scope of the exclusion intended by the italicised wording above. This difficulty can probably be overcome only if the wording is read as referring to the other types of *force majeure* delay (arising, for example, by reason of the buyer's default) which, while extending the delivery date, do not arise from *force majeure* events and are not therefore intended to count towards the 210-day limit.

38. Note that in *Bremer Handelsgesellschaft m.b.H.* v. *Vanden Avenne-Izegem P.V.B.A.* [1978] 2 Lloyd's Rep. 109, the House of Lords held that a clause in a commodity contract requiring a seller to give notice "without delay" of circumstances entitling him to rely upon a *force majeure* clause was an innominate term, i.e. whether the seller was precluded from invoking the clause where he had delayed in giving notice depended upon the effect of the failure upon the purchaser. The obligation to notify "without delay" was, however, considerably less specific than the 10-day time limit imposed by the SAJ form. See further pp. 99–100, above and p. 300, below.

39. Unreported, C.A., 4 December 1981.

40. This date will nevertheless usually be extended by any periods in which the buyer is in default of his own obligations.

It should also be noted that, on a strict reading of Article VIII.4, the buyer's right of rescission appears to accrue if there occur 210 days of delay "on account of the causes specified in paragraph 1", regardless of whether the builder has in fact claimed an extension of the delivery date for any or all of the same. It is clear, however, from *K/S Stasupply A/S* v. *Dae Dong Shipbuilding Co. Ltd.*[41] that the reference to "delay" must be taken to mean delay for which the builder is actually seeking a postponement of the delivery date.

In *Stasupply*, the contract, which was on terms identical to those of the SAJ form, provided that the purchasers should be entitled to rescind if the "total accumulated time of all [*force majeure*] delays amounts to 100 days or more". The purchasers, who were seeking to justify their purported rescission of the contract, contended that in computing the relevant period of delay, account should be taken of all non-overlapping events of delay regardless of their impact on the vessel's completion. The shipbuilders, who argued that the effect of individual delays would vary depending upon their impact upon the critical path of the vessel's construction, contended that "all delays" meant delays which actually extended the time needed for her completion.

Hobhouse J. preferred the shipbuilder's interpretation of the article, holding that:

"There can be no doubt that what is being referred to is delay in the sense of being delayed by a certain period. It is delay which involves comparison with a norm[42] and if the norm is achieved, then there has been no delay in the sense that that word is used in this Contract. That fits in with both the commercial and factual reality of using critical path analysis. In my judgment the ordinary meaning of 'the total accumulated time of all delays' is the total of the delays which are causing and are going to cause delay in the delivery of the vessel."

This decision, while plainly correct, highlights a difficulty for the buyer in seeking to use clauses of this type as the basis for rescission of the contract. If it is the effect upon the vessel's completion, rather than the duration of the event initially causing the delay, which counts for the purposes of such a clause, it follows that the builder may, by retrospectively waiving claims for *force majeure* delay, effectively determine whether or not a right of rescission will accrue to the buyer.

SIMON CURTIS

41. See fn. 36 above.
42. i.e. delivery upon the date originally agreed in the contract.

CHAPTER 8

WAR CLAUSES IN TIME CHARTERPARTIES

The subject matter of this chapter may seem to be one only for a small number of specialist maritime lawyers. However, time charterparties[1] almost invariably contain a clause which either brings the contract to an end or gives one of the parties an option to do so if one or more of a number of specified states become "involved" in a "war" or if a war breaks out between them during the currency of the charterparty.[2] Whether the clause applies thus depends on identifying whether the relevant event constituted a "war" and, if so, whether the specified state or states were "involved" in that war or that it had broken out between them. Decisions, often involving very large sums of money, are likely to have to be taken very quickly and, from what was written by some at the time of the Gulf War in 1991, it seems that there is some confusion on the subject. Furthermore, the principles which apply to charterparties may apply to other commercial contracts, although every contract must be considered by reference to its own wording and commercial background.

Over the last half century or so the nature of disputes between states which might amount to a war has altered, as has the manner in which a state may be involved in a war. Although there are almost no decided cases directly on the meaning of "war" in a commercial contract, and the word is often used in company with others, such as "warlike events", "civil commotion" and "armed hostilities", the existence of a war may have important consequences for the parties outside the terms of their contract.

Until the twentieth century there would probably have been no doubt whether a state was involved in a war. The state of facts which constituted a war seems to have been clearly recognised and principles of international law purporting to lay down rules of war emerged. In this century some of these rules have been formalised in the Hague Conventions. How far the rules of international law have much relevance today must be arguable, but if the state of facts amounts to a war in inter-

1. A time charterparty is a contract by which one party (the owner) makes available the services of a vessel and her crew to another (the charterer) for a period of time which may be specified in the charterparty or for the length of an event, such as specified voyage. (The "owner" named in the contract may himself be her time charterer from her registered owner. In such a case he is often referred to as the "disponent owner" but, most confusingly, this expression is sometimes used to refer to a time charterer who has not subchartered the vessel out.)

2. A reason for such a clause may be that the owner may want to make his ship available to his government's war effort or to avoid disputes with the charterer should the vessel be requisitioned by the state the flag of which she flies. It is also a harsh commercial fact that charter hire rates have been known to harden significantly when war breaks out.

national law there seems little room for doubt that this would in most instances be conclusive as to whether a war existed for the purposes of a war cancellation clause in a commercial contract.

1. THE PUBLIC INTERNATIONAL LAW VIEW OF "WAR"

According to the classical statements of public international law, wars only exist between states: "War is a contention between two or more states through their armed forces, for the purpose of overpowering each other and imposing such conditions of peace as the victor pleases".[3] Many definitions of war have been propounded: "War is the state or condition of government contending by force".[4] The state of war itself was defined in English law by Matthew J. in *Driefontein Consolidated Gold Mines Ltd.* v. *Janson*[5] who quoted from Hall on *International Law*[6]: "When differences between states reach a point at which both parties resort to force, or one of them does acts of violence, which the other chooses to look upon as a breach of the peace, the relation of war is set up, in which the combatants may use regulated violence against each other, until one of the two has been brought to accept such terms as his enemy is willing to grant."

Although there is no unanimity of definition, the following would appear necessary: a violent struggle through the application of armed force; use of armed forces, not private individuals; and war between states, not an internal civil war. It also seems to be generally agreed that a war can only exist if one of the belligerents has formally declared war on the other or otherwise formally indicated that a state of war exists between it and its opposing state. Article 1 of The Hague Convention 1907[7] declares that states must " . . . recognise that hostilities between them must not commence without previous and unequivocal warning, which shall take the form either of a declaration of war, giving reasons, or of an ultimatum with a conditional declaration of war".[8]

The outbreak of a war[9] may, at common law, bring about several important results so far as the parties to a contract are concerned. For example, if one of the parties is a subject of the Crown in the United Kingdom and the other becomes an enemy alien, further performance of the contract will be illegal.[10] The counterparty

3. *Oppenheim's International Law*, Vol. II, 7th Edn., p. 202.
4. Westlake, *International Law*, II, p. 1.
5. [1900] 2 Q.B. 339, at p. 343.
6. 4th Edn., p. 63.
7. This was agreed after the Sino–Japanese war in 1904, which Japan commenced without warning.
8. It may be questioned whether this aspect of the classical definition of war in public international law still holds good in every respect today. Has there been any declaration of war since the second world war? There was none at the beginning of the fighting in Korea or Vietnam in the 1950s and 1960s but if these events were not wars in the eyes of public international law, some might ask whether public international law has kept up with the times. Armed conflicts since the second world war have many differences from those which occurred before 1945.
9. At common law there either is a war or there is not a war. "The law recognises a state of peace and a state of war, but . . . it knows nothing of an intermediate state which is neither one thing nor the other—neither peace nor war" *per* Lord Macnaghten in *Janson* v. *Driefontein Consolidated Gold Mines Ltd* [1902] A.C. 484 at p. 497, quoted in McNair and Watts, *The Legal Effects of War* at p. 35.
10. *Esposito* v. *Bowden* (1857) 7 El. & Bl. 763 at p. 783 and see now the Trading With The Enemy Act 1939, s.l.

cannot sue or be sued. In these circumstances the contract will be frustrated. Other examples of the effect at common law of the outbreak of war include the bringing into play of the law of prize.[11] In these contexts the word "war" appears to have the meaning it has in public international law.

2. THE CONSTRUCTION OF TIME CHARTERPARTY WAR CANCELLATION CLAUSES

Most time charterparties are concluded on standard forms. Examples of war cancellation clauses in standard charter forms in current use are:

"In the event of the nation under whose flag the Vessel sails becoming involved in war, hostilities, warlike operations, revolution, or civil commotion, both the Owners and the Charterers may cancel the Charter . . . " (Baltime,[12] clause 21(E))

"In the event of the outbreak of war (whether there be a declaration of war or not) between any two or more of the following countries . . . either the Owners or the Charterers may cancel this Charter Party." (NYPE 93,[13] clause 32)

"If war or hostilities break out between any two or more of the following countries . . . both Owners and Charterers shall have the right to cancel this charter." (Shelltime 4,[14] clause 33)

What is significant about clauses of this type is that their operation does not depend on the vessel being affected by the war: the clause applies if the specified states become "involved" (or whatever verb the clause uses) in a war.

The only directly relevant English authority on the correct meaning of a charterparty war cancellation clause is *Kawasaki Kisen Kabushiki Kaisha of Kobe* v. *Bantham Steamship Company Limited (No. 2)*.[15] In that case the charterparty pro-

11. Enemy merchant ships may be taken and destroyed by warships as "prize", the crews of which ships becoming prisoners of war. The laws of prize are international in substance and prize courts are set up to determine whether ships so taken are indeed prize. Prize may be taken in high seas or enemy waters but not internal waters or neutral territory. Neutral vessels are not subject to prize unless performing unneutral services. They are, however, subject to rights of search to determine the nature of their cargo. Should a prize court find a neutral merchantman guilty of such unneutral services then the ship is liable to one of the following results: "(1) vessel and cargo may be condemned, or (2) the vessel alone may be condemned, or (3) the cargo alone may be condemned, or the vessel and cargo may be released either (4) with, or (5) without, costs and damages, or (6) subject to the payment of the captor's costs of the proceedings." *Oppenheim's International Law*, Vol. II, 7th Edn., p. 872.

12. The Baltime form was the most commonly used time charter form for dry cargoes and is still in frequent use.

13. NYPE 93 is intended to replace NYPE 1946. Whether and to what extent it does so remains to be seen.

14. Shelltime 4 is a typical charter form for use in the mineral oil trade.

15. [1939] 2 K.B. 544. It was applied by Mustill J. in *Spinney's (1948) Ltd.* v. *Royal Insurance Co. Ltd.* [1980] 1 Lloyd's Rep. 406 who made an extended consideration of the authorities in order to decide what was a civil war for the purposes of an insurance policy. His conclusion that there must be two clear sides is surely open to doubt, especially after the nature of the fighting that took place in Liberia in 1989–1990 and in Somalia in 1991. In any event, was an approach *via* the authorities really consistent with that which the Court of Appeal in *Bantham* said should be applied? Perhaps for an insurance policy, but not for a charterparty. The reasoning in *Bantham* was adopted by Sellers J. in a different context in *Luigi Monta of Genoa* v. *Cechofracht Co. Ltd.* [1956] 2 Q.B. 552. See also *New York Life Insurance Co.* v. *Bennion* 158 F. 2d 260 (1946); *New York Life Insurance Co.* v. *Durham* 166 F. 2d 874 (1948); and *Pan American World Airways Inc.* v. *Aetna Casualty and Surety Co.* [1974] 1 Lloyd's Rep. 207 (S.D.N.Y. 1973), affirmed [1975] 1 Lloyd's Rep. 77 (2d Cir). Although the US cases are very valuable, their reasoning would not, perhaps, always be accepted by an English court.

vided that "Charterers and Owners to have the liberty of cancelling the charterparty if War breaks out involving Japan". The owners purported to cancel the charterparty on the ground that such a war had broken out and that Japan was involved. The charterers contended that the cancellation was wrongful and claimed damages. Pursuant to the terms of the charterparty, the dispute was submitted to arbitration in London.

The umpire found that in the Shanghai area of China about 50,000 Japanese soldiers, supported by a fleet and aircraft, were engaged in battle with Chinese forces of over $1\frac{1}{2}$ million men, with heavy casualties on both sides. In North China three Japanese armies, numbering over 100,000 men, were advancing in the teeth of the opposition of Chinese armies numbering 300,000. Japan was maintaining a naval blockade over a 1,000 mile stretch of the coastline of China. The umpire held that, if and so far as it was a question of fact, war had broken out involving Japan.

However, the umpire also found that no declaration of war had been made by either country in relation to the other, that diplomatic relations between the two countries continued uninterrupted and that the Government of the United Kingdom was (in the words of a letter from the Foreign Office) "not at present prepared to say that in their view a state of war existed".[16] These facts, the charterers contended, led to the conclusion that as a matter of law, there was no war in which Japan was involved. The Court of Appeal, upholding the judgment of Goddard J.,[17] rejected the argument that, for the purpose of the construction of the clause, the word "war" had any technical meaning derived from international law. The views of the United Kingdom Government were not conclusive. The matter was to be decided in a "common sense way". What would a commercial person, exercising common sense, say if asked whether the nation in question was involved in a war? On the facts he would say that Japan was involved in a war.

From this case it is possible to draw certain important conclusions for the construction of a commercial contract, such as a charterparty:

(a) The question whether a country is involved in a war is to be answered by the application of common sense and not by applying rules of public international law:

(b) That no declaration of war has been made is not conclusive. Nations may, from time to time, claim that they are in a state of war with each other, without there being any actual fighting on the ground, at sea or in the air. Such was the position for many years between Egypt and Israel until their final peace treaty in 1979. Yet surely common sense would have said that there was not a war between them, save for the obvious times in 1956, 1967 and 1973 when there were periods of heavy fighting which everyone agreed were periods when the two nations could be described as being at war with each other[18];

16. The Foreign Office suggested (as was held by the courts) that the question whether Japan was involved in a war should be answered by reference to the context of the commercial contract from which the question arose rather than by the Foreign Office.

17. (1938) 67 Ll.L. Rep. 131.

18. In Miller, *Marine War Risks* (1990), it is suggested at p. 43 that "throughout the entire period from 1948 to 1979 the two countries were at 'war' in the sense with which we are concerned, if only because they both considered themselves to be at war and acted accordingly". *Sed quaere*.

(c) The view of Her Majesty's Goverment, however formally expressed, that a particular state is or is not at war is not conclusive of the question whether that state is or is not at war.[19] Today many governments are not prepared to make any admission that they are engaged in a war, preferring to use one of a number of euphemisms,[20] at least unless they are the victim of aggression from another[21]; and

(d) That diplomatic relations are not broken off is not a conclusive factor against the existence of a war.

The decision in *Kawasaki Kisen Kabushiki Kaisha* v. *Bantham* is of clear assistance in that what is a war has to be decided by the application of common sense and not by reference to the test of public international law. However, it does not directly assist on what is a war for the purpose of a war clause. Whereas a war seems customarily to have started with some form of declaration by at least one of the parties that it regarded itself as being in a state of war with the other, such is no longer the case. When hundreds of thousands of troops are actually fighting, common sense leads easily to the conclusion that war is in progress. But in many situations of armed conflict since the second world war it might not have been easy, at least in their early stages.

3. WHEN DOES A WAR START?

Before one of the parties starts belligerent acts against the other there is sometimes a period of "shadow boxing" or "eye-ball-to-eye-ball" during which the potential contestants prowl around each other, confront each other and make highly belligerent noises. It may well be that the countries doing this are not involved in a war at that stage. Behind the scenes they may even be negotiating. Both may be secretly doing all they can to make sure that no belligerent act will actually take place. Even the act of mobilising and of moving troops or armaments around the world may not mean that the nation in question is at war, notwithstanding the making of all the normal pronouncements made in a war. On the other hand, there may be wars which take place with very little publicity but with vicious fighting on both sides.

Sometimes a state seems to have slipped gradually into a state of war. The American military action in what is universally referred to as the "Vietnam War" is

19. Although no case decides the point, it must follow from the reasoning of the courts that, for the purposes of construing a commercial contract, a statement of Her Majesty's Government is not conclusive of the question whether the UK is involved in a war. The value of such a statement will, like a similar statement made by any other government, depend on the circumstances in which it was made. In other contexts the view of Her Majesty's Government may be of great importance or even conclusive. In *Spinney's (1948) Ltd.* v. *Royal Insurance Co. Ltd.* [1980] 1 Lloyd's Rep. 406, at p. 426, Mustill J. said that among the matters on which the court would treat the response of the Secretary of State as conclusive was the question whether the UK was at war. While this may be so for many purposes, for the construction of a private commercial contract is surely cannot be.

20. For example, Her Majesty's Government refused to say that the United Kingdom was involved in a war in Egypt in 1956.

21. A state which is invaded by another may well assert that the invader has started a war. Such statements must be treated with caution and may be worthless.

perhaps in this category.[22] The action of combined army, naval and airforce personnel in recapturing the Falkland Islands after an Argentinian invasion in 1982 had several unusual features but common sense would surely say that at least around the islands there was a war. However, British ships traded into Argentinian ports and vice versa, the nationals of each state in the other were not treated as enemy aliens nor was their property sequestrated. It was as if the armed forces of the two nations were engaged in a war in the South Atlantic but elsewhere the nations were not at war. Would this be sufficient for a war cancellation clause?

Some recent events which end in what common sense would probably have described as a war started with a blockade.[23] Some blockades do not end in war[24]; they may even avert it. A naval or air blockade[25] may be intended as a sanction intentionally falling short of war. If so, the state imposing the blockade could not properly be described as being involved in a war. Some blockades are intended to enforce a policy, probably backed by an appropriate United Nations resolution, which is related to a war but it could not be said that those states enforcing the blockade were at war with the state blockaded. The blockade of Serbia in 1993 is an example of such a blockade. Other blockades are intended to enforce a policy, probably also backed by an appropriate United Nations resolution, which is wholly unrelated to any war. The blockade of Haiti by the United States in 1994 to try to enforce the return of President Aristide is an example. In all these instances the state blockaded could not be described as being in a war unless it sought by armed force to break the blockade and the blockading states replied with force. However, a blockade can sometimes be a deliberate act in furtherance of an intention to win a war then in existence, notwithstanding that armed hostilities had not started because one state was still preparing its assault on the territory in dispute.[26] This is why, however much owners and charterers want a quick reply, it is not usually possible to answer the apparently simple question, "Is a naval blockade a warlike operation?" without knowing the full facts.

4. IS AN INVASION ALWAYS A WAR?

When one state invades another, does this *ipso facto* mean that the two states are involved in a war? The answer must surely be, "Not always. Wait and see what happens next". Thus, it seems likely that when the United States captured Grenada

22. Nevertheless, in *Hammond* v. *National Life and Accident Insurance Co.*, (1971) La. App. 243 S.O. 2nd 902 it was held that there was no "time of war" in Vietnam for the purposes of an insurance policy. Perhaps this case can be best understood by appreciating that if the court had decided otherwise, the plaintiff, a soldier injured while playing football in an army camp in Vietnam, would otherwise have been unable to recover under the policy.

23. For example, the blockade of Iraq which preceded the military action which recaptured Kuwait after the Iraqi invasion in 1990.

24. For example, the blockade imposed by the United States on the supply of missiles to Cuba in October 1962.

25. For its own reasons the United States sometimes prefers to refer to what the United Kingdom would refer to as a "blockade" as an "interdict".

26. The blockade of Iraq in 1990 was, however, probably not such a blockade because the intention was to enforce an Iraqi withdrawal of Kuwait rather than a deliberate act of war. Those blockading lacked any *animus belligerendi*.

in October 1983 in order to oust its then government the United States was not involved in a war. The same may hold good for the Argentinian invasion of South Georgia and the Falkland Islands in April 1982 and for the invasion of Kuwait by Iraq in 1990 (although both invasions were soon followed by war). If the invasion of Panama by the United States in December 1989 to oust the government of General Noriega had been a war, its significance is not hard to see in the light of the fact that even the most modern war cancellation clauses often apply in the event of war between, *inter alia*, the United States and the country of the vessel's flag. When there is no armed resistance other than token, it is hard to characterise the situation as a war, however much the invaded state claims that a war is in progress. Still less would it be correct to say that just because its armed forces have been engaged in some belligerent activity a state has necessarily been involved in a war.[27]

5. IS THERE A TOUCHSTONE?

The above considerations lead to only one conclusion: there is no touchstone by which it can be decided for the purposes of a war cancellation clause whether a state of war exists. The question must be decided as a question of fact[28] to be determined by reference to whether a reasonable well-informed person would say there was a war in progress.

6. EVIDENCE OF WAR

One most important source of evidence is the manner in which newspapers and other organs of the media describe the situation.[29] Headlines in newspapers such as "Britain in Gulf War", and reports and articles in the press, or on the radio or television, could be highly material. Of course, the occasional exaggeration is likely and what is said in countries where the media are government-controlled or controlled by a pan-global corporation may be of little value. Nevertheless, if there is a general agreement in media that are free to express their own views that a particular country is or is not involved in a war, this may be very significant evidence.

27. Any act of self defence by a "peace keeping" force could not mean that the state from which the force was drawn was involved in a war. Even such belligerent acts as air strikes by United States war planes in Bosnia in 1994, designed to prevent further attack on Sarajevo, surely did not mean that the United States was at war. On the same reasoning it could not be said that the United States was involved in a war in Somalia in 1992.

28. There can be no room for doubt that a finding of an arbitration tribunal on whether any particular state was involved in a war would be treated as a finding of fact (see *Pioneer Shipping* v. *B.T.P. Tioxide (The Nema)* [1982] A.C. 724) open to challenge only within the limited area explained in *Edwards* v. *Bairstow* [1956] A.C. 14.

29. In *Kawasaki Kisen Kaisha* v. *Bantham* Sir Wilfred Greene M.R. said (at p. 553) that if a court were unable to take judicial notice of whether this country was at war, that question could only be answered by reference to the executive. But can this still be regarded as correct, especially if the British Government were unwilling, for sound diplomatic reasons, to state what to a reasonable man of business would seem obvious?

7. WHEN IS A STATE "INVOLVED" IN A WAR?

Even if it is proved that a war was in existence at the relevant time, it is still necessary to prove that the specified state or states were involved in the war or (as appropriate) that war had broken out between them. Until recently this would probably have presented no problem but matters are not now so straightforward. Wars may now be fought by troops wearing the blue beret of the United Nations under the ultimate command of the Security Council, or, as in the case of the Gulf War in 1991, by an uncertain alliance, in that war referred to as "the coalition" but never defined. Perhaps the most interesting question is to ask which states were involved in that war. Clearly, the United States, the United Kingdom, Saudi Arabia, France, Kuwait and other Gulf States on one side and Iraq on the other. Italian aircraft took part in an early air strike (one pilot became a prisoner of war). Belgium had warplanes in Turkey and naval ships in the Gulf but none fired a shot. A Belgian medical team stood by in Cyprus to receive casualties, but none came. Ammunition, weapons and cash were contributed to those actually fighting. Would a commercial person applying common sense have said, for example, that Belgium was "involved" in the war? Perhaps not.

If a state such as Belgium presents problems, what of those whose contribution to the war effort was to make substantial payments towards the expense of the forces of the principal members of the coalition? Traditional thinking is that a state could not be involved in a war without at least its armed forces being involved. However, might the Japanese taxpayer not say with some justification that his country was deeply involved? Although it could not contribute armed forces, it contributed huge sums of money to help pay for the armed forces of others. Why is this not a sufficient involvement? Is it now good law to say: "They also serve who only stand and pay"?

8. WHEN MUST NOTICE OF TERMINATION BE GIVEN?

It is arguable that in law the notice of termination under a war clause has to be served while the alleged war is still in existence. Even if that is wrong, the option to terminate probably must be exercised before such time has elapsed as would lead the other party to think that no notice of termination would be served. In any event, a party who gives notice of termination after the alleged war has ended will probably elicit little sympathy from either arbitrators or a court.

9. "WARLIKE OPERATIONS"

Finally, it is necessary to sound a word of warning. Some contracts use the words "war or warlike operations". In the context under discussion in this chapter, the expression "warlike operations" has not been defined[30] or even considered. In the

30. Nor, in the light of *Bantham*, should it be.

context of an insurance policy[31] the expression was defined by Atkinson J. in *Clan Line Steamers Ltd.* v. *Liverpool and London War Risks Insurance Association Ltd.*:

"A warlike operation is one which forms an actual or intended belligerent act or series of acts by belligerent forces. It may be performed preparatory to the actual act or acts of belligerency, or it may be performed after such act or acts, but there must be a connection sufficiently close between the act in question and the belligerent act or acts to enable a tribunal to say . . . that it formed part of acts of belligerency."[32]

This passage was cited with approval by Mustill J. in *Spinney's (1948) Ltd.* v. *Royal Insurance Co. Ltd.*,[33] who stressed that the acts in question "must be done in the context of a war".[34]

To reason from "warlike operations" to "war" may lead to the wrong result. The only safe course to take is to ask whether an ordinary commercial man or woman, applying common sense, would say that there was a war and, if so, whether it had the relationship with the specified state or states required by the contract.

BRIAN DAVENPORT Q.C.

31. The cases on the f. c. and s. clause in the old form of marine policy which considered whether a ship was lost in "consequence of a warlike operation" are not only often of doubtful validity in their own field but are a siren song in the present context. The meaning of the clause, accepted in such cases as *Commonwealth Shipping Representative* v. *Peninsular and Oriental Branch Service* [1923] A.C. 191, was that any ship carrying war stores was engaged in a warlike operation but the question under a charterparty war clause must be answered by asking whether a commercial man or woman, applying common sense and not cases of doubtful authority in a different context, would consider that the country in question was engaged in a warlike operation. He or she would surely not say that a country which charters a ship in time of peace to carry, say, army ambulances is thereby engaged in a warlike operation. This illustrates the irrelevance of the f. c. and s. line of cases, of which some sense was made in *Yorkshire Dale S.S. Co. Ltd.* v. *Minister of War Transport (The Coxwold)* [1942] A.C. 691. The cases are probably beyond consistent analysis but in the present context they are irrelevant: the construction of a different clause in a different context cannot be used to answer the question that a business man or woman must answer, using common sense.

32. [1943] K.B. 209 at p. 221.

33. [1980] 1 Lloyd's Rep. 406 at p. 437.

34. In *Pan American World Airways Inc.* v. *Aetna Casualty and Surety Co.* [1975] 1 Lloyd's Rep. 77 at p. 95 the court stressed that there was no warrant for reading "warlike operations" so as to include the activities of non-governmental bodies in places far away from any war. In the context of this chapter this could not be directly relevant because the charterparty war clause is concerned with whether a nation is engaged in warlike activities. But it might be argued that a nation acting against belligerent non-governmental bodies (usually described by their enemies as "terrorists" and their friends as "freedom fighters") was engaged in a warlike operation. On both the English and the American authorities (in so far as material) the argument would fail.

PART IV

APPLYING THE PRINCIPLES: INDUSTRIAL ACTION AND BUILDING CONTRACTS

CHAPTER 9

THE PRIVATE LAW EFFECTS OF INDUSTRIAL ACTION

1. INTRODUCTION

Many contracts are unperformed because industrial protest impairs one party's capacity to perform them. Such industrial protest may arise within the non-performing contractor's own workforce, or within that of some third party such as a supplier on whose deliveries the contractor depends for performance of his obligations. In such an event, the law may be required to decide which contracting party should bear the resultant loss. Should it be the party whose performance is impaired, or should that party be relieved from the obligation to perform, leaving the other to absorb the cost of non-performance as best he can? Such questions involve the critical application of concepts of frustration and *force majeure*.[1]

One might, of course, question whether industrial action merits special treatment in this context. Contracts can be disrupted by physical, economic or political events, and in each case the considerations determining the resultant allocation of responsibility are essentially the same: did the contractual obligation extend to the events which have occurred, has that obligation been frustrated, is the employer vicariously liable for any wrongdoing which has occurred, and does the contract contain any material exculpatory term? At first sight, there seems no reason why the judicial approach to industrial action as a factor affecting civil obligations should differ from the approach to other adverse phenomena.

To an extent, this argument is persuasive. There may be little difference in principle, for example, between the dislocation of a charterparty by an external strike among stevedores and its dislocation by detention, fire or explosion. It is submitted, however, that a contractor's liability for disruption by industrial protest occupies a special category for several reasons.

First, it is an example of potential liability for the deliberate acts of others. This is most obviously true of domestic industrial action: a strike among the employer's workforce may cause him to miss delivery dates, a work-to-rule may cause damage to customers' property, a picket or mass occupation may block access to money or goods. More rarely, the question might arise in relation to external industrial protest: an employer's trading policies, for example, may provoke a strike among his supplier's workforce, producing a potential breach of the employer's contract with a customer. Although the issues are far from congruent, the policy considerations

1. As to whether, and in what circumstances, a strike constitutes *force majeure* under French law, see Nicholas, above pp. 25–26.

which have produced a special body of authority affecting tortious liability for independent human conduct[2] might justify some individuality of approach towards an employer's contractual liability for such conduct.[3]

Secondly, a party whose interests are threatened by industrial protest may have alternative remedies against the relevant employees or their trade unions and union officials. Such redress may be available to a customer of the employer[4] or to the employer himself. Labour law remedies are beyond the scope of this chapter, but they clearly cannot be disregarded in assessing a contractor's common law liability to his customers. For example, the contractor might argue that his customer's failure to take injunctive action against the protesters is a failure to mitigate loss.[5] More realistically, the customer might point to the contractor's own failure to take action against the protesters as a ground for depriving him of some defence otherwise open to him: for example, a *force majeure* clause.[6] Again, the statutory immunity of his workforce or their trade union may affect an employer's common law liability. The discovery of such immunity might lead to the conclusion that no tort was committed by the protesters, and thus that no vicarious liability can be attached to their employer.[7] Conversely, a denial of such immunity may render the employer vicariously responsible to a wider range of claimants than his immediate contractual neighbours. This possibility may prove especially significant in a case of economic duress. If, for example, it is accepted that a particular act of duress by the

2. *Smith* v. *Littlewoods Organisation Ltd.* [1987] A.C. 241. And see McKendrick (1989) 18 I.L.J. 161.

3. The questions are, of course, distinguishable on several grounds. For example, contractual liability is normally strict, whereas that in tort is normally fault-based. But that does not mean that the results produced by the two forms of obligation may not coincide in a given case. For example, in a case where the contractor's performance is threatened by industrial protest in a supplier's workforce, the lack of control which might justify exonerating the contractor from liability in tort for the protesters' conduct might also indicate that his contractual undertaking did not extend to performance in the events which occurred, or that an explicit *force majeure* clause exonerates the contractor from such liability. More generally, of course, a detailed commercial contract may be construed as prescribing the exclusive sum of the contractor's obligations in tort as well as in contract: below, pp. 178, 193.

4. Note particularly in this context s. 22 of the Trade Union Reform and Employment Rights Act 1993, adding a new section (s. 235A) to the Trade Union and Labour Relations (Consolidation) Act 1992. Under s. 235A(1) of the 1992 Act, an individual may now apply to the High Court (or the Court of Session) for an appropriate order wherever he claims that (a) a trade union or other person has done or is likely to do an unlawful act to induce any person to take part (or to continue to take part) in industrial action, and (b) an effect or likely effect of the industrial action is (or will be) to (i) prevent or delay the supply of goods or services, or (ii) reduce the quality of goods or services supplied, to the individual making the claim. Entitlement to an order does not depend on the applicant's entitlement to be supplied with the goods or services in question: s. 235A(3). The applicant may apply to the Commissioner for Protection Against Unlawful Industrial Action for assistance in relation to proceedings under s. 235A: see generally s. 235B, 235C of the 1992 Act.

5. See especially s. 235A of the Trade Union and Labour Relations (Consolidation) Act 1992 (above fn. 4).

6. Cf. *Oosten* v. *Hay Haulers', Dairy Employees' and Helpers' Union* 45 Cal. 2d 784; 291 P. 2d 17 (1955).

7. Cf., however, those authorities which suggest that the mere existence of a procedural bar to the recovery of damages in tort from the employee does not preclude the imposition of vicarious liability upon the employer: *Broom* v. *Morgan* [1953] 1 Q.B. 597; *Smith* v. *Moss* [1940] 1 K.B. 424; and see *Imperial Chemical Industries Ltd.* v. *Shatwell* [1965] A.C. 656 at 686 *per* Lord Pearce; *Parker* v. *Commonwealth* (1968) 118 C.L.R. 271 at 276 *per* Windeyer J.; cf. *Shaddock (L) and Assoc Pty Ltd.* v. *Parramatta City Council* (1981) 150 C.L.R. 225 at 251 *per* Mason J. Further, in an action against a contractual defendant for breach of a non-delegable duty (such as that owed by a bailee to his bailor) it may be immaterial whether the employee whose act actually causes the relevant damage has committed a tort against the claimant or not: see, e.g., *R.M. & R. Log Ltd.* v. *Texada Towing Company Ltd., Minette and Johnson, The Coast Prince* [1967] 2 Lloyd's Rep. 290.

workforce or their trade union both constitutes an independent tort and falls beyond the relevant statutory immunity, the employer may be vicariously liable for that tort.[8] Even in the absence of such liability, he may be disabled from enforcing a negotiated settlement with his customers if the settlement was procured by economic duress emanating from his employees and the employer knew that such duress was being exerted.[9] In short, where a protest centres on the conduct of the employer's customers (or where his workforce otherwise perceive those customers as the appropriate parties to relieve their complaint) the employer may find it imprudent to wash his hands of the matter and leave his workforce and his customers to fight it out.

For the present, only two observations are offered. Clearly, no decision concerning the pursuit of redress against the immediate authors of an industrial protest can be fully informed without first analysing the effects of that protest upon the employer's legal relations with his commercial neighbours. Moreover, it seems desirable for the policies bearing upon each issue and the resultant solutions to correspond.

This brings one to the third reason for special treatment. When granting remedies in an industrial context, judges have sometimes paid regard to the enhancement of industrial relations or to the avoidance of industrial strife. Admittedly, such references are commoner where discretionary remedies are sought, such as an injunction to command the delivery up of goods immobilised by industrial action.[10] But even in damages cases one can detect an occasional preference for a result which promotes industrial harmony over one calculated to foster discord. In *Morris* v. *Ford Motor Co. Ltd.*,[11] Roberts (a Ford employee) negligently injured Morris (an employee of Cameron Cleaning Services) while Morris was working on Ford's premises. Morris recovered damages from Ford, who were legally answerable for

8. The question whether acts of economic duress are independently actionable in tort is a controversial one, which cannot be examined in detail here. In *Universe Tankships Inc.* v. *International Transport Workers' Federation, The Universe Sentinel* [1983] 1 A.C. 366, Lord Scarman held that economic duress did constitute a tort, a position tentatively supported by Neill L.J. in *Dimskal Shipping Co. S.A.* v. *International Transport Workers' Federation, The Evia Luck* [1990] 1 Lloyd's Rep. 319 at 324 (dissenting); cf. however, the decision on appeal to the House of Lords [1992] 2 A.C. 152, where no opinion was considered to be necessary on this point, but Lord Goff of Chieveley emphasised (at 169) that "conduct does not have to be tortious to constitute duress for the purpose of English Law; this is so even at common law, and still more so if one has regard to the equitable doctrine of undue influence as an extended form of duress". See also at 170 *per* Lord Lowry. The proposition that economic duress is *per se* a tort is vigorously contested by Wedderburn: see Clerk and Lindsell, *Torts* (18th Edn.), paras. 15–06, 15–15, 15–20, 15–29, and Wedderburn's letter to *The Times*, 8 April 1982. In *Banque Financière de la Cité S.A.* v. *Westgate Insurance Co. Ltd.* [1990] 1 Q.B. 665 at 780, C.A., Slade L.J. observed that: "Since duress and undue influence as such give rise to no claim for damages, we see no reason in principle why non-disclosure as such should do so." The point as to duress was not mentioned on appeal: [1990] 2 All E.R. 947; [1991] 2 A.C. 249, H.L. For a general analysis of the difficulties of Lord Scarman's position, see Carty and Evans [1983] J.B.L. 218.

9. *Chitty on Contracts*, (27th Edn., 1994), para. 7–012.

10. E.g., *Harold Stephen & Co. Ltd.* v. *Post Office* [1977] 1 W.L.R. 1172; cf. *Howard E. Perry & Co. Ltd.* v. *British Railways Board* [1980] 2 All E.R. 579, and see *Parker* v. *Camden London Borough Council* [1986] Ch. 162, especially at pp. 173–174 *per* Donaldson M.R. (who accepted the proposition advanced by Geoffrey Lane L.J. in *Harold Stephen* v. *Post Office*, above, that a court should only in very rare and most extreme circumstances "interfere by way of mandatory injunction in the delicate mechanism of industrial disputes and industrial negotiations", but went on to hold that this was an exceptional case meriting injunctive relief); but cf. *Taylor* v. *N.U.M. (Yorkshire Area)* [1984] I.R.L.R. 445, at p. 450, where Nicholls L.J. refused to follow dicta of Geoffrey Lane L.J. in *Harold Stephen*.

11. [1973] Q.B. 792.

Roberts' conduct. Ford in turn recovered those damages from Cameron, because Ford's contract with Cameron required Cameron to indemnify Ford for any liability Ford suffered towards Cameron employees. Cameron now sought to recover those damages in turn from Roberts, whose negligence had caused the injury in the first place. The Court of Appeal held that they could not succeed.

There was no doubt that Ford could, in theory, have sued Roberts. He broke his contract of employment with them by injuring Morris, and Ford could have recovered damages equivalent to what Morris had recovered from them.[12] But it was clear that Ford would not have done so; although not represented in the action, they firmly opposed this action by Cameron. Their labour relations officer testified that Ford never sued their employees because to do so would be to invite a strike, and that if Cameron themselves could sue a Ford employee serious industrial repercussions would follow. The court's decision that Cameron could not recover was variously rationalised,[13] but Lord Denning M.R., at least, remarked that the resultant threat to industrial harmony made the extension of the remedy unthinkable:

"Fords would never, for a moment, have dreamt of suing their own servant Roberts. If they did so, all the men would have come out on strike . . . If [Cameron] are right in their contention . . . it would imperil good industrial relations. If the man himself is made to pay, he will feel much aggrieved . . . If the servant is to bear the risk, his wages ought to be increased to cover it . . . Everyone knows that risks such as these are covered by insurance. To make the servant personally liable would not only lead to a strike. It would be positively unjust."[14]

James L.J. hinted at a similar view, observing that the argument on which Cameron sought to hang their alleged right "was inoperative in an industrial setting in which [it] would be unacceptable and unrealistic".[15]

2. EXCULPATORY TERMS

Often, responsibility for industrial action will be dictated by purely commercial considerations. Especially in a case of domestic action, the contractor may find it expedient to absorb the cost of non-performance, whatever the strict legal position. It is not intended to explore such decisions in this chapter; they are the preserve of the businessman rather than the lawyer. But parties entrusted with them will clearly make them more effectively if they are informed as to the underlying legal position. Moreover, those negotiating a compromise in the aftermath of an industrial protest will bargain more effectively if they understand its legal implications.

Other contractors will prefer to distribute responsibility in advance. In such a case, the question is largely one of construction. Subject to the normal con-

12. Cf. *Lister* v. *Romford Ice & Cold Storage Co. Ltd.* [1955] A.C. 555. The decision itself is an example of the difficulties which can follow where a court disregards the demands of industrial harmony in identifying common law obligations. It was followed by the Report of an Inter-Departmental Committee (1959) and a gentlemen's agreement among insurance companies. Unfortunately, that agreement did not extend to situations like that in *Morris* v. *Ford Motor Co. Ltd.* [1973] Q.B. 792 (above).

13. See the discussion in Birds, *Modern Insurance Law* (3rd Edn., 1993) pp. 296–297.

14. [1973] Q.B. 792, at p. 798; and see at p. 801.

15. *Ibid.*, at p. 815. Cf. *Canadian Brotherhood etc.* v. *B.C. Airlines Ltd.* [1971] 1 W.W.R. 39, at p. 44, *per* Dohm J.

straints,[16] contracting parties can fashion their bargain as they choose.[17] If one party assumes responsibility for industrial action, that assumption is normally binding; the same is true of any other distribution which the parties choose to adopt. The party who fears that his delivery of goods or services will be affected by industrial action may, for example, purport to disclaim the responsibility to perform, or to limit his liability to an acceptable amount, or to recover that liability from another party: perhaps the other contractor himself. In such a situation, the conventional considerations apply.[18] Foremost among such considerations are the language of the contract, its surrounding circumstances, and the intentions which can be derived from it.

Unfortunately, references to contractual autonomy fall short of providing a complete solution. It does not always occur to the parties to provide explicitly for this eventuality. Even where the question has occurred to them, they may prefer to leave the position unstated rather than to articulate it in a manner which may give cause for regret. Further, the use of standard forms (many of which include industrial action among the excepted events)[19] may fit the facts uneasily. The effect of the adopted stereotype may be hard to square with the reality of the event which has occurred, or with the parties' intentions in that event.

There is a further aspect to the problem. When parties expressly provide for defective performance resulting from industrial action, that provision may march under one of several banners. It may take the form of an exception or limitation of liability, it may operate as an indemnity, or it may qualify as a *force majeure* clause. An exception clause may be demarcatory, pre-empting the relevant obligation, or defensive, admitting the obligation but raising a procedural bar to the recovery of damages for its breach.[20] Each of these types of exculpatory term has its peculiarities, and the effects of each can differ bewilderingly. For example, we are told that clauses purporting to exclude liability outright merit more sympathetic treatment now that statute has reduced the need for meticulous construction.[21] Even so, the applicable principles of construction appear more exacting than those governing limitation clauses.[22] Virtually no authority exists as to where an insurance clause,[23]

16. *Viz.*, the principles of illegality, mistake, fraud, misrepresentation, duress and undue influence, and the principles dictating the construction of contractual terms in general.

17. *Compagnie Commerciale Sucres et Denrées* v. *C. Czarnikow Ltd.*, *The Naxos* [1990] 1 W.L.R. 1337, H.L.

18. See generally Lewison, *Interpretation of Contracts* (1989).

19. For examples, see pp. 9–10 above.

20. Coote, *Exception Clauses* (1964); Palmer and Yates (1981) 41 C.L.J. 108; pp. 10–18 above.

21. E.g., *Photo Production Ltd.* v. *Securicor Transport Ltd.* [1980] A.C. 827, at p. 851, *per* Lord Diplock; *EE Caledonia Ltd.* v. *Orbit Valve Co. Europe* [1994] 2 Lloyd's Rep. 239, at p. 247, *per* Steyn L.J., cf. *Schenker & Co. (Aust.) Pty. Ltd.* v. *Malpas Equipment and Services Pty. Ltd.* [1990] V.R. 834, esp. *per* McGarvie J.A.; and see *Macy* v. *Qazi* (1987) *The Times*, 13 January.

22. *Ailsa Craig Fishing Co. Ltd.* v. *Malvern Fishing Co. Ltd.* [1983] 1 W.L.R. 964; *The Antares (No. 2)* [1987] 1 Lloyd's Rep. 424 but cf. *Darlington Futures Ltd.* v. *Delco Australia Pty. Ltd.* (1986) 161 C.L.R. 500, where such differential treatment was disapproved. See generally, as to the Australian approach to construing exclusion and limitation clauses, *Schenker* v. *Malpas* (above); *Nissho Iwai Australian Ltd.* v. *Malaysian International Shipping Corp. Bhd.* (1989) 63 A.L.J.R. 468; *Shoard* v. *Palmer* (1989) 98 F.L.R. 402; *The Antwerpen* [1994] 1 Lloyd's Rep. 213.

23. As in *Mark Rowlands Ltd.* v. *Berni Inns Ltd.* [1986] Q.B. 211; *Scottish Special Housing Association* v. *Wimpey Construction U.K. Ltd.* [1986] 2 All E.R. 957; cf. *Norwich City Council* v. *Harvey* [1989] 1 All E.R. 1180; *Surrey Heath Borough Council* v. *Lovell Construction Ltd.* (1990) 48 Build. L.R.

or a limited indemnity clause, fits into this scale of interpretative techniques.[24] Similar uncertainty attends the construction of *force majeure* clauses. Recent authority[25] suggests, for example, that the ability of a *force majeure* clause to relieve the *proferens* from liability for events caused by his negligence is dictated by principles akin to those governing defensive exclusion clauses.[26] But if a *force majeure* clause operates at the logically prior stage of determining the relevant obligation, it may be preferable to discard those artificial principles in favour of a simpler technique directed to the ordinary commercial meaning of the term.[27] The scant available evidence suggests that this is the judicial approach to clauses which, by requiring one party to insure, impliedly relieve the other of responsibility for negligence.[28]

Some of the problems of establishing the contractual identity of *force majeure* clauses have been explored in an earlier chapter.[29] In this context, it is sufficient to remark that anti-commitment clauses remain the subject of extensive judicial supervision and intervention, and that there are many modern cases where such terms have failed.[30] One cannot, therefore, be sure that a disclaimer will prove universally effective. If it fails, the court must resort to determining whether, irrespective of the clause, there existed an obligation to perform in the precise events which occurred.

The challenges of drafting a clause which will safeguard the contractor against liability for domestic industrial action are exemplified by two modern decisions of the Court of Appeal. In *B. & S. Contracts and Design Ltd.* v. *Victor Green Publications Ltd.*[31] the plaintiff company contracted for the erection of certain exhibition stands at Olympia. Employees of the subsidiary company to whom they allocated this task were informed some two months before the date of performance that they were to be made redundant shortly after the Olympia contract had been performed. Certain of these employees waited until immediately before the performance date, and then refused to carry out the erection of the exhibition stands unless extra sums by way of severance payment (totalling some £9,000) were paid to all members of the subsidiary company which the plaintiffs were planning to

113; *National Oilwell (U.K.) Ltd.* v. *Davy Offshore Ltd.* [1993] 2 Lloyd's Rep. 582; *National Trust for Places of Historic Interest or Natural Beauty* v. *Haden Young Ltd.* (1994) *The Times*, 11 August (C.A.); [1994] B.L.M. (September) 8.

24. Palmer (1982) 45 M.L.R. 327.

25. *Sonat Offshore S.A.* v. *Amerada Hess Development Ltd.* (1987) 39 Build. L.R. 1; *J. Lauritzen A.S.* v. *Wijsmuller B.V.* (*The Super Servant Two*) [1990] 1 Lloyd's Rep. 1, at pp. 6–7, *per* Bingham L.J.; and see at p. 12, *per* Dillon L.J.

26. *Canada Steamship Line Ltd.* v. *The King* [1952] A.C. 192, at p. 208, *per* Lord Morton of Henryton; cf. *Lamport & Holt Lines Ltd.* v. *Coubro & Scrutton (M. & I.)* (*The Raphael*) [1982] 2 Lloyd's Rep. 42; *EE Caledonia* v. *Orbit Valve Co. Europe* [1994] 2 Lloyd's Rep. 239 (indemnity clause).

27. See pp. 12–14 above.

28. *Scottish Special Housing Association* v. *Wimpey Construction U.K. Ltd.* [1986] 2 All E.R. 957; cf. *Mineralimportexport and Ors.* v. *Eastern Mediterranean Maritime Ltd.* (*The Golden Leader*) [1980] 2 Lloyd's Rep. 573; *Surrey Heath Borough Council* v. *Lovell Construction Ltd.* (1990) 48 Build. L.R. 113.

29. See pp. 10–18 above.

30. E.g., *Dorset County Council* v. *Southern Felt Roof Co.* (1989) 48 Build. L.R. 96; and see the *Surrey Heath* case, above; *Ackerman* v. *Protim Services Ltd.* [1988] B.T.L.C. 353; [1988] 2 E.G.L.R. 259.

31. [1984] I.C.R. 419, affirming the decision of Sir Douglas Frank Q.C. [1982] I.C.R. 654; noted by Palmer and Catchpole (1985) 48 M.L.R. 102. Cf. *Reader* v. *South Eastern and Chatham Railway Co.* (1921) 38 T.L.R. 192; *MacMillan Bloedel Ltd.* v. *British Columbia Hydro and Power Authority* (1992) 98 D.L.R. (4th) 492.

close down. The plaintiffs communicated their dilemma to the other contracting party (the defendants) who, fearing for their interests if the work were not undertaken, offered to pay half of the demanded sum. A cheque for £4,500 was forwarded and the work proceeded according to plan, but on presentation of the plaintiffs' final account the defendants deducted £4,500. In response to the plaintiffs' action for that amount, the defendants argued (a) that their promise to pay it was unsupported by consideration from the plaintiffs, because the plaintiffs were undertaking no more in return for that payment than they were already legally bound to do under the original contract; and (b) that, whether the plaintiffs had furnished the necessary consideration or not, the payment had been extorted from the defendants in circumstances amounting to economic duress, thereby rendering their agreement to pay the extra £4,500 voidable in law.[32]

It is the first defence which mainly concerns us at this stage. The plaintiffs contended that they had an answer to this defence in a term of the contract which was prefaced with the words "*Force majeure*". Broadly stated, this clause declared that while "every effort will be made to carry out a contract based on an estimate", its due performance was "subject to variation or cancellation owing to . . . strikes . . . work-to-rule or go-slow or overtime bans, lock-outs . . . or any other cause beyond (the plaintiffs') control". According to the plaintiffs, this clause entitled them to resile from the contract once the labour dispute occurred. Thus, when they agreed to continue performance in spite of the clause, they were undertaking to do something which they were not legally obliged to do. They had, therefore, supplied consideration for the promise of additional payment.[33]

The Court of Appeal rejected this argument and held that the *force majeure* clause did not entitle the plaintiffs to abandon the contract. The reason was to be found in the wording of the clause itself. It stated that every effort would be made to carry out a contract such as this. That constituted, according to the court, a binding promise to which the ensuing exemption from liability was subordinate. Taken as a whole, the clause obliged the plaintiffs, even in the event of industrial action, to exercise reasonable efforts to ensure that the contract was performed. Only

32. *Quaere*, whether this second argument was logically dissociable from the first. If there were no justification for the plaintiffs' withdrawal from the original transaction, such withdrawal would constitute a breach, thereby affording the necessary threat of unlawful conduct for the purposes of establishing economic duress. It is an open question whether such duress could have existed had the plaintiffs' decision to withdraw been justified by the *force majeure* clause (see below). It is generally accepted that a mere threat *not* to contract with the threatened party (or to re-contract, following a valid release) does not constitute economic duress, because (*inter alia*) a mere failure to contract is not illegitimate or unlawful conduct: see generally *Smith* v. *William Charlick Ltd.* (1924) 124 C.L.R. 38; but cf. *The Medina* (1876) 1 P. 272; *The Port Caledonia and The Anna* [1903] P. 184. In extreme cases it might be argued that the promisor's commercial vulnerability amounts to a special disability or incapacity, sufficient to justify relief from the resultant contract on the ground of the other party's unconscionable dealing: see generally *Boustany* v. *Pigott* (1993) 42 W.I.R. 175 (P.C.); *Louth* v. *Diprose* (1993) 67 A.L.R. 95 (H.C. Aust.); *Commercial Bank of Australia Ltd.* v. *Amadio* (1983) 151 C.L.R. 447 (H.C. Aust.); cf. *Fry* v. *Lane* (1888) 40 Ch.D. 312. But such relief appears improbable in a commercial context.

33. Of course, even in the absence of the excuse for withdrawal afforded by an effective *force majeure* clause, continued performance might constitute consideration if the decision of the Court of Appeal in *Williams* v. *Roffey Bros. & Nicholls (Contractors) Ltd.* [1991] 1 Q.B. 1 is followed. See generally Adams and Brownsword (1990) 53 M.L.R. 536; Treitel, *Law of Contract* (8th Edn.) pp. 89–90. This assumes, of course, that (as was accepted in *Williams* itself) the promisee has exerted no economic duress.

when such efforts had been made and proved unavailing were the plaintiffs released from the duty to perform.

Here, no such efforts had been made. The plaintiffs had failed to settle the dispute from their own resources when it would have been reasonable to expect them to do so. As the court observed, the dispute involved no significant issue of principle on which the employer might reasonably find it necessary to "take a stand"; and there would have been no risk of further industrial ransom through a concession by the plaintiffs on this occasion, because the workforce were about to be dismissed in any event.[34] The defendants had even originally offered to advance the plaintiffs half of the demanded sum of £9,000 by way of temporary loan in order to tide them over the contract period, so continued performance was economically possible. And if the fault for the dilemma lay anywhere as between the parties to the litigation, it lay with the plaintiffs, who had precipitated the threat of industrial action at a time when they knew this important contract would need to be performed.[35]

The Court of Appeal went on to hold that the agreement regarding continued performance resulted from economic duress and could be avoided by the defendants. It made no difference that the suggestion as to payment of the £4,500 had emanated originally from the defendants and not from the plaintiffs.[36] The plaintiffs had effectively "painted the defendants into a corner" by presenting a situation which left them no realistic option but to assume the cost of resolving the dispute. All the necessary ingredients for a plea of economic duress[37] were satisfied here: the dilemma had coerced the defendants to the extent of "vitiating their consent" to the revised arrangement; the threat presented to them by the plaintiffs was a threat to do something unlawful (*viz.*, to commit a breach of contract); the defendants had protested about having to comply with the agreement at the time of doing so; and they had taken sufficiently prompt steps to disavow it afterwards.

It is submitted that *B. & S. Contracts* is notable for several reasons. First, of course, it shows that a clause directed to alleviating the liability of a contracting party for losses caused by industrial action can fail by virtue of inadequate wording. But it also shows that courts are willing, when they consider it necessary, to make judgments about what is or is not a "reasonable" response to domestic industrial action on the part of the beleaguered contractor. These are delicate matters, and one wonders whether judges are equipped to quantify the desirability of compliance with industrial demands.[38] Of course, if the contract demands this analysis,

34. [1984] I.C.R. 419, at pp. 424–425, *per* Eveleigh L.J., pp. 426–427, *per* Griffiths L.J., p. 428, *per* Kerr L.J. But both Eveleigh and Griffiths L.JJ. did not deny that in principle a *force majeure* clause could apply in a situation of this kind.

35. *Ibid.*

36. *Ibid.*, at p. 424, *per* Eveleigh L.J., and p. 426, *per* Griffiths L.J.; but cf. *Williams* v. *Roffey Bros & Nicholls (Contractors) Ltd.* [1991] 1 Q.B. 1, at p. 21, *per* Purchas L.J.

37. See generally *Atlas Express Ltd.* v. *Kafco (Importers and Distributors) Ltd.* [1989] 1 All E.R. 641; Chitty, *op. cit.* above, paras. 7–001 *et seq*.

38. For strong judicial expression of a comparable reluctance in the context of the Trade Disputes Act 1906, see the speech of Lord Scarman in *Express Newspapers Ltd.* v. *McShane* [1980] A.C. 672, at p. 694: "It would be a strange and embarrassing task for a judge to be called upon to review the tactics of a party to a trade dispute and to determine whether in the view of the court the tactic employed was likely to further, or advance, that party's side of the dispute . . . It would need very clear statutory

the court must conduct it; that was the view taken in *B. & S. Contracts*, by virtue of the prefatory words about "every effort". But it is arguable that these words imposed a stricter obligation of performance than one limited to the pursuit of "reasonable" measures, and that notions of reasonable behaviour were thus irrelevant to the plaintiffs' immunity in that case. On this analysis, it was only if the plaintiffs had made "every effort" (i.e., more than reasonable effort) to perform the contract that their release from liability would apply.[39] On a more general level, it might be argued that if a contract itself does not expressly define the parties' obligations in terms of reasonable effort and no more, the difficulties of identifying reasonableness in the context[40] of industrial action should persuade the courts to hold that certain obligations, at least, are strict in nature. Such an approach would render redundant any consideration as to whether, for example, it would be reasonable for the employer on a given occasion to "give in" to a demand from his workforce (and thus safeguard some outside contract), or to "stand up" to such a demand (and put that contract in peril). Either the acts undertaken by the contractor would have been performed, or they would not; if they were not, the contract would be broken, irrespective of the cause of the breach.[41]

A third observation is that if conduct such as that in *B. & S. Contracts* can be stigmatised as unreasonable for the purpose of deactivating a *force majeure* clause, it might also be regarded as unreasonable in other contexts: for example, for the purpose of showing that the contractor has failed to attain a standard of reasonableness inherent in his implied obligations under the contract,[42] or for the purpose of enabling the other party to bring a direct action for negligence when unreasonable action by the defaulting contractor has caused a dispute among his employees to damage that other party's interests. The latter prospect is admittedly remote,[43] but it may be imprudent to discount it entirely.

Finally, it is notable that a further argument does not seem to have been advanced in *B. & S. Contracts*. The plaintiffs might have maintained that, irrespective of the explicit *force majeure* clause, their obligations did not (as generally construed) extend to a duty to perform in the circumstances which occurred: that such circumstances were beyond the parties' contemplation and beyond the range of the plaintiffs' undertaking. The argument appears questionable, not least because an ineffective specific exemption would appear inconsistent with an effective implied one.[44]

language to persuade me that Parliament intended to allow the courts to act as some sort of backseat driver in trade disputes." The other members of the House fell some way short, however, of sharing Lord Scarman's reluctance: cf. Lord Diplock at pp. 687–688.

39. Cf. the position regarding the defence of frustration; below, p. 185.

40. Including the possible adverse consequences to industrial relations: above, p. 167.

41. See generally *Raineri* v. *Miles* [1981] A.C. 1050, at p. 1086, *per* Lord Edmund-Davies; p. 3 above.

42. See, for example, ss. 13, 14, Supply of Goods and Services Act 1982.

43. For two reasons: first, actions in negligence for economic loss are unlikely to succeed, other than in special circumstances, following *Murphy* v. *Brentwood District Council* [1991] 1 A.C. 398; secondly, modern courts look askance at supplementary or discordant tortious obligations between parties who are contractually related: see below, pp. 193–194. But, of course, the question of a tort claim can arise between two parties who are not contractually related, and in respect of physical damage. Cf. *Woolfall* v. *Knowsley Borough Council* (1992) unreported, 8 June, C.A.; below, p. 184.

44. Cf. *Placer Developments Ltd.* v. *British Columbia Hydro and Power Authority* (1984) 16 D.L.R. (4th) 197; (below, p. 180) where there was no *force majeure* clause.

It has already been remarked that a court which is squarely confronted with the task of assessing the reasonableness of an employer's response to industrial action has no choice but to make that assessment. In *Channel Island Ferries Ltd.* v. *Sealink Ltd.*[45] this exercise was conceded to be necessary, even though the relevant clause contained no prefatory words requiring "every effort". Instead, the clause, referred to events beyond the control of either party. The defendant ferry operators were sued for failing to supply two of their vessels on bareboat charter to a newly formed company, British Channel Island Ferries. The vessels represented Sealink's promised contribution to a joint venture agreement between themselves and Channel Island Ferries Ltd. The original occasion of Sealink's failure to deliver was industrial action (including sit-ins) by the crews of their vessels when the joint venture agreement was announced. These protests escalated to the point of a national strike, and the dispute was not settled until Sealink concluded agreements with the relevant unions by which, *inter alia*, bareboat charters were wholly embargoed. This settlement disabled Sealink from delivering the vessels to British Channel Island Ferries on the terms originally agreed, and Channel Island Ferries sued them in respect of that failure.

Sealink relied, *inter alia*, on a *force majeure* clause, whereby:

> "A party shall not be liable in the event of non-fulfilment of any obligation arising under this contract by reason of Act of God, disease, strikes, lock-outs, fire and any accident or incident of any nature beyond the control of the relevant party."

Sealink conceded[46] that a successful invocation of this clause required them to establish two facts: (i) that their failure to bareboat charter the two nominated vessels resulted from circumstances beyond their control, and (ii) that there were no steps which they could reasonably have taken in order to avoid the strike or to mitigate its consequences. These concessions were evidently accepted as well founded both by Hirst J. at first instance[47] and by Ralph Gibson L.J. in the Court of Appeal.[48] Hirst J. held that the settlement between Sealink and the unions represented a completely new causative event in their disablement from performing the joint venture agreement, and that Sealink's entry into that settlement agreement, far from being an act beyond their control, represented a "genuine choice" on their part.[49] It would have been otherwise had their conclusion of the settlement been the result of duress, or had Sealink been able to show that they faced financial ruin if they had declined to settle on the stated terms. But there was some evidence at least to show that Sealink's employees might have "drifted back" to work in any event, or that the unions might ultimately have settled the dispute on other terms. An agreement which represented so positive and independent an act of policy on the part of an employer could hardly be said to qualify as an "accident" or "incident" within the meaning of the *force majeure* clause.

45. [1987] 1 Lloyd's Rep. 559; [1988] 1 Lloyd's Rep. 323 (C.A.).
46. Relying on *B. & S. Contracts and Design Ltd.* v. *Victor Green Publications Ltd.* [1984] I.C.R. 419; above, pp. 170–172.
47. [1987] 1 Lloyd's Rep. 559, at p. 570.
48. [1988] 1 Lloyd's Rep. 323, at p. 327.
49. [1987] 1 Lloyd's Rep. 559, at pp. 570–571, distinguishing the Vancouver strike cases: *Reardon Smith Line Ltd.* v. *Ministry of Agriculture, Fisheries and Food* [1961] 1 Lloyd's Rep. 385; [1962] 1 Q.B. 42.

Having held that Sealink failed on the first limb of *force majeure*, Hirst J. went on to conclude that they had, in any event, failed to satisfy the requirements of the second.[50] The manner in which they prepared their labour force for the introduction of the arrangements contemplated by the joint venture agreement was quite inadequate to forestall, or to minimise the risk of, industrial action. Although the adoption of additional preparatory precautions would not necessarily have averted the strike, it might well have made that strike easier to settle and would have enabled Sealink to avoid the "tragic miscalculation" represented by their "brutal" introduction of the agreement without prior consultation. Hirst J. considered that it would have been "most unjust" if Channel Island Ferries had had to bear the brunt of Sealink's "improvidence" in this regard.[51]

In holding that Sealink had failed to demonstrate reasonable steps to avoid or to mitigate the strike, Hirst J. made two further observations. First, he rejected Sealink's assertion that omissions on their part during the period before their conclusion of the joint venture agreement should be disregarded for the purpose of the second limb of the *force majeure* defence, on the ground that "there is no tort of negligent contracting". Whereas Hirst J. did not find it necessary to acknowledge the existence of such a tort, he did discover authority[52] which supported his inclusion of such inactivity on the part of Sealink within his evaluation of reasonable preventive measures on their part. To adopt Channel Island Ferries' own submission on this point, Channel Island Ferries could reasonably have expected that Sealink would, on the occasion of their concluding the joint venture agreement containing the *force majeure* clause, have conducted reasonable enquiries and exercised reasonable precautions, in order to ensure the availability of the vessels which they had undertaken to supply.

Secondly, Hirst J. appears to have attached little weight to Sealink's contention that the court should be chary about passing judgment on the conduct of industrial disputes by opposing parties.[53] He considered that, as in *B. & S. Contracts*, the task could not be avoided when the contract put it squarely before the court. Moreover, the omission which formed the substance of Channel Island Ferries' principal complaint in the instant proceedings related less to Sealink's conduct of the dispute once it had arisen than to their failure to prepare for it in the first place.

Hirst J.'s reasoning was endorsed almost without reservation by the Court of Appeal.[54] The only area of doubt concerned the argument that Sealink's pre-contractual improvidence disabled them from relying on the clause. Parker L.J.,[55] while observing that a decision on this point was unnecessary to the result, declined to construe Hirst J.'s judgment as stating a general principle that a party who has been improvident in concluding a contract is thereby disabled from invoking the

50. [1987] 1 Lloyd's Rep. 559, at pp. 571–576. Hirst J. regarded his conclusion as entirely consistent with *B. & S. Contracts* (above), pp. 170–172.

51. Especially since CIF were in no way jointly responsible for Sealink's industrial relations and had never been consulted about the introduction of Sealink's policy, but were merely informed on progress from time to time: *ibid.*, at p. 576. It would be interesting to hear argument as to why the legal position should differ when such consultation has taken place.

52. *The Angelia* [1973] 1 W.L.R. 210.

53. [1987] 1 Lloyd's Rep. 559, at p. 575.

54. [1988] 1 Lloyd's Rep. 323.

55. *Ibid.*, at p. 328.

terms of that contract in his defence. Such a principle would, in Parker L.J.'s opinion, be open to debate, but Hirst J. had intended no such generalisation in this case; he had merely been making a specific decision on the wording of a particular contract. Ralph Gibson L.J.[56] was less inclined to dismiss the general proposition out of hand. He believed that it could be both logical and just for a court, in conducting the necessary investigation as to whether a contractor had taken all reasonable steps to avert the strike, to pay regard to pre-contractual omissions, "for example, in this case preliminary discussions with Union representatives". In Ralph Gibson L.J.'s view, the difficulty lay rather in understanding how Sealink's failure to insist that the contract terms be modified, or their failure to refrain from entering into the agreement at all, could necessarily be equated with a failure to take reasonable steps to avoid or mitigate the consequences of the strike. Arguably, the conclusion of the contract was an event causally independent of the preceding omissions. If the *force majeure* clause had otherwise been applicable to the events which occurred (that is, if the settlement agreement had not been deemed to be a novel causative factor in Sealink's failure to perform), it might have been legitimate to conclude that it was not displaced by the pre-contract omission. Certainly, it was not alleged that Sealink had misrepresented the facts before contracting, and there was no allegation of any material implied term. The issue remains open, and seems almost certain to recur in litigation involving contracts impaired by industrial protest.

Both *Channel Island Ferries* and *B. & S. Contracts* involved domestic industrial action. The construction of *force majeure* clauses is inevitably more tendentious in such circumstances, because it raises directly the question whether the occurrence or non-resolution of the dispute was within the defendant's control, or whether he took reasonable measures to prevent or settle it. Such questions can theoretically arise in relation to external disputes: for instance, where employees of the defendant's supplier protest about some remediable aspect of the defendant's trading policy or employment practices, thereby disabling the defendant from performing his contracts. Suppose, for example, that employees of Company A (the supplier) embargo deliveries to Company B (the contractor) because of the latter's policy of trading with Libya. Company B decides against altering its policy, essentially because its contracts with Libyan customers are worth more than its contracts with English customers. Such a decision may be reinforced by the consideration that maintaining Company B's Libyan business is more likely to preserve jobs (for employees of Company B, if not for those of its English customers). Company C (an English customer) sues for non-delivery and Company B relies on a *force majeure* clause. It would be interesting to hear judicial opinion as to whether Company B should reasonably yield to the demands of the employees of Company A. The impossibility of making a satisfactory assessment of the competing moral, social, economic and managerial demands confronting Company B might induce the court, wherever this is remotely feasible, to construe Company B's obligation towards Company A as strict, rather than as tempered by notions of reasonable effort. Such an analysis would leave the court free to conclude that the essential

56. *Ibid.*, at pp. 328–329. Cf. *J. Lauritzen A.S.* v. *Wijsmuller B.V.* (*The Super Servant Two*) [1990] 1 Lloyd's Rep. 1, at p. 6, *per* Bingham L.J.

issue was one of actual, rather than reasonable, control. The issue would then become a simple one as to whether Company B could, by any means, have forestalled or detonated the event which it now invokes as relieving it from its contract with Company A. An analysis along these lines would have the further advantage of corresponding broadly to the modern approach to "self-induced" frustration.[57] Of course, it would largely emasculate the *force majeure* clause in cases where an industrial dispute (whether domestic or external) stems from some objectionable and remediable conduct on the part of the *proferens* himself,[58] but that (it is submitted) is preferable to the alternative. Moreover, such an analysis would still leave the clause a sufficient subject matter, even in the area of industrial protest, by confining it to cases of irremediable industrial action unconnected with the contractor's own behaviour.

Most cases of external industrial action will, however, be unpreventable by the contractor, and his *force majeure* clause will founder or flourish on less tendentious issues of construction. Such decisions have correspondingly less to contribute to questions of general principle and are rarely interesting.[59]

One consideration which appears to have been conspicuously absent from decisions like *Channel Island Ferries* and *B. & S. Contracts* is the application of the Unfair Contract Terms Act 1977. Modern legislation has created an elaborate and uncertain scheme of control over anti-commitment clauses. This control is by no means limited to consumer transactions. For example, section 3 of the Act subjects to a requirement of reasonableness any term which (i) is contained in a contract concluded on one party's written standard term of business, and (ii) purports to exempt that party from liability for breach of contract, or to entitle him to offer a different contractual performance from that which the other party reasonably believed that he was undertaking, or to offer no performance at all. Although the application of section 3 to *force majeure* clauses may be debatable,[60] its existence can only cast further doubt on the efficacy of exculpatory terms to protect a contractor in this situation.

Aside from such questions, modern authority amply demonstrates the fallibility of anti-commitment clauses in the context of industrial action. The clause may founder on one of several grounds: that the contractor took insufficient care to avert the protest or its consequences, that the relevant event was within the contractor's objective control, or that the language of the clause was otherwise inadequate to deny redress.

57. Below, pp. 186–187.

58. Of course, the question of remediability itself may pose almost intractable problems for the court. Even so, it is submitted that the task of answering them is less pernicious than the task of quantifying the reasonableness of the employer's response.

59. For examples, see *Caltex Oil (Australia) Pty. Ltd.* v. *Howard Smith Industries Pty. Ltd.* [1973] 2 N.S.W.L.R. 89 (where the clause failed); *Matsoukis* v. *Priestman & Co.* [1915] 1 K.B. 681 (where the clause was held capable of extending to a universal coal strike). See further *W. Young & Son (Wholesale Fish Merchants) Ltd.* v. *British Transport Commission* [1955] 2 Q.B. 177; *Boskalis Westminster Construction Ltd.* v. *Liverpool City Council* (1983) 133 N.L.J. 576; *MacMillan Bloedel Ltd.* v. *British Columbia Hydro and Power Authority* (1992) 98 D.L.R. 492.

60. See above, p. 11; and cf., as to a substance-orientated approach, to the 1977 Act, *Johnstone* v. *Bloomsbury Health Authority* [1992] Q.B. 333; *Phillips Products Ltd.* v. *Hyland and Hamstead Plant Hire* [1987] 2 All E.R. 620; MacDonald (1991) 107 L.Q.R. 555; McKendrick (1992) 5 J.C.L. 6, esp. at pp. 22–25.

It seems that a contractor who fails on such grounds will rarely find it profitable to augment his defence by alleging some implicit qualification on his duty to perform. In theory, he might discard the specific clause and claim that his duty is tempered or excluded by the general language or provenance of the contract; or, he might claim that the contract is frustrated. But the first device sits uneasily alongside the perception of commercial contracts as exclusive codes,[61] while the second jars with the judicial reluctance to treat foreseeable events as frustratory.[62] It is notable that neither in *B. & S. Contracts* nor in *Channel Island Ferries* was any auxiliary defence pleaded; the *force majeure* clause was the sole defence.

Different considerations apply where a contract contains no express exculpatory term. In that event, the entire contract and its attendant circumstances must be examined to ascertain the scale of the contractor's obligation and its application to the instant facts. The remainder of this chapter examines some of the authorities where this exercise was conducted and the lessons which they hold for litigants.

3. WHEN PERFORMANCE IS DISRUPTED BY EXTERNAL INDUSTRIAL ACTION (THAT IS, BY ACTION NOT AMONG THE CONTRACTOR'S OWN PERSONNEL)

In the absence of an explicit exculpatory term, the contractor must seek protection from contractual liability along two principal routes. Either he must show that the external industrial action has frustrated the contract, or he must show that some implied qualification on his nominal contractual obligations relieves him of the duty to perform in the situation prevailing.

(a) Frustration

There seems no reason in principle why a strike or other labour dispute which renders the defendant's contractual promises impossible to perform, or transforms performance so as to render it a wholly different commercial phenomenon from performance as originally undertaken, should not be regarded as frustrating the contract. Illustrations are relatively rare, but the defence can be observed in *Pioneer Shipping Ltd.* v. *B.T.P. Tioxide (The Nema)*.[63] There, shipowners were held to be released from performance of a long-term charterparty because the port at

61. *Greater Nottingham Co-operative Society Ltd.* v. *Cementation Piling and Foundations Ltd.* [1989] Q.B. 71; *Hendy Lennox (Industrial Engines) Ltd.* v. *Graham Puttick Ltd.* [1984] 1 W.L.R. 485. But cf. *Sonat Offshore S.A.* v. *Amerada Hess Development Ltd.* (1987) 39 Build. L.R. 1.

62. Below, p. 179. It is not, however, the case that the presence of a *force majeure* clause will inevitably exclude the operation of the defence of frustration. Rather, its presence will make it much harder to invoke the defence because it will be arguable either that express provision has been made for the event or that the event itself was foreseeable. See further Chapter 3.

63. [1982] A.C. 724; see also *The Penelope* [1929] P. 180, discussed by McElroy, *Impossibility of Performance* (1941), p. 180, pp. 228–229; *Organisation Danske Slagterier pro Jydske Andelsslagteriers Konservesfabrik AmbA (JAKA)* v. *Lanbrugsministeriet* [1994] 1 C.M.L.R. 729, at p. 738, per M. Jean Mischo (Advocate General), at p. 753, per the E.C.J. Cases where the defence has failed include *Ropner* v. *Ronnebeck* (1914) 20 Com. Cas. 95; *Braemont* v. *Weir* (1910) 15 Com. Cas. 101. The court's traditional reluctance to regard strikes as frustrating contracts stems from the possibility that a strike might be suddenly and unexpectedly terminated: *Metropolitan Water Board* v. *Dick, Kerr & Co.* [1917] 2 K.B. 1, at p. 35, *per* Scrutton L.J.

which the ship was due to call had been brought to a standstill by a long-standing strike among waterfront workers. The House of Lords agreed with the arbitrator that these events rendered performance so radically different from that which the parties originally contemplated that the shipowners were entitled to regard the contract as frustrated.

There are, however, several reasons why frustration may prove inappropriate in this context. It requires contractual performance to have become impossible, or wholly transformed, as a result of the adverse event. It is not enough merely to show that performance has become more difficult or costly than originally envisaged: "It is trite law that disappointed expectations do not of themselves give rise to frustrated contracts."[64] Further, there are serious difficulties in applying the defence to an event which was foreseeable to the parties when the contract was concluded.[65] In such a case, it may well be inferred that the parties impliedly wrote the prospective event into their formal distribution of responsibility, and that they intended the burden of performance in such an event to lie where it falls. Moreover, no event can constitute frustration if it (or its consequences) was within the control of the party invoking the defence.[66] Although the importance of this limitation is much slighter here than in cases where it is argued that a contract has been frustrated by domestic industrial action, it survives as a significant ingredient of the defence even in cases of external labour disputes.

(b) Limitation or qualification of the obligation

The alternative is for the contractor to establish some tacit limitation on the superficially absolute character of his promise to perform. A suitably drafted contract may enable him to argue that no obligation to perform exists in the industrial situation which has occurred, or that the obligation to perform requires him merely to do what is reasonable in the circumstances. Sometimes, the primary obligation will simply not extend to the events which have occurred. An example is *L.R.E. Engineering Services Ltd.* v. *Otto Simon Carves Ltd.*[67] There, OSC were contractors for works being carried out at the British Steel Plant at Port Talbot, and LRE were subcontractors. LRE were unable to gain access to the site because of a picket organised by steel workers. LRE claimed that this amounted to a repudiatory breach of OSC's obligation, under clause 24(1) of the relevant subcontracts, to afford "access to and possession of the site". Robert Goff J. held that this undertaking merely obliged OSC to provide LRE with the physical means of access to the site (viz., the use of sidings, gates and roadways) and with the opportunity to enter by means of that access. It did not constitute an absolute, universal guarantee that

64. *J. Lauritzen A.S.* v. *Wijsmuller B.V.* (*The Super Servant Two*) [1990] 1 Lloyd's Rep. 1, at p. 9, *per* Bingham L.J.

65. See generally Treitel, *Law of Contract* (8th Edn.), pp. 799–803.

66. *J. Lauritzen A.S.* v. *Wijsmuller B.V.* (*The Super Servant Two*) [1990] 1 Lloyd's Rep. 1; below, Chapter 3.

67. (1981) 24 Build. L.R. 127; Emden, *Construction Law* (1990) paras. I, 21–30. See further *Usher* v. *Intasun Holidays Ltd.* [1987] C.L.Y. 418 (Cardiff County Court); below pp. 193–194. Cf. *Marburg Management Pty. Ltd.* v. *Helkit Pty. Ltd.* (1990) 100 F.L.R. 458 (Sup. Ct. Aust. Capital Territory); *Rapid Building Group Ltd.* v. *Ealing Family Housing Association Ltd.* (1984) 29 Build. L.R. 5.

LRE would be able to take advantage of that opportunity irrespective of the conduct of any external agency, such as a picket line or a mob.

On other occasions, the primary obligation may survive the relevant event, subject to an implied qualification requiring no more than reasonable exertions or endeavours. Presumably, like any other term which is sought to be implied at common law, either this qualification must represent a term of habitual implication into the type of contract under debate, or it must satisfy the twin criteria of being both essential to lend commercial efficacy to the contract and consonant with its express terms: a formidable standard.[68] Yet, notwithstanding this, there is at least one modern decision[69] where the court has been willing to detect such an implied qualification and to relieve the contractor for a non-performance induced by his fears of industrial retaliation. The court arrived at this conclusion by construing the contractor's undertaking to supply the contractual services as an obligation merely to do what was reasonable to attain such supply; in other words, a comparable level of obligation to that which the court discovered (and the plaintiffs were held not to have satisfied) in the *B. & S. Contracts* case.

In *Placer Developments Ltd.* v. *British Columbia Hydro and Power Authority*[70] the plaintiff company were undergoing a particularly violent labour dispute, in the course of which poles carrying the power supply to their works were cut down. The defendants (who were under contract to supply power to the plaintiffs) refused to repair the lines and to resume the supply, or to permit the plaintiffs to reinstate the poles themselves. The defendants' refusal was prompted by the fear that, if they complied, they would become (under the British Columbia Labour Code) the "allies" of the plaintiffs, thereby entitling the strikers to set up a lawful picket of the defendants' own premises. The defendants also feared that a co-operation with the plaintiffs would expose them to the hazard of illegal picketing, whether they became allies of Placer or not. They were thereupon sued for breach of their contract to supply the power.

Perhaps surprisingly, frustration of contract does not appear to have been argued. Instead, argument centred upon whether the defendants' duty to perform the contract was qualified by a requirement of reasonableness and whether, if this qualification were legitimate, the defendants had satisfied the requirement by doing all that was reasonable to perform. The Court of Appeal of British Columbia held unanimously that the duty to supply power to the plaintiffs was not strict but merely obliged the defendants to take reasonable measures to maintain the supply. In the current circumstances, it was not reasonable to expect the defendants to incur the peril of co-operating in the resumption of the supply. The action accordingly failed.

One particular fact (apart from the violence of the labour dispute) needs to be emphasised about this case, for it suggests that the decision may be exceptional. The defendants were a public utility, and, as such, served a large proportion of the population of the province in which the dispute occurred. One member of the

68. As to the general criteria for implied terms, see *B.P. Refinery (Westernport) Pty. Ltd.* v. *Hastings Shire Council* (1977) 52 A.L.J.R. 20 at p. 26, *per* Lord Simon of Glaisdale; applied in *Rosehaugh Stanhope Properties plc* v. *Redpath Dorman Long Ltd.* (1990) 50 Build. L.R. 69 at p. 87, *per* Bingham L.J.

69. *Placer Developments Ltd.* v. *British Columbia Hydro and Power Authority* (1984) 16 D.L.R. (4th) 197 (below).

70. (1984) 16 D.L.R. (4th) 197.

Appeal Court in particular (Anderson J.A.)[71] drew specific attention to the possibility that an ordinary commercial contractor might not receive the same clemency of treatment with regard to the definition of the level of effort required under the contract: in short, that the qualification of "reasonableness" may be inapplicable in cases where the defendants are not a public utility. Further, the peculiar status of the defendants in this case made it possible for the court to declare that considerations wider than the mere losses suffered by the plaintiffs should be taken into account in quantifying the defendants' contractual duty. The threat of disruption to defendants' plant could easily have resulted in the loss of power to all their other customers. The defendants were, it seems, entitled to take this peril into account as an unacceptable risk of their compliance with the plaintiffs' demands; and this prospect was a material factor in determining the level and scope of the defendants' obligation to supply the power.

Three observations are suggested. In the first place, the *Placer* decision cannot be taken as universal authority for the proposition that, in the absence of a specific exculpatory term, a contracting party's obligation to perform his contract in the teeth of adverse industrial circumstances affecting a third party is merely a duty to do whatever is reasonable to discharge the stipulated task. Such a conclusion will depend upon propitious contractual terms. Occasionally (it seems) it may also depend on other circumstances, such as the status of the contractor, although this can hardly be a satisfactory general criterion. Ultimately, however, everything depends upon what the contract, as properly construed, obliged the defaulting party to do. In this respect, almost every contract may have its own story to tell.

Secondly, it is to be noted that the court in *Placer* expressly referred to the inability of the defendants, because of local unionisation, to obtain independent labour for the performance of repair work on the lines.[72] There may be a suggestion here that a contractual requirement of "reasonable endeavour" in carrying out the contract can include an obligation (where otherwise appropriate) to resort to non-union labour.[73] But the results of such a solution may well prove no better than those of non-performance, and there is some judicial recognition that the possible exacerbation of a dispute which will result from the use of outside labour relieves the contractor of any duty to resort to this means of performance.[74]

Thirdly, modern English authority affords some support for the view that a public institution, at least, may be entitled to judge the cost of remedying the particular default of which the plaintiff complains against the inconvenience or cost which the

71. *Ibid.*, at p. 209.

72. *Ibid.*, at p. 200, *per* Seaton J.A.

73. An obligation to employ such labour, if to do so offered the only practical means of performing the relevant duty, was evidently upheld by the Court of Appeal in *Woolfall* v. *Knowsley Borough Council* (1992) unreported, 8 June; see below, p. 184. In that case, the relevant duty was that of a local authority to take steps to protect members of the public who were using the highway, from dangers on adjoining land occupied by the authority. The court held it to be no defence to the authority's failure to alleviate the danger that such alleviation would have necessitated the engagement of private contractors, thereby aggravating the existing industrial dispute.

74. *Harold Stephen & Co. Ltd.* v. *Post Office* [1977] 1 W.L.R. 1172 (where the plaintiffs were seeking not damages but an injunction, which may be significantly different); *W. Young & Son (Wholesale Fish Merchants) Ltd.* v. *British Transport Commission* [1955] 2 Q.B. 177, at p. 194; and see *The Arawa* [1977] 2 Lloyd's Rep. 416, at p. 426, affirmed on a different point [1980] 2 Lloyd's Rep. 135; *Bartlett* v. *Department of Transport* (1984) 83 L.G.R. 579, at pp. 592–593, *per* Boreham J.

granting of the immediate remedy will occasion to other members of the institution's "clientele". Such an approach was taken by Lord Denning M.R., at least, in the injunction case of *Harold Stephen & Co. Ltd.* v. *The Post Office*[75] and is reflected by the decision of Boreham J. in *Bartlett* v. *Department of Transport*.[76] There, the Department of Transport were sued by the widow of a motorist under section 44 of the Highways Act 1959. She claimed that the failure of the Department's delegate (a county council) to grit or clear a particular trunk road during a period of heavy snow caused her husband's death. The defendants admitted that the county council had accepted that this particular road would not receive treatment against ice, but argued that this acquiescence was an essential feature of an arrangement whereby members of the National Union of Public Employees (employed by the council and in dispute with it) had agreed to grit or clear all other roads in the county. In upholding the defence, the judge accepted that the interests of users of other roads within the county were a material consideration in assessing the defendants' overall obligation under the Act.[77]

More will be said of this case later.[78] For the present, it is simply observed that the duty was not contractual but statutory. Whereas, however, this distinction may justify applying different principles of construction in order to gauge the alleged obligation against the relevant adverse event, the task in each case is essentially the same. That task is to examine the formulation of the duty to ascertain whether, on proper principles of construction, it applies in the given situation or not.

Many contractual duties traditionally impose an obligation of reasonable effort or achievement and no more. A typical example is the term in contracts for the supply of skill and labour that the contractor will (in the absence of express or inferable agreement) perform the task within a reasonable time.[79] In such a case, it may be legitimate to treat an external strike (for the outbreak of which the contractor is not responsible, and the effects of which he has taken reasonable steps to mitigate) as a factor in determining what is a reasonable period for performance. The result may be to extend the term allowable before the contractor falls into default.[80]

4. WHEN PERFORMANCE IS DISRUPTED BY INTERNAL INDUSTRIAL ACTION (THAT IS, BY ACTION AMONG THE CONTRACTOR'S OWN PERSONNEL)

The legal considerations bearing upon this situation correspond largely with those outlined in the preceding section. If the contract contains no express exculpatory term, a contractor whose performance is impaired by domestic industrial difficulties must normally resort to the following defences: (*a*) that the obligation to perform was not an absolute one, but was qualified in some manner which does not

75. [1977] 1 W.L.R. 1172, at p. 1179; cf. *Parker* v. *Camden Borough Council* [1986] Ch. 162, esp. at pp. 173–174, *per* Donaldson M.R.
76. (1984) 83 L.G.R. 579.
77. Cf., however, *Woolfall* v. *Knowsley Borough Council* (1992) unreported, 8 June, C.A.; below, p. 184.
78. Below, p. 183.
79. S.14, Supply of Goods and Services Act, 1982.
80. See, for example, *Hick* v. *Raymond and Reid* [1893] A.C. 22.

demand performance under the particular conditions; or (*b*) that the dispute has frustrated the contract.

(a) Qualified obligation

Certainly, some contractual duties are conditioned by notions of reasonable effort or attainment.[81] In relation to these, a court may well hold that it was unreasonable to expect performance in the circumstances at issue or that the offered performance satisfied the standard of reasonable attainment or endeavour. If so, the contractor will have committed no breach.

There appears to be no decisive modern authority raising this question in the context of domestic industrial protest. There are, however, authorities addressing the application of two other heads of civil obligation in the event of such protest: statutory duty and common law tort.

The principal decision on breach of statutory duty is *Bartlett* v. *Department of Transport*.[82] There, Boreham J. held that the duty owed by the defendants under section 44 of the Highways Act 1959 was not an absolute one. Liability would follow only if the council had been "blameworthy" in the occurrence or continuation of its employees' industrial action, which meant (apparently) if the council had condoned it. The plaintiff failed to establish any such blameworthiness or unreasonable contribution by the defendants to their employees' internal industrial action. The defendants must, therefore, be taken to have fulfilled their statutory duty.

There is, however, at least one decision concerning the particular obligation in *Bartlett* which holds that the duty imposed by section 44 of the Highways Act 1959 is absolute[83] and that it is no defence to show that the default occurred through the action of striking local authority employees.[84] Apart from this specific conflict, *Bartlett* suggests more general difficulties.

There can be little doubt that, if a contractual obligation has been pitched at the level of reasonable endeavour, the court must measure the contractor's response against that standard, however delicate or unpalatable such a task may be.[85] But, as a glance at *B. & S. Contracts* shows, no court should embark on this enquiry unless the language of the contract compels it. In particular, courts should be circumspect about construing duties, which would ordinarily be regarded as strict, as exacting mere obligations of reasonable endeavour in the context of industrial action. They should be equally reluctant, perhaps, to judge the reasonableness of the contractor's endeavours by some subjective standard, derived (for example) from his particular industrial relations policy or history, as against more objective causative criteria. The judicial assessment of reasonableness in this context (as in that of a specific *force majeure* clause) is a difficult and arguably mischievous exercise: it may involve stigmatising as unreasonable or misguided conduct by employees or trade unions who are not parties to the litigation, and this could fan industrial resent-

81. E.g., ss.13, 14, Supply of Goods and Services Act, 1982.

82. (1984) 83 L.G.R. 579, discussed above, p. 182.

83. Subject to the statutory defence provided by the Highways (Miscellaneous Provisions) Act 1961, s.1.

84. *Ellis* v. *Tyne and Wear County Council* [1984] C.L.Y. 1022 (H.H. Judge Percy, Newcastle-upon-Tyne County Court).

85. Above, p. 172.

ment. Further problems might arise concerning the admissibility of the court's conclusion as to the behaviour of the workforce or their trade union in later proceedings between them and the employer. As between customer and contractor, it might be preferable to allow the loss to fall upon the party whose staff precipitated the alleged breach of duty, whether that party's efforts to counteract the industrial action were reasonable or not. Again, however, the ultimate question is the language of the contract and the formulation of the particular undertaking.

A decision which stands in contrast to *Bartlett* is *Woolfall* v. *Knowsley Borough Council*.[86] A twelve-year-old pedestrian was injured by an aerosol can which was propelled from land adjoining the highway. The cause of the propulsion was a fire among accumulations of rubbish on the land. The land was owned and occupied by the council, which had been using it as a temporary rubbish tip during a strike of dustmen. The victim sued for breach of the council's duty (as occupier of adjoining land) to take steps to protect users of the highway from dangers. The council's defence that any further action on its part (e.g., by clearing the tip) would have required them to engage outside contractors, thereby exacerbating the dispute, was roundly rejected by Woolf L.J. Having observed that the point was "of some general interest", Woolf L.J. quickly (and without reference to authority) concluded that there was nothing in it:

> "I cannot accept that submission and I conclude without hesitation that the learned judge was right to reject it. The situation is that, if you are under a duty to take steps for protecting the public using the adjoining highway, it can be no answer to an allegation that you have failed to perform that duty to say that, for reasons of industrial relations, you have deliberately not taken those steps which are required to avoid the breach of duty . . . [W]hile it is understandable that a local authority should not wish to aggravate industrial relations by taking precipitous action, they remain under a duty, as does any other private individual, to take action to fulfil the duties which they owe to the public. Just as an employer is required to take action to protect his employees in the case of industrial action occurring in factory premises, so, in my judgment a landowner—and that was what the defendants were—who occupies land adjoining the highway remains under a duty to protect the public who could be endangered from activities which are occurring on his land, notwithstanding that he may at the time have problems with regard to industrial relations."

The council's defence that it had made a reasonable decision in leaving the tip uncleared therefore failed. Woolf L.J. further held that, even if that decision were "understandable", there were alternative steps which the council could have taken to alert the public to the danger.

There is, of course, a difference between a clearly formulated statutory duty and a general common law duty in tort. Even so, there is much in *Woolfall* which is at odds with *Bartlett*, and one cannot be certain that the result in *Woolfall* would have differed had the failure to clear the tip resulted from some agreement with the disaffected workforce whereby other public dangers were removed. There is also room for speculation as to whether (in appropriate conditions) injunctive relief should have been issued to require the council to abate the tort, bearing in mind the Court of Appeal's characteristic reluctance to intervene by injunction in the delicate process of industrial negotiation.[87]

86. Unreported, 8 June 1992 (C.A.).

87. *Parker* v. *Camden Borough Council* [1986] Ch. 162, *per* Sir John Donaldson M.R. who, as Lord Donaldson M.R., was a member of the court in *Woolfall*.

(b) Frustration

Suppose, then, that the contractor seeks his defence outside the verbal perimeter of the contract, arguing that the action of his employees has frustrated it. Of course, the same general difficulties will apply here as in a case of external industrial action.[88] More particularly, the contractor may lose his defence if the protest can be regarded as an event for which he was responsible; for then he may be regarded as having induced the relevant event. As Lord Sumner once remarked, "reliance cannot be based on a self-induced frustration".[89]

Until recently, this principle was characteristically expressed in terms of fault.[90] No defendant could invoke an event as constituting frustration if it resulted from his fault or default. Analysis in terms of fault caused difficulty at a general level: did fault extend to negligent as well as to deliberate conduct, and was negligence in this context limited to the breach of an actionable duty? Such uncertainties could cause almost insuperable problems for a court required to consider whether a particular act of domestic industrial protest, or the adverse consequences of that act, resulted from the fault of the defendant employer. For example, it might be argued that the contractor unreasonably provoked or otherwise precipitated the industrial protest, or allowed it to persist when a reasonable contractor in his position would have settled it. Such assertions would raise a broad spectrum of contentious issues concerning the employer's proper response to domestic industrial action, and would invite similar reservations to those expressed in relation to *B. & S. Contracts*. The resultant judicial task could involve an almost Herculean balancing of diverse obligations.

Nor, it is submitted, would the difficulty end there. The question might also arise as to how "personal" the employer's fault must be. A disappointed customer might seek, for example, to reinforce his claim by contending that the relationship between the employer and his protesting workforce (or, more specifically, the relationship between the work which the employees were engaged to perform and the acts of protest) was sufficiently intimate to justify equating the employees' conduct with that of their employer for the purposes of identifying self-induced frustration. It would follow that, irrespective of whether the employer had been personally at fault, he would be affixed with the same responsibility for the effects of the protest as if he had directly promoted it.

At first sight, it seems remarkable that an employer can be legally responsible for an act which is directed towards harming him. But, of course, industrial action can be aimed at an employer other than the protesters' own, as where employees of Company A conduct a work to rule in order to protest against the conduct of Company B. There is, in any event, slender modern authority for the view that an act of industrial protest can occur in the course of the protesters' employment for the purposes of rendering the employer vicariously liable in tort.[91] If a particular act of

88. Above, p. 178.

89. *Bank Line Ltd.* v. *Arthur Capel & Co.* [1919] A.C. 435, at p. 452.

90. See generally Treitel, *Law of Contract* (7th Edn.) pp. 699–702; and cf. now (8th Edn.) pp. 803–807.

91. *The Arawa* [1977] 2 Lloyd's Rep. 416; on appeal, not involving this point [1980] 2 Lloyd's Rep. 135. Cf. *J. Lauritzen A.S.* v. *Wijsmuller B.V.* (*The Super Servant Two*) [1990] 1 Lloyd's Rep. 1, at pp. 7–8, *per* Bingham L.J.

protest is one for which the employer would be vicariously liable in tort, it is arguable that that act should also qualify as one induced by his fault for the purposes of frustration. Unfortunately, the decisions concerning vicarious liability for industrial action offer no clear message. That authority is considered later in this chapter.[92]

Sufficient has been said to show the problems which can result from an uncritical introduction of notions of fault into the concept of self-induced frustration. Given these problems, the decision of the Court of Appeal in *J. Lauritzen A.S.* v. *Wijsmuller B.V.* (*The Super Servant Two*),[93] represents a welcome development. There, Bingham L.J. rejected the defendants' argument that an allegedly frustratory event would be deemed to have been induced by the fault of the defendant only if the party pleading frustration had acted deliberately, or in breach of some actionable duty, in causing the event. In Bingham L.J.'s view, such a test merely clouded the real issue, which was one of externality and control:

> "*Wijsmuller*'s test would, in my judgment, confine the law in a legalistic strait-jacket and distract attention from the real question, which is whether the frustrating event relied upon is truly an outside event or extraneous change of situation or whether it is an event which the party seeking to rely on it had the means and opportunity to prevent but nevertheless caused or permitted to come about. A fine test of legal duty is inappropriate: what is needed is a pragmatic judgment whether a party seeking to rely on an event as discharging him from a contractual promise was himself responsible for the occurrence of that event."[94]

It seems clear from Bingham L.J.'s reliance[95] on Griffiths L.J.'s judgment in *The Hannah Blumenthal*[96] that he was employing the notion of "responsibility" not as an independent legal question (was the defendant legally responsible for what occurred?) but as a conclusion of law following automatically from the discovery that the supervening event was not external to the defendant and was susceptible to the defendant's control:

> "The essence of frustration is that it is caused by some unforeseen supervening event over which the parties to the contract have no control and for which they are *therefore* not responsible. To say that the supervening event occurs without the default or blame or responsibility of the parties is . . . but another way of saying that it is a supervening event over which they have no control."[97]

This qualification is necessary, for otherwise the court, having ejected all issues as to the propriety or reasonableness of the defendant's response to industrial action by discarding the question of fault, might find such considerations re-admitted by the scarcely preferable notion of responsibility.

Thus construed, the test of the contractor's liability is an objective one: could he in fact have prevented the relevant event or its resultant harm? If he could, the contract continues to bind him and the supervening event does not frustrate it. Whether the event or its consequences could have been prevented only by unreasonable effort is immaterial. The criterion is one of actual, not reasonable, control.

This analysis has obvious implications for a contractor whose obligations are

92. Below, p. 189.
93. [1990] 1 Lloyd's Rep. 1. See generally McKendrick, Chapter 3, above, pp. 46–52.
94. *Ibid.*, at p. 10; cf. at pp. 13–14, *per* Dillon L.J.
95. *Ibid.*, at p. 10.
96. [1983] 1 A.C. 854, at p. 882.
97. *Ibid* (emphasis added).

imperilled by domestic industrial action. If the action is taken to enforce some demand by his workforce which the contractor is capable of satisfying, neither the action itself nor its consequences are beyond the contractor's control. Moreover, the action is not an external event. The contractor cannot, therefore, invoke it as frustratory. On this analysis, domestic industrial action will rarely, if ever, release a contractor from his obligations in the absence of some specific exculpatory term.

It is submitted that this approach is greatly preferable to one which requires the court to determine whether the contractor acted unreasonably in precipitating or prolonging the dispute. Further, it would be helpful if the judicial approach to *force majeure* clauses (while, admittedly, governed by different principles from those which govern frustration) were aligned with this analysis. Had it not been for the defendants' concession in *Channel Island Ferries*, for example, the court might have felt able to conclude that the sole question raised by the clause was whether the disruptive events were objectively within the defendants' control. Certainly, the qualification of reasonable endeavour emerged no more compellingly from the language of the clause in *Channel Island Ferries* than it did from the language of the clause in *B. & S. Contracts*. And whatever the historical approach to *force majeure* clauses, every contract term must ultimately stand or fall on its own language: there are no precedents in contractual construction.[98]

An interesting and persuasive parallel can be drawn from the decision of Parker J. in *Dairyvale Foods Ltd.* v. *Intervention Board for Agricultural Produce*.[99] This litigation arose from a Civil Service strike in the early 1980s. Under EC legislation relating to the Common Agricultural Policy, certain exporters of agricultural produce from the UK were entitled to receive monetary compensation amounts ("m.c.a.'s") from the government. The proper government agency to make these payments was the Intervention Board for Agricultural Produce, the defendants in the present case.

Dairyvale and several other companies became entitled to the payment of m.c.a.'s amounting to some £4.5 million. The board refused to pay the m.c.a.'s because 18 civil servants (computer technicians at their computer centre at Guildford) refused to operate the computer. The board claimed that this strike action made payment (temporarily) impossible; and they grounded their defence on certain EEC regulations made in 1975 and 1981. These provided a defence to non-payment in cases of "*force majeure*". Parker J., relying on Continental authority,[100] rejected the defence. He held that proof of *force majeure* depended on the

98. *Ashville Investments Ltd.* v. *Elmer Contractors Ltd.* [1989] Q.B. 488, at p. 495, *per* May L.J.; cf. at p. 505, *per* Balcombe L.J., and *Surrey Heath Borough Council* v. *Lovell Construction Ltd.* (1990) 48 Build. L.R. 113, at pp. 117–118, *per* Dillon L.J.

99. [1982] 3 C.M.L.R. 497. Cf. *Re Late Budget Payments: EEC Commission* v. *Greece* [1989] 1 C.M.L.R. 441; [1990] 1 E.C.R. 2849, discussed at p. 349 below and see generally Chapter 17; followed in *Organisationen Danske Slagterier pro Jydske Andelsslagteriers Konser vesfabrik AmbA (JAKA)* v. *Landbrugministeriet* [1994] 1 C.M.L.R. 729.

100. Case 4/68, *Schwarzwaldmilch* v. *Einfuhr-und Vorratsstelle für Fette* [1968] E.C.R. 377, [1969] C.M.L.R. 406; Case 25/70, *Einfuhr-und Vorratsstelle für Getreide and Futtermittel* v. *Koster, Berodt & Co.* [1970] E.C.R. 1161, [1972] C.M.L.R. 255; Case 42/79, *Milch-Fett-und Eierkontor G.m.b.H.* v. *Bundesanstalt für Landwirtschaftliche Marktordnung* [1979] E.C.R. 3703; *S.p.A. Ferriera Valsabbia & Ors.* v. *E.C. Commission* [1980] E.C.R. 907, [1981] 1 C.M.L.R. 613. And see further the unreported decision of Popplewell J. in *R.* v. *Intervention Board for Agricultural Produce, ex parte Nicolas Falise N.V.* (1989) 22 March. See generally Nicholas, above, Chapter 2.

establishment of two ingredients. These were: (i) an external event, the occurrence of which was beyond the control of the party relying on it, and (ii) consequences from that event which could not have been avoided by the party invoking the defence. The first ingredient required the court to apply an objective test. It was immaterial whether the defendant could reasonably have prevented the disruptive event; the only issue was whether he could possibly have done so. It was therefore unnecessary to examine whether either party to the strike had acted unreasonably in allowing it to develop. In addition, no event could be "external" for the purpose of the first ingredient if it occurred (as did the present strike) within the defendant's own workforce.

As regards the second ingredient, Parker J. was less certain as to whether the test imposed was objective or subjective.[101] His preference, again, was for an objective test,[102] but he remarked that, even if this preference were misguided, the defendant had failed to satisfy the second ingredient as a subjective requirement. It is significant that, in relation to each ingredient, Parker J. grounded his preference for an objective assessment of the avoidability of the disruption on the fact that this would obviate any need to delve into the "rights and wrongs" of the industrial dispute.[103]

It is unfortunate that this authority, distinguishable though it was, was not cited in *B. & S. Contracts*. Certainly, it seems likely that similar logic will prove influential in later disputes where a contractor relies on his domestic labour difficulties as constituting frustration. Of course, *force majeure* and frustration are distinguishable concepts, and there may be difficulty in applying the control analysis to individual cases. One such case might arise where the aim of those conducting the domestic industrial action is to protest against some past and irremediable act on the part of the employer, rather than to remedy a current grievance. On the one hand, it could be argued that if the employer's catalytic act had been voluntary, the entire series of subsequent events was within his control: he did not have to perform the catalytic act if he did not want to. Further, a protest can hardly be external when it takes place within the employer's own enterprise. On the other hand, courts may wish to set limits to the extent to which they will allow a contractor's past behaviour to deprive him of contractual defences to current claims: what, for example, should be the judicial reaction to a one-day strike called in response to the discovery that the contractor traded with a South African company in 1952? Further potential difficulties concern the position of a contractor in relation to employees of his independent contractors and the juridical nature of the requirement that the event relied upon as constituting frustration must be "external". If this were an independent ground for depriving the contractor of the defence, additional to that of "control", the result could be to deny the defence to a contractor whose alleged breach of contract results from a domestic industrial protest which is directed not against the contractor's own policies but against those of another employer, or against some political initiative. It is submitted, on balance, that lack of externality should be regarded as a synonym for want of control rather

101. [1982] 3 C.M.L.R. 358, at pp. 363–364.
102. *Ibid.*
103. *Ibid.*, at p. 363.

than an independent disqualification; but the question awaits authoritative resolution.

Whatever its attendant difficulties, however, the test of objective control seems greatly preferable to the alternative. No court should embark lightly on the exercise of identifying those demands which an employer should concede and those which he should resist. Nor should a court willingly advise as to the proper conduct of industrial relations, especially when such advice is necessarily retrospective. The stigmatisation of particular demands as unreasonable, and the identification of those which an employer should resist as a matter of principle, is contentious enough in litigation directly involving the immediate disputants. In cases where the employees are not parties, the cause of industrial harmony is unlikely to be advanced by such pronouncements.

5. VICARIOUS LIABILITY FOR INDUSTRIAL ACTION

If an objective test of control represents the proper approach to contractual liability for domestic industrial action, a disappointed customer will rarely need to assert that the employer is vicariously liable for such action. The employer, having had control over the dispute, will be answerable in any event. Vicarious liability may be a constructive alternative to a contract claim, however, where there is no contract between the litigants, or where the domestic industrial action which impairs a contractor's performance is directed not against him but against a third party. In such a case, the event and its consequences may not be within the contractor's control (although they are still hardly "external"). Can the claimant counteract the possible success of a defence of frustration by arguing that the contractor is vicariously liable for the acts of his employees?

In *The Arawa*,[104] industrial action took the form of a "go-slow" in the unloading of the plaintiffs' frozen meat from a vessel. Meat was shipped on a refrigerated vessel from New Zealand to London. The shipowners engaged a wharfage firm named Chambers to load the meat into lighters and store it for collection by the cargo owners. Employees of Chambers operated a go-slow, with the result that the unloading was delayed and the meat became unfit for consumption. The cargo owners sued. Brandon J. held that the deliberate delay in unloading was an act of negligence by Chambers' employees against the cargo owners, and that Chambers would have been vicariously liable to the cargo owners because it occurred in the course of the loaders' employment.[105] The defendants in this case were the shipowners and they, according to Brandon J., were equally liable as common law bailees for reward.[106] By entrusting the task to Chambers they impliedly undertook responsibility for any fault in performance on Chambers' part, even a fault which took the form of industrial action by Chambers' employees and which the shipowners (possibly even Chambers themselves) were powerless to prevent. The

104. *Producers Meats Ltd.* v. *Shaw Savill & Albion Co. Ltd.* (*The Arawa*) [1977] 2 Lloyd's Rep. 416; on appeal, without reference to this point, [1980] 2 Lloyd's Rep. 135.

105. [1977] 2 Lloyd's Rep. 416. at p. 420.

106. *Ibid.*, at p. 424, applying *British Road Services Ltd.* v. *Arthur V. Crutchley & Co. Ltd.* [1968] 1 Lloyd's Rep. 271. See generally Palmer, *Bailment* (2nd Edn., 1991) pp. 1346 *et seq.*

decision thus neatly combined both the doctrine of vicarious liability (by Chambers) and the doctrine of strict contractual performance (by the shipowners) in one situation. The fact that the damage to the meat was caused by unauthorised and unpreventable industrial action was no defence at all.

The implications of *The Arawa* were profound, because it recognised that conduct in protest against an employer could nevertheless qualify as conduct for which that employer was answerable to third parties. Moreover, if (as we have remarked) such action could be treated as the employer's for purposes of vicarious liability, it might also have qualified as "fault" on the employer's part for purposes of denying him the defence of frustration (indeed, it is uncertain whether this aspect of fault, if doctrinally legitimate, has survived the transition to an objective test of control). Of course, much industrial action would be incapable, almost as a matter of law, of occurring in the course of employment. But the question whether such action can ever be the subject of vicarious liability was answered in the clear affirmative by Brandon J.

That being said, it is important not to overstate the decision. Brandon J. made no reference to the effect of the loaders' conduct on their contract of employment, and there is little indication that vicarious liability was extensively argued. More significantly, the Privy Council has recently refused to treat a go-slow by firemen as constituting a tort in the course of their employment. In *General Engineering Services Ltd*. v. *Kingston and St. Andrew Corporation*[107] the appellants' premises caught fire around 5.45 a.m. and a neighbour called the fire brigade. A journey which normally took about $3\frac{1}{2}$ minutes took the fire brigade some 17 minutes on this occasion. The reason was a go-slow policy operated by the firemen in support of a dispute with the corporation, their employer. The go-slow involved stopping and restarting the fire engine at short intervals. By the time the brigade arrived, the appellants' premises had burned down.

The appellants alleged that the respondent corporation were vicariously liable to them. In the proceedings, the respondents appear to have made an important concession. It was, they conceded, a clear inference from their conduct that the firemen had decided to let the premises burn. As Lord Ackner expressed it, the effect of the firemen's unauthorised and wrongful act was " . . . *so to prolong* the time taken by the journey to the scene of the fire, as to ensure that they did not arrive in time to extinguish it before the building and its contents were destroyed".[108] It seems that the firemen not only contemplated but intended that the premises should be destroyed.

The lower courts rejected the claim and the Privy Council upheld them. The way in which the firemen drove to the fire was not sufficiently connected with the acts which they were authorised to perform as to constitute merely an unauthorised mode of performing those acts. The acts which the firemen were authorised to perform were essentially threefold: to answer the alarm immediately, to drive to it as expeditiously as possible, and to extinguish it on arrival. What happened was so far removed from those acts as to be incapable of being classed simply as an unauthorised mode of performing them.

107. [1988] 3 All E.R. 867; McKendrick (1989) 18 I.L.J. 161.
108. [1988] 3 All E.R. 867, at p. 869 (emphasis added); and see at p. 868.

Lord Ackner made two further points. First, he said that so far as the practical consequences of their action were concerned, the firemen might just as well have stayed in the station after getting the alarm call or arrived punctually and watched the building burn.[109] Clearly, that sort of negligence[110] would not have approached closely enough to the firemen's authorised activities as to represent a method of performing those activities; why should the present case, where the physical effects were the same, attract any different legal result? Whereas the types of misconduct listed by Lord Ackner might have been morally indistinguishable, however, one should guard against taking this sort of argument too far. In practical terms, there may be little difference between suffering a deliberate injury and suffering one caused by negligence. There seems, nevertheless, to be a distinction between the principles on which vicarious liability is imposed for deliberate wrongdoing and those on which it is imposed for cases of negligence.[111] It is, of course, another matter whether this distinction should be maintained.

Secondly, Lord Ackner commented on the state of the corporation's contractual relations with its employees. In his view, the firemen's misconduct was " . . . a wrongful repudiation of an essential obligation of their contract of employment".[112] This amounted both to a criminal offence and to "the very negation of any performance of authorised acts".[113] It seems relatively unusual for a court concerned with issues of vicarious liability to measure the distance of the employee's departure from the course of his employment according to the seriousness of his breach of the employment contract. In some cases, the question will be immaterial because the employee will have committed no breach: a tort against the third party will not necessarily constitute a breach of contract against the employer. In others, it may be thought unsatisfactory for a court to pronounce on the employee's contractual position in proceedings where the employee is not sufficiently represented; *a fortiori*, perhaps, where such pronouncement interferes unnecessarily with the delicate mechanism of industrial action and negotiation. Of course, in extreme cases the question may have to be answered, because no employee whose contract has ended by virtue of his repudiation can possess a course of employment within

109. *Ibid.*, at p. 869.

110. There is, in fact, considerable room for speculation as to whether the firemen's conduct in *General Engineering* (consisting substantially, as it did, of omissions) genuinely constituted the tort of negligence towards the plaintiffs. If it did not, it is difficult to identify any other tort on their part; and if no such tort were committed, the grounds for imposing vicarious liability appear (at best) highly questionable. If, however, the firemen were personally guilty of negligence, it is arguable that their misconduct consisted merely in doing an authorised act (viz., travelling to the fire) in an unauthorised manner (viz., at a snail's pace). In that event, the argument in favour of rendering the employers answerable appears appreciably stronger. See McKendrick (1989) 18 I.L.J. 161, who suggests an analogy with *Limpus* v. *London General Omnibus Co.* (1862) 1 H. & C. 526, and also raises the possibility that the employer might be liable in negligence by virtue of his "control" over the employees (relying on *Smith* v. *Littlewoods Organisation Ltd.* [1987] A.C. 241, especially *per* Lord Goff of Chieveley).

111. *Morris* v. *C.W. Martin & Sons Ltd.* [1966] 1 Q.B. 716; *The Ocean Frost* [1986] A.C. 717; *Heasmans* v. *Clarity Cleaning Ltd.* [1987] I.R.L.R. 286; *Irving* v. *The Post Office* [1987] I.R.L.R. 289; *Makanjuola* v. *Commissioner of Police for the Metropolis* (1989) *The Times*, 8 August; McKendrick (1989) 18 I.L.J. 161.

112. [1988] 3 All E.R. 867, at p. 869.

113. *Ibid.*, at p. 870.

which to act.[114] At this level, the case may be largely indistinguishable from that of an employee who is alleged to have left his employment when the relevant misconduct occurred (as, for example, where the miscreant returns to the workplace after having resigned and steals property belonging to customers of the employer).[115] But there was no suggestion that the firemen's contracts had actually terminated in the *General Engineering* case.

Reliance on the precise terms of the employment contract in this context suggests other problems. Suppose, for example, that the contract provides that conduct which would otherwise constitute a breach of the employee's contract shall not do so.[116] Will such a provision necessarily involve the employer in liability to third parties for such conduct, or is there a supplementary test which enables a work-related act to be placed beyond the course of the employee's employment even though it does not technically constitute a breach of contract on his part? And would the position differ if the relevant exclusion clauses, instead of defining certain conduct as beyond the realm of contractual obligation altogether, had simply allowed such conduct to stand as a nominal breach of the contract but had provided that no damages were recoverable for that breach? Again, suppose that the employment contract provides that certain items of conduct on the part of employees (such as the negligent driving of company vehicles) shall automatically be regarded as repudiatory. Can the employer insulate himself from vicarious liability to third parties in this way, however minor the misconduct? It may, of course, be objected that the mere prescription within the contract of employment of certain types of conduct as repudiatory will not necessarily make them so as between employer and employee. This may be particularly true when the allegedly repudiatory act is an inadvertent rather than a deliberate one. But it could be most unsatisfactory for a court to have to delve into the legislative and contractual complexities of the employer–employee relationship in order to answer these questions according to a strict technical analysis of the contractual implications of the employee's behaviour. Moreover, Lord Ackner himself appears to accept that it may be permissible to regard deliberate and negligent conduct as carrying equivalent legal consequences if the practical consequences of both types of conduct are the same.[117] Such considerations suggest that it may be preferable, wherever possible, to disregard the exact terms of the contract of employment in assessing vicarious liability in tort.

The more immediate question is whether *General Engineering* now prevents, as a matter of principle, any act of industrial protest from falling within the protesters' course of employment for the purposes of vicarious liability in tort. It is submitted that it does not. The facts of *General Engineering* were extreme and the speech of Lord Ackner offers little guidance on the broader issue. Further, *The Arawa*[118] was

114. Although it is necessary for the employee's repudiation to be accepted by the employer before the employment will terminate, such acceptance will be readily inferred where the employee simply walks off the job.

115. Cf. *Darling Ladies' Wear Ltd.* v. *Hickey* [1949] 2 D.L.R. 420; [1950] 1 D.L.R. 720; *Kooragang Investments Pty. Ltd.* v. *Richardson & Wrench Ltd.* [1981] 3 All E.R. 65.

116. Cf. *Torquay Hotel Co. Ltd.* v. *Cousins* [1969] 2 Ch. 106, at pp. 137–138, *per* Lord Denning M.R.; Carty (1988) 104 L.Q.R. 250.

117. [1988] 3 All E.R. 867, at p. 869.

118. *Producers Meats Ltd.* v. *Shaw Savill & Albion Co. Ltd.* (*The Arawa*) [1977] 2 Lloyd's Rep. 416; on appeal, without reference to this point, [1980] 2 Lloyd's Rep. 135; above, p. 189.

not cited. This omission may not subvert the conclusion in *General Engineering* itself, but it does suggest that *The Arawa* should not be discarded unless clearly incompatible with it. Nothing in *General Engineering* decisively excludes the possibility that less dramatic go-slow operations might fall within the course of employment. A work-to-rule, or a work-to-grade, might also qualify for this purpose, notwithstanding the possibility that it will involve the employee in a breach of the implied duty of co-operation.[119] An employee's refusal to perform one particular aspect of his contractual responsibilities (as, for example, where university teachers refuse to mark examination papers or to release results)[120] raises more difficult questions, but even here the result in *General Engineering* might be distinguishable on particular facts.

There is, however, a crucial point of distinction between the position of the defendant in *General Engineering* and that of a contractor whose performance is impaired by domestic industrial action. That distinction is, of course, the presence in the latter case of a contractual relationship between the claimant and the defendant. Where such a relationship exists, there are strong arguments in favour of looking exclusively to the employer's contractual duty towards his customer and of allowing the express or implied definition of that duty to dictate the sum of his responsibility. What, exactly, has he promised? Has he undertaken to be responsible for performance in the situation prevailing, or is the expectation of such responsibility unjustified, having regard to the language and provenance of the contract? Is it essential to business efficacy that the employer should (or should not) be accountable for defective performance in the events which have occurred?

The pursuit of such an analysis may well suggest that there should be no implied contractual exemption for losses caused by the contractor's domestic industrial problems, even in those rare instances where the supervening event might otherwise have constituted frustration. Contractual terms may displace the frustratory effect of a particular event, leaving the contract in force despite its occurrence.[121] Conversely, the lack of control which a contractor may enjoy over the labour relations of his sub-contractor in respect of the contractual services may justify the conclusion that the contractor undertook no responsibility for the continued performance of the contract in the event of a strike among the sub-contractor's personnel. An example of such an approach is the county court decision in *Usher* v. *Intasun Holidays*

119. *Secretary of State for Employment* v. *A.S.L.E.F. (No. 2)* [1972] 2 Q.B. 455.

120. A threat of legal action by students over the 1989 AUT marking boycott was reported in (1989) *The Sunday Times*, 5 February; the claim does not seem to have materialised. Contrast two earlier reports of threatened action by parents of pupils in relation to the 1985 teachers' pay dispute: (1985) *The Times*, 9 February; (1985) *The Observer*, 17 February; cf. *Meade* v. *Haringey London Borough Council* [1979] 2 All E.R. 1016. Contrast, however, *Bartlett* v. *Department of Transport* (1984) 83 L.G.R. 579, at p. 591, where the plaintiff had argued that the refusal by the defendants' employees to work on one particular road (the A34) constituted a wrong for which the defendants were vicariously liable. Boreham J. said: "This strikes me as a very harsh proposition. Of course, an employer is liable for the acts or omissions of his employees, which constitute a wrong done to the plaintiff and which are done in the course of the employees' employment. In this case, however, the plaintiff does not rely on anything done by employees in the course of their employment: they had refused to work on that particular road. In any event, assuming that the employees were acting unlawfully or in breach of their duty in withdrawing their labour, they were not in breach of duty to the plaintiff. Their breach was of their duty to their employers. In my judgment, of that, the plaintiff cannot complain unless, perhaps, that breach was induced, or condoned, by the employers." It seems clear that Boreham J.'s approach to the instant allegation of vicarious liability was not inconsistent with discovering such liability in other cases on less extreme facts.

121. Treitel, *op. cit.*, pp. 795–799.

Ltd.,[122] where the defendant tour operators were held not liable for the disruption of the plaintiffs' honeymoon as a result of industrial action and technical problems affecting the airline engaged by the defendants to carry the plaintiffs.

The adoption of a duty-orientated approach could also render redundant any collateral enquiry as to whether the contractor's conduct of a domestic labour dispute renders him liable in tort to his customers. There is substantial authority for the general proposition that commercial contracts, at least, should be regarded as defining the full measure of the parties' obligations, and should not be outflanked or supplemented by an independent liability in tort. This approach has been advocated both in regard to a contracting party's personal liability for negligence,[123] and in regard to his liability for the delinquencies of his employees.[124] The same attitude should govern the full spectrum of obligations owed by a contractor in the event of internal industrial strife. There is at least one judicial suggestion that a contractor who entrusts his bailor's goods to a sub-contractor when industrial action appears imminent among that sub-contractor's workforce may be sued for negligence if the action materialises and the goods are damaged.[125] It is true that Brandon J. dismissed this claim, but only (it appears) on the grounds that the industrial action was unforeseeable. In future, it may well be desirable to allow the contract to represent a full definition of the contractor's duties: not only in a case of external industrial action, but in a case where the impending industrial action involves the contractor's own employees.

6. DISCRETIONARY REMEDIES

There is one final point. This chapter has been limited to claims for damages. But many claimants will prefer a discretionary remedy, such as specific performance of the affected contract or an injunction to command the delivery up of goods immobilised by industrial action. The pursuit of such remedies raises somewhat different issues from a simple damages claim, particularly perhaps when the industrial action is merely threatened as a consequence of the contractor's future performance. In such cases, the court may be required not only to quantify the reality and potential consequences of the risk but also to identify the weight which is to be given, in any exercise of its discretionary jurisdiction, to threats of unlawful behaviour. Should a court, for example, be influenced by the potentially adverse consequence of its ordering the defendant to perform his contract or to deliver up the plaintiff's goods? Such dilemmas are significant, and have attracted a substantial volume of authority; not all of it, perhaps, consistent.[126] But that is another story.

NORMAN PALMER

122. [1987] C.L.Y. 418 (Registrar, Cardiff County Court). Cf. *Compton* v. *I.L.G. Travel* [1990] C.L.Y. 625 (Registrar, Winchester County Court).

123. *Tai Hing Cotton Mill Ltd.* v. *Liu Chong Hing Bank Ltd.* [1986] A.C. 80; *Greater Nottingham Co-Operative Society Ltd.* v. *Cementation Piling and Foundations Ltd.* [1989] Q.B. 71.

124. *Photo Production Ltd.* v. *Securicor Transport Ltd.* [1980] A.C. 827, at p. 848, *per* Lord Diplock.

125. *The Arawa* [1977] 2 Lloyd's Rep. 416, at p. 426, *per* Brandon J.

126. See the authorities listed in Halsbury, *Laws of England* (4th Edn.), vol. 45, paras. 1485, 1486; *Parker* v. *Camden Borough Council* [1986] Ch. 162. The most interesting modern analysis of this problem is that of Rogers J., Chief Judge of the Commercial Court, Common Law Division, Supreme Court of New South Wales, in an unpublished paper delivered at Melbourne on 5 July 1990.

CHAPTER 10

FRUSTRATION AND FORCE MAJEURE IN BUILDING CONTRACTS

1. INTRODUCTION

In building contracts, no less than other types of contracts, party objectives can be defeated without fault through unforeseen changes. Situations may change so rapidly from tender to taking possession of the site that a party acting prudently would simply not have bid on the contract had he known of these changes when entering into the contract. The changes could be economic, legal or natural. The building contract in this way may become a complete liability. Such changes do occur and it is not surprising that judicial and contractual mechanisms have arisen purporting to address them. The contractual means include price escalation or variation clauses, *force majeure* clauses, hardship clauses and others. The judicial means include doctrines such as frustration and commercial impracticability in Anglo-American law. However, this judicial evolution has still not kept up with the pace of change today and has left contractors with inadequate solutions.

A small number of commentators have now critically assessed the foundation of the doctrine of frustration in English law and concluded that it is misunderstood. John D. Wladis[1] argues that the leading case of *Paradine* v. *Jane*[2] is usually cited for a proposition for which the case does not stand and which the judge had no intention of establishing; likewise, *Krell* v. *Henry*[3] "was really a creature of unique circumstances rather than the foundation of a new principle of impossibility law".[4] The point in adverting to this is to introduce a call for flexibility in one's approach to both the law and these contractual doctrines. Hence, by pointing to doctrinaire views as to the bases of the doctrine of frustration and the concept of *force majeure*,

1. "Common Law and Uncommon Events. The Development of the Doctrine of Impossibility of Performance in English Contract Law", (1987) 75 Georgetown L.J. 1575; cf. W.H. Page, "The Development of the Doctrine of Impossibility of Performance", (1920) 18 Michigan L.R. 589.

2. (1647) Aleyn 26, 82 E.R. 897, Style 47, 82 E.R. 519 where the court held that dispossession of a lease by Royalists during the English civil war did not excuse the lessee's obligation to pay rent.

3. [1903] 2 K.B. 740 (C.A.), one of the so-called "coronation cases" in which a short-term lessee of a flat along the coronation route of Edward VII was excused from paying rent when the coronation was postponed. See generally R.G. McElroy and Glanville Williams, "The Coronation Cases—I", (1940) 4 M.L.R. 241 and, by the same authors, "The Coronation Cases—II", (1941) 5 M.L.R. 1.

4. *Op. cit.* Wladis, fn. 1, 1576. Others reiterate this view, see, e.g., Norman R. Prance, "Commercial Impracticability: A Textual and Economic Analysis of Section 2–615 of the Uniform Commercial Code", (1986) 19 *Indiana Law Review* 457, at p. 460; Richard A. Posner and Andrew M. Rosenfield, "Impossibility and Related Doctrines in Contract Law: An Economic Analysis", (1977) 6 *Journal of Legal Studies* 83, at p. 97; John Henry Schlegel, "Of Nuts, and Ships, and Sealing Wax, Suez, and Frustrating Things—The Doctrine of Impossibility of Performance", (1969) 23 *Rutgers Law Review* 419, at p. 420.

perhaps a greater willingness to re-examine these subjects in the future may accrue. Put bluntly, "do our courts really have no good reason for re-examining the concept of frustration in order to see whether or not the standard textbook view continues to be justifiable?".[5]

2. THE TEXTBOOK VIEW

"As a general rule contractual obligations are absolute in that a party is not absolved merely because performance becomes more expensive or even proves to be impossible. A party who contracts to do the impossible is liable for failing to do it, unless he excludes such liability."[6]

One may trace the authority for this proposition directly to *Paradine* v. *Jane*[7] and, although it is questionable authority for such a proposition, it has been applied to building contracts. *The Company of Proprietors of the Brecknock and Abergavenny Canal Navigation Co.* v. *Pritchard and others*[8] involved an agreement to construct and then maintain a bridge for a period of years. The bridge was completed but was subsequently washed away by a flood. The declaration sought by the plaintiff was that the defendants were still obliged to repair the bridge. The defendants in response argued that a flood was an extraordinary event and that impossibility should discharge the performance of their contract. The court rejected this argument and held the defendants liable to rebuild the bridge. Thus the foundation was laid for the application of the *Paradine* principle in subsequent building contract cases.

A series of cases followed in which *Paradine* was again applied, although only a few of these cases involved actual impossibility on a strict or textbook view.[9] Thus this textbook view, notwithstanding lines of authority that would develop into exceptions, continues to have an effect in the area of building contracts which is disproportionate to its validity.

3. INTO THE AGE OF EXCUSE

The erosion of the strict view of the *Paradine* principle and the consolidation of doctrines excusing non-performance can conveniently be referred to as commencing with the case of *Taylor* v. *Caldwell*.[10] The case involved a contract to let a garden and music hall for a concert. Following the accidental burning of the hall the court had to consider whether the contract was discharged. The court held that the contract was discharged. The rationale for this was that the parties' liabilities were excused through implying into the contract a condition that they would only be

5. A.D.M. Forte, "Economic Frustration of Commercial Contracts: A Comparative Analysis with Particular Reference to the United Kingdom", (1986) *Juridical Review* 1, at p. 3.
6. John Uff, *Construction Law* (5th Edn., 1991), p. 102.
7. *Op. cit.*, fn. 2.
8. (1796) 6 T.R. 750, 101 E.R. 807.
9. See Wladis, *op. cit.*, fn. 1, for a careful review of these cases.
10. (1863) 3 B. & S. 826, 122 E.R. 309. Illustrations of early cases subsequent to *Paradine* which were viewed as exceptional would include personal service contracts where the promisor died or was permanently incapacitated, e.g. *Hyde* v. *The Dean and Chapter of Windsor* (1596) Cro. Eliz. 457, 78 E.R. 710; and cases of supervening illegality, e.g. *Atkinson* v. *Ritchie* (1809) 10 East 530, 103 E.R. 877.

bound if the hall were standing. The spirit of these exceptions, motivated at times by Roman and civil law,[11] furthered the articulation of general rules of discharge or excuse which, for our purposes, included the doctrine of frustration.[12]

In the United States the change was heralded with the case of *Mineral Park Land Co.* v. *Howard.*[13] In that case, a contractor agreed to remove gravel which subsequently was discovered to be mostly below water and thus prohibitively expensive to extract. The contractor declined to remove the submerged gravel even though he was contractually bound to do so. In an action for breach of contract the court reasoned that the continued existence of the gravel was an implied condition of the duty of perform and that the difficulty in removing it rendered the gravel non-existent. Non-performance was excused on this basis: "A thing is impossible in legal contemplation when it is not practicable; and a thing is impracticable when it can only be done at an excessive and unreasonable cost."[14] Thus began the move in the evolution of the doctrine of impossibility of performance to impracticability of performance in American law. Prior to *Mineral Park*, cases involving an increase in costs formed no basis for excusing non-performance.[15] The result was a change in focus. "Over the course of the scholarly and judicial debate surrounding this excuse, most authorities re-characterised the impossibility . . . excuse as the doctrine of impracticability of performance."[16]

The purpose of referring to the American law is to raise one alternative course of direction for English law. As Harold Alexander Lewis wrote, "the doctrine of com-

11. The civil law authorities referred to by Mr. Justice Blackburn derive from the writing of the French jurist Pothier, see *Traité des obligations selon les règles tant du for de la conscience que de for exterieur*, Part 3, Chapter 6, art. 3, 668; Roman law addressed the effect of supervening circumstances on contractual obligations in the Digest of Justinian published in 533 A.D. at, e.g., 45.1.23 and 45.1.33. See generally R.G. McElroy, "Frustration and Force Majeure: The Common Law and the Common Market", (1963) 1 N.Z.L.J. 185.

12. The term frustration is often broadly used to describe the failure of any contractual purpose. However, the origins of the term are narrower and initially, *post Taylor*, were limited to cases involving a "frustration of the adventure" which usually arose from supervening or inordinate delay in charterparties and without fault on either part; see, e.g., *Jackson* v. *Union Marine Insurance Co. Ltd.* (1874) L.R. 10 C.P. 125 at p. 148, *per* Lord Bramwell. Later cases, e.g. *F.A. Tamplin Steamship Co. Ltd.* v. *Anglo-Mexican Petroleum Products Ltd.*, [1916] 2 A.C. 397 at p. 404, *per* Lord Loreburn and *Joseph Constantine Steamship Line Ltd.* v. *Imperial Smelting Corporation Ltd.* [1942] A.C. 154 at p. 168, *per* Viscount Maugham, drew upon "impossibility" to explain the term: Forte, *op. cit.* fn. 5, 1: "The modern view is to regard frustration as an omnibus concept covering supervening impracticability, supervening illegality and frustration of purpose." This accords with the usage of the term in this chapter, as the writer wishes to draw some broad comparisons to American doctrine.

13. 172 Cal. 289, 156 P. 458 (1916).

14. *Ibid.*, p. 293.

15. E.g. *Leavitt* v. *Dover* 67 N.H. 94, 32 A. 156 (1892); *International Paper Co.* v. *Rockefeller* 161 App. Div. 180, 146 N.Y.S. 317 (1914).

16. Harold Alexander Lewis, "Allocating Risk in Take-or-Pay Contracts: Are *Force Majeure* and Commercial Impracticability the Same Defense?" (1989) 42 *Southwestern Law Journal* 1047, at p. 1053, and accompanying notes. A considerable body of literature is devoted to this evolution, particularly in the context of section 2-615 of the Uniform Commercial Code, see further Chapter 16 and also Richard W. Duesenberg, "Impossibility: It Isn't Good Code Language", (1981) 1 *Journal of Law and Commerce* 29; Benjamin N. Henszey, "U.C.C. Section 2-615—Does 'Impracticable' Mean Impossible?" (1977) 10 *Uniform Commercial Code Law Journal* 107; Stephen J. Sirianni, "The Developing Law of Contractual Impracticability and Impossibility", (1981) 14 *Uniform Commercial Code Law Journal* 30. However, in the view of many commentators, notwithstanding the apparent intention of the drafters of section 2-615 and its express language, the section has been restrictively interpreted, see Norman R. Prance, *op. cit.*, fn. 4.

mercial impracticability is rooted in the English law doctrine of impossibility"[17]; and, arguably, so too may any future English doctrine of commercial impracticability be rooted in American law. What then is the English law in this respect?

The principal English case in support of the proposition that impracticability is not an excuse for non-performance is *Davis Contractors Ltd.* v. *Fareham U.D.C.*[18] Contractors agreed to construct 78 houses for the defendant local authority over a period of eight months at a cost of £94,000. Owing to serious labour shortages the work took 22 months and the cost increased to £115,000. The contractors alleged that the contract had been frustrated and claimed an increased sum on a *quantum meruit* basis. The House of Lords refused the claim and stated that the delay was within the ordinary range of commercial probability and that there had been no fundamental change of circumstances.[19]

However, in contrast to *Davis*, a series of cases may be put forward concerning matters such as delay, express contractual provision, construction and intent that lend support to the view that performance of a contract may be excused by frustration on the ground of impracticability. Although it has been argued that these cases are explicable on other grounds and, as such, do not support a rule that impracticability alone is sufficient to discharge the performance of a contract in English law,[20] the view taken here is that such a rationalisation of these cases will only serve to postpone their eventual critical evaluation.

(a) Destruction of the subject matter of the contract

The scope of the doctrine of frustration is usually approached by reference to different types of frustrating events. According to *Chitty on Contracts*,[21] this is "because of the accidents of litigation and of law reporting". While the doctrine can also be approached on the basis of the different types of contract involved, there are too few cases in the area of building contracts alone to provide an accurate portrayal in this way. In relation to the destruction of the subject matter of the contract, the classic case is, of course, *Taylor* v. *Caldwell*. "The principle seems to us to be that, in contracts in which the performance depends upon the continued existence of a given person or thing, a condition is implied that the impossibility of performance arising from the perishing of the person or thing shall excuse the performance."[22] While the mechanism of using an implied term as the theoretical foundation for the doctrine was criticised and later abandoned, the *Taylor* principle has remained.[23] The criticism of the implied term theory, as it came to be known, centred upon the fact that it would be unlikely for parties to a contract to hold a common view on any particular frustrating event. The anomaly is highlighted in building contract cases where a distinction can be drawn between agreements to

17. *Ibid.*, p. 1052.
18. [1956] A.C. 696.
19. See, generally, Lord Radcliffe at p. 729, discussed further at pp. 42–44.
20. Treitel, *The Law of Contract*, (8th Edn.), pp. 780–783.
21. (26th Edn., 1989) para. 1642.
22. (1863) 3 B. & S. 826, 839 (122 E.R. 309, 314).
23. See Robert L. Birmingham, "Why is there *Taylor* v. *Caldwell*? Three Propositions About Impracticability", (1989) 23 *University of San Francisco Law Review* 379; see also Lord Denning's comment in *The Eugenia* [1964] 2 Q.B. 226, at p. 238, that "the theory of an implied term has now been discarded by everyone, or nearly everyone, for the simple reason that it does not represent the truth".

build and agreements to repair buildings. In the former case, where risk is on the builder until completion, the destruction of the building without fault on the part of the builder will not excuse performance. However, in the latter case the existence of the building is assumed for the purposes of the agreement, thus the destruction of the building would frustrate the contract.[24] So, a contract to manufacture and install machinery in a factory was held to be frustrated, when a fire destroyed the factory prior to the completion of the installation, on the ground that the factory was necessary for the performance of the contract.[25]

Apart from the destruction of the subject matter of the contract, the operation of the doctrine of frustration may be examined under a variety of other headings. As the focus of this chapter is upon building contracts, the headings which have been chosen have particular relevance to this context. The first heading to be considered is delay.

(b) Delay

The unavailability of a person or thing that is essential for the purpose of performing a contract may, for present purposes, be equated with delay. A series of cases stemming from *Taylor* established the parameters which apply when unavailability for a period of time, such that it becomes unreasonable to expect performance of the contract, is permitted as an excuse for non-performance. The rationale for the excuse is understandable. If it appears from the contract that it was to be performed during a specified time, and this does not happen, there will then be "unavailability". The first cases to consider unavailability involved charterparties[26] designated with reference to a point in time. *Jackson* v. *Union Marine Insurance Co. Ltd.*[27] is perhaps the most important of these charterparty cases. *Jackson* involved a suit by a shipowner against his insurer for losses allegedly suffered while under charterparty and sailing to load. The charterer had purported to cancel the charterparty when confronted with a lengthy period of time for repairs. The issue before the court was whether or not the charterer had the right to cancel the charterparty because of the delay arising from the repairs. The insurer took the view that performance within a reasonable time was irrelevant. The court disagreed and implied a condition that the vessel should arrive in a reasonable time.[28] *Jackson* involved a charter for a specific voyage, although the principle has since been extended to time charterparties where no particular voyage was involved.[29]

The reasoning in *Jackson* has been applied in one of the leading building contract

24. See *Appleby* v. *Myers* (1867) L.R. 2 C.P. 651. The English view is premised upon the implied condition that the thing exists or will continue to exist, whereas the American view proceeds on the basis of a warranty by the employer that it shall exist; see *Butterfield* v. *Byron* 153 Mass. 517 (1890), 27 N.E. 667 (1891).

25. *Appleby* v. *Myers* (1867) L.R. 2 C.P. 651.

26. See, for example, *Geipel* v. *Smith* (1872) L.R. 7 Q.B. 404; *Jackson* v. *Union Marine Insurance Co.* (1874) L.R. 10 C.P. 125 and *Dahl* v. *Nelson, Donkin & Co.* (1881) 6 App. Cas. 38 (H.L.).

27. (1874) L.R. 10 C.P. 125.

28. *Ibid.*, p. 145, *per* Baron Bramwell: "There is then a condition precedent that the vessel shall arrive in a reasonable time. On failure of this, the contract is at an end." As to what constitutes a reasonable time, see Andrew J. Bateson, "Time as an Element of Frustration" (1954) *Business Law Review* 173.

29. See *Bank Line Ltd.* v. *Arthur Capel & Co.* [1919] A.C. 435; see also *Hirji Mulji* v. *Cheong Yue S.S. Co. Ltd.* [1926] A.C. 497.

cases, *Metropolitan Water Board* v. *Dick, Kerr & Co.*[30] The case concerned an engineering contract for the construction of a water reservoir with a period of completion set at six years. Approximately one and a half years into the project a stop work order was issued by the government because of war. Notwithstanding a clause in the contract permitting extensions of time for delay for any cause, and in lieu of other remedies, the court held that the contract had been frustrated because of a delay which was stated to have been beyond the contemplation of the clause.[31] The decision is exceptional in that the event which delayed the project was actually provided for in the contract. In the normal course, a court will hold in such a case that the doctrine of frustration is not applicable because the parties have addressed their minds to the event. However, the circumstances here, examined prospectively, were such that, by the time the statutory legal impediment could have been removed, there would have been such a total change in conditions as to have entailed new performance.[32]

(c) Subsequent legal changes and supervening illegality

Subsequent changes in the law or in the legality of the acts of parties to contracts may precipitate frustration. The legal position of contractors may be affected either by express legislative change or through the exercise of administrative power. A subsequent legal change may, for instance, forbid the act undertaken in the contract, as in the case of wartime regulations prohibiting the trading of timber.[33] Conversely, wartime regulations have also been held not to frustrate a lease.[34] Changes in municipal plan legislation or alterations to restrictive covenants could also form

30. [1918] A.C. 119 (H.L.), discussed further at pp. 35–36. See also *Wong Lai Ying* v. *Chinachem Investment Co. Ltd.* (1979) 13 B.L.R. 81 (P.C.) applying *Metropolitan Water Board* to a case involving a landslip, discussed further below, pp. 206–207.

31. *Ibid.*, p. 126, Lord Finlay wrote: "Condition 32 does not cover the case in which the interruption is of such a character and duration that it vitally and fundamentally changes the conditions of the contract, and could not possibly have been in the contemplation of the parties to the contract when it was made." The case is also susceptible to analysis from several other perspectives, for example illegality or statutory prohibition, war-requisitioning and impracticability.

32. Additional cases entailing delay in the context of contractual provisions for events are also discussed below pp. 206–210.

33. *Denny, Mott and Dickson Ltd.* v. *James B. Fraser & Co. Ltd.* [1944] A.C. 265 (H.L.); *Wahda Bank* v. *Arab Bank plc* (1992) *The Times*, 23 December. The outbreak of war itself will not frustrate a contract. Rather, it is the intercourse with an enemy that provokes the frustration. See *Finelvet A.G.* v. *Vinava Shipping Co. Ltd.* [1983] 1 W.L.R. 1469; *Fibrosa Spolka Akcyjna* v. *Fairbairn Lawson Combe Barbour Ltd.* [1943] A.C. 32 and *Ertel Bieber & Co.* v. *Rio Tinto Co. Ltd.* [1918] A.C. 260; see generally Arnold D. McNair, "Frustration of Contract by War", (1940) 56 L.Q.R. 173.

34. *Cricklewood Property & Investment Trust Ltd.* v. *Leighton Investment Trust Ltd.* [1945] A.C. 221. A recent application of the holding in this case may be found in *John Lewis Properties plc* v. *Viscount Chelsea* [1993] 2 E.G.L.R. 77. Briefly, the plaintiff was *prima facie* in breach of a building covenant to demolish and rebuild certain buildings on leased properties and sought declarations to clarify its legal position. Subsequent to assuming the obligation under the covenant, the subject buildings were listed as special interest premises and thus required planning authority consent to be demolished. Evidence was led that such consents were given in only about two per cent of the applications and so, even though no such application was in fact made, frustration was alleged as a ground for excuse. However, the case turned instead, in the judge's view, upon impossibility of performance. Mummery, J. stated (at p. 82): "On the high authority of these dicta [in *Cricklewood*] and as a matter of principle, I hold that there may exist lawful excuses for non performance of a building covenant in a long lease and such excuses would provide a defence to an action for forfeiture of breach of covenant, even though they would not provide a defence to a claim for rent". By reason of the listing of the buildings it became impossible to perform the rebuilding obligations and the plaintiff was therefore not in breach of the building covenant.

the basis for discharge under this heading. In the case of *Baily* v. *De Crespigny*,[35] a lessor was relieved from an alleged breach of a restrictive covenant that neither he nor his assigns would build on land adjoining the leased premises when a railway company compulsorily acquired the land and did build upon it.[36] Supervening illegality may even arise where the issuance of an injunction restrains performance of the contract as originally envisaged.[37]

These illustrations involve cases of supervening illegality; that is, illegality arising subsequent to the formation of the contract. However, if at the time the parties enter into the contract the illegality already exists, this antecedent illegality will not entail frustration. This point, while simply made, nevertheless entails considerable complexity because in the former case the contract is discharged on the ground of frustration (supervening illegality), whereas the latter example involves a consideration of the impact of the doctrine of illegality on the formation of a contract.[38] On certain fact situations it may be difficult to decide into which category the case falls. In the context of building contracts the importance of this determination is a function of the all-pervasive statutory control affecting the industry. The paradigm case arises when the contract can only be lawfully performed with administrative approval, as in the case of permits or licences. Whether there is lawful performance here may be approached on the basis of the parties' intentions. For instance, in the event that the parties are intent from the outset on performing without a required licence, such a contract is void or illegal *ab initio*. Conversely, where the parties are intent from the outset that the licence shall be obtained in advance of construction, then it is properly a condition precedent to performance, the failure of which should preclude formation of the contract and may absolve either party from paying damages. With building contracts in particular, approvals such as these usually stand in addition to express contractual terms providing for compliance with statutory provisions.[39]

35. (1869) 4 L.R. (Q.B.) 180.

36. See generally *Studholme* v. *South Western Gas Board* [1954] 1 W.L.R. 313 where nationalisation under the Gas Act 1948 frustrated a contract between a solicitor and a gas company, and *Brown* v. *The Mayor, etc. of London* (1862) 13 C.B., (N.S.) 828, 143 E.R. 327 where the statutory transfer of tolls rendered a condition in a bond to pay an annuity therefrom impossible. This context is particularly relevant today in view of the increasing number of concession and build and operate transfer agreements in building projects. See also *Islwyn Borough Council and Another* v. *Newport Borough Council* (1993) *The Times*, 28 June (C.A. Hirst L.J. dissenting) for an unsuccessful attempt by one of three borough councils to end continuing obligations toward two other councils on grounds of supervening illegality and frustration. The case suggests that courts will be very reluctant to find that subsequent legislation has frustrated a contract unless it is clear from the words of the statute that the contract was intended to fall within its scope and that further performance was rendered unlawful.

37. See *Codelfa Construction Pty. Ltd.* v. *State Rail Authority of New South Wales* (1982) 149 C.L.R. 337, and commented on by Jane P. Swanton, "Discharge of Contracts by Frustration: *Codelfa Construction Pty Ltd.* v. *State Rail Authority of New South Wales*", (1983) 57 A.L.J. 201.

38. M.P. Furmston, "The Analysis of Illegal Contracts", (1965–66) 16 *University of Toronto Law Journal* 267, devoted an article to this point in which he wrote, at p. 267: "The purpose of this paper is to show that the question of whether a contract is illegal is one of considerable complexity which demands precise analysis." See also Leon E. Trakman, "The Effect of Illegality in the Law of Contract: Suggestions for Reform" (1977) 55 Can.Bar Rev. 625 and Glanville Williams, "The Legal Effect of Illegal Contracts", (1942) 8 C.L.J. 51.

39. See, e.g., JCT Contract 1980 Edition and Clause 4, and the ICE Conditions, (6th Edn.), clause 26(3) discussed below; see generally Donald Keating, "Breach of the Building Regulations", (1984–85) *Construction Law Journal* 87.

(d) Ground conditions

The cases concerning ground conditions are strict and, save for contractual provisions to the contrary, performance will not be excused in a contract to build on a particular site as a result of the ground conditions rendering the construction impossible. The explanation for this is that the onus is upon the contractor to ascertain prior to tendering that the work may be effected on the site. By extension, where there is a risk to completion of the work due to the ground conditions, and if in consequence of the poor ground conditions part of the work is destroyed, the contractor will be required either to reinstate the work or to become liable in damages for failure to complete the contract.[40] If it is not the ground conditions *per se* but rather the method of constructing the works that gives rise to the impossibility of performance, then the contractors are obliged to adopt another method. The contractor is not entitled to abandon the contract simply as a result of any additional expense incurred in adopting an alternative method of construction.[41] The strictness of this rule is underlined in practice by the absence of express warranties or even express exclusions of liability concerning either the physical state of, or the information provided on, the ground conditions. When these situations combine with the absence of a warranty by the employer that the architect's design is even practicable, contractors have little room to manoeuvre.[42]

In sum, few areas of building law are as strict as that concerning ground conditions. Very often, the obligations to complete are unqualified and factual situations can preclude pre-site investigation by tendering contractors. Given that frustration is not an appropriate remedy in such a case, the implication by the courts of an appropriate warranty concerning practicability of design is called for.[43]

(e) Strikes[44]

One may begin with the general rule that, in the absence of a contractual provision granting relief in the event of a strike, strikes will afford no excuse for non-performance of the contract. The contractual provisions relating to time for completion of the work are regarded strictly. The consequences of a strike may differ depending on whether or not they stem from within one's own workforce or from without; for example, that of a third party. The courts may conclude that a contracting party cannot claim that a contract is frustrated where the strike is occasioned by his own workforce on the ground that a party cannot rely upon his own default as an excuse for his non-performance.[45] In such a case "frustration" has been held to have been "self-induced".[46] Conversely, in the case of a strike by a

40. *Emden's Construction Law* (1990) para. 431, citing *Bottoms* v. *York Corporation* (1892) 2 Hudson's B.C. (4th Edn.) 208, (C.A.); *McDonald* v. *Workington Corporation* (1893) 9 T.L.R. 230 (C.A.) and *Jackson* v. *Eastbourne Local Board* (1886) 2 Hudson's B.C. (4th Edn.) 81 (H.L.).

41. *Jackson* v. *Eastbourne Local Board* (1886) 2 Hudson's B.C. (4th Edn.) 81 (H.L.).

42. *Thorn* v. *The Mayor and Commonalty of London* (1876) 1 App. Cas. 120.

43. I.N. Duncan Wallace, *Hudson's Building and Engineering Contracts* (10th Edn.) (Supp.), 268–269 noting several American decisions that have not mitigated the strictness of these rules, for example *Bentley* v. *The State* (1889) 41 N.W. 338, *Penn Bridge* v. *City of New Orleans* (1915) 222 F. 733.

44. See generally Chapter 9.

45. *Budgett & Co.* v. *Binnington & Co.* (1890) 25 Q.B.D. 320, affirmed [1891] 1 Q.B. 35 (C.A.).

46. The concept of self-induced frustration is relatively obscure but is subjected to fuller analysis in Chapter 3.

third party and in the absence of a contractual provision on point, a contract may be frustrated if the change amounts to a radical change in the obligation.[47] The radical change may frustrate the commercial adventure through delay or through other means.[48] This situation may be contrasted with one where a contractual provision, very often a *force majeure* clause, has been incorporated into the contract and which does encompass strikes.[49] Thus, a *force majeure* clause may operate in circumstances which would be insufficient to discharge a contract on the ground of frustration.

(f) Weather

Outdoor construction, changes in the seasons, abrupt adverse weather conditions and the incidents of disparate regions and continents form the environment in which building contracts operate. Thus, it is perhaps not too surprising to see that, in the absence of express provision, such matters when operating to the contractor's detriment do not as a general rule excuse non-performance. The general rule is shortly illustrated by the early case of *Maryon* v. *Carter*.[50] An action was brought by a builder on a contract for a fixed price for the construction of a house. The builder also agreed, among other things, to pave a footpath to the house in return for a further sum. The builder agreed to complete the work by a certain date but needed an additional four days because of bad weather. As a result of the delay the purchaser refused to pay and the builder was forced to sue. Before the court it was held that, notwithstanding the bad weather which had prevented the builder from completing on time, the delay disentitled the builder from recovering the further sum.

In building contract cases the question of the weather is often inextricably linked to delays and how winter conditions may intervene either to increase cost or to affect access to or use of the site. This issue arose directly in *Bush* v. *Whitehaven Port and Town Trustees*.[51] Here, Bush contracted to lay pipes for Whitehaven over the summer months but, owing to Whitehaven's delay, the work had to be completed during the winter months with certain attendant cost increases. Bush sought recovery and the court upheld the claim. But the case has since been disapproved in *Davis Contractors*[52] and it runs contrary to other authorities.[53] A further case which raises similar issues is *Electric Power Equipment Ltd.* v. *RCA Victor Co. Ltd.*[54] The plaintiff contracted with the defendant to install power and communications cables

47. *Davis Contractors Ltd.* v. *Fareham U.D.C.* [1956] A.C. 696 at p. 729, *per* Lord Radcliffe.

48. Several illustrations involving charterparties or strikes by dockworkers may be given, for example, *Hick* v. *Raymond and Reid* [1893] A.C. 22 (H.L.); *The Penelope* [1928] P. 180 and *The Nema* [1982] A.C. 724.

49. The application of *force majeure* clauses to industrial action is discussed in more detail in Chapter 9, above. In *MacMillan Bloedel Ltd.* v. *British Columbia Hydro and Power Authority* (1992) 98 D.L.R. (4th) 492 (B.C.C.A.) the court held the word "strike" in a *force majeure* clause when given its natural and ordinary meaning included a work stoppage for political reasons.

50. (1830) 4 Car. & P. 295. N.P., 172 E.R. 711.

51. (1888) 52 J.P. 392, 2 Hudson's B.C., (4th Edn.), p. 122.

52. *Davis Contractors* v. *Fareham U.D.C.* [1956] A.C. 696.

53. Indeed, in *McAlpine Humberoak Ltd.* v. *McDermott International Inc.* (1992) 48 B.L.R. 1, 18–19 the Court of Appeal agreed with the view expressed in *Hudson on Building Contracts* (10th Edn.) at p. 573 that *Bush* may now be taken to have been overruled.

54. (1963) 41 D.L.R. (2d) 727.

at various sites in northern Canada. A completion date was stipulated as 15 December. This date was predicated on the defendant preparing the sites. The contract contained the following condition:

"1. It is agreed that the Contractors proposal is based on working conditions normally encountered during the months of September and October. In the event that snow or temperature conditions are such as to hinder or delay the progress of the work, the additional costs of continuing the work under such conditions when so directed by the Engineer, in writing, will be at the expense of RCA Victor."[55]

Although the contract was executed in early October the work did not commence until November when winter conditions made the anticipated mode of installation unworkable. The consequence was that a slower and more expensive alternative had to be employed. Verchere J. held, relying upon *Davis Contractors* v. *Fareham U.D.C.*,[56] that the contract was not frustrated and that the plaintiff's *quantum meruit* claim failed. He stated that:

"Neither can the existence then or the realization of the prevalence in the near future of weather conditions unlike those 'normally anticipated in September and October' have the effect of destroying the basis of the contract so as to entitle the plaintiff to payment upon a *quantum meruit* basis."[57]

One final case may be referred to. In *Klein* v. *Sanderson*[58] the plaintiff operated as a custom-combiner or someone who threshes crops for others on a one-off contractual basis. It was common ground that the sole point upon which the parties had actually reached agreement was that the whole crop should be threshed. There was no written agreement, no precise timeframe and not even a price for the work. Following commencement of the threshing, a snowstorm stopped the threshing indefinitely. Harvey C.J. stated that "the question for consideration here is whether when it is the act of God in the interposition of bad weather which prevents [the] continuance"[59] of the threshing, the thresher is relieved from liability to continue the threshing. After a review of a number of authorities he concluded:

"It seems . . . that the contract to thresh the whole crop is based on the assumption of conditions remaining such as will permit of that being done with nothing more than temporary interruption and while it would not be determined by a slight storm, a permanent break in the weather making threshing impossible for an indefinite period would determine it."[60]

In coming to this conclusion Harvey C.J. placed reliance upon *Krell* v. *Henry*[61] and the effect of the perishing of a state of things or condition essential for performance of the contract. His Lordship clearly viewed weather conditions as being within the scope of this principle and he was prepared to hold that, on the facts, the contract was discharged. The decision, though exceptional, may be understood if one examines the policy reasons behind it. These reasons included the importance of the full utilisation of threshing capacity during peak harvest times and the fact that crops

55. *Ibid.*, pp. 731–732.
56. [1956] A.C. 696.
57. (1963) 41 D.L.R. (2d) 727, at p. 751.
58. (1928) 3 D.L.R. 284.
59. *Ibid.*, p. 287.
60. *Ibid.*
61. [1903] 2 K.B. 740.

left standing over the winter in the district in question had become a source of difficulty.[62]

(g) Inflation, price and cost increases

Building contracts, with the vast number of inputs they comprise, are particularly susceptible to inflationary pressures and price and cost increases. Although some of the most flexible contract mechanisms which seek to redress these factors are found in building contracts, these mechanisms often fall short of the changes which confront parties. Where the mechanisms do fall short, can it be argued that the contract has been frustrated? The leading case on whether inflation can constitute a frustrating event is *Wates Ltd.* v. *Greater London Council.*[63]

Wates was the successful tenderer in 1969 on a housing project. The conditions of contract were based upon the JCT Standard Form of Building Contract and contained a clause for the adjustment of the contract sum in the light of increases in wage rates and materials. Following a period of high inflation, the parties agreed that the adjustment mechanism was falling short of fully compensating Wates. The parties thus agreed, in a signed supplemental agreement, upon a substitute mechanism to be based upon the then Ministry of Housing and Local Government's "housing cost yardstick". This mechanism was used generally to assess allowable costs on various housing projects and was updated by circulars issued by the Ministry. In fact, the supplemental agreement itself contained a default mechanism to adjust the contract sum if the circulars were not issued or if it otherwise became impossible to ascertain the housing cost yardstick. Wates alleged that such a default had taken place, inasmuch as the Ministry had failed to issue circulars in a timely manner. This failure resulted in financial loss to Wates which, they argued, frustrated the contract. The Court of Appeal rejected this claim. Purchas L.J. relied upon *Davis Contractors* v. *Fareham U.D.C.* and held that, in the circumstances, Wates' obligation was not radically or fundamentally altered as a result of the alleged frustrating event. It is true that the contract had become more expensive for Wates to perform by virtue of the inflation but this alone was insufficient. As Stephenson L.J. stated:

> "I agree . . . that the contract was not frustrated. Things may have turned out differently from what the parties contemplated in that inflation increased not at a trot or a canter, but at a gallop. But that difference in degree and tempo was not so radical a difference from the inflation contemplated and provided for as to frustrate the contract."[64]

The reasoning of the court was influenced by the fact that the parties had actually provided for the circumstances which had occurred and this undermined Wates' argument that the contract had been frustrated.

Wates is the successor to a long list of authorities which hold that the courts will not relieve parties from imprudent bargains, nor will they grant relief where performance of the contract has become more expensive or onerous. Typical and best known of these authorities are those that arose out of the closures of the Suez Canal in 1956 and 1967. In cases decided both in America and in England pleas of

62. (1928) 3 D.L.R. 284, at p. 285.
63. (1983) 25 B.L.R. 1 (C.A.).
64. *Ibid.*, p. 35.

frustration were rejected in the face of cost increases of 100% and more as ships were rerouted via the Cape of Good Hope and elsewhere.[65] For present purposes, these cases raise the difficult question: at what point in time does inflation or price and cost increases amount to a radical difference in the obligation? At the moment, there is no clear answer to this question. In fact, even if an exact answer could be given, it would not be a panacea but rather only one step in the development of a more consistent theoretical approach to the ascertainment of the limits of the doctrine of frustration.

4. THE ROLE OF FORESEEABILITY

Hudson argues that, to found relief on the ground of frustration in a building contract case, the supervening event which occurs must be so unexpected and beyond the contemplation of the parties that neither party can be said to have accepted the risk of the event taking place at the time of contracting.[66] Thus it is said that frustration can only very rarely occur in building contract cases since, by their nature, their performance is, through reasonable foresight, hedged with uncertainties and more likely to be prevented by physical difficulties than in the case of other types of contract. Foresight or foreseeability thus plays a pre-eminent role in delimiting the scope of the doctrine of frustration.

In deciding whether or not a contract has been frustrated, a court may begin by looking at the contract to ascertain whether express provision has been made for the eventuality. Courts may differ on this point. Where it is determined that a building contract does not make such express provision, the court will often turn to the foreseeability of that risk based on a construction of the contract. If the risk is foreseen, the court will infer that the parties contracted with reference to it. One unfortunate consequence of the latitude open to the court in construing the contract is that there are dicta in numerous cases which support the view that a contract cannot be frustrated by a risk that was either foreseen or foreseeable,[67] as well as dicta from other cases where the courts have acceded to frustration even though there was foreseeability.[68] Given this state of affairs it seems hasty to conclude either that foreseeability precludes the operation of the doctrine of frustration or that it does not.

Wong Lai Ying and Investment v. *Chinachem Investment Ltd.*[69] illustrates this problem. The case arose out of two building contract cases which were taken on appeal from Hong Kong to the Privy Council. They concerned contracts for the sale

65. See, for example, *Tsakiroglou & Co. Ltd.* v. *Noblee Thorl G.m.b.H.* [1962] A.C. 93; *Palmco Shipping Co.* v. *Continental Ore Corp.* [1970] 2 Lloyd's Rep. 21; *Glidden* v. *Hellenic Lines Ltd.*, 275 F.2d 253 (1960); *Transatlantic Finance Corp.* v. *U.S.A.*, 363 F.2d 312 (1966).

66. *Op. cit.*, fn. 43, p. 349.

67. *Baily* v. *De Crespigny* (1869) L.R. 4 Q.B. 180; *F.A. Tamplin Steamship Co. Ltd.* v. *Anglo-Mexican Petroleum Products Co. Ltd.* [1916] 2 A.C. 397 (H.L.); *Cricklewood Property and Investment Trust Ltd.* v. *Leighton's Investment Trust Ltd.* [1945] A.C. 221 (H.L.).

68. *Bank Line Ltd.* v. *Arthur Capel & Co.* [1919] A.C. 435 (H.L.); *W.J. Tatem Ltd.* v. *Gamboa* [1939] 1 K.B. 132; *The Eugenia* [1964] 2 Q.B. 226.

69. (1979) 13 B.L.R. 81 (P.C.).

and purchase of flats. By the terms of the contracts Chinachem, as the developer and builder, were to complete the flats within 18 months after going into possession of the site. Wong, a purchaser, paid the entire purchase price as a deposit. Seven months after the issuance of the original building permit, and well into the foundation work on the site, a major landslip occurred which obliterated the works. Within three months the building permit lapsed and it took approximately one and a half years for a second permit to be issued. In fact, owing to the overall instability of the site, no further building works took place for three and a half years. Material terms in the contracts included a "time shall be of the essence" clause and an "extension of time" clause with regard to delay caused by a variety of factors. However, this latter clause was limited to an extension of 365 days and thus was outside the instant facts. Clause 22 became the key provision; it read in part: "It is further agreed that notwithstanding anything herein contained should . . . any unforeseen circumstances beyond the Vendor's control arise whereby the Vendor becomes unable to sell . . . the Vendor shall be at liberty to rescind this Agreement forthwith . . . "[70] The purchasers sought to uphold the contracts while the vendors argued that the contracts had been discharged on the ground of frustration. Although both the lower and first instance appeal courts in Hong Kong held that the landslip was a frustrating event, the courts differed on whether or not clause 22 provided for it.

On the purchasers' appeal to the Privy Council, it was held that clause 22 was literally wide enough to cover the landslip but that upon its true construction it should not be given this effect. Lord Scarman stated that: "The unforeseen character of the event is not in dispute. Clause 22 cannot, in their Lordships' opinion, be construed as making provision for the possibility of this particular unforeseen contingency."[71] This case is as remarkable for what it did decide as for what it did not. Initially, and in the context of foreseeability, the case demonstrates that, even where contractual provision is made for an event, the provision itself may nevertheless be so narrowly construed as not to apply to the particular event which has occurred. It must be remembered that this was a building contract and hence one where the ordinary risk of the work is on the builder until completion. It must also be borne in mind that the site was in Hong Kong, where it would seem reasonable to assume that the local conditions prevailing might be taken to include the risk of landslip. If these factors are coupled with the point that, at the time of the decision, the doctrine of frustration was thought generally not to be applicable to leases the case is even more remarkable. Apart from these points the case may also be thought of as authority in relation to when delay is of such a nature as to make performance of the contract radically different from that originally undertaken and how supervening illegality and the builders' inability to secure a further building permit for one and a half years could operate to frustrate a contract. These latter, alternative bases for the decision are premised upon the fact that the court would consider the positions of the parties at the time of the event and not subsequently. Thus, at that time or shortly thereafter the prospect of completing the contract at all was remote.

70. *Ibid.*, pp. 89–90.
71. *Ibid.*, p. 95.

A more recent case which considered the issue of express provision and foreseeability in relation to a contract is *McAlpine Humberoak Ltd.* v. *McDermott International Inc. (No. 1)*.[72] The plaintiff was invited by the defendant to tender on the construction of deck pallets for an offshore oil rig. Negotiations took place for some time and when a contract was eventually signed it was stated to take effect from a date approximately four months earlier. The work did not proceed smoothly. There were additional drawings provided and changes made. The plaintiff alleged that the new drawings and changes had considerably delayed its work and that it was entitled to additional compensation. At trial, even though it had not been argued, the judge held that the sheer volume of the changes and their impact on the contract work had made the thing undertaken different from that contracted for and thus the contract had been frustrated. However, on appeal the court strongly disapproved of both the judge's reasoning and his conclusion:

"The revised drawings did not 'transform' the contract into a different contract, or 'distort its substance and identity'. It remained a contract for the construction of four pallets . . . . The contract, when signed, provided expressly . . . that the receipt of drawings would constitute change instructions . . . [and] that the plaintiffs' rights to time and recompense were covered elsewhere in the contract . . . [and] that recompense for additional work not being carried through on revised drawings to fabricate was covered by the variation order clauses and the contractors' right to claim."[73]

Lloyd L.J. concluded that:

"If we were to uphold the judge's finding of frustration, this would be the first contract to have been frustrated by reason of matters which had not only occurred before the contract was signed, and were not only well known to the parties, but had also been provided for in the contract itself."[74]

It can be seen from the above illustrations that express provisions in contracts can displace the doctrine of frustration. However, the courts still reserve considerable discretion to themselves in determining whether or not the clauses in fact encompass the events. The language of choice used by the courts in making those determinations often comprises foreseeability. One analysis of how foreseeability rose to its present level of importance is carried out by Halpern.[75] He argues that the primary issue involved in constructing a complete doctrine of excuse is the allocation of risk in the face of contractual silence.[76] Just as the courts replaced actual intent with presumed intent, the ensuing need to base the doctrine on some objective basis saw the courts develop the fiction of foreseeability.[77] Foreseeability thus came to dominate much of the judicial opinion in the area of frustration. This pre-

72. (1992) 58 Build.L.R. 1 (C.A.).
73. *Ibid.*, at p. 18.
74. *Ibid.*
75. "Application of the Doctrine of Commercial Impracticability: Searching for the 'Wisdom of Solomon' " (1987) 135 *University of Pennsylvania Law Review* 1123. See also Paul T. Wangerin, "The 'Wisdom of Solomon': Reliance, Unconscionability and Excuse in the Law of Contracts" (1992) 5 J.C.L. 241.
76. *Ibid.*, p. 1140.
77. *Ibid.* A simpler explanation is that of Rodman Elfin, "The Future Use of Unconscionability and Impracticability as Contract Doctrines", (1989) 40 *Mercer Law Review* 937, at p. 953, who suggests: "[p]erhaps because of their great familiarity with the tort concept of foreseeability in the context of proximate cause, courts have chosen to concentrate on . . . foreseeability."

occupation has been subjected to wide-ranging critiques.[78] One critique is that there is a complete absence of proof that either foreseeability or contractual silence is relevant to intent or to the situating of risk by the courts on the promisor.[79] In practice there are a multitude of factors which influence a party's willingness to draft and either include or exclude excuse provisions in a contract. These factors range from the unlikeliness of the event's occurrence to the perceived effects that the inclusion of a broad excuse clause may have on the completion of the negotiations.[80] These factors, coupled with the view of those who suggest that "foreseeability . . . is possible in almost every case",[81] invite the formulation of a more convincing theoretical basis for the doctrine of frustration than solely in terms of foreseeability.

A more recent theoretical framework for the doctrine of frustration has been proposed by Phang.[82] Phang begins by setting out how one theory may be put forward to address matters of impracticability, frustration of purpose and impossibility of performance; namely through an enquiry into them, which, he argues, is the same in substance.[83] He develops two themes, the first substantive and the second attitudinal, toward the doctrine. With regard to the first, drawing upon both English and American caselaw,[84] he begins: "if . . . the alleged supervening event upon which the argument of frustration is based is in fact within the reasonable control of at least one of the parties, the doctrine cannot be successfully invoked".[85] He then equates this to the principle of radical change in the obligation as understood in the case law and in particular to *Davis Contractors* v. *Fareham U.D.C.*[86] With regard to the second theme, relying upon the judgment of Bingham L.J. in

78. E.g., Michael D. Aubrey, "Frustration Reconsidered—Some Comparative Aspects", (1963) 12 I.C.L.Q. 1165; E. Allan Farnsworth, "Disputes over Omissions in Contracts", (1968) 68 *Columbia Law Review* 860; Charles G. Brown, "The Doctrine of Impossibility of Performance and the Foreseeability Test", (1975) 6 *Loyola University of Chicago Law Journal* 575.

79. Norman R. Prance, *op. cit.*, fn. 4 at p. 485: "An abandonment of the standard of foreseeability by the courts would represent a dramatic but beneficial departure from the past." Farnsworth, *op. cit.*, fn. 78 at p. 887: "the principle of foreseeability has no merit as a general rule and should be discarded."

80. See Leon E. Trakman, "Frustrated Contracts and Legal Fictions", (1983) 46 M.L.R. 39 at p. 43. Beyond the question of whether or not parties will even include excuse clauses in their agreements may be the more topical issue of whether the parties will then even invoke it. An increasing number of commentators in certain contract areas suggest they will not, see e.g. David Campbell and Donald Harris, "Flexibility in Long-term Contractual Relationships: The Role of Co-operation", (1993) 20 *Journal of Law and Society* 166; Christopher T. Wonnell, "The primacy of cooperation, rational bargaining, and an economic theory of part of the common law", (1992) 15 *Harvard Journal of Law and Public Policy* 771.

81. Comment, "Supervening Impossibility of Performance as a Defense", (1936) 5 *Fordham Law Review*, 322, at p. 331.

82. Andrew Phang, "Frustration in English Law—A Reappraisal", (1992) 21 *Anglo-American Law Review* 278.

83. *Ibid.*, p. 281. cf. Paul T. Wangerin, "The 'Wisdom of Solomon': Reliance, Unconscionability and Excuse in the Law of Contracts", (1992) 5 J.C.L. 241 at pp. 241–242 who writes that "mistake, impracticability [also used interchangeably with impossibility] and frustration . . . are mirror images of each other and that the standard for invocation of each is, or should be, exactly the same".

84. See, for example, *J. Lauritzen A.S.* v. *Wijsmuller B.V. (The Super Servant Two)* [1990] 1 Lloyd's Rep. 1; *Nissho-Iwai Co. Ltd.* v. *Occidental Crude Sales Inc.* 729 F.2d 1530 (1984).

85. *Op. cit.*, note 82, p. 282. What constitutes an event beyond the control of one party is not always easy to discern. In the case of *Scott Lithgow Ltd.* v. *Secretary of State for Defence* (1989) 45 Build.L.R. 1, the House of Lords held that defaults by suppliers or subcontractors in a works and services context may be a cause beyond the contractor's control.

86. [1956] A.C. 696.

The Super Servant Two,[87] he observes that the doctrine is not lightly to be invoked.[88] The scope of the role for foreseeability is tempered by a sound pragmatic approach: "foreseeability in an absolute sense is unrealistic"[89] and "[t]he determination must thus be, in the final analysis, one of degree."[90]

5. A RE-EVALUATION

Typically, construction contracts anticipate and allocate risk in predictable ways. What the draftsman seeks to achieve is an acceptable balance which allocates ordinary commercial risks among the parties. However, this approach leaves exceptional risks unaddressed. If an exceptional risk occurs and the matter goes to court, the court, by its decision, effectively allocates the risk. The decision of a court as to whether or not to invoke the doctrine of frustration allocates risk in a similar way, that is, after the fact.[91] If one accepts that courts do in fact perform this function, the question becomes whether this is an effective way to allocate risk. It is suggested that it is not, because the consequences of ending a contract in this way, often on an all-or-nothing basis, may not always accord with the wishes or with the best interests of the parties.[92]

(a) A comparative perspective

The value of a comparative point of view is plain when it is seen that "the concept of 'frustration' is different in each legal system".[93] In German law, the equivalent concept to frustration is construed very broadly and encompasses solely economic factors.[94] In contrast to this, French law, although without a doctrine of frustration as such, regulates the subject-matter of frustration under concepts of *force majeure* and *cas fortuit*.[95] From a practical point of view these two French concepts are syn-

87. [1990] 1 Lloyd's Rep. 1.
88. *Op. cit.*, note 82, p. 283.
89. *Ibid.*, p. 291.
90. *Ibid.*, p. 293. These views actually accord quite closely with those of the present writer.
91. A.D.M. Forte, *op. cit.*, fn. 5, at p. 4 fn. 13, although he concedes that in English law frustration is thought to turn upon the construction of the contract; cf. the American view discussed by Speziale, "The Turn of the Twentieth Century as the Dawn of Contract 'Interpretation': Reflections in Theories of Impossibility" (1978–9) *Duquesne Law Review* 555, at p. 588, fns. 114–115.
92. A.D.M. Forte, *op. cit.*, fn. 5, at p. 19. The subject admits of considerable complexity, see generally Randy E. Barnett, "The Sound of Silence: Default Rules and Contractual Consent", (1992) 78 *Virginia Law Review* 821; Clayton P. Gillette, "Commercial Relationships and the Selection of Default Rules for Remote Risks", (1990) 19 *Journal of Legal Studies* 535; and Jason S. Johnston, "Strategic Bargaining and the Economic Theory of Contract Default Rules", (1990) 100 *Yale Law Journal* 615.
93. A.H. Puelinckx, "Frustration, Hardship, *Force Majeure*, Imprevision, Wegfall der Geschäftsgrundlage, Unmöglichkeit, Changed Circumstances", (1986) *3 Journal of International Arbitration* 47. See generally Hans Smit, "Frustration of Contract: A Comparative Attempt at Consolidation" (1958) 58 *Columbia Law Review* 287.
94. See Puelinckx *op. cit.*, fn. 93 at pp. 59–61 and Forte *op. cit.* fn. 5 at pp. 7–10. See also Peter Hay, "Frustration and Its Solution in German Law", (1961) 10 *American Journal of Comparative Law* 345.
95. Code Civil, article 1148: "There is no occasion for damages where, in consequence of *force majeure* or *cas fortuit*, the debtor has been prevented from conveying or doing that to which he was obliged, or has done what he was debarred from doing." See further Chapter 2 and Rene David, "Frustration of Contract in French Law", (1946) 28 *Journal of Comparative Legislation and International Law* 11.

onymous.[96] French law also supplements these two concepts by a general doctrine of *imprévision* which may excuse non-performance on solely economic grounds.[97] Scots law also admits of a doctrine of frustration. Indeed, some would argue that Scots law permits the judicial adjustment of contractual obligations following frustration.[98] These examples from different countries serve to introduce the range of means whereby supervening events are addressed; in some instances, they include a form of judicial adjustment of contractual obligations. In one commentary, focusing primarily upon the law of Sweden,[99] seven bases supporting contractual adjustment are analysed.[100] Apart from these countries, American doctrine and jurisprudence possess an abundance of analysis on the subject.[101]

(b) The United States

In the United States the doctrine of frustration is the subject of widespread theorising and analysis. A divergence of views has arisen. For example, it has been argued that impossibility cases "are a special breed of contract law" because they involve situations for which the parties have not expressly contracted.[102] Further, it has been suggested that, in the case of international trade, a distinct regime of frustration should be applicable.[103] These are minority views which must be rejected for two reasons. First, it is submitted that the law which should be applied in cases where it is alleged that a contract has been frustrated is that normally applicable in contract cases. This accords with the overall development of the doctrine of frustration within and as a part of conventional contract law.[104] Secondly, they also appear to be inconsistent with the way in which the courts, rightly or wrongly, resort to general contractual presumptions in analysing frustration cases and, in particular, in cases in which it is alleged that a building contract has been frustrated.[105] American views also differ on whether frustration should be treated as a

96. In *ancien droit*, *force majeure* encompassed acts of man while *cas fortuit* concerned acts of nature, but today the two are synonymous, particularly if analysed in terms of their effects. See further p. 23 and Mazeaud, *Leçons de Droit Civil*, *Paris* 1956, vol. 2, p. 516, no. 573. This is discussed by Daniel Jacoby, "Réflexions sur le concept de cas fortuit", (1972) 32 *Revue de Barreau* 121., who also notes that the law of Quebec is to like effect: P.B. Mignault, *Droit Civil Canadien*, 1901, vol. 5, 668; L. Faribault, *Traité de Droit Civil du Québec*, 1959, vol. 8, 631, no. 798.

97. See further pp. 28–29 and A. von Mehren and J. Gordley, *The Civil Law System* (2nd Edn., 1977), pp. 545–551 and 1059–1064. Thus, the adoption has been in French *droit administratif*. This view of the civil courts is not without detractors: Mazeaud, *Traité Théorique et Pratique de la Responsabilité Civile, Délictuelle et Contractuelle* (6th Edn., 1970) and Planiol et Ripert, *Traité Pratique de Droit Civil Français* (2nd Edn., 1952).

98. William M. McBryde, "Frustration of Contract", (1982) 25 (N.S.) *Juridical Review* 1 and Forte, *op. cit.*, fn. 5, both referring to the case of *Wilkie* v. *Bethune* (1848) 11 D. 132.

99. Knut Rodhe, "Adjustment of Contracts on Account of Changed Conditions" (1959) 3 *Scandinavian Studies in Law* 153.

100. *Ibid.*, pp. 159–172, namely, the doctrines of economic impossibility; the underlying assumptions of the contract; the implied condition; unjust enrichment; good faith; important reasons and lost identity.

101. See, for example, the commentators noted at fn. 16.

102. Marcia J. Speziale, *op. cit.*, fn. 91, p. 557.

103. See Harold J. Berman, "Excuse for Non-performance in the Light of Contract Practices in International Trade", (1963) 63 *Columbia Law Review* 1413.

104. See Michael G. Rapsomanikis, "Frustration of Contract in International Trade and Comparative Law", (1979–80) 18 *Duquesne Law Review* 551, at p. 562.

105. See Sheldon W. Halpern, *op. cit.*, fn. 75, 1123, at p. 1127.

separate concept from commercial impracticability and physical impossibility. It is suggested here that a preponderance of doctrine supports one theoretical framework in the analysis of these three concepts.[106]

One theoretical approach to the problem of frustration is that of Professor J. H. Schlegel who, after embarking upon a socio-economic analysis, concludes simply that: "an event should be held frustrating when it is not one within that narrow range of events normally incidental to the . . . contract".[107] Unfortunately, this conclusion is problematic in its application to building contract cases because it is no easy task to decide whether a given event is "incidental" to the contract. But Professor Schlegel's theory has been taken further in the economic analysis of frustration. The main proponents of an economic analysis of frustration are Richard Posner and Andrew M. Rosenfield.[108] Their thesis is that only with economic efficiency as a criterion can a proper basis for the application and understanding of doctrines of contractual excuse be gained. In cases involving frustration, Posner and Rosenfield would allocate the risk to the "superior risk bearer". This allocation is based on the assumption that that is what the parties would have done had they had the opportunity to consider the matter. The superior risk bearer may be either the obligor or the obligee. Where it is the obligor, then, according to this theory, the case falls to be treated as one of breach of contract. Where it is the obligee, then it is appropriate that the contract simply be discharged without any liability for breach. By articulating this view Posner and Rosenfield have made efficiency the decisive factor rather than foreseeability. Whether or not the exclusive focus is justified is the subject of commentary elsewhere,[109] though by raising it here, a further alternative to frustration as presently formulated is raised.[110]

Apart from legal commentators, the American judiciary has at times advanced novel theoretical and practical approaches to the application of the doctrine of frustration, and no case has divided opinion as sharply as the case of *The Aluminum Co. of America (ALCOA)* v. *Essex Group Inc.*[111] In 1967 ALCOA agreed for a period of 16 years to smelt alumina supplied by Essex and to redeliver it to Essex as aluminium. This service was performed under a complicated cost formula which worked well for almost 10 years but became outdated because of certain non-labour costs. The result was an anticipated loss by ALCOA over the remainder of the contract of approximately US$75 million. ALCOA sued on the basis that the contract had, broadly, become frustrated and they sought reformation or adjustment of it. The court agreed with ALCOA and adjusted the contract.

Judge Teitlebaum adopted an approach that centred upon hardship. He stated that: "The focus of the doctrines of impracticability and of frustration is distinctly

106. Richard A. Posner and Andrew M. Rosenfield, *op. cit.*, fn. 4, Stephen J. Sirianni, *op. cit.*, fn. 16; Christopher J. Bruce, "An Economic Analysis of the Impossibility Doctrine", (1982) 11 *Journal of Legal Studies*, 311.

107. *Op. cit.*, fn. 4, pp. 419 and 447.

108. *Op. cit.*, fn. 4.

109. Proponents include Alan O. Sykes, "The Doctrine of Commercial Impracticability in a Second-Best World", (1990) 19 *Journal of Legal Studies*, 43; Michelle J. White, "Contract Breach and Contract Discharge Due to Impossibility: A Unified Theory" (1989) 17 *Journal of Legal Studies* 353; Bruce, *op. cit.*, fn. 106. Opponents include Halpern, *op. cit.*, fn. 75, and Sirianni, *op. cit.*, fn. 16.

110. Other theories could equally have been discussed, see Farnsworth, *op. cit.*, fn. 78, at p. 860.

111. 499 F. Supp. 53 (1980, U.S. Dist. Ct., W.D. Pa., *per* Judge Teitlebaum), discussed in more detail at pp. 321–323 below.

on hardship . . . Performance may be impracticable because extreme and unreasonable difficulty, expense, injury, or loss to one of the parties will be involved."[112] Taking this approach, Judge Teitlebaum argued that the potential loss to ALCOA outweighed any community interest in contract enforcement. Although the ALCOA case is exceptional in American law, it has raised the level of debate on the issue of whether or not there should be judicial adjustment of contracts.[113] Ten years later, and by way of contrast, we can now turn to the English law.

(c) English law—time for judicial adjustment of contracts

"The English courts have no power to adapt a long-term contract to an uncontemplated fundamental change. That was decided by the House of Lords in *British Movietonews Ltd.* v. *London and District Cinemas Ltd.* In accordance with English legal technique, the case is treated as concerning principles of interpretation, the 'contest between words and spirit', as Mr. Justice Kerr expresses it, but in reality it concerns the power of the court to adapt contractual provisions to uncontemplated changed circumstances of a fundamental nature."[114]

The reasons for this refusal to adapt contracts are plain: the sanctity and the absolute basis of contractual obligations. These reasons are synonymous with the *Paradine* principle, but they are not immutable.

The case for the judicial adjustment of contracts is strengthened in England in a number of respects. The first is the passage of the Law Reform (Frustrated Contracts) Act 1943[115] which empowers judicial reformation of contracts in certain cases. The enactment of this legislation proceeded upon the basis that recovery only upon the basis of a *total* failure of consideration could entail occasional hardship for contractors. It is also consistent with the view that the Act enacts a scheme of mutual restitution,[116] or, alternatively, that it permits the courts to engage in the apportionment of losses.[117] The second reason is the influence of European Community law which embraces, in numerous jurisdictions, notions of equitable adjustment.[118] The third and most compelling reason is that judicial adjustment will often better accord with the interests and wishes of the contractors.[119] While it is clearly heresy, courts can and do make contracts; if one can accept this, will there not also be instances where contracts are equally deserving of adjustment so as to enable them to continue in the changed circumstances?

112. *Ibid.*, at p. 72.

113. Sheldon W. Halpern, *op. cit.*, fn. 75, at p. 1176, argues that: "Judge Teitlebaum simply went too far too soon and with too little, laying no solid conceptual groundwork to support his fragile structure."

114. Clive M. Schmitthoff, "Hardship and Intervener Clauses", [1980] J.B.L. 82, pp. 82–83, (footnotes omitted).

115. Law Reform (Frustrated Contracts) Act 1943 is discussed in more detail in Chapter 11. For a recent critique of this Act and other statutory bases of adjustment see Andrew Stewart and J.W. Carter, "Frustrated Contracts and Statutory Adjustment: The Case for a Reappraisal", (1992) 51 C.L.J. 66 where the authors suggest that the statutes either be repealed or substantially modified by legislation or excluded altogether by individual contractors themselves.

116. See the judgment of Robert Goff J. in *B.P.* v. *Hunt* [1979] 1 W.L.R. 783.

117. A.M. Haycroft and D.M. Waksman, "Frustration and Restitution", [1984] J.B.L. 207. These issues are also addressed in Chapter 11.

118. For example, France, Germany, Italy and Greece. See *Adaptation of Contracts* (1979) International Chamber of Commerce publication No. 326.

119. See fns. 78–81 and associated text.

6. FORCE MAJEURE

Force majeure is the concept whereby the law recognises that a contracting party may, without fault on its part, provide an excuse for non-performance when circumstances beyond its control render performance impossible.[120] Thus, the clause itself seeks to define, in advance of certain stipulated events, the mutual rights and duties of the parties if those events, which, by definition, are beyond their control, occur. While these clauses frequently occur in practice, their scope and drafting vary considerably in terms of objects and effects.[121]

The purpose of including a *force majeure* clause in one's contract is to seek to limit one's exposure to damages for non-performance. Hence the purpose is to provide a legal standard against which future risks may be allocated. The motivation for parties may be the fear that the court will neither imply a term into a contract excusing performance nor employ the doctrine of frustration.

Most *force majeure* clauses are drafted in two parts. The first part will provide for a list of specified events whose occurrence will excuse performance; examples may include strikes,[122] accidents to machinery,[123] war,[124] licence restrictions[125] or acts of God.[126] The second part of the clause will usually purport to address all other causes howsoever arising.[127] The specificity of the drafting will vary depending upon the circumstances. Current usage may also see the operation of the clause in

120. In *Lebeaupin* v. *Richard Crispin & Co.* [1920] 2 K.B. 714, at p. 719, a definition of *force majeure* was attempted in the following terms: "This term is used with reference to all circumstances independent of the will of man, and which it is not in his power to control . . . Thus war, inundations and epidemics are cases of *force majeure*." However, the view of Donaldson J. in *Thomas Borthwick (Glasgow) Ltd.* v. *Faure Fairclough Ltd.* [1968] 1 Lloyd's Rep. 16 at p. 28 that "the precise meaning of this term, if it has one, has eluded lawyers for years" is more accurate.

121. The term is used interchangeably in American law with *force magesture*, *Fogg* v. *Van Saun Coal Co.* 12 N.J. Misc. 680, 174 A. 419 (1934); *fuerza mayor*, *American Sur. Co.* v. *Batangan*, 19 Philippine 110 (1911) and *vis major*, *Pacific Vegetable Oil Corp.* v. *C.S.T.*, 29 Calif. 2d 228, 174 P. 441 (1946): A.M. Squillante and F.M. Congalton, "Force Majeure" (1975) 80 *Commercial Law Journal* 4, cf. the English cases which suggest that *vis major*, which includes acts of God and the Queen's enemies, is broader than *force majeure*: *Simmons* v. *Norton* (1831) 7 Bing. 640, at p. 649, 131 E.R. 247, at p. 251 *per* Tindal C.J.; see also Konstantin D. Magliveras, "*Force Majeure* in Community Law", (1990) 15 *European Law Review* 460.

122. See, for example, *Matsoukis* v. *Priestman & Co.* [1915] 1 K.B. 681.

123. *Ibid.*

124. See, for example, *Tennants (Lancashire) Ltd.* v. *C.S. Wilson & Co. Ltd.* [1917] A.C. 495 (H.L.); *Peter Dixon & Sons Ltd.* v. *Henderson, Craig & Co.* [1919] 2 K.B. 778, (C.A.).

125. *Walton (Grain and Shipping) Ltd.* v. *British Italian Trading Co. Ltd.* [1959] 1 Lloyd's Rep. 223. See generally David Yates and J.W. Carter, "Export Licences, Standard of Duty and *Force Majeure*" (1989) 1 J.C.L. 57.

126. Acts of God are extraordinary and unforeseeable events or accidents that usually take place without human intervention, such as floods (*Nichols* v. *Marsland* (1876) 2 Ex. D. 1, (C.A.)) or storms (*River Wear Commrs.* v. *Adamson* (1877) 2 App. Cas. 743, (H.L.)). For a legal and theological critique of the concept of "act of God" see C.G. Hall, "An Unsearchable Providence: The Lawyer's Concept of Act of God", (1993) 13 O.J.L.S. at p. 227 who argues that the concept should not turn upon the harmful magnitude of the occurrence but rather upon notions of foreseeability and reasonableness. See generally B. Barrett, "Common Law Liability for Flood Damage caused by Storms", (1992) 142 *New Law Journal* 1608; and M. Flynn, "Construction Contracts and Contractors: Hurricane Andrew reteaches Consumers", (1993) 17 *Nova Law Review* 1093.

127. On drafting such clauses, see generally Chapters 4 and 5 and Bernard J. Cartoon, "Drafting an Acceptable *Force Majeure* Clause", [1978] J.B.L. 230. See also David Yates, "Drafting *Force Majeure* and Related Clauses", (1991) 3 J.C.L. 186; and H.O. Hunter "Commentary on 'Pitfalls of *Force Majeure Clause*'", (1991) 3 J.C.L. 214.

two stages. Thus, the contract may provide for a set time frame, which, in the case of a stipulated *force majeure* event occurring, is automatically extended by a further set period of time. This parallels notice provisions in building contracts.

The courts construe *force majeure* clauses strictly. In *Lebeaupin* v. *Richard Crispin & Co.*[128] Mr Justice McCardie stated: "I take it that a *force majeure* clause should be construed in each case with a close attention to the words which precede or follow it, and with a due regard to the nature and general terms of the contract."[129] Thus, by applying a strict rule of interpretation, here the *ejusdem generis* rule, the court denied that the event which was alleged to fall within the compass of the *force majeure* clause did fall within its compass.[130] The criticism of a strict approach to the construction of *force majeure* clauses is that it may not reflect the true intent of the parties or the risks either intended to assume. The reason for this is that many factors are involved in the negotiation of a contract which may preclude either party from being able to draft an all-inclusive clause which provides for every possible event.

Apart from utilising strict rules of interpretation to limit *force majeure*, the law imposes other requirements which reduce the scope of *force majeure* clauses. For example, the obligor must not be at fault[131] and the occurrence of the event must be beyond his control. Obligors must also show that there was no reasonable action that could have been taken to prevent or mitigate the outcome. Thus, where a party to a joint-venture agreement failed to establish that it had taken all reasonable steps to avoid a strike, that party was held to be precluded from relying upon a *force majeure* clause in the agreement.[132]

One last factor that circumscribes the scope of *force majeure* may be referred to, which is that the specific event alleged must be the actual cause of the non-performance. Contractors will be familiar with the difficulty of trying, for example, to attribute delay to discrete events! The cumulative effect of these limitations by the courts is to define very narrowly the ambit of operation of *force majeure*.

One result of these limitations is that contractors are forced to devote additional time to negotiations over their contractual provisions and their eventual length, in effect creating a "battle of the forms". To win in this battle requires contractors to see that "any foreseeable calamity, however remote, [is] . . . anticipated by careful

128. [1920] 2 K.B. 714. Similar illustrations may be found in Canadian law, e.g. *In re an Arbitration between the Podar Trading Co. Ltd., et al.*, [1949] 2 K.B. 227, at p. 286, and in American law, e.g. *Excelsior Motor Mfg. & Supply Co.* v. *Sound Equipment* 73 F. 2d 725 (7th Cir. 1934).

129. *Ibid.*, p. 720.

130. See Charles G. Brown, "The Doctrine of Impossibility of Performance and the Foreseeability Test", 6 *Loyola University of Chicago Law Journal* 575, at p. 580, critiquing such construction. Under an *ejusdem generis* approach, when general words follow specific words the general words are confined to only those types of things as the specific words address.

131. *J. Lauritzen A.S.* v. *Wijsmuller B.V. (The Super Servant Two)* [1990] 1 Lloyd's Rep. 1, cf. McKendrick, "The Construction of *Force Majeure* Clauses and Self-Induced Frustration", [1990] L.M.C.L.Q. 153 and see further pp. 46–50 above.

132. *B. & S. Contracts and Design Ltd.* v. *Victor Green Publications* [1984] I.C.R. 419, (C.A.) and see also *Channel Island Ferries Ltd.* v. *Sealink U.K. Ltd.* [1987] 1 Lloyd's Rep. 559, affirmed in [1988] 1 Lloyd's Rep. 323 (C.A.), discussed in more detail at pp. 170–178 above. For the American view, see *Nissho-Iwai Company Ltd.* v. *Occidental Crude Sales, Inc.* 729 F. 2d 1530 (1984) commented on by Katherine M. Gal, "Nissho-Iwai Company, Ltd. v. Occidental Crude Sales, Inc.: Curtailing the effectiveness of the *Force Majeure* Clause", (1986) 12 *Brooklyn Journal of International Law* 243.

'tiger-day' clauses in the drafting of the contract".[133] The difficulty in achieving this may also be exacerbated where standard forms are modified because this can then give rise to further difficult questions of interpretation.[134]

7. STANDARD FORM BUILDING CONTRACTS—FORCE MAJEURE AND FRUSTRATION

There are a number of the standard forms of building contracts which expressly incorporate clauses on *force majeure* or frustration or address similar subject-matter. Three such standard forms—the Conditions of Contract and Forms of Tender, Agreement and Bond (known as the ICE Conditions of Contract (6th Edn.)),[135] the Fédération Internationale des Ingénieurs-Conseils' (or FIDIC's) Conditions of Contract for Works of Civil Engineering Construction (4th Edn.)[136] and the Joint Contracts Tribunal for the Standard Form of Building Contract (or JCT Contract 1980 Edition)[137]—may be referred to.

The JCT Contract expressly refers to *force majeure*. Pursuant to clauses 25.4.1 and 28.1.3.1, when *force majeure* occurs then either an extension of time or the determination of the contract may take place.[138] The references to *force majeure* are without qualification and thus the court may be expected to construe the clause according to the principles of construction which have been elaborated in this chapter.

In contrast to the JCT Contract, neither the ICE Conditions nor the FIDIC Conditions expressly refer to *force majeure*, although their approach is similar. Both standard forms first refer to adverse physical obstructions or conditions that would impact upon performance.[139] According to their own terms, they exclude from the list of excusing events weather or climatic conditions as well as events which could have reasonably been foreseen.[140] The adverse physical obstructions are qualified though by references to "physical or legal impossibility".[141] Whether or not these references mean impossibility as understood in the doctrine of frustration is an open question; the better view is that they do.

"It is tentatively suggested that . . . what is aimed at . . . is a state of affairs

133. Celia Battersby, "Frustration: a limited future", (1990) 134 S.J. 354.

134. See, for example, *Pagnan S.p.A.* v. *Tradax Ocean Transportation S.A.* [1987] 3 All E.R. 565 (C.A.) where a seller's obligation to "provide [an] export certificate" was held to be absolute and overrode a GAFTA standard form *force majeure* clause, even where a subsequent government export quota was imposed; cf. *Tradax Export S.A.* v. *André & Cie. S.A.* [1976] 1 Lloyd's Rep. 416, and *Cook Industries* v. *Tradax Export S.A.* [1983] 1 Lloyd's Rep. 327 where *force majeure* did operate when an export prohibition was imposed.

135. This form is issued and approved by the Institution of Civil Engineers, the Federation of Civil Engineering Contractors and the Association of Consulting Engineers, 1991.

136. (4th Edn.) 1987.

137. The Joint Contracts Tribunal publishes this contract.

138. *Ibid.*

139. Clause 12(1) ICE Conditions, clause 12.1 FIDIC.

140. *Ibid.*, this further reference to foreseeability reinforces the significance of the concept in relation to matters of excuse and which has been discussed above.

141. Several cases have considered the meaning of legal or physical impossibility under the standard forms, including *Holland Dredging (UK) Ltd* v. *The Dredging and Construction Co. Ltd.* (1987) 37 Build.L.R. 1; *Yorkshire Water Authority* v. *Sir Alfred McAlpine & Son (Northern) Ltd.* (1986) 32 Build.L.R. 114; and *A.E. Farr Ltd.* v. *Ministry of Transport* [1960] 3 All E.R. 88.

affecting the works as a whole which would give rise to frustration under English law."[142] Following these initial references "excepted risks" are enumerated and assigned to the employers.[143] Many of these excepted risks would normally fall within a *force majeure* clause; for instance, war, rebellion, invasion and even the forces of nature. This wording thus enables parallels to be drawn with *force majeure*. Where certain of these risks, which now include exceptionally adverse weather conditions, occur, the contractor becomes entitled to an extension of time under the standard forms[144] and may be excused from any liability whatsoever in the event of the risks also being classified as "special".[145] The enumeration and allocation of special risks in this way should remove them from the general operation of the doctrine of frustration, as the doctrine is generally inapplicable where the parties have expressly provided for the event.[146]

The ICE Conditions and the FIDIC form do expressly include clauses on frustration.[147] The clauses are virtually identical and purport to cover frustration by war or otherwise. In the event that the contract is frustrated, the clauses provide for calculations of the amounts to be paid by the employer to the contractor.

The references to *force majeure*, frustration or other related events has not yet advanced the articulation of a uniform approach to addressing supervening events. Allusions to old concepts, which may or may not have been well and truly tested against the intentions of the contractors, continue to persist. Having said this though, in the most recent FIDIC Client/Consultant Model Services Agreement, the term "*force majeure*" was replaced by "changed circumstances".[148] The effect of such a change may be to introduce greater equity into a court's assessment of the obligation assumed by a party, perhaps even a contractual justification for a court to resort to the adjustment of the contract.[149] If this were to occur, it would move courts toward a reconciliation with the powers they exercise after the fact under the Law Reform (Frustrated Contracts) Act 1943.

8. CONCLUSION

This chapter began by asking whether our courts have no good reason for examining the concept of frustration to see if the standard textbook view continues to be justifiable. The short answer at the end of the chapter is no. The doctrine of frustration has always been and continues today to be rooted in and, indeed, equated with impossibility, notwithstanding its critical reassessment. The consequence of this equation is to circumscribe the operation of the doctrine. This may be clearly seen,

142. I.N. Duncan Wallace, *The International Civil Engineering Contract. A Commentary on the FIDIC International Standard Form of Civil Engineering and Building Contract*, (1974) at p. 45.

143. Clause 20(2) ICE Conditions and clause 20.4 FIDIC.

144. Clause 44(1) ICE Conditions and clause 44.1 FIDIC.

145. For example, clauses 65.1 and 65.2 FIDIC.

146. *The Eugenia* [1964] 2 Q.B. 226, at p. 239, *per* Lord Denning.

147. Clause 64 ICE Conditions and clause 66 FIDIC.

148. S. 26, 1990 edition.

149. A.H. Puelinckx, *op. cit.*, fn. 93 at pp. 62–63 on the interpretation of the doctrine of changed circumstances in German and Japanese law. See generally Albert Bohemier and Francis Fox, "De l'effet des changements de circonstances sur les contrats en Common Law", (1962) 12 *Themis* 145.

not only in the broad spectrum of contract cases in general, but also in more particular applications such as building contract cases. The limitations observed in general contract cases have become the inherent limitations of building contract cases. Apart from the continued grounding of the doctrine of frustration in impossibility, the most significant other limitation is the absence of a sound theoretical basis for the doctrine. The implied term theory, which was the first to be advanced, has disappeared over time. Other explanations have been advanced to replace it. American writers especially have devoted considerable scholarship to the task. Some of those efforts have been referred to, notably in terms of economic theory and risk allocation. In England theories have also been put forward and may be seen in the judicial opinions on the subject. Two theories that are central in this respect focus upon the foundation of the contract and the construction of the contract.[150] While all of these theories have their supporters, in this writer's view they are still wanting. The main reason for this is the use by the courts of foreseeability to limit the doctrine of frustration and maintain it on the outermost reaches of excuse, both in the United States and in England. This is so notwithstanding statutory initiatives in the United States that have sought to reduce the significance of foreseeability.

If one accepts that the courts have been unduly restrictive in considering the application of the doctrine of frustration, one may ask how this could be overcome. It is suggested here that refocusing the theoretical foundation of the doctrine upon the concept of hardship may assist. A review of the approach adopted in a number of civil jurisdictions leads to this conclusion and to the acceptance of Judge Teitlebaum's view that this is an appropriate way to reconcile frustration and commercial impracticability[151] and, in this writer's view, it can also reconcile frustration and imprévision or changed circumstances. By focusing on the hardship that is entailed in being forced to complete a contract in the face of supervening changes, it can be seen that completion of the contract according to its original terms is neither likely to be in accordance with the best interests of the parties nor with their original intentions. The enactment of the Law Reform (Frustrated Contracts) Act 1943 itself suggests that this is implicitly true. If the concept of hardship is made the theoretical underpinning of the doctrine of frustration, the courts may more readily move toward invoking their equitable jurisdiction to adjust the obligations of the parties. New support for this view may be found in the Draft UNIDROIT Principles for International Commercial Contracts.[152] The draft principles were released by a working group of eminent jurists who laboured on the project for more than ten years. The principles are put forward as nonbinding suggestions on the law of contract. They are valuable for numerous reasons, including the fresh vocabulary they occasionally bring to the subject and their tilt toward a more comprehensive approach to risk allocation.[153] It is telling that the working group singled out hardship for special attention: "the working group has happily seen fit in at least one case, namely the rules relating to hardship, to disregard the dominant

150. *F.A. Tamplin*, *op. cit.*, fn. 67; *W.J. Tatem Ltd.* v. *Gamboa*, *op. cit.*, fn. 68.
151. *Op. cit.*, fn. 111.
152. UNIDROIT 1992, Study L—Doc 40 Rev 10.
153. Richard Hyland, "On setting Forth the Law of Contract", (1992) 40 *American Journal of Comparative Law* 541 at pp. 543 and 547.

view in domestic law."[154] The working group appears to have affirmed the similarities that exist with other related concepts as well, such as *force majeure*.[155] In fact, in examining the criteria indicated in the principles to invoke either hardship to justify adaptation of the contract or *force majeure* to support an excuse for non-performance, three of the four criteria noted overlap.[156] They are, first, whether the event arose after the conclusion of the contract; secondly, that the event could not reasonably have been taken into account; and thirdly that the event was beyond the control of the party. The second criterion may be a reformulation of foreseeability which, if it is, would move us closer to practice and the research results which suggest there are important reasons why parties to contracts do not always address every event that may arise in the course of negotiations leading up to the conclusion of a contract.[157] That the event must be beyond the control of the party also picks up on recent work redefining frustration in these terms.[158] The effects of hardship are clear; a right is given to the court to adapt the contract if it is reasonable to do so. Adaptation of contracts may seem far from the proper role of the court in contract cases, but for some judges at least the courts already exercise such a role. As Lord Denning has stated: "In these frustration cases . . . the courts really exercise a qualifying power—a power to qualify the absolute, literal or wide terms of the contract—in order to do what is just and reasonable in the new situation."[159]

J. A. MCINNIS

154. *Ibid.*, at p. 542.

155. See Dietrich Maskow, a member of the working group, "Hardship and Force Majeure", (1992) 40 *American Journal of Comparative Law* 658 at p. 663 and also citing Fontaine, *Droit des contrats internationaux. Analyse et redaction de clauses* (1989) at p. 238.

156. *Ibid.*, p. 662. In looking at the criteria they also overlap with other organising assumptions in related civilian concepts such as Wegfall der Geschäftsgrundlage and imprévision, *ibid.* p. 661 and fn. 93 above.

157. See, for example, pp. 206–210.

158. See, for example, Andrew Phang, "Frustration in English Law—A Reappraisal", (1992) 21 *Anglo-American Law Review* 278.

159. *British Movietonews* v. *London and District Cinemas* [1951] 1 K.B. 190, at p. 200.

PART V

FRUSTRATION, REMEDIES AND RE-APPRAISAL

CHAPTER 11

THE CONSEQUENCES OF FRUSTRATION—THE LAW REFORM (FRUSTRATED CONTRACTS) ACT 1943

1. INTRODUCTION

Where contracting parties elect to incorporate into their contract a *force majeure* clause they can make provision, not only for what constitutes a *force majeure* event, but also for the consequences of such an event. For example, provision can be made for extensions of time, the suspension or variation of the contract or even the termination of the contract. The variety of such clauses and their flexibility are such that the consequences of the occurrence of a *force majeure* event must depend primarily upon the proper interpretation of the clause at issue, although in certain cases, where the *force majeure* clause itself does not deal with all eventualities, it may be possible to have resort to common law rules.[1] But in the case of frustration the story is a rather different one; here greater reliance has, historically, been placed upon the general law, both common law and statute, rather than upon contractual terms negotiated by the parties. For example, a contract which is discharged on the ground of frustration is brought to an end automatically by the operation of a rule of law, irrespective of the wishes of the parties.[2] On the other hand, it must be conceded that contracting parties generally remain free to make provision in their contract for what would otherwise be a frustrating event, thereby excluding the operation of the doctrine of frustration.[3] It is also true that contracting parties remain free to deal with the *consequences* of a contract which has been frustrated.[4]

But contracting parties appear to be reluctant to embark upon the task of making provision for the consequences of the frustration of their contract and it has been left largely to legislatures, both in England and elsewhere in the Commonwealth, to undertake this task. In England it is the Law Reform (Frustrated Contracts) Act 1943 which is the principal source of the law relating to the remedial consequences of the frustration of a contract.[5] The influence of this Act extends far beyond

1. One example might arise where the effect of the *force majeure* clause is to terminate the contract between the parties. Where the contract is terminated and one party has paid money or otherwise conferred a benefit upon the other party prior to the termination of the contract and the *force majeure* clause makes no provision for the return of money paid, it may be possible to argue that money paid is recoverable upon a total failure of consideration, on which see below pp. 224–226.

2. *Hirji Mulji* v. *Cheong Yue S.S. Co.* [1926] A.C. 497.

3. *Paal Wilson & Co. A/S* v. *Partenreederei Hannah Blumenthal* [1983] 1 A.C. 854, at p. 909.

4. See s. 2(3) of the Law Reform (Frustrated Contracts) Act 1943 discussed below, pp. 240–242 and see also pp. 117–119 above.

5. The assumption is therefore made that the contract has been frustrated. The principles which are applied by the courts in deciding whether or not a contract has been frustrated do not form the subject-matter of this chapter.

England; it has acted as a model for legislation enacted in New Zealand,[6] the state of Victoria in Australia,[7] and it was used by the Commissioners on Uniformity of Legislation in Canada as the basis for a model Act,[8] which was subsequently enacted in every Canadian Province with the exceptions of Nova Scotia, British Columbia and Saskatchewan. But despite the influence and apparent popularity of the 1943 Act it has, in recent years, been subjected to considerable criticism by various Commonwealth law reform committees.[9] British Columbia was the first to reject the model of the 1943 Act when it enacted its Frustrated Contracts Act in 1974. Legislation has since been enacted in New South Wales in 1978[10] and South Australia in 1988.[11] These three Acts all differ from the 1943 Act and, indeed, they all differ from each other. No Act has yet been able to escape harsh criticism. The failure of legislatures to achieve an acceptable solution to the problems which arise on the frustration of a contract suggests that contracting parties should, in future, give greater consideration to the possibility of including within their contracts clauses which regulate the consequences of the frustration of their contract.

Therefore, as we analyse the 1943 Act and the problems to which it gives rise, we shall occasionally consider the alternatives proposed and enacted in British Columbia, New South Wales and South Australia and we shall also consider the extent to which it is open to contracting parties to make their own provision for the consequences of frustration.

2. THE COMMON LAW PRIOR TO THE 1943 ACT

Before analysing the 1943 Act, it is important to outline the position at common law. This is so for a number of reasons. The first is that it helps us to understand the reasons why the Act was thought to be necessary and it may also shed some light on the scope of the Act. The second is that the common law rules have not been displaced in some Commonwealth jurisdictions. Finally, certain contracts are not regulated by the 1943 Act and so continue to be regulated by the common law rules.[12]

The case which classically illustrates the deficiencies of the common law is *Chandler* v. *Webster*.[13] The defendant agreed to let rooms to the plaintiff for the

6. Frustrated Contracts Act 1944.
7. Frustrated Contracts Act 1959.
8. The Uniform Act [Frustrated Contracts Act], which was recommended in 1948.
9. See the New South Wales Law Reform Commission Report on Frustrated Contracts No. 25 (1976); Law Reform Commission of British Columbia "Report on the need for Frustrated Contracts Legislation in British Columbia" (Project No. 8); and the Seventy-First Report of the Law Reform Committee of South Australia Relating to the Doctrine of Frustration in the Law of Contract (1983). For academic discussion of these issues see Stewart and Carter, "Frustrated Contracts and Statutory Adjustment: The Case for a Reappraisal" [1992] C.L.J. 66, and Stewart, "The South Australian Frustrated Contracts Act" (1992) 5 J.C.L. 220.
10. Frustrated Contracts Act 1978.
11. Frustrated Contracts Act 1988.
12. See s. 2(5) of the 1943 Act. For example, advance freight continues to be governed by a rule "analogous to what we all know as the rule in *Chandler* v. *Webster* [1904] 1 K.B. 493" (*per* Robert Goff J. in *The Lorna I* [1981] 2 Lloyd's Rep. 559, 560; affd. [1983] 1 Lloyd's Rep. 373). Advance freight is discussed further by Howard at pp. 124–127 above.
13. [1904] 1 K.B. 493.

purpose of enabling the plaintiff to view the coronation procession of Edward VII. The contract was frustrated when the coronation procession was cancelled because of the illness of the King. Under the contract the sum of £141 15s was declared to be payable before the moment in time when the procession was cancelled. The plaintiff had, however, only paid £100 and he sued to recover that £100. The defendant counterclaimed for the balance payable of £41 15s. The Court of Appeal held that the plaintiff was not entitled to recover the £100, but that the defendant was entitled to recover the remaining £41 15s. The reason for this was held to be that, while the effect of frustration was to release both parties from their obligations to perform in the future, frustration did not affect the obligations which had accrued prior to the date of frustration. The plaintiff's obligation to pay the £141 15s therefore remained enforceable and, although money paid was recoverable upon a total failure of consideration, the Court of Appeal held that such a total failure could only arise when the contract was set aside *ab initio*. The plaintiff in *Chandler* could not contend that the contract had been set aside *ab initio*; therefore there was no total failure of consideration and no ground upon which he could seek recovery of the money paid. The plaintiff was obliged to pay £141 15s but received nothing in return; the injustice was apparent.

The result in *Chandler* was also unsatisfactory because the crucial issue on which the rights of the parties hinged was whether the obligation to pay had accrued before the date of the frustrating event. Had the obligation to pay arisen after the date of the frustrating event, the plaintiff would have been released by the frustrating event from his obligation to pay. In *Krell* v. *Henry*,[14] which was another "coronation case", the balance of £50 was payable *after* the date of frustration and therefore ceased to be payable. Given that a frustrating event is, by definition, an unforeseen event, it was perverse to select the date of the frustrating event as the date for ascertaining the rights of the parties.

The conclusion of the court in *Chandler* aroused much concern. It was subjected to harsh criticism by two Scottish Law Lords, Lord Dunedin and Lord Shaw of Dunfermline, in *Cantiere San Rocco S.A.* v. *Clyde Shipbuilding and Engineering Co.*[15] As a result of their Lordships' criticisms, a Law Revision Committee[16] was asked to report on the state of the law and duly made proposals for reform. But the committee's terms of reference were extremely narrow; it was simply asked whether the rule laid down in *Chandler* required modification. It was not asked to engage in a wide-ranging consideration of the state of the law.

The committee reported in 1939 but its report was not enacted immediately; and, more importantly, before the enactment of the Law Reform (Frustrated Contracts) Act in 1943, the House of Lords reversed *Chandler* in the case of *Fibrosa Spolka Akcyjna* v. *Fairbairn Lawson Combe Barbour Ltd.*[17] The House of Lords there held that money paid prior to the frustration of a contract was recoverable upon a

14. [1903] 2 K.B. 740.

15. [1924] A.C. 226, on which see Evans-Jones, "Unjust Enrichment, Contract and the Third Reception of Roman Law in Scotland" (1993) 109 L.Q.R. 663.

16. The Law Revision Committee "Seventh Interim Report (Rule in *Chandler* v. *Webster*)" Cmnd. 6009.

17. [1943] A.C. 32, although it should be noted that the House of Lords expressly stated that their decision did not affect the law in relation to advance freight, thus preserving the rule which is "analogous" to the now discarded rule in *Chandler* v. *Webster*. See further fn. 12.

total failure of consideration. But they overruled *Chandler* v. *Webster*[18] and rejected the proposition that a total failure of consideration could arise only when a contract was set aside *ab initio*; it arose whenever money (or, impliedly, goods or services[19]) was paid on a basis which wholly failed.[20] In *Fibrosa* the respondents agreed to manufacture machines for the appellants and to deliver them to Gdynia in Poland. However, before the respondents completed the manufacture of the machines, the contract was frustrated when Gdynia was occupied by the German army. The appellants had paid £1,000 on the signing of the agreement (although the agreement actually provided that £1,600 was payable) and they sought to recover the £1,000 from the respondents. The House of Lords held that the appellants were entitled to recover the money because it had been paid for a consideration (or on a basis) which had wholly failed.

While it is true to say that *Fibrosa* represented an improvement upon the rule established in *Chandler*, it did not leave the law in an entirely satisfactory state.[21] The first defect was that the payer could only recover money paid upon a total failure of consideration; where the failure was only partial he could not recover.[22] The second defect was that the House of Lords held that the payee could not set off against the money to be repaid any expenditure which he had incurred in the performance of the contract.[23] For example, on the facts of *Fibrosa*, the respondents incurred expenditure in making the machines (although it was, admittedly, unclear whether that expenditure had been wasted), yet they were unable to retain any part of the prepayment.

These defects meant that *Fibrosa* could not prevent the enactment of the Law Reform (Frustrated Contracts) Act 1943. However, it is important to note that, although the Act is based upon the recommendations of the Law Revision Committee, it is wider in its scope than their recommendations. In the light of this, it is perhaps no surprise to learn that in *B.P. Exploration Co. (Libya) Ltd.* v. *Hunt (No. 2)*[24] Robert Goff J. held that the committee's report should not be used as an aid to the interpretation of the Act.

3. THE SCOPE OF THE 1943 ACT

The scope of the 1943 Act is identified in section 1(1) which states:

"Where a contract governed by English law has become impossible of performance or been

18. [1904] 1 K.B. 493.

19. Total failure of consideration is logically applicable both to money claims and to non-money claims; see Birks, *An Introduction to the Law of Restitution* pp. 230–231. Although this is the position which is dictated by logic, it must be conceded that this proposition has not yet been embraced by the judiciary, who still tend to conceive of total failure of consideration as a money claim only.

20. See Birks, "Restitution and the Freedom of Contract" 1983 *Current Legal Problems* 141.

21. For a fuller analysis of the decision of the House of Lords in *Fibrosa*, its implications for the common law rules and an assessment of the relevant common law principles see McKendrick, "Frustration, Restitution and Loss Apportionment" in Burrows (ed.), *Essays on the Law of Restitution* (O.U.P. 1991), p. 147.

22. *Whincup* v. *Hughes* (1871) L.R. 6 C.P. 78.

23. Although it can be argued that the common law position was not as bleak as their Lordships in *Fibrosa* made it appear; see McKendrick *op. cit.* fn. 21 at pp. 151–152.

24. [1979] 1 W.L.R. 783, 798.

otherwise frustrated, and the parties thereto have for that reason been discharged from the further performance of the contract, the following provisions of this section shall, subject to the provisions of section two of this Act, have effect in relation thereto."

Two points should be noted about this provision. The first is that the Act applies to contracts which are "governed by English law". That is to say, the crucial question is whether the law applicable to the contract is English law.[25] The Act, therefore, does not apply to contracts which are governed, for example, by Scots law. It does, however, seem rather strange that the draftsman has elected to use the law applicable to the *contract* as the decisive factor when we are here concerned with an independent restitutionary claim which is, of course, distinct from an action on the contract. On the other hand, Rule 201(2)(a) in *Dicey and Morris*[26] states that "if the obligation [to restore the benefit of an enrichment obtained at another's expense] arises in connection with a contract, its proper law is the law applicable to the contract". Thus it can be argued that the obligation to restore a benefit received in the course of performance of a contract which is subsequently frustrated is an obligation which "arises in connection with a contract".[27] But such reasoning is difficult to reconcile with the proposition that an action to recover the value of a benefit conferred is an independent restitutionary claim and, on principle, one would think that the applicable law should be the law of the place where the unjust enrichment takes place[28] or the law of the country where the plaintiff's loss and the defendant's gain occurs.[29] It is also instructive to note that British Columbia, Victoria and South Australia in their respective Frustrated Contracts Acts have not included a choice of law provision. The principal reason for rejecting the approach contained in section 1(1) of the 1943 Act was best expressed by the Law Reform Commission of British Columbia when they pointed out that there are dangers in "tinkering with the law of conflicts on a piecemeal basis" and that it is "unnecessary and unwise to interfere with the general operation of the rules of private international law".[30]

The second point to note is that the Act applies to contracts which have become "impossible of performance or been otherwise frustrated". The Act makes no attempt to define frustration; on that point resort must be had to the common law. One possible point of doubt here is whether the Act applies to contracts affected by

25. See, for example, *B.P. Exploration Co. (Libya) Ltd.* v. *Hunt* [1976] 1 W.L.R. 788 where there was an argument before Kerr J. as to whether or not the proper law of the contract was English law.

26. *The Conflict of Laws* (12th Edn.) and see more generally Bennett, "Choice of Law Rules in Claims of Unjust Enrichment" (1990) 39 I.C.L.Q. 136.

27. In *Fibrosa Spolka Akcyjna* v. *Fairbairn Lawson Combe Barbour Ltd.* [1943] A.C. 32 the House of Lords applied English law, being the law applicable to the contract, but the point did not not seem to have been contested. There does, however, appear to be a tendency on the part of the courts to resort to the law applicable to the contract in a restitutionary claim (see further *Dimskal Shipping Co. S.A.* v. *International Transport Workers' Federation* [1992] 2 A.C. 152). See further Dicey and Morris, *op. cit.*, fn. 26, pp. 1474–1476 and for criticism see Burrows, *The Law of Restitution*, pp. 492–493 (although note his support for the reasoning of the House of Lords in the *Dimskal Shipping* case at pp. 499–500).

28. *Re Jogia (A Bankrupt)* [1988] 1 W.L.R. 138.

29. This suggestion is put forward by Burrows, *op. cit.*, fn. 27 at p. 492 and, while it is true to principle in that it emphasises both the "enrichment" and the "at the expense of" stage of the restitutionary enquiry, it does seem more likely to give rise to difficult practical problems (see, for example, the problems which this test experiences when applied to the facts of *Re Jogia (A Bankrupt)* [1998] 1 W.L.R. 138, discussed by Burrows at pp. 497–498).

30. *Op. cit.*, fn. 9, p. 52.

supervening illegality.[31] Goff and Jones content themselves with saying that contracts determined by supervening illegality are "probably frustrated contracts within the Act".[32] However, the generally accepted view is that the Act does apply to cases of supervening illegality. On the other hand, it is clear that the Act does not apply to contracts which are discharged by breach or to contracts which are *initially* impossible of performance. The latter case is truly one of common mistake and not frustration and hence is outside the scope of the Act. Finally, the Act does not apply to the discharge of a contract under an express provision of the contract, such as clause 22 of the GAFTA forms which provides for automatic cancellation of a contract on the occurrence of a specified event.[33]

4. THE PURPOSE BEHIND THE 1943 ACT

It is important to seek to identify the purpose which lies behind the 1943 Act because not only does it help in seeking to ascertain the limits of the Act, but it also helps us to understand some of the criticisms which have been levelled against it. In *B.P.* v. *Hunt*, Robert Goff J. stated that the "fundamental principle underlying the Act itself is prevention of the unjust enrichment of either party to the contract at the other's expense".[34] Its purpose was not to "apportion the loss between the parties".[35] However, in the Court of Appeal, Lawton L.J. noted this view and stated that the court got "no help from the use of words which are not in the statute".[36] The purpose behind the Act, therefore, remains a matter of doubt and some commentators have challenged the validity of the analysis of Robert Goff J. and asserted that the "real basis of the Act is that it is designed to provide a flexible machinery for the adjustment of loss".[37]

But the view that the Act is designed to "provide a flexible machinery for the adjustment of loss" is difficult to accept, especially when the Act is compared with the legislation enacted in British Columbia, New South Wales and South Australia, all of which clearly seek to engage in loss apportionment. The fundamental feature of the 1943 Act is that the court must first identify the benefit which the defendant has obtained at the expense of the plaintiff; in the case of section 1(2) the benefit is money and in the case of section 1(3) the benefit is a non-monetary one. The only point at which loss apportionment can be said to enter into the equation is when the court exercises its discretion to allow the plaintiff to recover so much of the benefit as appears to it to be "just". But even here, as we shall see, it is possible to rationalise this discretionary power in restitutionary terms.

The restitutionary focus of the 1943 Act should be contrasted with the broader focus of the legislation enacted in British Columbia, New South Wales and South

31. See McNair (1944) L.Q.R. 160, 162–163.
32. *The Law of Restitution* (4th Edn.), p. 450.
33. Discussed in greater detail at pp. 293–299 below.
34. [1979] 1 W.L.R. 783, 799.
35. *Ibid.*
36. [1982] 1 All E.R. 925, 983.
37. Haycroft and Waksman, "Restitution and Frustration" [1984] J.B.L. 207, 225.

Australia. Thus, in the case of British Columbia[38] and South Australia,[39] losses are to be apportioned equally between the parties, while the New South Wales Act[40] provides a more complex scheme for the adjustment of losses. As we shall see, this failure to consider the issue of loss apportionment is one of the great failures of the 1943 Act.[41]

5. THE RECOVERY OF MONEY: SECTION 1(2)

Section 1(2) of the Act provides that:

> "All sums paid or payable to any party in pursuance of the contract before the time when the parties were so discharged (in this Act referred to as 'the time of discharge') shall, in the case of sums so paid, be recoverable from him as money received by him for the use of the party by whom the sums were paid, and, in the case of sums so payable, cease to be payable: Provided that, if the party to whom the sums were so paid or payable incurred expenses before the time of discharge in, or for the purpose of, the performance of contract, the court may, if it considers it just to do so having regard to all the circumstances of the case, allow him to retain or, as the case may be, recover the whole or any part of the sums so paid or payable, not being an amount in excess of the expenses so incurred."

There is, perhaps rather surprisingly, no reported case on the operation of section 1(2), although in *B.P.* v. *Hunt*[42] Robert Goff J. did express an opinion on the effect of the subsection, even though it was not necessary for the resolution of the case. Its principal effect is to entitle a contracting party to recover money paid to the other contracting party prior to the frustrating event and it also relieves such a party of the obligation to pay any monies which were payable prior to the frustrating event but which had remained unpaid. Further, money paid is recoverable even upon a partial failure of consideration, the common law rule limiting the right of recovery to cases of *total* failure of consideration having been abolished in the case of frustration by this subsection. The effect of this subsection may also be to rescue the payer from his bad bargain because the prepayment is recoverable irrespective of the consideration which he would have received had the contract been performed.[43] Three further points should be noted about this subsection.

(a) Sums paid or payable "before the time of discharge"

The first point is that it only applies to sums paid or payable "in pursuance of the contract" and "before the time of discharge". Two points arise here. The first is that the payment must be made as a result of a contractual obligation to pay. Thus,

38. Frustrated Contracts Act 1974, s. 5(3).
39. Frustrated Contracts Act 1988, s. 7(2)(c).
40. Frustrated Contracts Act 1978, ss. 9–15.
41. However, it should be noted that the claim that loss apportionment has a role to play in these cases has been the subject of some criticism recently: see Burrows, *op. cit.*, fn. 27, pp. 286–287 and Stewart and Carter, *op. cit.*, fn. 9, pp. 86–89 and 109–110.
42. [1979] 1 W.L.R. 783, 800.
43. *Ibid.*

it has been argued that the subsection has no application to money deposited by a customer with his bank because, in such a case, the customer is "not obliged" to deposit the money with the bank.[44] The second point is that the sum must be paid "before the time of discharge" so that the subsection has no application to sums paid after the date of discharge and, in such a case, resort must be had to the common law.[45] Where, after the frustration of the contract, the parties enter into a fresh contract in relation to the work done, then that contract will govern the relationship between the parties and so will regulate any entitlement to recover any sum paid. But if, as is likely to be the case, no fresh contract is concluded the only action available to a plaintiff would appear to be a restitutionary one to recover the value of any post-frustration payment. Such a claim will only be available within narrow confines. A plaintiff could seek recovery on the ground of total failure of consideration but, in most cases, such a claim will be barred because the plaintiff will have received some part of the bargained-for performance.[46] An alternative ground of recovery might be mistake but here too plaintiffs are likely to encounter difficulties. Where the payment is made after the time of discharge because the plaintiff was unaware of the frustrating event, then the payment may be recoverable on the ground that it was conferred under a mistake of fact.[47] Greater difficulty arises where a payment is made because the plaintiff, although aware of the frustrating event itself, was unaware that the event amounted in law to frustration. In such a case the payment may not be recoverable because benefits conferred under a mistake of law are generally irrecoverable,[48] although the mistake of law bar is difficult to defend on any rational basis and there are indications that it might soon be removed and the rules relating to mistake of law assimilated with those applicable to mistake of fact.[49]

(b) The proviso

The second point to note is that, in comparison with *Fibrosa*, section 1(2) improves the lot of the payee because the proviso to section 1(2) states that the payee may be entitled to set off against a claim by the payer "the amount of any expenses

44. *Libyan Arab Foreign Bank* v. *Banker's Trust Co.* [1989] Q.B. 728, at p. 772.

45. Contrast s. 5(4) of the New South Wales Frustrated Contracts Act 1978 and s. 7(6) of the South Australia Frustrated Contracts Act 1988, both of which specifically bring within the control of the Act post-frustration conduct.

46. Although an argument can be made out that money should be recoverable upon a partial failure of consideration, English law has not yet reached that position.

47. See Goff and Jones, *op. cit.*, fn. 32, Chapter 3.

48. See Goff and Jones, *op. cit.*, fn. 32, Chapter 4.

49. The Law Commission has proposed that the mistake of law bar be abolished (Consultation Paper No. 120 "Restitution of Payments Made Under a Mistake of Law") and it has been abrogated by the judiciary in Canada (*Air Canada* v. *British Columbia* (1989) 59 D.L.R. (4th) 161), Australia (*David Securities Pty. Ltd.* v. *Commonwealth Bank of Australia* (1993) 175 C.L.R. 353) and South Africa (*Willis Faber Enthoven Pty. Ltd.* v. *Receiver of Revenue* (1992) (4) S.A. 202). In *Woolwich Equitable Building Society* v. *Inland Revenue Commissioners* [1993] A.C. 70, 154 Lord Keith stated that the mistake of law bar was too deeply embedded in English law to be uprooted judicially, but Lord Slynn (at p. 199) was of the opinion that the present rule was open to review in the House of Lords. Lord Goff (at p. 164) and Lord Jauncey (at p. 192) noted the criticisms which have been levelled against the present rule but preferred to leave the matter to the Law Commission. So, notwithstanding the views of Lord Keith, the present standing of the mistake of law bar cannot be said to be secure.

incurred before the time of discharge . . . in, or for the purpose of, the performance of the contract". It is this proviso which gives rise to most of the difficulties of interpretation and here of course we are impeded by the lack of case law. We shall focus upon three particular difficulties.

The first difficulty lies in ascertaining the principle which underpins the proviso. In *B.P.* v. *Hunt* Robert Goff J. was of the opinion that the proviso constituted a "statutory recognition of the defence of change of position".[50] Until recently English law did not recognise the existence of such a defence. But in the landmark decision of the House of Lords in *Lipkin Gorman* v. *Karpnale Ltd.*[51] their Lordships took the vital step of recognising the existence of the defence, although they did not establish its limits. Thus Lord Goff stated that:

> "[a]t present I do not wish to state the principle any less broadly than this: that the defence is available to a person whose position has so changed that it would be inequitable in all the circumstances to require him to make restitution, or alternatively to make restitution in full. I wish to stress however that the mere fact that the defendant has spent the money, in whole or in part, does not of itself render it inequitable that he should be called upon to repay, because the expenditure might in any event have been incurred by him in the ordinary course of things."[52]

A hypothetical example will illustrate the potential scope of the defence. Suppose that X mistakenly pays £10,000 into Y's bank account. Y, who is ignorant of the mistake and who believes that the £10,000 is a birthday present from a benevolent uncle, spends £5,000, which he would not otherwise have spent, on a luxury cruise. X, who has now discovered his mistake, demands the return of the £10,000. Can Y resist the claim on the ground that he has "changed his position" as a result of the receipt of the £10,000 by spending £5,000 on a cruise which he would not otherwise have embarked upon? This is the issue raised by the change of position defence. It can be seen that there are similarities between the position of Y in our hypothetical example and the position of the payee in a case such as *Fibrosa*.

But there are difficulties with the view that the proviso constitutes a rationalisation of the defence of change of position. The first is that English law has only recently recognised the defence of change of position and, as has been noted, its scope remains uncertain. There are inevitable difficulties in drawing an analogy with a defence which itself has not yet established its parameters or its underlying principle. The second difficulty is that it is not clear that the wording of the proviso corresponds with the version of the defence recognised by the House of Lords in *Lipkin Gorman*. In one respect the proviso is more restrictive because it is not sufficient that the defendant has changed his position; he must have done so "in, or for the purpose of, the performance of the contract". So the defendant who changes his position by incurring expenditure on some purpose unrelated to the contract would not be able to invoke the proviso, but such expenditure (such as the money spent on the cruise in our hypothetical case) might fall within the general defence of change of position recognised in *Lipkin Gorman*. Secondly, it remains unclear whether the defendant who invokes the *Lipkin Gorman* version of the defence

50. [1979] 1 W.L.R. 783, at p. 800.
51. [1991] 2 A.C. 548.
52. [1991] 2 A.C. 548 at p. 580.

must show that the change of position was incurred *in reliance upon* the payment.[53] However, there is no such doubt in relation to the proviso because it contains no requirement that the expenditure be incurred in reliance upon the payment. The expenditure could be incurred before the receipt of the payment and the payee may nonetheless invoke the proviso. Therefore, in the absence of a settled definition of the defence, the invocation of the language of change of position may lead to confusion in application.[54] The rationalisation may, however, be of some assistance in identifying the purpose which underpins the subsection, a point to which we shall return.[55] But it may be of little assistance in interpreting the precise wording of the subsection. The function of the court is to interpret the proviso as it stands, not to distort its wording in an effort to accommodate it within a version of the defence of change of position which has been recognised by the House of Lords in another context, or one which has been advocated by academic commentators, courts or legislatures in other jurisdictions.

The second difficulty with the proviso lies in identifying the relevant "expenses" to be taken into account. The first point to note here is that expenses include a reasonable sum for overhead expenses and for work or services personally performed.[56] Secondly, the expenses must have been incurred "in, or for the purpose of, the performance of the contract". Thus pre-contract expenditure is unlikely to be included because, at the time of the expenditure, there was no contract for the expenses to be incurred in "the performance of", although it is arguable that where the expenditure is incurred in the reasonable belief that a contract will be concluded it may be brought into account.[57]

The third difficulty with the proviso lies in calculating the sum which a court will allow the payee to recover or retain. Suppose that a payee, having received £50,000 from the plaintiff prior to the frustration of the contract, has incurred expenditure of £25,000 in performing the contract. How much of the £50,000 can the payee retain? There are two principal approaches which could be adopted. The first is to argue that the payee should be entitled to retain £12,500 so that the consequences of frustration are divided equally between the contracting parties, so that they both lose £12,500. Professor Glanville Williams has supported such a construction on the ground that the "situation with which the Act is concerned is the familiar one in which one of two parties has to suffer loss for which neither is responsible" and that in the "normal case" the just course "would be to order the retention or repayment of half the loss incurred".[58] Such an approach has been expressly adopted in section 5(3) of the British Columbia Frustrated Contracts Act 1974.

The second approach is to argue that the payee should be entitled to retain £25,000, that is the full amount of the expenditure incurred in the performance of

53. Goff and Jones, *op. cit.*, fn. 32, p. 741, citing the approach adopted in s. 142 of the American Restatement of Restitution, would not appear to restrict the scope of the defence in this way but, as they acknowledge, such a limitation was recognised by the Supreme Court of Canada in *Rural Municipality of Storthoaks* v. *Mobil Oil of Canada Ltd.* (1975) 55 D.L.R. (3d) 1, at p. 13. The point therefore remains an open one in English law.

54. See further Burrows, *The Law of Restitution*, p. 285.

55. See pp. 232–233 below.

56 S. 1(4).

57. See the examples given by Goff and Jones, *op. cit.*, note 32, p. 452.

58. *The Law Reform (Frustrated Contracts) Act 1943*, pp. 35–36.

the contract. This would appear to be the conclusion reached by the application of the change of position rationalisation, at least where the expenditure is, in fact, wasted. Such a conclusion was also reached by the English Law Revision Committee on the ground that it is "reasonable to assume that in stipulating for prepayment the payee intended to protect himself against loss under the contract".[59] However, this assumption is open to challenge. It may be true to say that the payee, in stipulating for a prepayment, intended to protect himself against any loss which would otherwise be incurred as a result of the payer's breach, but is it also true to say that he intended to protect himself against the effects of frustration, especially when it is conceded that, by definition, frustration is an unforeseen event?

It therefore remains unclear which of these alternatives (or, indeed, if any other alternatives) will be adopted by the courts and it is unsatisfactory that Parliament should have left the law in such an uncertain state. In the absence of any English authority or any legislative guidance, an instructive approach might be to ask upon whom the onus of proof rests in relation to the proviso. In *Lobb* v. *Vasey Housing Auxiliary*,[60] decided under the Victorian Frustrated Contracts Act 1959 which, in turn, was modelled on the 1943 Act, it was held that the onus was on the defendants to show that it was just in all the circumstances of the case for them to retain any part of the prepayment. The consequence of the adoption of such an approach may be that, where the defendant fails to satisfy the onus,[61] any loss lies on him but that, where he does satisfy the onus, he is entitled to retain or recover all the expenditure incurred in or for the purpose of the performance of the contract. On the other hand, it can be argued that such an interpretation ignores the fact that the court is also given a discretion in relation to the *proportion* of the prepayment which the payee can retain or recover.[62] It can also be argued that this discretion is ignored in the change of position rationalisation and, further, that the equal division of the loss advocated by Professor Glanville Williams unduly circumscribes the court's discretion.

The uncertainty which surrounds the interpretation of the proviso and the basis of the payee's claim to have his expenditure brought into account underlines the fact that this subsection is not well drafted and that inadequate consideration has been given to the apportionment of any losses between the parties.

(c) Does the payee have a cause of action?

The third point to note about section 1(2) is the question whether a payee can use the subsection to recover money from the payer or whether section 1(2) confers a cause of action only upon the payer. The general answer is that, subject to one

59. *Op. cit.*, note 16, p. 7.
60. [1963] V.R. 239.
61. For example, it would be difficult for a payee to satisfy the onus where his expenditure resulted in a product which he could use in the performance of another contract, as in *Davis and Primrose Ltd.* v. *Clyde Shipbuilding and Engineering Co. Ltd.* 1917 1 S.L.T. 297. See also Treitel, *The Law of Contract* (8th Edn.) pp. 810–811 and for a slightly different argument to the same end see Williams, *op. cit.*, fn. 58, p. 39, who argues that expenses in s. 1(2) means "expenses after deduction of gains resulting from those expenses".
62. Cf. *National Carriers Ltd.* v. *Panalpina (Northern) Ltd.* [1981] A.C. 675, 707, where Lord Simon of Glaisdale did not think that the court was empowered by the Act to engage in loss apportionment and that, in consequence, there would often be an "all-or-nothing" situation.

exception, the subsection gives a cause of action to the payer and not to the payee. The one exception arises in the case where money payable by the "payer" to the payee before the time of discharge remains unpaid; in such a case the payee can invoke section 1(2) to recover so much of his expenses, not exceeding the amount of the prepayment due, as is just. This is because the proviso states that the payee may be able to "recover" in whole or in part any sums which are "payable" to him.

However, a problem does arise where no money is paid or is payable to the payee prior to the frustrating event but the payee nevertheless incurs expenditure in, or for the purpose of, the performance of the contract. In such a case, the payee cannot recover under section 1(2) (although a claim may be made under section 1(3) where the expenditure results in a valuable benefit being obtained by the other party). Such sums are, section 1(3) apart, deemed to be spent at the risk of the payee. Therefore, it is clear that it is vitally important to require that a prepayment is made before embarking upon performance of the contract because not only will it provide protection in the event of the default of the other party, it will also provide some protection in the event of the contract being frustrated.

6. RECOVERY IN RESPECT OF NON-MONETARY BENEFITS: SECTION 1(3)

Section 1(3) states that

"Where any party to the contract has, by reason of anything done by any other party thereto in, or for the purpose of, the performance of the contract, obtained a valuable benefit (other than a payment of money to which the last foregoing subsection applies) before the time of discharge, there shall be recoverable from him by the said other party such sum (if any), not exceeding the value of the said benefit to the party obtaining it, as the court considers just, having regard to all the circumstances of the case and, in particular—

(a) the amount of any expenses incurred before the time of discharge by the benefited party in, or for the purpose of, the performance of the contract, including any sums paid or payable by him to any other party in pursuance of the contract and retained or recoverable by that party under the last foregoing subsection, and
(b) the effect, in relation to the said benefit, of the circumstances giving rise to the frustration of the contract."

This is the most controversial and difficult section in the Act and its effect was critical in the case of *B.P.* v. *Hunt*.[63] Before analysing the judgment of Robert Goff J. in *B.P.* v. *Hunt*, some profit may be gained by examining the structure of the subsection without regard to the judgment of Robert Goff J. The first point to note is that the Act does not provide a definition of what constitutes a "benefit". This should be contrasted with the legislation enacted in British Columbia[64] and New South Wales[65] which clearly identifies what counts as a benefit. The second point is that the Act does not identify with sufficient precision the point in time at which the benefit is to be valued. The subsection refers to a valuable benefit being obtained "before the time of discharge" and it can be argued that that is the time at which

63. [1979] 1 W.L.R. 783.

64. Frustrated Contracts Act 1974, s. 5(4). Provision is also made for the calculation of the benefit in ss. 6–7.

65. Frustrated Contracts Act 1978, ss. 9–15.

the benefit is to be valued. But the point is, as we shall see, by no means clear. In short, the subsection was enacted after insufficient consideration of the relevant issues and, in consequence, it is shoddily drafted.[66] It is further suggested that these points have been largely obscured in the criticisms which have been levelled against the judgment of Robert Goff J.

Returning to *B.P.* v. *Hunt*, the proper approach to the construction of the subsection was held by Robert Goff J. to be a three-stage one. At the first stage the valuable benefit must be identified; at the second stage the benefit must be valued and, finally, at the third stage the court must consider the award of a just sum.

(a) Identification of the benefit

The first question to be resolved is, therefore, what constitutes a "benefit". Section 1(3) is of course concerned with non-monetary benefits and Robert Goff J. stated that, either the "end-product" of the services could be identified as the valuable benefit,[67] or it could be the services themselves which are to be recognised as the benefit.[68] The latter view, it is suggested, is closer to the rule at common law where services can constitute a benefit, even in the absence of an end-product.[69] As a matter of principle, this latter approach was the one favoured by Robert Goff J.[70] But he felt constrained by the wording of section 1(3) to conclude that "in an appropriate case" it was the end-product which was to be regarded as the benefit. This reference to "an appropriate case" suggests that Robert Goff J. did not unequivocally rule out the possibility of a court having regard to the services themselves in identifying and valuing the benefit. There are two particular cases where it is likely that the court will have regard to the services themselves in identifying the benefit.

The first case arises where the service by its very nature does not result in an end-product, for example, "where the services consist of doing such work as surveying, or transporting goods".[71] In such a case Robert Goff J. conceded that the court would simply have to consider the benefit which the defendant has obtained by virtue of the plaintiff's contractual performance, which presumably would be calculated by reference to the value of the services performed by the plaintiff under the contract. The conclusion that the existence of an end-product was a necessary ingredient of a section 1(3) claim would have led to ridiculous arguments as to what constitutes an "end-product". Thus, Professor Birks has argued that "there is no purpose in insisting on an end-product if one which is eccentric and worthless will suffice. Whitened coal might be said to be the end-product of coal whitening, whereas book burning arguably leaves no product at all. It would be absurd to say

66. See further, on the process leading up to the enactment of the 1943 Act, McKendrick *op. cit.*, fn. 21 at pp. 152–154.

67. See Keener. *Quasi Contracts*, pp. 253–258.

68. See Woodward, *Quasi Contracts*, pp. 182–184.

69. Contrast Beatson "Benefit, Reliance and the Structure of Unjust Enrichment" in *The Use and Abuse of Unjust Enrichment: Essays on the Law of Restitution*, p. 21. But see Burrows, *op. cit.*, fn. 27, pp. 291–292, who doubts the importance of the distinction between the services themselves and the end-product of the services, choosing to focus on the point in time that the benefit is received by the recipient.

70. *Cf.* Beatson, *op. cit.* fn. 69, especially pp. 39–44.

71. [1979] 1 W.L.R. 783, at p. 802.

that a maximum award can be calculated for whitened coal simply because a visible end-product can be identified when the work is done. It would lead to ridiculous inventiveness in the identification of end-products".[72] This "ridiculous inventiveness" can be avoided by having regard to the services themselves in identifying and valuing the benefit.

The second case arises where the services performed result in an end-product which has no objective value. Robert Goff J. gave the example of a plaintiff who commences "the redecoration, to the defendant's execrable taste, of rooms which are in good decorative order".[73] In such a case, the work of the plaintiff may even reduce the value of the defendant's property, but Robert Goff J. nevertheless held that the services must be regarded as a benefit because they were requested by their recipient. He did not, however, say how the benefit should be valued, although surely the primary point of reference must be the value of the services provided under the contract.

There is a third case in which it has been argued that the court should regard the services themselves, rather than the end-product, as the benefit. This arises where the end-product of the services is destroyed by the frustrating event. However in such a case, Robert Goff J. stated that the plaintiff has no claim under section 1(3) because the value of the benefit is reduced to zero by the frustrating event.[74] Robert Goff J. sought to justify this conclusion on the ground that "benefit" in section 1(3)(b) clearly refers to the end-product of the services rather than the services themselves. Although section 1(3)(b) undoubtedly refers to the end-product of the services, the words immediately preceding paragraphs (a) and (b) ("having regard to all the circumstances of the case, and in particular") appear to be directed to the assessment of the just sum and not to the identification of the valuable benefit.[75] On the other hand, there are arguments which can be adduced in favour of the construction adopted by Robert Goff J. The first is that section 1(3), in its opening words, does draw a distinction between the plaintiff's performance and the defendant's benefit as if the defendant's benefit cannot be the value of the plaintiff's performance. The second is that the Newfoundland Supreme Court in *Parsons Bros Ltd.* v. *Shea*,[76] a case decided under the similarly worded Newfoundland Frustrated Contracts Act 1956, reached the same conclusion as Robert Goff J. This case is, of course, in no way binding upon an English court, but it is of some value because the Newfoundland Frustrated Contracts Act 1956 was based upon the 1943 Act. Finally, it is interesting to note that, fearful that the interpretation adopted by Robert Goff J. would prove to be the correct one, the British Columbia Frustrated Contracts Act 1974 provides that a benefit is "something done in the fulfilment of contractual obligations whether or not the person for whose benefit it was done received the benefit".[77] This provision has been rightly criticised on the ground that it gives the word "benefit" an unnatural and artificial meaning, but it does show that the wording of section 1(3) had given rise to cause for concern before the judg-

72. *Op. cit.*, fn. 19, p. 252.
73. [1979] 1 W.L.R. 783, at p. 803.
74. Thus, the result of *Appleby* v. *Myers* (1867) L.R. 2 C.P. 651 would be unaffected by s. 1(3) of the Act.
75. Treitel, *op. cit.*, note 61, pp. 813–814.
76. (1966) 53 D.L.R. (2d) 86.
77. S. 5(4).

ment of Robert Goff J. This point of construction is undoubtedly an extremely difficult one but it is suggested that the construction adopted by Robert Goff J. accords more closely with the literal wording of section 1(3), although it is capable of reaching conclusions which are, in principle, undesirable.

(b) Valuing the benefit

Once the benefit has been identified, the next step is to value the benefit and, here too, issues of great complexity can arise. These difficulties flow largely from the conclusion that it is the end-product and not the services themselves which are to be regarded as the benefit. Had the benefit been identified as the services themselves then many of these difficulties would not have arisen. The principal problem is that there is no necessary relationship between the services and the end-product: a small service may confer an enormous benefit, conversely, a substantial service may confer a small benefit. Where a small service confers an enormous benefit then the benefit is to be valued at that large sum, although it must be remembered that the plaintiff can only recover under section 1(3) a "just sum", which may be considerably less than the value of the benefit. And in the case where the service results in a benefit of no objective value, as in the example given above of the defendant who has rooms which are in good decorative order decorated to his own execrable taste, then the primary reference point in valuing the benefit is likely to be the value of the services performed under the contract.

Two further problems arise in valuing the benefit. The first is the date on which the benefit is to be valued. In *B.P.* v. *Hunt* Robert Goff J. held that the benefit must be valued as at the date of the frustrating event. The difficulty with this proposition is that section 1(3) applies where "a valuable benefit has been obtained *before* the time of discharge". This suggests that the date of the valuation should be before the time of discharge[78] and the point may yet be open for further argument. The second problem relates to the role of section 1(3)(a). The expenses could either be deducted from the benefit or from the just sum. Robert Goff J. held that the expenses were to be deducted from the value of the benefit and not from the just sum. But, as we have already noticed, the words immediately preceding paragraph (a) suggest that the expenses should be deducted from the just sum and not from the valuable benefit and, once again, the point may yet be open for further argument.[79]

(c) The just sum

Finally, the court must consider the principles to be applied in the assessment of the just sum. Robert Goff J. sought to put the assessment of the just sum on a principled basis when he said that the aim of the court in assessing the just sum ought to be the "prevention of the unjust enrichment of the defendant at the plaintiff's

78. It should also be noted that Robert Goff J. concluded (at p. 804) that the Act does not make allowance for the time value of money, so that the benefit is valued at the date of the frustrating event without regard to the money which the defendant may have obtained by selling the benefit before the date of the frustrating event (although he did award interest from the time of frustration under the Law Reform (Miscellaneous Provisions) Act 1934).

79. See Haycroft and Waksman, *op. cit.*, fn. 37, p. 220.

expense"[80]. But the Court of Appeal appeared to reject this approach. Lawton L.J. concluded that "[w]hat is just is what the trial judge thinks is just" and he held that an appellate court is not entitled to interfere with the assessment of the just sum by the trial judge "unless it is so plainly wrong that it cannot be just".[81] This leaves the issue virtually to the untrammelled discretion of the trial judge and it is regrettable that the Court of Appeal did not establish guidelines to assist trial judges in the exercise of their discretion and to ensure a measure of consistency in decided cases and out of court settlements.

It is therefore extremely difficult to give advice with any degree of certainty in relation to the assessment of the just sum. There are, however, certain points which ought to be borne in mind. The first is that the value of the benefit acts as a ceiling on the sum which the court can award so that, were the "just sum" to be greater than the value of the benefit, the plaintiff can only recover the value of the benefit. The second point is that the contractual allocation of risk is likely to be an important factor in the assessment of the just sum. In this context a difficult issue arises where the plaintiff has entered into a bad bargain. We have already noted that a payer can use section 1(2) to escape from the consequences of his bad bargain: does the same principle apply in the case of section 1(3)? Robert Goff J. thought it was "likely" that in most cases the plaintiff's claim would be limited to a rateable proportion of the contract price so that section 1(3) could not be used to escape the consequences of a bad bargain.[82] The third point is that the process of assessing the just sum may bear some resemblance to the enquiry conducted by the court in an action for a *quantum meruit* or a *quantum valebat*.[83] Indeed, this type of enquiry can be seen at work in the judgment of Robert Goff J. in *B.P.* v. *Hunt* when he said that his task was essentially to "assess a just sum in respect of the services rendered by B.P.".[84] But this principled approach has been put at risk by the *ad hoc* approach adopted by the Court of Appeal so that it is now impossible to know exactly how a trial judge will exercise his discretion to award a just sum.

(d) No discharge of obligations prior to date of discharge

There are one or two other problems which surround the interpretation and scope of section 1(3). The first is that the subsection does not make any provision for the discharge of obligations which had not been fulfilled at the date of frustration. We have already noted that section 1(2) expressly relieves a promisor from an obligation to pay monies which were payable prior to the frustrating event but which had remained unpaid. There is no such provision in section 1(3) and Professor Treitel has termed this a "*casus omissus*".[85] Thus, an obligation to provide goods or services, while being discharged from the moment of frustration, remains enforceable

80. [1979] 1 W.L.R. 783, at p. 805.
81. [1982] 1 All E.R. 925, at p. 980.
82. [1979] 1 W.L.R. 783, at p. 806
83. *Ibid.*, p. 805.
84. *Ibid.*, p. 825.
85. Treitel, *op cit.*, fn. 61, pp. 814–815. In this respect it is instructive to note that the New South Wales Frustrated Contracts Act, the British Columbian Frustrated Contracts Act and the South Australian Frustrated Contracts Act all make provision for the discharge of all obligations which remain unperformed (in ss. 7(1), 5(2) and 6 respectively).

prior to that date. Therefore, a party who has failed to perform an obligation, other than one to pay money, can be liable for the consequences of his non-performance of that obligation and he will be unable to offset any liability in respect of the non-performance by invoking section 1(3) because the subsection only encompasses benefits obtained "before the time of discharge".

(e) Obligations performed after the date of discharge

Where a non-money benefit is conferred after the date of the frustrating event, section 1(3) can have no application because it only applies to benefits which were obtained "before the time of discharge". Where the parties enter into a fresh contract in relation to the provision of post-frustration services or goods then that contract will govern the obligation to pay for the work or goods. Where no such contract has been concluded it may be possible for the party performing the obligation to bring a restitutionary claim in respect of any benefit conferred on the other party. But such a claim has two difficult obstacles to surmount if it is to succeed. The first is to show that the recipient was enriched by the performance of the obligation. This task is not an easy one where non-money benefits are concerned because the law of restitution does not generally employ an objective test of enrichment. A provider of goods or services has, essentially, two routes to establishing that the recipient was enriched. The first is to show that he was incontrovertibly benefited. English law has not yet firmly established the tests which are to be applied in determining whether or not a party has been incontrovertibly benefited, but generally it can be said that a person is incontrovertibly benefited when he has been saved a necessary expense[86] or when he has obtained a realised[87] or, possibly, a realisable[88] benefit. The second route lies in showing that the defendant requested[89] or bargained for[90] or possibly freely accepted[91] the goods or services in the knowledge that they were to be paid for. The difficulty which a provider of goods or services may encounter in the latter route is that, where only part of the goods has been delivered or the service has been only partially performed, the recipient may be able to argue that he has not been enriched at all because what he requested was complete performance and not partial performance and that his request is not pro-ratable.[92]

Once over the enrichment hurdle, the provider of the service must then point to a relevant unjust factor. The most obvious one is mistake. Where the mistake is one of fact (relating to the occurrence of the frustrating event) then recovery should fol-

86. Goff and Jones, *op. cit.*, fn. 32, pp. 22–23; Burrows, *op. cit.*, fn. 27, p. 11; Birks, *op. cit.*, fn. 19, pp. 117–121.

87. Birks, *op. cit.*, fn. 19, pp. 121–124. For a middle view see Burrows, *op. cit.*, fn. 27, pp. 10–11.

88. Goff and Jones, *op. cit.*, fn. 32, pp. 23 and 175–176. Some support for this view can be found in the judgment of Judge Bowsher Q.C. in *Marston Construction Co. Ltd.* v. *Kigass Ltd.* (1989) 46 Build. L.R. 109, p. 126.

89. Goff and Jones, *op. cit*, fn. 32, p. 19.

90. This is the phrase preferred by Burrows, *op. cit.*, fn. 27, pp. 14–15.

91. Goff and Jones, *op. cit.*, fn. 32, pp. 18–22: Birks, *op. cit.*, fn. 19, pp. 114–116. For criticism of the view that free acceptance is an appropriate test to use to estabish an enrichment, see Burrows, *op. cit.*, fn. 27, pp. 11–14.

92. It can be argued that *Appleby* v. *Myers* (1867) L.R. 2 C.P. 651 is an example of such a phenomenon because the defendant was not enriched by part performance of the contracted-for service: see McKendrick, *op. cit.*, fn. 21, p. 150.

low[93] but, as we have already noted,[94] considerable difficulties arise where the mistake is one of law (the provider of the service was aware of the event but did not realise that it constituted a frustrating event). An alternative (but, in theoretical terms, more controversial) unjust factor is "free acceptance", that is to say, the recipient freely accepted the benefit of the post-frustration performance, in the sense that he knew that the performance was being rendered non-gratuitously and elected to accept the performance, having had the opportunity to reject it.[95] In such a case the plaintiff may be able to recover the reasonable value of the goods supplied or services performed.[96] It has been argued that such cases are better classified as examples of recovery based upon (total) failure of consideration,[97] but the English judiciary have steadfastly refused to recognise that failure of consideration can generate a claim in anything other than a claim to recover money.

7. SEVERABILITY: SECTION 2(4)

Section 2(4) of the Act provides:

"Where it appears to the court that a part of any contract to which this Act applies can properly be severed from the remainder of the contract, being a part wholly performed before the time of discharge, or so performed except for the payment in respect of that part of the contract of sums which are or can be ascertained under the contract, the court shall treat that part of the contract as if it were a separate contract and had not been frustrated and shall treat the foregoing section of this Act as only applicable to the remainder of that contract."

A contract, rather than being "entire", may be divided into severable and distinct obligations. Where this is the case and the severable obligation has been completely performed, the Act has no application to that obligation (treating it as a separate contract), although it does apply to those severable obligations which have not been completely performed. It is the application of the Act to those several obligations which have not been completely performed that constitutes the significant change from the common law position, where no recovery was possible in respect of money paid or benefits conferred in the performance of a severable obligation which had not been completely performed.[98]

8. CONTRARY INTENTION: SECTION 2(3)

Section 2(3) provides:

"Where any contract to which this Act applies contains any provision which, upon the true construction of the contract, is intended to have effect in the event of circumstances arising which operate, or would but for the said provision operate, to frustrate the contract, or is

93. See Goff and Jones, *op. cit.*, fn. 32, Chapter 5.
94. See fns. 48 and 49 and associated text.
95. See further on free acceptance Birks, *op. cit.*, fn. 19, Chapter X.
96. *Société Franco Tunisienne D'Armement* v. *Sidermar (The Massalia)* [1961] 2 Q.B. 278, overruled on another point in *Ocean Tramp Tankers Corporation* v. *V/O Sovfracht (The Eugenia)* [1964] 2 Q.B. 226. See also *Codelfa Construction Pty. Ltd.* v. *State Rail Authority of New South Wales* (1982) 149 C.L.R. 337.
97. See Burrows, *op. cit.*, fn. 27, pp. 260–261 and 293–299.
98. *Stubbs* v. *Holywell Rly. Co.* (1867) L.R. 2 Ex. 311.

intended to have effect whether such circumstances arise or not, the court shall give effect to the said provision and shall only give effect to the foregoing section of this Act to such extent, if any, as appears to the court to be consistent with the said provision."

We have already noted that, in a number of respects, the drafting of subsections 1(2) and 1(3) is unsatisfactory. Section 2(3) therefore gives to contracting parties the opportunity to eliminate these problems by contracting out of the Act. It would, however, be a mistake simply to exclude the operation of the Act[99] because, in the absence of a clause in the contract making provision for the consequences of frustration, a court would presumably have resort to the common law rules as expounded in *Fibrosa*. And, as we have noted, *Fibrosa* did not leave the common law in a satisfactory state.[100] So the parties must go further and make their own provision for the consequences of the frustration of their contract. It should be noted that we are here concerned with a clause which seeks to regulate the *consequences* of the frustration of a contract and not with a clause which seeks to make provision for an *event* which would otherwise frustrate the contract; where the parties make provision for what would otherwise be a frustrating event, the effect of such a clause is to exclude the operation of the doctrine of frustration completely and the Act does not apply to a contract which has not been frustrated.[101]

But parties who wish to include in their contract a clause which regulates the consequences of frustration should make such provision clearly and expressly. Although it has been stated that, in deciding whether the parties have made such provision, a court will apply "ordinary principles of construction"[102] it has also been said that "where there is no clear indication that the parties did intend the clause to be applicable in the event of frustration, the court has to be very careful before it draws the inference that the clause was intended to be applicable in such radically changed circumstances".[103] More difficulty arises where there is no express provision for the consequences of frustration but it is argued that the contract impliedly makes provision for the consequences of such an event. For example, what is the effect of a clause which provides that one contracting party is under an obligation to maintain insurance against the consequences of the frustrating event? Such a clause would appear to be effective to exclude the operation of the Act so that the party upon whom the obligation to insure is imposed cannot bring a claim under the Act.[104] Similarly, what is the effect of a clause which states that payment is not due until the work is complete, or of a clause which provides a date for payment but that date is after the date of the frustrating event? In *B.P.* v. *Hunt* Robert Goff J. held that the fact that the contract is entire should not "automatically preclude an award of damages under section 1(3)"[105] and it is only "if

99. Although this appears to be the view of Stewart and Carter, *op. cit.*, fn. 9, p. 112.

100. See above, p. 226.

101. See s. 1(1), discussed above pp. 226–228. It is true that s. 2(3) states that it applies to any provision which "would but for the said provision operate" to frustrate the contract, but these words would appear to be unnecessary because when the contract is not frustrated the Act does not apply.

102. [1979] 1 W.L.R. 783, 806.

103. *Ibid.*, p. 829.

104. *Ibid.*, p. 807A, although it should be noted that s. 1(5) provides that "the court shall not take into account any sums which have, by reason of the circumstances giving rise to the frustration of the contract, become payable to that party under any contract of insurance unless there was an obligation to insure imposed by an express term of the frustrated contract or by or under any enactment".

105. *Ibid.*, p. 807.

upon a true construction of the contract the plaintiff has contracted on the terms that he is to receive no payment in the event which has occurred, will the fact that the contract is 'entire' have the effect of precluding an award under the Act".[106]

One final point should, however, be noted in relation to the scope of section 2(3). It is that the party seeking to rely upon section 2(3) must demonstrate that the clause was intended to operate in the circumstances which have actually happened; where the circumstances which have occurred are so devastating and unusual as to fall outside the ambit of the clause in question, then the Act will not have been excluded.[107] It was this point which was crucial on the facts of *B.P.* v. *Hunt*[108] because, while it could be shown that B.P. had taken a risk that there would be no oil in the field, it could not be shown that they had taken the political risk that the oil fields would be expropriated by the Libyan government. Therefore the parties had not contracted out of the operation of the 1943 Act.

But, given the failure of subsections 1(2) and 1(3) to address the issue of loss apportionment, it should not be difficult for the parties to devise a clause which achieves a more equitable solution than the one adopted by the 1943 Act (for example the clause could state that "in the event of the frustration (for whatever reason) of this contract it is agreed that each party shall make restitution for all benefits conferred (with an agreed method of identification and valuation of the benefit) and that any loss caused by the frustration of the contract shall be divided equally between the parties").

9. PRIOR BREACH BY THE PLAINTIFF

One other difficult question which was considered by Robert Goff J. in *B.P.* v. *Hunt* was the relevance to a claim under the 1943 Act of the fact that the plaintiff had, prior to the frustrating event, broken the contract between the parties. Robert Goff J. held that the effect of such a prior breach is that the defendant may have an accrued right to damages which may, in turn, be the subject of a set-off or counterclaim. But a prior breach by the plaintiff has no other impact upon the operation of either section 1(2) or section 1(3).[109]

10. EXCEPTED CASES

There are certain contracts which are excluded from the ambit of the 1943 Act. Thus section 2(5) provides that the Act does not apply

> "(a) to any charterparty, except a time charterparty or a charterparty by way of demise, or to any contract (other than a charterparty) for the carriage of goods by sea; or

106. *Ibid*.

107. For example, where the events which have occurred are particularly devastating or unusual, the courts have in the past been prepared to conclude that general words in a clause which, *prima facie*, are wide enough to encompass an event of the type which has occurred do not in fact cover that event; see, for example, *Metropolitan Water Board* v. *Dick, Kerr & Co. Ltd.* [1918] A.C. 119 and *Wong Lai Ying* v. *Chinachem Investment Co. Ltd.* (1979) 13 B.L.R. 81.

108. [1979] 1 W.L.R. 783.

109. *Ibid*., p. 808.

(b) to any contract of insurance, save as is provided by subsection (5) of the foregoing section; or
(c) to any contract to which section 7 of the Sale of Goods Act 1979 (which avoids contracts for the sale of specific goods which perish before the risk has passed to the buyer) applies, or to any other contract for the sale, or for the sale and delivery, of specific goods, where the contract is frustrated by reason of the fact that the goods have perished."

The exceptions contained in paragraphs (a) and (b) reflect well-established rules,[110] although paragraph (c) is rather puzzling because it excludes from the Act cases where the cause of the frustration is the fact that the goods have perished, but it does not exclude cases where the cause of frustration is some other cause, such as illegality. It has been strongly argued by Goff and Jones[111] that section 2(5)(c) should be repealed and that the Act should apply to all contracts for the sale of goods which are frustrated, and such a proposal has in fact been adopted in the South Australia Frustrated Contracts Act 1988, which applies to contracts which are avoided under the South Australian equivalent to section 7 of the Sale of Goods Act 1979.[112]

11. THE FUTURE

It is now clear that the Law Reform (Frustrated Contracts) Act 1943 suffers from a number of deficiencies and that the Law Reform Commission of British Columbia was right to conclude that the Act "was not well thought out or well drafted".[113] The British Columbia Frustrated Contracts Act 1974, the New South Wales Frustrated Contracts Act 1978 and the South Australia Frustrated Contracts Act 1988 all represent considerably more sophisticated attempts to deal with the remedial consequences of the frustration of a contract.

The fact that other jurisdictions have enacted solutions which are preferable to those contained in the 1943 Act is likely to be of little comfort to contracting parties in England or to parties whose contracts are governed by English law. The gloom is unlikely to be lifted in the foreseeable future by Parliamentary intervention to remedy the 1943 Act, nor are the uncertainties inherent in the Act likely to be resolved by the judiciary because of the almost complete lack of case law. In any event, the Court of Appeal in *B.P.* v. *Hunt* displayed little or no interest in providing any guidance for those concerned with the proper interpretation of the 1943 Act. The solution, if any, must therefore lie in the hands of the parties themselves. It will not suffice simply to exclude the operation of the Act, because that will only throw the parties back on to the common law as expounded in *Fibrosa*, which, as we have seen, suffers from a number of deficiencies. Nor will it suffice to place sole reliance upon a *force majeure* clause because a contract may be frustrated despite the presence of a *force majeure* clause in the contract[114] and, when the contract has been

110. Although, in relation to s. 2(5)(a), note the point made at p. 128 above, in relation to the rise of time charter trips, which has significant consequences for the scope of the 1943 Act.
111. *Op. cit.*, note 32, pp. 466–468.
112. See the definition of "frustration" in s. 3(1) which specifically states that it "includes avoidance of the contract under section 7 of the Sale of Goods Act, 1895".
113 *Op. cit.*, note 9, p. 7.
114. See further on the relationship between *force majeure* clauses and frustration, Chapter 3.

frustrated, the *force majeure* clause cannot regulate its consequences. So contracting parties must go further and, if they wish to avoid being subject to the operation of the 1943 Act, they must make express provision in their contract for the consequences of the frustration of that contract.

EWAN MCKENDRICK

CHAPTER 12

FRUSTRATION AND ESTOPPEL

The operation of the doctrine of frustration is one of the least successful of the efforts of lawyers to meet the needs of commerce. Unforeseen occurrences are surely a common event. Yet the response of the law of contract is both uncertain and inadequate.

Ordinarily an event which may frustrate a contract will not be expressly in contemplation or the subject of an express provision in an agreement. However, as Mahoney J.A. said in *Beaton* v. *McDivitt*[1] "There is, in my opinion, nothing in the doctrine of frustration which will prevent it operating where the parties have contracted on an expressed assumption which in the event proves false."

The suggestion in this note is that a more satisfactory result may have been available, in a number of the leading decisions, both in England and Australia, if resort had been had to the doctrine of estoppel rather than frustration. This suggestion is bottomed on the rapid development in Australia of the doctrine of estoppel exemplified by the decisions of the High Court of Australia in *Walton's Stores (Interstate) Ltd.* v. *Maher*[2] and even more recently in *The Commonwealth* v. *Verwayen*.[3]

In England the decision which founds the modern doctrine of frustration is *Davis Contractors Limited* v. *Fareham Urban District Council*.[4] With their tender, the contractors sent a covering letter stating, *inter alia*, that "our tender is subject to adequate supplies of material and labour being available as and when required to carry out the work within the time specified. It is also based on the present published market prices of materials delivered to site and existing established rates of wages in the various trades for the district."[5] Subsequently, a building agreement was executed which incorporated the tender and various other documents[6] and provided for a fixed price of £92,425.

Because of lack of skilled labour, the work took not the eight months called for by the contract but 22 months. The contractors contended that, owing to the long delay, the contract price had ceased to be applicable and that they were entitled to a payment of an additional £17,651 on a *quantum meruit* basis. The dispute went to arbitration. The arbitrator found that, at the time of entering into the agreement, both parties anticipated that there would be available in the building industry a suf-

1. (1987) 13 N.S.W.L.R. 162 at p. 177.
2. (1988) 164 C.L.R. 387.
3. (1990) 170 C.L.R. 394.
4. [1956] A.C. 696.
5. *Ibid.*, p. 698.
6. *Ibid.*, p. 700.

ficient labour force and a sufficient supply of materials to enable the work specified in the agreement to be carried out substantially within the time stipulated within the agreement. However, there was a serious shortage of skilled labour in the industry. The claimants were unable to obtain an adequate supply of skilled labour, and there was difficulty in obtaining adequate supplies of bricks, timber and plumbers' goods.

Viscount Simonds said:

"It may then be said that they made the contract on the 'basis' or on the 'footing' that their expectations would be fulfilled. Nor presumably were the expectations, or at least the hopes, of the respondents in any way different. Let it said, then, of them, too, that they contracted upon the same 'basis' or 'footing'. But it by no means follows that *disappointed expectations lead to frustrated contracts*."[7].

Lord Morton agreed with Lord Justice Morris, in the Court of Appeal, that:

"Though the basis or footing of the contract was removed in the limited sense that the anticipations of the parties were not realised, the facts found do not require an implication in the contract that it was to come to an end if those anticipations were not realised."[8]

I would hazard the respectful observation that most commercial people would find it an offensive conclusion that, having entered into a contract on the basis of a common assumption or with shared acceptance of a certain state of affairs, when those assumptions are falsified by subsequent events the parties should nonetheless be held strictly to their contract.

For Australia the law on frustration is set out in the judgment of the High Court in *Codelfa Construction Pty. Ltd.* v. *State Rail Authority of N.S.W.*[9] There was a similarity between the underlying factual situation in *Davis* and *Codelfa*. Although, ultimately, the result in *Codelfa* was different, this was only after the dispute had dragged its way through an arbitration, two visits to the Supreme Court, one to the Court of Appeal and two to the High Court—not a scenario calculated to endear the system to the commercial consumer. The contractor, Codelfa, entered into a contract for the excavation of tunnels. Work was to be completed within 130 weeks. Three shifts a day were worked. Local residents obtained an injunction prohibiting work between 10pm and 6am and on Sundays. The contractor sought to be paid the resultant increase in costs. The ensuing dispute was submitted to arbitration. It is important, for the present discussion, to note the findings of the arbitrator.[10] He found that the parties had each entered into the contract "on the common and mutual understanding and on the basis" that: first, work should and would be carried out on a three-shift continuous basis six days a week, and without restriction as to Sundays. Secondly, the work to be performed was inherently of a noisy and disturbing nature, and was to be carried out in close proximity to areas of residential neighbourhood. Thirdly, that no injunction or other restraining order could or would be granted against the contractor in relation to noise or other nuisance arising out of the carrying on of the works on such basis. He found that the last mentioned matter "was represented by the Principal to the Contractor, and was

7. *Ibid.*, pp. 714–715 (emphasis added).
8. *Ibid.*, p. 717.
9. (1982) 149 C.L.R. 337.
10. *Ibid.*, pp. 339–340.

accepted as the situation by the Contractor prior to and at the time of entering into the Contract".[11] He found that the work could not be carried out within the agreed period otherwise than by working the hours contemplated by the parties.

The arbitrator and the courts below the High Court all found for the contractor on the basis of implied terms in different terms which it was said were to be included in the contract. The High Court firmly rejected the proposition that there was any term to be implied in the contract.

Mason J. (with whom Stephen J. agreed) said:

"To say that the maintenance of three eight hour shifts a day for six days a week was a matter of common contemplation between the parties is not enough in itself to justify the implication of a term. This is not a case in which an obvious provision was overlooked by the parties and omitted from the contract. Rather it was a case in which the parties made a common assumption which masked the need to explore what provision should be made to cover the event which occurred. In ordinary circumstances negotiation about the matter might have yielded any one of a number of alternative provisions, each being regarded as a reasonable solution."[12]

Mason J. defined the issue on frustration as follows:

"The critical issue then is whether the situation resulting from the grant of the injunction is fundamentally different from the situation contemplated by the contract on its true construction in the light of the surrounding circumstances. The contract itself did not require that the work be carried out on a three shift continuous basis six days a week without restriction as to Sundays. But it required completion of the work within 130 weeks. And Codelfa with its tender had submitted a construction programme which involved a three shift continuous basis six days a week.[13] . . . The finding [of the Arbitrator] contained in par. 16 proceeds on the footing that the contract work could not be carried out as contemplated by the contract once injunctions were granted, the effect of which was to prohibit the continuous three shifts a day operation six days a week. Performance by means of a two shift operation, necessitated by the grant of the injunctions, was fundamentally different from that contemplated by the contract."[14]

In the event, what the High Court decided was that a conclusion that the contract had been frustrated was open, and the court remitted the case to the arbitrator for the purpose of reaching a final determination on whether the facts warranted the conclusion of frustration. As matters fell out, for reasons it is not necessary to canvass, subsequently the court itself concluded that the contract had been frustrated. At this point it may be worth mentioning that, if a prudent legal advisor had originally suggested that a *force majeure* clause might be advisable, in all likelihood the parties would have responded by saying that the position was quite clear by reason of their shared assumption.

It may be suggested that, in commerce, completing a contract in 22 months instead of eight and at an additional cost of over 18% of the fixed price as in *Davis Contractors* was as fundamentally different from that contemplated by the contract as was working two shifts instead of three shifts a day. The effect of the decision in *Davis*, using the language of risk allocation, was that the risk of labour and materials shortages was borne by the promisor.

11. *Ibid.*, p. 339.
12. *Ibid.*, pp. 354–356.
13. *Ibid.*, p. 360.
14. *Ibid.*, p. 366.

Once it is held that the contract is frustrated, it is open to the contractor, in such circumstances, either to claim additional payment on a *quantum meruit* basis, or to make a claim pursuant to the provisions of the Frustrated Contracts Act 1978 (N.S.W.).[15] The difficulty is that, as demonstrated by *Davis Contractors*, in the eyes of lawyers, where the allegedly frustrating event merely makes performance more onerous, the contract remains on foot.

It is of some interest to note that in US law impossibility of performance is now generally classified as commercial impracticability. Focus is not directed to actual impossibility of performance, but to a comparison between what performance would have cost had circumstances not changed, and the actual, or likely, cost of performance.

To return to the point in hand, what would have been the position had the contractors in *Davis* and *Codelfa* argued that the owner was estopped by the shared expectation of the parties from contending that the contract remained on foot? The advantage would have been that the contractor would not have had to show that the contract became fundamentally different. It would have been sufficient to show that the parties entered into the contract on the basis of common assumptions, and that those assumptions, having been falsified by subsequent events, meant that the contractor should no longer be required to abide by the terms of the contract.

In *The Commonwealth* v. *Verwayen*[16] the plaintiff was a sailor on *HMAS Voyager* in 1964 when, in the biggest peacetime disaster experienced by the Royal Australian Navy, it was accidentally sunk by the aircraft carrier *HMAS Melbourne*. The plaintiff did not issue a Statement of Claim until 1984. By its defence, filed in 1985, the Commonwealth did not plead the Limitation of Actions Act. In correspondence between the solicitors for the plaintiff and the Crown Solicitor it had been confirmed that the Statute of Limitations would not be relied upon. As well, a number of statements were made by Ministers of the Crown confirming that fact. For some reason, in November 1985 the Commonwealth reconsidered its policy, and in 1986 sought and obtained leave to amend its defences to rely on the Statute. Four members of the High Court held that the Commonwealth was not entitled to rely on that defence. Two of the judges, Deane and Dawson J.J., held that an estoppel had arisen. The two other members of the majority held that the Commonwealth had waived its statutory rights. Even some members of the minority held that there was an estoppel. Where the difference between the majority and the minority lay in this regard was whether the equity which had arisen, by reason of the Commonwealth's unconscionable conduct in seeking to renege on its promise not to rely upon the Statute, could be satisfied otherwise than by precluding reliance upon the Statute. The most exhaustive analysis of the doctrine of estoppel appears in the judgment of Deane J. His Honour is the foremost advocate in Australia of the view that promissory estoppel is not a separate proposition and distinct doctrine but an emanation of the general doctrine of estoppel by conduct. His Honour enumerated in eight propositions[17] the conceptual foundations for the doc-

15. The Frustrated Contracts Act 1978 (N.S.W.) being the Act which regulates further the consequences of frustration in New South Wales. The consequences of frustration are discussed further in Chapter 11.

16. (1990) 170 C.L.R. 394.

17. *Ibid.*, pp. 443–446.

trine of estoppel by conduct. The central principle of the doctrine is that the law will not permit an unconscientious departure by one party from the subject matter of an assumption which has been adopted by the other party, as a basis of some relationship, course of conduct, act or omission which would operate to that party's detriment, were the assumption not to be adhered to for the purposes of the litigation. Now it can be clearly seen that, in the case of a common assumption, such as existed in the *Davis* case and *Codelfa*, the doctrine would operate so as to make it unconscientious for one party to seek to suggest that, in the case of *Codelfa*, two shifts a day, or in the case of *Davis*, 22 months required for fulfilment were in accordance with the previous common assumption of the parties. As Mason C.J. pointed out in *Verwayen*,[18] equity was concerned merely to do the minimum necessary to prevent the suffering of the detriment. To do more would sit uncomfortably with the general principle whose underlying foundation was the concept of unconscionability. Nonetheless, it followed that: "In appropriate cases, that will require that the party estopped be held to the assumption created even if that means the effective enforcement of a *voluntary* promise."[19]

It can be seen, therefore, that the advantage of recourse to principles of estoppel is that some of the restrictions on the principles of frustration would go by the board. Equally, the remedy would be no more and no less than was required to do justice between the parties. Thus, for example, one would not have frustration invoked by the party other than the one likely to suffer from the frustrating event. There would be a more accurate reflection in the remedy granted of the detriment suffered.

Delivering the judgment of the Court of Appeal in *J. Lauritzen A.S.* v. *Wijsmuller B.V.* (*Super Servant Two*)[20] (and speaking of frustration), Lord Justice Bingham said: "The object of the doctrine was to give effect to the demands of justice, to achieve a just and reasonable result, to do what is reasonable and fair, as an expedient to escape from injustice where such would result from enforcement of a contract in its literal terms after a significant change in circumstances."[21] It is self-evident that the purpose of the doctrine of estoppel is the same. What is suggested is that estoppel would implement the identical purpose more adequately than does frustration.

It is sometimes suggested that the invocation of estoppel in such circumstances would result in an unacceptable degree of uncertainty in commercial transactions. But these criticisms seem misconceived when it is remembered that the aim of the intervention of equity is to do the minimum necessary to present the suffering of the detriment. In the context of equitable estoppel Australian courts have devoted a great deal of effort to the examination of the minimum remedy required to overcome unconscionability. In that vein, Mason C.J. pointed out in *Verwayen*:

"There is but one doctrine of estoppel, which provides that a court of common law or equity may do what is required, but not more, to prevent a person who has relied upon an assumption as to a present, past or future state of affairs (including a legal state of affairs), which assumption the party estopped has induced him to hold, from suffering detriment in reliance

18. *Ibid.*, p. 411.
19. *Ibid.*, p. 412 (emphasis added).
20. [1990] 1 Lloyd's Rep. 1.
21. *Ibid.*, p. 8.

upon the assumption as a result of the denial of its correctness. A central element of that doctrine is that there must be a proportionality between the remedy and the detriment which is its purpose to avoid. It would be wholly inequitable and unjust to insist upon a disproportionate making good of the relevant assumption."[22]

The same point was made by Brennan J. in *Walton's Stores (Interstate) Ltd.* v. *Maher* in the following terms:

"The element which both attracts the jurisdiction of a court of equity and shapes the remedy to be given is unconscionable conduct on the part of the person bound by the equity, and the remedy required to satisfy an equity varies according to the circumstances of the case. However, in moulding its decree, the court, as a court of conscience goes no further than is necessary to prevent unconscionable conduct. As Robert Goff J. said in *Amalgamated Property Co.* v. *Texas Bank* [1982] QB 84, 103: 'of all doctrines, equitable estoppel is surely one of the most flexible'."[23]

It was the application of these principles which led to the difference of opinion in the High Court in *Verwayen* as to the appropriate outcome. A number of the judges thought that the detriment to the plaintiff in allowing the Commonwealth to plead the limitation point after its repeated assertions that it would not be relied upon could be adequately and sufficiently overcome by a recompense in costs thrown away. The majority considered that the only way the detriment could be met was by holding the Commonwealth to the assumption which its conduct induced in the plaintiff.

In a subsequent decision in *Commonwealth* v. *Clark*,[24] the Appeal Division of the Supreme Court of Victoria unanimously held that the Commonwealth should be held to the assumption which it had engendered. The basis on which the court was able to come to that conclusion was evidence led to show that the plaintiff suffered and would suffer in the future more than simply costs thrown away if the amendment were permitted in circumstances otherwise identical with *Verwayen*. In contrast, one must remember the warning in *Verwayen* by Deane J. that: "There could be circumstances in which the potential damage to the allegedly estopped party was disproportionately greater than any detriment which would be sustained by the other party."[25]

The foregoing illustrates the careful balancing that is required to be carried out by the court in determining the minimum relief which it is necessary to afford the injured party to compensate for the conduct by the party estopped. It is true that at the end of the day there is a judgment call by the judges as to the extent of the remedy. The necessary consequence is a degree of difficulty on the part of legal advisers in evaluating likely outcomes. In commercial contracts that is undoubtedly a factor to be reduced to the minimum level. That having been said, is the uncertainty truly any greater than that arising in connection with the determinations required to be carried out under section 1(3) of the Law Reform (Frustrated Contracts) Act 1943?

A further objection to the frustration doctrine is that it determines a contract automatically at the time of the frustrating event.[26] The court may, therefore, hold that the contract was frustrated even though the parties for some time after the

22. (1990) 170 C.L.R. 394, at p. 413.
23. (1988) 164 C.L.R. 387, at p. 419.
24. Unreported.
25. (1990) 170 C.L.R. 394, at p. 441.
26. *B.P. Exploration (Libya) Ltd.* v. *Hunt* [1979] 1 W.L.R. 783, at 809, aff'd [1983] 2 A.C. 352.

event go on behaving as if the contract still existed.[27] Presumably, estoppel would not call for that result.

Again, frustration may be invoked by either party and not only by the party likely to suffer from the frustrating event. Thus, where a ship under charter is requisitioned, frustration is sometimes paradoxically claimed by the shipowner even though the charterer is perfectly willing to pay the agreed hire.[28] This, of course, stands in vivid contrast to estoppel. In *Isle of Mull*[29] and *Nickoll & Knight* v. *Ashton Eldridge & Co.*,[30] where the market price of the goods rose above the contract price so that the seller seems to have made a profit out of frustration, nonetheless the rule of automatic termination was used to enable a party to profit from frustration.

It is of some interest to look at the leading authorities on frustration in the light of modern day thinking as to the reach of estoppel. It may be that the issues before the court in those cases may have been more appropriately decided on the basis of estoppel as understood today rather than on the basis of frustration.

An interesting decision on which to test this theory is *Hirji Mulji* v. *Cheong Yue Steamship Company Limited*.[31] The respondents, owners of the steamship *Singaporean*, entered into a time charter with the appellants bearing the date 17 November 1916. The ship was to be placed at the appellant's disposal on 1 March 1917 for ten months. Shortly before that date the ship was requisitioned by the government. The owners thought that they would recover possession of the ship after a few months and, on 5 April 1917, wrote to the charterers to ask whether they would be prepared to take up the charter after the release of the vessel. The charterers replied on 12 May that they would require the vessel when released. There was some further inconclusive correspondence in the next few months, and then from 11 October 1917 to March 1919 there was silence. The government released the ship in late February 1919, and on 2 March 1919 the owners informed the charterers of that fact and enquired as to who would take delivery of the ship at Singapore. The charterers replied that delivery was now useless, the charter having long since expired. This was a clearly incorrect contention because the charter did not run from any specified date but from the date on which the ship was placed at the disposal of the charterers.

The advice of the Privy Council was delivered by Lord Sumner, who said:

"Counsel admitted before the Board, and rightly on the materials, that the communications which passed on April 5 and May 12, 1917, did not amount to a new contract or in any way vary the contract contained in the charter-party. No new promise was made nor, if there had been any new promise in form, was there any consideration to support it. The parties were over sanguine. If they thought that the delay would not frustrate the charter, events showed that they were wrong, and their error left their position unaffected."[32]

Relevantly for present purposes, their Lordships stated:

"Throughout the line of cases, now a long one, in which it has been held that certain events

27. Cf. *The Agathon* [1982] 2 Lloyd's Rep. 211 at 213.
28. *Bank Line Ltd.* v. *Arthur Capel & Co.* [1919] A.C. 435.
29. (1921) 278 F. 131.
30. [1901] 2 K.B. 126.
31. [1926] A.C. 497.
32. *Ibid.*, pp. 500–501.

frustrate the commercial adventure contemplated by the parties when they made the contract, there runs an almost continuous series of expressions to the effect that such a frustration brings the contract to an end forthwith, without more and automatically. They are too numerous to be cited exhaustively, but there are few expressions to the contrary and none in recent cases."[33]

A little later in the advice their Lordships said: "An event occurs, not contemplated by the parties and therefore not expressly dealt with in their contract, which, when it happens, frustrates their object."[34] What their Lordships appeared to be saying was that, although the parties themselves expressly stated that the contract should remain on foot, the law should hold their contract to have been frustrated. When was it frustrated? It certainly would not have been in the beginning when the charterers specifically stated that they would accept the charter when the ship became available. Their Lordships explained this by saying:

"Evidently, therefore, whatever the consequences of the frustration may be upon the conduct of the parties, its legal effect does not depend on their intention or their opinions, or even knowledge, as to the event, which has brought this about, but on its occurrence in such circumstances as showed it to be inconsistent with further prosecution of the adventure. . . . Frustration is then complete. It operates automatically. What the parties say and do is only evidence, and not necessarily weighty evidence, of the view to be taken of the event by informed and experienced minds."[35]

This decision highlights what a blunt weapon frustration is. When it does operate it does so without regard to the wishes and intentions of the parties. The first citation from the judgment of Lord Sumner,[36] in so far as it relies on absence of consideration, may be usefully contrasted with the statement by Mason C.J. in *Verwayen* that the party estopped may be held to the assumption created, "even if that means effective enforcement of a *voluntary* promise".[37]

The point I am considering clearly arose for decision in *B.P. Exploration Co. (Libya) Limited* v. *Hunt (No. 2)*.[38] In that case, it was contended that even if the contract between BP and Mr Hunt had been frustrated, BP had waived the frustration or was estopped from relying on it against Mr Hunt. At first instance, Robert Goff J. said:

"First, it is well established that, if a contract is frustrated, it is forthwith determined as a matter of law. It follows that, as a matter of law, the legal relationship between the parties under the contract so frustrated comes to an end, apart from any provision of the contract which may, on its true construction, be held to continue to apply in the events which have occurred; although of course, following frustration, one or both of the parties may have the right to claim restitution under the Act of 1943. That being the case, it is somewhat difficult to talk in terms of one party in such circumstances 'waiving frustration of the agreement or any right to rely thereon' or being 'estopped from relying thereon' against the other party. Frustration is not a right; it is a legal doctrine, the effect of which is to determine the rights and obligations arising under the contract which has been frustrated. Of course, following frustration, the parties may agree to enter into a fresh contract, possibly on the same terms as the old; and such new agreement may be either express or may be implied from the conduct of the parties. Again, insofar as there is a legal relationship surviving the frustration of

33. *Ibid.*, p. 505.
34. *Ibid.*, p. 507.
35. *Ibid.*, p. 509.
36. See fn. 32 above.
37. (1990) 64 A.L.J.R. 540, at p. 546 (emphasis added). See also fn. 19 and associated text.
38. [1979] 1 W.L.R. 783.

the contract, and one party has any rights against the other arising under that legal relationship (for example, the right to claim restitution under the 1943 Act), he may preclude himself from enforcing those rights by virtue of the principle of equitable estoppel. But such circumstances apart, it is difficult to see how, in law, the doctrine of waiver of estoppel can be invoked by a party faced with a claim under the Act of 1943."[39]

With the greatest respect I would question whether in 1995 the last sentence from the judgment any longer correctly states the law.

Further light is thrown on the question by the decision of the Court of Appeal in *Kissavos Shipping Co. S.A.* v. *Empresa Cubana de Fletes (The Agathon)*.[40] This was one of the many cases that arose from the detention of ships in Shatt-al-Arab waterway in 1980. However, this ship was in a slightly different position. The crew abandoned the vessel between 30 September 1980 and 8 November 1980. Then arrangements were made for the crew to return and they discharged her cargo. The discharge was completed on 10 December 1980. The owners claimed hire for the period up to that date. The question which arose was whether the charterparty had been frustrated. Robert Goff J., who heard the matter at first instance, thought that there was not even an arguable case to that effect. The judge came to that clear-cut conclusion primarily on the basis that there was no suggestion as between the parties of frustration and "all communications before the court are only consistent with the parties regarding the charter party as continuing in existence throughout". Before the Court of Appeal it was argued that if there had been frustration the parties would have recognised it themselves in October or November 1980. Not having recognised it themselves, they went on with the contract as though it was clearly in existence. Lord Denning and Lord Justice May both guided themselves by the words of Lord Roskill in *The Nema*, where he said:

"Secondly, in some cases where it is claimed that frustration has occurred by reason of the happening of a particular event, it is possible to determine at once whether or not the doctrine can be legitimately invoked. But in others, where the effect of that event is to cause delay in the performance of contractual obligations, it is often necessary to wait upon events in order to see whether the delay already suffered and the prospects of further delay from that cause, will make any ultimate performance of the relevant contractual obligations 'radically different', to borrow Lord Radcliffe's phrase, from that which was undertaken by the contract. But, as has often been said, business men must not be required to await events too long. They are entitled to know where they stand."[41]

I do not suggest that in all instances where frustration may have been thought to be the appropriate remedy to invoke, estoppel is a more appropriate source of relief. What this note has endeavoured to do is to call attention to developments in the operation of the doctrine of estoppel, and raise for discussion and argument whether, in at least some cases, it would be rewarding to the ends of justice to substitute for the relatively blunt weapon of frustration, the more selective rapier of estoppel.

ANDREW ROGERS Q.C.

39. *Ibid.*, p. 809.
40. [1982] 2 Lloyd's Rep. 211.
41. [1982] A.C. 724, at p. 752.

PART VI

FRUSTRATION AND FORCE MAJEURE—INTERNATIONAL AND COMPARATIVE ASPECTS

CHAPTER 13

FORCE MAJEURE AND FRUSTRATION UNDER INTERNATIONAL SALES CONTRACTS

1. FRUSTRATION

A contract, quite in order when made, becomes incapable of performance as a result of a supervening event. In English law the principles evolved by the courts to regulate this situation have come to be known as those dealing with "frustration" of the contract.

Frustration was a relatively late arrival on the contractual scene. For centuries the courts took the view that a promise was a promise. If it could not be performed, the promisor was in breach of contract. If he sought relief from the consequences of his non-performance he was refused, for he should have foreseen the situation that arose, however unforeseeable, and negotiated an express term in the contract. This was actually said by the court in the case of *Paradine* v. *Jane*[1]: "when the party by his own contract creates a duty or charge upon himself, he is bound to make it good, if he may, notwithstanding any accident by inevitable necessity, because he might have provided against it by his contract."[2]

It was not until the second half of the nineteenth century, in *Taylor* v. *Caldwell*,[3] that supervening impossibility arising without the fault of either party was seen to excuse both parties from performance. Thereafter, a number of cases applied the doctrine of frustration, though there was always a reluctance to do so: "Frustration is not to be lightly invoked as the dissolvent of a contract."[4]

2. SALE OF GOODS

In relation to contracts for the sale of goods, the law of frustration was partially codified, in a sketchy way, in the Sale of Goods Act 1893 (now re-enacted as the Sale of Goods Act 1979). Section 7 of the 1979 Act reads as follows: "Where there is an agreement to sell specific goods and subsequently the goods, without any fault on the part of the seller or buyer, perish before the risk passes to the buyer, the agreement is avoided." It will be remembered that in codifying the law of sale of goods, Chalmers was not attempting to codify the general principles of the law of contract. Indeed, section 62(2) provides that: "The rules of the common law,

1. (1647) Aleyn 26; 82 E.R. 897 (lease of land).
2. But note the phrase "if he may".
3. (1863) 3 B. & S. 826; 122 E.R. 309 (use of a music hall).
4. *Davis Contractors Ltd.* v. *Fareham U.D.C.* [1956] A.C. 696, at p. 727 *per* Lord Radcliffe.

including the law merchant, except in so far as they are inconsistent with the provisions of this Act, and in particular the rules relating to . . . the effect of fraud, misrepresentation, duress . . . , mistake, or other invalidating cause, apply to contracts for the sale of goods."

For the purpose of this chapter, we are concerned with "mistake, or other invalidating cause". One aspect of the rules relating to mistake was codified in section 6 of the Act, in a provision that closely parallels section 7. Section 6 reads: "Where there is contract for the sale of specific goods, and the goods without the knowledge of the seller have perished at the time when the contract is made, the contract is void." Why did Chalmers not seek to codify the general principles of mistake and frustration? There are several reasons. One is that finite limits had to be drawn so as to sever rules peculiar to contracts of sale, legitimately the topic of the codification, from those rules applicable to contracts generally. Another is that in 1890, when Chalmers first published his digest of the law of sale in book form, the rules relating to mistake and frustration—and particularly the latter—were still evolving. Sections 6 and 7 were indeed based on a particular fact situation that had already given rise to litigation: the destruction of specific goods.[5]

3. SPECIFIC GOODS

Both sections 6 and 7 are limited to contracts for the sale of specific goods. This term is defined in section 61(1) of the Act: " 'specific goods' means goods identified and agreed on at the time a contract of sale is made". *Elphick* v. *Barnes*[6] affords an example of a sale of specific goods: the sale of a horse, with the very horse the subject matter of the contract delivered to the buyer on sale or return; the risk would not pass to the buyer until the property passed (see now section 20(1)); the horse died before the property passed under what would now be Rule 4 of section 18. Thus the specific goods perished—an apt word in relation to animals—before the risk passed to the buyer.[7]

It should not be assumed that frustration by reason of the goods perishing can only occur when the goods are specific. If S sells to B "100 tons of wheat out of the 200 tons in the hold of" a named ship, and the ship goes down so that all 200 tons are lost before the risk passes to B, the contract for the sale of the wheat will be frustrated by reason of the perishing of the goods, even though the 100 tons are unascertained goods.[8]

It appears that in drafting section 7 Chalmers had in mind *Howell* v. *Coupland*.[9] This case involved a contract to sell 200 tons of potatoes to be grown on land

5. S.6 was based on *Couturier* v. *Hastie* (1856) 5 H.L. Cas. 673 (cargo of corn had deteriorated and been disposed of by carrier before the contract of sale was made) and s.7 on *Elphick* v. *Barnes* (1880) 5 C.P.D. 321 (death of a horse).

6. (1880) 5 C.P.D. 321.

7. The application of s.7 depends on the horse dying after the making of an agreement to sell. Where goods are delivered on sale or return, is there a contract of sale where the buyer does not "adopt the transaction"? The Act does not explicitly give the answer to this question, but the structure of s.18 suggests that Chalmers assumed that there was.

8. Despite the similarity to *Couturier* v. *Hastie* (1856) 5 H.L. Cas. 673, the case posed would not be covered by s.7: see the next two paragraphs.

9. (1876) 1 Q.B.D. 258.

belonging to the seller, land which was expected to produce over 400 tons. Disease attacked the potatoes and the crop failed: the land produced less than 80 tons, all of which were delivered to the buyer. The buyer sued for damages for the non-delivery of 120 tons. It was held, applying the principle of *Taylor* v. *Caldwell*,[10] that the seller was not liable for breach of contract.

Despite Chalmers' apparent view that such a case would have been covered by section 7, it seems clear that the goods that did not exist at the date of the contract could not be identified at that date and so could not be specific within the statutory definition.[11] If the goods were not specific, section 7 would not apply.[12] Whether the result arrived at by the common law was identical to that which would have resulted had section 7 applied will be considered below when we look at "avoidance".

4. THE GOODS PERISH

The other requirement in section 7 (and also section 6) is that the goods must perish. This term is not defined in the Act. It clearly covers the physical destruction of the goods, and would be apt to describe the loss of a cargo at sea. But could it be said that the cargo of corn in *Couturier* v. *Hastie*[13] had perished? The corn had been sold, and was no longer in the seller's possession, but until it was consumed it continued to exist. The answer may be that, as far as the parties to the contract were concerned, the goods had perished—they were no longer in their sphere of influence. This may follow from *Barrow, Lane and Ballard Ltd*. v. *Phillip Phillips & Co. Ltd*.,[14] where 700 bags of nuts in a warehouse—identified and agreed upon, and therefore specific—were sold; in fact at the date of the contract 109 bags had been stolen, so that there were only 591 bags in the warehouse. It was held that the parcel of 700 bags had ceased to exist, and thus "perished", and that section 6 applied so that the contract was void. Logically, the loss of even one bag of nuts would have the effect that there was no longer a parcel of 700 bags in existence, though this would no doubt be subject to the *de minimis* principle. It may well be that as a general rule goods that are stolen would be treated as having perished, even though they may physically exist somewhere unknown.[15]

Another situation where there seems to be widespread agreement that goods would be treated as having perished even though their material substance remains is where they have been impregnated by a foreign substance or so changed their nature, as a result, for example, of soaking in water, as to be no longer saleable under the contract description. Examples include the dates contaminated by sewage,[16] and cement soaked and turned into concrete.

It is of interest to see how these problems are dealt with in the current American

10. (1863) 3 B. & S. 826; 122 E.R. 309; above at fn. 3.
11. Note the expression "goods sold ex-bulk" used by the Privy Council in *Re Goldcorp Exchange Ltd*. [1994] 3 W.L.R. 199, 208.
12. *Re Wait* [1927] 1 Ch. 606, *per* Atkin L.J. at p. 630.
13. (1856) 5 H.L. Cas. 673.
14. [1929] 1 K.B. 574.
15. *Contra* P.S. Atiyah, *The Sale of Goods* (8th Edn.) 1990, p. 83.
16. *Asfar & Co. Ltd*. v. *Blundell* [1896] 1 Q.B. 123.

codification of the law of sales, article 2 of the Uniform Commercial Code. In that legislation, the English sections 6 and 7 are merged into a single provision in section 2–613 of the Code:

"Where the contract requires for its performance goods identified when the contract is made, and the goods suffer casualty without fault of either party before the risk of loss passes to the buyer . . . then
(a) if the loss is total the contract is avoided; and
(b) if the loss is partial or the goods have so deteriorated as no longer to conform to the contract the buyer may nevertheless demand inspection and at his option either treat the contract as avoided or accept the goods with due allowance from the contract price for the deterioration or the deficiency in quantity but without further right against the seller."

It will be seen that this section is not confined to the "perishing" of the goods. The term "suffer casualty" is not defined in the Code, but would presumably include any damage to the goods. If they do indeed "perish" in the English sense, this would no doubt be a total loss within section 2–613(a), leading to avoidance; but a partial loss would not, under paragraph (b), automatically lead to avoidance. It could no doubt be argued, if the facts of *Barrow, Lane and Ballard Ltd*. v. *Phillip Phillips & Co. Ltd*,[17] were to arise under section 2–613, that the loss was total under paragraph (a), since the parcel of 700 bags had ceased to exist, but it is thought that most courts would rule that the loss of 109 bags was a partial loss so that paragraph (b) would apply. If this is so, it improves the position of the buyer; under the English provision applicable to the *Barrow, Lane* case, the contract was void, so that the seller could have taken advantage of the theft of part of the parcel to get out of the contract with the buyer if the price of nuts had risen; under the American provision, only the buyer could opt to avoid the contract.

The Uniform Commercial Code includes another relevant section which deals with "Excuse by failure of presupposed conditions". This is section 2–615:

"Except so far as a seller may have assumed a greater obligation and subject to the preceding section on substituted performance:
(a) Delay in delivery or non-delivery in whole or in part by a seller who complies with paragraphs (b) and (c) is not a breach of his duty under a contract for sale if performance as agreed has been made impracticable by the occurrence of a contingency the non-occurrence of which was a basic assumption on which the contract was made or by compliance in good faith with any applicable foreign or domestic governmental regulation or order whether or not it later proves to be invalid.
(b) Where the causes mentioned in paragraph (a) affect only a part of the seller's capacity to perform, he must allocate production and deliveries among his customers but may at his option include regular customers not then under contract as well as his own requirements for further manufacture. He may so allocate in any manner which is fair and reasonable.[18]
(c) The seller must notify the buyer seasonably that there will be delay or non-delivery and, when allocation is required under paragraph (b), of the estimated quota thus made available for the buyer."

This section applies to a wide range of circumstances.[19] The Official Comment

17. [1929] 1 K.B. 574, at fn. 14 above.
18. Contrast the approach of the Privy Council in *Maritime National Fish Ltd*. v. *Ocean Trawlers* [1935] A.C. 524, discussed in more detail at pp. 47–48 above.
19. S. 2–615 is discussed in greater detail in Chapter 16.

states that "The additional test of commercial impracticability (as contrasted with 'impossibility', 'frustration of performance' or 'frustration of the venture') has been adopted in order to call attention to the commercial character of the criterion chosen by this Article."

5. AVOIDANCE

How far does section 7 of the Sale of Goods Act bring about a resolution similar to that occurring under the common law doctrine of frustration? Where section 7 applies, the contract is avoided. Frustration leads to discharge of the contract. In most circumstances, the effect is the same. A party who has not performed will no longer be obliged to perform. If the buyer has paid in advance, and the seller can no longer deliver, the buyer will in both cases be entitled to recover the price on a total failure of consideration. What if there is only a partial failure of consideration, as where part of the goods have been delivered and the rest perish? This might lead to frustration at common law, but it is not certain that any money paid can be recovered back: there may be a distinction between a partial failure of consideration and a total failure of part of the consideration, possibly depending on whether the contract is severable.[20]

6. EFFECT OF FRUSTRATION

The common law effect of frustration is well illustrated by the *Fibrosa* case[21] which concerned a contract for the international sale of goods. A contract for the sale of machinery provided for delivery in Poland. The outbreak of the Second World War and the enemy occupation of Gdynia rendered performance of the contract illegal and impossible: it was held that the contract was discharged and that the buyer could recover an advance payment because there was a total failure of consideration, notwithstanding that the seller had incurred expense in starting to manufacture the goods. As is well known, in consequence of a report of the Law Reform Committee Parliament changed the law by enacting the Law Reform (Frustrated Contracts) Act 1943.

One result of the 1943 Act is to fragment the law, for section 2(5)(c) provides that the Act does not apply "to any contract to which section 7 of the Sale of Goods Act 1979 . . . applies, or to any other contract for the sale, or for the sale and delivery, of specific goods, where the contract is frustrated by reason of the fact that the goods have perished". In the *Fibrosa* case the contract was frustrated otherwise than by the perishing of the goods, so the 1943 Act would now apply; if the goods had perished, section 7 would apply. No one knows what the last part of section 2(5)(c) means, or whether it is possible for a contract of sale to be frustrated by the perishing of the goods without section 7 of the Sale of Goods Act applying.[22]

The essential difference between the 1943 Act regime and the Sale of Goods Act

20. Cf. P.S. Atiyah, *op. cit.*, p. 336.
21. *Fibrosa Spolka Akcyjna* v. *Fairbairn Lawson Combe Barbour Ltd.* [1943] A.C. 32, H.L.
22. See P.S. Atiyah, *op. cit.*, pp. 333–336. See also p. 243 above.

regime is that under the 1943 Act the court has a discretion to permit money paid in advance to be retained up to the amount of any expenses incurred in performance of the contract.[23] (Where the goods have perished before the risk passed to the buyer it may be unlikely—though it is not impossible—that a party will have obtained a valuable benefit (see section 1(3) of the 1943 Act).[24] There is no power under section 7 to order payment for such a benefit.)

There is of course plenty of scope for the application of the 1943 Act to contracts for the sale of goods. As we have seen, it would apply to the facts of the *Fibrosa* case itself, both because the goods were not specific and because they did not perish.

7. PROBLEMS WITH FRUSTRATION

There are a number of situations where a party is effectively prevented from performing his contract by the occurrence of outside events, or where a change of circumstances leads to the elimination of the profit expected from the contract, but where the legal view is that there has been no frustration, so that the contract is still binding. Such situations include the drying up of the source of supply,[25] the introduction of a licensing or quota scheme which prevents a party satisfying all his customers,[26] delay for a prolonged period where it is, however, impossible to say that the delay has deprived the party of substantially the whole benefit of the contract,[27] the incurring of extra expense,[28] and even a disastrous movement in the market. Another problem arises out of the interrelation between negligence, or fault, and frustration.[29]

It is, therefore, to be expected that, in an attempt to distribute risks fairly between them, the parties might attempt to regulate the issue of supervening illegality, impossibility or inconvenience by contractual provisions. This brings us to the *force majeure* clause.

8. FORCE MAJEURE

In English law there is no readily recognised concept of *force majeure* other than that dealt with by the doctrine of frustration considered above. Contract clauses dealing with *force majeure* may differ substantially, and everything will turn on the precise words adopted in the contract.[30] In one case, the phrase "subject to *force majeure* conditions" was held to be too vague and uncertain to have any meaning,

23. 1943 Act, s.1(2), discussed further at pp. 229–234 above.
24. On which see Chapter 11.
25. *Blackburn Bobbin Co.* v. *Allen* [1918] 2 K.B. 467.
26. *Maritime National Fish Ltd.* v. *Ocean Trawlers* [1935] A.C. 524; cf. text at fn. 18 above.
27. Cf. *Hongkong Fir Shipping Co.* v. *Kawasaki Kisen Kaisha* [1962] 2 Q.B. 26.
28. *Tsakiroglou* v. *Noblee & Thorl* [1962] A.C. 93; *Davis Contractors Ltd.* v. *Fareham U.D.C.* [1956] A.C. 696.
29. E.g. *Joseph Constantine Steamship Line Ltd.* v. *Imperial Smelting Corporation Ltd.* [1942] A.C. 154 (H.L.), discussed further at pp. 50–52 above.
30. See further pp. 7–10 above.

so that the purported contract containing these words never came into existence.[31] In another case,[32] "*force majeure*" was given some meaning by its context, but was held not to apply to facts substantially similar to those of *Howell* v. *Coupland*.[33]

For present purposes it may be sufficient to look at just one case to see how a commonly used *force majeure* clause—the prohibition clause (clause 19) in GAFTA Contract Form 119[34]—was treated by the court. This clause reads as follows:

"*Prohibition*—In case of prohibition of export, blockade or hostilities or in the case of any executive or legislative act done by or on behalf of the government of a country of origin, or of the territory where the port or ports of shipment named herein is/are situate, restricting export, whether partially or otherwise, any such restriction shall be deemed by both parties to apply to the Contract to the extent of such total or partial restriction to prevent fulfilment whether by shipment or by any other means whatsoever and to that extent this contract or any unfulfilled portion thereof shall be cancelled. Sellers shall advise Buyers without delay with the reasons therefor, and if required, Sellers must produce proof to justify the cancellation."

The clause was relied on in *Pagnan S.p.A.* v. *Tradax Ocean Transportation S.A.*[35] A contract was entered into for the sale of tapioca to be exported from Thailand and imported into Italy. Tapioca, used in animal feed, is an important crop in Thailand but there is virtually only one market for it, the EEC. According to Bingham L.J., "the reason for this is that tapioca pellets . . . compete with grain, but grain is cheaper almost everywhere in the world . . . It is only in the EEC, where the price of grain is artificially maintained, that Thai tapioca can effectively compete." As the result of an EEC–Thai agreement, the quantity of tapioca exported from Thailand was controlled.

Accordingly, the sale contract included a special condition, typed and not in any standard form. It imposed on the sellers an absolute obligation to obtain an export certificate from the Thai authorities. The sellers could not obtain an export certificate. Were they in breach of contract? They were in breach of the special condition, but were they protected by the prohibition clause? This depended on whether the special condition and the prohibition clause could be reconciled. If they were inconsistent, the contract expressly provided that the special condition should prevail. But the Court of Appeal held they were not inconsistent.

The question was whether effect could be given to both clauses, and the court concluded that this could be done. As Bingham L.J. put it, "The natural construction of this contract . . . is that the sellers were to provide for the export certificate, but in case of prohibition of export . . . the unfulfilled portion of the contract was to be cancelled." He pointed out that this construction did not deprive the special condition of effect. The obligation to obtain the export certificate remained on the sellers. "If the certificate was not provided . . . as a result of oversight, error, mishap, bureaucratic inefficiency or delay . . . the sellers would remain liable. But if the sellers were unable to provide . . . the certificate because of any impediment

31. *British Electrical & Associated Industries* v. *Patley Pressings Ltd*. [1953] 1 All E.R. 94.
32. *Podar Trading Co. Ltd*. v. *Tagher* [1949] 2 All E.R. 62.
33. (1876) 1 Q.B.D. 258. See above, text at fn. 9.
34. GAFTA is the Grain and Feed Trade Association. Form 119 is the Association's general FOB contract form.
35. [1987] 3 All E.R. 565, C.A.

falling within the carefully-defined ambit of clause 19, they were relieved of their contractual obligation . . . ."[36]

9. UNFAIR TERMS?

Everything, then, turns on the actual wording of the *force majeure* clause and, sometimes, on its relationship to other terms of the contract in which it is incorporated.[37] There is a further question: does the court have the power to control the *force majeure* clause if it is found to be unreasonable?

On the face of it, the answer appears to be yes.[38] Section 3 of the Unfair Contract Terms Act 1977 provides as follows:

"(1) This section applies as between contracting parties where one of them deals . . . on the other's written standard terms of business.
(2) As against that party, the other cannot by reference to any contract term
(a) . . .
(b) claim to be entitled . . .
(ii) in respect of the whole or any part of his contractual obligation, to render no performance at all,
except in so far as . . . the contract term satisfies the requirement of reasonableness."

Clearly, it depends on the facts of the particular case whether the clause can be considered to be part of the standard terms of business of the party relying on it, and it depends on the wording of the clause whether it entitles that party to render no performance; a clause providing for cancellation of the contract (like the prohibition clause in the GAFTA contract just referred to) would undoubtedly fall within section 3(2)(b)(ii) and be subject to the reasonableness test in the 1977 Act.

However, there are two reasons why judicial control of *force majeure* clauses will not often be a threat to their validity. The first is that in the context of the subject matter of this chapter, most *force majeure* clauses will be free of supervision. This is because section 26 of the 1977 Act provides that section 3 and the reasonableness test do not apply to international supply contracts. The definition of an international supply contract is that it is a contract of sale of goods with the following characteristics: the places of business of seller and buyer are in different countries and either (i) the goods are being carried, or will be carried, from one country to another, or (ii) the acts of offer and acceptance were done in different countries, or (iii) if offer and acceptance were effected in the same country, the goods are to be delivered in another country.

This definition may not in fact embrace every contract that may reasonably be thought of as an international sale, so there will probably be some such contracts that include clauses subject to the reasonableness test. Even for those, however, the risk of invalidity is slight, because there is a marked tendency in the courts to uphold as reasonable clauses in contracts promulgated by trade associations representing both buyers and sellers. Once again, it may be emphasised that everything turns on the precise wording of the clause in question, but there is, for example, no

36. *Ibid*., p. 575.
37. And, it seems, the intention to act upon the clause: *The Marine Star* [1993] 1 Lloyd's Rep. 329, at p. 331.
38. For an alternative view see at pp. 10–11 above.

reason to doubt that the prohibition clause in the GAFTA contract above would survive scrutiny.

10. VIENNA CONVENTION

Reference has been made to the provisions contained in the American Uniform Commercial Code. These provisions had their origin in the English Sale of Goods Act or the common law. It is of interest to see a different statutory provision owing more to the civil law and to accepted notions of *force majeure* in those systems. This is to be found in Article 79 of the United Nations Convention on Contracts for the International Sale of Goods of 1980[39]:

"(1) A party is not liable for a failure to perform any of his obligations if he proves that the failure was due to an impediment beyond his control and that he could not reasonably be expected to have taken the impediment into account at the time of the conclusion of the contract or to have avoided or overcome it or its consequences.

. . .

(4) The party who fails to perform must give notice to the other party of the impediment and its effect on his ability to perform . . . .

(5) Nothing in this Article prevents either party from exercising any right other than to claim damages under this Convention."

This provision is of greater significance than the provisions of the Uniform Commercial Code previously cited, for the Code no longer applies to international contracts of sale of goods within the 1980 Vienna Convention. The ratification of the Convention by the United States has supplanted the Uniform Commercial Code for such contracts as from the time the Convention came into force on 1 January 1988. As can be seen, Article 79 of the Convention goes far beyond the common law concept of frustration or the statutory provisions found in or based on section 7 of the Sale of Goods Act.

11. CONCLUSION

The common law approach to frustration has always been either to deny the possibility of relief or to restrict the ambit of the relief as far as possible. Contracts are to be performed, and a relieving power would introduce uncertainty, and the possibility of dispute, in too many cases. This is not what business people desire. They are willing to recognise that outside events may alter the nature of the obligation. Thus the Vienna Convention reflects commercial reality more than the common law and the Sale of Goods Act do.

We have seen how a not-untypical *force majeure* clause, the GAFTA prohibition clause, afforded relief in circumstances where the common law would have found a breach of contract. Many *force majeure* clauses in practice are wider and vaguer than the GAFTA clause. It will suffice to conclude by citing part of a clause promulgated by the United Nations Economic Commission for Europe in its General Conditions of Sale for the Import and Export of Durable Consumer Goods and of

39. Discussed in greater detail in Chapter 14.

other Engineering Stock Articles (No. 730). This is headed "Reliefs", and paragraph 1 is as follows:

> "Any circumstances beyond the control of the parties intervening after the formation of the contract and impeding its reasonable performance shall be considered as cases of relief. For the purposes of this clause circumstances not due to the default of the party invoking them shall be deemed to be beyond the control of the parties."

AUBREY DIAMOND

CHAPTER 14

EXEMPTIONS AND IMPOSSIBILITY UNDER THE VIENNA CONVENTION

The problems marshalled by common lawyers under frustration and impossibility of performance and corresponding concepts in other systems are dealt with in the Vienna Convention on International Sales[1] under the rubric of "Exemptions", continuing a usage which has persisted not only through the immediate *travaux préparatoires* of the Convention but which also appeared in its predecessor, the Uniform Law on International Sale of Goods (ULIS) and its *travaux préparatoires*.[2] Put briefly, it is now provided that if either party is prevented from performing any of the obligations of their contract by an uncontrollable "impediment" which could not reasonably have been foreseen when the contract was concluded or could not have been avoided or circumvented, then, provided they give notice of this to the other, they are freed from liability in damages, but remain subject to other remedies which may be available to the other party.

An English lawyer will notice that this differs markedly from his familiar concepts in that the impediment does not necessarily affect liability on the contract as a whole but may afford partial relief, leaving other terms of the contract operative, and when an "impediment" does operate it does not effect a total discharge but merely releases the non-performing party from liability in damages.

It also seems clear that since Article 79(5) preserves all remedies under the Convention other than damages, the non-performance resulting from the impediment is a breach of contract, fundamental if it substantially deprives the other party of what he was entitled to expect under the contract,[3] otherwise non-fundamental. The significance of the distinction is that fundamental breach entitles the victim to the drastic remedy of avoidance of the contract,[4] releasing both parties from their obli-

1. In force since 1 January 1988. Many important trading nations have acceded. Under Art. 99(3) states which are parties to the Hague Uniform Laws on Formation and Sales must denounce either or both if they accept the corresponding provisions of the Vienna Convention. For notes of criticism see Hobhouse J., "International Conventions and Commercial Law: The Pursuit of Uniformity" (1990) 106 L.Q.R. 530 and Simon Fisher and Michael Hains "Futures market law and practice and the Vienna Sales Convention" [1993] L.M.C.L.Q. 531; also the comments of the Law Society cited in Robert G. Lee "The U.N. Convention on the International Sale of Goods: O.K. for the U.K.?" [1993] J.B.L. 131 at p. 132.

2. The Vienna Convention has been described as "a radically revised version" of The Hague Uniform Laws on Sales (ULIS) and Formation, embodied in United Kingdom legislation by the Uniform Laws on International Sales Act 1967. Hence the 1964/7 Uniform Laws and their *travaux préparatoires* may be relevant to the interpretation of the Vienna Convention. See Barry Nicholas, "The Vienna Convention on International Sales Law" (1989) 105 L.Q.R. 201, at p. 203.

3. For definition see Art. 25.

4. See Arts. 26, 49(1), 64(1).

gations and entailing restitution of whatever may have been supplied or paid under the contract,[5] as well as to other remedies.

1. EXCLUSION AND MODIFICATION OF ARTICLE 79

The principal provision in the Vienna Convention is Article 79. It has been remarked that, though this is one of the longer articles and much time was devoted to its preparation, it is still in many respects unsatisfactory.[6] Fortunately its shortcomings may not manifest themselves too insistently in practice, since it has also been said that though this was one of the most discussed provisions it may also be the least often applied, since almost all standard form contracts used in international sales, however rudimentary, contain *force majeure* clauses dealing in detail with events which would otherwise fall within Article 79.[7] Because of the general freedom accorded to parties by Article 6 to exclude the application of the Convention in whole or in part these *force majeure* clauses will normally supersede Article 79.[8]

This is a forceful reminder that, although Article 79 and its satellite, Article 80, are grouped together as Section IV of Chapter IV of the Convention, they cannot be considered in isolation from very many other provisions. They must, as with the rest of the Convention, be read subject to the provisions of Part I, delimiting the sphere of application of the Convention, both in terms of the subject matter of the contracts it governs and of transnational relationships between the parties. Hence, if Article 79 has not been excluded and some hindrance to the performance of an international contract at first sight appears to present an instance of an "impediment" within the article, it will be necessary initially to consider a number of these rules in Part I to determine whether the contract answers to the definition of a contract for the international sale of goods governed by the Convention and is, therefore, subject to the article. If it does, it will then be necessary to resolve questions relating to the detailed application of Article 79. These preliminaries include Article 4, dissociating the Convention from problems of the validity of the contract, the general guidelines for interpretation in Articles 7 and 8, Article 9 on the applic-

5. See Arts. 81, 82, 83 and 84.

6. Nicholas, above, fn. 2 at p. 234. See also Nicholas in N. Galston and H. Smit, eds., *International Sale* (New York 1984) Chapter 5, "Impracticability and Impossibility in the U.N. Convention on Contracts for the International Sale of Goods".

7. Jan Hellner, "The Vienna Convention and Standard Form Contracts", Chapter 10 of Peter Sarcevic and Paul Volken, eds., *International Sale of Goods: Dubrovnik Lectures* (New York, 1985) p. 353; John Honnold, *Uniform Law for International Sales under the 1980 United Nations Convention* (2nd Edn.) (Deventer, 1991) pp. 125–134 and 538–542. There is doubt as to how far implied exclusion may be effective, Nicholas above, fn. 2, p. 208. See also Honnold, pp. 126–129, who concludes that ordinary rules of interpretation apply and that the Convention can be excluded either by express agreement or by an agreement that is clearly implied in fact. A "theoretical or fictitious" implied agreement will not be enough. Fisher and Hains, fn. 1 at p. 555 recommend that futures markets should amend their rules to exclude the Convention and that consideration should be given to amending the Convention itself to exclude these contracts since they conclude that at present it does apply to such contracts when they relate to goods as distinct from financial futures. See pp. 540–541. M. G. Bridge [1991] L.M.C.L.Q. p. 134 also favours implied exclusion.

8. Whilst the Convention can be excluded there is no provision corresponding to Art. 4 of ULIS allowing it to be adopted where it would otherwise not apply. Honnold, above, fn. 7, pp. 125–134 esp. pp. 129–134, thinks the Convention can be adopted when it is otherwise appropriate.

ability of usages and Articles 11, 12 and 13 on proof and the restricted circumstances in which writing may be required. Key issues arising from these will be considered before turning to the text of Article 79 itself.

2. FREEDOM FROM FORMALITIES

There are a number of rules as to form and interpretation which may be of particular significance in cases in which Article 79 may be in question, in addition to the general provision allowing exclusion or modification. For example, Article 11 provides that normally a contract need not be in writing, is not subject to requirements of form and may be proved by any means, including witnesses.

Another provision on freedom from formality is Article 29. In its first paragraph it provides that a contract may be modified or terminated by mere agreement between the parties and in its second that if a contract is in writing and contains a term requiring modification or termination to be in writing, that will have full effect unless a party is precluded by his conduct from relying on the term and then it will be displaced to the extent that the other party has relied on the waiver.[9]

3. CONTRACTS NOT WITHIN THE CONVENTION

Article 3 of the Convention lists a number of specific contracts to which it is not to apply. These include consumer sales, auctions, sales by authority of law, sales of stocks, shares, securities, negotiable instruments and money, sales of ships, hovercraft and aircraft and of electricity. Furthermore, Article 3 effectively provides that the Convention is not to apply to contracts for the supply of work and materials and Article 79 will, therefore, not apply to an impediment to the performance of any of these excluded contracts.

4. GENERAL PRINCIPLES OF INTERPRETATION

In interpreting the Convention regard is to be had to its international character, to the need to promote uniformity in its application and to the observance of good faith in international trade. Moreover, problems within the scope of the Convention but which are not expressly covered in it are to be settled in conformity with the general principles on which it is based or, if no such principles are relevant, then

9. Arts. 11 and 29 and any other provision of Part II of the Convention allowing freedom of form are subject to Art. 12, excluding their operation when a state whose legislation requires contracts of sale to be embodied or evidenced in writing makes a declaration under Art. 96 to apply these requirements when one of the parties has his place of business there. The parties cannot contract out of this. Whatever the effect of informality on validity in such case, it would seem that the Convention, and with it Art. 79, would not apply to impediments in performance if the applicable law required writing and this was not provided. Informal notices of impediment under Art. 79(4) would also be ineffective. Arts. 12 and 96 were introduced at the instance of the USSR and have been regarded as creating a trap for the unwary. See Nicholas, above, fn. 2, pp. 211–212 and 242. Honnold, above, fn. 7, pp. 187–188. "Writing" includes telegram and telex. Art. 13.

in conformity with private international law,[10] thus indicating the law applicable to the contract. These provisions may well be of practical significance in dealing with problems associated with Article 79 since, although English courts in common with those of many other systems have long recognised that the maintenance of international uniformity must be taken into account in interpreting conventions,[11] it is also clear that considerable differences exist between the approaches of different systems to interruption of contractual performance. Thus, English frustration and impossibility of performance differ from French *force majeure* and *imprévision* and both in turn differ from German failure of the foundation of the contract.[12] Hence, these provisions of the Convention may be a needed reminder to tribunals that they must not be unduly swayed by their own local attitudes or principles. The ultimate reference to private international law provides a possibility of a final solution which is not available under ULIS.[13]

A further provision which may be of importance in applying Article 79 is contained in Article 8 of the Vienna Convention. In its first paragraph it provides that statements made by and other conduct of a party are to be interpreted according to the intent of the maker when the other party knew or could not have been unaware what was that intent. In its second paragraph it provides that, if the first does not apply, then statements and conduct are to be interpreted as a reasonable person of the same kind as the other party would have done, due consideration being given to "all relevant circumstances of the case including the negotiations, any practices which the parties have established between themselves and any subsequent conduct of the parties".[14] This clearly may operate in determining the existence and terms of notice of the existence of an impediment to performance of the contract which the party impeded is required to give under Article 79(4).

Yet another general provision bearing on the operation of Article 79 is Article 4(a) providing that "except as otherwise expressly provided in the Convention it is not concerned with:

(a) the validity of the contract or of any of its provisions or of any usage."

This would seem to exclude from the ambit of Article 79 both initial and supervening illegality and their consequences, these aspects of frustration being dealt with by conflict rules.[15] A somewhat more difficult problem arises when under the applicable law, as in English law, a frustrating event wholly discharges the contract, thus depriving it of validity,[16] or an initial "impediment" such as the non-existence

10. Art. 7. Honnold, above, fn. 7, pp. 135–161; Nicholas, above, fn. 2, pp. 209–10 noting that the place of good faith was subject to controversy, but some writers contend for wide application.

11. *Fothergill* v. *Monarch Airlines* [1980] A.C. 25; *Buchanan* v. *Babco* [1978] A.C. 141; *Stag Line* v. *Foscolo Mango* [1932] A.C. 328. See Honnold, above, fn. 7, pp. 138–145.

12. See further Chapter 2 and see also Barry Nicholas, *French Law of Contract* (2nd ed. Oxford 1992) pp. 200–210; Nicholas, "*Force Majeure* and Frustration" (1979) 27 Am.J.Comp.L. 231 at pp. 237–238; Honnold, fn. 7, pp. 533–534.

13. See ULIS, Art. 2.

14. The reference to subsequent conduct conflicts with *Miller* v. *Whitworth Street Estates* [1970] A.C. 583. See Nicholas, fn. 2, p. 211.

15. Nicholas, fn. 2, p. 207. Winship in Galston-Smit, above fn. 6, 1–37 says "in the abstract the issue of validity is potentially the most troublesome" and thinks it includes "at least" error, mistake, fraud, duress and illegality.

16. Sale of Goods Act 1979, s.7 (goods perishing before risk passes to buyer, contract "avoided"). See P. S. Atiyah, *Sale of Goods*, (8th Edn., London, 1990) pp. 327–341; *Benjamin's Sale of Goods* (4th Edn., London 1992) Chapter 6.

of the subject-matter nullifies consent and renders the apparent contract void from the outset.[17] Some commentators contend that the solution lies in asking "whether the domestic rule is invoked by the same operative facts that invoke a rule of the Convention"[18] and, if so, the Convention prevails. Applying this test, it is said that it would not be possible to have recourse to the applicable law where the goods had perished before the conclusion of the contract since the "operative facts" are covered by Article 30 (seller's duty to deliver) and Article 79 (impediment excusing a party from damages).[19]

By the same criterion, supervening impossibility which answered to the definition of "impediment" would fall to be dealt with under Article 79 rather than under the applicable law. Here an anomaly would seem to threaten, since some commentators also seem agreed, on the basis of *travaux préparatoires*, that frustration in the sense of "a radical change in circumstances", not rendering performance literally impossible but merely impracticable, does not fall within Article 79[20] and, since there do not seem to be any appropriate general principles, it would then appear to be dealt with under the applicable law. Very frequently the same set of facts could be described indifferently as either supervening impossibility (in a com-

17. Sale of Goods Act 1979, s.6 (unknown to seller goods perished before contract, contract "void"). Sometimes the seller may be taken to warrant the existence of the goods, *McRae* v. *Commonwealth Disposals Commission* (1951) 84 C.L.R. 429.

18. Honnold, fn. 7, pp. 111–118, 119–124, 313–318; Nicholas, fn. 2, pp. 207–208.

19. Nicholas, fn. 2, p. 208. See also Peter Schlechtriem, *Uniform Sales Law* (Vienna 1986) p. 33. But M. J. Bridge in [1991] L.M.C.L.Q. at p. 134 says of the question whether non-existent goods are a problem of mistake rendering a contract void and so going to validity for the applicable law or a condition precedent preventing performance and so within Art. 79: "The answer will obviously depend on the doctrinal approach of individual legal systems." This reasoning can clearly be extended. Also D. Tallon in C. M. Bianca and M. J. Bonell (eds.), *Commentary on the International Sales Law* (Milan 1987), pp. 577–578, thinks non-existent goods are governed by the applicable law and at pp. 591–592 thinks it debatable whether the Convention covers *imprévision*. (This applies to contracts under *droit administratif* and allows effect to failure of the economic basis as well as physical and legal impossibility. See p. 28 (above) Nicholas, *French Law of Contract*, fn. 12, pp. 208–210). However, at p. 594 Tallon concludes against leaving *imprévision* (in the broad sense of economic difficulty modifying obligation) to the applicable law as this would imperil uniformity and render Art. 79 useless in countries which admit this form of release. F. Enderlein and D. Maskow, *International Sales Law* (New York 1992), p. 323, do not agree with Tallon on non-existent goods being subject to the applicable law. See below, fn. 64 where "radical change" resulting from initially temporary impediment is to be left to the applicable law.

20. Honnold, fn. 7, pp. 543–544 (now allowing that economic dislocations comparable to non-economic barriers may perhaps excuse, in particular if they result in state laws requiring contract modification, these being effective under the applicable law); Nicholas, fn. 2, pp. 235–236. "Radical change in circumstance" may denote a Continental doctrine but it also describes the basic English principle underlying frustration. See Lord Radcliffe in *Davis Contractors* v. *Fareham* [1956] A.C. 696 at p. 728 (circumstances in which performance called for "would render it a thing radically different from that which was undertaken"); P. S. Atiyah, *Introduction to the Law of Contract* (4th Edn., Oxford, 1989), p. 257 " . . . the basis of the doctrine is that to enforce the contract after a radical change of circumstances is to enforce obligations quite different from those undertaken by the parties". More precisely, perhaps, the English doctrine now hinges on "radical change in the obligation". *Chitty on Contracts* (27th Edn., Vol. I, London, 1994) paras. 23–008–23–009. But see Schlechtriem fn. 19, p. 102 fn. 422a who thinks it imperative to treat radically changed circumstances as "impediments" within Art. 79 to avoid courts having recourse to domestic law but concedes that Vischer in *Lausanner Colloquium* 177 thinks this unavoidable. Enderlein-Maskow, fn. 19 p. 324, say the Convention does not make it clear whether considerably increased difficulty may amount to an impediment but think that insistence on unchanged performance in such a case would be a breach of the requirement of good faith in Art. 7(1). They recommend that parties should cover the matter by agreement. See to the same effect Lee fn. 1 pp. 143–144 and fn. 32 noting the absence of provision for frustration and suggesting *force majeure* clauses.

mercial sense) or a radical change in circumstances,[21] and it would be strange if the legal outcome depended on the arbitrary attachment of a label. In any event, leaving initial and supervening illegality to the applicable law, initial and supervening impossibility to Article 79 and frustration (perhaps) to the applicable law produces a muddled mosaic.

If it be argued that a contract affected by a radical change should stand valid under the Convention, the answer seems to be that to enforce such a contract when the change of circumstances would have terminated the contract under the applicable law would seem to be a contradiction of Article 4(a). The proposed "operative facts" rule of interpretation is said to be based on the requirement of Article 7(1) that in interpretation of the Convention "regard is to be had to its international character and the need to promote uniformity in its application".[22] This paragraph is not cast in unqualified imperative language and whilst the proposed rule may be a helpful guide to many topics, such as conformity of the goods,[23] when it does produce what seems to be clear conflict with the legislative text, as in upholding the validity of contracts which by their applicable law are wholly discharged by impossibility or frustration, then the rule of interpretation[24] seems open to query in this context, even if at the cost of some loss of uniformity. The exclusion of validity from the ambit of the Convention seems to be an imperative rule of law, not one of construction or interpretation, therefore not yielding to Article 7(1) and, since the Convention itself does not attempt any definition of "validity", the definition and application of this concept would appear to be for the applicable law under Article 7(2). To attempt to use the principle that interpretation should favour uniformity as a general principle to divert to Article 79 cases which under the most obvious application of the validity rule would be dealt with under the applicable law might be self-defeating. Decisions might well be more unpredictable and diverse under the unspecific language of the Article than under the applicable law. Formal uniformity might well promote practical uncertainty and diversity.

5. USAGE AND CUSTOM

The reference to usage and practice in Article 8 is confirmed and expanded in Article 9 which provides that the parties are bound by any usage which they have agreed and by practice which they have established between themselves, this corresponding to the English "course of dealing". Moreover, in the absence of agreement to the contrary, they are to be regarded as having impliedly made applicable to their contract "a usage of which the parties knew or ought to have known

21. Honnold, *ibid.*, p. 542 (business standard; cf. *Asfar* v. *Blundell* [1896] 1 Q.B. 123); Nicholas, fn. 2, p. 236, puts a case of "enormous cost increases" which might arguably be both a radical change in circumstances and an impediment within Art. 79.

22. Honnold, fn. 7, p. 122. But see p. 544, fn. 19 at end conceding that the applicable law should apply to validity "when agreement is barred no matter how clearly it is stated".

23. *Ibid.*, pp. 301–318, especially pp. 311–318.

24. *Ibid.*, pp. 148–156, also Honnold, *Documentary History of the Uniform Law for International Sales* (Deventer 1989) pp. 218, 243, 323, 407, 583. Only the Secretariat Commentary in these sources at p. 407 contemplates the Convention prevailing over national law. See also Schlechtriem, fn. 19, p. 102, fn. 422a, citing Vischer in *Lausanner Colloquium* 177, above, fn. 20.

and which in international trade is widely known to and regularly observed by parties to contracts of the type involved in the trade concerned".

This is similar to the test of notoriety for the implication of commercial custom in English contracts and may well have relevance to problems trenching on Article 79,[25] particularly in determining what may be expected by way of avoiding or circumventing an "impediment". Thus in some trades and ports if a trader receives sufficient goods to fulfil only part of his commitments it may be the practice to "pro-rate" or ration such goods as are available amongst his buyers, and compliance with such a usage would be secured by Article 9.[26]

6. PASSING OF RISK

Another topic associated with impediments and imperfect performance is the passing of risk. As with impossibility itself, the passing of risk is usually covered in standard form contracts and, as with Article 79, it may well be that the provisions of the Convention will rarely operate, at least in unmodified form.[27]

Under the Convention both the underlying rule for passing of risk and its consequences, including its relationship to impossibility of performance, differ markedly from English law.

The articles dealing with risk first cover a number of cases involving carriage and then provide a residual rule that risk passes either on the delivery of the goods to the buyer or on the placing of them at his disposal. Unlike the English Sale of Goods Act which *prima facie* links passing of risk to the passing of property, it could be said that, broadly speaking, the Convention links the passing of risk to the goods passing from the control of the seller.[28]

As to the consequences of risk passing, Article 66 provides that loss or damage after that does not discharge the buyer from his obligation to pay the price, unless

25. See Honnold, fn. 7, pp. 173–180 noting at p. 179 that an applicable usage has the force of contract and prevails over the Convention by virtue of Art. 6. In English law the customs of a trade or locality may be implied in relevant contracts even if they are of very recent origin. See Lord Mansfield C.J. in *Noble* v. *Kennoway* (1780) 2 Doug. 510 at p. 513 (one year may suffice provided it is well-known) cf. Honnold, pp. 175–176, fn. 4, who does not seem to make clear the distinction between ancient local custom in land law, an original source of law, and commercial custom adopted in contract. See Salmond, *Jurisprudence* (12th Edn., London 1966) pp. 189–203. See also Aleksandar Goldstajn, "Usages of Trade and Other Autonomous Rules of International Trade According to the UN (1980) Sales Convention", Chapter 3 of *Dubrovnik Lectures*, above, fn. 7 and Fisher and Hains fn. 1 pp. 544–545 citing *Nelson* v. *Dahl* (1879) 12 Ch.D. 568 at p. 575; *Con-Stan Industries of Australia Pty. Ltd.* v. *Norwich Winterthur Insurance (Australia) Ltd.* (1986) 160 C.L.R. 266 at p. 236.

26. Law Commission Working Paper No. 112: *Rights to Goods in Bulk* pp. 67–68, Q11 p. 68, n. 142.

27. Nicholas, fn. 2, p. 237. See also Lee, fn. 1, pp. 142–143 to the same effect, citing INCOTERMS. For English law see Atiyah, fn. 16, pp. 320–321; Benjamin, fn. 16 Chapter 6.

28. Nicholas, fn. 2, p. 240; Honnold, above, fn. 7, p. 451. Art. 67 prescribes risk is to pass on delivery to a carrier when the contract involves carriage. If a place of delivery to the carrier is specified it passes there, retention of documents by the seller not affecting the passing of the risk. The goods must be identified to the contract. Under Art. 68, if goods are sold when in transit, risk presumptively passes when the contract is concluded but may pass retrospectively from the start of the journey. Under Art. 69, if the carriage rules do not apply, risk passes when the buyer takes delivery or when he ought to take delivery but in breach of contract fails to do so. If delivery is to be elsewhere than at the seller's place of business risk passes when the buyer knows the goods are available for him at that place. Again the goods must be identified. Identification may raise problems with sales of undivided shares in bulk. Nicholas, fn. 2, p. 240.

the loss or damage is due to an act or omission of the seller. Since an impediment within Article 79 merely releases a party from damages and not from other remedies, after the passing of risk, the buyer is prevented by such an impediment from performing his duties of taking delivery or paying the price, he will be freed from any liability in damages but will still be liable in an action for the price or to take delivery.

As to the seller, Article 70 provides that if the seller has committed a fundamental breach of contract, substantially depriving the buyer of what he was entitled to expect under the contract, the fact that risk has passed to the buyer under the three preceding articles will not impair the buyer's remedies for that breach. If the fundamental breach results from an "impediment" within Article 79, the seller will not be liable in damages but will be subject to the other remedies listed in Article 45, such as avoidance.

7. PREPARATORY QUESTIONS

Thus when some event occurs which might at first sight seem to indicate reference to Article 79 to exempt a party from liability for breach it is therefore necessary to ask a number of questions before going to the Article itself.

In the first place, is the contract one within the ambit of the Convention? If it is, have the provisions of the Convention been excluded or modified by the terms of the contract, by any course of dealing or applicable trade usage or custom? Do special national requirements as to written evidence or the embodiment in writing of the contract or any notice given under the Convention have any part to play? Do municipal rules as to nullity of contracts affected by mistake or to the discharge of frustrated contracts go to validity and hence remove the contract from the ambit of the Convention? Have the provisions as to risk been excluded, or modified by usage on the contract? Only when these questions have been answered, at any rate provisionally, should one turn to the text of Article 79 itself.

8. ARTICLE 79

The first and key paragraph of Article 79 reads:

"A party is not liable for a failure to perform any of his obligations if he proves that the failure was due to an impediment beyond his control and that he could not reasonably be expected to have taken the impediment into account at the time of the conclusion of the contract or to have avoided or overcome its consequences."

The corresponding provision in Article 74 of ULIS reads:

"Where one of the parties has not performed one of his obligations, he shall not be liable for such non-performance if he can prove that it was due to circumstances which, according to the intention of the parties at the time of the conclusion of the contract, he was not bound to take into account or to avoid or overcome; in the absence of any expression of the intention of the parties regard shall be had to what reasonable persons in the same situation would have intended."[29]

29. The final part of this paragraph is now covered by Art. 8 of the Vienna Convention.

9. IMPEDIMENT v. CIRCUMSTANCES

The chief difference between these formulations is that whilst ULIS speaks of "circumstances," the Vienna Convention employs the term "impediment". This change was intended to ensure that exemption from liability did not include defective performance and in particular the supply of non-conforming goods.[30]

The UNIDROIT (Rome) Draft of a Uniform Law of 1956 had in its Article 85 made exemption dependent on "an obstacle" to performance,[31] but this wording was questioned at The Hague Diplomatic Conference of 1964,[32] especially by the Federal German Government, who considered that this term would cover only supervening and external events, would bar exemption based on radical change in economic circumstances and would exclude exemption in respect of defects in the goods which did not result from the seller's fault.[33] The inclusion of this last point was expressly mentioned by Professor Tunc as the explanation for the adoption of the word "circumstances".[34]

The issue was reopened by representatives of common law countries when preparing the Vienna Convention, and the replacement of "circumstances" by "impediment" was confirmed at the Diplomatic Conference in order to exclude absence of fault as a ground of exemption.[35] The underlying policy consideration was that whilst impossibility was ordinarily based on events of general notoriety, and easy of proof, such as storms, crop failures, pestilence and the like, exemption based on absence of fault might involve long, uncertain and expensive investigations into the manufacturing and storage methods not only of the immediate selling party but also into those of a lengthy string of suppliers behind him.[36] An early appearance of the term "impediment" reveals that members of a preparatory Working Group in 1984 felt that the terminology of ULIS was insufficiently stringent.[37] They said that grounds for exemption were not restricted to physical or legal

30. Nicholas, fn. 2, p. 235. But for doubt whether this was achieved see Nicholas (1979) 27 Am.Jo. Comp. L. at p. 240; Honnold, fn. 7, pp. 534–536 (exemption may apply to any of a party's obligations). See also Nicholas in Galston-Smit, fn. 6, citing Professor Huber, 5–11 to 5–15. Schlechtriem, fn. 19, p. 101, fn. 416a, thinks defects are included but the seller will rarely be excused, and at fn. 417 says that despite Nicholas' doubts, "German jurists should not, and most likely will not, read the fault principle into the text of Article 79." See also Tallon, fn. 19, pp. 579–580; Enderlein-Maskow, fn. 19, pp. 320–321, share doubt as to whether the change from "circumstances" to "impediment" has made a real difference. Tallon, p. 583, considers the impediment must be the sole cause of non-performance but Enderlein-Maskow, p. 322, disagree and would admit an impediment which operates with other causes.

31. See *Records and Documents of the Diplomatic Conference on the Unification of Law Governing the International Sale of Goods, The Hague 1964*. The Netherlands Ministry of Justice (The Hague, 1966) Vol. II, p. 21.

32. *Ibid.*, Vol. I, pp. 121–122; Vol. II, p. 351.

33. Honnold, fn. 7, pp. 534–535.

34. *Records and Documents of the Hague Conference*, Vol. I, p. 384.

35. *Documentary History*, fn. 24, p. 631 (contribution to discussion by Professor Honnold).

36. Honnold, fn. 7, pp. 536–537. For the link between "defects" and "fault" see Nicholas in Galston-Smit, fn. 6, 5–11 to 5–16.

37. *Documentary History*, fn. 24, p. 185. It also appears that "impediment" was chosen "as suggesting an event which was both subsequent to the conclusion of the contract and external to the seller and the goods". Nicholas, fn. 2, p. 235. But see Schlechtriem, fn. 19, p. 101, who thinks it irrelevant whether the impediment was pre-existing or subsequent, citing the Secretariat Commentary. See *Documentary History*, fn. 24, p. 445, para. 4. Tallon fn. 19 pp. 577–579 thinks the Article would not apply to already existing impediments known to the defaulting party.

impossibility or to cases where there had been a radical change of circumstances[38] but could embrace situations where performance had become unexpectedly onerous, as with an unforeseen rise in prices. Hence exemption, they thought, "should only be available on the occurrence of an objective obstacle or impediment". One observer remarked that Article 74 of ULIS could be invoked when damage was caused by a hidden defect in the goods and that it was desirable to prevent this. Some representatives also recognised that the central issue was allocation of risk of unforeseen events, but others, whilst accepting this analysis, thought it would be difficult to draft in terms of risk.

Some commentators remarked that the ULIS Article 74 owed much to common law ideas, especially in reducing the problem to one of interpreting the intention of the parties.[39] Moreover, although the "impediment" under the Convention must be "beyond [the party's] control" and such that he could not reasonably be expected to have taken into account, or have avoided or overcome, in this reflecting the French rule that *force majeure* must be "unforeseeable, insurmountable and irresistible", it is recognised that this requirement of externality should not cause problems for lawyers familiar with the types of events which bring the English doctrine of discharge by impossibility of performance into play.[40]

The language of Article 79 is broad and flexible[41] and should readily accommodate almost, if not all, the types of events just mentioned, but there are many other features of Article 79 which, as has already been seen, depart considerably from the common law position. Thus if the English doctrine operates, the contract is discharged in its entirety. The Vienna Convention, following ULIS, both being in accord with French law, regards component obligations of a contract as being available for exemption. Again, English impossibility of performance or frustration wholly discharges the contract, leaving only adjustment under the Law Reform (Frustrated Contracts) Act 1943, whereas exemption under Article 79 merely excludes the remedy of damages, leaving all other contractual remedies on foot. Again, English frustration releases both parties whereas Article 79 only exempts the non-performing one.[42]

10. IMPOSSIBILITY v. FRUSTRATION

A question has, indeed, been raised as to whether frustration in the sense of discharge by a radical change of circumstances, leaving performance literally possible

38. *Documentary History*, fn. 24, p. 185.

39. R. H. Graveson, E. J. Cohn and Diana Graveson, *The Uniform Laws on International Sales Act 1967*; *A Commentary* (London 1968) pp. 94–96; the United Kingdom in a comment to The Hague Conference also thought Art. 74 of ULIS resembled frustration but they overlooked very significant differences, Nicholas, 27 Am.Jo.Comp. L. at p. 233.

40. Nicholas, fn. 2, p. 235, though the nullifying effect of English frustration may perhaps take a frustrated contract governed by English applicable law outside the Convention by virtue of Art. 4(a). See above fns. 15–24. See also Nicholas in Galston-Smit, fn. 6, pp. 5–6, pointing out that despite strictness of language, individual French decisions may be much more lenient than they would be in England.

41. But this may lead to it being handled with wide variation in national courts, *ibid.*, fn. 2, p. 235. Also 27 Am. Jo. Comp. L. p. 249 "the word 'impediment' is all that emerged in the end from a lengthy attempt to escape from the elasticity and imprecision of the ULIS requirement that non-performance be 'due to circumstances . . .'".

42. Nicholas, 27. Am. Jo. Comp. L. at pp. 233–239. For a discussion of the Law Reform (Frustrated Contracts) Act 1943 see Chapter 11.

but wholly different from what it had been intended to be, as distinct from outright impossibility, does apply under Article 79. Professor Nicholas thinks that this is not the case, on the ground that, when a proposal was made that the Convention should expressly declare that an exempted party should be wholly discharged if, at the end of a temporary impediment, "circumstances had so radically changed that it would be manifestly unreasonable to hold him liable", this was rejected, it seems, as he says, on the ground of reluctance to discuss frustration and *imprévision*.[43] On the other hand, Professor Honnold took the view that, whilst it would be a serious breach of Article 7 to have unrestricted recourse to municipal methods of handling interruptions of performance, nonetheless the language of the Convention was sufficiently broad and flexible to accommodate the concept of frustration in the sense of radical alteration of circumstances. This, however, was to be achieved by relying on a broad interpretation of the contract under the freedom given by Article 8 to construe in accordance with the intent of the parties rather than by adopting a forbidden general rule from a municipal system. He now takes the view that "extreme price and (especially) currency dislocations" may result in state law or regulation requiring contract adjustment and that the Convention does not affect the validity of such laws or regulations or, more broadly, general economic difficulties will only exempt under Article 79 if they amount to a barrier to performance comparable to other exempting causes.[44] This seems to be a significant increase in the stringency of his opinion.

Professor Honnold was also at pains to point out that those who drafted the Convention carefully avoided a test of "impossibility" since this has been subject to a process of erosion in national systems in response to commercial realities.[45] In avoiding or circumventing an impediment he thinks a party would not be expected to run a blockade, but from this extremity there is a continuum in which it might be difficult to draw a line.[46] Perhaps the answer is that within Articles 7 and 8, which direct attention to the promotion of international uniformity and good faith and govern the attribution of intent to the parties, the court will have to impose the just solution, as in older English approaches to these problems. Just as English courts interpret "perish" not in a strict scientific sense but rather in a commercial sense,[47]

43. Nicholas, fn. 2, pp. 235–236. This was a Norwegian proposal and, though it was certainly rejected, the records give no indication of the reason, so that this may be an insufficient ground on which to exclude "radical change" from the category of "impediment". *Documentary History*, fn. 24, pp. 706–707. See also Schlechtriem, fn. 19, pp. 102–103, giving same reasons as Nicholas. See also Lee, above, fn. 1, p. 144, fn. 32 accepting that there is no provision for frustration.

44. Honnold, fn. 7 (1st Edn., 1981), pp. 442–443; (2nd Edn., 1991) fn. 7, pp. 543–544. And see Schlechtriem, fn. 19 and above, fn. 20, who thinks it imperative that "change of circumstances" be regarded as an "impediment" in order to exclude recourse to domestic law while admitting others think this unavoidable.

45. This is borne out by Nicholas, 27 Am. Jo. Comp. L. at p. 240, who says that the word "impossible" was rejected because if it was interpreted in the common law sense it would have given too narrow an "exemption" but if interpreted in the German sense it would have admitted "economic impossibility". "Radical change" would have been familiar to common lawyers but equally would not exclude "the deceptive width of economic impossibility". The draftsmen returned to basically the ULIS formula "which has the unambitious virtue that its elasticity is reasonably obvious on its face". But, it may be asked, if it is so elastic, can it exclude these perhaps undesirable approaches to exemption?

46. Fn. 7 (1st Edn.), p. 433; (2nd Edn.) p. 542 indicating the questions of degree within domestic rules of impossibility.

47. *Asfar* v. *Blundell* [1896] 1 Q.B. 123. And see Schlechtriem, fn. 19, who thinks the standard of performance should be that of a reasonable person within Art. 8. For a discussion of Arts. 7 and 8 see

so, too, the overcoming or circumvention of an impediment should be handled not in terms of what might be theoretically possible but rather in terms of what might be commercially expected from a man acting in good faith. Guidance on this could be obtained from the study of contract forms which Honnold recommends, especially from the detailed terms of *force majeure* clauses.[48]

11. OPERATION OF THE IMPEDIMENT

For the impediment to operate it must be beyond the control of the party seeking exemption and *either* he could not reasonably be expected to have taken it into account at the time of the conclusion of the contract *or* to have avoided or overcome its consequences. The first question that arises is the stringency of these requirements. In respect of control, is it what is theoretically possible or what is commercially realistic? It has been seen that Professor Nicholas has suggested that this formulation reflects the French rule that *force majeure* must be "unforeseeable, insurmountable and irresistible". This requires that performance should be impossible, not merely more onerous. "No doctrine of change of circumstances or economic impossibility or disappearance of the foundation of the contract or frustration of the adventure has been admitted by the civil courts."[49] The fact, however, that there are verbal similarities between the text of the Convention and the codes of a national legal system, whilst it may provide general guidance, such as indicating a more stringent or a more flexible approach, should not lead to precise adherence in all circumstances to the solutions of that system, since to follow that course would be to disregard the injunction in Article 7 to have regard to the international character of the Convention, the promotion of uniformity and perhaps the observance of good faith. Since it has been pointed out that "virtually all of the Convention's provisions may be described as rules for interpreting international contracts of sale",[50] in order that they may more effectively fulfil this role, the proper course would seem to be to study not merely contract forms, as when attempting to estab-

above, fns. 10–14. See also Honnold, fn. 7, p. 542, citing Nicholas in Galston-Smit, pp. 5–9. Enderlein-Maskow, fn. 19, p. 324, would accept that the requirement of good faith in Art. 7(1) may provide a solution, though they do not attack the possibility of "changed circumstances" amounting to an impediment. See above, fn. 20.

48. Honnold, fn. 7, pp. 537–542. But Tallon, above, fn. 19, p. 595, criticised the comparative approach on the ground that it might arouse the nationalism of judges since they might conclude that their own domestic systems were the most satisfactory. Honnold, p. 538, acknowledges this risk but despairs at the power of words to express the questions of degree instrinsic to the present problem and says all possible help is needed. Enderlein-Maskow, fn. 19, p. 320, express agreement with Tallon's criticism but approve derivation of ideas of contractual interpretation from contractual practice. Lee, above, fn. 1, p. 147, points out that there is no process to determine the status of national decisions or for continuing review of the text of the Convention. Maurer (1988) 15 Syracuse Jo. Int. Law and Com. 361 at p. 383 thinks courts will draw heavily on their own approaches even though this will compromise uniformity and certainty.

49. Nicholas, *French Law of Contract* (2nd Edn.) pp. 202–203. But see Nicholas in Galston-Smit, fn. 6, pp. 5–6, cited above, fn. 40, pointing out the leniency of individual French cases. Views differ as to the affinity of the Convention regime with national systems. Whilst Nicholas sees French influence, Jelena Vilus, *Dubrovnik Lectures*, fn. 7, pp. 253–254, says a chief problem is that Art. 79 attempts to combine *force majeure* and frustration. Tallon, fn. 19, p. 592, accepted by Honnold, fn. 7, p. 542, says the Convention stands somewhere between the most strict and most liberal domestic systems.

50. Honnold, fn. 7 (1st Edn.) p. 259. See above, fn. 48, for criticism of this approach. For a proposal that publicity be given to arbitral awards see 18 Can.Bus. Law Jo. 16–43.

lish an abstract statement of standard, but the practice not only of national courts but also of arbitral tribunals to discover what the international commercial community regards as just and reasonable in this field. Thus by a reflex process the rather general and elastic wording of the Convention might be given that additional content which would not leave its interpretation to the whim of the particular tribunal which happens to be hearing a case.

Some more detailed points of language arise on this paragraph. The point of time at which the non-performing party's obligation to take into account an existing or prospective obstruction to performance operates is the conclusion of the contract and this may require reference to the formation provisions in Part II (Articles 14–24). The obligations are alternatives, so that it would seem to follow that, if some hindrance to performance could not be foreseen at that time but was relatively trivial, it would have to be avoided or overcome. If it was more serious but still unforeseeable then it would be an impediment if it could not be avoided or overcome when it happened. The paragraph operates not only on the impediment itself but also on "its consequences".

"Beyond control" would seem to emphasise that a party is not to escape liability for merely defective performance, such as non-conformity,[51] or for what is done by his servants and employees, a conclusion which would seem to follow *a fortiori* from Article 79(2) which imposes liability in respect of the failure of third parties who have been engaged "to perform a whole or a part of the contract", who would appear to be independent contractors. "Taking into account" seems to suggest more than merely foreseeing but also to require some measure of forethought and prior planning towards the avoidance or reduction of the harm if it strikes. It has been suggested that "avoiding or overcoming" should, like other elements, be subject to a criterion of commercial feasibility rather than theoretical possibility.[52]

12. FAILURE OF A THIRD PARTY

Article 79(2) then goes on to provide that even if a party is *prima facie* exempt under the first paragraph, he will be deprived of that exemption if his failure results from the failure of a third party whom he has engaged to perform "the whole or a part of the contract" unless that third party would in his turn be exempt from liab-

51. As to which see *ibid*. (2nd Edn.) pp. 534–537, but above, fn. 30.

52. As to which see above fns. 45–47. Schlechtriem, fn. 19, p. 101, considers that a party may be liable for uncontrollable impediments if he could foresee them. These should be covered by exclusion clauses. *Sed quaere*. "Taking into account" is an alternative to "avoiding or overcoming" so that even if a party can "take account" he should still be protected by Art. 79 if he cannot "avoid or overcome". In English law some foreseeable events may have frustrating effect. Treitel, *Law of Contract* (8th Edn.) pp. 799–803. At p. 102 Schlechtriem says the general view was that economic difficulties, "unaffordability", could constitute an impediment, but an obligor is generally taken to guarantee his financial capability. More detailed points are raised by Enderlein-Maskow, fn. 19, pp. 322–323. Are fires (when precautions have been neglected) and strikes matters beyond control? Tallon, fn. 19, p. 582, thinks a contract for generic goods would not come within Art. 79 unless a source of supply was stopped. Supervening illegality would doubtless also be enough. Fisher and Hains, fn. 1, do not discuss the application of Art. 79 to futures contracts but these points seem relevant. Cain (1983) 57 Conn.B.Jo. 327–328 thinks strikes will not excuse and thinks the expenses of avoidance or overcoming impediments are not to be taken into account. He prefers the corresponding provisions of the Uniform Commercial Code and recommends using "strike"clauses.

ility under Article 79(1). It has been said that such a rule is not only not found in ULIS but not, it would seem, in any domestic system.[53] It might be added, however, that during the course of preparing ULIS persistent attempts were made to include similar terms, which suggests that delegation must frequently have been advanced as an excuse for unsatisfactory performance.[54] The working party in its draft Convention used the term "sub-contractor" but this was replaced by the less economical wording because of the close association of the term "sub-contractor" in some systems with building and engineering.[55]

It was said in the *travaux préparatoires* that it seemed clear that a seller would not be exempt from liability by failure of a supplier since a supplier would not be described as a person engaged to perform any portion of the seller's contract.[56] There seems, however, no good reason why the failure of a supplier, if it otherwise answers to the concept of impediment, should not have exempting effect, even if that might only be temporary whilst substitutes were obtained elsewhere, without the seller having to prove that the supplier in his turn suffered an impediment.[57] Article 79(2) would thus be confined to the case of a third party with whom the seller had close commercial relations and whose efficiency he can assess.[58]

13. TEMPORARY INTERRUPTION

The problem of temporary interruption is addressed in Article 79(3) which reads: "The exemption provided by this article has effect for the period during which the impediment exists." This differs markedly from the corresponding provision of ULIS, Article 74(2), which provides that in the case of a temporary impediment the party in default "should be permanently relieved of his obligation if, by reason of the delay, performance would be so radically changed as to amount to the performance of an obligation quite different from that contemplated by the contract".

This is cast in terms not unfamiliar to English lawyers who will recognise the concept of delay giving rise to frustration[59] and the criterion of a radical change for determining whether frustration operates.[60] It seems, however, that this infusion of

53. Nicholas, fn. 2, pp. 236–237.

54. *Records and Documents of The Hague Conference* (1964) Vol. II, p. 104 (Federal German Government), p. 201 (Note on the Observations of the Governments), p. 350 (Federal German Government), Vol. I, p. 121 (Federal German Government); p. 168 (German amendment withdrawn).

55. *Documentary History*, fn. 24, pp. 349, 446, 631–634. See Honnold, fn. 7, pp. 544–547. And see Schlechtriem, fn. 19, who distinguishes between those engaged to fulfil directly the seller's duty to the buyer to whom Art. 79(2) applies, and those, such as suppliers, whose performance is a mere precondition of the seller's performance, who are not within the paragraph. Both Tallon, fn. 19, p. 585 and Enderlein-Maskow, fn. 19, p. 328 are agreed that the fact that a "sub-contractor" is imposed by the buyer should not alter the seller's liability.

56. *Documentary History*, fn. 24, p. 349, para. 449, p. 446, para. 12.

57. Honnold, fn. 7, pp. 545–547. See also Nicholas, fn. 2, p. 237.

58. *Ibid.*, p. 546, citing Tallon, fn. 19, p. 585, saying that there must be an "organic link" between the main contract and the subcontract but not expressly accepting Tallon's further points that the subcontractor should know that he is a means of performing the main contract and that his action relates only to the performance of that contract. Enderlein-Maskow, fn. 19, pp. 329–330, reject Tallon's suggestion that the third party subcontractor must have been properly chosen, saying this is irrelevant if an impediment has occurred.

59. *Metropolitan Water Board* v. *Dick, Kerr & Co.* [1918] A.C. 119.

60. *Davis Contractors* v. *Fareham U.D.C.* [1956] A.C. 696 at pp. 728–729.

discharge by frustration was felt to match uneasily with other elements of the article based on *force majeure,* hence it has been deleted in the Vienna Convention.[61] As article 79(3) now stands it is, says Nicholas, "logical but limited",[62] dealing only with exemption from liability in damages. This led him to consider critically a number of possible solutions when the impediment does effect "a radical change".[63] The approach of the Law Reform (Frustrated Contracts) Act 1943, involving a substantial element of judicial discretion, was, he thought, perhaps the best from the point of view of ideal justice but it involved much uncertainty and would thus be unsuitable for international trade. Another approach, which appears in ULIS, would require the buyer to return the goods or to account for benefits. Yet another would permit the seller to claim the amount of the benefit to the buyer, so long as this does not exceed a proportionate part of the purchase price. No final solution was achieved, the matter being left to the law applicable to the contract, and the resulting uncertainty seems the less significant since it would appear that problems of this kind will not occur frequently in international sales,[64] and in any event will usually be dealt with under *force majeure* clauses.[65]

14. NOTICE

The next requirement is notice. Article 79(4) reads: "The party who fails to perform must give notice to the other party of the impediment and its effect on his ability to perform. If the notice is not received by the other party within a reasonable time after the party who fails to perform knew or ought to have known of the impediment, he is liable for damages resulting from such non-receipt." This did not appear in ULIS, though attempts by the International Chamber of Commerce and Hungary were made to include such a provision.[66] These proposals were questioned by the Special Commission which prepared for the 1964 Hague Diplomatic Conference,[67] who thought that whilst the idea was superficially attractive it might raise difficult questions as to the notification of impending or imminent obstruction of performance. If successive threats of interruption were posed, was a party under a duty to give successive notices of his fears? The original proposal of the International Chamber of Commerce explicitly required notice both of the commencement and cessation of the obstacle to performance, but the present wording of the Convention in requiring notice of the effect of the impediment on the non-

61. 27 Am.Jo.Comp. Law at p. 241. And see Nicholas in Galston-Smit, fn. 6, 5–17, 5–18, pointing out that the word "only" was deleted after "effect" to allow the initially temporary impediment to become permanent when appropriate, but he thinks courts would need the help of preparatory materials to reach this conclusion. Feltham, "The U.N. Convention on Contracts for the International Sale of Goods" [1981] J.B.L. 346 at p. 359 prefers ULIS and thinks relief when the impediment becomes permanent is left to the applicable law.

62. *Ibid.*, p. 241.

63. *Ibid.*, pp. 241–245.

64. *Ibid.*, p. 244. If the results of "radical change" are left to the applicable law there would seem to be merit in leaving the whole operation of "radical change" to the applicable law.

65. Hellner, above, fn. 7, p. 353. Tallon, fn. 19, p. 588, points out that Art. 79(3) deals with a temporary impediment but not with one affecting part of the performance. Honnold, fn. 7, pp. 548–550, poses a number of problems and suggests that the Convention provides ample resources for solutions.

66. *Records and Documents of The Hague Conference 1964*, Vol. II, pp. 115, 349–350.

67. *Ibid.*, p. 202.

performing party's "ability to perform" would seem to cover this. It would seem that Article 11 stating that a contract governed by the Convention need not be concluded or evidenced in writing, "is not subject to the other requirements as to form" and may be proved by any means including witnesses, would apply also to notice under Article 79(4). There seems no reason why Article 8, requiring interpretation in the light of the known understanding of the recipient or of a reasonable person of the same kind and in the light of custom and practice, should not apply to notices under Article 79(4). On the other hand, in putting risk of loss or delay in communication on the sender, Article 79(4) constitutes an exception to the general principle for notices and requests embodied in Article 27 that the sender may rely on them even if undelivered. This requirement of notice is a further point of difference between the English law of frustration and impossibility and the regime established by Article 79. In English law frustration determines the contract automatically at the time of the frustrating event, "its legal effect does not depend on [the parties'] opinions, or even knowledge, as to the event",[68] hence Article 79(4) poses an additional demand for caution, unless the nullifying effect of English frustration does take a contract governed by English law outside the ambit of the Convention.[69]

15. REMEDIES

Article 79(5) finally provides, as already mentioned, that an operative impediment merely excludes damages and not any other remedy, the Article in this respect differing strikingly from the discharging effect of English frustration. It has been remarked that some of these remedies are scarcely appropriate for a breach partially excused on grounds of impossibility[70] and the *travaux préparatoires* show that attempts were made, but without success, to exclude some of the more apparently incongruous, such as requiring performance.[71]

68. Treitel, *Law of Contract* (8th Edn., 1991, London) p. 807; *Hirji Mulji* v. *Cheong Yue S.S. Co. Ltd.* [1926] A.C. 497, at p. 505; *B. P. Exploration (Libya) Ltd.* v. *Hunt* [1979] 1 W.L.R. 783, at p. 809, but see R. B. McElroy and Glanville L. Williams, *Impossibility of Performance* (1941, Cambridge) at pp. 221–227, especially pp. 227–232 questioning English authorities and supporting a requirement of notice. Notice is required under UCC 2–615(c). Tallon, fn. 19, pp. 586–587, considers that Art. 79(4) only requires notification of an actual, not an anticipated, impediment and also points out that the event which impedes may also impede notification, in which case non-notification would be excused.

69. Above, fns. 15–20.

70. Nicholas, fn. 2, p. 236, pointing out that the Convention does not attempt any such adjustment as is found in the Law Reform (Frustrated Contracts) Act 1943 nor, it could be added, does it attempt anything like the pro-rating provision of UCC 2-615(b). Also Nicholas, 27 Am. Jo. Comp. L., pp. 241–242. Enderlein-Maskow, fn. 19, p. 321, would approve pro-rating where there is a partial failure of supplies. Feltham, fn. 61, p. 359, finds requiring performance of an impeded party "a strange result".

71. *Documentary History*, p. 349. It was pointed out that requiring performance could render exemption from damages worthless. Under Art. 28 a court is not bound to decree specific performance unless it would have done so in a contract of sale not within the Convention. This was to meet the needs of common law countries where specific performance in sale is very rare. In many civil law countries, though formally a primary remedy, it is only employed exceptionally in commercial cases. Honnold, fn. 7, pp. 267–277. Cf. ULIS Art. 74(3) which preserved avoidance and reduction of price only. Schlechtriem, fn. 19, p. 103, points out that in case of absolute impossibility domestic doctrine would debar performance being decreed but in case of impracticability a court might impose heavier penalties for non-performance than sums payable as damages. This paradox results from civil law theory that without a right to performance there would be no obligation and ancillary obligations would also fail. See p. 102,

(a) Remedies for buyer

Remedies for breach of contract by the seller are listed in Article 45 and, apart from damages, are specified in Articles 46 to 52.[72]

Article 46 allows the buyer to require performance. In the context of an impediment this may be appropriate when the impediment is either temporary or partial, after it has ceased to operate or in respect of obligations not covered by it. Whether or not non-conformity or an impediment causing lack of conformity come within Article 79, the buyer may demand substituted performance if the lack of conformity amounts to fundamental breach and notice is given under Article 39. The buyer may require goods to be repaired and under Article 47 may fix an additional reasonable period of time for performance and during that time may not exercise remedies.

Even after the date for delivery under Article 48 the seller may at his own expense remedy any failure to perform if this can be done without undue delay, inconvenience or the imperilling of reimbursement of expenses already paid by the buyer to the seller. In an ordinary case the buyer can still claim damages but this would be excluded if the seller's non-performance was initially caused by a temporary impediment. They might be available if the impediment was only partial. The seller may ask the buyer if he will accept performance and if the buyer does not reply within a reasonable time the seller may proceed to performance.

The most radical of the remedies available to the buyer is avoidance[73] which may be employed either when the seller has committed a fundamental breach, substantially depriving the buyer of what he was entitled to expect under the contract, or when he has failed to perform within a period of extra time fixed by the buyer. This remedy must be exercised within a reasonable time. If goods do not conform with the contract then, whether or not the price has already been paid, the buyer may reduce the price in proportion to the value that the goods actually delivered bear to the value that conforming goods would have had. If the seller remedies his performance in accordance with Articles 37 and 48 then the price may not be reduced.[74]

If the seller delivers only part of the goods or part only fail to conform then the buyer may only exercise his remedies in respect of the missing or defective part. He may only avoid the contract as a whole if the failure to provide full performance amounts to fundamental breach of the whole contract.[75]

(b) Remedies for seller

The remedies for breach of contract by the buyer are listed in Article 62 and, apart from damages, are set out in Articles 62 to 65. Article 62 first provides that the

fn. 426. Also Nicholas in Galston-Smit, fn. 6, 5–19, 5–20. Schlechtriem, p. 105, points out that whether an impediment exempts from penalties and liquidated damages will depend on domestic law. Tallon, fn. 19, p. 589, thinks liquidated damages are governed by the applicable law. Enderlein-Maskow, fn. 19, p. 332, also think penalties are excluded from the Convention.

72. For detailed treatment of remedies under the Convention see Honnold, fn. 7, pp. 356–405 (for buyer), pp. 433–446 (for seller) and pp. 557–574 (effects of avoidance). Neither a court nor an arbitral tribunal can grant a period of grace to a seller when a buyer sues for breach of contract. Art. 45(3).

73. Art. 49. For the effects of avoidance see Arts. 81–84 and below, fn. 77.

74. Art. 50.

75. Art. 51.

seller may require the buyer to pay the price,[76] take delivery or perform his other obligations, unless the seller has resorted to some inconsistent remedy. Then under Article 63 the seller may fix an additional period of time for fulfilment of the buyer's obligations. If the seller does so, he may not have recourse to any other remedy during that period of time unless the buyer has told him that he will not perform during that period of time. Finally, under Article 64, the seller may declare the contract avoided if the failure of the buyer to perform constitutes a fundamental breach or the buyer fails to perform within an additional period fixed by the seller. Where the buyer has paid the price the seller loses his right to avoid unless, in respect of late performance, he does so before he is aware that performance has been provided and in other cases unless he exercises it within a reasonable time.

The effects of avoidance are detailed in Articles 81 to 84. It releases both parties from their obligations under the contract, subject to any damages which may be due.[77] It does not affect any provision for the settlement of disputes, normally an arbitration clause, nor does it affect any special agreement between the parties as to their rights after avoidance. If, however, one party has performed their part of the contract in whole or in part, then they may claim restitution and if both parties are obliged to make restitution then they must do so concurrently. Restitution is not confined to a party in default.

Article 82 provides that as a general rule a buyer loses the right to declare the contract avoided or demand substitute goods if he cannot return the original goods in substantially the same condition as that in which he receives them. This, however, does not apply if the alteration in the goods is not due to the buyer's act or omission, or if it results from examination provided for under Article 38 to ascertain if they conform with the contract or if they have been sold or consumed in the normal course of business or use.

The fact that this complex and formidable array of remedies remains operative even after the "impediment" has operated and that some of these remedies may render the exemptions worthless means that the exempting effect of Article 79 appears narrow in the extreme, at least to common lawyers.

This may, however, give some indication as to the stringency to which exemption should be subject. The total and sweeping effect of common law frustration is balanced by a declared unwillingness on the part of the courts to find that it has occurred.[78] The fact that an exempting impediment under Article 79 has such relatively limited absolving effect, coupled with the fact that the Convention in no way essays any such balancing of the rights of the parties as is attempted in the Law Reform (Frustrated Contracts) Act 1943[79] may indicate that a less stringent approach to finding that an impediment has operated may be appropriate.

76. See *Documentary History*, p. 349, for a contention that a buyer should never be allowed to plead an impediment to the payment of the price and the countervailing argument that such a plea should be allowed in cases such as the outbreak of war or imposition of exchange controls.

77. Even in an impediment context there may be damages if the impediment was only partial. Art. 51.

78. *Per* Lord Radcliffe in *Davis Contractors* v. *Fareham* [1956] A.C. 696, at p. 727: "Frustration is not to be lightly invoked as the dissolvent of a contract."

79. Nicholas, fn. 2, p. 236.

16. DEFAULT IN CO-OPERATION

Article 80, which appears together with Article 79 in the section headed "Exemptions", provides: "A party may not rely on a failure of the other party to perform, to the extent that such failure was caused by the first party's act or omission." This does not deal with self-induced frustration, which is covered by a party's obligation to foresee, avoid or circumvent hindrances to performance, but with the case where one party by a failure to co-operate (e.g. failing to supply specifications for goods to be manufactured or processed) makes it impossible for the other to perform. On the basic principle that a party must not be allowed to take advantage of their own wrong, the defaulting party is not allowed to exercise remedies against the non-performing party.

At the Vienna Conference it was suggested that this situation was covered by the general principles of the Convention, but this Article was included to remove any doubt and, despite the fact that it appears with Article 79 in "Exemptions", is of general application.[80]

17. CONCLUSIONS

A survey of Article 79 seems to lead to the following conclusions:

(1) The obvious flexibility of its language leaves considerable freedom for courts and arbitral tribunals to apply varying principles and standards to the evaluation of an alleged impediment. It seems by no means clear, given the views of distinguished commentators who themselves played leading roles in the preparation of the Convention, that the change in wording from the "circumstances" of ULIS to the "impediment" of the Convention has effectively excluded lack of conformity from the ambit of the article.[81] Again, the commentators are not at one on whether the "change of circumstances" may constitute an impediment within the article.[82] These are only the most striking of many uncertainties. It may take long for generally accepted standards of application to emerge and this process may be delayed by the fact that the deficiencies of Article 79 will lead to its regular exclusion, thus preventing the creation of a guiding body of case law and practice.

(2) A further serious problem is the relationship of Article 79 to Article 4(a) and its exclusion of nullity from the scope of the Convention. When a national rule of frustration renders a contract null and void and the Convention expressly excludes nullity, it seems at least open to query that the

80. Honnold, fn. 7, pp. 553–556. Cf. ULIS Art. 74(3) at end which may be more restricted.

81. See Nicholas, fn. 2, p. 235 (to exclude questions of non-conformity); 27 Am. Jo. Comp. L. p. 240 (the advantage of impediment was that it was thought to exclude non-conformity "but this seems very doubtful"; Honnold, fn. 7, pp. 534–536 (defective performance excluded); Schlechtriem, fn. 19, p. 101 (included).

82. Nicholas, fn. 2, pp. 235–236, fn. 60 (no) but Honnold, fn. 7, pp. 543–544 (yes, if general economic difficulties and dislocations are comparable to other types of exempting cause); Schlechtriem, fn. 19, p. 102 (yes). In a different context one of the chief complaints of Fisher and Hains, fn. 1, p. 555, is that the uncertainty which the Convention creates is undesirable in the futures industry.

proposed "operative facts" rule of interpretation should be invoked to keep the nullified contract in being for Article 79 to work on it.[83]

(3) The exempting effect of an impediment is narrow and leaves in being a battery of remedies more appropriate for ordinary rather than excused breach. There is no provision for equitable adjustment of the rights of the parties and some of these remedies could render exemption illusory.[84]

(4) The requirement of notice, though apparently reasonable, may, as the framers of ULIS foresaw, provide ample scope for contention.[85]

From this it would seem that Professor Hellner's prophecy is only too likely to be fulfilled and *force majeure* clauses continue to rule the field. This may well make little difference to larger traders who are members of trade associations with ready access to tried and proven standard form contracts. Those unfortunates who may be compelled to face the prospect of exploring in detail the demerits of Article 79 may be smaller traders, perhaps from the developing countries, and those engaged in "one-off" transactions who have not properly adapted a standard form contract to their dealing.

If these conclusions seem unduly gloomy, they derive support from no less an authority than Professor Honnold himself. He confesses that "in spite of strenuous efforts of legislators and scholars we face the likelihood that Article 79 may be the Convention's least successful part of the half-century of work towards international uniformity. This prospect calls for careful, detailed contract drafting to provide solutions to fit the commercial situation at hand."[86] Elsewhere, after saying that "general legal rules, domestic or international, can scarcely provide clear and satisfactory answers to all these problems", he goes on effectively to commend *force majeure* clauses, saying that "in important transactions and in a wide variety of standard contracts explicit provision is made for the consequences of serious impediments to performance. The contracts can (and do) take account of the conditions and needs presented by various types of transactions."[87]

These passages are the more significant since Professor Nicholas has gone so far as to say that, if there is a weakness in Professor Honnold's work, it derives from the fact that he was "to a substantial extent the midwife of the Convention and indeed indirectly the progenitor of important parts of it" and has, therefore, sometimes been less willing than other commentators "to acknowledge its shortcomings".[88] At least on Article 79 Professor Honnold now seems entitled to an acquittal but equally the crucial and indispensable role of *force majeure* clauses in international sales seems to be incontestably confirmed.

A. H. HUDSON

83. Above, fns. 15–24.

84. Nicholas, fn. 2, p. 236; 27 Am. Jo. Comp. L. pp. 241–242 (pointing out the special unsuitability of avoidance). The problem of remedies is exacerbated by the fact that an American proposal to extend a duty of mitigation from damages to all remedies was rejected. See Honnold, fn. 7, pp. 518–522. This was designed to prevent specific performance causing needless waste and hardship.

85. Above, fns. 66–69.

86. Honnold, fn. 7, p. 543.

87. *Ibid.*, p. 532. See to the same effect Lee, fn. 1, p. 144, suggesting *force majeure* clauses, and Bassindale and Fletcher (1992) 3 I.C.C.R. 10 at pp. 14–15; Albert H. Kritzer, *Guide to the Practical Application of the United Nations Convention on Contracts for the International Sale of Goods* (Boston-Deventer 1989) pp. 502 and 519.

88. [1987] L.M.C.L.Q. p. 534.

CHAPTER 15

THE 1973 MISSISSIPPI FLOODS: "FORCE MAJEURE" AND EXPORT PROHIBITION

1. INTRODUCTION

An unswerving adherence to the maxim "*genus numquam perit*" would compel resistance to the idea that a contract for the sale of unascertained goods could ever be frustrated or become impossible to perform as a result of supervening events. Nevertheless, such an outcome is perfectly possible. The contractual description of unascertained goods might, for example, so shrink the universe of generic goods available to satisfy the contract as to permit proof of the seller's inability to perform.[1] And, of course, express contractual provision might be made for supervening events to an extent that is more generous to the handicapped seller than would be made by the general law. It is important to remember, however, that an express provision may be limited in effect so that any outstanding issues have to be remitted to the general law.

This relationship between general law and express contract is highlighted in a lengthy series of cases decided in the wake of the 1973 Mississippi floods and the ensuing American governmental prohibition of export. The cases involve dealings in American soya bean meal, an important component in animal feeding stuffs and hence in the production of beef for human consumption, and concern the GAFTA 100 standard form, which formed the basis of the contractual dealings in question. Two clauses[2] in particular stand out in the welter of litigation following the floods: clause 22, giving relief to a seller whose intended performance is delayed, though not necessarily permanently prevented,[3] by an event conforming to the description of "*force majeure*"; and clause 21, justifying contractual cancellation in the event of a governmental prohibition of export affecting the contract or any outstanding executory part. Clause 21 emerged as rather the more contested of the two provisions in a series of cases which, despite their impenetrable,[4] even repellant,[5] character,

1. *Howell* v. *Coupland* (1876) 1 Q.B.D. 258. Cf. *Blackburn Bobbin Co. Ltd.* v. *T.W. Allen & Sons Ltd.* [1918] 2 K.B. 467 (C.A.).

2. Their antecedents were cll. 18–19 of form 6 of the now defunct Corn and Feed Trade Association: *Tradax Export S.A.* v. *André & Cie. S.A.* [1975] 2 Lloyd's Rep. 516, at p. 529 (Donaldson J).

3. After a stipulated period, delayed delivery gives way to cancellation of the contract.

4. *Tradax Export S.A.* v. *Cook Industries Inc.* [1982] 1 Lloyd's Rep. 385, at p. 387 (C.A.) ("the cognoscenti in this recondite field").

5. *André & Cie. S.A.* v. *Tradax Export S.A.* [1983] 1 Lloyd's Rep. 254, at p. 258 (C.A.) ("unattractive piece of forensic history").

nevertheless repay study for the light they throw on contractual dealings in agricultural commodities. In particular, these cases display the tension between the individual contracts of traders and the structural integrity of linked contracts concerning the same goods entered into by many such traders. Indeed, the cases demonstrate the artificiality of any commitment to the doctrine of privity of contract taking the form of a refusal to examine the contractual world in which a particular contract is grounded.

To demonstrate the above points, it is necessary to say a little about the way individual commodity contracts are entered into before being pieced together to form a contractual string.[6] American soya bean meal is imported into Europe on c.i.f. terms, through a variety of ports such as Rotterdam and Bremen, by traders based in the United States and a variety of European countries. Contractual dealings in feeding stuffs are commonly entered into on the GAFTA 100 form, a c.i.f. contract issued by the Grain and Feed Trade Association, a London-based[7] trade association which, among its various functions, promulgates and edits standard form contracts for use by the trade. The current version[8] of the GAFTA form is a revised version of the one in use when the 1973 events occurred, but the essential nature of contractual dealings and the way that they are connected to produce the string remains unaltered. GAFTA forms, and FOSFA[9] forms for that matter too, provide for arbitration in the City of London and for the application of English law as the law applicable to the contract. An individual contract may well have no physical connection at all with England. Other contracts in the same string, however, might have a connection, and the contract forms themselves contain a domicile clause deeming the contract to have been entered into in England.[10]

At the time when the events in question occurred, a c.i.f. consignment of soya bean meal could well have been the subject of 30 separate contracts, and in certain instances the sales chains might run to a 100 or so contracting parties. Sales chains of such length, facilitated by the documentary character of c.i.f. contracts, are hardly needed to move soya bean meal from American ports to European feed mills. The existence of a very large number of linked paper transactions, where only the end buyer will take physical delivery of the goods themselves, is a characteristic of speculative dealings. Speculation commonly occurs on organised futures markets where investors deal according to the rules of the market, which include the provision by investors of margin deposits for each transaction and possibly governmental limits on the volume of speculative dealings by individual investors.[11] Nevertheless, where the physical market in goods of a particular type is subject to price fluctuations, it tends to be invaded by speculative activity that is not con-

6. See also Bridge, "International Private Commodity Sales" (1991) 19 Can. Bus. L.J. 485.

7. GAFTA House, 6 Chapel Court, Chapel Place, Rivington Street, London EC2A 3DQ.

8. Effective 1 April 1987. There is also for dealings in soya bean meal a specific form: GAFTA 97. Standard clauses, like those pertaining to *force majeure* and prohibition, are uniform throughout the various GAFTA forms dealing with c.i.f. contracts.

9. Federation of Oils, Seeds and Fats Associations Ltd., 20 St. Dunstans Hill, London EC3R 8HL.

10. GAFTA contracts also deem performance to have occurred in England, however effective that is supposed to be.

11. D. Courtney & E. C. Bettelheim, *An Investor's Guide to the Commodity Futures Market* (1986). For a discussion of the activities of the London Metal Exchange, see *Shearson Lehman Hutton Inc.* v. *Maclaine Watson & Co.* [1989] 2 Lloyd's Rep. 570.

strained by margin deposit and other controls.[12] The number of paper transactions correspondingly increases and a bull market in commodity prices may then emerge.

Traders entering into sales contracts for forward delivery will operate on a broad front, which requires them to match up their various purchase commitments with their resale commitments. A trader who has sold goods for July delivery will, therefore, become the purchaser of corresponding July goods. On a rising market, a trader will make money if his purchase commitment is given before his resale commitment; on a falling market, the opposite of course is true. All of this supposes that the trader wishes to balance his books for July in advance. Traders who do not incur a market risk forgo the chance of gain. Consequently, they may decide to run a further risk by taking a "long" or "short" position for July. They will be "long" if they anticipate a rising market, since their purchase entitlement for July exceeds their resale obligations. Conversely, they will be "short" if they anticipate a falling market by committing themselves to resales that exceed their purchases. A "long" or "short" seller will of course be able to go to the market in July itself seeking immediate performance, to buy the deficiency or sell the surplus as the case may be. In such a case, the trader's activities will be affected by market movement within the month of July itself.

When forward delivery contracts are entered into, details of the eventual shipment cannot be known, so provision has to be made for the seller to pass this vital information on to the buyer at a later date by a communication known as a notice of appropriation (GAFTA forms) or declaration of shipment (FOSFA forms). The notice or declaration will state the name of the vessel, the approximate shipment quantity and the date of the bill of lading.[13] It is the transmission of this information that permits myriad unconnected contracts to be linked together in a contractual string, in which all traders will be both buyer and seller, apart from the original seller and the final buyer.[14] Information emanating from the original seller will be passed on by succeeding parties, each step in the process adding to the chain.

The rules relating to the timely transmission of information are strict and are treated as contractual conditions by the courts,[15] the reason being that a tardy trader would otherwise be given an unfair speculative advantage over other traders if able to achieve unduly advantageous contractual matches in a moving market. The various contracts will commonly be for different amounts, since soya bean meal traders are prepared to break up shipments into separate parcels, based on units of 220 tonnes, the carrying capacity of Rhine barges. In lengthy sales strings it

12. A. Slabotsky, *Grain Contracts and Arbitration* (1984), pp. 57–58. For the emergence of informal commodities exchanges based upon multiple dealings among the major grain traders, see D. Morgan, *Merchants of Grain* (1980, Penguin), pp. 276–280.

13. For example, GAFTA 100 (also GAFTA 97) (c.i.f. soya bean meal), cl. 10, and FOSFA 24 (c.i.f. soya beans), cl. 11.

14. The goods may have been sold to the first c.i.f. seller on different terms: *Continental Grain Export Corp.* v. *S.T.M. Grain Ltd.* [1979] 2 Lloyd's Rep. 460 (North American Export Grain Association form no. 2 (f.o.b.)). The goods may be disposed of in numerous ways on discharge.

15. *Toepfer* v. *Lenersan-Poortman N.V.* [1980] 1 Lloyd's Rep. 143 (C.A.). See *State Trading Corp. of India* v. *M. Golodetz Ltd.* [1989] 2 Lloyd's Rep. 277, at p. 283 *per* Kerr L.J. (importance of time in string contracts); *Cie. Commerciale Sucres et Denrées* v. *C. Czarnikow Ltd.* [1990] 1 W.L.R. 1337 (H.L.). But see *Phibro Energy A.G.* v. *Nissho Iwai Corp.* [1991] 1 Lloyd's Rep. 38 (C.A.), where the seller had five days in which to inform the buyer whether its nomination of a ship was acceptable. This duty of the seller was treated as an intermediate stipulation but (*semble*) the seller's breach (in taking 14 days) went to the root of the contract.

is not uncommon for the same party to appear more than once. To abbreviate the settlement process, the contract forms contain circle clauses dispensing with the tender of shipping documents. What happens is that parties intervening between the two appearances of the same party are circled out, and a series of bilateral monetary settlements effected based upon the mean contract quantity and the lowest contract price in the circle. Each buyer will pay his seller the difference between their agreed price and the lowest of the prices paid by the various buyers in the circle.[16] The receipts of successful buyers will, therefore, exceed their outgoings.

2. THE EVENTS OF 1973

The trouble began with severe floods in the upper Mississippi valley after the 1973 spring thaw. The river and its tributaries became unnavigable in the upper reaches and several locks were closed for lengthy periods. This led to shipping delays in the Gulf ports, but the trouble appeared to have cleared up by the end of May. These events undoubtedly gave to sellers of soya bean meal the right to invoke the *force majeure* provision of the GAFTA 100 contract[17] which in consequence produced a large number of arbitrations.[18] But this was nothing in comparison with the arbitrations[19] and case law brought about by the intervention of the American Department of Commerce (the USDC), which was described as a "man-made disaster" with more far-reaching consequences than the floods.[20]

Although the soya bean crop eventually turned out to be a very good one, the USDC evidently feared a domestic shortage[21] and took the following steps to reduce the overseas shipment of soya bean meal. It should be understood that the USDC's concern was with the first export contract affecting a consignment of soya bean meal, and not at all with the succession of paper contracts making up the sale string. First of all, in Bulletin 84(a) (13 June), exporters were advised in a general way of the possibility of future quota restrictions and required to report anticipated exports for monitoring purposes. Secondly, in Bulletin 86 (27 June), an immediate embargo on the export of soya bean meal was announced with the promise of an export licensing system to be published on 2 July. This bulletin, in what later came to be described as one of the "loopholes", excepted from the embargo goods bound for export and already on a lighter vessel or in the course of being loaded on an exporting vessel. There is some suggestion that this panic measure was, to a degree at least, prompted by the cancellation on 20 June of a huge contractual commitment[22] owed by the Minnesota-based Cargill Inc. to a subsidiary, Tradax Export.[23]

In the third announcement, Bulletin 88 (2 July), the USDC introduced its licensing system. Exporters who had reported anticipated exports pursuant to Bulletin

16. For example, GAFTA 100, cl. 28, FOSFA 24, cl. 22. See Slabotsky, fn. 12 above, pp. 60–62.
17. *Toepfer* v. *Cremer* [1975] 1 Lloyd's Rep. 406; [1975] 2 Lloyd's Rep. 118 (C.A.).
18. Donaldson J. mentioned 260 in *Toepfer* v. *Cremer* (Q.B.D.), above.
19. In *Tradax Export S.A.* v. *André & Cie. S.A.* [1975] 2 Lloyd's Rep. 516, Donaldson J. set the number at over 1000.
20. *Ibid.*, 526. The intervention of the USDC was described as "extremely damaging" to the reputation of the US as a reliable soya bean exporter and as giving a boost to the competing Brazilian soya industry: Morgan, fn. 12, above, p. 293.
21. *André & Cie. S.A.* v. *Tradax Export S.A.* [1981] 2 Lloyd's Rep. 355, at p. 356.
22. 28 million bushels.
23. Morgan, fn. 12 above, p. 293.

84(a) were invited to apply for an export licence entitling them to ship 40% of the unfulfilled balance under each contract, provided that the exporter obtained from its buyer the latter's written consent to delivery of this quantity. Fourthly, Bulletin 93 (19 July) introduced another "loophole" exemption concerning goods that, on 27 June, were "en route to port, or in port earmarked for loading on an export vessel". Bulletin 98 (10 September) then went on to announce a licensing scheme permitting the export of all the agreed goods in contracts concluded after 8 September. Finally, Bulletin 101 (24 September) announced the end of all export controls with effect from 1 October.

The intervention of the USDC had a predictable impact on the market price of soya bean meal. Between 10 May and 18 June, the price had already climbed from \$338 to \$452.50 per tonne. On 29 June, it stood at \$590 and had risen to \$650 by 6 July, whence it declined to \$635 by 10 July and \$585 on 11 July before falling further to \$475 on 18 July. Needless to say, sellers were keen in the circumstances to seek relief from the usual consequences of non-performance by invoking the *force majeure* and prohibition of export provisions of GAFTA 100. Whilst, apparently, it would be just as much in the interest of buyers to resist sellers, it should be remembered that intermediate string traders are buyers and sellers of the same goods, and so each is possessed of an interest in pressing the other's arguments[24] against the previous seller or subsequent buyer as the case may be. The volume of arbitrations and litigation, therefore, calls for some explanation. It would appear to be due not just to pressure or apprehended pressure from the end buyer but also to a belief by some buyers that their sellers were insufficiently forthcoming in making available "loophole" cargo and correspondingly keen to take advantage of the prevailing seller's market.

As stated earlier, the litigation following the USDC export embargo concentrated primarily on two clauses of GAFTA 100—clause 21, the prohibition clause, and clause 22, the *force majeure* clause. Other clauses were also discussed at some length in the litigation, namely clause 9 (shippers' right to extend the shipment period and subsequent sellers' consequent right to do likewise), clause 10 (appropriation of shipments), clause 23 (relaying of notices), clause 26 (default procedure and settlement) and clause 27 (circle procedure). These provisions will be referred to where appropriate. Considerations of space prevent any discussion of waiver and the pre-1979 arbitration procedure, the former of which received extensive treatment in the case law,[25] and the latter of which played a very great part in shaping the form and dictating the frequency of references to the Commercial Court.

3. FORCE MAJEURE

According to clause 22 of GAFTA 100 as it stood at the relevant time:

"Sellers shall not be responsible for delay in shipment of the goods or any part thereof occasioned by any Act of God, strike, lockout, riot or civil commotion, combination of work-

24. *Toepfer* v. *Cremer*, fn. 17 above, Donaldson J. (Q.B.D.) ("each has a lively appreciation of the merits of the other's points of view"), p. 415.

25. It alleviated quite significantly in a number of cases the onerous burden on a seller seeking to rely on cl. 21.

men, breakdown of machinery, fire or any cause comprehended in the term 'force majeure'. If delay in shipment is likely to occur for any of the above reasons, Shippers shall give notice to their Buyers by telegram, telex or teleprinter or by similar advice within 7 consecutive days of the occurrence, or not less than 21 consecutive days before the commencement of the contract period, whichever is later. The notice shall state the reason(s) for the anticipated delay. If after giving such notice an extension to the shipping period is required, then Shippers shall give further notice not later than 2 business days after the last day of the contract period of shipment stating the port or ports of loading from which the goods [were] intended to be shipped, and shipments effected after the contract period shall be limited to the port or ports so nominated. If shipment be delayed for more than one calendar month, Buyers shall have the option of cancelling the delayed portion of the contract, such option to be exercised by Buyers giving notice to be received by Sellers not later than first business day after the additional calendar month. If Buyers do not exercise this option, such delayed portions shall be automatically extended for a further period of one month. If shipment under this clause be prevented during the further one month's extension, the contract shall be considered void. Buyers shall have no claim against Sellers for delay or non-shipment under this clause provided that Sellers shall have supplied to Buyers, if required, satisfactory evidence justifying the delay or non-fulfilment."

It is important to understand at the outset that clause 22 has a dual aspect. First of all, it permits the seller to claim a time extension where the shipment has been "delayed", and secondly, when at the end of the extension period the shipment is "prevented", the contract is cancelled. Whilst the expression "*force majeure*" covers both delay and prevention, it by no means follows that a *force majeure* event sufficient to excuse "delay" will in the end prove strong enough to justify a "prevention". The case law under consideration here does not satisfactorily resolve this issue. Besides a number of specific events, clause 22 makes general mention of *force majeure*. It seems to be an uncontroversial proposition that the severe flooding was a *force majeure* event justifying delay, whether because it was an Act of God or because it fell within the saving words "any cause" following the list of events. Furthermore, the case law clearly established that a governmental prohibition of the kind that occurred was also such an event, even though specifically dealt with in clause 21 too.

Now, clause 22 afforded in the first place only temporary relief to a beleaguered seller, while clause 21, if satisfied, produced an immediate and automatic contractual cancellation. In one sense, any conflict between the two clauses could be resolved by using clause 22 as a gateway into clause 21. A seller, given an extension under clause 22, would be able to invoke clause 21 (as well as clause 22 itself if the shipment is "prevented") at the end of the extension if still prevented from performance by governmental prohibition. Nevertheless, the language of the two clauses does not match well enough to allow such an easy progression. Clause 22 speaks of a "*force majeure*" event causing initially a "delay in shipment", while clause 21 speaks of prohibition "preventing fulfilment" of the contract. This, as we shall see, affects the nature of the burden the seller must discharge to invoke the relevant clause. A more serious discrepancy between the two clauses involves contrasting the automatic effect of clause 21 and the elective effect of clause 22. May a seller, whether the original shipper or a later seller holding the coat tails of the original shipper, claim a voluntary clause 22 extension when the event in question is caught by the automatic cancellation provisions of clause 21? Events of the kind contemplated in clauses 21 and 22 can have a drastic impact on market prices, so the answer to this question is important in settling issues of damage quantification and in timing the buyer's decision to seek alternative goods in the market.

A seller contemplating a clause 22 extension would do well to consider his position at the end of the extension period, which will run automatically to a second month if the delay in shipment persists, unless the buyer moves to cancel the contract at the end of the first month's extension.[26] In *Alfred C. Toepfer* v. *Peter Cremer*[27] an effective two-month extension of an April shipment served to delay the seller's eventual default and carry damages assessment forward to a date at the peak of the market.[28] In later cases, concerned with clause 21 prohibitions and June shipments, a valid extension under clause 22 would have favoured the seller with a declining market. Mr Justice Donaldson in *Toepfer* referred to clause 22 as being neither pro-seller nor pro-buyer,[29] but as dealing (seemingly in a bipartisan way) with circumstances affecting both parties' performance, though he was alive to the danger of sellers improperly playing the market. Nevertheless, it is hard to see how the *force majeure* event has the same impact on a buyer's performance as on a seller's. Moreover, the treatment of clause 22 in later case law is consistent with its status as an exemption clause favouring the seller, in that the burden of satisfying the clause plainly rests upon the seller.[30] On the other hand, Lord Wilberforce has remarked that clause 22 is a codification of the law relating to *force majeure* events.[31] This must be read subject to the role of clause 21. In addition, Lord Wilberforce was concerned with defective compliance by a seller with the clause 22 notice requirements. A seller does not have to invoke clause 22 at all,[32] so it is difficult to see why a seller may not choose instead to go to the general law. Where performance is impossible, as it would have to be under the general law, it is no longer a matter of delayed performance but of prevented performance. But if a seller chooses to invoke clause 22, then the contract will be cancelled after one or two months as the case may be, if shipment is prevented (and not merely delayed) by the end of the extension.

The conflict between the automatic clause 21 and the elective clause 22, noted above, was played out in the cases. In *Tradax Export S.A.* v. *André & Cie. S.A.*, Donaldson J. took the point that a seller could not avail himself of clause 21 where

26. *Toepfer* v. *Cremer*, fn. 17 above; *Bremer Handelsgesellschaft m.b.H.* v. *Finagrain S.A.* [1981] 1 Lloyd's Rep. 224.

27. Fn. 17 above. Though able to claim a cl. 22 extension, the seller would later have to show "prevention" for cancellation under the same clause.

28. The precise fixing of the date of default (10 July instead of 11 July) was overturned by the House of Lords in *Bremer Handelsgesellschaft m.b.H.* v. *Vanden Avenne-Izegem P.V.B.A.* [1978] 2 Lloyd's Rep. 109. See also *Bunge S.A.* v. *Kruse* [1979] 1 Lloyd's Rep. 279. The point was a difficult one. Under, say, a June shipment, the seller would have the first 10 days of July to appropriate a shipment from a Great Lakes, Gulf or East Coast port, unless the contract were extended under cl. 9 or cl. 22 or both. Failing an extension, did the seller default on July 10, the last permissible date, or on July 11? *Bremer* v. *Vanden* favoured 11 July, since the seller had until midnight of 10 July to perform and so would not be in breach until the first moment of 11 July. Cf. the Sale of Goods Act 1979 rules on market damages for non-acceptance and non-delivery (ss.50(3) and 51(3)) which set damages according to the performance date (the last date in a range). The market in soya bean meal declined 50 dollars per tonne between 10 and 11 July.

29. [1975] 1 Lloyd's Rep. 406, at p. 417.

30. *Tradax Export S.A.* v. *André & Cie. S.A.* [1976] 1 Lloyd's Rep. 416 (C.A.).

31. *Bremer* v. *Vanden*, fn. 28 above, *per* Lord Wilberforce, at p. 116.

32. *Ibid.*, p. 115.

he was "obliged"[33] (*sic*) to operate clause 22. In the Court of Appeal, Lord Denning could see no reason why a governmental prohibition should not fall within both clauses.[34] Prohibitions, depending on the facts, might either delay shipment or prevent fulfilment of the contract. Further, clause 21 could pre-empt a clause 22 extension if circumstances of delay give way to impossibility within the "contract period", which in his view ran to 30 June in the case of June shipments.[35] This view was apparently rejected in the House of Lords in *Bremer Handelsgesellschaft m.b.H.* v. *Vanden Avenne-Izegem P.V.B.A.*,[36] where Lord Wilberforce contemplated a valid clause 22 notice, which the seller was not required to serve,[37] extending the "contract period".[38] In the circumstances consequent upon the 27 June prohibition of export, even the 2 July licensing of partial export, it could not be said for certain how long the governmental intervention would last. Any attempt to pre-empt a clause 22 extension with a clause 21 cancellation would, therefore, be circumstantially premature.

While a clause 22 extension cannot be prevented by clause 21, what of the seller who, within the extension period, becomes able to perform? Must that seller perform as soon as possible or within a reasonable time, or may that seller perform at any time up to the end of the extension period? The point was not fully argued in *Bremer* v. *Vanden Avenne-Izegem*. Nevertheless, Viscount Dilhorne thought the seller was protected by clause 22 only to the extent that he was still impeded by *force majeure*,[39] while Lord Russell invoked earlier authority[40] to give the seller the whole of the extension period.[41] The latter approach is less likely to attract litigation, appears to be the one contemplated by clause 22 itself, and so is to be preferred.

The extension of the shipment period under clause 22 at the expense of clause 21 left one difficulty unresolved. Clause 22 gives the seller a period of grace of two business days after the end of the contract period in which to avail himself of a clause 22 extension. This left the status of a June shipment contract in some considerable doubt between 30 June and 4 July.[42] If the seller elected not to extend under clause 22, then the contract had already been cancelled on 30 June if the requirements of clause 21 were satisfied. If the contract was extended in early July by the seller acting under clause 22, then a contractual nullity (if clause 21 was satisfied at the end of June) was apparently unilaterally revived. In *Bremer Handelsgesellschaft m.b.H.* v. *Finagrain Compagnie Commerciale Agricole et Financière S.A.*[43] Mr Justice Robert Goff plainly had difficulty with this problem[44] but ruled in

33. [1975] 2 Lloyd's Rep. 516, at p. 529. Cf. Lord Wilberforce in the House of Lords.
34. Fn. 30 above, at p. 421.
35. *Ibid.*
36. Fn. 28 above.
37. Cf. Donaldson J. at first instance. Cl. 9 extensions, which diminish the seller's price entitlement on a sliding scale, are also voluntary: *Tradax Export S.A.* v. *André & Cie. S.A.*, fn. 29; above; *Bremer* v. *Vanden*, fn. 28 above; *Tradax Export S.A.* v. *Cook Industries Inc.* [1982] 1 Lloyd's Rep. 385 (C.A.); *Bremer* v. *Finagrain*, fn. 26 above.
38. Fn. 28 above, at p. 115.
39. *Ibid.*, p. 120.
40. *European Grain & Shipping Co.* v. *J. H. Rayner & Co.* [1970] 2 Lloyd's Rep. 239.
41. Fn. 28 above, at p. 130.
42. 1 July 1973 was a Sunday.
43. Fn. 26 above.
44. *Ibid.*, p. 231.

favour of the clause 22 extension, diminishing a conceptual difficulty to the practical one of the buyer's ignorance of whether the contract was alive or not between the two dates. Not easy to justify in literal terms, this is a sensible resolution of a construction difficulty revealed by the rough edges of clauses 21 and 22 and still present in the current version of the GAFTA form.

Clause 22 requires the seller to point to a "delay in shipment". It has been asserted that the burden on a seller meeting the requirements of clause 22 is the same as that for clause 21.[45] But clause 21 speaks of prevention, not delay, and the clause 21 cases clearly demonstrate that the seller does not have to show that the prohibition of export prevented fulfilment of the particular contract. The cases on clause 22, on the other hand, require the seller to be somewhat specific.[46] In *Avimex S.A.* v. *Dewulf & Cie.*[47] the seller had to show that the *force majeure* event delayed shipment of the goods intended for the contract which, since the present seller was a string seller, meant that the string had to be traced back to an affected shipper. Furthermore, Mr Justice Robert Goff in *Tradax Export S.A.* v. *Cook Industries Inc.* made it quite plain that the original shipper had to have goods, intended for the first string trader, that were in fact delayed, and that such a delay would not be established unless the goods would have been shipped within the original contract period.[48] A seller able to show only that the shipper would have satisfied half his overall June commitments by the end of that month was, therefore, unable to demonstrate that his particular shipment had been delayed.[49]

Assuming that the seller was able to invoke clause 22 to justify a delay in shipment, it remained to consider the nature of the notice that had to be served. First of all, clause 22 appears to contemplate two notices, the first of which must have been served if the seller wished to remain free to extend at a later date. The first notice would be a forewarning of delay, and would have to be served 21 days before the commencement of the contract period or within seven days of the *force majeure* occurrence, whichever date was the later. On the facts of the Mississippi cases, most of which were concerned with June shipments, only the latter of the two above deadlines could have been relevant. Even then, a seller prompted by the 27 June prohibition to seek an extension would be unable to wait the full seven days, since his decision to avail himself of the clause could be exercised no later than 3 July.[50] Clause 22 was not designed for the catastrophic impact of the 1973 events,

45. *Bremer Handelsgesellschaft m.b.H.* v. *C. Mackprang Jr. (No. 1)* [1979] 1 Lloyd's Rep. 221, *per* Lord Denning M.R., at p. 224.

46. *Tradax Export S.A.* v. *André & Cie. S.A.* [1975] 2 Lloyd's Rep. 516, *per* Donaldson J., at p. 529 (but cf. [1976] 1 Lloyd's Rep. 416, *per* Browne L.J., at pp. 426–427); *Warinco A.G.* v. *Mauthner* [1978] 1 Lloyd's Rep. 151, *per* Megaw L.J., at p. 154; *Fairclough Dodd and Jones Ltd.* v. *J.H. Vantol Ltd.* [1956] 2 Lloyd's Rep. 437 (H.L.); *European Grain & Shipping Co.* v. *J.H. Rayner & Co.* [1970] 2 Lloyd's Rep. 239; *Avimex S.A.* v. *Dewulf & Cie.* [1979] 2 Lloyd's Rep. 57, *per* Robert Goff J., at p. 67; *Tradax Export S.A.* v. *Cook Industries Inc.* [1981] 1 Lloyd's Rep. 236, *per* Robert Goff J., at p. 242, [1982] 1 Lloyd's Rep. 385, *per* Kerr L.J., at p. 391; *Continental Grain Export Corp.* v. *S. T. M. Grain Ltd.* [1979] 2 Lloyd's Rep. 460, *per* Robert Goff J., at pp. 473–474.

47. Fn. 46 above.

48. Fn. 46 above, at p. 242.

49. *Tradax Export S.A.* v. *Cook Industries Inc.*, fn. 46 above. See also *Bremer Handelsgesellschaft m.b.H.* v. *C. Mackprang Jr. (No. 2)* [1980] 1 Lloyd's Rep. 210, [1981] 1 Lloyd's Rep. 292.

50. If he was the shipper. A string seller would also have to prove no delay in the transmission of notices down the string.

which prevented a relatively leisurely progression from warning notice to notification of extension. This is well recognised in the cases, which realistically declined to withdraw the protection of clause 22 from sellers issuing a combined warning notice and extension notification.[51]

An effective notice invoking clause 22 had to be given on time or was ineffectual,[52] a position consistent with the orthodoxy that time provisions in commercial contracts are of the essence of the contract.[53] A prerequisite to the validity of any shipper's clause 22 notice was that it take effect for, say, the month of June at any time before the end of business on 3 July. String sellers would also have to demonstrate that they and all prior string sellers had passed the notice on without delay. One difficulty concerned the effective date of the notice and whether it turned on the giving or the receipt of the notice. The buyers in *Bremer* v. *Vanden Avenne-Izegem*[54] argued that a notice was not given without delay when, under clause 23, dealing with the transmission of notices, it was deemed to have been received by them on the following day. This rather weak point was convincingly refuted by Lord Wilberforce[55] who, on a construction of clause 22, demonstrated its preoccupation with the transmission rather than the receipt of notices.

A notice defective for reasons of time could be the subject of a waiver by the buyer.[56] Waiver also surfaced more than once in relation to the nomination of a port or ports in the clause 22 notice. Clause 22 requires the notice to state "the port or ports of loading from which the goods were intended to be shipped" and requires the delayed shipper to ship from that port or ports. The use of the past tense, as well as the scope of clause 22 for dealing with a range of impediments, suggests a choice of port before the *force majeure* event and rules out a change of mind, even where it seems this might be for the benefit of both parties. The cases at this point relaxed somewhat the proposition dealt with above that clause 22 is concerned with specific shipments. Donaldson J. plainly saw the commercial sense of refraining from probing inchoate shipping plans and let pass a nomination of "Mississippi river port(s)".[57] He gave the seller more leeway still in *Tradax* v. *André*[58] when letting through "the usual ports on the Lakes, East Coast, Gulf", which all happen to be ten-day ports for the purpose of appropriating the bill of lading under clause 10. The Court of Appeal,[59] however, disagreed with a ruling that subjected the seller to practically no control at all.

In *Bremer* v. *Vanden Avenne-Izegem*[60] a defective notice of "the usual ports on the Lakes/East Coast, Gulf" was waived by the buyer. Dissenting on the validity of

51. See for example *Tradax Export S.A.* v. *André & Cie. S.A.*, fn. 46 above.

52. *Tradax Export S.A.* v. *André & Cie. S.A.*, fn. 46 above, *per* Donaldson J., at p. 524, *per* Lord Denning M.R., at pp. 423–424; *Avimex S.A.* v. *Dewulf & Cie*, fn. 46 above, at p. 67; *Bremer Handelsgesellschaft m.b.H.* v. *Westzucker m.b.H.* [1981] 1 Lloyd's Rep. 207, *per* Robert Goff J., at p. 211. Cf. advices under cl. 21, below.

53. Fn. 15 above.

54. [1978] 2 Lloyd's Rep. 109 (H.L.).

55. *Ibid.*, p. 116.

56. *Bremer* v. *Vanden*, fn. 54 above; *Toepfer* v. *Cremer* [1975] 1 Lloyd's Rep. 406.

57. *Toepfer* v. *Cremer*, fn. 56 above. See, in the Court of Appeal, Lord Denning's example of alternative ports: [1975] 2 Lloyd's Rep. 118, at p. 123.

58. Fn. 46 above.

59. Fn. 46 above.

60. Fn. 54 above.

the notice, Lords Salmon[61] and Russell[62] would have allowed the nomination,[63] since the general prohibition made it an irrelevant matter which port the seller had in mind. Lord Wilberforce,[64] with whom Lord Keith concurred, and Viscount Dilhorne[65] disapproved of the notice for different reasons. Viscount Dilhorne asserted that clause 22 was not concerned with original shipment intentions but with the shipper's intention at the time of seeking the extension, but in his view an undiscriminating notice like the present one could not be said to be nomination at all.[66] Truer to the literal reading of clause 22, Lord Wilberforce declared it was concerned with the original intention and, unlike the dissentients, declined to give it a differential reading according to the particular *force majeure* event. In his view, the mention of East Coast ports plainly contradicted this shipper's original though inchoate intention and so the notice was bad. On the whole, while the cases do not force the shipper to show a firm choice of original port, they demonstrate that it is original intentions or dispositions that count, not subsequent possibilities.

4. PROHIBITION OF EXPORT

At the time of the 1973 events, clause 21 stated:

"In case of prohibition of export, blockade or hostilities or in case of any executive or legislative act done by or on behalf of the Government of the country of origin or of the territory where the port or ports of shipment named herein is/are situate, preventing fulfilment, this Contract or any unfulfilled portion thereof so affected shall be cancelled. In the event of shipment proving impossible during the contract period by reason of any of the causes enumerated herein, Sellers shall advise Buyers without delay with the reasons therefor. If required, Sellers must produce proof to justify their claim for cancellation."

This clause gave rise to numerous difficulties. A seller seeking to take advantage of clause 21 so as to claim the contract automatically cancelled had to prove first of all that shipment from the country of origin[67] had become impossible. If that seller was also the shipper of the goods, he would also have to prove that he had no "loophole" cargo available to satisfy the contract. The loopholes permitted by the USDC concerned cargo in the process of being loaded on an export vessel or on a lighter barge ready for loading, supplemented later by goods earmarked for loading but still in port or in transit to the port. It seems to have been understood that shippers would normally have appropriated such cargoes to particular contracts but, given the common practice of appropriating c.i.f. contracts once afloat, this is not an irresistible inference.

Most of the cases involve string sellers and deal with the intricate business of tracing the sales string back to an affected shipper. A seller physically unable to trace the shipper, or reaching an earlier seller who had taken a short position and had not

61. Fn. 54 above, at pp. 123–124.
62. Fn. 54 above, at p. 130.
63. Even though the seller, before the embargo, had soya bean meal in, or in transit to, certain Lakes and Gulf ports, but not East Coast ports.
64. Fn. 54 above, at pp. 115–116.
65. Fn. 54 above, at p. 119.
66. *Quaere* "the usual Mississippi ports"?
67. All ports had to be knocked out: *Tradax Export S.A.* v. *André & Cie. S.A.*, fn. 46 above, *per* Donaldson J., at p. 529; *Warinco A.G.* v. *Mauthner*, fn. 46 above.

yet entered into a contract leading back to an affected shipper,[68] would be unable to rely upon clause 21. In the course of the multiple litigation following the prohibition, numerous other loopholes emerged, some of which were valid and some of which were judicially dismissed. These loopholes and sellers fell outside the reach of the USDC's bulletins, which dealt with the parties to the export contract, namely the shipper and the first buyer.

Apart from the intricate business of tracing the string and plugging the loopholes, a number of other points were discussed in the clause 21 cases. First of all, the argument of buyers that sellers, in the light of the warning bulletin of 13 June, ought to have performed their contracts before the embargo of 27 June, was tried and failed. The issue concerned the seller's obligation of due diligence[69] and the findings of fact in one case showed there was no real likelihood of an embargo at all, still less a strong likelihood.[70]

Another issue concerned the giving of advice of prohibition "without delay". It was argued that in this regard time was of the essence, but the argument failed largely because of the generality of the wording.[71] The authoritative view is that the duty to advise without delay is an intermediate stipulation that might in an appropriate case produce a breach going to the root of the contract.[72] It seems more sensible and more faithful to the language of clause 21, however, to regard the seller's duty to advise as distinct and consequential upon a cancellation already effected,[73] as concerned rather with the consequences of a frustrated contract.[74]

Another argument raised by sellers was that clause 21 could be relied upon despite the contract in question having been circled out under clause 27, predictably rejected on the ground that the seller's duty to deliver had been commuted to a perfectly practicable duty to pay a sum of money by the relevant date.[75] Conversely, the buyer was unable to invoke the circle clause against a seller successfully closing the loopholes, since the circle clause explicitly and understandably defers to the terms of the prohibition clause.[76] However, the buyer was able to resist a defaulting seller's attempt to bring in the circle clause to his advantage[77] once the prohibition defence had failed.

Some difficulty arose in respect of the application of clause 21 to partial prohibi-

68. See *Bremer Handelsgesellschaft m.b.H.* v. *C. Mackprang Jr. (No. 2)*, fn. 49 above, at p. 301; *Bunge S.A.* v. *Deutsche Conti Handelsgesellschaft m.b.H.* [1979] 2 Lloyd's Rep. 435.

69. *Ross T. Smyth & Co.* v. *W.N. Lindsay Ltd.* [1953] 2 Lloyd's Rep. 378; *Tradax Export S.A.* v. *André & Cie. S.A.*, fn. 46 above (C.A.). The c.i.f. seller's freedom to ship or procure or adopt shipment on any day within the agreed range is abridged where the shipment is prevented for part of the period and the seller is able with due diligence to perform within the remainder of the period.

70. *Continental Grain Export Corp.* v. *S. T. M. Grain Ltd.* [1979] 2 Lloyd's Rep. 460, at pp. 474–475.

71. *Bremer* v. *Vanden*, fn. 54 above, reversing on this point *Tradax Export S.A.* v. *Andre & Cie. S.A.*, fn. 46 above.

72. *Bremer* v. *Vanden*, fn. 54 above, *per* Lord Wilberforce, at p. 115, *per* Lord Russell, at p. 130; *Bunge S.A.* v. *Kruse* [1979] 1 Lloyd's Rep. 279, *per* Brandon J., at pp. 290–291.

73. *Bremer* v. *Vanden*, fn. 54 above, *per* Viscount Dilhorne (*semble*), at p. 121.

74. *Bremer* v. *Vanden*, fn. 54 above, *per* Lord Salmon, at p. 128. At the relevant time, FOSFA contracts did not contain an advice provision, so there was nothing to impede an automatic cancellation: *Continental Grain* v. *S. T. M. Grain*, fn. 70 above. See now the current text of FOSFA 24, cl. 20 ("Sellers . . . shall advise buyers with due despatch").

75. *Tradax Export S.A.* v. *Giuseppe & Figli* [1981] 1 Lloyd's Rep. 353.

76. *Bremer Handelsgesellschaft m.b.H.* v. *Westzucker G.m.b.H. (No. 2)* [1981] 1 Lloyd's Rep. 214.

77. *Tradax Export S.A.* v. *Cook Industries Inc.* [1981] 1 Lloyd's Rep. 236, [1982] 1 Lloyd's Rep. 385; *Cook Industries Inc.* v. *Tradax Export S.A.* [1983] 1 Lloyd's Rep. 327.

tions of the present type. Clause 21 provides that, in the event of a prohibition "preventing fulfilment . . . this Contract or any unfulfilled portion thereof so affected shall be cancelled". Countervailing interpretations were advanced that the clause could only apply where the prevention was complete—hence it would be inapplicable to 60% embargoes—and that the seller could be excused in full if his performance had become only partly impossible. These arguments were rejected[78] as courts preferred sense to literalism by holding that a seller could be partly excused to the extent of a partial prohibition.[79]

It was firmly established at an early date that the seller bore the burden of demonstrating that the terms of clause 21 had been satisfied.[80] The presence of the loopholes meant that it was insufficient for the seller merely to show the embargo.[81] Initially, there was some doubt as to what more the seller had to prove. In *Tradax* v. *André*, Lord Denning spoke of a string seller having "to prove that the shipper, at the head of the string, had goods ready to ship and that shipment was prevented by the prohibition of export".[82] But many such instances would have fallen within the loopholes in the bulletins and the House of Lords in *Bremer* v. *Vanden Avenne-Izegem* preferred to lighten the seller's load. It was for the seller to establish the embargo and fill in the necessary loopholes, leaving it then to the buyer to show that shipment would not have taken place in any event for whatever reason.[83] It was not enough for a seller merely to show that its purchase and sale commitments were balanced, for that merely showed it had not taken a long position.[84]

As stated above, the burden on a string seller was heavier than that on the shipper in that the former also had to trace back to the shipper. These efforts should be appraised against a general statement of the seller's responsibilities, applicable whether or not the seller is in string. In the event of a prohibition, the seller must prove that he has no goods of the contract description available to fulfil the contract and cannot by reasonable means procure such goods.[85] This means that the seller must still show the impact of the embargo on his intended source of supply[86] to

78. *Bremer* v. *Vanden*, fn. 54 above.

79. *Ibid.*; *Continental Grain* v. *S. T. M. Grain*, fn. 70 above, at p. 471; *André & Cie. S.A.* v. *Tradax Export S.A.* [1981] 2 Lloyd's Rep. 355, *per* Mocatta J., at pp. 358–359.

80. *Tradax Export S.A.* v. *André & Cie. S.A.* [1976] 1 Lloyd's Rep. 416 (C.A.); *Bremer* v. *Vanden*, fn. 54 above.

81. *Bremer Handelsgesellschaft m.b.H.* v. *C. Mackprang Jr. (No. 1)* [1979] 1 Lloyd's Rep. 221 (C.A.); *André & Cie. S.A.* v. *Ets. Michel Blanc & Fils* [1979] 2 Lloyd's Rep. 427 (C.A.); *Bunge S.A.* v. *Deutsche Conti Handelsgesellschaft m.b.H.* [1979] 2 Lloyd's Rep. 435 (C.A.).

82. [1976] 1 Lloyd's Rep. 416, at p. 423. Counsel for the buyer in *Bremer* v. *Vanden*, fn. 54 above, sought to tighten the screw by asserting that the seller could not rely on a cl. 9 extension that it might have exercised but for the intervening embargo: see *Continental Grain* v. *S. T. M. Grain*, fn. 70 above, at p. 470.

83. *Bremer* v. *Vanden*, fn. 54 above; *André & Cie. S.A.* v. *Ets. Michel Blanc & Fils* [1977] 2 Lloyd's Rep. 166; *Cook Industries Inc.* v. *Meunerie Liégeois S.A.* [1981] 1 Lloyd's Rep. 359, at p. 363. Robert Goff J. in *Continental Grain* v. *S. T. M. Grain*, fn. 70 above, at p. 471 would not even have given the buyer the opportunity of showing that the seller could not have performed in any event (*sed quaere*, since the clause refers to governmental intervention "preventing", not "prohibiting", fulfilment?).

84. *Bremer Handelsgesellschaft m.b.H.* v. *C. Mackprang Jr. (No. 2)* [1981] 1 Lloyd's Rep. 292 (C.A.).

85. *Ross T. Smyth & Co.* v. *W. N. Lindsay Ltd.*, fn. 69 above; *Continental Grain* v. *S. T. M. Grain*, fn. 70 above, at p. 473.

86. *Cook Industries Inc.* v. *Meunerie Liégeois S.A.*, fn. 83 above, at p. 363; *Bremer Handelsgesellschaft m.b.H.* v. *C. Mackprang Jr. (No. 1)*, fn. 81 above.

demonstrate that the embargo prevents fulfilment of the contract and that no loophole cargo is available. This is because clause 21 focuses on the reasons for non-shipment and not upon a seller's reasons for non-delivery. In the process, the string seller has to recreate the string.[87]

In the case of linked contracts that proceed to due performance, the string can be traced through the notices of appropriation, which identify the carrying vessel and the contract quantity. It may, however, be physically difficult to follow a lengthy string to its source. Moreover, when performance of the various contracts is interfered with before the notices of appropriation are served, it becomes more difficult to trace the string, and recourse has to be had instead to other communications between sellers and buyers, namely, notices of extended shipment under clause 9 and of *force majeure* under clause 22, and any advice of prohibition under clause 21.

But there is a substantial practical problem associated with tracing the string through these alternative communications. It lies in the practice of traders cautiously relaying these various communications to all of their buyers, instead of selecting their buyers individually. As these various communications work their way down the distribution chain, it is not a series of discrete strings that is produced but a lattice of interconnected contracts.[88] A buyer down the distribution chain is, therefore, faced with a maze if he is to trace a path to the shipper, and it may be "impossible for one trader to trace a notice back to the shipper who originally set it in motion".[89] Such a buyer is not permitted by *ipse dixit* to select any one of these possible shippers and establish the embargo and the absence of loopholes in relation to that shipper.[90] In particular, a seller may not treat the shipper of the permitted 40% as the shipper of the prohibited 60%.[91] It is, after all, common practice in the soya bean meal trade to break up shipments into separate parcels appropriated to different contracts.[92] Consequently, the string seller has to account for all relevant or notional shippers, namely, all those from whom notices of appropriation were due,[93] even if not every link in the chain can be proved.[94] Failing all attempts to identify the relevant shippers, a string seller would be driven to identify and eliminate all possible shippers,[95] an arduous task that failed in one case because of the seller's inability to discover the name of an unidentified shipper on a "mystery ship",[96] which might have contained June cargo.

A successful identification of the relevant shipper or shippers is not properly accomplished if the notices lead back to one trader, three-quarters of whose total

87. *Bremer Handelsgesellschaft m.b.H.* v. *Continental Grain Co.* [1983] 1 Lloyd's Rep. 269, *per* Mustill J., at p. 274.

88. *Cook Industries Inc.* v. *Meunerie Liégeois S.A.*, fn. 83 above, at pp. 363–365.

89. *Bremer* v. *Continental Grain*, fn. 87 above, at p. 273. Clearly, a June shipment cannot be traced back to a July shipper: *Continental Grain* v. *S. T. M. Grain*, fn. 70 above.

90. *Continental Grain* v. *S. T. M. Grain*, fn. 70 above.

91. *Bremer* v. *Mackprang (No. 2)*, fn. 84 above; *Bremer* v. *Continental Grain*, fn. 70 above.

92. See the excellent and concise description of trading conditions of the board of appeal in *André & Cie*. v. *Tradax Export S.A.* [1983] 1 Lloyd's Rep. 254, at pp. 259–260.

93. *Cook Industries Inc.* v. *Meunerie Liégeois S.A.*, fn. 83 above.

94. *Bremer* v. *Continental Grain*, fn. 87 above.

95. *Cook Industries Inc.* v. *Tradax Export S.A.*, fn. 77 above; *Bremer Handelsgesellschaft m.b.H.* v. *Westzucker G.m.b.H. (No. 3)* [1989] 1 Lloyd's Rep. 582.

96. *Bremer* v. *Westzucker (No. 3)*, fn. 95 above, at p. 585.

contractual commitments were to be settled by its own shipments and one-quarter by purchases in string,[97] for this leaves unaccounted for the identity of the shipper of shippers in respect of that one-quarter. Identifying the shipper on the balance of probabilities[98] did not involve an arithmetical comparison of the seller's commitments and sources of supply. Thus a seller failed whose established practice it was to retain complete freedom when appropriating to contracts goods that it had shipped or that came to it from another shipper.[99]

The task of the string seller was not completed when the relevant shipper was found and the effect of the embargo on the shipper demonstrated. It had to be shown that the shipper had no loophole cargo in transit or on a lighter barge.[100] In a July shipment case, the seller's efforts were destroyed when the transit loophole appeared on 19 July and the seller was unable to plug it.[101] A string seller would also have to show that he was not long,[102] for nothing in the bulletins prevented him from appropriating more than 40% to a contract. Likewise, he would also have to show that the relevant shipper was not long in unappropriated goods[103] shipped before 27 June. Logically, a string seller should have had to establish that no prior sellers were long, but this impracticably onerous requirement was rejected as an unwelcome innovation.[104]

A similar infusion of judicial common sense met the contentions of certain buyers that sellers had to scour the high seas in search of unappropriated goods afloat. If already shipped before 27 June, these would have escaped the embargo and their existence was perfectly possible, given the prevalence of sales afloat of c.i.f. cargoes. It takes little imagination to realise the effect on a rampant market of large numbers of traders chasing relatively modest quantities of goods as prices escalated dramatically. Any such requirement was roundly rejected by the authorities[105] on practical rather than logical grounds[106] which appeared not to depend on the construction of the contractual provision itself.[107] The requirement was also rejected even in respect of a variant of the standard soya bean meal, which was not traded in the same volume and which did not attract the same degree of speculative interest.[108] Reasoning of a similar kind relieved the seller from having to compete

97. *Bremer* v. *Continental Grain*, fn. 87 above.

98. *Vanden Avenne-Izegem P.V.B.A.* v. *Finagrain S.A.* [1985] 2 Lloyd's Rep. 99. In *Tradax Export S.A.* v. *Cook Industries Inc.*, fn. 77 above, the court declined to go behind a board of appeal finding that did not state the underlying evidence.

99. *Bremer Handelsgesellschaft m.b.H.* v. *Bunge Corp.* [1983] 1 Lloyd's Rep. 476 (C.A.).

100. *Bremer* v. *Westzucker (No. 2)*, fn. 76 above (seller successful).

101. *Raiffeisen Hauptgenossenschaft* v. *Louis Dreyfus & Co.* [1981] 1 Lloyd's Rep. 345.

102. *Cook* v. *Meunerie Liégeois S.A.*, fn. 83 above, at pp. 365–366; *Tradax* v. *Cook*, fn. 77 above; *André* v. *Tradax*, fn. 92 above. A seller did not for present purposes become long when September cargo was released for export: *André* v. *Tradax*, *ibid.* See also *Cook* v. *Tradax*, fn. 77 above.

103. *Tradax* v. *Cook*, fn. 77 above.

104. *André* v. *Tradax*, fn. 92 above, at p. 263.

105. *Tradax Export S.A.* v. *André & Cie. S.A.* [1976] 1 Lloyd's Rep. 416 (C.A.); *Bremer* v. *Vanden*, fn. 54 above; *Bremer Handelsgesellschaft m.b.H.* v. *Finagrain S.A.* [1981] 1 Lloyd's Rep. 224; *Bunge* v. *Kruse*, fn. 72 above, *per* Brandon J., at p. 292. Cf. *Tradax* v. *Cook*, fn. 77 above, *per* Robert Goff J., at p. 245.

106. *Bremer* v. *Vanden*, fn. 54 above, *per* Lord Wilberforce, at p. 115.

107. See *Tradax* v. *Cook*, fn. 77 above, *per* Robert Goff J., at p. 245, where he laid emphasis on the seller in *Bremer* v. *Vanden*, fn. 54 above, also being a shipper.

108. *Bremer* v. *Finagrain*, fn. 105 above. Contracts with a protein content other than 44% are now catered for by GAFTA 98.

for unappropriated cargoes on lighter vessels[109] or having to search the world for spare soya bean meal on shore in silos.[110]

The course of identifying relevant shippers and plugging loopholes brought to light in certain cases the existence of cargoes eligible to satisfy a number of competing contracts. This raised the related issue of whether a cargo that had to be subdivided into small amounts should be ignored for present purposes. A mechanical application of frustration principles might have it that a seller choosing to appropriate spare cargo to one contract could not claim to be correspondingly discharged from the other contracts, since his inability to perform would stem from his voluntary action and not from any supervening event. But these cases concern the application, not of frustration principles as such, but of an express clause in a commodities contract.[111] A seller cannot be held to be the cause of non-fulfilment of a particular contract if he has acted in a way that is both reasonable and implicitly sanctioned by the contract.[112] The soya bean meal cases are more generous to the seller than the general law of frustration, but it is not clear whether the somewhat tentative expressions of the position lend support to a seller who appropriates spare cargo in any reasonable way or to a seller who apportions spare cargo *pro rata* among all his various buyers.[113] The better view would appear to support any reasonable action on the seller's part,[114] bearing in mind the seller's duty by reasonable means to procure loophole cargo.[115] It should be remembered that trading activity in this field is volatile and fast-moving and does not tolerate extensive and expensive enquiries.[116] Trade practice could well prove a fruitful source of judicial assistance in the matter. Finally, any apportionment exercise that would only yield trivial rewards for a particular buyer would, on that ground alone, be dismissed as "an exercise in logic destructive of commercial reality"[117] and the seller would be released on *de minimis* grounds.[118]

5. CONCLUSION

These cases reveal more about trade practice and understanding than about legal principle. A disenchanted reader might say that they should be commemorated by

109. *Bunge S.A.* v. *Kruse* [1979] 1 Lloyd's Rep. 279, [1980] 2 Lloyd's Rep. 142.
110. *André & Cie. S.A.* v. *Ets. Michel Blanc & Fils* [1979] 2 Lloyd's Rep. 427.
111. Cf. *J. Lauritzen A.S.* v. *Wijsmuller B.V.* [1990] 1 Lloyd's Rep. 1 (C.A.), discussed in greater detail by McKendrick at pp. 46–50 above. See also Treitel, *The Law of Contract* (8th Edn., 1991), pp. 774–776.
112. *Westfälische Central Genossenschaft G.m.b.H.* v. *Seabright Chemicals Ltd.* (unreported, but discussed in *Bremer* v. *Continental Grain*, fn. 87 above).
113. See *Bremer* v. *Vanden*, fn. 54 above, *per* Lord Wilberforce, at p. 115; *Intertradex S.A.* v. *Lesieur-Tourteaux S.A.R.L.* [1978] 2 Lloyd's Rep. 509 (C.A.), *per* Lord Denning M.R., at p. 513; *Bremer* v. *Mackprang (No. 1)*, fn. 81 above, *per* Lord Denning M.R., at p. 224, *per* Stephenson L.J., at p. 228; *Continental Grain* v. *S. T. M. Grain*, fn. 70 above, at p. 473; *André* v. *Tradax*, fn. 92 above, *per* Kerr L.J. at p. 263; *Bremer* v. *Continental Grain*, fn. 87 above, *per* Mustill J., at pp. 280–281, *per* Ackner L.J., at pp. 291–292.
114. See *Westfälische* v. *Seabright*, fn. 112 above, cited with approval in *Bremer* v. *Continental Grain*, fn. 87 above, at pp. 292–293.
115. *Ross T. Smyth* v. *W.N. Lindsay*, fn. 69 above, cited in *Continental Grain* v. *S. T. M. Grain*, fn. 170 above, at p. 473.
116. *Bremer* v. *Continental Grain*, fn. 87 above, *per* Mustill J., at pp. 280–281.
117. *Bremer* v. *Vanden*, fn. 54 above, *per* Lord Russell, at p. 131.
118. *Bremer* v. *Vanden*, fn. 54 above; *Bremer* v. *Continental Grain*, fn. 87 above.

the erection in St. Mary Axe in the City of London of a tomb dedicated to the unknown shipper. Representatives of the various soya bean meal traders still solvent might be called upon to lay wreaths every year on 27 June. Certainly, the tension between seeing each trading contract as a separate entity and seeing the connected contracts as an integral whole, evident throughout the GAFTA and other commodities forms, led in this instance to a body of litigation producing arguments of byzantine complexity. It is possible that the post-1979 arbitration law will reduce the likelihood of similar disputes escaping the bonds of trade arbitration. It should also be asked to what extent the present draft of the GAFTA forms represents a useful reaction to this experience.

It seems fair to say that the cases on *force majeure* and clause 22 clarified the meaning of the clause to a point where it would not have been productive to conduct an extensive overhaul.[119] Indeed, the present version of the clause (now renumbered clause 23) contains no significant changes to the version discussed above. But a major service would be provided to the trade and the legal system if the present prohibition clause (now clause 22) released sellers from making endless, futile enquiries in an attempt to recreate sales chains and plug all possible loopholes. The prohibition provision in the present GAFTA forms reads as follows:

> "In case of prohibition . . . restricting export, whether partially or otherwise, any such restriction shall be deemed by both parties to apply to this contract and to the extent of such total or partial restriction to prevent fulfilment whether by shipment or any other means whatsoever and to that extent this contract or any unfulfilled portion thereof shall be cancelled . . ."

This provision would appear to rule out any search for loopholes, whether provided by the unhelpful assistance of a governmental department or emerging in other ways. By deeming export restriction to amount to preventing the fulfilment of the contract, it lets off the hook the short string seller and liberates shippers and sellers with unappropriated cargo to seek higher market prices than the cancelled contract allows. That seems a small price to pay for getting rid of the evidential intractability of the old prohibition clause. Had it not been revised, the learning acquired in the prohibition clause cases would simply have sharpened arbitrations; it would not have helped to diminish their number.

MICHAEL BRIDGE

119. Doubt remains concerning the difference between a shipment initially delayed and one that is ultimately prevented at the end of the period. It is a question of moving from the particular to the general.

CHAPTER 16

THE APPLICATION OF COMMERCIAL IMPRACTICABILITY UNDER ARTICLE 2-615 OF THE UNIFORM COMMERCIAL CODE

1. INTRODUCTION

In the United States, the doctrine of commercial impracticability under article 2-615 of the Uniform Commercial Code (the code)[1] incorporates a number of features which seemingly bear little, if any, resemblance to the English doctrine of frustration. Indeed, it may be said that it is the scope, the application, the principles used and the kinds of remedies available under the code that provide the distinction. Thus the doctrine is imbued with a general policy "to use equitable principles in furtherance of commerical standards and good faith".[2] In English law, the doctrine of frustration provides limited contractual excuse and English courts are not receptive to the idea of expanding the scope and application of the doctrine or to recognising a doctrine of commercial impracticability.[3] This is evident in the rejection of claims based upon increased costs in performance, commercial impracticability and partial allocation of goods.[4] Consequently, whereas the refusal of equitable notions in commercial agreements in English law serves to reinforce a strict judicial approach in considering cases involving the doctrine of frustration, it is the adoption of these notions under the doctrine of impracticability in the United States that serves to promote a more receptive and flexible judicial approach.

This chapter discusses the role and function of article 2-615 and some related principles of legal excuse. The main emphasis, however, is on claims involving commercial impracticability and commercial hardship. It will examine the meaning of both concepts and the types of claim that constitute inpracticability or hardship in the US courts. Since it appears that there is a considerable contrast between United

1. Hereinafter the Uniform Commercial Code will be abbreviated to the code.

2. See Comment 6 of art. 2-615; Comment 2 of art. 2-209 and arts. 1-106(1), 1-203, 2-103 of the code. See also fns. 29, 37–44, 179 below.

3. Cf. In the context of contractual excuse and express provisions (e.g. *force majeure* clauses), English courts are more inclined to be flexible and to adopt a broader approach. In the *Soya Bean Meal* cases, the courts not only adopted a commercially realistic standard and acknowledged that the duty to purchase goods afloat was absolved, but also conceded the notion of impracticability. See for example *Tradax Export S.A.* v. *André & Cie S.A.* [1976] 1 Lloyd's Rep. 416; *Bremer Handelgesellschaft m.b.H.* v. *Vanden Avenne-Izegem* [1978] 2 Lloyd's Rep. 109; *Cook Industries Inc.* v. *Tradax Export S.A.* [1983] 1 Lloyd's Rep. 327. See, however, *Coastal (Bermuda) Petroleum Ltd.* v. *VTT Vulcan Petroleum S.A. (The Marine Star)* [1993] 1 Lloyd's Rep. 329, at p. 332. See also fn. 4 below and the discussion of these cases in Chapter 15.

4. Cf. The position of the parties where contractual excuse is based on the express provisions of the contract, *Intertradex S.A.* v. *Lesieur-Tourteaux* [1978] 2 Lloyd's Rep. 509; *Continental Grain* v. *S.T.M. Grain Ltd.* [1979] 2 Lloyd's Rep. 460; *Pancommerce* v. *Veecheema* [1982] 1 Lloyd's Rep. 645, at p. 652.

States and English doctrines of excuse, particularly as certain US cases have no parallel in English law, as, for example, *Florida Power & Light Co.* v. *Westinghouse Electric Corp.*[5] and *Aluminum Company of America* v. *Essex Corp. Inc. (ALCOA)*,[6] consideration will be given to the degree to which this contrast is reflected in practice. There will follow a comparative case study of the approach and application of the US doctrine of impracticability and the English doctrine of frustration. The final sections will consider this application of the doctrine in circumstances where the method of performance (express or contemplated) or failure or unavailability of the source of supply (express or contemplated) renders performance of the contract impossible or impracticable.

2. THE CONDITIONS OF ARTICLE 2-615 OF THE UNIFORM COMMERCIAL CODE

Article 2-615 of the code specifically applies to contracts for the sale of goods. It states:

> "Except so far as a seller may have assumed a greater obligation . . . :
>
> (a) Delay in delivery or non-delivery in whole or in part by a seller . . . is not a breach of his duty under a contract for sale if performance as agreed has been made impracticable by the occurrence of a contingency the non-occurrence of which was a basic assumption on which the contract was made or by compliance in good faith with any applicable foreign or domestic governmental regulation or order whether or not it later proves to be invalid.[7]

Since the doctrine of impracticability is adopted separately by each state,[8] it is formulated in different ways and subject to a variety of interpretations. However, under article 2-615, the courts have generally agreed that the seller[9] has to satisfy three basic conditions.[10]

The first condition is that the seller must not have assumed the risk of the supervening event. The determination of this condition involves a complex analysis. The courts are required to consider different kinds of factors: the contract terms,[11] sur-

5. 826 F. 2d 239 (US Court of Appeals for the 4th Cir. 1987).

6. 499 F. Supp. 53 (W.D. Pa. 1980).

7. Translation taken from *Uniform Laws Annotated, Uniform Commercial Code*, Vol 1B (1989) St. Paul, Minn., West Publishing Co., p. 195.

8. See Farnsworth, E.A., *Contracts* (1982) Little, Brown & Company, p. 27; White, J.J., and Summers, R.S., *Handbook of the Law Under the Uniform Commercial Code* (2nd Edn., 1980) West Publishing Company, § 3. pp. 7–8.

9. It has been said that the code cannot be invoked by a buyer; see *Northern Indiana Public Service Company (NIPSCO)* v. *Carbon County Coal Company* 799 F. 2d. 265 (7th Cir. 1986). Although art. 2-615 mentions only the 'seller' and not the buyer, it appears that a buyer may be able to bring a claim under the statutory and common law doctrines of excuse. See Comment 9 of art. 2-615 and fn. 167 below. See also White, J.J., and Summers, R.S., *Uniform Commercial Code, op. cit.*, § 3–9, p. 128.

10. Cf. Merhige J. in *In the Matter of Westinghouse Electric Corporation Uranium Contracts Litigation, Florida Power and Light Company* v. *Westinghouse Electric Corporation* 517 F. Supp. 440, at p. 451 (E.D. Va. 1981); *Opera Company of Boston* v. *WolfTrap Foundation for the Performing Arts* 817 F. 2d. 1094, at p. 1102 (4th Cir. 1987) *per* Russell J.

11. See arts. 1-102(2)(b) and 1-201(3) and Comment 8 of art. 2-615 of the code. See also White, J.J., and Summers, R.S., *Uniform Commercial Code, op cit.*, § 4, pp. 9–21.

rounding circumstances,[12] intentions of the parties,[13] importance of trade usage and custom,[14] and the likelihood and foreseeability of the supervening event.[15] Foreseeability, in particular, seems to play a significant role in this area.[16] Although absolute "non-foreseeability" of the event was once held to be an essential condition to the applicability of the legal principles and rules of excuse,[17] it is now settled that foreseeability is to be viewed as a question of degree and not as an absolute bar to contractual relief from the consequences of non-performance of the contract.[18]

The second condition of article 2-615 is that the non-occurrence must have been a basic assumption underlying the contract[19] and it enables the courts to determine whether or not the contract was actually made on any particular basis or assumption.[20] Occasionally, for example, the courts seek to distinguish between the occurrence of an event which amounts to a "mere expectation" and one which amounts to a "basic asumption".[21] In practice, this condition can also be used in determining the application of the rules of strict impossibility and the principle of physical impossibility.[22]

The last condition, that the supervening event must have rendered the performance commercially impracticable, demonstrates the "new" standard required under the code. It is said to be used deliberately as a contrast to the standard of impossibility.[23]

Ultimately, the task of determining a claim under the doctrine of commercial impracticability does not depend on the establishment of only one of these conditions, but on all of them.[24] It is said that commercial impracticability is an objective

12. See art. 1-201(3) and Comment 8 of art. 2-615 of the code. See also White, J.J., and Summers, R.S., *Uniform Commercial Code, op cit.*, § 4, pp. 9–21.

13. See Comment 8 of art. 2-615 of the code. See also White, J.J., and Summers, R.S., *Uniform Commercial Code, op. cit.*, § 4, pp. 9–21.

14. See art. 1-102(2)(b); Comment 2 of art. 1-102; Comment 8 of art. 1-201(3) and arts. 1-205 and 2-615 of the code. See also White, J.J., and Summers, R.S., *Uniform Commercial Code, op. cit.*, § 4, pp. 9–21.

15. See fn. 17 below.

16. *Id.*

17. See the comments of Harlington Wood J. in *Waldringer Corp.* v. *C.R.S.* 775 F. 2d. 781, at pp. 786–787 (1985). See also *Eastern Air Lines* v. *McDonnell Douglas Corp*. 532 F. 2d. 957, at p. 992 (5th Cir. 1976).

18. *Transatlantic Financial Corporation* v. *U.S.* 363 F. 2d. 312, at p. 318 (1966) *per* Skelly Wright J.; *Waldringer* v. *C.R.S.* 775 F. 2d. 781, at p. 786 (1985); *Opera Company of Boston* v. *WolfTrap* 817 F. 2d. 1094, at pp. 1100–1102 (1987).

19. See Prance, N.R., "Commercial Impracticability: A Textual and Economic Analysis of Section 2-615 of the Uniform Commercial Code" (1986) 19 Ind. L. Rev. 457, at p. 484 and Judge Merhige in *Florida Power and Light Company* v. *Westinghouse Electric Corporation* 517 F. Supp. 440, at pp. 454–455 (1981); *U.S.* v. *Wegematic* 360 F. 2d. 674, at p. 676 (2d Cir. 1966) *per* Friendly J. For the position in English law see *Krell* v. *Henry* [1903] 2 K.B. 740 where the coronation procession was a "basic assumption" of the contract. Cf. *Herne Bay Steamboat Co.* v. *Hutton* [1903] 2 K.B. 683 where the hired boat trip to view the naval review and to cruise around the fleet was merely "an expectation"

20. For example *Aluminum Company of America* v. *Essex Corp. Inc. (ALCOA)* 499 F. Supp. 53, at p. 70 (1980).

21. See fn. 56 below.

22. See Farnsworth, E.A., *Contracts, op. cit.*, p. 686. See also *Restatement of the Law Second, Contracts 2d.*, Vol. 2 (1981) St. Paul, Minn., American Law Institute Publishers, Chapter 11, "Impracticability of Performance and Frustration of Purpose", introductory note. Hereinafter referred to as the "*Restatement Second, Contracts*". See also fn. 57 below.

23. See fn. 34 below.

24. For a general analysis of the conditions in art. 2-615, see Farnsworth, E.A., *Contracts, op cit.*, Chapter 9, Section C, § 9.5–9.9; White, J.J., and Summers, R.S., *Uniform Commercial Code, op. cit.*, § 3–9, p. 128. For cases see *Iowa Electric Light and Power Co.* v. *Atlas Corp.* 467 F. Supp. 129, at p. 134

test[25] but, in practice, the courts often consider cases both on an objective[26] and subjective basis.[27] Indeed, it is arguable that US courts generally place more emphasis than English courts on the subjective factors of a case. For example, they seem to be readier to examine the reason behind a party's excuse or defence.[28] The provisions of the code encourage the courts to take subjective factors into account and to examine the merits of each case by discerning the real motive of the contracting parties. The "obligation of good faith" which the code imposes in the performance and enforcement of every contract or duty[29] is such an example. This yardstick of "good faith" can be used not only to determine whether the claim or defence of commercial impracticability should be upheld, but also as to which remedy should be given.[30] Where bad faith can be established, or where the absence of good faith is manifestly obvious, a claim of commercial impracticability will carry less force than it otherwise might. For example, allegations of a party's bad faith or the absence of good faith may be used in argument to affect the merits of the claims or the remedies sought.[31]

The role and function of article 2-615

Since its inception, the scope and construction of article 2-615, as well as the Official Comments,[32] have been the subject of much discussion. An issue of contention has been whether the code should be construed narrowly or broadly. On the one hand, it is said that the code has its roots in the common law doctrine of

(ND Iowa 1978); *Louisiana Power & Light Company* v. *Allegheny Ludlum Industries, Inc. and Allegheny Ludlum Steel Corporation* 517 F. Supp.1319, at p. 1323 (1981); *Opera Company of Boston* v. *Wolf-Trap* 817 F. 2d. 1094, at p. 1102 (1987).

25. *Natus* v. *U.S.* 371 F. 2d. 450, at p. 457 (1967); *Florida Power and Light Company* v. *Westinghouse Electric Corporation* 517 F. Supp. 440, at pp. 454–455 (1981); *International Mineral & Chemical Corp.* v. *Llano* 770 F. 2d. 879, at p. 887 (1985); *Opera Company of Boston* v. *Wolf Trap* 817 F. 2d. 1094, at p. 1099 at fn. 8; *Alimenta (U.S.A.) Inc.* v. *Cargill Incorporation* 861 F. 2d. 650, at p. 652 (11th Cir. 1988). See Farnsworth, E.A., *Contracts, op. cit.*, § 9.6, p. 688. See also Hurst, T.R., "Freedom of Contract in an Unstable Economy: Judicial Reallocation of Contractual Risks Under UCC Section 2-615" (1976) 54 N.C.L. Rev. 545, at p. 557.

26. See Farnsworth, E.A., *Contracts, op. cit.*, § 9.6, pp. 688–689. See also fn. 25 above.

27. *Id.*

28. See fn. 31 below.

29. Art. 1-203 concerns the obligation of good faith which states that "Every contract or duty within this Act imposes an obligation of good faith in its performance or enforcement". Translation taken from *Uniform Laws Annotated, Uniform Commercial Code*, Vol 1, *op. cit.*, pp. 109. See also art. 2-302(1) concerning unconscionable contracts or clauses, which states: "If the court as a matter of law finds the contract or any clause of the contract to have been unconscionable at the time it was made the court may refuse to enforce the contract, or it may enforce the remainder of the contract without the unconscionable clause, or it may limit the application of any unconscionable clause as to avoid any unconscionable result." Translation taken from *Uniform Laws Annotated, Uniform Commercial Code*, Vol 1A, *op. cit.*, p. 15.

30. See fn. 31 below.

31. In *Fratelli Gardino S.p.A.* v. *Caribbean Lumber Co.* 587 F. 2d., 204, at p. 208 (1979) the court agreed with the buyer's contention that a seller acting in bad faith "is not able to reap the fruits of his misdeeds". See *Alimenta (U.S.A.) Inc.* v. *Cargill Incorporation* 861 F. 2d. 650 (1988) where it was alleged that the sellers had not acted in good faith in allocating a quota of the contract goods to the buyers; *Roth Steel Products and Toledo Steel Tube Company* v. *Sharon Steel Corporation* 705 F. 2d. 134 (1983).

32. The official comments do not have the same legislative force as the text, and although they have not necessarily been enacted into law by state legislatures, they are influential as regards the interpretation of the code. (1986) 19 Ind. L. Rev. 457, at p. 463. For cases see *International Minerals* v. *Llano* 770 F. 2d. 879, at p. 885, fn. 2, (1985) (contract to purchase natural gas) where the Federal Court of Appeal regarded the official comments to the code as persuasive authority.

impossibility.[33] Therefore, since the latter has been construed strictly, both the common law rule and the statutory doctrine should be construed in like manner. On the other hand, it is said that the ethos and philosophy of the code envisage a marked departure from the orthodox rule of impossibility. It is to be construed liberally and that this is so is evidenced by the express provisions and official commentary of the code, and the intentions of its original draftsmen.[34]

There are a number of reasons which can be put forward in support of the conclusion that the doctrine is designed to operate in a different manner from the common law rule of impossibility.[35] Firstly, Official Comment 3 of article 2-615 itself distinguishes commercial impracticability from other rules concerning the discharge of the contract. This comment states: "The first test for excuse under this Article in terms of basic assumption is a familiar one. The additional test of commercial impracticability (as contrasted with 'impossibility,' 'frustration of performance' or 'frustration of the venture') has been adopted in order to call attention to the commercial character of the criterion chosen by this Article."[36]

Secondly, the scope of the doctrine, in recognising claims based on hardship (for example, increased costs in performance) is much wider. Thirdly and perhaps most importantly, the general philosophy of the code and, in particular, provisions such as articles 1-102,[37] 1-103,[38] 1-106,[39] 1-203[40] and 2-302[41] demonstrate that the doc-

33. See for example *Eastern Air Lines* v. *Gulf Oil Corp.* 415 F. Supp. 429, at p. 438 (1975); *Louisiana* v. *Allegheny* 517 F. Supp. 1319, at p. 1323 (1981); *Opera Company of Boston* v. *WolfTrap* 817 F. 2d. 1094, at pp. 1099–1102 (1987).

34. See White, J.J., and Summers, R.S., *Uniform Commercial Code, op. cit.* For articles see Hawkland, W.D., "The Energy Crisis and Section 2-615 of the Uniform Commercial Code" (1974) 79 Com.L.J. 75; Schmitt, M.A., and Wollschlager, B.A., " 'Commercial Impracticability': Making the Impracticable Practicable" (1976) 81 Com.L.J. 9; Wallach, G., "The Excuse Defense in the Law of Contracts: Judicial Frustration of the U.C.C. Attempt to Liberalize the Law of Commercial Impracticability" (1979) 55 Notre Dame Law. 203. For cases see *Transatlantic* v. *U.S.* 363 F. 2d. 312, at p. 315 (1966); *Natus* v. *U.S.* 371 F. 2d. 450, at p. 456 (1967); *Neal-Cooper Grain Co.* v. *Texas Gulf Sulphur Co.* 508 F. 2d. 283, at p. 293 (1974) (contract to supply and deliver potash); *Iowa* v. *Atlas* 467 F. Supp. 129, at p. 134 (1978); *Eastern Air Lines* v. *McDonnell* 532 F. 2d. 957, at p. 991 (1976); *Aluminum Co. of America* v. *Essex* 499 F. Supp. 53, at p. 76 (1980); *International Minerals* v. *Llano* 770 F. 2d. 879, at p. 886 (1985) *Opera Company of Boston* v. *WolfTrap* 817 F. 2d. 1094, at pp. 1099–1102 (1987). See further fn. 70 below.

35. See, however, *Mineral Park* v. *Howard* 172 Cal. 289 (1916). The case involved commercial impracticability at common law and the Supreme Court of California accepted the claim of impossibility (and impracticability) and excused the defendant for refusing to perform the contract on the basis that to do so would have involved "an expense of ten or twelve times as much as the usual cost". See "Contractual Flexibility in a Volatile Economy: Saving U.C.C. Section 2-615 from the Common Law" (1978) 72 Nw. U.L. Rev. 1032, at p. 1036.

36. Translation taken from *Uniform Laws Annotated, Uniform Comm. Code*, Vol 1B, *op cit.*, p. 195.

37. Arts. 1-102(1), (2) and (3) of the code state: "(1) This Act shall be liberally construed and applied to promote its underlying purposes and policies. (2) Underlying purposes and policies of this Act are (a) to simplify, clarify and modernize the law governing commercial transactions; (b) to permit the continued expansion of commercial practices through custom, usage and agreement of the parties; (c) to make uniform the law among the various jurisdictions. (3) The effect of provisions of this Act may be varied by agreement, except as otherwise provided in this Act and except that the obligations of good faith, diligence, reasonableness and care are prescribed by the Act may not be disclaimed by agreement but the parties may by agreement determine the standards by which the performance of such obligations is to be measured if such standards are not manifestly unreasonable." Translation taken from *Uniform Laws Annotated, Uniform Commercial Code*, Vol 1, *op. cit.*, p. 12. See also fns. 2 and 179.

38. See fn. 43 below.

* For footnotes 39, 40 and 41 see p. 310.

trine of impracticability is designed to provide a more distinctive and flexible approach to supervening circumstances which prevent the parties from performing contractual obligations.[42] Article 1-103 which states that "Unless displaced by the particular provisions of this Act, the principles of law and equity, including the law merchant . . . shall supplement its provisions" is said to be "probably the most important single provision in the Code".[43] By specifying that the "principles of law and equity" are supplementary, it not only highlights the working relationship of general legal principles and equitable principles, but also authorises the use of equitable principles (and notions) in the context of commercial agreements.[44] The significance of this becomes apparent by the manner in which courts approach claims based upon the doctrine of impracticability and the factors considered both in applying the doctrine and determining the remedy available.

3. ARTICLE 2-615 AND RELATED PRINCIPLES OF LEGAL EXCUSE

The doctrine of commercial impracticability[45] under article 2-615, and the common law doctrines of impossibility[46] and frustration of purpose[47] are not mutually independent.[48] Although the latter two doctrines are codified within sections 261–265[49] of the Restatement Second, Contracts and apply in the general field of contract, they are supplementary to the code.[50]

By virtue of the Restatement Second, Contracts the common law doctrine of "impossibility" has now also adopted the principle of impracticability in preference to the principle (and term) impossibility.[51] However, the US courts, like the Eng-

39. See art. 1-106 of the code which states: "(1) The remedies provided by this Act shall be liberally administered to the end that the aggrieved party may be put in as good a position as if the other party had fully performed but neither consequential or special nor penal damages may be had except as specifically provided in this Act or by other rule of law. (2) Any right or obligation declared by this Act is enforceable by action unless the provision declaring it specifies a different and limited effect." Translation taken from *Uniform Laws Annotated, Uniform Commercial Code*, Vol 1, *op. cit.*, pp. 54–55.
40. See fn. 29 above.
41. *Id.*
42. See fn. 34 above.
43. Translation taken from *Uniform Laws Annotated, Uniform Commercial Code*, Vol 1, *op cit.*, p. 20. See also Farnsworth, E.A., *Contracts, op. cit.* See White, J.J., and Summers, R.S., *Uniform Commercial Code, op. cit.*, s.3 § 2 at p. 7.
44. See also Comments 6–8 of art. 2-615 of the code.
45. References to the doctrine of commercial impracticability are in the context of art. 2-615. See fns. 52–54 below.
46. See fns. 33, 34 and 49.
47. See Ryan, J.G., "U.C.C. art. 2-615: Excusing The Impracticable" (1980) 60 B.U.L. Rev. 575, at p. 587. See also s.265 of the *Restatement Second, Contracts*.
48. The statutory and the common law doctrines of impracticability and the common law doctrine of frustration form an interesting relationship. In the *ALCOA* case 499 F. Supp. 53 (1980) it was held that the doctrine of frustration includes "frustration of the purpose to earn money or to avoid losses", p. 78 and that (p. 73) "the doctrine of impracticability and of frustration focus on different kinds of disappointment of a contracting party".
49. See *Restatement Second, Contracts*. The statutory doctrine of impracticability under art. 2-615 of the code has undoubtedly influenced the *Restatement Second, Contracts*. See the discussion in the Tentative Draft No. 9 of the *Restatement Second, Contracts*, 1974.
50. See fns. 8 and 51.
51. Farnsworth, E.A., *Contracts, op cit.*, p. 677 states that the code "promises to have a substantial influence on the law of contract generally and has been adopted by the Restatement Second". See s.261 of the *Restatement Second, Contracts*, and the Reporter's Note to the Introductory Note, p. 312; s.261,

lish courts, are not always clear in their application and terminology in this area.[52] In certain cases, claims may be based not only on the statutory claim of impracticability but also on the common law doctrines of impossibility or frustration of purpose.[53] In this respect, the common law term "impossibility" and the statutory term "impracticability" are sometimes used synonymously.[54] Where both common law and statutory principles are used, this process may be somewhat more understandable; but where a particular case relies solely upon common law principles of discharge or solely upon the statutory principles of article 2-615, little justification, if any, can be given.

In discussing the application of both of these principles (common law impossibility and the statutory principles of impracticability) the courts use not only "the basic assumption upon which the parties contracted" test,[55] but also virtually the same test as that employed by Lord Radcliffe in *Davis Contractors* v. *Fareham U.D.C.*,[56] namely that performance must have been rendered "so vitally different from what was anticipated that the contract cannot be reasonably thought to govern". There are many similarities between the US common law principles of impossibility and English rules of impossibility.[57] However, since the US common law doctrine of impossibility now appears to have changed its ambit to cover instances of "supervening impracticability",[58] its application is potentially wider than that of the English rules of impossibility. Accordingly, it is probable that greater differences between these respective rules will gradually emerge.

Comment d, Impracticability and Official Comment 4 of art. 2-615 of the code. See also Merhige J. in *Florida Power and Light Company* v. *Westinghouse Electric Corporation* 517 F. Supp. 440, at p. 451 (1981) stating that "common law impossibility . . . is equivalent to impracticability under the Code".

52. See *Transatlantic* v. *U.S.* 363 F. 2d. 312, at p. 320 (D.C.Cir. 1966); *U.S.* v. *Wegematic* 360 F. 2d. 674, at p. 676 (2d. Cir. 1966); *Eastern Air Lines* v. *Gulf* 415 F. Supp. 429 (S.D.Fla. 1975); *Eastern Air Lines* v. *McDonnell* 532 F. 2d. 957, at p. 991 (1976); *Hancock Paper Co.* v. *Champion Int'l Corp.* 424 F. Supp. 285, at p. 290 (E.D.Pa. 1976); *Florida Power and Light Company* v. *Westinghouse Electric Corporation* 517 F. Supp. 440, at p. 451 (1981); *Opera Company of Boston* v. *WolfTrap* 817 F. 2d. 1094, at p. 1099 (1987).

53. *Northern Indiana Public Service Company (NIPSCO)* v. *Carbon County Coal Company* 799 F. 2d. 265 (7th Cir. 1986).

54. For example *Asphalt International* v. *Enterprise Shipping Corp.* 667 F. 2d. 261 (1981); *ALCOA* 499 F. Supp. 53 (1980). See fn. 52 above.

55. [1956] A.C. 696, at p. 729.

56. See the comments of Gorman, J.J., "Commercial Hardship and the Discharge of Contractual Obligations Under American and British Law" (1980) 13 Vand. J. Transnat'l L. 107, at p. 137 as to the relevance of the notion of "basic assumption" in relation to the US doctrine of impracticability and the English doctrine of frustration. In practice, the tests used in the United States and English courts so as to determine the legal principles and rules of contractual excuse are similar. For US cases see *Mishara Construction Company* v. *Transit-Mixed Concrete Corporation* 310 N.E. 2d. 363, at p. 367 (1974); *Eastern Air Lines* v. *McDonnell* 532 F. 2d. 957, at p. 991 (1976); *Asphalt International* v. *Enterprise Shipping Corp.* 667 F. 2d. 261, at p. 266 (2d. Cir. 1981); *Louisiana* v. *Allegheny* 517 F. Supp. 1319, at pp. 1323–1324 (1981); *Waldringer* v. *C.R.S.* 775 F. 2d. 781, at p. 786 (1985). For English cases see *Davis Contractors Ltd* v. *Fareham U.D.C.* [1956] A.C. 696; *Kissavos Shipping Co. S.A.* v. *Empresa Cubana de Fletes (The Agathon)* [1982] 2 Lloyd's Rep. 211; *Pioneer Shipping Ltd.* v. *B.T.P. Tioxide Ltd. (The Nema)* [1982] A.C. 724.

57. For example supervening illegality, legal impossibility, strict impossibility of performance (such as the death or illness of the performing party) and physical impossibility (destruction of the subject-matter which forms the basis of the contract).

58. See fn. 34 above.

Frustration of purpose

Frustration of purpose is categorised separately in the Restatement Second Contracts.[59] It is analysed in contradistinction to the rules of impossibility and can be viewed in the same context as the English principle of frustration of purpose. US courts sometimes refer to this specific principle as the "doctrine of frustration", but the doctrine is only applicable in the context of the *Krell* v. *Henry*[60] principle. It is not a general legal doctrine which encompasses the various principles of excuse which are now commonly ascribed to the English doctrine of frustration. The US common law test of the principle of frustration of purpose is strikingly similar to the statutory test of article 2-615: "Where, after a contract is made, a party's principal purpose is substantially frustrated without his fault by the occurrence of an event the non-occurrence of which was a basic assumption on which the contract was made, his remaining duties to render performance are discharged, unless the language or the circumstances indicate the contrary."[61]

Frustration of purpose is not only recognised in common law but also within article 2-615 of the code. The courts have conceded that parties may be excused on this basis. In addition they have, at least in principle, recognised that failure to make a profit may amount to the frustration of the purpose of the contract.[62] By contrast, English judges have largely rejected the principle of frustration of purpose in commercial transactions.[63]

4. THE SCOPE OF COMMERCIAL IMPRACTICABILITY

The term "impracticability" rather than "impossibility" is adopted to indicate that article 2-615 covers a wider range of supervening circumstances than those traditionally encompassed within the common law doctrine of impossibility.[64] Official Comment 2 to the code states that: "The present section deliberately refrains from any effort at an exhaustive expression of contingencies and is to be interpreted in all cases sought to be brought within its scope in terms of its underlying reason and purpose."[65] Thus, the doctrine includes commercial hardship and even the prin-

59. S.261 of the *Restatement Second, Contracts* incorporates a general rule of discharge under the heading of "supervening impracticability". The *Restatement Second, Contracts* under ss.262–265 also includes separate rules of discharge on grounds of supervening circumstances preventing contractual performance.

60. [1903] 2 K.B. 740.

61. See *Restatement Second, Contracts*, § 265. Translation taken from *Restatement of the Law Second, Contracts 2d.*, Vol 2, *op. cit.*, pp. 334–335.

62. *ALCOA* 499 F. Supp. 53, at p. 78 (1980); *Everett Plywood Corp.* v. *U.S.* 651 F. 2d. 723, at pp. 728–729 (1981) *per* Nichols J.; *Printing Industries* v. *International Printing and Graphic Communications Union* 584 F. Supp. 990 (1984); *International Mineral & Chemical Corp.* v. *Llano* 770 F. 2d. 879, at p. 887 (1985).

63. See *Herne Bay Steamboat Co.* v. *Hutton* [1903] 2 K.B. 683; *Chandler* v. *Webster* [1904] 1 K.B. 493; *Amalgamated Investment & Property Co. Ltd.* v. *John Walker & Son Ltd.* [1977] 1 W.L.R. 164. Cf. *Krell* v. *Henry* [1903] 2 K.B. 740.

64. See s.1 above.

65. Translation taken from *Uniform Laws Annotated, Uniform Commercial Code*, Vol 1B, *op. cit.*, p. 195.

ciple of frustration of purpose.[66] On occasions, the US courts have sought to distinguish the principle of frustration of purpose from commercial impracticability.[67] However, frustration of purpose is included within the doctrine of commercial impracticability.[68] This suggests that the scope and the application of the US statutory doctrine of impracticability is wider than that of the English doctrine of frustration.

As claims arising under article 2-615 can be based upon a variety of grounds and circumstances, the scope and meaning of the doctrine of impracticability is not always easy to discern. It has been said that "the term 'impracticable' has, over the years, acquired a fairly specific meaning".[69] This "fairly specific meaning" will now be investigated.

(a) Commercial impracticability and commercial hardship

The judicial determination of claims based on hardship has been criticised.[70] US courts sometimes use "hardship" and "impracticability" interchangeably. This can result in considerable confusion because claims of commercial impracticability may arise out of different kinds of supervening events—hardship is only one of these.[71] Thus, a claim based on hardship is a separate tenet encompassed within the doctrine of commercial impracticability. The courts tend to give the impression that all claims under the doctrine of impracticability are analysed in the same way. In *Gulf Oil* v. *Federal Power Commission* (*F.P.C.*)[72] the court said: "The crucial question in applying that doctrine to any given situation is whether the cost of performance has in fact become so excessive and unreasonable that the failure to excuse performance would result in grave injustice."[73] However, this analysis is only relevant to claims involving hardship. It is not necessarily relevant to every claim based upon a supervening circumstance rendering performance of the contract impracticable.[74]

66. See for example *NIPSCO* v. *County Carbon* 799 F. 2d. 265, at p. 277. Cf. Farnsworth, E.A., *Contracts, op. cit.*, p. 690, at fn. 4, the "doctrine of impracticability does not operate to discharge a duty to pay money merely because its performance has become impracticable".

67. See *Everett* v. *U.S.* 651. F. 2d. 723, at p. 729 (1981).

68. See for example *ALCOA* 499 F. Supp. 53, at p. 78 (1980); *Sabine Corporation* v. *Ong Western Inc.* 725 F. Supp. 1157 (U.S. District Court, W.D. Oklahoma 1989); *Everett* v. *U.S.* 651 F. 2d. 723, at pp. 728–729 (1981). US courts sometimes use the term frustration to denote the application of the principle of the frustration of purpose and the doctrine of frustration. For US common law position see also fn. 48 above.

69. *International Minerals* v. *Llano* 770 F. 2d. 879, at p. 886 (1985) *per* Barrett J.

70. See for example "Comments—Commercial Frustration: A Comparative Study" (1967–68) 3–4 Tex. Int'l L. Forum 275; Forte, A.D.M., "Economic Frustration of Commercial Contracts: A Comparative Analysis with Particular Reference to the United Kingdom" (1986) Juridical Rev. 1; Triantis, G.G., "Contractual Allocations of Unknown Risks: A Critique of the Doctrine of Commercial Impracticability", (1992) 42 Univ. of Toronto L.J. 450; Trimarchi, P., "Commercial Impracticability in Contract Law: An Economic Analysis" (1991) 11 Int'l Rev. of Law and Ec. 63; Walt, S., "Expectations, Loss Distribution and Commercial Impracticability" (1990) 24 Ind.L.R. 65. See fn. 34 above.

71. In the *NIPSCO* case 799 F. 2d. 265, at p. 275 (1986) the court questioned whether the contracting party had suffered any "hardship" within the notion of the code. See fn. 72 below.

72. 563 F. 2d. 588 (1977). See the test which the court applied in *ALCOA* 499 F. Supp. 53, at p. 76 (1980). See also *Mineral Park* v. *Howard* 172 Cal. 289 (1916); *Gulf* v. *F.P.C.* 563 F. 2d. 588 (3rd Cir. 1977) cert. denied 434 U.S. 1062, 98 S. Ct. 1235 (1978).

73. 563 F. 2d. 588, at p. 599 (1977).

74. See *Opera Company of Boston* v. *WolfTrap* 817 F. 2d. 1094 (1987).

(b) Article 2-615 and increased costs in performance

During the past four decades, political and economic crises have given the US courts ample opportunities to address new problems. Examples were the closure of the Suez Canal,[75] the development of private nuclear power in the early 1970s[76] and the sharp increases in fuel costs as a result of the Arab oil embargo in the 1970s.[77] These events all sufficiently disrupted the flow of trade, so as to hinder, prevent, or delay the performance of contractual obligations. The following analysis will show that whilst (in cases giving rise to analogous facts and circumstances) the approach of US courts differs from English courts, there is not, in practice, a substantial difference in the outcomes.

Claims of increased costs in performance or hardship[78] under article 2-615 must be viewed against the particular context and framework of US commercial agreements. Accordingly, the various types of cases, the magnitude of the losses or profits involved and the status and bargaining power of the parties concerned demonstrate that the range of cases concerning commercial impracticability can be very wide. Given these characteristics, it is difficult to draw any analogy in the way in which the English doctrine of frustration considers claims of increased costs in performance and hardship in English commercial agreements.

Official Comment 4 of article 2-615[79] provides that financial and economic difficulties can afford a contracting party an excuse:

"Increased cost alone does not excuse performance unless the rise in cost is due to some unforeseen contingency which alters the essential nature of the performance. Neither is a rise or a collapse in the market in itself a justification, for that is exactly the type of business risk which business contracts made at fixed prices are intended to cover. But a severe shortage of raw materials or of supplies due to a contingency such as war, embargo, local crop failure, unforeseen shutdown of major sources of supply or the like, which either causes a marked increase in cost or altogether prevents the seller from securing supplies necessary to his performance is within the contemplation of this section."[80]

A "marked increase in costs" might, therefore, provide an excuse under the code. Added costs *per se* will not. Many cases involving impracticability often include increased costs as *one* of the factors in the claim. For example, in the *Suez* cases[81] (decided in the US courts) the parties contended that performance had been

75. See fn. 87 below.

76. See for example *In re Westinghouse Elec. Corp. Uranium Contract Litigation* 405 F. Supp. 316 (J.P.M.D.L. 1975); *Iowa Electric Light & Power Co.* v. *Atlas Corp.* 467 F. Supp. 129 (N.D.Iowa 1978), rev'd on other grounds, 603 F. 2d. 1301 (8th Cir. 1979); *Florida Power and Light Company* v. *Westinghouse Electric Corporation* 517 F. Supp. 440 (1981); *Florida Power and Light Co.* v. *Westinghouse Electric Corp.* 826 F. 2d. 239 (U.S. Court of Appeals for the 4th Cir. 1987).

77. See for example *Eastern Air Lines* v. *Gulf Oil Corp.* 415 F. Supp. 429 (S.D. Fla. 1975); *Publicker Ind.* v. *Union Carbide* 17 UCC Rep. Serv. (Callaghan) 989 (E.D.PA. 1975) (contract to supply ethanol); *Iowa* v. *Atlas* 467 F. Supp. 129 (1978); *ALCOA* 499 F. Supp. 53 (1980); *Louisiana Power* v. *Allegheny* 517 F. Supp. 1319 (E.D. La. 1981).

78. See fns. 70–74 below.

79. Translation taken from *Uniform Laws Annotated, Uniform Commercial Code*, Vol 1B, *op cit.*, pp. 195–196.

80. It is arguable that this section only applies where the source was contemplated only by a seller. Official Comment 5 deals with the situation where "a particular source of supply is exclusive" and is expressly stated in the contract or contemplated by both parties. See also fns. 166–174 below.

81. *Transatlantic Financing* v. *U.S.* 363 F. 2d. 312, at pp. 315, 319 (1966); *American Trading & Prod. Corp.* v. *Shell Int'l Marine Ltd.* 453 F. 2d. 939 (2d. Cir. 1972). See fn. 87 below.

rendered impossible not only because the canal was closed,[82] but also on the basis of increased expenditure which would be incurred in adopting an alternative route. The US courts, like the English courts, held that performance had not been rendered impossible.[83] The extra expenditure was not substantial: it did not amount to a risk so large that it went beyond the terms of the contract. In the US cases, the actual principle of increased costs (amounting to commercial impracticability) was not rejected: it was simply not applicable in the circumstances.

(c) What constitutes excessive cost and excessive hardship?

Initially there was doubt amongst courts and legal scholars as to whether increased cost, no matter how excessive, could ever provide a legal excuse.[84] Skelly Wright J.'s notable comments in *Transatlantic Financing Corporation* v. *U.S.*[85] suggested that a claim based on increased costs might suffice to provide an excuse for non-performance. His dictum soon became a basis for many of the claims of hardship brought under both the common law and the code: "The doctrine [of impossibility] ultimately represents the ever-shifting line, drawn by courts hopefully responsive to commercial practices and mores, at which the community's interest in having contracts enforced according to their terms is outweighed by the commercial senselessness of requiring performance."[86] To the extent that this dictum encouraged the admission of a new standard (impracticability rather than impossibility), relief by operation of the law did seem to offer something new. The doctrine was now to be applied when performance of the contract no longer proved to be commercially viable. In other respects, the dictum did not affect the stringency with which the doctrine was applied. This later became clear when courts continued to apply the common law and statutory doctrines of excuse sparingly.

The *Suez* cases were the first major series of cases involving increased costs in performance as the basis of contractual relief.[87] English and US courts both reached the same results—both refused to excuse the parties and both held that the parties would not have suffered any excessive or severe hardship[88]—but their

82. As in the analogous *Suez* cases in English law, shipment via the canal was claimed to be the intended route.

83. See *Transatlantic Financing* v. *U.S.* 363 F. 2d. 312 (D.C. Cir. 1966)—this was a pre-UCC case but the same principle would have been applied under the code.

84. See however the comments of McManus J. in *Iowa* v. *Atlas* 467 F. Supp. 129, at p. 134, fn. 7 (1978).

85. 363 F. 2d. 312 (D.C. Cir. 1966). See Teitelbaum J. in the *ALCOA* case 499 F. Supp. 53, at p. 76 (1980) who stated that Wright J.'s approach was "more in keeping with the spirit and purpose of the Uniform Commercial Code." Cf. "Contractual Flexibility in a Volatile Economy: Saving U.C.C. Section 2-615 from the Common Law" (1978) 72 Nw. U.L. Rev. 1032, at p. 1043 where it is stated: "Although Judge Wright's approach in *Transatlantic* uses the formal gloss of section 2-615 language, the substance of his analysis is firmly wedded to the old common law tests of impossibility and foreseeability." See also *ALCOA* 499 F. Supp. 53, at pp. 89, 91.

86. 363 F. 2d. 312, at p. 315 (1966). See generally Arnold, M.W., "Impracticability of Performance—Is It Grounds For Breach?" [1977–78] L.M.C.L.Q. 346.

87. *Glidden Co* v. *Hellenic Lines Ltd.* 275 F. 2d. 253 (2d. Cir. 1960) (the contract expressly provided for shipment "via Suez or Cape of Good Hope"); *Transatlantic* v. *U.S.* 363 F. 2d. 312 (1966); *American Trading and Production Corp.* v. *Shell International Marine Ltd. (The Washington Trader)* 453 F. 2d. 939 (1972), [1972] 1 Lloyd's Rep. 463.

88. See for example *American Trading and Production Corp.* v. *Shell International Marine Ltd. (The Washington Trader)* 453 F. 2d. 939 (1972), [1972] 1 Lloyd's Rep. 463, at p. 467.

approach to the issue differed. The English courts refused to excuse the parties primarily on the basis that hardship was not recognised within the doctrine of frustration, and, therefore, increased costs could not afford contractual relief.[89] The US courts refused to excuse the parties on the basis that, although hardship could in principle excuse the parties, the hardship was not excessive or unreasonable in law so as to provide an excuse.[90] It was said that:

"While it may be an overstatement to say that increased cost and difficulty of performance never constitute impracticability, to justify relief there must be more of a variation between expected cost and the cost of performing by an available alternative than is present in this case, where the promisor can legitimately be presumed to have accepted some degree of abnormal risk, and where impracticability is urged on the basis of added expense alone."[91]

Whilst US courts and writers have realised that hardship is essentially relative[92] and peculiar to the facts of each case,[93] they have continued to analyse the issue in terms of actual percentages of increase that can or can not bring the doctrine in to operation. It has been held that increases between 10.4%,[94] 15%,[95] 38%,[96] 50–50.8%[97] and over 100%[98] of production costs over the contract price are not excessive within the context of common law or statutory doctrines of excuse. The doctrine is not invoked merely because "costs have become more expensive than originally contemplated",[99] the anticipated profits have not materialised, or there

89. See fn. 87 above.
90. See fn. 87 above.
91. *Transatlantic* v. *U.S.* 363 F. 2d. 312, at p. 319 (1966) *per* Skelly Wright J.
92. See for example Joskow, P.L., "Commercial Impossibility, the Uranium Market and the Westinghouse Case" (1977) 6 J. Legal Stud. 119, at p. 160 stating that "it appears, then, that moderate increases in cost of up to 100 percent do not satisfy the requirement, while extreme increases of 1,000 percent or more do", and Ryan, J.G., "U.C.C. s. 2-615: Excusing The Impracticable" (1980) 60 B.U.L. Rev. 575, at p. 592.
93. *Florida Power and Light Company* v. *Westinghouse Electric Corporation* 517 F. Supp. 440, at p. 454 (1981).
94. *Maple Farms* v. *City School District* 76 Misc. 2d. 1080 (1974).
95. *Roth Steel Products and Toledo Steel Tube Company* v. *Sharon Steel Corporation* 705 F. 2d. 134 (1983).
96. *Louisiana* v. *Allegheny* 517 F. Supp. 1319 (1981).
97. *Iowa* v. *Atlas* 467 F. Supp. 129 (1978).
98. See *Maple Farms* v. *City School District* 76 Misc. 2d. 1080 (1974) where the court held that it was not aware of any cases where anything less than 100 per cent cost increase has been held to make a seller's performance "impracticable". *Publicker* v. *Union Carbide* 17 UCC 989, at p. 992 (1975). Cf. Denning L.J. in *Brauer & Co. (GB) Ltd.* v. *Clark (James) (Brush Materials)* [1952] 2 All E.R. 497, at p. 501.
99. *Jennie-O Foods* v. *U.S.* 580 F. 2d. 400, at p. 409 (1978) (contract to sell processed turkeys); *Roth Steel* v. *Sharon Steel* 705 F. 2d. 134 (1983); *U.S.* v. *Southwestern Electric Cooperative, Inc.* 869 F. 2d. 310 (7th Cir. 1989). See also contracts for the sale and production of specified goods made with the US Government and usually in accordance with the US Government's specifications. Such contracts generally incorporate a "changes clause" or a "changes article" which allows an adjustment of the contract price for increased costs of performance due to defective specifications given by the government or where supervening events have rendered the contract impracticable. Reliance upon these clauses is often very difficult. The standard of proving impracticability is often equated with the standard that a party must show under the general law of impossibility. See for example *Natus Corp.* v. *U.S.* 371 F. 2d. 450 (1967); *The Clark Grave Vault Company* v. *U.S.* 371 F. 2d. 459 (1967); *Foster L.W. Sportswear Company Inc.* v. *U.S.* 405 F. 2d. 1285 (1969); *Piasecki Aircraft Corporation Island Road* v. *U.S.* 667 F. 2d. 50 (1981); *Laka Tool and Stamping Company* v. *U.S.* 639 F. 2d. 738 (1980); *Koppers Co. Inc.* v. *U.S.* 405 F. 2d. 554 (1968).

has been a contract loss.[100] Excuse will not be provided because performance has become "economically burdensome or unattractive"[101] so that it "requires a departure from the least costly to the most costly means of operation".[102] Where such losses are especially severe and unreasonable or where contractual performance is "economically unrealistic"[103] or "economically prohibitive",[104] the doctrine may be applied.[105]

An example of hardship in law is provided by the case of *Florida Power & Light Company* v. *Westinghouse*.[106] Briefly stated, Westinghouse, the contractors, agreed with Florida, an electric company, to supply uranium, to dispose spent fuel discharged by Florida's plant reactors and to supply Florida with a pressurised water reactor (PWR) nuclear power installation. They further agreed to provide the uranium, at a fixed price, for the first 10 years of the plant's operations and to grant an option to exercise one of three options for the disposal of the spent fuel discharged by the plant's reactors (also for the first 10 years of the plant's operations). Both at the time of the contract and when the option was exercised, reprocessing spent fuel constituted the only method of disposal. Westinghouse had assumed that this was to be the case and had begun negotiations with the Allied General Nuclear Services (AGNS) to construct a reprocessing plant for the purpose of securing reprocessing of Florida's spent fuel. Subsequently, in order to promote commercial reprocessing, the government issued a policy statement assuring the nuclear power industry that if commercial reprocessing were not made available when these facilities were needed, they would provide reprocessing services for any commercial nuclear power plants. Governmental policy changed and by 1975 the government had discontinued the reprocessing services for such commercial

100. In *Eastern Airlines* v. *Gulf* 415 F. Supp. 429, at pp. 440, 441 (1975) the "costs" in the production of crude oil to which Gulf adverted as substantiating their claim of commercial impracticability were held to be unlike any costs that might arguably afford ground for any relief. The court stated that the so-called costs in fact reflected a lower profit margin than originally contemplated. Gulf's so-called increased costs per barrel were not the kind of costs against which to measure hardship "real or imagined, under the Uniform Commercial Code" (p. 441). The court was adamant that "under no theory of law can it be held that Gulf is guaranteed preservation of its intra-company profits," (p. 441). Thus Gulf had to distinguish and prove its real costs from its costs "inflated by its internal profits at various levels of the manufacturing process and located in various foreign countries" (p. 441). See *Gulf Oil* v. *Federal Power Commission* 563 F. 2d. 588 (1977); *Louisiana* v. *Allegheny* 517 F. Supp. 1319 (1981). See also ALCOA 499 F. Supp. 53 (1980); *Florida* v. *Westinghouse* 826 F. 2d. 239 (1987); *Sabine Corporation* v. *Ong Western Inc.* 725 F. Supp. 1157 (U.S. District Court, W.D. Oklahoma 1989).

101. *Neal-Cooper Grain* v. *Texas* 508 F. 2d. 283, at p. 293 (1974) *per* Pell J.; *Day, Day Oil. Ltd. and Day Exploration, Inc.* v. *Tenneco Inc. and Tennessee Gas Pipeline Co.* 696 F. Supp. 233 (S.D. Miss. 1988) (purchase of gas); *U.S.* v. *Southwestern Electric Cooperative, Inc.* 869 F. 2d. 310 (7th Cir. 1989) (contract to purchase electric power).

102. *Natus* v. *U.S.* 371 F. 2d. 450, at p. 457 (1967); see also fn. 87. In *Gulf Oil Corp.* v. *F.P.C.* 563 F. 2d. 588 (1977) (delivery and supply of natural gas) the court found that what in fact Gulf meant by "exorbitant costs" was a depreciation in the contractual profits from that which they had originally contemplated. Accordingly it was held that (p. 600) Gulf would "probably suffer no loss, and certainly not a severe and devastating loss". See fn. 172 below.

103. *Natus* v. *U.S.* 371 F. 2d. 450, at p. 458 (1967) *per* Collins J.

104. *The Clark Grave Vault Company* v. *U.S.* 371 F. 2d. 459, at p. 461 (1967) *per* Collins J.

105. *ALCOA* 499 F. Supp. 53 (1980); *Florida Power and Light Co.* v. *Westinghouse Electric Corp.* 826 F. 2d. 239 (1987).

106. 826 F. 2d. 239 (1987). The court also had to consider whether Westinghouse's further claim of impracticability also constituted an excuse. As The Nuclear Waste Policy Act 1982 had, *ipso facto*, provided an alternative means of performance, Westinghouse might have been able to perform their contractual obligations.

nuclear power plants. Consequently, no reprocessing facilities for spent fuel discharged by private nuclear power plants existed. Westinghouse informed Florida that it could not perform its obligations, and claimed that it was excused under article 2-615 as well as under the common law doctrine of impossibility. In 1982, Congress passed an Act—The Nuclear Waste Policy Act (NWPA)—providing for expedient development of permanent depositories for nuclear waste. Whilst these were being developed, the government stated that commercial nuclear plants should, if possible, continue re-racking the spent fuel in on-site storage; that is, to use the method of disposing the spent fuel which had been authorised since 1975. Westinghouse alleged that notwithstanding the method of re-racking, performance had been rendered both impossible and impracticable.[107] Florida brought an action seeking damages for breach of contract.

The court had to determine whether, in spite of the method of performance being different from that which the parties had initially contemplated, Westinghouse was obliged to perform or whether Westinghouse could successfully rely on the defence of commercial impracticability on the ground of excessive and unreasonable hardship. The court analysed what the financial position of Westinghouse would have been had it been able to effect performance when the contract was made, and also when performance had subsequently become due in 1975. In this connection, it not only considered the purpose and objectives of the parties in making the contract, the effect of the supervening event on both parties, and the actual practicalities involved in adopting the new method of performance, but also the costs involved in effecting performance and the profits that would have been made. The court held that since Westinghouse had relied on these government assurances to provide effective reprocessing facilities, and since at the time of performance no such facilities were available, the contract had been rendered impossible. Thus Westinghouse was excused its future obligations to perform, first, on the basis that the particular method of performance which subsequently became available was not a method which the parties had originally anticipated at the time of contracting, and secondly, on the basis that the adoption of this new method of performance (when subsequently available) would involve severe and substantial costs. The court stated that: "Assuming the storage is finally provided, it would not only fail to yield a profit of some $18,000,000 to $20,000,000 to Westinghouse, as contemplated by the parties when this contract was signed, but would, if the district court's decision is affirmed, cost Westinghouse at least well over $80,000,000. The difference here is not 50% as the district court reasoned but percentages in the hundreds range."[108]

The approach of the court in *Florida* v. *Westinghouse* was different from that employed in other cases dealing with claims of hardship and impracticability. For example, in *Alimenta* v. *Cargill* Nesbitt J. said that commercial impracticability under article 2-615 focused "upon 'the reasonableness of the expenditure, not upon the ability of a party to pay the commercially unreasonable expense' ".[109] However, these factors can be important as is evidenced by *Florida* v. *Westinghouse*. Westinghouse was excused from its obligation to dispose of the spent fuel because

107. See fn. 106 above.
108. 826 F. 2d. 239, at p. 277 (1987).
109. *Alimenta (U.S.A.) Inc.* v. *Cargill Incorporation*, 861 F. 2d. 650, at p. 652 (11th Cir. 1988).

"as a matter of law" the promise of future storage (as made by the government under the NWPA but as yet unavailable) was not a reasonable alternative. Florida was not entitled to recover from Westinghouse the cost of future storage in a government storage facility that was to be built later.[110] The US Court of Appeals affirmed the decision that the costs of re-racking the spent fuel on site (which Westinghouse had been obliged to carry out by virtue of Option C) was to be divided between Westinghouse and Florida. In making this decision the court stated that it was aware that in all probability Florida would be permitted to recover its costs from its ratepayers. In the words of the court, they knew of "no case where the use of the alternative not only wiped out the expected profit but resulted in a loss some four or five times greater than the expected profit and that was not found to be so excessive as to justify the application of the impossibility doctrine."[111]

Commercial hardship was also successfully invoked in *Aluminum Co.* v. *Essex* (ALCOA).[112] This case involved a long-term contract[113] whereby Aluminum agreed to process alumini supplied by Essex into molten alumini. This was to be used by Essex in the manufacture of aluminum wire products. The processing was to be conducted at a plant owned by Aluminum in Indiana. The price escalation clause in the contract was based on a complex indexing system. It reflected a projected variation of costs which would give Aluminum an anticipated profit of between $0.01 per pound and $0.07 per pound. Aluminum's own target profit was $0.04 per pound. As a result of the energy crisis in 1973, electricity costs greatly increased and Aluminum's costs escalated well over that contemplated by the escalation clause. Although by late 1974 Aluminum had earned a profit of $27.6 million, at the time of the trial its profits had decreased to $9 million. However, due to a 500 per cent variation of actual costs to indexed costs, it was now anticipated that if Aluminum were compelled to perform, it would lose $60 million over the rest of the contract. During this time Essex had reaped a so-called "windfall" by reselling the converted aluminum.[114]

Aluminum brought an action seeking, *inter alia*, a revision or an equitable adjustment of the agreement. In a surprisingly innovative decision, the District Court applied Indiana law,[115] and granted Aluminum relief by revising the contract so as to allow an adjustment on the basis of a specially designed formula.[116] The court concluded that, since the parties had incorporated a carefully detailed escalation clause in their contract, they had taken all the necessary measures in protecting themselves against the risk of foreseeable price deviations. The parties had only

110. The judgment of the District Court in its third opinion in assessing such costs against Westinghouse was reversed. The US Court of Appeals then specifically addressed the issue of the increase in costs of performance and the alternative method of performance (p. 277).

111. 826 F. 2d. 239, at p. 277 (1987).

112. 499 F. Supp. 53 (1980). The court viewed the contract as one for services and accordingly applied the *Restatement Second, Contracts* and not the Uniform Commercial code.

113. Signed in 1967, for 17 years, and known as a "toll conversion service contract".

114. Although it had paid Aluminum $364 per pound for the alumini, the open market price had now increased to $733 per pound.

115. As provided under the specific provisions of the contract. See 499 F. Supp. 53, at pp. 59–60 (1980).

116. This formula was devised without the agreement of the contracting parties. Subsequently the parties reached an agreement on the adjustment and settled the dispute before the appeal to the US Court of Appeals was decided.

assumed closely calculated risks and not risks arising from unforeseen circumstances such as those which caused a severe imbalance in the exchange.[117] It was said that the risk of the contingency was not only unforeseen but far beyond the kind of risk that the contracting parties could have envisaged.[118]

In considering the case, the court examined the effect the energy crisis had had on both parties,[119] the amount of the increased costs and losses involved,[120] and the "windfall" gained by Essex.[121] It was said that the merits of Aluminum's claims were distinguishable from other cases[122] where a party sought to rely upon increased costs or substantial losses in the performance of the contract—because the degree of loss (the prospective loss of $60 million) here was much greater.[123] In concluding that continued performance of the contract had been rendered "commercially senseless and unjust", the court held that the most appropriate method of relief was not to cancel the contract,[124] but to grant equitable reformation of the price term.[125] Contractual adjustment was more fitting to the "new spirit"[126] of the contract.

The court held that Aluminum was also entitled to contractual redress on the basis of the doctrine of frustration.[127] The fact that Aluminum's claim of frustration was "a frustration of the purpose to earn money or to avoid losses",[128] that is "for the conversion of an expected profit into a serious loss",[129] did not, in the court's view, give rise to any "legitimate doctrinal problem".[130] Although the remedial relief available, within Restatement Second, Contracts § 285, did not specifically provide for equitable adjustment in circumstances of frustration of purpose, the court, nonetheless, allowed "reformation" of the contract on the basis of the "more general rules of equitable restitution".

117. See 499 F. Supp. 53, at pp. 68, 69 (1980).

118. 499 F. Supp. 53, at p. 63. In distinguishing *Transatlantic Financing Corp.* v. *U.S.* 363 F. 2d. 312 (1966), the court held (p. 75) that "ALCOA's loss is more than a thousand times greater than the carrier's loss. And the circumstances surrounding the contract show a deliberate avoidance of abnormal risks".

119. The important point is that the court not only considered the fact that the energy crisis had directly resulted in a substantial gain for one party (Essex) and a substantial loss for the other (Aluminum), but that part of the Essex's substantial gain had actually been reaped at the expense of Aluminum. See fn. 121 below.

120. The prospective loss of $60 million.

121. See 499 F. Supp. 53, at p. 59 where the court was influenced by the facts that a significant fraction of Essex's profit was directly attributable to the corresponding out-of-pocket losses that ALCOA suffered, and that ALCOA had shown that without judicial relief or economic changes it stood to lose in excess of $75,000,000 during the remaining term of the contract.

122. For example *Transatlantic Financing Corp.* v. *U.S.* 363 F. 2d. 312 (1966); *Maple Farms* v. *City School District* 76 Misc. 2d. 1080 (1974). *Publicker* v. *Union Carbide Corp.* 17 UCC Rep. 989 (1975); *Eastern Air Lines Inc.* v. *Gulf Oil Corp.* 415 F. Supp. 429 (1975); *Iowa Electric Light and Power Co.* v. *Atlas Corp.* 467 F. Supp. 129 (1978); *Louisiana* v. *Allegheny* 517 F. Supp. 1319 (1981).

123. 499 F. Supp. 53, at p. 63.

124. *Ibid.*, p. 79. See Ryan, J.G., "U.C.C. s. 2-615: Excusing The Impracticable" (1980) 60 B.U.L. Rev. 575, at pp. 596, 597.

125. The equitable adjustment related to future performance under the contract and not past performance.

126. 499 F. Supp. 53, at pp. 73, 89, 91.

127. The court considered whether the case involved impracticability, frustration of purpose or both (p. 73).

128. *Ibid.* p. 78.

129. *Ibid.*, p. 76. See also *Florida* v. *Westinghouse* 826 F. 2d. 239 (1987).

130. *Ibid.*, p. 78.

The decision in the ALCOA case has received little support. In appealing to the "new spirit of commercial law",[131] the judge implied that courts should specifically consider the peculiarities and practicalities of each case in question and should not be reticent in using alternative solutions in dealing with claims of commercial impracticability.[132] Yet, in so doing, it appeared that courts were now given a much wider basis to frame the most suitable remedy. Many legal writers expressed concern that the scope of this remedy was too broad.[133] It was said that the decision was too extreme to be of any real use or precedent in dealing with other kinds of contractual agreements or in other areas of contract law.[134] Accordingly, Teitlebaum J.'s plea to follow the "new spirit of commercial law" lost much of its momentum. It was not only clear that modification of the contract was extremely difficult to invoke, let alone justify,[135] but also that the criticisms and controversy it raised were sufficient in themselves substantially to undermine its application.

Florida v. *Westinghouse* and *Aluminum Co*. v. *Essex* both demonstrate that claims involving hardship and excessive costs in performance compel the courts to make a very detailed and complex enquiry into the facts and circumstances of each case. The assumptions and the eventual decisions seem very arbitrary. Consideration will now be given to some cases in which such claims have been raised but have not succeeded.

In *Eastern Air Lines* v. *Gulf Oil Corp*.,[136] the sellers, Gulf, made a contract in 1972 to supply jet fuel to Eastern Air Lines for a period of five years. The price was tied to the price of "West Texas Sour"—this was a crude oil bought and sold in large volume and which was thought to be a reliable indication of the market value of crude oil generally. Whilst the contract was in force, the price of foreign oil increased significantly. During September 1973 and January 1974, it rose over 400 per cent. As a result, the US Government implemented a series of price controls affecting the oil industry, which culminated in the introduction in the autumn of 1973 of the "two-tier" price controls.[137] One tier related to the "old" price-controlled oil and the other to the "new" price-unregulated oil. Accordingly, the price of the old oil remained fixed by the government. Consequently, there was an increase in the market price of foreign crude oil and certain domestic crude oil which affected the contract price, rendering it substantially below the market price at the time of delivery.

131. *Ibid*., p. 89.
132. *Ibid*., p. 91.
133. See fns. 134 and 135 below.
134. See Halpern, S.W., "Application of the Doctrine of Commercial Impracticability: Searching for the 'Wisdom of Solomon' " (1987) 135 U.Pa.L.Rev. 1123; Wuorinen, S.E., "*Northern Indiana Public Service Company* v. *Carbon County Coal Company*: Risk Assumption in Claims of Impossibility, Impracticability, and Frustration of Purpose" (1989) 50 Ohio St. L.J. 163.
135. See also Farnsworth, E.A., *Contracts, op. cit*., p. 705; Murphy, E.J., and Speidel, R.E., *Studies in Contract Law* (3rd Edn., 1984) Mineola, New York, The Foundation Press, Inc., pp. 951–961; White, J.J., and Summers, R.S., *Uniform Commercial Code, op. cit*., pp. 42 *et seq*. For articles see Dawson, J.P., "Judicial Revision of Frustrated Contracts: Germany" (1983) 63 B.U.L. Rev. 1039, Dawson, J.P., "Judicial Revision of Frustrated Contracts: The United States" (1984) 64 B.U.L. Rev. 1; Trakman, L.E., "Winner Take Some: Loss Sharing and Commercial Impracticability" (1985) 69 Minn. L. Rev. 471; Triantis, G.G., "Contractual Allocations of Unknown Risks: A Critique of the Doctrine of Commercial Impracticability", (1992) 42 Univ. of Toronto L.J. 450.
136. *Eastern Air Lines Inc*. v. *Gulf Oil Corp*. 415 F. Supp. 429 (1975).
137. *Ibid*., pp. 433–434.

As a result of the 400 per cent increase in the market price of foreign crude oil and the US Government's fixed price measures, Gulf contended that its obligation to deliver crude oil had become commercially impracticable within the meaning of article 2-615. The court rejected Gulf's claims and held that Gulf had not sufficiently established hardship. In reaching this conclusion the court focused on the foreseeability of events,[138] and said that the events associated with the energy crisis were reasonably foreseeable at the time the contract was made.[139] On this basis, the court held that since the risk of the events and risk of their consequences were outside the scope of article 2-615, it followed that the increase in costs was a risk that was assumed (or deemed to be assumed) by the promisor.

Another example of a case in which a claim of hardship and impracticability failed is *Northern Indiana Public Service Company (NIPSCO)* v. *Carbon County Coal Company*.[140] A long-term contract[141] was made between NIPSCO and Carbon County for the sale of coal at a price of $24 a ton subject to various provisions for escalation.[142] The coal was to be used to generate electricity for sale to NIPSCO's customers. Due to a sharp decline in fuel prices, NIPSCO, realising that it could buy electricity at a much cheaper rate, decided to stop purchasing coal from County Carbon. In seeking a declaration to excuse it from its obligations to purchase from Carbon County, NIPSCO relied upon the doctrines of impossibility, impracticability and frustration of purpose[143] and the *force majeure* clause contained in the contract.[144] County Carbon counterclaimed for breach of contract and sought specific performance of the contract. The US Court of Appeals in uphold-

138. *Ibid.*, pp. 441–442.
139. *Ibid.*, pp. 441–442. See also *Restatement Second, Contracts*, Chapter 11, Introductory Note.
140. 799 F. 2d. 265 (7th Cir. 1986). See *Day, Day Oil. Ltd. and Day Exploration, Inc.* v. *Tenneco Inc. and Tennessee Gas Pipeline Co.* 696 F. Supp. 233 (S.D. Miss. 1988) (purchase of gas); *U.S.* v. *Southwestern Electric Cooperative, Inc.* 869 F. 2d. 310 (7th Cir. 1989); *Goodrich B.F. Co.* v. *Vinyltech* 711 F. Supp. 1513 (1989); *Kaiser-Francis Oil Company* v. *Producer's Gas Company* 870 F. 2d. 563 (10th Cir. 1989); *Sabine Corporation* v. *Ong Western Inc.* 725 F. Supp. 1157 (U.S. District Court, W.D. Oklahoma 1989).
141. The contract period was 20 years.
142. By 1985 the escalation clause had driven the price up to $44 per ton.
143. It would seem that the court here viewed the common law doctrine of frustration as synonymous with the statutory doctrine of impracticability.
144. NIPSCO's rates were regulated by the Indiana Public Service Commission IPSC. The latter had directed NIPSCO by virtue of "economy purchase orders" to make a good faith effort to find and wherever possible buy from utilities that would sell electricity at prices lower than its costs of internal generation (which was estimated to be more expensive than buying from neighbouring utilities). In 1983, NIPSCO requested permission to raise its rates to reflect increased fuel charges. Some of NIPSCO's customers opposed the increase on grounds that NIPSCO could reduce its overall costs by buying elsewhere. Thus NIPSCO was not allowed to pass on fuel costs to its ratepayers in the form of higher rates if it could buy electricity cheaper than it could generate electricity internally using County Carbon's coal. Accordingly, it was held that the effect of the increased costs was a burden which had to rest "squarely on the shoulders of NIPSCO management" (p. 267), and that even if the risk which NIPSCO took was deemed to be excessive, the matter was one between NIPSCO and the Public Service Commission. The court concluded that the appropriate course of action would, therefore, be to seek judicial review of the economy purchase orders. See also *U.S.* v. *Panhandle Eastern Corp.* 693 F. Supp. 88 (U.S. District Court, D. Delaware, 1988), 868 F. 2d. 1363 (3rd. Cir. 1989) (natural gas purchase contract) where the party was not excused under the *force majeure* provisions as a result of economic hardship or market fluctuations. Compare *Atlantic Richfield Company, d/b/a Arco Oil and Gas Company* v. *ANR Pipeline Company* 768 S.W. 2d. 777 (14th Cir. Court of Appeals of Texas, Houston, 1989) (gas purchase contract) where the party was excused under the *force majeure* provisions as a result of the Federal Energy Regulatory Commission Order No. 380 which permitted gas pipeline customers to refuse to pay

ing, in part, the decision of the US District Court,[145] said that NIPSCO was in breach and was liable in damages for $181 million.[146] It was held that since NIPSCO had entered into a fixed price contract, it had taken the risk that the market price of coal could fall as well as rise. The ensuing loss suffered by NIPSCO was a factor which the courts deemed to be an assumed risk under the contract.[147] NIPSCO's "losses" were merely the result of an incorrect forecast of the market. Thus, "locked into a disadvantageous contract", the buyer "has only himself to blame and so cannot shift the risk back to the seller by invoking impossibility related doctrines".[148] The court concluded that specific performance was not appropriate,[149] and notwithstanding that the contract had become "uneconomical", NIPSCO could not escape liability. Given that the contract was for a fixed price, had included escalation provisions,[150] and would have involved a sum of "$1 billion (the estimated amount that NIPSCO would have owed over the life of the contract if the contract had not been cancelled)",[151] damages of $181 million reflected the appropriate measure of liability.

The court's approach was again different from other kinds of cases, such as *Florida* v. *Westinghouse*, that had, in one form or another, also involved hardship. In *Northern Indiana Public Service Company* (*NIPSCO*) v. *Carbon County Coal Company*, the court was more concerned with the extent of the actual risks that had been assumed by the parties than NIPSCO's position and its inability to sustain the risks. The court emphasised that NIPSCO had assumed the risk and was liable in damages for $181 million, despite the fact that it was specifically prevented from passing the loss on to its ratepayers.[152] In *Florida* v. *Westinghouse*, on the other hand, the court was primarily concerned with the effect that its decision would have on the contracting parties and whether the parties themselves were actually in a position to sustain the particular losses. Thus the court decided that the costs of reracking could be divided between both parties—both parties were deemed to be equally able to carry the costs. Florida was in a position to sustain some of the costs

for gas not taken. It was held that (p. 781) "the term *force majeure* included any act (including the failure to take gas) of a purchaser of substantial quantities of gas from ANR which is excused by any event constituting *force majeure and* any orders or regulations of any governmental body".

145. Since the case was first heard in the US District Court for the Northern District of Indiana, Indiana law was applied. The court applied the Indiana version of art. 2-615 of the code, that is, the Burns Ind. Stat. Ann. § 26-1–2-615 and the Indiana Comments. There was some difference in the provisions and interpretation between art. 2-615 and the Official Comments of the Code and those adopted within the Indiana Federal State. One major difference related to whether a buyer could invoke the protection of the statutory doctrine of impracticability. There was also some dispute as to whether Indiana law recognised the common law doctrine of frustration (the alternative claim of the buyer).

146. Nonetheless, specific performance was not granted. It was said that since the breach was both "efficient" and "cost-justified", the remedy of damages was sufficient.

147. See 799 F. 2d. 265, 279 (1986).

148. *Ibid.*, p. 278.

149. *Ibid.*, pp. 279–281.

150. *Ibid.*, p. 278. See Halpern, S.W., "Application of the Doctrine of Commercial Impracticability: Searching for the 'Wisdom of Solomon' " (1987) 135 U. Pa. L. Rev. 1123; Wuorinen, S.E., "*Northern Indiana Public Service Company* v. *Carbon County Coal Company*. Risk Assumption in Claims of Impossibility, Impracticability, and Frustration of Purpose" (1989) 50 Ohio St. L.J. 163.

151. 799 F. 2d. 265, at pp. 268–269.

152. *Ibid.*, at pp. 274–275.

of re-racking because "in all probability" it would be "permitted to recover its costs from its ratepayers".[153]

The cases in this area show that, although article 2-615 clearly recognises that claims of hardship may provide some measure of relief, this kind of claim has not in practical terms been readily received or widely accepted. To some degree, this is attributable to the fact that the courts have not really been able to establish any firm guideline as to what is sufficient in law to constitute "excessive hardship". Despite the endorsement of hardship within article 2-615, the courts still tend to view the application of the doctrine of commercial impracticability to contracts for the sale of goods with much caution. In deciding cases involving the doctrine of impracticability, the courts have not used one particular approach, or placed emphasis upon any one particular criterion, but, rather, have emphasised different approaches and criteria.

It is evident from the cases where claims of impracticability have been successfully upheld, that the supervening event must not only have resulted in substantial additional expenses, but also in a substantial change to the whole performance of the contract. For example, in *Florida* v. *Westinghouse* the supervening event (the government policy) not only affected the monetary obligations of the party, but also changed the whole contract—the method by which the contract was to be executed. Westinghouse was excused on the basis of impracticability precisely because the alternative method of performance involved excessive and severe increases in costs *and* was not a method contemplated by the parties at the time the contract was made.

5. A COMPARISON BETWEEN THE US DOCTRINE OF IMPRACTICABILITY AND THE ENGLISH DOCTRINE OF FRUSTRATION

The US and English legal principles of contractual excuse do not necessarily recognise the same grounds for contractual relief. Whilst the English doctrine of frustration demonstrates that commercial impracticability, commercial hardship and frustration of purpose or object of the contract will not be given effect in international contractual agreements,[154] such bases of relief have not only been accepted by US courts, but they have also been incorporated as a statutory doctrine under article 2-615 of the code (and under the US common law). For example, in certain cases in the US, claims have been upheld under the principle of frustration of purpose, commercial impracticability and commercial hardship[155] and the courts have even discussed the extent of the increases or losses in performance which have to be sustained before a party can be excused.

US courts, by virtue of article 2-615, are able to grant a much wider range of

153. 826 F. 2d. 239, at p. 279 (1987). See also fn. 110 above.

154. The principle of frustration of purpose, as recognised in *Krell* v. *Henry*, is of limited application. The case of *Krell* v. *Henry* involved a contract to hire a flat and was made between two domestic parties. See fns. 59–63 *above*.

155. See *ALCOA* 499 F. Supp. 53 (1980); *Florida Power & Light Co.* v. *Westinghouse Electric Corp.* 826 F. 2d. 239 (1987).

remedies than that provided under the English doctrine of frustration. Articles 2-615 and 2-616 of the Uniform Commercial Code deal with the remedial consequences which may follow once it has been concluded that performance of the contract has been rendered wholly or partially impracticable. Provision is made not only for the termination of the contract and discharge of the parties' liabilities, but also for the modification and adjustment of the contract,[156] statutory assignment of rights[157] and in circumstances whereby performance of the contract has been rendered partially impracticable.[158]

A comparative case analysis

In view of some of the apparent differences between the application of the US doctrine of impracticability and the English doctrine of frustration, an analysis will now be made to illustrate how English courts would have approached a case such as *Florida* v. *Westinghouse*. The objective is to show whether or not the same result would be reached as was reached by the US court, and if so, on the same or on an entirely different basis. The case will be considered in the light of the English doctrine of frustration.

It would seem that an English court would only assume that "reprocessing" formed the "basis" of the contract if there was a clear indication in the terms of the contract, expressly or impliedly, that the parties contemplated that "reprocessing" constituted *the* method of performance rather than *a* method of performance. The distinction is important as it would determine whether Westinghouse would be obliged to adopt another, alternative method of performance. In English law, the first conclusion is only likely to be drawn if "reprocessing" amounted to a term of fundamental importance and constituted a method which is exclusive.[159] It is submitted that, on the facts of *Westinghouse*, the criteria would not be satisfied. Thus, an English court would hold that "reprocessing" merely constituted *a* method of performing the contract and that Westinghouse would be obliged to adopt an alternative method.

Since the unavailability of "reprocessing" would not necessarily frustrate the contract, and Westinghouse would be obliged to adopt an alternative method of

156. See fn. 135 above.

157. *InterPetrol, Bermuda Ltd.* v. *Kaiser Aluminum International Corp.* 719 F. 2d. 992 (1983). See Bermingham, J.P.. "Extending Good Faith: Does the U.C.C. Impose a Duty of Good Faith Negotiation Under Changed Circumstances?" (1987) 61 St. John's L. Rev. 217.

158. See arts. 2-615 (b), (c); Comment 11 of art. 2-615 and art. 2-616. For cases see *Roth Steel Products* v. *Sharon Steel Corp.* 705 F. 2d. 134 (1983); *Cosden Oil & Chemical Company* v. *Karl O. Helm Aktiengesellschaft* 736 F. 2d. 1064 (1984); *Alimenta (U.S.A.), Inc.* v. *Cargill, Incorporated.* 861 F. 2d. 650 (11th Cir. 1988) Cf. For the position of the parties in English law see fn. 4 and pp. 45–50 above.

159. *Nickoll and Knight* v. *Ashton, Eldridge & Co.* [1901] 2 K.B. 126. See *Benjamin's Sale of Goods* (4th Edn.), Sweet & Maxwell, para. 19-030/1. See also *Tsakiroglou* v. *Noblee & Thorl* [1962] A.C. 98, 112 *per* Viscount Simonds. In the light of Lord Simonds' statement, it may appear that the doctrine of frustration will not apply even when both parties contemplate a particuar method of performance and intend that method to be exclusive. It is suggested that, notwithstanding this statement, if the particular method is specified and if the parties show, expressly or impliedly, that they intend that method to be exclusive, the doctrine might apply. Cf. *Jon-T Chemicals Inc.* v. *Freeport Chemical Co.* 704 F. 2d. 1412 (U.S. Court of Appeals, 5th Cir. 1983) where the sellers were not liable to adopt an alternative method of performance on the basis of the particular clause contained in the contract.

performance, it would appear that they could only be excused if they could prove either of the following. First, that although they were *prima facie* obliged to adopt an alternative method, no alternative method in fact existed. Therefore there was no real or practical alternative for them to adopt in that the initial unavailability of "reprocessing" had rendered performance of the contract impossible. Secondly, on the basis that an alternative method existed, the alternative method would be fundamentally different from that originally contemplated. In the US decision, the court concluded that the enactment of the Nuclear Waste Policy Act (NWPA) did (at least theoretically) provide an alternative method. The court, in excusing Westinghouse, did so not necessarily on the basis that the alternative method of performance was impossible, but on the basis of the excessive and unreasonable expenditure (impracticability). Whilst such a claim would not generally succeed in an English court,[160] it is prudent, given the degree of expenditure involved in *Florida* v. *Westinghouse*, to consider whether such a claim cloud be entertained within the English doctrine of frustration. Given that this kind of claim has not been fully explored, and given that expenditure of this magnitude has never been put forward as the basis of a claim, the claim is undoubtedly worth advancing.

It would appear that Westinghouse would, perhaps, be more likely to satisfy the first of the two alternatives mentioned—namely that no alternative method of performance existed. Thus, leaving aside impracticability and increased costs, the question for consideration is whether English courts would deem (as did the US court) the method provided under the statute (the Nuclear Waste Policy Act) as a "real" alternative method of performance, or whether they would deem it as providing no alternative method, theoretically or otherwise. On the one hand, English courts could conclude that, although storage within the terms of the NWPA was not immediately available, it did provide an alternative method. On this basis, the immediate unavailability of the method might be construed as merely temporary—such temporary unavailability would not, therefore, be sufficient to frustrate the contract. On the other hand, given the facts of the case and given that there was no actual certainty as to the date when such storage facilities would, if ever, be available,[161] it would appear more likely that an English court would not construe such unavailability as temporary. On this basis, the unavailability might be construed to be of such uncertain duration[162] as not to present any alternative method of performance at all, or as to render the contract radically different from that contemplated

160. *Tsakiroglou* v. *Noblee Thorl* [1962] A.C. 93, at pp. 118, 128, 129 *per* Lord Reid: "I need not consider what the result might be if the increase had reached an astronomical figure" and Denning L.J. in *Brauer & Co (GB) Ltd.* v. *Clark (James) (Brush Materials)* [1952] 2 All E.R. 497, at p. 501 where he stated that 100 per cent over the contract price would amount to the frustration of the contract. Cf: *Davis Contractors Ltd.* v. *Fareham U.D.C.* [1956] A.C. 696; *Amalgamated Investment & Property Co. Ltd.* v. *John Walker & Son Ltd.* [1977] 1 W.L.R. 164. See also Treitel, G.H., *The Law of Contract* (8th Edn.) Sweet & Maxwell, pp. 779–785.

161. See 826 F. 2d. 239, at p. 277: "The site for storage has not been selected . . . it may be as late as 2010 before storage is available and even that estimate is not firm."

162. As, for example, cases where supervening events have resulted in delay of such an uncertain duration as to frustrate the contract. In *Embiricos* v. *Sydney Reid & Co.* [1914] 3 K.B. 45, at p. 54 Scrutton J. stated that commercial men must be entitled to act on reasonable commercial probabilities at the time when they are called upon to make up their minds: *Pioneer Shipping Ltd.* v. *B.T.P. Tioxide Ltd. (The Nema)* [1982] A.C. 724, at p. 752; *National Carriers Ltd.* v. *Panalpina (Northern) Ltd.* [1981] A.C. 675, at pp. 688, 706. See further on this point pp. 129–138.

by the parties at the time of contracting. In reaching either conclusion, the courts would not even have to consider the question of impracticability or increased costs as an additional ground of discharge.

So it would appear that, had *Florida* v. *Westinghouse* been decided under English law, Westinghouse may have been excused within the doctrine of frustration, although the approach taken by an English court would have been rather different from the United States Court of Appeals. There is one important aspect of the case which would have caused great difficulty if it had been litigated before an English court: the decision of the US court to divide the costs of re-racking the spent fuel on site between the parties.[163] In this respect, it is not only the approach, but, arguably, also the result which would have been different. Given the limited relief available under the doctrine of frustration and the fact that the issue of "loss apportionment" within the Law Reform (Frustrated Contracts) Act 1943 remains unclear,[164] it is unlikely that an English court would have been able to adjust the parties' liabilities in the same manner as the US court. In the final analysis, since it appears that Westinghouse would have been excused from its liability to perform, it would seem to follow that Florida would probably have had to sustain the risk of re-racking the spent fuel.[165]

6. ARTICLE 2-615: THE METHOD OF PERFORMANCE AND FAILURE OR UNAVAILABILITY OF THE SOURCE OF SUPPLY

Where supervening circumstances render the method of performance impossible, or a failure or unavailability of the source of supply renders the method of performance impracticable, article 2-615 provides an excuse for non-performance of the contract. There are, however, separate guidelines where the seller himself is to grow the contracted goods.[166]

At first glance it appears that in the United States a seller is, by virtue of Official Comments 4 and 5 of article 2-615, afforded a greater measure of protection than

163. This particular part of the decision was affirmed by the US Court of Appeals, notwithstanding the fact that neither Westinghouse nor Florida had actually appealed against this part of the judgment from the US District Court. See fn. 110 above.

164. See *Chandler* v. *Webster* [1904] 1 K.B. 493 reversed in *Fibrosa Spolka Akcyjna* v. *Fairburn Lawson Combe Barbour Ltd.* [1943] A.C. 32; *B.P. Exploration Co. (Libya) Ltd.* v. *Hunt (No. 2)* [1983] A.C. 352. See further and Chapter 11; *Benjamin's Sale of Goods, op. cit.*, paras 6-048-6-056; Goff, R., and Jones, G., *The Law of Restitution* (4th Edn.), Sweet & Maxwell, pp. 447–468. See fn. 110 above. Furthermore, it may be argued that, the Law Reform (Frustrated Contracts) Act 1943 would not necessarily be relevant on the basis, *inter alia*, that the contract had expressly provided for the risk of supervening events (s.2(3) of the Law Reform (Frustrated Contracts) Act 1943). See, however, *B.P. Exploration Co. (Libya) Ltd.* v. *Hunt (No. 2)* [1983] A.C. 352 where the House of Lords accepted that the clause was not of the kind that applied in the event of frustration and that it was only intended to affect the parties' contractual rights and obligations under the contract.

165. Subject to any claims under ss.1(2) and 1(3) fo the Law Reform (Frustrated Contracts) Act 1943.

166. Official Comment 9 of art. 2-615: "The case of a farmer who has contracted to sell crops to be grown on designated land may be regarded as falling either within the section on casualty to identified goods or this section, and he may be excused, when there is a failure of the specific crop, either on the basis of the destruction of identified goods or because of the failure of a basic assumption of the contract." Translation taken from *Uniform Laws Annotated, Uniform Commercial Code*, Vol 1B, *op cit.*, pp. 196–197.

under English law.[167] For example, under Official Comment 4, the seller may be excused notwithstanding the absence of a specific reference to the source or supply, or the fact that he alone contemplated that source. Under Official Comment 5,[168] it appears that, where both parties have contemplated a particular source, a seller may still be excused although that particular source is not exclusive. In practice, the courts have been very reluctant to excuse a seller in such circumstances. Often relief is denied on the ground that the seller has failed to show that he tried to perform in every way possible.[169] An example of a case in which relief has been denied is where a seller has failed to establish that the goods could not be obtained elsewhere.[170] Consequently, it has been held that the doctrine of impracticability will not apply when the failure of the method of performance or the failure or unavailability of the source of supply is due to the fact that the seller has miscalculated the contract goods, underestimated the anticipated market value of the goods or over-contracted in anticipation of supplies.[171] Thus, in *Gulf*

167. See also art. 2-613 of the code on "Casualty to Identified Goods". This provision applies where goods are "identified" when the contract is made and "suffer casualty without fault of either party before the risk of loss passes to the buyer". Cf. the position of the contracting parties in English law: *Benjamin's Sale of Goods, op cit.*, para. 19-109; Treitel, G.H. *The Law of Contract, op. cit.*, pp. 770–779. For cases see *Blackburn Bobbin Co. Ltd.* v. *Allen T.W. & Sons Ltd.* [1918] 2 K.B. 467; *Tsakiroglou & Co. Ltd.* v. *Noblee Thorl G.m.b.H.* [1962] A.C. 93; *J. Lauritzen A.S.* v. *Wijsmuller B.V. (The Super Servant Two)* [1990] 1 Lloyd's Rep. 1 (C.A.).

168. Official Comment 5 states: "Where a particular source of supply is exclusive under the agreement and fails through casualty, the present section applies rather than the provision on destruction or deterioration of specific goods. The same holds true where a particular source of supply is shown by the circumstances to have been contemplated or assumed by the parties at the time of contracting . . . There is no excuse under this section, however, unless the seller has employed all due measures to assure himself that his source will not fail . . . In the case of failure of production by an agreed source for causes beyond the seller's control, the seller should, if possible, be excused since production by an agreed source is without more a basic assumption of the contract." Translation taken from *Uniform Laws Annotated, Uniform Commercial Code*, Vol 1B, *op. cit.*, p. 196. There are a number of difficulties relating to the construction of this comment. The first is that it is unclear whether a seller is able to seek excuse if he alone has contemplated a particular and exclusive source of supply. The second is that it is uncertain whether "failure of production by an agreed source" is a matter which can only be inferred when parties have expressly provided for it, or whether it can be inferred when both parties merely contemplated it. The third is that, given the absence of the word "exclusive" in the case where the source of supply is merely contemplated by the parties, it is arguable that a seller may be excused where the source is contemplated and is not intended to be the exclusive source. Cf: the position in English law—where the source is not expressed and is merely contemplated by one party—the result is similar to the parallel situation in which one party has contemplated a particular method of performance. In either context, the doctrine does not apply (*Blackburn Bobbin* v. *Allen* [1918] 2 K.B. 467).

169. *Natus Corp.* v. *U.S.* 371 F. 2d. 450 (1967); *Neal-Cooper Grain Co.* v. *Texas Gulf Sulphur Co.* 508 F. 2d. 283 (1974); *Publicker* v. *Union Carbide Corp.* 17 U.C.C. Rep. 989 (1975); *Jennie-O Foods Inc.* v. *U.S.* 580 F. 2d. 400 (1978); *Fratelli Gardino S.p.A.* v. *Caribbean Lumber Co.* 587 F. 2d. 204 (1979); *Luria Brothers & Co. Inc.* v. *Pielet Brothers Scrap Iron & Metal Inc.* 600 F. 2d. 103 (1979); *International Minerals* v. *Llano* 770 F. 2d. 879, at p. 885 (1985). See also the *Suez* cases held in the United States; in *Glidden Co.* v. *Hellenic Lines Ltd.* 275 F. 2d. 253 (2d. Cir. 1960) the contract expressly provided for shipment "via Suez or Cape of Good Hope". It was held that the contract was not frustrated. In *Transatlantic Financing Corporation* v. *United States* 363 F. 2d. 312, at p. 317 (1966) the court said that "in some cases, even an express expectation may not amount to a condition of performance".

170. *Luria Brothers & Co. Inc.* v. *Pielet Brothers Scrap Iron & Metal Inc.* 600 F. 2d. 103 (1979).

171. See *Jennie-O Foods* v. *U.S.* 580 F. 2d. 400 and that is unless both parties knew that the goods were only to be purchased or grown from a specified source. In contracts which can be performed in a number of alternative methods, a party must ensure that these alternative methods are no longer commercially practical or possible. See *Transatlantic Financing Corp.* v. *U.S.* 363 F. 2d. 312 (1966); *Natus* v. *U.S.* 371 F. 2d. 450 (1967); *Roth Steel* v. *Sharon Steel* 705 F. 2d. 134, at p. 150 (1983) (contract to sell steel). In *Alimenta (U.S.A.) Inc.* v. *Cargill Inc.* 861 F. 2d. 650 (11th Cir. 1988) (contract to sell peanuts) it was held that the failure to supply the full quantity of goods was not due to a miscalculation of the

v. *F.P.C.*[172] the sellers (who were also suppliers) had contracted to supply natural gas. Although no specific source was mentioned in the contract, the sellers had contemplated using one of their own large reserves. Due to overestimation of this reserve, they could not deliver the contracted quantity and contended that they were only bound to deliver what was practically available. They also maintained that, even if their contractual obligations to supply were taken to be "unconditional on the face of the contract", they should still be excused on the basis that: "(1) even facially unconditional obligations are subject to economic limitations; and (2) '[w]here performance has been rendered impracticable, even though not impossible, and such impracticability was the result of unforeseen events, as here, a party will be excused from performance.' "[173] The court found that the sellers had not merely contracted to sell but had *warranted* to deliver the necessary quantity required by the buyers. The sellers were held liable because "a warranty by its very nature precludes relief on a theory of commercial impracticability resulting from the unavailability of gas" and "even in the absence of an express and unconditional warranty, the doctrine of commercial impracticability would not apply to this case".[174]

6. CONCLUSIONS

Although the doctrine of commercial impracticability has been tried and tested in a number of different cases and contracts, it is still a doctrine in its judicial infancy. As a result, it is rather difficult to delineate its exact scope and impact: its potential remains to be realised. Nonetheless, this has not precluded legal scholars from discussing a wide range of issues ranging from when, how and in what circumstances article 2-615 is applied, to when, how and in what circumstances particular solutions and remedies may be given.[175] Unfortunately, their endeavours have not always been successful.[176] One main reason is that many have sought to extract specific answers and solutions from provisions of the code which, of themselves, are only designed to provide broad and rather general guidelines. Legal scholars, therefore, have only been able to make speculative comments and conclusions about the scope and application of article 2-615. In this respect many scholars have become disillusioned with article 2-615.[177]

The courts have experienced difficulties in applying the doctrine of impracticability. They have not construed it consistently and have employed a variety of different approaches. Some of the decisions by the US courts appear to be more innovative than those given by English courts. This is attributable as much to the philosophy and flexibility of article 2-615 of the code as it is to the nature, type and

anticipated goods by the sellers. The court disregarded the fact that the sellers had already made numerous contracts even before the peanuts had been grown, on the ground that "pre-harvest forward sales contracts are customary in the peanut industry".

172. *Gulf* v. *F.P.C.* 583 F. 2d. 588 (1977). Gulf sought judicial review of an order concerning its obligation to deliver gas.

173. *Ibid.*, p. 597.

174. *Ibid.*, p. 599.

175. See arts. 2-614–2-616 of the Code.

176. See fns. 34 and 70 above.

177. *Id.*

peculiarity of US commercial contracts. It may be said that the US courts have a much greater opportunity to address claims of impracticability and hardship and amongst a much broader range of contractual agreements[178] than the English courts are ever likely to encounter. Given the general standards imposed by the various provisions of the code, such as "the obligations of good faith, diligence, reasonableness and care",[179] the US courts seem to adopt a more interventionist role than English courts. In so doing, they often assess the wider ramifications which would result from applying or denying a claim of impracticability. These are not merely policy considerations[180] but also financial considerations, such as the ability of the parties to pay,[181] and considerations relating to the status of the contracting parties.[182] The English doctrine of frustration is particularly inadequate regarding the kind of relief that is available, as, for example, in circumstances resulting in the "partial frustration" of the contract. Even the concept of "reasonableness" regarding a contracting party's partial allocation of available goods, or election to perform one or some of his contracts, fails to persuade the courts to introduce an element of flexibility in determining claims of frustration.

Thus the US courts have been able to use "good faith" in determining whether or not a contracting party can be afforded any contractual relief under article 2-615. The code's "good faith" obligation enables US contracting parties to advance some interesting arguments. In some cases, these arguments have been influential. By way of contrast, since English law has not recognised any general obligation to act in good faith,[183] the courts have not been able, at least not ostensibly, to take this into account in applying the doctrine of frustration. English contracting parties have therefore not been able to employ arguments based upon good faith in the same fashion as their US counterparts. Accordingly, it would appear that want of good faith does not bear the same significance in the application of the English doctrine of frustration.

There are still a number of important points that remain unresolved in relation to the scope of article 2-615, such as the circumstances in which the courts will impose a solution such as the modification of the contract, or the extent to which increased costs in performance is sufficient to invoke the doctrine of impracticability. Whereas a 10- to 12-fold increase has been upheld in one instance,[184] the general trend has been to deny relief in cases, particularly where the increased costs do not run into millions of dollars. On the analysis of the cases in this area, losses or added expenditure of millions of dollars (anticipated or prospective) do not appear to be the only prerequisite to the successful invocation of a claim based on increased costs. It would seem that the contract itself must be of a long-term nature primarily

178. For example *Asphalt* v. *Enterprise Shipping* 667 F. 2d. 261 (1981).

179. Art. 1-102 of the code. See also arts. 1-203 (good faith) and 2-302 (unconscionable contract or clause).

180. *ALCOA* 499 F. Supp. 53 (1980); *Florida Power & Light Co.* v. *Westinghouse Electric Corp.* 826 F. 2d. 239 (1987); *NIPSCO* v. *Carbon County* 799 F. 2d. 265 (1986).

181. See fn. 180 above.

182. *NIPSCO* v. *Carbon County* 799 F. 2d. 265 (1986); *Florida Power & Light Co.* v. *Westinghouse Electric Corp.* 826 F. 2d. 239 (1987). These cases can be compared with cases where both contracting parties are private commercial parties, *ALCOA* 499 F. Supp. 53 (1980).

183. See *Walford and Others* v. *Miles and Another* [1992] 2 A.C. 128; *Nicolene Ltd.* v. *Simmonds* [1952] 2 Lloyd's Rep. 419, at p. 425, *per* Sellers J.

184. *Mineral Park* v. *Howard* 172 Cal. 289 (1916). See fn. 35 above.

involving service industries, large-scale corporations and public utilities. This suggests that courts are only prepared to consider claims of commercial hardship in long-term contracts of supply or services. Claims of commercial hardship in the context of contracts of sale of goods are neither very promising nor likely.

SUKHNAM DIGWA-SINGH

CHAPTER 17

FORCE MAJEURE IN EU LAW[1]

1. THE DOMESTIC POSITION IN THE UK

It would not be unfair to suggest that a treatise on the subject of *force majeure* under English law could be produced with considerable speed. The amount of case law generated by this topic is relatively small and has attracted little enthusiasm on the part of academics, practitioners and judges. In 1915, Mr Justice Bailhache in *Matsoukis* v. *Priestman*[2] reflected this apparent lack of enthusiasm when he uttered the following classic statement: "The words *force majeure* are not words which we generally find in English contracts. They are taken from the Code Napoleon . . . In my construction of the words . . . I am influenced to some extent by the fact that they were inserted by this foreign gentleman."[3]

However, Mr Justice Bailhache did apply his mind to the meaning of *force majeure* when he went on to state:

" . . . I cannot accept the argument that the words are interchangeable with *vis major* or Act of God. I am not going to attempt to give any definition of the words *force majeure*, but I am satisfied that I ought to give them a more extensive meaning than Act of God or *vis major*. The difficulty is to say how much more extensive . . . I think that the complete dislocation of business . . . as a consequence of the universal coal strike . . . did come within the reasonable meaning of the words *force majeure* . . . As to delay due to breakdown of machinery it comes within the words *force majeure*, which certainly cover accidents to machinery. The term *force majeure* cannot, however, in any view, be extended to cover bad weather, football matches, or a funeral."[4]

A similar aversion to the use of "foreign" terminology subsequently appeared in the judgment of Mr Justice Sankey in *Hackney Borough Council* v. *Doré*[5] when he stated that: "I regret the introduction of foreign words into English statutes and orders without any definition of them being given."[6] The underlying premise in English law is that both parties are to stand by their contractual obligations even though this may appear to be unreasonable or unjust in certain circumstances. The view is taken that the parties should have made appropriate provisions in the contract. For this reason, a large number of commercial contracts contain *force*

1. The law is stated on the basis of materials available as at 1 July 1994.
2. [1915] 1 K.B. 681.
3. *Ibid.*, at p. 685.
4. *Ibid.*, at pp. 686–687.
5. [1922] 1 K.B. 431.
6. *Ibid.*, at p. 437.

majeure clauses and it is in the context of construing those clauses that what little case law English law has produced has arisen.

2. THE IMPORTANCE OF FORCE MAJEURE IN EU LAW

In the EU context, the principle of *force majeure* is very much alive and vibrant and has produced a great deal of jurisprudence over the past 25 years. To understand why this should be the case, it is necessary to comprehend how *force majeure* slots into the scheme of operations in the European community. In particular, it arises most frequently in aspects of the exportation of agricultural produce, although *force majeure* is relevant to a number of different areas of EU law.

To facilitate certain areas of trade in the agricultural sector, the individual agencies in each member state of the EU distribute licences, export refunds and various other forms of subsidies. The intention is three-fold. First, the governments in non-EU countries are frequently found to be providing similar types of subsidies and the EU therefore wishes to try to guarantee equality of trading opportunity for companies within the member states. Secondly, it is an integral part of the Treaty of Rome that there will be equality of trading opportunity between exporters in the member states themselves. Thirdly, the Commission is committed to trying to keep to a minimum the notorious mountains and lakes of EU produce. The sums provided by the EU are substantial. In general, these sums are paid in advance to exporters by the various EU agencies with the exporters providing security to cover the possibility of their failing to satisfy any of the various regulatory obligations.

The problems arise where the exporters fail to satisfy the obligations which are strict and numerous. For example, in certain cases goods are required to be exported from the EU within a very strict timetable and, in others, exporters have to ensure that the goods are placed on the home market of the country of destination. In such cases, exporters can easily find themselves technically in breach of their obligations through no fault of their own. In such instances, the EU agencies will nevertheless turn to the exporters and demand repayment in full of any EU refunds paid at the outset and will normally seek to impose a penalty of up to 20 per cent regardless of the degree of personal fault on the exporter's part. This can result in the transactions producing enormous and crippling losses. In such instances, *force majeure* instantly comes to the minds of exporters and they are likely to make a very prompt application to the EU agency, seeking confirmation that their circumstances qualify for *force majeure*. Equally, the bankers and insurers of such exporters stand by, awaiting the outcome of the application with a considerable degree of self-interest.

It is useful to quote sample extracts from regulations to see the precise type of provisions to which exporters turn. For example, article 9 in Regulation 2730/79 reads:

"Without prejudice to the provisions of Articles 10, 20 and 26, the refund shall be paid only upon proof being furnished that the product in respect of which customs export formalities have been completed has, within 60 days from the day of completion of such formalities:

— In the case specified in Article 5, reached its destination unaltered,

or

— In other cases, left the geographical territory of the community unaltered.

When the exporter is unable by reason of *force majeure* to comply with the time limit specified in the preceding sub-paragraph, such time limit may at his request be extended for such a period as the competent agency of the member state in which customs export formalities were completed considers necessary in view of the circumstances invoked."

Similarly, article 10 in the same regulation reads:

"In the following circumstances payment of the refund shall be conditional not only on the product having left the geographical territory of the community but also—save where it has perished in transit as a result of *force majeure*—on its having been imported into a non-member country and where appropriate into a specific non-member country:

(a) Where there is serious doubt as to the true destination of the product; or
(b) Where by reason of the difference between the rate of the refund on the exported product and the import duties applicable to an identical product on the day when customs export formalities are completed it is possible that the product may be re-introduced into the community . . .

If a product, after leaving the geographical territory of the community, has perished in transit as a result of *force majeure*, the amount paid shall be:

— in the case of a refund which varies according to destination, the part thereof specified in Article 21.
— in the case of a refund which does not so vary, the total amount thereof."

Subsequently, exporters have had to turn to Regulation 3665/87. Similar words to those quoted above are set out in, *inter alia*, articles 4 and 5 of Regulation 3665/87. Article 21 in Regulation 3665/87 is also worth setting out and states:

"The provisions of this Article shall apply where the product is exported on submission of an export licence or advance-fixing certificate specifying a compulsory destination . . . Where, as a result of *force majeure*, the product is delivered to a destination other than that in respect of which such licence or certificate was issued, a refund shall be paid at the request of the exporter if he furnishes proof of *force majeure* and proof of the actual destination of the product . . . "

3. THE DIFFERING PERSPECTIVES OF EXPORTERS, BANKERS AND THE INSURANCE INDUSTRY

It is easy to understand why the concept of *force majeure* should be so important to exporters. It is not, however, quite so immediately apparent why bankers and insurers (or insurance brokers) should be so interested. It is, therefore, useful to highlight, by means of the following examples, the way in which *force majeure* affects the perspective of these differing interests:

(a) The exporter

During transit of the goods from the EU to the ultimate destination, the exporter's customer goes into liquidation and the goods are brought back within the EU. The exporter was dealing with a long-standing customer whose liquidity problems were not known to him and over whom he could not possibly have exercised control. It would not have been possible to predict this occurrence and he therefore turns to the EU agency in his member state and applies for *force majeure* to prevent the agency from claiming payment of 120 per cent of the export refund.

(b) The banker

The banker's favourite customer comes to him, indicating that he is about to export a large quantity of grain. The customer wishes to pre-finance the transaction and asks his banker to provide security on his behalf to the EU agency for the available export refund plus 20 per cent. During transit from the exporter's warehouse to the dock, however, the goods are stolen by the haulage contractor. The banker then finds that his customer has gone into liquidation and the EU agency turns to the bank for repayment of the export refund plus the 20 per cent penalty. The banker immediately seeks to invoke *force majeure*.

(c) The insurer/insurance broker

An exporter comes along indicating that he is about to export a large quantity of grain. The export documents including the sales invoice indicate that the c.i.f. value of the cargo is, say, US$1 million. The exporter, however, indicates that the export is attracting substantial refunds and he is concerned that these may have to be returned together with the appropriate penalty if the goods are lost during transit or if they are rejected on arrival at the ultimate destination. Should he prudently insure such a risk and, if so, how should he fix the premium?

It will be seen from the examples set out in section 6 below that neither the exporter nor the banker is likely to succeed in their attempts to invoke *force majeure*. The answer to the situation posed in the insurer's or insurance broker's case is that they should positively advise the exporter to insure the risk.

4. DEFINITION

Practitioners are always expected to define concisely and accurately the subject-matter of their discussions. Any lawyer considering the concept of *force majeure*, however, is instantly faced with the difficulty that the European Court has over the last 25 years been trying to devise a definition or test with which it is satisfied itself. The court has received considerable assistance from some eminent Advocates General such as Mancini, Caportorti, Gulmann and Slynn, who have been involved in a large proportion of the cases on *force majeure*.

The court began to tackle the problem of *force majeure* in the *Schwarzwald-milch*[7] case in 1968. The court's judgment contains the following much-quoted passage:

> "As the concept of *force majeure* is not identical in the different branches of law and the various fields of application, the significance of this concept must be determined on the basis of the legal framework within which it is intended to take effect. Thus, the interpretation of the concept of *force majeure* used in the regulation in question must take into account the particular nature of the relationships in public law between the importers and that national administration, as well as the objectives of that regulation.

7. [1968] E.C.R. 377.

The public interest which requires the most accurate forecast possible of the future development of imports in each member state and warrants the lodging of a deposit on the issue of an import licence must be reconciled with the need, which is also a matter of public interest, for trade between states to remain unhampered by obligations which are too rigid. The threat to the loss of the deposit is intended to encourage the importers to whom the licence has been issued to fulfil the obligation to import and thus to ensure the accuracy of the forecast of the future development of imports in the general interest.

It follows therefore that an importer who has shown the necessary diligence is in principle released from the obligation to import within the meaning of Article 6 of Regulation 136/64 EEC when circumstances outside his control make it impossible for him to effect the importation within the required period."[8]

Then in 1970 the court in *Internationale Handelsgesellschaft* v. *Einfuhr-und Vorratsstelle*[9] adopted a more flexible approach and moved away from the idea of impossibility being an integral part of *force majeure*. In its judgment, the court stated that:

"The concept of *force majeure* adopted by the agricultural regulations takes into account the particular nature of the relationships in public law between traders and the national administration as well as the objectives of those regulations. It follows from those objectives as well as from the positive provisions of the regulations in question that the concept of *force majeure* is not limited to absolute impossibility but must be understood in the sense of unusual circumstances outside the control of the importer or exporter, the consequences of which in spite of the exercise of all due care, could not have been avoided except at the cost of excessive sacrifice."[10]

Having introduced some degree of flexibility, the court then appeared to move back towards the notion of absolute impossibility in *Office Belge de L'Economie et de L'Agriculture* v. *Corman* and *Valsabbia* v. *Commission*.[11] In the *Valsabbia* case the court stated that " . . . recognition of circumstances of *force majeure* presupposes that the external course relied on by individuals has consequences which are inexorable and inevitable to the point of making it objectively impossible for the persons concerned to comply with their obligations . . ."[12]

Nevertheless, the court is then to be seen in *De Jong* v. *VIB*[13] trying to reconcile the two positions. The court stated:

"As regards the question whether that requirement can be waived on grounds of *force majeure*, it is clear from the objectives and the provisions of the relevant legislation that the concept of *force majeure*, within the meaning of Article 18(2) of Regulation 232/75, must be understood as meaning absolute impossibility caused by abnormal circumstances beyond the control of the purchaser of the butter the consequences of which could not have been avoided without unreasonable sacrifices, despite the exercise of all due care."[14]

It did, however, seem difficult to accept that it was possible to have such a reconciliation when the definition of *force majeure* contained references to absolute impossibility. reasonableness and due care all within one sentence. It has, however, subsequently been stated unequivocally that the concept of *force majeure* is not limited to absolute impossibility. Having seemingly disposed of the issue of ab-

8. *Ibid.*, at p. 385.
9. [1970] E.C.R. 1125.
10. *Ibid.*, at p. 1137.
11. [1985] E.C.R. 3039, [1980] E.C.R. 907.
12. [1980] E.C.R. 907 at p. 1022.
13. [1985] E.C.R. 2061.
14. *Ibid.*, at p. 2111.

solute impossibility, which was becoming a conceptual distraction, the court purported to concentrate on the two principal issues, namely, whether the circumstances were abnormal and unforeseeable and whether they were beyond the control of the party seeking to invoke *force majeure*. In practice, however, it is difficult not to suggest that the requirement of absolute impossibility lingers on, despite protestations to the contrary by the European Court of Justice (ECJ).[15] In *An Bord Bainne Cooperative Limited and Another* v. *The Intervention Board for Agricultural Produce*[16] ("IBAP") two EU exporters had entered into contracts with a Soviet state-owned importer for the supply of large quantities of butter oil of a specified quality. That butter oil was to be processed from intervention butter sold to the two exporters by IBAP. In the process of tendering for the purchase of the butter, the exporters provided to IBAP bank guarantees by way of security to ensure that they would perform their contractual obligations to take delivery of the butter.

However, after the tendering procedure had been followed through but before the butter had been collected, the Soviet authorities radically altered the quality requirements for the first time in 30 years in such a way as to make it impossible for the EU exporters to satisfy them. In his opinion, Advocate General Gulmann reiterated that there was no need to establish absolute impossibility and he proposed that *force majeure* should be granted provided that a prudent and careful exporter and any party to a contract with an exporter had not foreseen, and had no reason to foresee, that change, and also provided that the effect of the change could not in fact have been avoided despite the exercise of all due care. It was also proposed that the national court should be left to determine whether those conditions had been satisfied. He also made it plain that his sympathies lay firmly with the exporters, indicating that IBAP were adopting an unduly strict interpretation of the concept of *force majeure* and that its interpretation would impose an onerous burden on commercial activity which had not been shown to be necessary to ensure compliance with the objectives of the relevant community rules.

IBAP had argued that the exporters had failed to take reasonable precautions either through incorporating suitable contractual provisions or by taking out appropriate insurance cover. The Advocate General, however, suggested that:

"... in the real world it may be impossible or at any rate very difficult for a trader to persuade the other contracting party to agree to assume the risk of events constituting *force majeure*. Likewise, it will undoubtedly also be difficult for traders to take out insurance cover for loss resulting from events constituting *force majeure* and normally such cover will presumably be expensive."[17]

The court, however, subsequently took a remarkably contrasting view of "the real world" and decided that the change in regulations imposed by the Soviet authorities was a normal commercial risk that an EU exporter had to accept in dealing with state-owned customers, directly subject to the public authority of that state. Furthermore, the court commented that a prudent exporter should have taken

15. For example see *Organisationen Danske Slagterier pro Jydske Andelsslagteriers Konservesfabrik A.m.b.A. (JAKA)* v. *Landbrugsministeriet (Ministry of Agriculture)* [1994] 1 C.M.L.R. 729, considered in further detail at p. 347 below.

16. [1993] 3 C.M.L.R. 856.

17. *Ibid.*, at p. 872.

appropriate precautions either by inserting a suitable clause in the contract of sale or by taking out specific insurance, thus essentially accepting IBAP's view. Having said all this, the court did stress that the concept of *force majeure* is not limited to cases of absolute impossibility but if, in practice, that is the case, it is submitted that it is difficult to comprehend why the court's view should be so dramatically opposed to that of the Advocate General. On any analysis, it would seem that, in practice, *force majeure* will only be granted in very rare cases.

Certainly the court has strictly applied a theory of vicarious liability when exporters have delegated or subcontracted their obligations to third parties. In *Anthony McNicholl* v. *Minister for Agriculture*[18] Advocate General Mischo said:

> "In my opinion, therefore, it may reasonably be concluded in the present case that if the purchaser of the beef in question, instead of carrying out the required exportation himself, instructs a third party to do so, he is not thereby released from his obligation to export; he continues to bear, with regard to the intervention agency, all the risks which a diligent trader can and should reasonably foresee and consequently he must be responsible for any misconduct or negligence on the part of that third party.
>
> I would go so far as to say that the above principle is all the more valid in this case in which the purchaser has not re-sold the products in question but has merely instructed a transport undertaking to take charge of their exportation."[19]

In its judgment in this case, the court applied the same reasoning, stating that:

> "It follows that a trader who, on purchasing the goods, entered into a contractual obligation to export them cannot escape that obligation by claiming *force majeure* where the goods are stolen as a result of fraud or negligence on the part of his own employee.
>
> In a case involving the misappropriation of a consignment of butter from intervention stocks purchased for the purpose of exportation (*Case No. 42/79, Milch-Fett-und Eierkontor G.m.b.H.* v. *BALM*), the court held that if the first purchaser decides to re-sell the product to a third party for the purpose of exportation he thereby assumes, with regard to the agricultural intervention agency, all the risks which a diligent trader can and should reasonably foresee in the context of that transaction, including that of misappropriation of the product through the fraudulent conduct of a duly authorised agent of the third-party purchaser. The same rule applies where the first purchaser entrusts the exportation of the goods to a third party and that third party concludes a contract of carriage for that purpose with a fourth undertaking. In such a case, the purchaser must therefore be answerable to the intervention agency for any unlawful conduct or negligence on the part of those other two undertakings. Such circumstances cannot be regarded as unforeseeable in contractual relations and are therefore an inherent part of the commercial risk.
>
> It follows that the purchaser must also be answerable for the conduct of an independent contractor to whom the transport of the goods was sub-contracted even if, by taking that course of action, the first carrier was in breach of his own contractual obligations."[20]

At present, the academic lawyer is faced with a wealth of opportunity to analyse the theory and application of *force majeure*. From case to case the court and, for that matter, the Advocates General and the Commission have looked at different cases in different ways, applying *force majeure* with differing degrees of emphasis. Insofar as practitioners and exporters are concerned, however, this produces little more than frustration and uncertainty. It therefore appears to be more constructive

18. [1988] 2 C.M.L.R. 275.
19. *Ibid.*, at p. 279.
20. *Ibid.*, at p. 284.

to extract the bare bones of the definition and then look in detail at a number of the decisions on *force majeure* to detect a pattern to be able to advise on how individual cases would be viewed by the ECJ.

The key elements are:

(a) The burden of proof is on the party seeking to rely on *force majeure*.[21]
(b) The circumstances must be abnormal and unforeseeable.
(c) The consequences should not have been avoidable except at the cost of excessive sacrifice and in spite of the exercise of all due care.
(d) The circumstances must be extraneous.
(e) The nature of the EU benefit concerned and the legal context in which it is to operate must be analysed.[22]

5. EUROPEAN COMMISSION NOTICE C.(88) 1696

Before turning to a series of examples of cases concerning *force majeure*, it is worth noting that the Commission has issued guidelines in an effort to explain the working of *force majeure* and to ensure consistency. The notice is, however, in some ways defeatist. In its first paragraph it states that " . . . the attempt to set out in such legislation an exhaustive list of circumstances which constitute *force majeure* has long since been abandoned". The conclusion reached in the notice is that "the *force majeure* clause should be interpreted restrictively". It is hopefully not too disrespectful to suggest that *force majeure* has, almost without fail, always been applied in this way regardless of the manner in which the concept itself has been defined.

The notice extracts its definition from the *Internationale Handelsgesellschaft*[23] case when it states: " . . . the concept of *force majeure* is not limited to absolute impossibility but must be understood in the sense of unusual circumstances, outside the control of the trader, the consequences of which, in spite of the exercise of all due care, could not have been avoided except at the cost of excessive sacrifice."[24] Nothing contained in the notice is particularly controversial. What is interesting is the fact that such a notice has been published. This is a clear response to the demands of the EU agencies, exporters and other interested parties in the different member states to whom *force majeure* is frequently of importance. Exporters in particular have complained about lack of consistency on the part of the different agencies, whilst both the exporters and the agencies have complained to each other about a lack of comprehension of when *force majeure* can properly be granted. It is to be doubted whether the notice will necessarily solve any of these problems but at least its publication shows that the Commission is willing and able to respond constructively to groundswell opinion.

21. *Schwarzwaldmilch* (fn. 7 above).
22. *Butter-und-Eier-Zentrale Nordmark* v. *Hauptzollamt Hamburg-Jonas* [1980] E.C.R. 643; *An Bord Bainne Cooperative Ltd. and Another* v. *IBAP* [1993] 3 C.M.L.R. 856 at p. 877.
23. [1970] E.C.R. 1125 (fn. 9 above).
24. *Ibid.*, at p. 1137 (fn. 10 above).

6. CASE EXAMPLES

(a) Union Française des Céréales *v.* Hauptzollamt Hamburg-Jonas[25]

In this case, the exporter was seeking payment of EU accession compensatory amounts. The vessel carrying his goods had sunk during the voyage to the country of destination. The EU agency argued that this was not a case of *force majeure* since, they asserted, the loss arose out of a normal commercial risk against which the exporter should have insured. The court, however, found in favour of the exporter, holding that the loss was abnormal and unforeseeable. In reply to the assertion that the trader could have avoided the consequences of the loss by taking out insurance, the court firmly rejected this on the basis that, if this were the case, the trader would be placed in an unfavourable competitive position.

(b) Butter-und-Eier-Zentrale Nordmark *v.* Hauptzollamt Hamburg-Jonas[26]

In this case, the facts were similar to those in the *Union Française*[27] case in that goods were lost when the carrying vessel ran aground. However, in the *Nordmark* case, the exporter's application was in relation to monetary compensatory amounts (mca's). The application failed. The court distinguished between mca's and accession compensatory amounts (which were similar, in purpose, to export refunds). The Commission stated that:

> " . . . the objectives of the two systems are different: the system of monetary compensation seeks to prevent currency fluctuations from disturbing the market or deflecting traditional trade, whereas the aim of the system of accession compensatory amounts is that of permitting free movement of agricultural products in the enlarged community before the entry into force of uniform agricultural prices and therefore of facilitating such a deflection within that larger community. In the granting of accession compensatory amounts fundamental importance is thus attached to the principle of community preference, while that principle does not play an essential part in the system of monetary compensatory amounts.
>
> The Commission considers that . . . it is proper to recognise an entitlement to an accession compensatory amount in a situation such as that underlying case 6/78 [i.e. the *Union Française* case], where the product has been exported from a member state having a higher price level. In order to prevent possible abuses in such cases, it is sufficient to require proof that the product was in fact destined for the specified new member state.
>
> The Commission goes on to state that the legal position with regard to monetary compensatory amounts is totally different. Two independent amounts, for which different qualifying conditions apply, are involved. The matter is not merely one of preventing, by means of the obligation to provide proof of importation, the perpetration of fraudulent practices in certain cases; quite simply in the absence of importation, there is no entitlement to the compensatory amount."[28]

The Commission went on to distinguish between mca's and refunds in other ways and these distinctions were accepted by the court.

The *Nordmark* case is of considerable interest to exporters in the way in which it analysed the *Union Française* decision. In referring to that case, the Commission stated that it:

25. [1978] E.C.R. 1675.
26. [1980] E.C.R. 643 (fn. 22 above).
27. Fn. 25 above.
28. *Ibid.*, at p. 650.

"... concedes that, were the principle of community preference to play an essential part in the present case also, as was the position in [the *Union Française* case], the German authorities would have to pay the monetary compensation for the United Kingdom. In its opinion, however, as between the system of accession compensation and that of monetary compensation, there are important differences which make impossible the straightforward transposition to monetary compensation of the principles formulated by the Court in regard to accession compensation."[29]

The Commission went on to say that:

"The granting of export refunds and the granting of accession compensatory amounts have a common objective, namely, that of opening the markets of non-member countries and of member states which are not yet fully integrated into the community to certain goods which would not be sold on those markets because their basic price is too high."[30]

Advocate General Capotorti similarly distinguished the *Union Française* case, reiterating the opinion expressed by him in that case that:

"Refunds are intended to cover the difference between quotations and prices for those markets within the community and on the world market . . . in order to attain that goal it is thought necessary that provision must be made for varying the amount of the refund according to the destination of the products since markets in the countries of destination are at varying distances from community markets and special conditions apply to imports in certain countries of destination."[31]

The question of insurance was tackled by the Advocate General. He stated that if the exporter was expected to insure this potential risk he:

"... would thus suffer a real loss, in order to avoid which he would in future have to take out *ad hoc* insurance. From this would flow an increase in costs and a corresponding rise in price. Quite different, however, is the situation of sellers in non-member countries exporting to the community. They insure their goods at world market prices which are lower than those of the community, and the lower cost of insurance is reflected in the level of prices quoted by them. Accordingly it appears to me to be sensible to have recourse to analogy in order to avoid similar distortions in competition, detrimental to intra-community trade."[32]

In dealing with the same point the court reiterated that:

"Above all, the principle of community preference, which was the basis both of accession compensatory amounts and refunds on exports to third countries, does not play an essential part in the system of monetary compensatory amounts.

In fact, the system of refunds on exports to non-member countries was introduced in order to ensure that, subject to special considerations relating to the different products, community exporters would enjoy a level of prices similar to that within the community market and accordingly certain market products, significantly higher than the level of prices on the world market.[33]

Dealing with the proposition that the exporter could simply have insured against the potential risk, the court commented: "Whether he bore that risk himself or whether he had insured against that risk, the exporter would be in an unfavourable competitive position in relation to a seller in a non-member country, which is precisely what the system of refunds is intended to prevent."[34]

29. *Ibid.*, at p. 650.
30. *Ibid.*, at p. 651.
31. *Ibid.*, at p. 660.
32. *Ibid.*, at p. 664.
33. *Ibid.*, at pp. 654–655.
34. *Ibid.*, at p. 655.

(c) De Jong Verenigde *v.* VIB[35]

In the *De Jong case*, the trader purchased butter subject to stipulated terms and on-sold the goods, incorporating those terms in the contract of sale. However, the ultimate purchaser failed to comply with those terms which related to the processing of the goods. As a result, the trader was *prima facie* liable to various penalties and sought to invoke *force majeure*. The court, however, rejected this, stating that:

"The failure by a subsequent buyer to comply with the processing obligation is not therefore, as far as the successful tenderer is concerned, an unforeseeable and unavoidable circumstance which might constitute *force majeure*. Indeed, no provision of community law prevents the successful tenderer from including in his supply contract with a subsequent buyer terms enabling him to verify whether the subsequent buyer complies with his undertakings in requiring the subsequent buyer to bear the financial consequences of any failure to comply with his undertakings and to provide securities or other guarantees in that regard."[36]

(d) E. D. & F. Man (Sugar) Limited *v.* Intervention Board for Agricultural Produce[37]

In the *E. D. & F. Man* case, the exporter was some three or four hours late in making the requisite application for an export licence. The reason was that the employee of the company reponsible for making it had simply too much work to carry out at that time and had failed to meet the stipulated deadline. In such circumstances, E. D. & F. Man clearly acknowledged that the facts did not support a claim for *force majeure*—clearly appreciating that the circumstances were neither particularly abnormal nor unforeseeable. Furthermore, they were within the direct control of the company itself.[38]

(e) Anthony McNicholl *v.* Minister for Agriculture[39]

In this case (mentioned above), the Irish exporter was required to ensure that a consignment of meat left the territory of the EU within a prescribed period. Sub-contracted hauliers were engaged to take the goods to an appropriate port but during transit the driver absconded with the load and the exporter was faced with an unimpressed Department of Agriculture in Dublin seeking repayment of the export refund together with the appropriate penalty. The exporter argued that he had done everything possible and that any fault lay with the independent contractors for whom he could accept no legal responsibility. The European Court, however, firmly rejected the trader's argument and the thrust of the court's decision was that, if a trader seeks to subcontract part of his obligations, he must accept the consequences if the subcontractor's acts or omissions result in a *prima facie* breach of the trader's regulatory obligations.

35. [1985] E.C.R. 2061 (fn. 13 above).
36. *Ibid.*, at p. 2112.
37. [1985] E.C.R. 2889.
38. Nevertheless, it is worth noting that the company achieved the relatively rare success of invoking the principle of proportionality—they persuaded the court that the potential penalty was so far out of proportion to their technical breach that it should not be imposed.
39. [1988] 2 C.M.L.R. 275.

(f) Greece *v.* Inter-Kom[40]

In the *Inter-Kom* case, the Advocate General proposed that the exporter (who had failed to ensure that certain produce had left the community within the prescribed period) might not be liable for the consequences of a delay in exporting goods when it was due partly to a power failure which temporarily prevented his supplier from delivering the goods and partly to a period of bad weather. This view was adopted by the court in deciding that the circumstances were at least capable of constituting *force majeure*. The court did, however, determine that the national courts should investigate in detail whether the surrounding circumstances were, in fact, abnormal.

(g) Belgium *v.* Nationaale Instituut voor Landbouwkrediet[41]

In this case the exporter was seeking to invoke *force majeure* on the basis that its customer failed to import goods because it had gone into liquidation. The case was, however, withdrawn and hopefully it would not be improper to suggest that the exporter realised that it would, in that case, have experienced considerable difficulty with its plea.

(h) Buitoni *v.* Forma[42]

The trader asked the court to hold either that a provision that the whole deposit would be lost if certain documents were not produced within six months of importing the goods was invalid or, if it was valid, that he was the victim of *force majeure* on the ground of internal administrative disorder during the holiday period. Advocate General Caportori stressed that: "The concept of *force majeure* refers to abnormal circumstances beyond the control of the individual . . . an internal malfunction within a commercial company during the summer holiday period cannot be deemed to be a case of *force majeure*."[43]

(i) Denkavit France *v.* Fonds d'Orientation[44]

The trader in the *Denkavit* case failed to provide the EU agency with any of the requisite documentation proving arrival at the ultimate destination. The trader was waiting to receive certain transit documents which had been lost by the customs authorities of the country of destination. The trader sought to invoke *force majeure* on the basis that, as must have been correct, the acts of the customs authorities were entirely outside his control and that the customs authorities were in fact agents for the EU agency. The court, however, rejected this submission on the basis that alternative provision was made in the applicable regulation for the trader to lodge all other available documents in the interim.

40. Case 71/87 (unreported).
41. Case 132/87.
42. [1979] E.C.R. 677.
43. *Ibid.*, at p. 689.
44. [1987] 3 C.M.L.R. 202.

(j) Molkerei Zentrale *v.* BALM[45]

In this case, the trader had failed to supply proof within the stipulated period that butter had been processed in another member state. The trader sought to invoke *force majeure.* It was held by the ECJ that there may be a presumption of *force majeure* within the meaning of article 22(4) of Commission Regulation (EU) No 262/79 on the sale of butter at reduced prices for use in the manufacture of pastry products, ice cream and other foodstuffs where the failure to comply with the time limit for the production of proof that butter has been processed in another member state is attributable to delay on the part of the administrative authorities of that other state in verifying that the butter had been processed and in returning the control copy to the state of origin. Such a trader would also have to show that he had demonstrated diligence in requesting the administrative authorities of the state in which the goods are processed to complete those transactions, or in ensuring that they have been requested to do so. The fact that the trader has failed to make an application for other documents to be accepted as equivalent may be held against him only if it was the conduct of the administrative authorities in question which prevented him from safeguarding his rights through that procedure.

(k) Ministerio delle Finanze *v.* Esercizio Magazzini Generali S.p.A.[46]

In this case, *force majeure* arose in the context of the payment of customs duties. After clearance into the community, goods were stolen and the importer sought to invoke *force majeure* to avoid having to pay import duties. However, after construing the relevant parts of the applicable Directive, the court stressed that the underlying purpose of import duties relates to the entry of the goods into the community commercial circuit. The court assumed that, having been stolen, the goods would undoubtedly enter the commercial circuit in this way and that, therefore, theft of the goods, even though there was no fault on the importer's part, did not extinguish the obligation to pay duty.

On close analysis, this case may well have more relevance to the meaning of "loss" in the context of import duties rather than to the pure context of *force majeure*. Nevertheless, it is illustrative of the way in which *force majeure* constantly appears in cases relating to the movement of goods.

(l) Erpelding *v.* Secrétaire d'État à l'Agriculture et à la Viticulture[47]

In this case, it was accepted in principle that a fall in the milk production of a herd caused by chronic mastitis and flu could fall within the definition of *force majeure*.

(m) Bayer AG *v.* EC Commission[48]

Here Bayer received notification of the Commission's decision to impose a fine for violating Article 85 of the Treaty of Rome. The notice contained a postal acknow-

45. Case C50/92.
46. [1983] E.C.R. 2951.
47. [1988] E.C.R. 2647, discussed more fully at p. 350.
48. [1993] 4 C.M.L.R. 30, discussed further at pp. 351 and 352.

ledgement and a second acknowledgement form. Bayer incorrectly treated the two month period for lodging the appeal as commencing on the date the second form was returned. This was crucial because there was a delay of six days before the legal department received the notice caused by a series of bureaucratic errors within the company. Furthermore, the legal department compounded these errors by failing to deduce that the postal acknowledgement had been returned. This case is more noteworthy for the observation made about the principle of excusable error covered in section 10 below but Bayer also sought to invoke *force majeure*. This application was, however, swiftly rejected by the ECJ because the circumstances were neither abnormal nor extraneous.

(n) R. *v.* IBAP ex parte Tara Meat Packers Limited[49]

In this case, the UK exporter had received advanced payment of subsidies subject to the provisions of Regulation 3665/87 and therefore had to ensure that the exported produce was cleared for home consumption in the country of destination—in this case, Egypt. However, whilst awaiting clearance through Egyptian Customs in Alexandria Harbour, the cargo was destroyed by fire. The exporter made an application for *force majeure* and this was indeed granted by IBAP—a view implicitly accepted by the ECJ when subsequently dealing with the article 177 reference.

This case is, however, extremely noteworthy because, even though *force majeure* was granted, the exporter was still required to return the export refund. The decision centred around the interpretation of article 20 of Regulation 3665/87. The key part of this article reads:

"1. . . . a part of the refund shall be paid upon proof being furnished that the produce has left the customs territory of the community.
2. The part of the refund referred to in paragraph 1 shall be calculated:
(a) In the case of exports where the refund has not been fixed in advance at the lowest rate applicable on the date of acceptance of the export declaration . . ."

Under the scheme of the common agricultural policy, it is only exports to certain named destinations that qualify for export subsidies and, therefore, in other cases the rate of subsidy is zero. The ECJ held, applying a strict interpretation, that on this basis "the lowest rate applicable" would have been zero. Counsel for Tara Meats had argued that article 20.2 must have been referring to the lowest positive rate applicable but this was rejected by the court. This judgment highlights some of the dangers to which exporters are exposed. Some exporters insure this risk—as did Tara Meats in this case. This judgment, therefore, should have a significant bearing on the level at which insurers assess the appropriate level of premium since it was previously thought that they could bring a subrogated claim against the relevant EU agency to recover the amount of the subsidies. The only consolation for Tara Meats and any other exporter in the same situation was that, having been granted *force majeure*, the 20% penalty in addition to the export subsidy was not payable. Other exporters do not insure this risk and must accept the consequences.

49. [1993] 3 C.M.L.R. 130.

(o) Organisationen Danske Slagterier pro Jydske Andelsslagteriers Konservesfabrik A.m.b.A. (JAKA) ("ODS") *v.* Landbrugsministeriet (Ministry of Agriculture)[50]

This case was referred to the ECJ by the Eastern High Court in Denmark. A member of ODS had entered into a commitment to export tinned ham 12 days after notice had been given that 80 per cent of Danish workers would be going on strike. Although ODS had been aware of this, it had not anticipated that it would have any effect on its ability to export the ham within the regulatory period. However, when it became plain to ODS that it would not in fact be able to export the ham in due time, it applied to the Danish ministry for an extension on grounds of *force majeure*. That extension was not granted and the ECJ held that the ministry had acted correctly. Whilst the court agreed that the strike had been beyond the control of ODS's member, it went on to hold that: " . . . a strike which was preceded by the required statutory notice and in respect of which it was announced that it would spread to sectors affecting the activities of the holder of the licence does not constitute an abnormal and unforeseeable event".[51]

ODS pointed out to the court that in only three of the last 13 instances had a strike occurred where statutory notice had been given. The court, however, was not persuaded that this made it in any way abnormal or unforeseeable that the 14th notice should be followed by the fourth strike.

As is clear from a number of such cases, the court placed great weight on the fact that the ODS's member had two options. It could either apply for the export subsidy applicable on the date of exportation or it could seek to have that rate fixed several months in advance. As is very frequently the case, the member had elected for the latter option on grounds of commercial certainty. The *quid pro quo*, however, was that, in the view of the court, the member accepted the serious consequences that followed if the produce was not exported in due time. This view was suitably summarised when the court stated: "Whilst economic operators obtain considerable advantages in that way from the system of advanced fixing, it is justified that they should also bear the risks arising from it."[52]

7. APPLICATION OF FORCE MAJEURE BY ANALOGY OR IMPLICATION

In almost every case of *force majeure* considered by the European Court, express reference to *force majeure* has been made in each appropriate regulation or directive. The principle, therefore, appears to have developed that, in the absence of such a reference, *force majeure* should not be applied. Indeed, in the Commission's notice it is stated that: "*Force majeure* is not a general principle of law, but can be regarded, in exceptional cases, as an embodiment of the principle of proportionality, in the strict conditions laid down by the court's decisions."[53]

The court has, however, shown some flexibility from time to time. In the *Union*

50. [1994] 1 C.M.L.R. 729.
51. *Ibid*., at p. 753.
52. *Ibid*., at p. 754.
53. C(88) 1696

Française[54] case, there was no *force majeure* provision in the applicable Regulation. Instead, the court incorporated the applicable article[55] in Regulation 192/75 which related to export refunds. The court stated its ground for doing so as follows:

"It is common ground that if the exporter were refused the grant of accession compensatory amounts in circumstances such as those in the present case after goods have perished as a result of *force majeure*, he would suffer a real loss, as the insurance taken out in favour of the purchaser pursuant to the c.i.f. clause would cover only the value of the goods in terms of the prices prevailing in the importing country, and not in terms of the higher common prices prevailing in the exporting country.

If it were accepted that the exporter had to bear that loss, or that he had to insure himself against the risk, he would be in an unfavourable competitive situation in relation to a seller in a third country.

Such a result would be incompatible with the principle of community preference, which the Act of Accession was intended to promote.

Therefore there is an omission in Regulation No. 269/73 in that it does not provide for the granting of accession compensatory amounts in cases of *force majeure*, and this omission should be made good by applying article 6(1) of Regulation 192/75 by analogy.

Such an application by analogy is also justified by the numerous parallels which exist between the detailed rules for the application of export refunds, on the one hand, and of accession compensatory amounts, on the other."[56]

A few years previously in the *Reich*[57] case the court similarly decided that there were grounds for allowing a plea of *force majeure*, holding that: "To make, in respect of imports of cereals from third countries, special regulations that provide for the case of *force majeure*, is justified by reasons of equity."[58] Both cases are strong authority for the proposition that in appropriate cases the court may imply a provision for *force majeure* into a regulation. It is, however, to be expected that these cases will be extremely rare.

8. TWO-WAY PROCESS

The overwhelming bulk of EU regulations place numerous and onerous obligations on traders. It is, therefore, very much the case that traders see the concept of *force majeure* as being solely designed for their potential benefit. A number of cases within this decade have, however, shown that the various agencies may themselves sometimes seek to invoke *force majeure*. It is worthwhile reviewing three of these cases by way of illustration, although in each case the agency was unsuccessful. The first case was *Dairyvale* v. *Intervention Board for Agricultural Produce*[59] which was a decision of the English High Court. Substantial payments were being withheld from exporters due to a civil servants' strike in the UK in 1981. IBAP, the UK agency responsible for distributing EU agricultural subsidies, was sued by a number of traders and sought to rely on the strike as justifying the delay in making payment on the basis of *force majeure*. The exporters applied to the High Court for an order

54. Fn. 25 above.
55. Art. 6(1) provided that refunds would exceptionally be granted when goods had perished in transit as a result of *force majeure*.
56. [1978] E.C.R. 1675 at p. 1683.
57. *Reich* v. *Hauptzollamt Landau* [1975] E.C.R. 261.
58. *Ibid.*, at pp. 268–269.
59. [1982] 3 C.M.L.R. 497, discussed more fully at pp. 187–189.

for interim payment and the court rejected IBAP's attempts to invoke *force majeure* on the basis that the strike was within its control (being internal) and, therefore, could not be attributed to external forces—i.e. it was not extraneous.

Similarly, in *Denkavit Belgie* v. *Belgium*[60] the Belgian State sought to invoke *force majeure* when it was late in paying mca's to exporters. It pleaded that the delays were due to staffing problems arising out of government cutbacks and to the complexity of the Commission legislation. The European Court, however, was quick to reject this application, pointing out that the staff shortages arose out of an entirely domestic situation wholly attributable to the Belgian State itself. It also indicated that there was nothing unusual or particularly unforeseeable about the notion of community legislation being complex.[61]

Referring to previous judgments, Advocate General Mischo said:

> " . . . I do not think that those judgments can be taken to indicate that the court draws a distinction according to whether the plea of *force majeure* is put forward by an individual or an undertaking or by member states. On the contrary, it seems to me that the judgments I have referred to must be applicable to anyone and that consideration of whether there has been *force majeure* cannot be affected merely by differences in the legal context in which that concept is to have effect."[62]

With regard to the complexity of community legislation he stated that: "Indeed it would scarcely seem possible to regard the complexity of community legislation which a member state has taken part in drafting as constituting an unusual and unforeseeable difficulty which has proved insurmountable for that state's staff despite all possible diligence in overcoming it."[63] With regard to staff shortages, he commented: "As for the lack of sufficient staff due to budgetary restrictions imposed by law, that too is something that cannot be regarded as an ingredient of *force majeure* because it is an element attributable to the Belgian State and is therefore hardly outside its control."[64] These views were incorporated by the court into its judgment.

Thirdly in *Re Late Budget Payments: EC Commission* v. *Greece*[65] a claim was brought by the Commission against the Greek State because it was late in paying its VAT contributions. The Greek State sought to invoke *force majeure*, claiming that the delay had been caused by a bank strike. However, the court again rejected the application. It was established that the bank was in fact owned by the state so that the circumstances were therefore not outside the control of the state. Furthermore, it was also shown that the likelihood of the strike occurring had been published in advance so that, if it had been prudent, the Greek State could have set payment in motion beforehand. In its judgment the court stated that: " . . . the strike relied on as an excuse by the Greek Government was not an event extraneous to it and the consequences of that strike were not inevitable since it was known in advance or was at least foreseeable that a strike would be called."[66]

60. [1988] 2 C.M.L.R. 679. Discussed further at p. 344.
61. *Denkavit France* v. *F.O.R.M.A.* [1986] E.C.R. 149; *Commission* v. *Belgium* [1970] E.C.R. 237; *Commission* v. *Italy* [1970] E.C.R. 961; *Commission* v. *Italy* [1985] E.C.R. 2629.
62. [1988] 2 C.M.L.R. 679 at p. 689.
63. *Ibid.*, at p. 690.
64. *Ibid.*, at p. 691.
65. [1989] 1 C.M.L.R. 441, [1990] 1 E.C.R. 2849.
66. *Ibid.*, at p. 447.

9. FORCE MAJEURE—A SHIELD AND NOT A SWORD

This sub-heading instantly instils a vision in any English common lawyer's mind of Lord Denning, *High Trees*[67] and promissory estoppel. The same principle, however, applies to *force majeure* in the EU law context. This point has most recently been stressed in *Erpelding* v. *Secrétaire d'État à l'Agriculture et à la Viticulture.*[68] Mr Erpelding is a dairy farmer in Luxembourg. As part of the common agricultural policy, milk producers are allowed to produce up to a stipulated quantity of milk and if they exceed that quantity, a levy is imposed and must be paid—normally by the producer. In calculating that quantity or limit, one of the factors taken into account is the amount of milk produced over a stipulated three-year period. In Mr Erpelding's case, the period in question covered a time when his herd had been afflicted either by chronic mastitis or Canadian flu—as a result of which his herd's yield had suffered a dramatic fall. He therefore sought to invoke *force majeure*. Mr Erpelding failed in this argument.

The applicable regulation contained a specific provision whereby it was stated that, if the yield in any one particular year was adversely affected by exceptional events, the authorities should make their calculations on the basis of another year within the prescribed three-year period. A list of the exceptional events covered by the regulation in this way was set out in the regulation itself and included the type of afflictions suffered by Mr Erpelding's herd. Mr Erpelding's problem, however, was that all of the three possible years had been relatively disastrous for him and he did not wish the calculations to be carried out by reference to any of the three years. Mr Erpelding was, therefore, in effect, claiming to be entitled to a higher figure than would *prima facie* be justified by reference to any of the three stipulated years—on the basis of *force majeure*. Other arguments arose in that case but in dealing with this point Advocate General Darmon commented that:

> "The solution advocated by the applicant is technically distinct from the traditional effects of *force majeure*, which are to free a party from the consequences of failure to perform or non-compliance with an obligation.
>
> . . . This case is not concerned with excusing the failure to perform an obligation but obtaining a different reference year from that resulting from the system provided for by the rules."[69]

The Advocate General went on to express his opinion that the concept of *force majeure* could not be used in such a way as to create an additional provision in a regulation—an "invented" provision, in the words of the Advocate General himself.

In its judgment, the ECJ adopted the Advocate General's analysis of *force majeure* and stated that: "Although the Court has consistently held that *force majeure* may excuse an operator from certain legal consequences which, under the applicable rules, would normally flow from the non-occurrence of a fact or the non-compliance with an obligation, it can never create for the benefit of that operator a

67. *Central London Property Trust Ltd.* v. *High Trees House Ltd.* [1947] K.B. 130.
68. [1988] E.C.R. 2647 (fn. 47 above).
69. *Ibid.*, at pp. 2660–2661. See also *Schertzer* v. *European Parliament* [1977] E.C.R. 1729 and *Orlandi* v. *EC Commission* [1979] E.C.R. 1613.

right not provided for in the relevant rules."[70] The theory behind this enunciation of principle has the apparent advantage of clarity but, it is submitted, may not always be easy to apply in practice. In a number of the cases described above, the trader could have argued that he was not seeking to rewrite the regulation in question but was seeking to avoid the imposition of a penalty as a consequence of a technical breach of the regulation as written. Equally, the EU agency or the member state could have argued the opposite. To that extent, therefore, the apparent clarity of the principle set out above may in fact do little to remove the cloud of uncertainty which can sometimes shroud the application of *force majeure*.

Instead it is submitted that a closer look should first be taken at the applicable part of the regulation in question. In *Erpelding* there was express reference to *force majeure*. A list of the instances in which *force majeure* would, in fact, be granted was set out. Furthermore, each EU agency was given a discretion to increase the reference quantity in specific cases and, again, those cases were listed and described in detail. It is relatively rare that regulations emanating from Brussels are so comprehensive in this respect and it is submitted that in such cases the European Court of Justice would almost invariably treat the applicable parts of any such regulations as being exhaustive in defining instances of *force majeure*. Where regulations are not drafted in this way, it can be expected that the clear principle set out above may find itself the subject of the level of flexibility which characterises (often to its credit) European Community law.

10. EXCUSABLE ERROR

Excusable Error—another EU concept novel to English common law—appears rarely in EU case law but has certain similarities to *force majeure* and is worthy of mention. When a party is *prima facie* in breach of a provision of EU law, that party can invoke Excusable Error as a defence in exceptional circumstances where the conduct of an institution within the Commission has been, either alone or to a decisive exent, such as to give rise to confusion in the mind of that party, acting in good faith and exercising all the diligence required of a normally experienced trader.

Excusable Error is a concept used to reflect the EU principle of legitimate expectation, primarily that parties are entitled to rely on representations made by the Commission. The difference between Excusable Error and *force majeure* is two-fold. First, no express provision is made in EU regulations for Excusable Error; it is only implied, whereas the opposite is almost invariably the case with *force majeure*. Secondly, with Excusable Error it is not necessary to establish that the circumstances were in any way abnormal, which is essential for *force majeure*.

Both concepts were invoked unsuccessfully in *Bayer A.G.* v. *EC Commission*.[71] In that case, the Commission had imposed a fine on Bayer, having been in direct correspondence with Bayer's legal department. The decision, however, was simply put in an envelope addressed to "Bayer A.G." at its registered office without any

70. *Ibid*., at p. 2572.
71. [1993] 4 C.M.L.R. 30. Discussed further at pp. 345 and 346.

reference to the legal department. It also contained an acknowledgement slip. Due to a sequence of administrative errors within Bayer, it took six days to be passed to the correct department, and then the department thought that the time for lodging an appeal ran from the date of returning the slip to the Commission. As a result, the appeal was lodged but out of time.

Bayer raised, *inter alia*, Excusable Error. This was, however, rejected by the Court of First Instance on two grounds. First, it was held that there had been no exceptional circumstances with the Commission simply addressing the envelope to Bayer's registered office. Secondly, the decisive factor was Bayer's own sequence of errors in its internal distribution and in not being aware of the regulatory provision regarding time bar. This second factor was also fatal to the plea of *force majeure*, which failed on the basis that the circumstances were not abnormal.

11. WAYS IN WHICH THE DIFFERING INTERESTS CAN PROTECT THEMSELVES

The differing interests involved in any export transaction should all be able to reappraise the risks they are running in the light of the problems highlighted above. Traders should be giving serious consideration to taking out increased insurance to cover these potential risks. Insurers and bankers should, on the other hand, be taking into account these risks in assessing premiums and charges.

There is, however, another possible method which may be in the interests of all concerned. There are increasing examples of exporters finding themselves in default of their obligations owing to a failure on the part of their customers in other countries to take delivery of the goods for various reasons. Whilst accepting that commercial realities may sometimes preclude this, this problem might be tackled in the following ways:

1. The exporter should insist on being provided with counter-security by his customer as a condition of entering into the contract of sale.
2. Contracts should only be on the basis of appropriate letter of credit arrangements ensuring payment against appropriate documentation.
3. Exporters should refuse to accept any *force majeure* conditions in the contract of sale which may be less favourable than the *force majeure* provisions in the applicable regulations.

With regard to *force majeure* clauses, these should be tailored to each individual contract, but a typical one would read as follows:

"If an event beyond the control of the contractor such as, for example, war, industrial dispute, fire, mobilisation, requisition, embargo, currency restrictions, insurrection, shortage of transport, general shortage of materials or restrictions in the use of power would delay, hinder or prevent the carrying out of this contract, either party is entitled to cancel this contract by giving one calendar month's written notice thereof to the other party."

Such a clause could easily be invoked by either party to the contract in cases where, as highlighted above, the exporter would have little or no prospect of success when faced with an EU agency demanding repayment of export refunds plus penalties. It is, therefore, in the interests of exporters to ensure that they at least explore the possibility of taking one or more of the steps mentioned above and it is similarly in the interests of bankers and insurers to encourage them to do so.

MICHAEL PARKER

INDEX

INDEX

INDEX

INDEX